Cronkite

ALSO BY DOUGLAS BRINKLEY

The Quiet World: Saving Alaska's
Wilderness Kingdom, 1879–1960

The Wilderness Warrior: Theodore Roosevelt
and the Crusade for America

The Great Deluge: Hurricane Katrina, New Orleans,
and the Mississippi Gulf Coast

Tour of Duty: John Kerry and the Vietnam War

Windblown World: The Journals of Jack Kerouac,
1947–1954 (editor)

Wheels for the World: Henry Ford, His Company,
and a Century of Progress, 1903–2003

Dean Acheson: The Cold War Years, 1953–71

The Mississippi and the Making of a Nation
(with Stephen E. Ambrose)

American Heritage History of the United States

The Western Paradox: Bernard DeVoto Conservation
Reader (editor, with Patricia Nelson Limerick)

Rosa Parks: A Life

The Unfinished Presidency: Jimmy Carter's Journey
Beyond the White House

John F. Kennedy and Europe (editor)

Rise to Globalism: American Foreign Policy Since 1938,
Ninth Edition (with Stephen E. Ambrose)

The Majic Bus: An American Odyssey

Driven Patriot: The Life and Times of James Forrestal
(with Townsend Hoopes)

FDR and the Creation of the U.N.

Cronkite

Douglas Brinkley

HARPER LUXE

An Imprint of HarperCollins*Publishers*

HarperCollins books may be purchased for educational, business, or sales promotional use. For information please write: Special Markets Department, HarperCollins Publishers, 10 East 53rd Street, New York, NY 10022.

FIRST HARPERLUXE EDITION

HarperLuxe™ is a trademark of HarperCollins Publishers

Library of Congress Cataloging-in-Publication Data is available upon request.

ISBN: 978-0-06-200243-3

12 13 14 ID/RRD 10 9 8 7 6 5 4 3 2 1

To Brian Lamb
and
David Halberstam
(1934–2007)

If we cannot produce a generation of journalists—or even a good handful—who care enough about our world and our future to make journalism the great literature it can be, then "professionally oriented programs" are a waste of time. Without at least a hard core of articulate men, convinced that journalism today is perhaps the best means of interpreting and thereby preserving what little progress we have made toward freedom and self-respect over the years, without that tough-minded elite in our press, dedicated to concepts that are sensed and quietly understood, rather than learned in schools—without these men we might as well toss in the towel and admit that ours is a society too interested in comic strips and TV to consider revolution until it bangs on our front door in the dead of some quiet night when our guard is finally down and we no longer kid ourselves about being bearers of a great and decent dream.

—HUNTER S. THOMPSON, *The Proud Highway*

The stalwart kingpin of CBS News . . . Walter Cronkite, who has earned for himself, and in turn for CBS that which we have wanted from the very start of our News Division: the highest degree of credibility in the world of journalism. . . . Walter has been so characterized—if not immortalized—with the oft-heard line: "If Walter says it, it must be so."

—WILLIAM S. PALEY

When the history of journalism is written about our era, it will be divided into separate eras—B. C. and A. C.—before Walter Cronkite and after Walter Cronkite. And the great division here is that Walter had in spades what today is lacking in huge proportion—and that is trust. It's probably hard for Walter himself to fathom how the profession of journalism has declined in public trust and, I'm bound to say, public esteem since he left it. But the decline has been sharp and precipitous. In a profession, as with currency, it's good to have a gold standard, and Walter is simply the gold standard of network, national, shared news experience.

—GEORGE F. WILL

Contents

Prologue

Walter Cronkite—for godsake, there are millions of people out there, 19, 20, 21, ridiculous ages like that, who think there has always been a Walter Cronkite. After the fashion of Franklin Roosevelt, Santa Claus, and the Easter Bunny. Every time there would be one of those great hulking Moments in History, an election, a national convention, a man in space, Kennedy's assassination, there would be the face of Walter Cronkite on TV, with his hair combed straight back over his sagittal suture and his mustache spreading out like Melvyn Douglas after a good rousing heigh-ho afternoon at the St. Regis barbershop and his head tilted with him holding an earphone over one ear and then his voice coming out flue-cured *Southern with the drawl trimmed off.*

—TOM WOLFE

When novelist Kurt Vonnegut heard that, on March 6, 1981, after nearly nineteen years of service, Walter Cronkite was retiring at sixty-four years old from his job as anchorman of the *CBS Evening News,* he wrote a heartfelt paean for *The Nation* titled "A Reluctant Big Shot." Vonnegut worried about what Cronkite's abdication meant for the future of American democracy. Over the years he had come to equate Cronkite, a fellow midwesterner, with a Father Christmas character who in self-deprecating fashion insisted that he was "only a newsman." Now Vonnegut fretted that the most trusted reporter, one who remained "as entranced by the unfolding of each day's news as a child with a new kaleidoscope," was sailing off into the retirement horizon. There were no consolation prizes for the American people. With cable TV news as the emergent driving force, Vonnegut worried that the era of *thoughtfulness* in news broadcasting was over. "The actual crisis is upon," Vonnegut lamented. "A subliminal message in every one of his broadcasts was that he had no power and wanted none.

So now we feel that a kindly and intelligent teacher is leaving our village. It turns out not to matter that the village happens to be as big as all outdoors."

Since the CBS heyday of Edward R. Murrow in the 1950s, no television broadcaster had been so omnipresent in American life as Cronkite. He was as familiar to TV watchers as the "Star-Spangled Banner" at the end of late-night programming before the static ruled. Whether it was chronicling astronaut John Glenn's orbit of Earth, lamenting the JFK assassination, sharing his post–Tet Offensive doubts about the Vietnam War, dubbing the Chicago police "a bunch of thugs" at the 1968 Democratic Convention in Chicago, or celebrating the nation's bicentennial, Cronkite was the clarion voice in network news. Instead of the error some TV anchors made of babbling constantly through special coverage of a presidential inauguration or a moon walk, Cronkite had mastered the intentional pause, the need for frozen seconds of long silence at certain historic moments. Nobody before or after Cronkite had mastered the art of communicating news on television nightly without ever becoming an irritant. What Murrow had been to radio, Cronkite was to TV—though they were as different in style as night and day, their overmastering legacies at CBS News represent high-water marks of twentieth-century electronic journalism. Cronkite trained himself to speak at a rate of 124 words per minute in broadcasts so that TV viewers could easily absorb the newscast. Americans typically average about 165 words a minute, and hard-to-understand speakers average 200. Blessed with a mellifluous voice, Cronkite slowed the verbiage down like an old muddy river, and TV viewers approved en masse.

As Cronkite prepared to step down as CBS News anchorman, on a Friday night, one network executive postulated that the broadcaster had come to represent "God, mother, the American flag, the four-minute mile, and Mount Everest" to an adoring public traumatized by Vietnam and Watergate. Every physical feature of Cronkite told the same story, from the glacial blue of his receptive eyes to the perfect grooming of his Walt Disney–like mustache. By all outward appearances, he looked like a serious man. His French-cuffed shirts, many bearing the monogram WLC (for Walter Leland Cronkite), were always starched. Only his large knot ties—some of them with fat stripes or polka dots—hinted toward humor. As a child of the Great Depression, Cronkite found that frugality came naturally. Even his best friends called him stingy. He hated picking up tabs or tipping. Committed to being a top-tier reporter in the 1940s, 1950s, and 1960s, Cronkite habitually worked ten to twelve hours a day.

Swirling around him were always scores of producers, writers, runners, typists, and cameramen—but only he was the calm eye of the news-gathering storm, creating an overall impression of gentility, equanimity, and decency. Cronkite, the quintessential team leader, perceived introspection as self-indulgent. "I never spent any time examining my navel," he boasted as an octogenarian. "And I'm bored with people who do."

Another chief factor of Cronkite's success was that he cared deeply about TV scripts. What Cronkite's key producers understood was that the veteran broadcaster had a full-bore ardor about certain issues such as civil rights, space travel, and the environment. The greatest moments in TV broadcasting history—Walter Cronkite on the Apollo missions, Dan Rather from Tiananmen Square, Peter Arnett from Baghdad, Christiane Amanpour from Bosnia-Herzegovina, Brian Williams during Hurricane Katrina, Anderson Cooper from Haiti, and others—all gelled because the scriptwriters felt the passion of the on-air reporter. Instead of being fully objective, they spoke from the heart. The intensity index was ratcheted up a few notches to garner dramatic effect.

Broadcasters are notorious for having big egos. Many conflate TV face time with being important figures in the same league with Washington, Lincoln,

and the Roosevelts. Cronkite wasn't like that. He had
a rather matter-of-fact, humble, and benevolent disposition that was borderline heroic. "It can be said of
three men that, in their time as communicators, this
nation hung on their words, waited in eager anticipation of what they were going to observe and report and
treat in their special way," H. D. Quigg, a senior UPI
editor, wrote. "Mark Twain, Will Rogers, and Walter
Cronkite." Obviously he had become more than a mere
TV anchorman to the American public. "You can't
overestimate Walter's life experience during World
War II working for the United Press," Roger Ailes,
the president of the Fox News channel explained. "He
had the voice, calmness, and organic writing style of
a wire reporter who knew what he was doing. There
was *something* comforting about his nuts-and-bolts
approach. Just seeing Walter—in person or on the air—
meant everything was going to be okay. He guided us
through the cold war with more steadiness than flare.
He had an enormous life."

At a 1981 seminar at Columbia University Fred
Friendly, Murrow's alter ego, offered an unvarnished
assessment of Cronkite upon his retirement from
anchoring. Friendly, a CBS News producer for decades
and president of CBS News from 1964 to 1966, compared
Cronkite to the erudite columnist Walter Lippmann—a

high compliment indeed. "Cronkite has the capacity to make people believe him," Friendly explained. "I hate it when people talk about his avuncular quality. I don't know how that ever started, but he was no more of a nice old man than Walter Lippmann was." As a journalist, Lippmann had the capacity to truly understand the complexity of an issue. Murrow had a marvelous ear for news. But Cronkite was *the* master of modern communication. His act in this regard has yet to be surpassed. "I don't suppose," Friendly wrote, "you'll see another Cronkite."

With torches and trumpets, Friendly claimed that Cronkite's greatest gift was for recognizing his own limitations, an unusual quality in the narcissistic broadcast medium. To Friendly, Cronkite was a genius at boiling down and clarifying complex issues for middle-class Americans, even physics and astronomy. He wasn't a great philosopher or writer. But he was a marvelous teacher and a willing student. This made it hard, Friendly believed, to judge Cronkite's stratagems in a historical way. You couldn't compare them to that of a brilliant polemicist such as Lippmann or a you-are-there reporter such as Murrow. How do you really classify Cronkite's anchorman coverage for CBS News of *Apollo 11* or President Nixon's resignation from the White House? Was it really journalism? Or was it neat-and-tidy showmanship? Or hand-holding? Or babysitting? The genius Cronkite showcased was the steadfast ability to reassure millions of TV viewers, in a manner at once authoritative and convincing, that no matter what, they could depend on him to calm the waters and convey the truth. As corny as it sounded, Pulitzer Prize–winning journalist Frances FitzGerald spoke for many reporters when she told *The Washington Post* in 1981 as Cronkite prepared to step down as CBS anchor, "I guess Dad is leaving us."

It was the assassination of President John F. Kennedy, Friendly believed, that turned Cronkite into this patriarchal figure for millions of TV watchers. "There's no way of explaining what he contributed," Friendly told the 1981 class of Nieman fellows, describing Cronkite's professionalism during the Dallas tragedy. "In many countries during four such traumatic days there would have been a revolution. Television, which stayed on the air for four straight days, played a role. All the things that are wrong in that billion-dollar penny arcade paid off in those four days, and that's the tragedy of television—at its best it is so very good. But television can make so much money doing its worst that it can't afford to be its best."

On March 3, 1981, just three days before Cronkite ceded the *CBS Evening News* spot to Dan Rather,

President Reagan sat down with the broadcast legend for an hourlong exclusive interview from the White House. Reagan had been a bona fide fan ever since Cronkite took over the anchor chair in 1962. The cordiality between the two was self-evident. Cronkite started out by asking Reagan about the Middle East, the Soviet Union, and the struggling economy. Toward the end of the interview Reagan, in a reversal, became the kindhearted inquirer. "I know you must be having a little nostalgia," he suddenly interjected with a smile, "the many presidents that you've covered in this very room . . ."

"Indeed so, sir," Cronkite replied. "I was counting back. It's eight presidents. It's been a remarkable period in our history."

And then Reagan said, with genuine warmth, "Well, may I express my appreciation. You've always been a pro."

The avalanche of press stories marking Cronkite's high-profile retirement that month was mind-boggling. *Newsweek* put Cronkite on the cover in a large box screen surrounded by the dwarfed faces of Dan Rather, John Chancellor, and Frank Reynolds. The banner read, "After Cronkite." CBS purchased more than fifty full-page newspaper ads featuring Cronkite with the headline, "Introducing Our Newest Correspondent"—a happy reminder that the retiring legend would get paid $1 million a year to occasionally host a *Special Report*. A thoughtful ABC News—Cronkite's third-place competitor (after NBC News)—countered with a full-page advertisement in *The New York Times* in tribute to his broadcast career. Other newspapers likewise printed their own "Thank you, Walter" ads before he went into eclipse.

From coast to coast Cronkite's good-bye broadcast was billed as if it were game seven of the World Series: must-watch TV. Accolades, telegrams, and special awards came pouring in full force from so many quarters that Cronkite, with amiable amusement, hired a special secretary for two weeks to manage the deluge of mail. When Betsy Cronkite was asked by *Parade* why her husband seemed to be liked by *everybody*, her answer was both funny and probably true. "I think," she said, "it's because he looks like everyone's dentist. Both his father and grandfather were dentists, you know."

Sixty-eight-year-old Eric Sevareid of CBS News, still the erudite Minnesota silver fox, appeared on ABC's *Good Morning America* to say that more media attention was being paid to Cronkite's departure than to Jimmy Carter's farewell address. "The image of Walter Cronkite is a national symbol," Mark Crispin

Miller and Karen Runyon wrote in *The New Republic.* "When it no longer appears at the anchor desk, it will be as if George Washington's face had suddenly vanished from the dollar bill."

Circumspect and unemotional, Cronkite, in the fullness of his fame, wasn't memorable on his farewell broadcast. The loyal *CBS Evening News* audience was hoping for a dramatic departure that March evening, with the venerable man-of-the-half-hour saying something worthy of *Bartlett's Familiar Quotations*. It was instead all business as usual. Cronkite's wife, children, and agent watched the public adieu in the studio. Dan Rather did the same, only on a TV set in the office of executive producer Sandy Socolow. The assumption was that the last broadcast would be a memory-lane affair, a triumphal procession of his greatest moments.

But Cronkite's last news story as anchorman was a NASA space shuttle update, his demeanor typically low-key. During the final commercial break, Cronkite told the crew, "Don't get nervous, everybody; we'll try to do it just like we rehearsed." Ironically, his last two minutes on the air as anchorman—simulcast by NBC News and ABC News—represented perhaps the first time that Cronkite was out of sync with his viewing audience. To his loyal fans he seemed visually awkward and self-conscious. Of his own accord, Cronkite turned to a shopworn cliché to close the broadcast: "Old anchormen, you see, don't fade away. They just keep coming back for more." Rather, time would prove, did not like those last seven words.

Cronkite told the TV viewers that his retirement was "but a transition, a passing of the baton" to a younger Turk. And with that, he uttered the trademark sign-off, "And that's the way it is," one last time, continuing, "Friday, March 6, 1981. I'll be away on assignment, and Dan Rather will be sitting in here for the next few years. Good night."

The CBS cameras pulled back, and the image of Cronkite got smaller. As a parting gesture, Cronkite reached across the desk to shake hands with Jimmy Wall, his beloved stage manager, in an emotional farewell. When the camera went dead, Cronkite, no longer an anchorman, shoved his glasses in his pocket, moved a pencil a few inches, glanced at a stopwatch, popped a stick of gum into his mouth, and threw his script in the air like confetti. "School's out!" he said. And then he left the building.

PART I

The Making of
a Reporter

1.

Missouri Boy

FIRST FLIGHT—DUTCH HERITAGE—SON OF THE SON OF A DENTIST—GREY LYING-IN HOSPITAL—A PONY EXPRESS TOWN—THE DOUGHBOYS—CITY OF FOUNTAINS—STREETCARS, MILKSHAKES, AND THE DEATH OF HARDING—KAYCEE BLUES—GOOD-BYE, CITY OF FOUNTAINS—APPLES DON'T GROW IN TEXAS

Of all Walter Cronkite's boyhood adventures, the one that was seared in his memory clearest was his first airplane flight, in 1923. For the seven-year-old Cronkite the near-death episode ironically engendered a compulsion toward risky endeavors. He liked having his adrenal gland working in overdrive. In this pre-Lindbergh era, prop airplanes had been flown recreationally for only a decade. "My father and I went up in an old Curtiss-Wright bi-plane with an OX-5 engine in it off of a grass field in Kansas City," Cronkite told David Friend, a reporter for *Life* magazine. "The engine failed just on take-off and the pilot put it down in a nearby field, running through a fence. Scared the devil outta Dad. I thought it was a great experience. Didn't know any better."

For Cronkite, the spectacular bird's-eye view of the Show-Me State's topography was an unforgettable thrill. In later years he enthusiastically recalled the flight over his birthplace of St. Joseph, perched along the Missouri River, and the clock tower at Union Station in downtown Kansas City jutting upward on the horizon like Oz. The perilous Curtiss-Wright flight was emblematic to Cronkite; it foreshadowed his intrepid career as a military aviation beat reporter for the United Press and CBS News. After admiring little Walter's contained bravery on the near-disastrous flight, Walter Cronkite Sr.—his father—proudly called his only child "The Flying Dutchman."

In *The Story of My Life*, Clarence Darrow bemoaned the fact that so many autobiographers and biographers "begin with ancestors" for the "purpose of linking themselves by blood and birth to some well-known family or personage." But in Cronkite's case, lineage mattered, for he *always* wanted to be associated with his Dutch (more so than his German) heritage. To the imaginative Cronkite, Dutch seafarers—libertarian, democratic, and worldly—were unflappable ocean explorers worthy of a Rijksmuseum full of Old Master oil portraits. One of the first educational documentaries Cronkite narrated after stepping down as CBS News anchorman in 1981 commemorated the bicentennial of America's friendship and unbroken diplomatic relations with the Netherlands. Cronkite filmed the documentary at the regal Van Cortlandt Manor in suburban Croton-on-Hudson, New York. "We Dutch are a very pragmatic people," Cronkite said at the film's outset, "quick to seize on things that will benefit us. Yes, I did say *we* Dutch. You see, back in 1642, when this town of New York was called New Amsterdam, there was a fetching young maiden named Wyntje Theunis. In the pragmatic Dutch manner she was courted by a gallant lad named Hercks. Now Hercks knew a good thing when he saw it. He married Wyntje and bestowed on her his family name: Krankheidt."

The future CBS newsman's pride in his Dutch heritage, an inheritance from his father, was profound. On Thanksgiving Day, Cronkite Sr. would talk at length about how the Pilgrims sailed from Holland to Cape Cod looking for a place to worship God without religious persecution. While young Cronkite wasn't taught to memorize all of America's state capitals or the chronological order of the U.S. presidents by his parents, he proudly knew that the Vanderbilt, Rockefeller, and Roosevelt families were of noble Dutch stock. His daughter Kathy remembered, "It took many years and a great deal of mixing of other ethnic influences to evolve the modern-day Cronkite family, but our Dutch ancestry is a valued legacy."

During his decades at CBS News, Cronkite would tell stories about his maternal grandparents, Edward and Matilda Fritsche—how they were part owners of the Continental Hotel in Leavenworth, Kansas, and had worked in the Kansas City pharmaceutical business during the days of Theodore Roosevelt. An engrossing chronicle could be written, he believed, about how his mother's grandparents both left Bavaria in the mid-nineteenth century for the green pastures of America. But his genealogical memory was tilted toward the Cronkite clan. Being of German descent— like the Fritsches—was frowned upon when you were born during World War I in the American Midwest.

Being Dutch was nobly different. What distinguished F. P. Cronkite (his paternal grandfather) from other Kansas dentists in the early twentieth century, he believed, was his passion that dentistry, as a medical profession, was of the *utmost* importance to the modern world. Restoration dentistry was all the rage in the early twentieth century. Medicine shows that sold potions, cure-alls, and great remedies were by then regulated by the federal government, and practitioners of dentistry required accreditation. The age of patent medicines and quack cures was drawing to an end with the passage of the Pure Food and Drug Act of 1906. Even Coca-Cola had to stop putting cocaine in its soft drink; some said quite tragically. Grandfather Cronkite made all the gold inlays, molds, and dentures his patients needed. The future CBS News anchorman insisted that his grandpa judged character by the shine of a person's teeth.

A national dental periodical called *Items of Interest: A Monthly Magazine of Dental Art, Science and Literature* featured Dr. F.P. Cronkite's practice in a glowing article in 1899. It even ran a photo spread of his seven-room office under the banner "Office and Cabatory of Dr. F. P. Cronkite, St. Joseph, Mo." The story suggested a meticulous Kansan who had definite opinions about modern dentistry and no faint pride in its bright future. A resourceful F. P. Cronkite not only owned the best dental equipment then available in the Midwest, but he also designed drill chairs himself. Convinced that dentists needed to cater to patients with come-ons such as waiting room magazines and alphabet blocks for kids, he was consciously concerned with the image his office projected. "The impressions we make upon our patrons," he advised in *Items of Interest*, "are powerful factors in our professional lives, and it behooves us to take advantage of this fact." He offered many tips on creating a good impression with patients. A famous F. P. Cronkite admonishment to his colleagues was that a dentist should never be caught reading the magazines in his own waiting room. A dentist needed to always be at the ready.

Apart from being lifetime boosters of their respective hometowns—St. Joseph and Leavenworth—the Cronkites and the Fritsches were similar in other ways. Despite heavily Dutch and Germanic surnames, both were thoroughly and even provincially Midwesterners, unwilling ever to criticize the U.S. government. All F. P. Cronkite wanted was to excel in the dental arts. He and his wife, Anna, enjoyed a spacious home in St. Joseph and a summer cottage on Lac Courte Oreilles (near Hayward, Wisconsin). If both sets of Cronkite's grandparents lived without variety or risk, they also lived without pretension, earning the right to be comfortably middle class (a term social scientists bandied about).

F. P. and Anna Cronkite had six children together. The oldest was Walter Leland Cronkite, who followed in his father's professional footsteps and graduated from Kansas City Dental College in 1914. His classmates there assumed Walter would go far, having a toehold in the family business and an inherited work ethic. Walter L. Cronkite—father of the future CBS News anchorman—was simultaneously gregarious and opaque, with piercing light blue eyes and a blond mustache. The two Walters shared a genuine intellectual curiosity as well as a fascination with Dickens and Balzac. By the time he turned eighteen, Cronkite Sr.'s bright future was seemingly guaranteed by his mastery of dental surgery techniques. He recognized that no matter how rotten the economy got, people would presumably still fix a decayed tooth. Sidestepping the chance to work alongside his father, he accepted a job as a staff dentist at the Leavenworth Federal Penitentiary.

As Cronkite Sr. settled into his new life in Leavenworth, he met Helen Fritsche, a Kansas girl who had spent time at college in Pennsylvania but never graduated. The two made a good match: they enjoyed dancing and nightlife and welcomed adult commitments. Both were twenty-two when they married in 1915, and soon moved in with the bride's family (the Fritsches) in the old cavalry town of Leavenworth.

In the fall of 1916, Helen was admitted to the Grey Lying-In Hospital in St. Joseph, a modest two-story clapboard residence at the corner of Fifteenth St. and Edmond St. that was later converted into medical offices. On November 4, she gave birth to Walter Leland Cronkite Jr. Helen boasted that her boy couldn't be more winning in appearance and personality. Like all mothers, Helen thought little Walter—"a warm berry"—was enshrined in a bell of sunshine. She remembered every tiny freckle on his skin with alert merriment. "It is unlikely that my parents pictured me with a mustache at that exultant moment at Dr. Grey's," Cronkite joked in his memoir, *A Reporter's Life.* "Much more likely they were thinking of the immediate bliss ahead as, now a threesome, they began a new life together."

Cronkite was proud of being born where the Pony Express had been founded in 1860. From St. Joseph, messengers once relayed news to more than 150 far-flung Pony Express stations scattered across the Great Plains through the Rocky Mountains and all the way to Sacramento. Cronkite liked to think of the Pony Express as the precursor to the wire services, TV news, and Federal Express. To Cronkite, who loved the 1939 film *Frontier Pony Express* starring Roy Rogers, the Pony Express was the romantic epitome of American can-do-ism.

When little Walter was born in 1916, the Great War raged in Europe. The United States desperately clung to its isolationist tradition. As tens of thousands of British soldiers died in the muddy trenches of France and Belgium, American life continued normally. Just three days after Walter's birth, his father voted at the Frederick Boulevard firehouse in St. Joseph for President Woodrow Wilson's reelection. Like Wilson, he was for staying out of the bloody conflict. But America wouldn't be able to play ostrich for long. Although President Wilson had championed "neutrality" with tedious regularity in his successful reelection bid, he was quickly being forced toward intervention. Certainly, the German navy's sinking of the *Lusitania* the year before, killing more than one hundred American citizens, suggested the gravity of the situation. U.S. entry into the cauldron of war was only a matter of time.

Cronkite Sr., ecstatic to be a father, was biding his time in St. Joseph during the winter of 1916–1917, working out of a small dental office in the same building as his father's larger seven-room suite. When the well-known auto racer Barney Oldfield came to St. Joseph with a new vehicle called the *Lightning*, Walter Sr. was on the scene with a camera, capturing gasoline-powered modernity in motion. Ever since Henry Ford started punching out Model Ts in 1908, automobile ownership had been exploding around the United States. For the burgeoning middle class, having one's own car was an opportunity to roam far beyond the provincial environs of one's hometown. Once Cronkite Sr. bought his first Ford in December 1916 he insisted that the locals call him Dr. Cronkite—the newly minted father of one was at last a community man of standing. Dr. Cronkite now dreamed of opening a dentistry office in Kansas City, the hard-charging metropolis fifty miles south of St. Joseph along the Kansas-Missouri border.

On April 2, 1917, the United States entered the Great War against Germany. President Wilson, abandoning his "neutrality" after winning reelection the previous November, called up the Doughboys (the nickname given to American soldiers during World War I). Although Dr. Cronkite asked the draft board to excuse him from service "on account of dependents"—wife Helen and little Walter—the board refused. The twenty-four-year-old Missourian was a physically fit dental surgeon and the U.S. Army demanded high levels of health and hygiene among the troops. "Report for examination for regular army service," he was told.

Dr. Cronkite convinced himself that he would be permanently stationed stateside, examining and treating draftees after basic training at Fort Sill. It proved to be a pipe dream. The Cronkites took up residence in Sapulpa, Oklahoma, a little glass-manufacturing town.

The hope was that they could all wait out the war in Sapulpa. But by the end of 1917, Dr. Cronkite had become a first lieutenant assigned to the 140th Infantry of the Thirty-fifth Division. He was headed to France to serve behind the lines, as a dental surgeon with the medical corps. A fellow Missouri soldier he befriended was Harry Truman. "To his credit, Dad, as far as I know, never claimed a close battlefield relationship with the thirty-third president of the United States," his son recalled. "Although, with a modesty probably meant to be becoming, he acknowledged having known the chap."

There wasn't much to do in Sapulpa except eat walnut pie—a local delicacy. Unable to communicate with her husband in Europe, Helen decided to move to Kansas City, where her brother Ed Fritsche had become a candy wholesaler in the Hospital Hill section of town. Helen took on odd jobs around Kaycee, from babysitting to bookkeeping, to help pay the household bills. She lived for the occasional Western Union telegram from her husband.

Dr. Cronkite returned from France in 1919, swollen with pride at having served America abroad with distinction. He was pleased that Helen had the gumption to move to Kansas City. When he spoke about the 140th Infantry in Europe fighting the Kaiser, it sounded like current news. Taking a new lease on life, the Great War veteran regaled little Walter with tales of German submarines, torpedo attacks, barbed-wire entanglements, grenades, bayonets, and gas masks. Places such as the Argonne Forest and Hindenburg Line became more historically important in Dr. Cronkite's house than Gettysburg or Antietam.

Embraced as a heroic returning Doughboy, Dr. Cronkite immediately opened his own dental practice in Kansas City. He made the wooden shingle himself. Like his father, he manufactured dental implants. He was deft with his hands and assiduous in keeping up with medical trends. After seeing the carnage in Europe, he was pleased that Kansas City—the Paris of the Great Plains—was rather insular. He rented a small apartment not far from his practice. He didn't really harbor any expectations of being part of Kansas City society—and that was all right by him. "I know exactly how they felt about all other walks of society," Cronkite later said of his parents circa 1920, "the lower classes as well as the upper. Unless you were a 32nd degree Mason living on Benton Boulevard in Kansas City, Missouri, and a white Protestant, there was something a little wrong with you."

The City of Fountains—another Kansas City nickname because of the Romanesque fountains in public places—mesmerized young Cronkite. He was also fascinated by the electric streetcars that rattled by their sparsely furnished apartment. In sun and rain alike he would time the streetcars' progress from one point to another, keeping careful records. He knew the trolley cars by number and knew all the drivers by name. "I played all kinds of imaginative games with myself," he recalled. "We had a swing on our front porch and that swing became everything from a submarine to an airplane. But mostly it was a streetcar!"

Cronkite's avid interest in Kansas City's transportation system offers perhaps the most telling window into his personality. Unlike school learning, monitoring streetcar activity gave Cronkite mathematical discipline and fed his excitement about how the world really worked. Whenever a streetcar ground past, he shouted "hello" at its passengers. Kansas City had the perfect geographical conditions for electrified cable traction (with an industrial district by a river and residential areas upon bluffs on either side of the Missouri River). For Cronkite, the Ninth Street trestle across the Argentine yards toward Union Depot was a kinescope into the Great Wide World. Whether it was streetcars, sailboats, race cars, airplanes, or rockets, Cronkite liked motion. Although the Cronkites were struggling to make ends meet, with Helen selling sets of the *World*

Book Encyclopedia door to door to help pay the rent, the family nevertheless bought a complete set (used) of the volumes for little Walter. His first instinct was to memorize the key facts about tinkerers like Thomas Edison and Robert Fulton. "I was always a researcher," Cronkite recalled, "and anything that interested me I'd go to the *World Book Encyclopedia* for information."

Following the Great War, everyone in Kansas wanted revelry and hijinks. Big band concerts at Fairmont Park's outdoor pavilion, American Legion parades down Grand Avenue, and zeppelins passing over the stockyards were all part of the pageantry celebrating victory in Europe. On November 21, 1921, the city dedicated the Liberty Memorial—a towering monument—with General John J. Pershing, who led the American Expeditionary Forces during World War I, as the main attraction. As the economy improved in Kansas City, the Cronkite family shared in the resulting prosperity. They were able to vacate their apartment and move into a humble bungalow on Kaycee's southeast side. The rich kids lived in Swope Parkway. The Cronkites resided in a "*middle* middle-class neighborhood." Only six blocks away was the Electric Park amusement grounds, which included a Ferris wheel and a roller coaster. Sometimes young Walter visited his paternal grandparents in St. Joseph for some fresh country air. "They had horses," Cronkite later said, "and a storm cellar that always smelled marvelously of apples."

The CBS News legend had lived in St. Joseph for only the first ten months of his life. He had no memory of Sapulpa. He considered Kansas City to be his hometown. In looking back on his childhood during the peak of his fame in the 1970s, he would hold court about the marvels of Kaycee during the 1920s Jazz Age. Never feeling underprivileged, he eagerly performed odd jobs in order to treat himself to a marshmallow sundae or Mrs. Stover's chocolates. By keeping twenty-five or thirty cents in his pocket, he always felt rich. Sometimes he would, with his mother's approval, tip street musicians who were playing blues-infused jazz and ragtime.

When Cronkite was nine, he became a paperboy for the *Kansas City Star* and dreamed of his own byline emblazoned above the fold. *Nothing* seemed more intoxicating to him than encountering his own name in print. It was a classic case of "Kilroy Was Here" syndrome. The paperboy job demanded that he travel to Union Depot by himself via streetcar and lug as many copies of the *Star* as he could back to his neighborhood to sell. Kansas City's bustling downtown thrived as a commercial hub after the Great War. Under the guise of working, Walter used to window-shop in Harzfeld's and Woolf Brothers. (His parents forbade him from ever going to Twelfth Street, where vice flowed as freely as the beer.) Radio hadn't yet become a commonplace commodity, so newspapers were still the town criers. Both Kansas City's *Journal* and *Star* were published in morning and afternoon editions and, when important stories were breaking, in special editions. Anyone who wanted to know the latest developments relied on a passing newsboy hawking a clutch of papers. It might have been child labor, but young Cronkite thrived on it. Not every newsboy becomes a journalist, but the early exposure to the pressures and satisfactions (and the remuneration) of the news business intrigued young Cronkite. He had no inkling that he had entered the journalism trade at the very bottom of the food chain, but he had. Besides peddling newspapers he also sold subscriptions door-to-door to *The Saturday Evening Post* and *Liberty* magazine.

Time magazine reporter James Poniewozik once singled out a telling anecdote about Cronkite's early years in Kansas City as indicative of Cronkite's journalistic instinct to avoid hyperbole and be wary of definitive statements. On August 3, 1923, the *Kansas City Star* ran the front-page story that President Warren G. Harding had died of a heart problem in San Francisco. Clutching the newspaper, young Walter sprinted over to a friend's house to break the dramatic news. "Look carefully at that picture," Cronkite told his pal. "It's the last picture you will ever see of Warren Harding." Years later, in *A Reporter's Life*, Cronkite reflected on this silly statement with self-deprecation. "I can't quite reconstruct today what led me to that foolish conclusion, but I record it here to establish my early predisposition to editorial work—the ability to be both pontifical and wrong."

In late 1926, Dr. Cronkite was invited to join the faculty of the Texas Dental School (now part of the University of Texas Health Science Center) in Houston. The school was a private institution, but the administration hoped to attach it to the Texas public university system. That would put the institution in rightful proximity to the state's medical school in Galveston. Dr. Cronkite, with his special expertise in the dental aspects of reconstructive surgery, felt he could grow professionally in that academic capacity and accepted the offer.

Ten-year-old Walter didn't want to leave Kansas City, where he had the Ninth Street line schedule memorized and where his friends were already made. For all his outward gregariousness, he was shy about changing schools and having to make new friends. Youthful pleas were made to stay in Missouri. They went nowhere. As a consolation, at least, he finagled getting both a saxophone and a clarinet for Christmas so he could learn Buddy Rogers songs. His father told him the instruments were gifted because he had behaved so "grown-up" about moving from Kaycee to Houston. As an adult Cronkite recalled with pride that the Kansas City of his youth spawned both Virgil Thomson (America's premier modern composer) and Charlie Parker (the great jazz musician).

In February 1927, the Cronkites packed up their meager belongings and drove their Ford toward the Ozarks. There weren't even a lot of teary good-byes. The three Cronkites—Walter Sr., Walter Jr., and Helen—sort of eased out of Missouri in a misty sleet without regrets. Texas was booming economically and plenty of well-heeled Houston folks wanted healthy teeth. If young Walter found any solace in leaving, it was that his grandparents were staying put in Missouri. They were his placeholders. For the next decade living in hot and humid Houston in the era before air-conditioning, he often dreamed about Buchanan County's apple orchards ripe with fruit. Someday, Cronkite vowed, he would return to his real home, Missouri, and pick those apples again.

2.
Houston Youth

ADJUSTING TO HUMIDITY—BUILDING A TELEGRAPH
SYSTEM—NO GUNS AND BRUSH FIRE—ODD JOBS—
1928 DEMOCRATIC CONVENTION—CONFRONTING
JIM CROW—THE POLITICS OF BOY SCOUTING—
DRIVING A DODGE—GREAT DEPRESSION WOES—AN
ALCOHOLIC FATHER—CHILD OF DIVORCE—
JOURNEYMAN HEROES—SCRIBING FOR THE *CAMPUS
CUB*—THE ORDER OF DEMOLAY—CUTTING HIS
TEETH AT *THE HOUSTON POST*—DATING BIT
WINTER—BALFOUR RING AT LAST

E ver since Cronkite was a skinny boy delivering
newspapers in Kansas City, he had pushed himself out into the world, hungry for opportunity. His

curiosity about Houston loomed large when, in 1927, the Cronkites moved into a rented bungalow at 1838 Marshall Street in the suburban-like Montrose neighborhood. In preparation for relocating to the Gulf South, Walter dutifully read up on Houston in his trusty *World Book Encyclopedia*. To his disappointment, Houston had no El Paso swinging-door saloons or Fort Worth rodeos. Just a lot of gnarled oaks, biting flies, mesquite groves, tangled thickets, and storm drainage canals called bayous. Cronkite had read that Houston was a huge cotton exchange, yet he didn't see a single boll. "I expected to see an ocean-going ship . . . right on Main Street," he recalled. "Of course, they were way out of town. It was weeks before we ever got out to the ship channel for me to see a ship. And that was disappointing. As a Midwest boy, I'd never seen a ship or the ocean. And there were no cowboys."

Perhaps Cronkite's most important growing-up moment in Houston, one that signaled a career in telecommunications, was when he erected a telegraph system connecting friends' houses in the Montrose neighborhood. Cronkite constructed telegraph lines in the same way some kids practice cello or piano five hours a day. Calling the hookup his most constructive hobby, Cronkite rigged the system from a simple blueprint that was published in a boys' magazine. "We communicated by Morse code and were pretty good at it when it all ended abruptly," Cronkite recalled. "The telephone company took what we considered to be unnecessary umbrage at our use of their poles to string our wires."

Once, Cronkite dug a tunnel on a vacant lot using the gunpowder from a package of firecrackers and started a raging fire. A fire department lieutenant arrived to snuff out the flames, full of reprimands. "If he hadn't stunted my enthusiasms," Cronkite later joked, "I might have grown up to help build the Lincoln Tunnel, or, at least, be a pyrotechnics guru like George Plimpton."

Two skyscrapers rose above Houston back then. One was the Gulf Oil headquarters; it attested to the pivotal role that "sweet" crude had played in Houston's fortunes since pay dirt was hit in Beaumont in 1901. Not long after that year, the salt dome oil field known as Spindletop was producing more than twenty million barrels a day, while sparking a regional boom as other fields also yielded black gold. Soon the dirt roads would be paved, world-class art museums built, and universities with large endowments founded. Not a single bank would fail in Houston during the Depression. More than forty oil companies had offices in Houston, and refineries sprang up just south of downtown near Galveston Bay. "The ship channel had been completed and the East Texas oil finds had come not so many years before," Cronkite recalled. "And the job boom was beginning."

Buffalo Bayou, a sleepy waterway that connected Houston with the Gulf of Mexico, became Cronkite's fishing hole, albeit not a very profitable one (except for bottom-feeders). Before too long the oceanside world of Galveston and League City had an impact on Cronkite's life that was both immediate and unending. Each summer, he and his family explored the sandy beaches along the Bolivar Peninsula, where Cronkite collected seashells and watched the mind-boggling array of wintering birdlife around the tidal marshes of Galveston Bay. Audubon's *Birds of America* was now his favorite book. An amateur ornithologist, Cronkite one day shot a bird with a BB gun and gave up killing animals for the rest of his life. Firearms, the very thought of them, became anathema to him. "I hit a sparrow," he recalled, "[that was] sitting on the telephone line in the back of our house. It fell to the ground. And I picked up the sparrow, who looked at me mortally wounded with this look like, 'Why did you want to do that?' You know it turned me all funny. I never—I didn't do it again."

While the Cronkite family, considered Yankees, loved Houston, one aspect of the city sickened them:

Jim Crow laws and rules. The Ku Klux Klan was thriving in America in the 1920s; more than two thousand
Houstonians were inducted in a single ceremony. The
KKK reflected the institutionalized racism and religious antagonism that existed throughout the nation.
Jews were disdained. Blacks were segregated from
whites in many aspects of daily life, from medical care
to sporting events and public transportation to education. While there had been black students at Cronkite's
Kansas City school, there were none in his new school
in Houston. Furthermore, by both law and tradition,
the facilities accorded to black people were inferior to
those for whites. Jim Crow made Houston an ugly new
world for the Cronkites, one that young Walter dutifully accepted but never fully understood. "My natural
sympathy," Cronkite recalled, "was with blacks."

As a liberal Jayhawker who considered John Brown
a hero of the Civil War era, not a terrorist, Dr. Cronkite
professionally refused to adhere to Jim Crow, taking
black as well as white patients. As his son later told Ron
Powers of *Playboy*, this ethic was reflected in a wrench-
ing episode on one of their first nights in Houston. Dr.
Finis Hight, president of the Texas Dental School, had
asked the Cronkite family to dinner at his River Oaks
home. After the steak-and-potatoes meal, the group
moved to the porch to savor the breeze and await the

delivery of homemade ice cream from a nearby drug-store. In those days, there was no air-conditioning and residential refrigeration options were limited. The Jim Crow "rules" of Houston said that African Americans could not approach the home of a Caucasian from the front. Years later, Cronkite recalled what happened next: "The black delivery boy drove up on his motorcy-cle and looked with his flashlight, clearly for some way to go to the back of the house." Not finding a driveway or alleyway to deliver the ice cream, the young man started up the sidewalk. When he hit the first step to the porch, Dr. Hight, in Cronkite's words, "jumped out of his chair like a cat, and hit him right in the middle of his face, wham!—knocked him back into the grass, ice cream cart spilling—and he said, 'That'll teach you, nigger, to put your foot on a white man's front porch!' My father said, 'Helen, Walter, we're leaving.'"

The three Cronkites marched out of Dr. Hight's house. When the embarrassed host tried to coax them into staying, Dr. Cronkite said "get lost" and kept walk-ing. After that incident, Dr. Hight had the long knives out for Dr. Cronkite because of his "pro-Negro" sym-pathies. "I was horrified about the incident," Cronkite recalled. "Terrified by the walk through the oak trees with their long Spanish moss dripping in them. It looked like a Walt Disney forest that I would expect all the animals jumping at us. We finally got a ride from somebody on a street corner. Got back to our hotel. But from that moment on I was wholly aware of the racial bigotry, prejudice, and treatment of blacks in that part of the world."

In the fall of 1927, Cronkite put on a uniform: that of a Boy Scout. Being a Scout in 1920s Houston primarily meant building fires, camping, and fishing. But when the Democratic National Convention convened there in 1928, Walter and other Boy Scouts worked the convention floor at Sam Houston Hall. They served as ushers for the delegates. Without proper ventilation in the hall, let alone air-conditioning, the heat was stifling. Cronkite was tasked with distributing hand-fans with the faces of Cordell Hull, Walter George, James Reed, and Houston's own favorite son, Jesse Jones, on them. The Democrats nominated Al Smith for president, the candidate of the "wets" (who promised to repeal the then ten-year-old Prohibition law). But Cronkite's heart was with the polio survivor FDR, who fought for Smith's nomination at the convention with oratorical zeal.

A month later Cronkite was able to observe the political process again, when Uncle Edward Fritsche took him to the GOP Convention in Kansas City. Cronkite witnessed the nomination of Herbert Hoover.

He remembered liking Hoover's campaign slogan a lot: "A chicken in every pot and a car in every garage." Not many people, and certainly few other eleven-year-olds, could boast of attendance at *both* 1928 conventions. "I got hooked on them for a singular reason," Cronkite recalled. "Somewhere in the convention hall would be a future president. The trick was in picking him out." When on Election Day (November 6), Hoover defeated Smith (444 electoral votes to 87) to become America's thirty-first president, Cronkite listened to the results on the radio with his father.

With its boomtown atmosphere in the 1920s, Houston devoted large amounts of money to modernizing its public school system. Forward-thinking educators adopted the system of creating separate junior high schools and hired one of the region's finest architects as a full-time employee to design them. Young Cronkite was lucky in this regard: in 1927 he was a first-wave student enrolled in the brand-new Sidney Lanier Middle School. The school served several affluent Houston neighborhoods, drawing prep-school-quality students. Lanier boasted a progressive environment from day one. The brightest Houston students chose it over all others. The ultimate compliment came from other Houston public school kids, who dubbed Lanier students "woodenheads" (i.e., nerds with minds full of facts).

Lanier offered a full range of extracurricular activities for the students, including a student newspaper called (like the school's mascot) *The Purple Pup.* Cronkite—who attended the junior high for three years—was on a reportorial team that won a statewide journalism contest for Lanier. Cronkite continued to take all sorts of odd jobs, including one with *The Houston Post* that trumped all others in educational value. The *Post* city room was just ten or twelve desks crowded into a crammed second-story office, the floor littered wih the wadded-up debris of rejected leads and spent cigarettes. But to Cronkite it was Yankee Stadium or Madison Square Garden. "It had a wonderful aura," he remembered, "the model of every newspaper movie you saw." Rather than peddle papers on a street corner, as he had in Kansas City, he delivered copies of the *Post* on a regular bicycle route to customers between West Alabama and Westheimer, Woodland, and Hazard. When his boss discovered that he was rolling the papers and throwing them from the bike instead of quietly placing them on front porches, he received a harsh reprimand. "I was a small boy and I guess the *Houston Post* was a small newspaper," Cronkite recalled in 1985, "although to me it was the *New York World,* the *Washington Star,* and the *Chicago Tribune* rolled into one."

During summer breaks from Lanier, Cronkite flipped hamburgers at Sylvan Beach, one of the resorts along nearby Galveston Bay. For a spell, he worked at the Sakowitz department store in downtown Houston, helping customers find appropriate toys for toddlers. After only a short time in Texas, his father could afford to buy a *second* car. At the age of about fourteen, Walter inherited the older model. "It was a great big black box of a Dodge," he recalled thirty-three years later in *Parade* magazine. "I could get more kids in that car. . . . There were usually about 12 passengers. I tell you, it made me the undisputed social leader."

After the onset of the Great Depression in the fall of 1929, Dr. Cronkite's life became more complicated. Edward and Matilda Fritsche were forced to close their drugstore and move to Texas to live with their daughter's family. Having two more mouths to feed put a new stress on Dr. Cronkite, as the Depression clawed away at middle-class bank savings and the Texas Dental School hovered on the verge of foreclosure. Enrollment started to dramatically decline, as did revenue from the school's clinic.

Still, Dr. Cronkite remained at the Texas Dental School, eking out a living; he had blown the meager family savings on the extravagance of two cars. Houston didn't have the impoverished Hoovervilles sprouting up on vacant lots common to other parts of America, but overnight dental implants had become luxury items. Walter Sr.'s personal life was also unraveling. Always prone to dulling life's edge with a swig from the bottle, Dr. Cronkite had, somewhere along the line, passed into alcoholism. His once formidable presence had shrunk. Sometimes he was aggressive and unpleasant in the evenings; at other times he was distant, looking out the parlor window or listening to poetry records and repeating the verses almost endlessly. Under these strained circumstances, young Walter naturally drew closer to his mother. They shared the secret of his dad's serious drinking problem. However, even as an adult, Walter remained convinced that his father was a perfect medical professional. Only at night, he explained, did Dr. Cronkite become intoxicated.

Everyday life got extremely tense in the Cronkite household in 1930. In general, Houston was a good place to weather the stormy economy, but not for the Cronkites. As Cronkite told Dan Carleton in an interview for the Archive of American Television in 1998, "Dad ran out of cash." Bills were left unpaid, piggy banks were emptied for loose grocery change. The cupboards were bare. Pitifully, Helen was forced to cook up a can of Ken-L Ration for dinner one evening; so much for Hoover's chicken in every pot. (Helen denied this happened, but her son insisted.) "We had actually run out of food," Walter recalled. "Thank goodness we didn't have to dine on dog food for long." The pressure on Dr. Cronkite was so unbearable he turned even harder to drink.

In 1932, Helen Cronkite, then thirty-nine years old, filed for divorce. When a broken-down Dr. Cronkite moved back to St. Joseph to reopen his practice, Helen and Walter stayed in Houston. It wasn't easy being a single parent. The alimony checks seldom came. Much like Ronald Reagan, who also had an alcoholic father, Cronkite bottled up his emotions about his dad. To his credit, he learned to be stoic about his parental abandonment—dad had done the best he could. And instead of finding dark clouds of pain in his childhood, he purposely remembered only the silver linings.

Even after his father left for Kansas City, Cronkite remained a good kid without any glint of rebellion. His mother instilled tolerance and liberalism in him. She also made him go to church most Sundays. When asked as a CBS News anchorman about his Christian upbringing, Cronkite explained that he had a "Presbyterian-Lutheran kind of Calvinist background." (As an adult, he became a token Episcopalian.) As a single mother, Helen doted on Walter. She established strict curfew hours. She grounded him for misdemeanors. Cronkite told a *Parade* magazine interviewer in 1981 that he once persuaded a Houston pharmacist to allow him to purchase a watch on credit. When Helen learned that her son had made a major purchase in that way, she confiscated the watch, paid the druggist a dollar for it, and kept it hidden until Walter could pay her back. "Don't you see?" she asked him. "You don't know how you're going to earn the money. There's no outright dishonesty here, but you're flirting with it. It's one of those gray areas, Walter. Be careful of gray—it might be grime."

Working on *The Purple Pup* at Lanier had kept Cronkite out of trouble. The idea of trying to teach reporting was a relatively new one in 1929—the nation's first journalism school had been established at the University of Missouri–Columbia in 1908. As more journalism schools opened through the 1920s, newsroom veterans debated whether a good reporter could be manufactured from classroom learning. Some said that journalism couldn't be taught and couldn't be studied; it was a natural bent. A former reporter in Houston, Fred Birney, strongly disagreed and set out to prove his point by teaching journalism part-time throughout the metropolitan area, including at San Jacinto High, where Cronkite had recently been named sports editor of the student paper, the *Campus Cub*.

Birney—in Cronkite's memory a "wiry man" and a "bundle of energy"—taught the class to write with economy and speed when necessary and with accuracy under any circumstances. The students were enthralled by Birney's tales from the world of print. "I had a sense," Cronkite said of Birney, "whenever I was in his presence that he was ordering me to don my armor and buckle on my sword to ride forth in a never-ending crusade for the truth." The metaphor might have been merely playful coming from almost anyone else, but it is obvious Birney set Cronkite's standards for decades to come. "He was so in love with his work," Cronkite recalled of Birney, "that he passed it on to all of us."

Not every article printed in the *Campus Cub* had to be seized with armor and a sword. A typical news flash, which might be attributed to Cronkite (or "Cronky," as he was sometimes called), covered the annual picnic for the journalism classes or a stray feline on school grounds. The Cronkite pieces in the *Campus Cub* don't stand out markedly from the others, but even so he was voted by his peers as best reporter. Cronkite found that he couldn't resist the excitement of editing the school rag. According to the 1933 San Jacinto yearbook, the *Campus Cub* had been able to maintain a "high standard of quality" in spite of the Great Depression, even while other high schools were forced to close shop.

Another teacher Cronkite took a shine to at San Jacinto was Sarah Gross Cory, who encouraged him to pursue a newspaper career. While Birney was a stickler for the rules, Cory saw young Walter through a more maternal and comical lens. "He was always running up and down the corridors with a little pad and pencil," she told *Parade* magazine fifty years later, "looking for news items." Besides writing for the high school paper, Cronkite joined the Houston chapter of the junior version of the Masons—the Order of DeMolay—to find fellowship. It soon followed that the Order of DeMolay of Houston had a mimeographed newspaper, edited by one "WLC"—inevitably, wherever Cronkite went, a newspaper byline would emerge.

While Cronkite was in high school in the 1930s radio became all the rage. The number of radios in use in the United States rose by two-thirds in the first half of the 1930s, to 30.5 million sets by 1935. This reflected the increasing potency of radio networks, which provided entertainment programming in the evening. The one laggard in radio was general news reporting. Although many of the most powerful stations in each city were owned by newspapers, interest in developing radio journalism was mixed. Inept in gathering and delivering straight news, radio invented what it called the news commentator: someone who would describe some current event with either style or authority or both and then editorialize lightly upon it. CBS signed the documentarian Lowell Thomas of Ohio as a news commentator–entertainer in 1932. In addition to delivering his own essays on current events, the energetic Thomas produced *The March of Time*, which reenacted news articles from the pages of *Time* magazine.

Cronkite took notice. Such live radio broadcasts gave listeners something they could not find in a newspaper: the present tense. Newspapers retaliated by joining together and insisting that wire services such as United Press and Associated Press no longer sell content to radio. The flow of wire service news to radio stopped in early 1933. Left in the lurch, stations and networks now had to gather their own news, which they were ill equipped to do. The radio broadcasting field was more crowded than that of newspapers, and like Hollywood, it demanded a certain charisma, which Cronkite tried to develop. With careful practice, he crafted a "radio voice." In true Lowell Thomas fashion, he interviewed anyone who would stand still and speak into whatever faux microphone prop he held. When FDR delivered his first "Fireside Chat" a week after his inauguration in 1933, he sounded incandescent, as if he'd been "dipped in phosphorous," as Lillian Gish put it. Cronkite, thinking about a career in radio for the first time, wanted to glow like FDR someday.

Continuing his apprenticeship in print, Cronkite, after his junior year, landed a summer job as "an exalted copy boy" at *The Houston Post*, one of the three largest dailies in the city and the one that Cronkite thought reigned supreme. His up-from-delivery duties were generally confined to running messages around the newsroom. Occasionally he was allowed to conduct research for a reporter. Darting around the desks, amid the shouts of the editors, he saw how the *Post* transformed a slate of random information into a neatly spaced line of fresh newspapers rolling off the presses. The urgency of the newsroom and the rush to fill the paper made him want to excel in a way that his schoolwork never did. "I wasn't really employed there; tolerated is more like it," Cronkite later recalled of his stint at a paper on the edge of bankruptcy. "I had discovered journalism to be my life's ambition."

When a little article that Cronkite wrote was published on June 29, 1932, he jumped for joy. Seeing his byline gave him an "ego-fulfilling" feeling that he had only dreamed of while selling copies of *The Kansas City Star* five years before. But now he had that feeling for real. "I could watch fellow passengers reading my story on the Mandellvine streetcar," Cronkite boasted.

He clipped the *Post* article out for his scrapbook; "Page 4," he wrote. "First story." And then, best of all: "No corrections."

In the fall of 1932, Cronkite began his last year at San Jacinto High. He was now the editor in chief of the *Campus Cub*, and under his aegis the paper leaned toward the humor of Harvard University's student-run *Lampoon*. It also gave in to the circulation-building habit of mentioning as many potential readers as possible, and it combined both tendencies by printing column after column of one-line witticisms. Under Cronkite's leadership, the *Campus Cub* was a good but not brilliant student paper. Sometimes Cronkite wrote his articles at hangout spots such as Ye Olde College Inn, where a friend of his mother waitressed. When Birney suggested books on journalism for his students, Cronkite sought them out and read them voraciously.

So it was that he happened to be perusing *Best News Stories of 1924* in the spring of 1933 as graduation approached. Whether Cronkite studied their style or simply enjoyed the stories in the book, he was unquestionably well versed in the major news of 1924 when he walked into a newswriting contest in the spring of his senior year. The contestants were to be given a random topic and a short time in which to write a story about it. When the moderator disclosed the subject of the news story in question, Cronkite had to smile. It was the sensational newspaper story of 1924: the Leopold and Loeb murder case originally published in *The Chicago Daily News*. Cronkite had read not only a riveting account of the trial the night before, but also the "best interview" of 1924, which was with none other than Nathan Leopold, and it really paid off. The only entrant with a plethora of just-studied facts in his brain, Cronkite won the contest easily. Luck had something to do with it, but so did diligence, a quality that remained with him as a journalism trademark. The contest taught the valuable lesson that the first rule to being a top-flight journalist is being well informed about the world at large.

Cronkite's high school sweetheart was Cornelia "Bit" Winter, who was a year behind him at San Jacinto. Bit was an extremely popular girl. Her picture appeared in *The Houston Press* in October 1931: she was the recipient of an American Legion youth medal. With curled auburn hair, perfect teeth, and an actress's flare, Bit was irresistible to Cronkite. He held on to her after school as if she were the living embodiment of a Miss America trophy. Not only did they date, but they also hatched plans to perhaps get married someday. Every dollar Cronkite earned in high school doing odd jobs went to filling up his car at the Texas Company (Texaco) station at Main and Bremond and then taking

Bit out for blue-plate dinners. In Winter's scrapbook she scrawled next to a picture of Cronkite, "Tall, very Blonde—Good Dancer . . . Good date."

That spring, as Cronkite approached graduation from San Jacinto High—which would also count among its alumni racecar driver A. J. Foyt, heart transplant pioneer Dr. Denton Cooley, and future mayor of Houston Kathy Whitmire—he couldn't afford to buy a Balfour class ring. It was the only time he felt pitiful. All his buddies were showing theirs off during the last week of high school, but Cronkite's hand was bare. His mother tried to compensate by getting him a cheaper department-store ring with a black onyx stone in the middle.

Later in life, Cronkite used to joke that graduation was his favorite high school memory. Like many of the 425 graduates in San Jacinto's class of '33, he was desperate to cut his own swath in the world. However, Cronkite never lost touch with his high school friends, and they occupied a special place in his heart. Every five or ten years, he would return to Houston for reunions to swap stories over cocktails. Perhaps out of all the class of '33 reunions Cronkite attended, the fortieth was the most fun. Everybody swarmed around the famous anchorman. Like all class reunions, everybody was checking out who was the baldest, heaviest, sickest, and richest, and Cronkite was targeted for a lot of the class of '33 humor jabs; it was their job to keep his ego in its place. A special 1973 edition of the *Campus Cub*, in fact, lampooned Cronkite as "the only man alive who can shuffle one piece of paper." Former assistant principal E. C. "Gumshoe" Gates held court about all the trouble Cronkite had supposedly raised. (Nobody could believe he remembered.) In reality, Cronkite had been respected in high school. "I used to see him in the hall," recalled Fay Shoss, who was two years Cronkite's senior. "People used to point him out as the smartest person in the school."

The highlight of the evening, however, was when the class of '33 gave the Credibility Gap Award to "the man Americans are most likely to buy a used car from." The razzing continued until Cronkite, winner of the National Press Club's very first Fourth Estate Award for outstanding contributions in both electronic and print media, took the floor for rebuttal. "There's nothing I would like to have more," he said, looking at his new faux gift, "except the money that went into this award."

It was noticed at the fortieth reunion that Cronkite was one of the few class of '33 graduates still without a proper ring. This lingering Depression-era defi-cit was rectified in 2004 when he narrated the PBS documentary *Proud to Serve*, about soldiers in the U.S. Army. Executive producer Andrew Goldberg hoped to get Balfour to sponsor the documentary because the company manufactured jewelry for the U.S. military. Reminiscing about his Houston youth one afternoon, Cronkite had told Goldberg he'd been too poor to purchase a Balfour class ring back in 1933. "It was quite moving," Goldberg recalled. "He went on for a while about just how broke his mother had been."

A few days later, Goldberg acted on a brainstorm: he invited a top Balfour salesperson to visit Cronkite at his CBS office in New York. Cronkite was eighty-seven years old, but he was excited to talk about the history of Balfour rings, which dated from World War I. The company, to Cronkite's surprise, presented him with a San Jacinto class of '33 ring, with a journalism seal on one side and the *Campus Cub* logo on the other. A black onyx stone was affixed in the middle, to honor Cronkite's mother.

3.

Learning a Trade

ROAD TRIP TO THE CHICAGO WORLD'S FAIR—TV
HAM—STRUGGLING LONGHORN—THE FAILED MINING
ENGINEER—GOOD-BYE TO BIT—FREELANCING AND
BOOKIE JOINTS—THE CURTAIN CLUB—SPORTS HACK
WRITER—VANN KENNEDY AND THE ART OF INS
MENTORING—K.C. DREAMING—THE VOICE OF
KCMO—FAUX FOOTBALL—THE NATURAL CADENCE
OF EDWARD R. MURROW—HIDING BEHIND WALTER
WILCOX—HOT JAZZ IN K.C.—COURTING BETSY
MAXWELL—FIRED FOR HONESTY

Upon graduating from San Jacinto High in May
1933, Cronkite went on a road trip in a late-model
Dodge with Houston buddies to the Chicago World's

Fair (officially, "A Century of Progress International Exposition"). The fair's motto was "Science Finds, Industry Applies, Man Adapts," and it was held on 427 acres on the Near South Side of Chicago, along Lake Michigan. While Cronkite enjoyed hearing the Andrews Sisters sing live and studied dwellings in a "Homes of Tomorrow" exhibit, it was the "See Yourself on TV" interactive display that owned his enthusiasm.

Standing stationary in front of a new-fangled contraption called television—really just a twitching little screen—Cronkite looked into the camera and mugged by playing two clarinets at once like Benny Goodman gone mad. Besides his clowning around, all that was noticeable about Cronkite on the display screen was some Texas barber's idea of a haircut. "They were inviting people to come up and be on television," Cronkite recalled. "Naturally, being the ham I've always been, I stepped up immediately." This thirty seconds of World's Fair camera time allowed Cronkite to comically boast that he was on the Tube long before Murrow, Brinkley, Sevareid, or anybody else.

When it came time for college, Cronkite, to the surprise of his friends in Houston, enrolled at the University of Texas at Austin for the fall semester. Most of his classmates assumed he would attend the University of

Missouri at Columbia; his father had opened a dental practice in Kansas City. But Fred Birney had advised him that *The Daily Texan* was an amazing college newspaper. And he was officially a resident of Texas, not Missouri; this meant his UT tuition was far more affordable. Cronkite's father offered some financial support if his son went the economical UT route. The real kicker was that Bit Winter would be finishing high school in Houston. By going to UT, he could see his "darling" on weekends.

Cronkite entered the mining engineering program instead of journalism (now, to the surprise of friends, deemed an extracurricular "flirtation"). Like many Houstonians, he dreamed of huge fortunes in the oil industry. Everyone in Texas was always only a Spindletop away from shopping at Neiman Marcus. Cronkite, to his detriment, was prone to sleeping late and soon discovered that learning the intricacies of hydraulics, mineral determination, and blasting was a complex business. By October 1933 it was brutally apparent that the $E = mc^2$ physics in Professor C. Paul Boner's class was too complicated for Cronkite to master. In the ne'er-do-well fashion of youth, Cronkite preferred attending stadium-rattling Longhorn football games and Dixieland stomps à la the Duke Ellington Orchestra to dull science classes.

Instead of living in a dormitory, Cronkite moved into the Chi Phi fraternity house at 1704 West Avenue in Austin. It was the former home of Colonel Edward M. House, Woodrow Wilson's closest advisor. The editor of *The Daily Texan* was a Chi Phi named D. B. Hardeman. Cronkite became fast friends with him. Determined to be the big man on campus, Cronkite went to every social function imaginable, usually with Vance Muse Jr., a former classmate at San Jacinto High who now wrote a *The Daily Texan* column called "Musings." In letters to his mom, Cronkite boasted of dating popular girls from the Kappa Alpha Theta sorority, including Louise Rhea, "the campus big shot of Fort Worth," whom he brought to his fraternity's formal dance one year. Later in Cronkite's life the humorist Art Buchwald took exception to the anchorman's overdrawn boast of prowess with Longhorn women, claiming his friend graduated from the University of Texas a "magna cum virgin."

Life, however, threw Cronkite a real curve ball in the fall of 1933. Quite unexpectedly, Bit Winter was yanked out of San Jacinto High by her mother and relocated to Anna, Illinois. Cronkite was devastated. He had chosen the University of Texas, in part, to be near her. During the Great Depression, with commercial air transportation minimal, the 750-mile distance between Austin and Anna was insurmountable. So he and Bit resorted to letter writing, with dreams of wild summertime adventure exploring America.

Encouraged by his fraternity brothers at Chi Phi, where he cut a popular figure, Cronkite ran his only political race—for freshman class vice president. His campaign slogan read: "Freshmen, Vote for the New Deal Ticket. For President—GEORGE ATKINS of North Texas, Halfback of Football Team. For Vice-President—WALTER CRONKITE of South Texas, *Daily Texan* staff. FAIR—SQUARE—INDEPENDENT." His ticket was beaten badly. What made the election licking unbearable was that Joe Greenhill, a friend from San Jacinto High School and his Chicago trip companion, was the ballot box victor. Losing punctured Cronkite's whole big-man-on-campus façade. The only consolation he ever gleaned from the defeat was Greenhill's success later in life as chief justice of the Texas Supreme Court from 1972 to 1982.

It was quite understandable that Cronkite, as a UT freshman in the early 1930s, made a temporary divestiture (sort of) from journalism. To make it in the fourth estate you had to develop a brand identity like Arthur Brisbane, Heywood Broun, or Walter Lippmann. Getting paid by the word was a hard racket during the deep Depression years. Studying the communications industry—learning how to be a radio operator, for example—made only slightly more job market sense. When a popular gossip columnist such as Walter Winchell of the New York *Daily Mirror* took to radio, beginning his broadcast with "Good Evening, Mr. and Mrs. North America and all the ships at sea," it was clear that a global radio revolution was under way. A well-rounded knowledge of world affairs, it seemed, was a prerequisite for an aspiring broadcaster. Cronkite was too lackadaisical with his studies to rise quickly in journalism. He never learned a foreign language. The day-to-day monotony of applying himself was unappealing. If UT stood for anything to Cronkite, it was partying at the Chi Phi house. "I missed a lot of classes," Cronkite admitted. "I should have spent a lot more time there and concentrated more on my studies."

When corresponding with Bit and his mother, Cronkite wrote about Hell Week, pledge hazing, tennis matches, bull sessions at the O.P.K. restaurant, and sleep deprivation. His waning grades were an embarrassment. "I still want to be a journalist and hope to specialize in political analysis," he told his St. Joseph grandparents. "Therefore my college tendencies are toward government, economics, English, and journalism. I am experiencing great difficulty in staying on the beaten path that leads to a degree."

Getting to write newspaper articles now became Cronkite's primary focus. While most of his articles for *The Daily Texan* were of the calendar event kind, he did score a coup with an interview of Gertrude Stein at the Driskill Hotel, located at the corner of Brazos and Sixth Street. Accompanied by Alice B. Toklas, her famous partner, Stein was in town to give a public lecture. If one were to pick a high point of Cronkite's journalism career in the 1930s, it would be his profile "Miss Stein Not Out for Show, But Knows What She Knows." Cronkite took a real shine to Stein, who was dressed in a "mannish blouse, a tweed skirt, a peculiar but attractive vest, and comfortable-looking shoes." Calling Stein a "modern," Cronkite enthused that the famed author of *Three Lives* was a twentieth-century-thinking woman visiting a nineteenth-century-thinking Austin. "She is genuine," Cronkite reported after his forty-five-minute interview with Stein, "the real thing in person."

Using his *Campus Cub* and *Daily Texan* clippings as bait, Cronkite secured a job at *The Houston Press* freelancing articles. He wore a suit to work—soft fabric with a vest, a shining watch chain (set on Kansas City time) across his vest, and two-toned wingtips (never polished). Developing a keen interest in politics, Cronkite, in time, was freelancing well-crafted columns about campus life and the legislature to several other Texas newspapers. These papers paid a pittance (for one column in a local paper, he received ninety cents). Others didn't pay at all. But college cost money, while journalism actually paid him. Writing columns on Lone Star governmental issues for two struggling newspapers was a start. It provided spending money for dating and drinking, hoots and sing-alongs.

From then on Cronkite focused on learning the gritty trade of journalism in a hands-on, tangible way, even as he took UT courses. But it didn't pay much. When a mysterious Mr. Fox offered him $75 a week (more than his father made as a dentist) to announce horse races at a bookie joint, he seized the opportunity. With piles of money at stake, it was a dangerous mob-related job. The sawdust-floor Texas establishment smelled of smoke and rye. Spurring horses toward the finish line out of a megaphone, he made acquaintance with shady characters—gamblers, swindlers, drunks, and con men. "Well, I'd never been in a place like this before, so I gave them the real Graham McNamee approach on this, described the running of the race and all," Cronkite recalled. "A mean character ran this place—a guy named Fox . . . came chasing into the room and asked me, 'What the hell do you think you're doing? We don't want entertainment! We just want the facts!' "

As Cronkite admitted about his Chicago World's Fair TV debut, he was a bit of a ham, a jocular egotist wanting to please and show off in front of adoring crowds. Unfortunately, people simply didn't see Cronkite as he saw himself. While he aspired to be the leading man in a UT Curtain Club production, he was instead cast as the stodgy, middle-aged university president born into squarely bourgeois circumstances. Cronkite considered himself a colorful card, even dashing; other people thought of him as the embodiment of Mr. Beige. During the play rehearsals that went on from 7:00 p.m. to midnight, Cronkite learned that to his peers he was a rather muted and mundane classmate.

What Cronkite came to understand, even in the improvident rush of those college days, was that he'd never become a Broadway or Hollywood star. He tacitly abandoned the stage in favor of a communications field in which everyone was then an adventurer. Broadcast radio was entering its own golden age during the Great Depression, with live programming on local stations all through the day. Stations needed singers, musicians, announcers, and whipcord personalities, along with Christian clergy for prayers and pundits on world affairs. Each local U.S. radio station created a carnival in its studio. The four preeminent radio networks—CBS, Mutual, NBC Blue, and NBC Red—provided regional or national programming in the evenings. Cronkite's best asset in 1934 was a budding reputation as something of an authority on sports—a boon in tackle-hard Texas. Years later he recalled that he failed his freshman engineering class at UT in part because he couldn't fathom the workings of a pulley. Yet he had a steel-trap memory for football rosters, baseball box scores, and horse racing numbers.

Scrambling for cash to stay afloat on his own in 1935, Cronkite was hired by KNOW, a major AM radio station in Austin, as "the man who gets behind the campus news." It was a heady prospect, since he would be not merely a reporter but the "talent"—earning a dollar a day. The fact that Cronkite landed the job at KNOW, whose studio was in an alley behind Sixth Street, without any real radio experience indicated that he could sell himself. Later, the station asked him to write and read a sports report every Tuesday and Friday at 5:15 p.m. As an added perk he got to drink free 3.2 percent beer. In his memoir, *A Reporter's Life*, Cronkite writes eloquently of how incredible it was to be alive in the "crystal days" of radio reading the Western Union baseball score ticker. "One could tell a wireless faddist," Cronkite recalled. "He or she was the one whose eyes were rimmed with dark circles from having stayed up all night when reception was best, bringing in distant stations."

At KNOW, Cronkite was shackled by the same conundrum that faced all radio at the time: corroborating facts was difficult. His boss, Harfield Weedin—later to become the general manager of Lady Bird Johnson's Austin radio station, KTBC, and then West Coast head of CBS Radio—warned Cronkite of misusing the airwaves with erroneous babble. Nevertheless, Cronkite was expected to read aloud sports scores with flare even though he didn't have the actual play-by-play color at his disposal. Because the wire services wouldn't pay for access to these game results, Cronkite had to be cunning and resourceful. A local Austin tobacconist, who encouraged patrons to linger in the shop and smoke, paid for a ticker service to provide up-to-date box scores, and Cronkite furtively looked at the ticker and memorized the teams, the scores, and the highlights for his broadcasts later. His modus operandi for collecting sports stories had its banana republic side, but it worked. Later in the year, the CBS network would form its own news service, organizing news sources, reporters, and stringers around the country. Radio news gathering was getting streamlined.

In the spring semester of 1935, after two years at the University of Texas, Cronkite dropped out. At the time, college was still considered a luxury, not a birthright, and given Walter's steadily diminished return, the family couldn't afford his UT tuition. He had squandered the opportunity to be a college-educated man. Antsy beyond words, Cronkite also didn't have the patience to sit still in UT classes. He preferred toiling in the newspaper field full-time, but later in life he told his daughter Kathy that he was embarrassed because he hadn't earned a degree at UT. Kathy pointed out that without a college diploma he had nevertheless become the best TV broadcaster in American history. "Yes," Cronkite shot back, "but if I had gotten a formal education, I could have been the Kaiser!"

Becoming a first-rate print reporter was more a pleasant daydream than a burning ambition for Cronkite in the mid-1930s. The newspaper industry that Cronkite entered looked primarily to one of the wire services—led by the Associated Press and the United Press—to obtain general news. The Hearst Corporation's International News Service (INS) was the third largest. What Cronkite soon learned about the fiercely competitive wire service industry held true for all journalism enterprises: internal corporate policy and budget requirements shaped the direction of news coverage.

The idea behind AP, founded in 1846, was that this association of newspapers would sometimes share reporting and otherwise underwrite the cost of gathering news in bureaus around the country and the world. The influence of the AP was tremendous, and its slant eastern and conservative.

Edward W. Scripps founded the United Press in 1907 as, in his words, "the people's news source," and any paper could buy its service—even those that were subscribers to AP. The United Press never grew quite as big as AP, but its brilliant reporting from Europe during World War I gave it a reputation for high standards. By the time Cronkite entered the newspaper field in the mid-1930s, the general feeling was that AP was a more prestigious place to work, but it was just a journalism job. By contrast, UP, where resources were thin, was sold to cub reporters as a sacred calling.

Cronkite's big Austin break came when Vann M. Kennedy of Corpus Christi hired him in 1934 to write stories for the Austin bureau of INS, in a small office "up with the pigeons" on the press wing of the state capitol. An Alabaman by birth, the stiff-necked Kennedy was a gifted mentor. An advocate of objective journalism, Kennedy, an expert wire transmitter, was fact-driven and judicious, believing that reporting was a dignified occupation. "I learned the principles of great journalism from him," Cronkite said, "because he lived them." As an assistant reporter, Cronkite was basically a gofer at INS. But Kennedy, wanting him to earn his medals, refusing to offer a soft landing, also assigned him the heady job of covering Texas government. Kennedy represented intelligent and principled journalism to Cronkite. "I have never found anything I like so much as working at the Capitol," Cronkite wrote in a letter home. "I go down a little after ten and work until one. . . . This week I met nearly all the Houston members of the legislature and worked the Teletype machine."

At INS Cronkite learned how to write in an adjective-free way and how to send a wire report. Journalism wasn't a conceit to Cronkite—it was a trade with stature, a concrete way to earn money in the Great Depression. Under Kennedy's watchful eye, Cronkite was taught how to get a story, how to write it, and how "ethics" mattered most of all. Competing head-on, the wire services undoubtedly made one another hungrier, and news in America stronger. Day in and day out, AP, UP, and INS raced one another for scoops with fanatical energy, commitment, and concentration. The battle for stories was brutal. The industry was not for the timid. Only an instinctive counterpuncher could prevail, one with a tough hide and a knack for making correct split-second judgments to scoop people. Cronkite of INS, patching together a living as a freelance writer in Austin, competed with the major wire services. "The columns to weekly papers over the state concerning the Capitol doings fell through," he wrote home. "It seems that those who are able to support such a column already get weekly Associated Press or United Press columns for a very nominal sum."

After a year at INS, Cronkite was hired as a rewrite man by *The Houston Press*, which was owned by Scripps Howard. He moved to Houston's Montrose neighborhood to live with his mother. "Hours," he wrote a friend soon after moving back to Houston, "7 a.m. to 3 p.m., salary, $15 per week. My duties consist of taking stories over the phone and whipping them into shape." The *Press* also asked Cronkite to organize the morgue (the newspaper archives). As a born bon vivant and lover of jazz, Cronkite soon owned the nightclub beat in Houston and Galveston Island—a truly great job for a hot-to-trot single man looking for a girlfriend. His journalism about music revues and movies was third-rate. And he drank too much whiskey.

When Cronkite wasn't judging the rollicking night-life in Galveston, he covered the sedate Methodist and

Baptist church news for the *Press*. For the first time he read the Bible with a sense of true understanding. He wasn't writing political analysis yet, as he had hoped, but then, he wasn't yet twenty. Time was on his side. He was generally happy with his *Press* work. But being desk-bound meant that "the poor old wanderluster"—himself—had no "means of wanderlusting." With a fedora on his head, scrawny as a ship mouse, trying to grow a pencil-thin mustache to look older, he repeatedly begged his editor for an oceangoing vessel assignment, with the promise that he would write fun articles about the Caribbean. *The Houston Press* wasn't interested—and in truth, even Cronkite wasn't that adventurous when push came to shove. In the summer of 1934, for his first paid vacation, he didn't book passage on a freighter out of Galveston to Jamaica, but went to Anna, Illinois, to see Bit Winter; the visit proved disastrous.

The saga of Bit Winter had turned sordid for Cronkite. During the summer of 1934 he learned that she had been two-timing him. Just weeks after Cronkite began his sophomore year, Bit, who had graduated from high school in Anna, married twenty-year-old H. E. Hunskaker. To break the news, the new Mrs. Hunskaker wrote Walter a letter about the surprise marriage. Chi Phi pledge Woody Williams told Cronkite, who had been at a college lecture by folklorist

J. Frank Dobie, that a letter from Anna was waiting for him at the frat house. Cronkite practically floated home to get it; he soon turned ill. "The old breath went out, the heart skipped a beat and sank as I read the parenthesized Mrs. H. E. Hunskaker," Cronkite wrote her back. "And as I delved into the contents of the letter I had a million different sensations ranging from depths of sadness, which really prevailed throughout, to the heights of happiness that I imagined I was sharing with you." Cronkite, in the same letter, went on to write a long, rambling, brokenhearted missive that read like a Hank Williams lyric. Bit had implied that he drank too much, and now, defending himself in a dust storm of temperance, he promised never again to "touch a drop." It was all in vain. By letter's end, Cronkite, recognizing that he had lost her heart, offered a melancholic good-bye. "Keep up the smoking though and maybe, when you're in a reminiscent mood, you'll see old Walt in those smoke rings and I can and will be seeing you in my dreams," he wrote. "Please don't forget me Bit. But don't feel under any obligation to write. I will understand."

Cronkite was beyond devastated. His stomach regularly did flips. He couldn't study. His heartbreak knew no bounds. He worried that his relations with women in general were vexed. After the fall semester, during the Christmas hiatus, Cronkite finally came to terms with the betrayal. Free of foul humor, he wrote Bit, expressing hope they could remain special friends. Bit filed for divorce in 1935. Cronkite once again had a flicker of hope that she could be his wife. But instead of marrying Cronkite, in a fever she married the ambitious Illinois lawyer John Paul Davis. Cronkite, playing the fool, had been stiffed again.

Although Cronkite never earned a degree from the University of Texas, completing only two years of classes before quitting in 1935, he considered himself an alumnus. Hook 'Em Horns forever. Because *The Daily Texan* had allowed him to write feature stories as a budding reporter, he remained beholden to the university once he made it big at CBS News. UT's burnt orange and white colors were his coat of arms. In the 1990s, he lent his signature voice, pro bono, to a whole host of public service announcements promoting the university. If you attended a Longhorn sporting event, you'd see the huge face of Cronkite suddenly appear on the Jumbotron, making appeals for financial support for UT. On a couple of occasions, asked who his best friend was, Cronkite would jokingly name Bevo, the university's Longhorn mascot.

But Cronkite's UT boosterism had its limits. He was a Texan by adoption only. Given a choice, he always claimed he was a Missourian first and foremost. During his later journalism career, Cronkite traveled to more than fifty countries, but he tended to keep his pocket watch on Kansas City time. Throughout his life, he romanticized the City of Fountains, and in 2000 he emceed Kansas City's 150th birthday celebration before a sold-out crowd at Arrowhead Stadium with rock 'n' roller Little Richard as cohost. Cronkite concurred with something painter Thomas Hart Benton once wrote about Kansas City people: "I have not met a really complete ass among them."

In May 1936, Cronkite drove from Austin to Kansas City to visit family. *The Houston Press* gave him two weeks off. His plan was to visit his father and have a secret rendezvous with the married Bit in Illinois, hoping she'd dump number two. But the scheme—chasing after a married woman—left him feeling duplicitous. While in Kansas City, Cronkite, without moral compunction, was drawn to the previously forbidden Twelfth Street music clubs. He had inherited his father's penchant for drink.

Cronkite was leisurely reading *The Kansas City Star* on the front porch of his grandparents' home on May 13, 1936, his eyelids heavy from a hangover, when an article caught his eye. It reported that a license had been granted to the new owners of the local radio station, KWKC, to begin broadcasting under a different set of call letters, KCMO (as in "K.C., Mo."). Despite Cronkite's steady job at *The Houston Press*, the item reignited his old interest in broadcast news and tempted him to take another crack at radio. As Cronkite perused the article, one name jumped out at him—Tom Evans, a family friend. This was his gold-star opportunity to enter the wireless medium.

KWKC had struggled since it went on the air in 1925. It had a weaker signal than other local stations, and so had trouble finding an audience. By 1932, a distant fourth among Kansas City's four commercial radio stations, it was forced to reduce its broadcast hours. And two years later the Internal Revenue Service (IRS) seized the station in lieu of back taxes. But at the beginning of 1936, as the article reported, three businessmen made an offer to purchase KWKC; one of them was Tom Evans, a principal in the city's Crown drugstore chain. At first the Federal Communications Commission (FCC), which regulated broadcasting, was in no hurry to approve the transfer of ownership from the IRS. So Evans asked Missouri first-term senator Harry Truman to sit in on a meeting with representatives of the IRS and the FCC. Evans had known Truman, who was from nearby Independence, since they ran retail stores in the same northside K.C.

neighborhood and attended KCDO meetings. Evans wasn't asking Truman to do anything unethical, only to help untangle the red tape in the two government agencies that had stalled the deal.

The nineteen-year-old Cronkite knew a good ride when he saw it. KCMO could be a fast-moving station in a growing industry. Because it was still at the bottom of the heap in Kansas City, it would probably have room for a fellow like him—especially if that fellow had an "in" with Tom Evans. Dr. Cronkite had attended the Kansas City College of Pharmacy at the same time as Evans's father. With things starting to fall into place, Cronkite canceled his visit with Bit (she would die a year later in a car crash). Full of excitement, he reported his big radio break to his mother in Houston. "Yesterday I went to K.C.M.O., a new station in the Commerce Trust Building and was given an audition," he enthused. "The program director, a Mr. Simmons, handed me some stuff to read. He stood in the other room listening over the amplifying system and when I had finished he came dashing into the studio, grabbed my arm and said, 'Come on, we're going to see the manager.' We got into the manager's office and Simmons said, 'Here is a man with the best radio voice I've heard in my years of radio.' "

During the following week, the station manager formally hired Cronkite. His strong yet relaxed voice would earn him twenty-five dollars per week, ten dollars more than *The Houston Press* had been paying him as a cub reporter and rewrite man. Knowing firsthand just how hard it was to research, write, rewrite, and edit—and then re-edit—a single article for a newspaper, Cronkite was intrigued to be in the more modern stream of media, in which he would be paid just to talk. Technically, he had applied for a job as a newsman—a role that barely existed in local radio at the time. News reporters scoffed that radio commentators were expositors of fact at best, prose thieves at worst. Joining the Ringling Bros. or entering into vaudeville was considered nobler work than radio. Newspaper journalists crashed through daunting obstacles to find the truth and confirm facts. To be a newspaper reporter—whether trained at college or in the school of hard knocks at an obituary desk—was to uphold high standards of clarity, accuracy, and objectivity that had made newspapers "the fourth estate" across America, and an adjunct to decent democratic government.

Radio news, by contrast, had no standards (except that curse words were verboten on the air). The new medium seemed rudderless and gimmicky in terms of integrity to something other than filling airspace. In radio, men with velvety baritones could earn a living by repeating news purloined from the daily paper, boiled down into two or three declarative sentences. By the most generous calculation, radio news was only fifteen years old in 1936, when KCMO had its license upgraded to increase its broadcasting range. A more steely analysis would conclude that in terms of news gathering, radio had yet to arrive. Later in life, Cronkite was asked what his greatest achievement was in his long, storied broadcasting career; his answer was "helping establish . . . news standards."

The hearty and pleasant Cronkite went on air at KCMO in 1936 with a modulated voice that was, if not quite velvety, surprisingly rich for a man his age. Having that airtime experience in Austin had proved helpful. And with a slight staccato-like delivery, as if typing out the news while talking, he was *very* distinctive.

Just as Cronkite was getting going on K.C. radio, executive vice president of CBS News Edward Klauber hired twenty-nine-year-old Edward R. Murrow as "Director of Talks" (which meant that he would arrange for scientists and scholars to broadcast on the radio for fifteen minutes on Sundays). Realizing that his clear voice was a resonant asset, Murrow, who had been studying elocution since college at Washington State in Pullman, majoring in speech, wanted a broadcasting career. Late in 1936 the young executive received permission from Klauber to step behind the microphone and deliver a news broadcast. At the time, the CBS network was not much more sophisticated than struggling KCMO in Kansas City: broadcasts consisted of a few lines for each story, with no original reporting or remote feeds. Murrow was nervous enough to solicit private coaching from Robert Trout, a North Carolinan with a dozen years of experience in radio. Unflappable in the extreme, Trout had taken to radio easily, and he tried to impart the importance of a natural cadence to the budding Murrow.

Murrow was assigned to Europe by CBS to broadcast cultural events such as Viennese waltzes and German operas. In March 1938, CBS journalist William L. Shirer told Murrow that the expected *Anschluss*, Hitler's annexation of Austria, had begun. German troops were pouring over the border. Springing to action, Murrow flew first to Berlin, then chartered a twenty-seven-seat Lufthansa transport at great expense to get to ground zero: Vienna. Taking a streetcar from the airport to downtown Vienna, he described on a shortwave radio the sacking of the Austrian city perched along the Danube River. On March 13, with Cronkite listening in Kansas City, Murrow broadcast his dramatic report from Austria for American listeners' edification. It was a leap into grown-up reality:

> *This is Edward Murrow speaking from Vienna. It's now nearly 2:30 in the morning and Herr Hitler has not yet arrived. No one seems to know just when he will get here, but most people expect him sometime after ten o'clock tomorrow. . . . I arrived here by air from Warsaw and Berlin only a few hours ago. From the air, Vienna didn't look much different than it had before, but nevertheless it's changed . . . they lift the right arm a little higher here than in Berlin and the "Heil Hitler" is said a little more loudly . . .*

Up until that Murrow broadcast, the most illustrious voice Cronkite knew was NBC's Lowell Thomas, an old boyhood hero. Murrow's *Anschluss* report turned Cronkite inside out like a sock. For the first time, Cronkite started listening regularly to CBS News. The whole CBS News "Round-up" crowd—from William L. Shirer in London, to Edgar Ansel Mowrer in Paris, to Pierre Huss in Berlin, to Frank Gervasi in Rome, to the indomitable Robert Trout everywhere—were major discoveries to Cronkite. How did CBS News present real-time history in the making with such dramatic flair? The tumultuous events in Europe were being routed via a shortwave transmitter in Berlin, onward to London, then to New York and straight to the American heartland.

Generally, radio news in 1936, during the lull between the two wars, was synonymous with such diligent and dapper men as Trout. He happened to be a good newsman, but first he had been a voice. A mesmerizing voice: that was the only thing that radio offered over newspapers at the time. Cronkite had, for all intents and purposes, abandoned print journalism—*Houston Press* style—for wireless entertainment. At first, talking to the microphone was fun for Cronkite. His star turn each week lay in broadcasting sporting events without seeing them. That was the accepted sleight-of-hand of radio, first learned in Texas bookie joints. Cronkite, fast on his feet, mastered the art of what he called "reconstructed games."

During the fall of 1936, Cronkite, broadcasting under the fictional name Walter Wilcox (Cronkite sounded too German), sat in the KCMO studio every Saturday and received via Western Union telegraph a running description of a preselected college football game. Cronkite had to rely on a nimble mind and a tireless imagination to create a fully believable and exciting live broadcast. Listeners were informed at intervals that the broadcast was a re-creation based on wire reports, yet Cronkite continued to hone the masquerade of play-by-play broadcasts. It was fake sports announcing by a fake Walter Wilcox. Four words on the ticker were turned into a solid minute of description over the radio. It was exactly the opposite of his work during the week, when he turned long newspaper articles into three- or four-sentence news briefs for the radio. "I didn't need many facts," Cronkite told *The Oklahoman* in 2002. "I just used my imagination."

Cronkite's KCMO sports broadcast re-creations were successful, even if the station was still by far the weakest on the Kansas City radio dial. The proof came when an official from the FCC told the station to increase the number of advisories that the broadcast was not actually live, but a re-creation from telegraph reports.

After Cronkite relocated to Kansas City, his mother returned there to be near her son. Walter didn't live with her, instead taking an apartment with his KCMO coworker Harry Bailey. Cronkite explored local bars and jazz haunts, sometimes with Bailey, who wrote commercials at KCMO. The waitresses at the

Chesterfield Club were naked, though that was not entirely uncommon in the clubs, where serving drinks and prostitution were often blended into one profession. At Chesterfield's, the waitresses' pubic hair was shaved to reflect the suits in a deck of cards: clubs and spades for the African American waitresses, hearts and diamonds for the Caucasian ones. That innovation seemed almost innocent when compared with the scheduled onstage sexual performances, at some clubs, that might feature any combination of humans—and animals. "The joints were shoulder-to-shoulder, and there wasn't any closing hour," Cronkite recalled. "There were girls in most, transvestites in a few and, the street's real glory, great jazz in many. . . . If there was anything comparable in Houston, it had certainly escaped my attention. I was nineteen when I hit Kansas City. The visits to Twelfth Street and the brief associations with its denizens helped me grow up in a hurry."

Soon after starting at the radio station in early 1936, having finally worked Bit Winter out of his emotional system, Cronkite met a beautiful young advertising copywriter at KCMO. Mary Elizabeth "Betsy" Maxwell was a recent graduate of the University of Missouri School of Journalism in Columbia. Cronkite couldn't take his eyes off her when she glided into the station. Although he wanted to flirt with Betsy, he was tongue-tied by her comeliness. "I watched her coming down the hall," he later recalled, "and I was stricken, absolutely stricken." But Betsy could feel Cronkite's gaze, and reciprocated with a smile worthy of Veronica Lake. "It was," she recalled, "love at first sight for both of us." The two began dating a few days later, and within months they were seriously considering marriage. "Betsy and I went from the studio to lunch, from lunch to dinner," Cronkite wrote, "and from KCMO through life together."

Betsy was bright, feisty, and rapt with words. A native of Kansas City, she was, in the parlance of the time, a *looker*. At the University of Missouri, while earning As in journalism courses, she became runner-up in the campus election of Agriculture Queen. About five foot four, with a lithe, nimble figure, slightly pale, with large eyes and a profusion of curl-ironed hair, Betsy exuded a girl-next-door allure. Blessed with a wicked sense of humor and the gift of putting everyone at ease, she was the unusual combination of homespun sweet and scorpion sting. After graduation, she took the job at KCMO, but her goal was to join the staff of a newspaper. The first time Walter and Betsy bonded was when they were co-reading a radio commercial script for the Richard

Hudnut Corporation, a cosmetics company. They performed together on air, selling makeup, courtesy of a come-on written by Betsy:

Cronkite: "Hello, Angel. What heaven did you drop from?"

Maxwell: "I'm not an angel."

Cronkite: "Well you look like an angel."

Maxwell: "That's because I use Richard Hudnut."

By the beginning of 1937, Betsy had found a new job, writing features for the women's page at the *Kansas City Journal-Post*, a lot of local-color copy on quilting bees and library functions. The paper was teetering on the edge of bankruptcy, but Betsy was pleased to be a "woman's section" writer. Before long she was assigned to write the "advice to the lovelorn" column. The future Mrs. Cronkite joked that she wasn't old enough to *read* some of the rather revealing letters sent into the paper, let alone to provide counsel on the problems. Betsy kept dating Walter, who was irresistibly attractive, but not handsome. "He used to be such a string bean," she recalled of their courting days, "that my mother insisted on having us over for dinner all the time to fatten him up. Also, for many years he wore his hair slicked back, as was the fashion—but it wasn't extremely flattering."

While Cronkite's love life was on the upswing, his professional life hit a roadblock. One day the wife of his boss, Jim Simmons, called the station to report that three firemen had been killed in a blaze in her neighborhood. Simmons rushed to Cronkite's desk, saying, "Get on the air with a flash! The new city hall is on fire, and three firemen just jumped to their deaths!" Cronkite, full of protestations and litanies, insisted on checking the facts himself with the fire department by telephone.

"You don't have to check on it," Simmons snapped at Cronkite. "My wife called and told me."

"I do too have to check on it," Cronkite said, remembering the fundamentals of journalism instilled in him at San Jacinto High, *The Houston Press*, and INS.

"Are you calling my wife a liar?" a ticked-off Simmons asked the young Lone Star hotshot.

"No," Cronkite said, evoking the Standard Model of Professional Journalism. "I'm not calling your wife a liar, but I don't know the details."

Simmons was now livid. "I've told you the details. The new city hall building's on fire, and three firemen have jumped."

With Cronkite resolutely refusing to go on air, Simmons, in a temperamental snit, headed to the microphone himself. Playing the fool, he went on the KCMO airwaves ad-libbing a breaking news bulletin about the supposedly burned firemen. Cronkite's sleuthing subsequently proved that the fire had been minor. There were no deaths. Nevertheless, the next day, Cronkite was summarily fired by the ego-bruised Simmons. Cronkite felt betrayed, clubbed over the head with the farce. "They felt," Cronkite recalled, "that I was getting a little bit too big for my britches."

This unsettling fire incident might have precipitated the split with KCMO, but it probably wasn't the only source of friction. Once the glamour of radio wore off—such as it was at a weak, 100-watt midwestern station—Cronkite began to chafe at the shallow radio version of events that passed for news. Even though he was unsure how his bills would get paid, he was relieved to be out of KCMO, uncontaminated by Simmons. With a snort of contempt, he remained proud of getting fired for refusing to go live without first triple-sourcing for confirmation of the fire's reality. And he got the last laugh. When Cronkite died in 2009, one blog told the story of how KCMO canned, for being ethical, the broadcaster who became the Most Trusted Man in America. The headline of the post was "KCMO: Stupid Enough to Fire Cronkite, Downhill Ever Since."

4.

Making of a Unipresser

UP TRADITION—NEWS AS COMMODITY—MISSOURI
METHOD OF JOURNALISM—THE WELL-PRESSED JOHN
CAMERON SWAYZE—TEXAS SCHOOL EXPLOSION—
PHONE BOOTH REPORTING FOR CBS—ACTION
ADDICT—WKY SOONERS SPORTSCASTER—LEARNING
TO AD-LIB—FLYING LOW WITH BRANIFF—MESSRS.
SMITH AND SEVAREID GO TO EUROPE—BEGGING FOR
THE UP JOB—THE HIGH-ALTITUDE KIDNAPPING
CAPER—SPELLBOUND BY MURROW—HITLER'S
RAMPAGE—POISED FOR WAR

After three months of uneasy post-KCMO unemployment, Cronkite gladly accepted a job as night editor with the Kansas City office of the United Press.

Located at the intersection of East Twenty-second and Oak Street, just two blocks from a burlesque joint, the UP bureau wasn't much more than a garret with typewriters, Teletype machines, and a water cooler. Cronkite was elated to be a Unipresser, as UP's wire service reporters were called. The *Chicago Tribune* got it right when it called UP a "scrappy alternative" to AP. UP's fighting underdog attitude fit Cronkite's indefatigable personality to a tee.

Unipressers such as Cronkite knew how to stretch a dollar, cheat a pay phone, use rented typewriters, and sleep in the backseat of a broken-down Ford instead of squandering money on a motel room. Unipressers were preternaturally hungry for scoops to sell to newspapers. At all times, UP tried to break news first, not just to beat AP, but all other media as well. In 1914, UP was the first to use the Teletype (invented that year), and in the 1930s it was the first to develop the International Unifax machine (the pioneering automatic picture receiver). Most important for Cronkite's career trajectory, UP, starting in 1935, was the first major news service to offer breaking news to radio stations. Before long, UP, a worldwide news wholesaler headed by a dynamic general manager, Roy Howard, also became the first North American news agency to offer wire service to newspapers in Europe, South America, and the Far East.

In *Fortune* magazine (May 1933), the artiste Stephen Vincent Benét explained the religious devotion Unipressers had to their company. "It is a business concern and its members work for profit," Benét wrote. "But there is another motive that drives them quite as strongly. You can call it pride of profession or professional zest or enthusiasm or self-hypnosis. But, whatever you call it, it is as common to the stockholding executives as to the lunch-money copy boy—it is indeed the strongest bond that holds U.P. together. And what it boils down to, when the sentiment and the wisecracks are both skimmed off, is an actual genuine love of the game."

A young Unipresser such as Cronkite, outposted in Missouri, had to dream of big national bylines. He had been jobless long enough to bring a new level of dedication to his UP work. Kansas City was his proving ground. With constant pressure to provide content for thousands of newspapers, especially in the Midwest, Cronkite found himself reporting, fact-checking, rewriting, editing, and even generating story ideas from his UP bureau desk. Although an individual newspaper, such as the *Kansas City Journal-Post* (where Betsy worked), naturally reflected a particular point of view—that of the locality, as the editors saw it—at a UP office, news was a commodity. When a major story hit Missouri or Kansas, the staff had to scramble to cover it, preferably with greater speed and style than the competing Associated Press or local reporters. Likewise, when mundane events occurred, UP still had to provide news of all types: from eye-catching headlines to incidental squibs to box scores to garden club announcements to instant obituaries. UP was in the wholesale business, and the marketplace didn't lie. Newspapers, Cronkite learned, voted allegiance with the amount of space accorded to UP-originated material. His reputation would be made by how many "Cronkite" stories sold per week.

A harmful trend to which the advent of the AP and UP wire services contributed was the decline of daily newspapers (or, as Max Lerner plugged it in *America as a Civilization*, the "thinning of the pipelines of communication" from coast to coast). In 1909, when Theodore Roosevelt was president, there were 2,600 daily newspapers operating in America. By the time Franklin Roosevelt was in the White House during the Great Depression, that number had been reduced to 1,750. An argument can be made, in fact, that the wire service led to many cities no longer having competing newspapers. To the detriment of America, news was getting streamlined into two main pipelines: UP and AP.

Kansas City in the year 1938 still had two fine newspapers: the *Star* and the *Journal-Post*; Cronkite intellectually gravitated to the second because of personal friendships. A lot of Betsy Maxwell's classmates from the University of Missouri–Columbia, it turned out, had worked on the *Columbia Missourian* in college and ended up at the *Journal-Post* after graduation. These budding Missouri reporters became lifelong friends of the Cronkites. Both Walter and Betsy were exposed to what was known as the "Missouri Method" of journalism: hands-on reporting in real-world local media market outlets, a kind of provincial baptism by fire that characterized the Missouri School of Journalism, the oldest J-school in the world. John Cameron Swayze was then a young columnist at the *Journal-Post*—he would become one of Cronkite's closest friends.

Though Swayze was perceived as a handsome dandy by NBC News viewers in the 1950s, Cronkite knew that Swayze was a true reporter at heart. The *Journal-Post* newsroom was just across a stairwell corridor in the same downtown building where UP rented offices. Almost daily, as Cronkite was punching out from his night shift, he'd bump into the meticulously groomed Swayze, with a pocket-square in his suit jacket, racing to make airtime (he had a 7:00 a.m. radio news show). Cronkite would hand Swayze the UP news copy, placed in metal-ringed notebooks, for him to speed-read before broadcast. He would sit at his desk and read over

Cronkite's tight UP copy, barely having time for a gulp of coffee. Then Cronkite, with amazement, would watch as the broadcast light went on and a suddenly cool and collected Swayze performed flawlessly. "Good morning, John Cameron Swayze here with the news from the *Kansas City Journal-Post* city room. Today . . ."

When Cronkite joined UP, he brought with him a good two years of Texas news-gathering experience, checkered though it was. He eagerly volunteered to substitute for vacationing editors and reporters in other UP offices around the region, a form of training that exposed him to other cities and, more important, to colleagues with a wide range of talents and tips. Such assignments, usually in the southeasterly direction, down secondary blacktop roads from the Ozarks to the Rio Grande Valley, kept Cronkite away from Kansas City for two- or three-week stretches. Betsy Maxwell, busy with her own career at the *Journal-Post*, was patient, although Walter's out-of-state absences to Oklahoma, Arkansas, and Texas severely tested their courtship.

Two months after starting at UP, Cronkite was assigned to work at the Dallas bureau for a brief spell, on loan from the Kansas City desk. On March 18, 1937, at 3:05 p.m. on a beautiful spring day, Cronkite was at his Dallas desk when there was a natural gas explosion at a consolidated public school in New London, Texas, causing 295 deaths, a majority of them children. A gas leak at the two-story school, a steel-formed building only a couple of years old, had caused a bomblike detonation that blew the edifice to kingdom come. Balls of rolling gas shot into the Texas sky like a fiery orange tornado and caused the ground to shake for miles around.

The area around New London—located in the northwest corner of Rusk County—was surrounded by ten thousand oil derricks; eleven had been fatally erected on school grounds. Governor James Allred called up the Texas Rangers, Texas Highway Patrol, and the Texas National Guard to pull out bruised and battered survivors. The New London boom's echo, it was said, had been heard a hundred miles away, in the stockyards of Fort Worth. Some students miraculously walked out of the rubble unscathed, dazed and confused but spared serious injuries.

Cronkite received a dispatch from the Houston UP bureau confirming the explosion, and off he raced in his Dodge to New London with Bill Baldwin, the manager of the UP bureau in Dallas. Just how horrific the tragedy was became vividly apparent when he saw a line of cars, ambulances, and trucks parked at the funeral home in Tyler, all unloading corpses. Makeshift morgues had been erected in Henderson, Kilgore, and Overton to accommodate the dead.

Cronkite flashed a United Press badge for access to the disaster zone. He hitched a ride on a fire department searchlight vehicle that had just arrived from Beaumont to help out in the impending nighttime rescue efforts. Cronkite searched for eyewitnesses who saw the school's roof blow off. "It is not easy," Cronkite quickly learned, "to approach someone in such distress to seek answers to the questions that need asking."

Nothing in his University of Texas journalism classes or the Missouri Method had prepared Cronkite for *this story*. Oil roughnecks had rushed to New London from the Permian Basin to look for lost children, to collect the charred and crushed bodies of the young. Cronkite's harrowing eyewitness UP features offered emotional images of what the reporter saw—and yet kept the reporter out of the articles. His eye for ironic detail—such as a surviving school wall with a blackboard on which someone had written, "Oil and natural gas are East Texas' greatest mineral blessings"—was superb. One of his UP reports read, in part, as follows:

OVERTON, TEX., MAR. 19 [1937]—(UP)

Take oil from this town and nothing would be left. The last census showed its population to be a little more than 500 yet 3,000 persons receive their mail at the general post office.

It is the capital of the East Texas oil field, the richest in the world, whose forest of derricks stretch [sic] 90 miles across the Texas hills on a line one to 15 miles wide.

Week days, its few streets are dotted by the toughest migratory workers in the world—the men who go from field to field where oil is gushing, who work hard and dangerously and live hard and gaily.

Saturday night, dressed in their silk shirts and pleated trousers, a week's pay in their pockets, the men come in for what diversions the town affords. They are strong men and hard men.

Today they were in town on another mission and beneath the flamboyant shirts, knotted shoulder muscles bent beneath unseen weights. Faces were heavy-jawed and screwed tensely.

They stood about in small knots, looking not into passing faces but toward their feet. They gathered at the curbs. From a distance they seemed to be chatting. But closer, the passerby heard men weep, heard rasp-like voices oddly strained in unaccustomed efforts to be tender.

Decades later, even after he was credited with helping end the Vietnam War, Cronkite called the New London tragedy his most memorable reporting assignment. Sleeping at the Overton Hotel, calling CBS

Radio News in New York from a pay phone to offer a nationwide listening audience a detailed eyewitness report, Cronkite earned his spurs that sad March week. Fifty years later—on March 18, 1987—reporter Harry Smith of *CBS Morning News* was preparing to do an anniversary segment on the Texas explosion and was surprised to discover after thorough research that Walter Cronkite of UP had been *the* premier reporter of the deadliest school disaster in U.S. history, one that practically wiped out a whole community. "I got some very good lessons in emergency coverage there," Cronkite recalled, "and wrote two or three stories that got some notice."

No sooner were the bodies buried in New London than Cronkite's managing editor assigned him to open a bureau in El Paso, where United Press was just starting to sell its service to KTSM radio (the voice of the Rio Grande Valley). Unbeknownst to Cronkite, he was walking into a media gunfight between the *El Paso Arrow Post* (owned by Scripps Howard) and KTSM (using UP reports extracted from Scripps Howard services). After a week in hot, contentious, and dusty El Paso, smack in the middle of a local press war, a month having passed since he'd seen Betsy, Cronkite simply drove home to Kansas City to let the chips fall where they may. With hours to kill behind the wheel, he felt odd thinking that New London had been more fun than El Paso. "I used to think life wasn't worth living," Cronkite later recalled, "if I couldn't be in on the action."

After a year with UP, unable to settle back comfortably into his K.C. job and more than a bit impetuous, Cronkite bolted back into radio broadcasting on WKY in Oklahoma City. After an interview in Dallas where he auditioned in an empty studio and was told to improvise a football game, Cronkite was hired. He grabbed the chance to do play-by-play coverage of live football games at the University of Oklahoma for the powerful NBC affiliate, which had acquired exclusive broadcast rights just before the season opener on September 26, 1937 (against the University of Tulsa Hurricanes). The Oklahoma locals were sports fanatics, and Cronkite came advertised on WKY as a "hot shot" in football broadcasting with a supposed track record at the University of Texas.

But once again Cronkite found himself in the danger zone of faking football plays on air. In anticipation of the first game in September, he hired spotters and had WKY concoct a costly electronic system to hook him up almost walkie-talkie style with his moles. The scheme was for the spotters to sit in the stands of Oklahoma Memorial Stadium (in Norman) and punch buttons on a WKY board, which in turn would indicate the formation, jersey number of the running back, and the tackler. Cronkite would be in a press booth, watch basic raw data appear on his electronic board, and then riff on air.

This system proved to be a complete disaster. Cronkite's electronic board went haywire. The spotters made mistakes. Wrong buttons were pushed. There were three or four technical glitches. Cronkite was a complete and utter bomb. "It was really one of the lowest moments of my life," he recalled. "When it was over I just wanted to go out and silently slip away. But I stayed in the press box waiting. I remember finally when there was no one there, walking slowly out." The moral of the WKY story for Cronkite was profound. "If you're going to be doing an ad-lib extemporaneous broadcast never depend upon anybody to do any part of your work. From there on out, I spent twelve hours a day learning the names and numbers of each player on each squad of the team we would play. And I knew their hometowns, their ages, their weight, and probably their mother and father's names and how many brothers and sisters they had."

Not long after football season, Cronkite accepted a job as a K.C. manager at Braniff Airlines—founded in 1928—whose corporate headquarters were in Dallas.

The job gave Cronkite a chance to stay close to Kansas City and seriously date Betsy Maxwell, whom he wanted to marry. The pay wasn't impressive, but it was higher than journalism offered. Although Cronkite was only twenty-two, he was a bona fide executive, with real coat-and-tie responsibilities. One part of the Braniff job was a seat at the Kansas City Chamber of Commerce. Cronkite could see how the powerful and rich held themselves and exerted their societal influence, and he learned how to approach them with ease. Cronkite never tried to hide his middle-class roots, but he didn't allow them to hold him down, and this coveted opportunity to mix with movers and shakers in K.C. was invaluable.

At some other juncture, it's possible Cronkite might have been lulled into a long career at an airline such as Braniff, with the good life in Kansas City it promised. But like millions of Americans, he was catching Edward R. Murrow's courageous reports from Europe on CBS Radio News and in his case his life was altered. Murrow wasn't a mindless recorder of facts like UP reporters. He was a voice—*the* voice—of America on the precipice of World War II. He was to electronic journalism what George Washington had been to the Revolutionary War: the deity. Murrow's father, a railroad worker, moved the family from Polecat Creek, North Carolina, to the Olympic Peninsula in Washington in 1914, when his son was still in britches. Tall, energetic, content to be alone in the evergreen wilderness, and steady-eyed about how the world worked, Murrow had fallen into radio by accident while he was a student at Washington State in Pullman. He had originally gone to Europe in 1932 to oversee the International Educational Association (which arranged student exchanges from European nations), a job that Wisconsin senator Joseph McCarthy would use to smear Murrow in the 1950s as a communist sympathizer. While working as CBS's director of talks in the 1930s, Murrow fell in love with Great Britain, wore suits cut in the English style, and took on the unflappable demeanor of the British in the face of the evil aggression of Adolf Hitler's Third Reich.

In the world of journalism, Murrow had created buzz by hiring ambitious young correspondents to broadcast for CBS News in the late 1930s. Cronkite was envious. Many of America's most aggressive journalists—like Eric Sevareid (formerly of the *Minneapolis Journal*) and Howard. K. Smith (a Tulane University graduate and Rhodes Scholar at Oxford University)—understood that working in Europe under Murrow was a hot ticket. Cronkite, stuck at Braniff, couldn't possibly compete with college-graduate world travelers such as Murrow, Smith, and Sevareid. In the first place, he never dreamed of foreign locales. He didn't even have a passport. As the folks of Kansas City learned, he was good at gumshoe reporting, investigating, editing, and announcing. But he wasn't a standout. His raw talent had not taken charge of his career like Murrow's and Shirer's had. While others in his generation of budding journalists were following their instincts and strategically positioning themselves for the rising tide of World War II, Cronkite was lagging behind as a Braniff meet-and-greet man. By 1939, Cronkite, ever the revolving-door opportunist, finally saw where he needed to be. He once again decided to embrace the news business, preferably at United Press. "I loved the United Press," he realized, "and I had missed it ever since I left."

The twenty-three-year-old Cronkite groveled at the UP altar to be rehired, throwing himself on the executives' mercy. "The management had not been happy about my leaving so precipitously a couple of years before," he said. "But they welcomed me back." Once again joining the Kansas City bureau, Cronkite picked up where he had left off as a junior reporter-editor, usually on the UP night desk. Virtually every day a new revelation about Tom Pendergast, chairman of the Jackson County Democratic Club, and his political machine, with its connections to mafiosi and grifters, shocked K.C. citizens. But Cronkite pursued a different journalistic track. A half year after returning to the UP office, he finally got a story with national potential. Circumstances worked in his favor; he received the reportorial assignment mainly because he happened to be working the night desk when it broke.

Before dawn on a Saturday morning, October 28, 1939, word arrived from rural Missouri of the overnight search for an airplane that had taken off and never returned. Cronkite rushed to the town of Brookfield, north of Kansas City, and started filing stories for the afternoon newspapers, hour by hour.

BROOKFIELD, MO., OCT. 28—(UP)

Officials of airfields throughout the nation were asked today to watch for a small yellow monoplane in which, state police believed, Carl Bivens, Brookfield flying instructor, was being held prisoner by a student.

A mysteriously-acting man who had been tentatively identified through an automobile drivers license as Larry Pletch took off yesterday from the instructor's private field and, after circling over the countryside in sight for 30 minutes, the plane disappeared in a southeastern direction.

Cronkite, playing Sherlock Holmes, talked with investigators and rummaged through Pletch's car himself. Working until he was good and tired, he spoke to employees at a local restaurant who thought they had seen the aviation student just before he took off. He also managed to interview the instructor's wife and son, both pilots. He learned that another son flew for Pan Am in South America. For papers with later editions, he rewrote his lede, indicating that the search was not for an airplane but, more narrowly, for a criminal.

BROOKFIELD, MO., OCT. 28—(UP)

State authorities appealed to airports and fliers through the country today for aid in hunting down a man they believed to be a flying kidnaper with no apparent motive.

Whoever he was, he had apparently made off with Carl Bivens, Brookfield flying instructor, and his new yellow monoplane, thereby precipitating a mystery that baffled local and state authorities.

State police officials said they had established a strong chain of circumstantial evidence that the mystery flier was Ernest Pletch, known to authorities throughout the Midwest as the "Lochinvar of the Air."

The "Lochinvar" bit came from an old Sir Walter Scott poem about an ardent lover. It gave Cronkite his hook for the story about romance, kidnapping, aviation, and mystery. Determined to grab notice, to have his UP articles appear in dozens of newspapers, Cronkite added vivid details about Ernest "Larry" Pletch, scion of a prosperous Indiana family, who had recently been arrested for absconding with a young woman. He had trapped her in an airplane and taken off, trying to force her at high altitude to agree to marry him. After hopscotching through the Midwest, he let her go. It had been assumed that this was merely an impulsive prank. In truth, Pletch was a dangerously disturbed man, as Cronkite's reporting on Saturday implied. All day, Cronkite worked every angle of the surefire cliff-hanger: a missing plane, a cloud of theories, and irresistible suspense.

Cronkite was competing against both the clock and the Associated Press. Both wire services broke the news that a farmer in northwest Missouri had announced that a yellow plane had landed on his property the night before, and that the pilot—in blood-spattered coveralls—had spent the night. The AP, however, topped Cronkite's coverage by interviewing members of the farm family. Cronkite wasn't licked yet, though. He calculated the range of the plane, with the gasoline available, and plotted a circle approximately that distance from the farmer's property. "I began calling airports in the circle," he later recalled, "On the second call I hit bingo." Workers at an airport in Indiana reported that they had helped a monoplane land in a nearby cornfield via radio; its gas tank was on empty. The employees at the airfield were excited that the infamous yellow mono-plane had come down in their neck of the woods. "I had a nice beat on the opposition," Cronkite said of his scoop.

In a matter of days, the Lochinvar case was resolved. The kidnapper was indeed Ernest Pletch, who con-fessed to having shot Bivens twice in the back of the head as they flew along. He did not offer any reason. Pletch pleaded guilty to murder and was sentenced to life in prison. Cronkite's aggressive reporting was well received by his bosses at United Press.

In August, two months before Pletch took his last flight, Eric Sevareid was in Paris mulling over the offer of a full-time job with United Press. Just then, Murrow offered Sevareid employment as a CBS News reporter, the fourth in all Europe. Both organizations—UP and CBS—were betting that war was imminent and were trying to snap up hot-to-trot journalists for the impending blanket radio coverage.

On September 1, 1939, the German army rolled into Poland, an overt act of aggression that seemed to demand a response from the rest of the world. Murrow waited impatiently for the next two days for Britain, or France, or any leading power to come to the defense of Poland. Everyone in free Europe was waiting for the same thing, and yet nothing was happening. Murrow, making daily broadcasts from London over CBS Radio, tried to reflect the defiant feeling on the street. He concluded his September 3 broadcast: "The general attitude seems to be, 'We are ready, let's quit this stalling and get on with it,'" he said. "As a result, I think that we'll have a decision before this time tomorrow. On the evidence produced so far, it would seem that that decision will be war. But those of us who've watched this story unroll at close range have lost the ability to be surprised."

Shortly after that Murrow broadcast, Britain, France, Australia, and New Zealand declared war on Germany. Americans, proclaiming neutrality for the time being, were desperate for raw, hour-by-hour news reports from Europe. Cronkite had become a compulsive listener to *CBS World News Roundup*, with reporters broadcasting live from London (Ed Murrow), Vienna, Paris, Berlin (William Shirer and Pierre Huss), and Rome (Frank Gervasi). Walter Cronkite and Betsy Maxwell could no longer wait for the morning newspaper: They wanted to hear CBS over the radio from

Europe in step-by-step real time. It was Murrow who made Cronkite realize that the days of stringers and passenger pigeons were over at UP. The wire service needed serious-minded and hard-boiled correspondents to cover every aspect of the gathering global conflagration. Cronkite fit the work-for-hire bill of the moment. In the United States alone, UP had more than 1,715 newspaper and radio clients, and nearly all of them would be running stories by Cronkite before long. (UP ended up sending 150 of its best reporters to cover World War II; five would be killed and over a dozen would be wounded, captured, or held as POWs in Germany, Italy, and Japan.)

Cronkite had been working on the UP night desk in Kansas City when the news of Germany's brutal invasion of Poland with tanks and *Stuka* dive bombers came across the wire that September morning. The regular night editor had gone home just before the alarming news from Europe came clickety-clacking through the Teletype machine. Cronkite had, as he later recalled, all the "excitement" of Hitler's blitzkrieg to himself.

PART II

The Second World War

5.

Gearing Up for Europe

MARRYING BETSY MAXWELL—THE NEWLYWEDS—
WIRELESS LISTENERS—POOR ROTTERDAM—COLOR
BLINDNESS—EDWARD R. MURROW LEAGUE—MR.
PALEY'S CBS—TRANSFER TO THE BIG APPLE—
DONNING THE FOREIGN CORRESPONDENT
UNIFORM—CAREER AHEAD OF MARRIAGE—AT A
BRITISH PORT—MISADVENTURES ON THE U.S.S.
TEXAS—SLINKING HOME ACROSS THE ATLANTIC—
LEARNING THE ROPES OF TRANSMISSION—CATCHING
A BREAK AT THE UNITED PRESS

Walter Cronkite married Betsy Maxwell on
March 30, 1940, in a formal ceremony at the
Grace and Holy Trinity Episcopal Cathedral in Kansas

City. Up until the vows, they had been courting covertly for four years, in violation of *Kansas City Journal-Post* employee policy. Because Cronkite's UP columns appeared in the newspaper, this strict standard applied to Betsy and him. So the Cronkite-Maxwell romance blossomed with an illicit edge to it. When Cronkite, not wanting to turn Betsy into a sexual outlaw, popped the big question, she said yes . . . with an engagement ring on her left hand . . . and a promise that they'd soon have a brood.

Cronkite's Kansas City wedding was very traditional. The church was bedecked in calla lilies and ferns, and the bride wore an old-fashioned white gown with a long train, and a gold locket that both her grandmother and mother had worn on their wedding days. Leaving at the rising of a pale blue prairie dawn, the Cronkites went on a whirlwind auto honeymoon to Houston, Galveston, El Paso, and Mexico, before heading back to western Missouri. Cronkite, procuring journalism contacts and future sources along the way, visited upstart United Press cubbyhole offices (the 1940s equivalent of stopping by Pony Express stations) far and wide. Thanks to his insatiable need for human company, the honeymoon became what Hemingway called a "movable feast." Betsy learned during all those road trip hours that despite any inner sadness, her new husband never stopped laughing. He had an infectious laugh. It wasn't coarse or hearty or even especially loud. It just had an amazing *ain't life somethin'* ring to it. "We were traveling with a little group," Cronkite fondly recalled of the honeymoon. "I'd keep inviting people to come along."

Once back in springtime Kansas City, the Cronkites moved into a Locust Street apartment in the southwest part of town. The quarters comprised four rooms—living area, bedroom, kitchen, and bathroom. There was a little alcove where Cronkite kept his *World Book Encyclopedia* set. The floors were inlaid wood, the wall panels rich oak; there were forest green silk tapestries and a pedestal wide enough to hold a huge Victrola radio. They became great friends with another young journalist, Frank Barhydt, who was a community writer-director and later a publicity director for WHB Broadcasting Co. in Kansas City, Missouri. Together, the Cronkites and Barhydt tried to make a movie in their spare time just for fun.

Betsy Cronkite, a stately figure for all her down-to-earth ways, continued her newspaper work as women's page editor of the *Kansas City Journal-Post*. Blessed with a wicked sense of droll humor, always dressed to the nines, she was beloved by colleagues at the paper. Her journalistic specialty was human interest stories of the sentimental variety. One of her duties was to continue writing an advice column for the lovelorn, "Ask Hope Hudson." Because there was real pain behind the letters she answered weekly, Betsy took even the most frivolous ones seriously. Betsy, it turned out, was a better natural writer than her husband, with a loose, breezy, and distinctive style all her own. Nevertheless, she downplayed her career in later years. "My journalism was really trivial," she said in a 1979 interview. "I just worked for the money."

Cronkite's United Press bureau was on the top floor of the same factory building occupied by the *Journal-Post*, so when work permitted, she and Walter sneaked off for a quick whisper, hug, or fool-around. Cronkite determined that his beloved Kansas City was the ideal town in which to raise a family. But those gathering CBS News broadcasts from Europe made him want to get in on the burgeoning war action. If radio news became too popular, even newspapers would become passé. A few of Cronkite's bosses in Kansas City advocated for UP to boycott any news delivery to radio companies. A press-versus-radio war had kindled, but Cronkite, hungry for income, declined to choose sides. He wanted paychecks from both print and radio companies. With CBS Radio News delivering real-time transmissions from overseas, Cronkite, the consumer, was a news junkie. He

couldn't get enough international reportage. No longer did he care when the American Newspaper Publishers Association (ANPA) scoffed about radio as a fad: he knew it was the future of the communications industry.

For Cronkite, early May 1940 was the most eye-opening moment of the war thus far—violating the neutrality of the Netherlands, Belgium, and Luxembourg, Nazi Germany unleashed the Luftwaffe fire. The Dutch did their best to thwart this air assault, but the bustling port of Rotterdam was soon reduced to rubble by the German Luftwaffe, and nearly a thousand people were killed. With no other choice at hand, Cronkite's ancestral homeland, under the threat of continued German bombing, surrendered; this led to five years of brutal occupation. More than 250,000 buildings had been destroyed. "The Dutch people would never be the same again," Cronkite believed. "When the reports of the bombing of Rotterdam came in, we could scarcely believe the stories of heartbreak and devastation."

Cronkite now hoped to join the Army Air Corps if the United States entered the European war to help the Dutch people. The Luftwaffe now had the ability, it was feared, to bomb London back to the preindustrial age. Both he and Betsy—big believers in Billy Mitchell's "Air Power Doctrine"—responded to a Roosevelt administration call for airplane pilots by signing up for flying lessons in Missouri. A huge aviation buff since childhood, Walter hoped to learn how to pilot the P-39s and P-40s, the best Army Air Corps fighters. A monkey wrench soon presented itself that changed the direction of Cronkite's life. One afternoon at flight school, Cronkite learned that he was color-blind. When asked to read a chart by a U.S. Army optometrist, he couldn't tell red from green. The condition meant he'd be exempt from the draft and ineligible for military service. It was a devastating blow to the ego of the young Unipresser. He felt neutered. While Betsy professed sadness at her husband's visual impairment, a secret part of her celebrated: his diagnosis would keep him out of combat. Forging onward, she ended up getting her pilot's license. It was Betsy's big one-up over her husband, who later would bundle honorary doctorates the way some men collected butterflies or coins.

Judging by all the press reporting from Great Britain, America would soon be pulled into World War II. Cronkite, wanting to help the Allied cause, refocused on his journalism career and campaigned for reassignment by the United Press to New York City. Kansas City was too cloistered from the gathering storm. If he couldn't pilot fighter planes, then he'd at least report on them. UP was known for moving journalists willy-nilly from bureau to bureau; as of 1933, the average tenure at one office was a year and a half. Cronkite had been at the Kansas City bureau for more than two years. At every opportunity when speaking with UP executives in New York, Cronkite mentioned his abiding interest in becoming a foreign correspondent who could report on military aviation.

The U.S. military draft was draining UP of a lot of young talent. When UP news manager Earl Johnson, at the wire service's New York office, irritably said *not now* to Walter's relocation requests, it churned up resentment in Cronkite. Nevertheless, he hunkered down in Kansas City, working harder than ever at his UP bureau job, which often took him out of state to meet sources who liked roadhouses and pool rooms. He got acquainted with pawn shops, burlesque theaters, blood-donor stations, and drab hotels offering dollar beds. "If I hadn't been trained as a journalist, we wouldn't have made it," Betsy Cronkite said of their marriage. "All the stories you hear about life with a newsman are true—chasing fire trucks, crazy hours and the company they keep, all for the sake of getting the whole story. During our first years of marriage, we were apart more than we were together."

Talking with fellow reporters at UP, Cronkite learned that Murrow, on CBS Radio, had become the new patron saint of journalism. Cronkite was a tad skeptical and a lot envious. As Cronkite learned from a telephone chat with Johnson, the *real* genius behind CBS's European operation was William S. Paley, the network's energetic president. Paley had started in radio in 1928, when he signed a fifty-dollar-a-week advertising contract between his family's cigar company and Philadelphia radio station WCAU for *The La Palina Hour.* The program was a winner: La Palina cigar sales shot through the roof, and Paley was hooked on broadcast radio. Before long he owned sixteen radio stations, which formed the nucleus of the Columbia Broadcasting System. He kept buying stations, and built his fledgling network into a powerful rival to NBC. By 1930 he owned seventy stations and earned a net profit of $2.35 million. Hence was born the intense competition between CBS and NBC in the late 1920s and early 1930s.

While Paley was on the march with CBS Radio, he worried that TV was too much of a "technological toy" instead of an "everyday necessity." He focused on attracting listeners with high-quality radio programs. Instead of following NBC's approach—whereby affiliates were charged fees for sustaining (unsponsored) programs but reimbursed for sponsored network programs—Paley made CBS's entire sustaining schedule available to affiliates free. This created a huge windfall, especially for smaller radio stations in midsize markets, because for twelve hours a day a CBS affiliate could use as many national programs, or as few, as it needed.

Word had gotten to the UP bureau that the Battle of Britain had begun on July 10, 1940. Cronkite, on the road in Lawrence, Kansas, found a college bar that was playing CBS News on the radio. Dressed in a pressed suit and subdued tie, surrounded by farmers and students, he learned that the Luftwaffe was bombing London nightly, while the Royal Air Force pushed back with all the fighters it could put in the air. Rumor had it that the Nazis were aiming to sabotage all British Broadcasting Corporation (BBC) transmission stations. Murrow, reporting from London, sometimes recorded his reports in CBS studios on Fleet Street—which were themselves periodically bombed out. Avoiding sitting-duck syndrome, he wisely broadcast from other, undisclosed locations. He made frequent use of portable shortwave transmitters that fed into long-distance networks connected to the United States. This made him CBS's appealing man of mystery to Americans catching his ethereal broadcasts on their big radio boxes at night. With London calling, the planned Main Street future, insofar as it spelled raising a happy family in Kansas City, no longer made sense to Cronkite.

When Hitler imposed a blockade of the British Isles in late August 1940, London became an even more difficult place to be, and Murrow seemed to relish this. Not only did he hitch a ride on over twenty-five combat missions for his CBS Radio reports, many not necessary, but he actually *wanted* to get into an aerial firefight, as if to prove his mettle. There was never a down moment for Murrow as long as the evil Third Reich existed; he was wired for action and opportunity. "There was," his CBS colleague Larry LeSueur recalled with nostalgia years later, "a perverse exhilaration to it all."

Newspaper reports from Europe might have offered more detail, but radio, Murrow brilliantly proved on CBS, could be as immediate as real life. For his broadcast of August 24, 1940, he stood in London's Trafalgar Square and, as his American audience heard air-raid sirens in the background, set the scene in a visceral, urgent, and elevated manner, a true civic feat that helped his fellow Americans cope with the urgency of the moment:

A searchlight just burst into action, off in the distance, one single beam sweeping the sky above me now. People are walking along quite quietly. We're just at the entrance of an air-raid shelter here and I must move this cable over just a bit so people can walk in. . . . There's another searchlight, just square behind [Admiral] Nelson's statue. Here comes one of those big red buses around the corner, double-deckers they are, just a few lights on the top deck; in this blackness, it looks very much like a ship that's passing in the night and you just see the portholes. . . . More searchlights come into action. You see them reach straight up into the sky and occasionally they catch a cloud and seem to splash on the bottom of it. . . . One of the strangest sounds one can hear in London these days, or rather these dark nights: just the sound of footsteps walking along the street, like ghosts shod with steel shoes.

What a dramatic radio bulletin for Cronkite to hear on the radio. Murrow's edgy broadcast was immediately imbued for Cronkite with the old atmosphere of democratic optimism—the same stiffening of the spine that his father had felt when President Wilson had declared war on Germany back in 1917. AP's report from London that same August 24 appeared in print, and was just as immediate. Drew Middleton, a twenty-six-year-old New Yorker, wrote for the Associated Press:

Off to the east, searchlights poked up through the sky. We could hear the German plane, but couldn't see it. We stood there. Presently a woman walked past. Tragic-eyed, dressed in nightclothes and a man's old greatcoat, she clutched a baby to her breast. There was silence while she passed. The men's faces reflected only a sober, fierce anger. A man came pounding up the street bawling, 'Stretcher party! Stretcher!' His cries soon brought four men carrying stretchers. One of the stretcher-bearers was immaculately clad in evening dress. In a few minutes they trudged past in the opposite direction, their stretchers occupied. A limp arm dangled from one.

Middleton's talent for the telling detail was as good as Murrow's, but the AP print journalist, even in a feature story like this, had to relate dramatic incidents in order to retain the interest of a reader. Middleton could not have made news of a red double-decker bus rumbling past Trafalgar Square as Murrow had. Murrow's bold reporting was what had Americans talking at the diners and churches that summer and fall. "There was an awful lot of clatter of showmanship in radio broadcasting," Cronkite explained in a 1973 *Playboy* interview. "The telegraphic ticker, the Walter Winchell approach, and a lot of the deep-voice announcer types, reading copy prepared by someone else. Ed [Murrow] squared that away pretty quickly by setting a tremendous example, fighting for the truth, honesty, integrity, and all the proper things. What we owe Ed is just absolutely immense."

United Press was operating a London bureau in 1940, in the News of the World Building just off Fleet Street. When German bombers struck London again in October, swooping right past Parliament at only four thousand feet in altitude, UP reporter Wallace Carroll was on duty. He logged detailed stories that Cronkite read over the wire machine in Kansas City. Cronkite was a long way removed from the London air-raid sirens that Murrow, Middleton, and Carroll experienced that fall. While life with Betsy was wholesome, he itched for more exciting assignments than Chamber of Commerce meetings and Missouri murder whodunits.

But by the fall of 1941 everything had started to unravel for Cronkite. Betsy, for starters, suffered a terrible career disappointment in October, when the *Journal-Post* was sold (the paper would cease publication entirely in March 1942) and she lost her job. Their shoestring budget was now missing a shoe. After the Japanese attacked Pearl Harbor on December 7, wiping out half of America's Pacific fleet, the Cronkites knew their world had changed.

UP was the first to report the surprise Japanese attack. The next afternoon, Walter, Betsy, and a gaggle of their journalist friends gathered around the big-box radio as FDR declared war on the Japanese Empire, saying the day of the strike on Pearl Harbor would "live in infamy." And so it did. Incredibly, by December, Germany had conquered most of Europe, even dealing Great Britain a crippling defeat at the battle of Dunkirk. Decades later, Cronkite, in a long National Public Radio interview, recalled how frustrated he was that when FDR declared war on Japan and Germany, UP had him working stateside in Missouri. "It was," he said, "a long year of waiting." What most concerned Cronkite was that the Japanese Mitsubishi Zero, or Zeke, fighters in the South Pacific traveled higher and farther than any comparable aircraft in the U.S. arsenal, a deficiency that needed to be remedied at once.

In January 1942, Cronkite finally received the UP transfer to New York that he'd been coveting. His longest bout of job stability—K.C. bureau chief—was at an end. He packed for the United Press headquarters on Park Row to train as a credentialed war correspondent. His unemployed wife was equally excited about the temporary move to the Big Apple. Neither had ever been to the East Coast before; Chicago was the swarming metropolis for all Midwesterners. Storing furniture in a K.C. relative's garage, Cronkite left for New York that month from Kansas City's Union Station, reading newspaper reports from Europe along the way. Betsy would arrive at Penn Station a few weeks later by train.

Cronkite was assigned the U.S. Navy office (at 90 Church Street in the financial district, just a few blocks from UP's headquarters) as his beat. He was tasked with building a Rolodex of naval officers for UP to rely on as sources during the war. Two *New York Times* staff members—Kip Orr and Oliver Gregg Howard—taught Cronkite the ropes of living in Manhattan, from using the YMCA to discovering the best all-night doughnuts-and-coffee shops. That winter, a life-long love affair began between Manhattan Island and Cronkite. (As it turned out, Walter and Betsy would raise three children on the Upper East Side.) "I'm convinced," Cronkite wrote his mother, "that New York is one of the finer spots on earth."

Cronkite now had a fixed vision about excelling as a UP war correspondent in the European Theater. Because of his 4-F status, which made him ineligible for the draft, Cronkite remained a prime candidate for a combat zone correspondent. Only poor eyesight kept him out of the military—he was still perfectly fit for acrobatics, long runs, and trail hikes. His vitals were strong. When Hitler had declared war on America in December 1941, he captured all the U.S. journalists operating in Germany and Italy and sent them to a detention camp at Bad Nauheim. A whole host of UP reporters Cronkite knew from their bylines had been a part of Hitler's reprehensible roundup. In March 1941, Richard C. Hottelet, then a UP correspondent and a future roommate of Cronkite's in Moscow after World War II, was arrested by the Germans for espionage.

Being a reporter in wartime was inherently dangerous, and Cronkite was worried about testing his personal courage should he go overseas and be exposed to the *real* European shooting war. Such existential concerns are common enough for anyone approaching the foxhole for the first time, but the nagging doubts may have been worse in Cronkite's case because he was a nonviolent man. The sight of blood made him wince. A nonhunter ever since shooting that sparrow in Houston, he couldn't kill any creature; even spiders and flies that entered his living quarters had to be "rehabilitated" (put outside) rather than swatted dead. Years after the war, at a Phoenix, Arizona, roast in his honor, Cronkite, a cat enthusiast, told an audience of more than a thousand journalists that he was a "nut animal-lover" who "carried an ant out of the house on a piece of cardboard rather than step on it."

Ostensibly the flow of information for a UP correspondent covering the war, such as Cronkite, was by way of the Office of War Information. The popular director of OWI was Elmer Davis, an ex-CBS radioman with an admiration for the wire services and Murrow. Working closely with the Librarian of Congress, the poet Archibald MacLeish, who headed the Office of Facts and Figures, Davis believed that *truth* was the smartest type of propaganda. This was in stark contrast to the Axis nations, which banned opposition newspapers, censored stories, and screened every dispatch. Fortunately, the Allied and Axis countries purportedly shared an adherence to the Geneva Convention, which stipulated that members of the press couldn't carry firearms. So when he finally shipped out, Cronkite, in essence, would be a civilian in uniform.

As the spring of 1942 wore on, Cronkite contrived to prepare for his first foreign assignment with UP. Proudly he donned an olive-drab "foreign war correspondent" uniform. On his left arm was a green felt identification embroidered on the side and a big C patch. Somehow the uniform made him seem more handsome. There were a spate of rules of engagement Cronkite was sworn to follow. He took the oaths proudly. When on combat missions, Cronkite would be limited to duffel-bagging only 125 pounds of luggage and a musette bag for his portable typewriter and other tools of the trade. He would be one of just 1,646 American news correspondents and photographers who covered the global war from 1936 to 1945. (He was blessed not to be one of the 37 killed or 112 seriously wounded. While war correspondents earned 203 Purple Hearts and 108 Silver Stars during the war, Cronkite would not be among their ranks.) "I did everything possible," he later admitted "to avoid getting into combat."

Cronkite exaggerated his pacifism to emphasize his Quaker-like aversion to war; he could easily have arranged with UP to stay in Kansas City or line-edit cable copy at a New York desk. Instead, that July, fully accredited by the U.S. Navy, he boarded the U.S.S. *Arkansas*, a battleship anchored off Staten Island. The *Arkansas* sailed through the submarine-infested waters of the North Atlantic, dodging torpedoes, in a convoy bound for Great Britain. It was escorting a little flotilla of heavily loaded cargo ships headed for English port towns. (For the August convoy, which was Cronkite's first assignment as a war correspondent, he was given the "simulated rank" of field-grade officer.) The cruise didn't exactly temper Cronkite for the hardships to come. "I occupied the admiral's cabin on the escorting battleship," he wrote in a letter home, "private bedroom, lounge with desk, and private bath, all on the main deck." For a while Cronkite felt that the men aboard the *Arkansas* treated him weirdly, always looking at him with downcast eyes. He soon found out why. "I could not help noticing how well-behaved the naval officers seemed to be in my presence: no swearing, no bawdy jokes, no talks about women. This was going to be an unrewarding journey, I thought. The reason, I soon learned, was the C on my uniform. They thought I was a chaplain."

According to Cronkite's own reporting, the convoy was the largest one sent to England up to that time. His UP story, slugged as "At a British Port," made a superlative of the size of the convoy, but because of censorship restrictions Cronkite couldn't mention the number of ships or their types, the personnel on board, or the destination of the cargo. Censorship was one of the many hurdles that made a war correspondent's job a catch-22—it wasn't easy to write about a convoy without saying anything about the convoy. Given that *Arkansas* had anchored safely in England, Cronkite used a bit of humor to distract from the many missing details in his article. He mentioned that one of the escort ships in the convoy had radioed the other ships that it had spotted a submarine and attacked it immediately. "But a derelict merchantman wreck had been mistaken for a submarine," Cronkite wrote, "and the only result of the bombing was that a 'slick' of lemon extract appeared on the surface."

While the *Arkansas* regrouped for the return trip to New York, Cronkite had ten days to acquaint himself with London. It was by no means the harried place of two summers before, during the first German blitz. But the ravages of war, as he wrote Betsy, were all around. Cronkite got his first real take on the horror of war when he interviewed a survivor of the failed raid of Dieppe (a costly August 19, 1942, Allied raid on the French port). Of the 6,086 Allied troops who went ashore at Dieppe, 3,623 British were killed, wounded, or captured, all without the Allied air force luring the Luftwaffe into open battle; the Allies lost 96 aircraft to Germany's 48. Two years later, in 1944, Cronkite would use the mistakes made in Dieppe to explain how the Allies strategically retooled to win the Battle of Normandy, thereby initiating the heroic liberation of Western Europe.

During the return trip on the *Arkansas* in October, the U.S.S. *Wakefield*, a former luxury liner commissioned for troop transport in 1941, caught fire. Cronkite was the only reporter within a hundred-mile radius. He therefore had a big scoop. But UP couldn't run his story until it was officially approved by U.S. Navy censors. During the delay, Cronkite wrote to his mother. "The cruise home was just like a cruise as far as the weather was concerned, in fact, it was a little boring," he confided. "We did get a little action, however, about which I'm sorry I can't tell you just yet. I've got a pretty good story on my hands when and if I can fight it through censorship."

Three days later, the censors cleared the *Wakefield* article. When Cronkite's editors dispatched it over the wire, they included a special biographical introduction about their talented twenty-five-year-old reporter. It was his first real exposure to a large national audience. "Walter Cronkite," the description ran, "United Press correspondent assigned to the Atlantic fleet, witnessed the burning of the big naval transport *Wakefield* and the rescue at sea of her crew and 840 passengers. His dispatch of this thrilling sea episode follows." Cronkite was happy to put himself in the story à la Murrow, since his bosses wanted to stress that this account of the burning seven-hundred-foot-long ship, all of whose passengers were rescued, was a UP exclusive. "I could see the rescue vessels crowd so close to the burning ship that, as we later learned," Cronkite recalled, "their paint was scorched and their hulls bruised as they bounced against the *Wakefield* to take off the passengers by means of rope ladders and improvised gangways." A week later, UP was printing unrelated Cronkite-bylined articles with the rather breathless reminder that he was the only reporter who had seen the *Wakefield* burn. The UP was overtly building Cronkite's brand name and reputation. His career was taking off.

After continuing to cover the convoys through late October, Cronkite was instructed to report to Norfolk, Virginia (the East Coast headquarters of the navy). No longer would he be assigned to a convoy. It turned out to be a hurry-up-and-wait a few weeks in a dockside Norfolk holding tank. "Once I entered the base, I was not permitted to leave, which meant that something was going on," he recalled. "I was told to report to the battleship *Texas* right away and that I'd be aboard the *Texas* until such time as the operation was completed."

Although the United States had been at war for almost a year, the army had yet to recapture so much as an acre from the Axis powers in Europe. Americans, including President Franklin D. Roosevelt and the young pipsqueak Walter Cronkite, were eager to start a ground offensive against Germany and Italy. The question was where to strike. Nazi fortifications in North Africa were the chosen target. In November 1942 the goal of the Allied fleet, of which the battleship *Texas* was a part, was to clear the Axis powers from Morocco, Algeria, and Tunisia; gain Allied control of the Mediterranean Sea; and prepare an invasion of Sicily, planned for the next year.

Cronkite was one of six UP correspondents covering the North African invasion. He watched the thunderous initial action from aboard the U.S.S. *Texas*. Fourteen-inch naval guns blasted away, their recoils rocking the vessel, sending anvil-shaped towers of black smoke 500 feetin the air. This bombardment was perhaps the best war news for the Allies since the pivotal Battle of Midway began on June 4, 1942. By reporting on the U.S. Navy assault on Vichy forces at Port Lyautey and by writing about Operation Torch (the invasion's code name), he could forever claim to have participated in the D-day of North Africa, a giant plume in any correspondent's cap.

The UP that prided itself on "the world's best coverage of the world's biggest news" put its faith in a half-dozen no-nonsense reporters in North Africa like Cronkite. It couldn't help but gloat that the AP and the INS had been given only four berths each with the expeditionary force. The amount of pettiness in journalism made college professors, by contrast, seem open-palmed generous. Five of the Unipressers—Philip Ault, Walter Logan, Chris Cunningham, John Parris, and Leo Disher—had all been toughened by years of experience covering the war; Cronkite was the new kid on the block. His principal instinct was hesitation.

While UP was a major news outlet, it was hard for reporters to gain much adulation because of the formulaic writing rules. But breaking news was breaking news. A UP reporter with an exclusive, Cronkite knew, could quickly become the toast of the fourth estate. At least for a few days.

The fighting in Morocco began early on November 8, 1942. Operation Torch met only halfhearted resistance from the French troops being commanded by the puppet government of Marshal Philippe Pétain in Vichy, France. Back in the United States, the Associated Press transmitted only the U.S. government's official announcement over the wire; it described the invasion plan in general terms. The United Press offered that too, but it also carried an eyewitness account of the landing, written by Chris Cunningham. The wonder was that he found a way to transmit it among the heavy bombardment—but then, the resourceful Cunningham was known to cultivate a chummy relationship with the telegraph detail in war zones.

The only news from the Northern Group, Cronkite's beat during the assault, came from a Vichy French radio service, a pro-Nazi propaganda fog machine. While the UP editors were awaiting a report from Port Lyautey in Morocco, the U.S.S. *Texas* plastered the French arsenal with a cavalcade of bombs. Within two days, the battle was over, as the last Vichy resistance collapsed; the city of Casablanca, the Lyautey airfield, the Moroccan rail yards, and a number of useful ports were all in Allied hands.

Having survived the ordeal with only a ringing in his ears, Cronkite went ashore at Port Lyautey with a gunnery officer to inspect the damage. He was amazed at how off-target the U.S. Navy's marksmanship had been. All the wrong buildings were in ruins. Unbeknownst to Cronkite, his dispatches on Operation Torch—all dutifully logged—had mysteriously not gotten through to New York. United Press hadn't publicly released an original Cronkite article on the action at Lyautey, though he had filed thirteen. He had filed them from the radio bridge of the *Texas*, via a British communication relay channel in Gibraltar, but the channel was giving preference to BBC reporters, so none of his pieces got through to London or New York. Determined to dominate the North African coverage, UP headquarters in New York took advantage of an agreement among the news organizations to pool stories during the first week and used an article from Robert G. Nixon, the INS man, regarding a flight he took over the Moroccan coastline. Censor approval of anything more specific demanded a delay of more than a week anyway. Still, when UP finally received permission to run an article on the Northern Group's assault, it was one written by Walter Logan. No Cronkite byline.

Algeria was a stalemate. But the Germans, in a counteraction, hurried reinforcements to neighboring Tunisia. Heavy combat would ensue there. Logan, Cunningham, and the other UP men moved on, too, heading to far more stubborn fighting to the east, in Tunisia. But no one in North Africa or New York knew where Cronkite had ended up. As it happened, he was back aboard the *Texas*, assuming it was sailing from Port Lyautey down to Casablanca.

Staring into the bracing, choppy pearl-gray waves as they broke, trying to keep his stomach straight, Cronkite realized he had made a tactical error. The African coast kept getting farther and farther away. He had accidentally "hitchhiked" an oceanic retreat trip back to the naval yards of Norfolk, Virginia, instead of to Casablanca. He obeyed the U.S. Navy directive for correspondents to remain with their ships, not realizing that this order was to be taken seriously *only* before and during action. Secretly, he did intend to break the rule and leave the ship when the *Texas* docked near Casablanca, a city so secure that a meeting between Franklin Roosevelt and Winston Churchill would be held there only two months later. Reporting from Casablanca after the Allied landings would have been a safe choice for Cronkite. But any UP article he wrote would have been more of a travelogue than an urgent war dispatch. In any case, the *Texas* sailed straight past Casablanca in heavy seas, turning westward into the spinning surf.

With every hour finding him farther from North Africa, anxiety swept over him. Was he in professional trouble? Could a foreign war correspondent be charged with dereliction of duty? Had cowardice influenced his retreating actions? Was an excoriating memo being written at UP headquarters with his name on it? A sort of nausea now held sway over him on that stuck-at-sea journey. If it were possible, he would have sucked down an entire keg of beer to numb the shame. And it wasn't just an existential crisis over what constituted being AWOL. Ever since press lord Edward Willis Scripps had founded UP in 1907, frugality was the reigning ethic in the bureau that had mastered skinflint journalism. How were Cronkite's tightwad bosses in New York going to perceive his leaving North Africa prematurely? Would they compute his travel blunders as money lost?

At this critical moment, not wanting to be declared dead or AWOL, practically in a panic, Cronkite charmed a ride on a reconnaissance plane that took off from the deck of the *Texas*; it shortened the trip home to America by a few days. When Cronkite finally arrived at United Press headquarters in New York at the end of November, full of regret, he was met by his editors with hands-on-hips reprimands. He was on shaky ground. Where have you been for six weeks, Cronkite? With his marvelous memory as get-out-of-a-jam helper, he explained every big scene and small nuance of his North African adventure that had been lost when his UP articles on Operation Torch were not received. He also learned that his bosses had presumed he was dead. Cronkite's editors, glad he had survived the North Africa ordeal, salvaged his reporting (and the six weeks that he'd devoted to it) by releasing his account of the assault on Lyautey—more than two weeks after the assault. The Cronkite article was unusually long, and composed of pieces from the stories he'd tried to file while overseas. The result was clumsy and disjointed. "It was enough to make a young wire-service reporter think about turning in his typewriter," Cronkite recalled, "and go into radio."

A major error of Cronkite's, in hindsight, was falsely assuming the UP articles he'd written on the radio bridge of the *Texas* had gotten patched through to his editors simply because he had handed them off to a U.S. Navy censor. There was, he learned, much more hustle to transmitting war reporting than pushing a magic "send" button. Not only did reporters have to cover the action, but it was also their sacred responsibility to guarantee that their copy got published. The importance of following up was incalculable; it constituted the difference between a pay raise and an enduring dark blot on one's name. Echoing his screwup when broadcasting his first football game for WKY in Oklahoma, the *Texas* experience taught Cronkite a cardinal journalism lesson: triple-check everything—especially your story transmission.

6.

The Writing Sixty-Ninth

Cronkite spent a few nights in New York making love with Betsy and taking walks around Central Park. They attended the lighting of the Christmas tree at Rockefeller Center and chatted incessantly about the war. Then, in early December 1942, United Press assigned Cronkite to the London bureau. Clearly, his shortcomings in reporting Operation Torch and his premature, unintended departure from North Africa hadn't derailed his career. Along with UP's Douglas Werner, who'd been in the Washington bureau, Cronkite left New York aboard the Dutch passenger ship *Westerland*. Both he and Werner would be available to UP around the clock in England to report on the anticipated escalation in the air war against Germany. Betsy, grateful for the fling with her husband, returned to Kansas City. She had been hired by an advertising office of the Hallmark Corporation, editing the in-house magazine. She had seen Walter off on December 11, with gifts to be opened on the holiday aboard the *Westerland*, including vitamins, stollen (German cake), chewing gum, cuff links, and some Max Brand and Zane Grey westerns. They would not see each other again for two years. "Like a lot of other people that year, we had to be apart on Christmas," she recalled. "There was a war going on, but all I could think of then was that Walter would be at sea on Christmas Day."

For Cronkite, the transfer to London presented a dramatic shift in his professional prospects. The United Press management was aware that the company did not have enough reporters to cover every hotspot in Europe, but it was determined to "compete toe-to-toe on the big stories of the day," as a company executive put it, "with a view to keeping a dominant position on the front pages." UP president Hugh Baillie was convinced, as were many others, that one of the biggest stories would be the Allied invasion of France from Britain. More than others, perhaps, Baillie believed it could occur in 1943, so UP made sure the London bureau was not short of good reporters.

Cronkite's journey across the Atlantic was fraught with danger. German *Unterseebooten* (U-boats) attacked the convoy, sinking a couple of sluggish freighters. The *Westerland* emerged unscathed, the only high note of a voyage "abominable from every other standpoint." After the convoy anchored in Glasgow, Scotland, on December 30, 1942, Cronkite made his way immediately to London by train, where he worked alongside Ed Beattie of UP, who handled many of the major articles and whom Cronkite later called his "hero."

Joe Alex Morris and other UP executives gave Cronkite the kind of break a budding journalism career needs, an opportunity to prove his mettle in the Fleet Street milieu. Cronkite didn't squander a minute of it. In his first weeks in London, he met Andy Rooney, an Army-enlisted man reporting for *The Stars and Stripes*, whose office was located in the Times of London

Building, near UP's bureau. Reporters from scads of news outfits, including United Press, congregated after work at the same nearby pub on Fleet Street, swapping information over tavern ale about everything from B-17 bomber raids to where to find the bombshells around Piccadilly Circus—the high-heeled prostitutes, not the ordnance. Once the pub closed, Cronkite started the habit of relocating to a private club, where cheap gin could be purchased by the bottle. "I thought Walter was one of the big guys," Rooney recalled. "I was four years younger, just a little guy at *Stars and Stripes*. We'd often get called about an upcoming bombing raid, so we'd go visit the bases together to get the scoop." The feisty, funny Rooney deemed Cronkite "a tough, competitive scrambler . . . in the old *Front Page* tradition of newspaper reporting."

Cronkite found lodging at the Park Lane Hotel, in a room he deemed a "cell," just across a park from Buckingham Palace. The American Bar at the hotel became his salon. On New Year's Eve he had "absolutely no desire for liquor," he wrote in a letter to Betsy. Nevertheless, he went on to describe the four cocktails he drank at a private club, as he began to get acclimated to wartime London. And by journalistic standards, four drinks was nothing. Sometimes it seemed that finishing a bottle of gin at Jack's Club or the Wellington Inn won respect from one's fellow newsmen. "Joe Morris and Ed Beattie were organizing a sort of party, but when they got around to inviting me they themselves were pretty well organized," Cronkite wrote. "I didn't feel like that kind of hilarity."

Worn out, plagued with a sinus infection, and home-sick for Betsy, Cronkite was in a funk his first week in London. Feeling dehydrated and exhausted from the transatlantic trip, already almost broke (a continual concern throughout the 1940s), Cronkite felt uprooted. Everything in London was so uncertain. UP not only hadn't given him marching orders, it hadn't so much as offered him a map. "What hours I'm going to be working and what I'm going to be doing I won't know till Monday," he wrote Betsy. "I'm hoping it will be big enough to keep me out of the office most of the time. I have no desire to sit on the desk writing cables."

Between 1943 and 1945, Cronkite wrote Betsy dozens of letters. Without direct telephone service, it was how the couple communicated. Whenever Betsy received a missive from her husband, she'd read it aloud back in Kansas City to her new Hallmark friends, circulate it around the family circle, and then read it again at bed-time. (While she saved all incoming correspondence from Europe, few copies of her own letters to Walter survived the war.) Five main themes emerged from

Cronkite's correspondence: the British weather was gloomy; he missed Kansas City; alcohol was a friend; holidays were a big deal; and the UP had put him on a woefully chintzy expense account. "I'm going through my meager funds like they were pennies in an amusement arcade," he wrote. "And unless Doug Werner and I get an apartment in a hurry I shall soon be sleeping in a Hyde Park air raid shelter."

Once Cronkite got acclimated to London, he was given a top-notch assignment, one he had coveted since 1941: covering the Allied air war against Germany. He hoped to go on bombing missions aboard a four-engine B-17 Flying Fortress or a B-24 Liberator. The U.S. Army Air Force had been pressured for a year by the British government to undertake strategic bombing of German industrial sites. Great Britain's own Royal Air Force (RAF) fleet of planes had been effectively bombing Germany on night raids. On January 28, 1942, the Eighth Air Force was officially activated at the National Guard Armory on Bull Street in Savannah, Georgia. A few months later, the Eighth was prepared to raid Germany as part of the air war preparation for the Allied invasion of the continent.

By August 1942 the U.S. Eighth Force Bomber Command—part of the Eighth Air Force—had been organized to carry out the daytime bombing missions over Germany, using British airfields at Alconbury and Molesworth, both in Cambridgeshire, as bases. But the Mighty Eighth, as the Eight Air Force came to be known after World War II, began slowly with sorties over France and Holland. By the end of 1942 it still hadn't flown any missions over Germany, which frustrated Prime Minister Winston Churchill. The British fear was that American delays in fully executing the air offensive were allowing the German economy to freely supply Hitler's war machine.

The key figure in Cronkite's London life was General Ira C. Eaker, who had grown up on a farm near Eden, Texas, and was now head of the Eighth Air Force's bomber wing. Like Cronkite's father, Eaker had enlisted as an infantry private right after the United States declared war on Germany in 1917. He rose to the rank of captain during the Great War. Eaker was involved with notable feats of early aviation that Cronkite heard about while working for Braniff (including Eaker's being the first pilot to fly coast to coast "blind," solely on instruments). Shortly after Pearl Harbor, Eaker, now a general, arrived in England to take over the Mighty Eighth's Air Force from General Carl Spaatz.

General Eaker quickly earned the respect of the British people by establishing effective Eighth Air Force Bomber and Fighter Groups at air bases across

East Anglia. At the Casablanca Conference in January 1943, Eaker was successful in convincing President Roosevelt and Prime Minister Churchill of the practicality of precision daylight bombing of vital targets deep inside Nazi Germany. With the Royal Air Force night attacks, American daylight missions under Eaker's command would provide "round-the-clock" bombing that would destroy German industrial and military targets as well as German morale. In a nutshell, Cronkite's job was to cover the Mighty Eighth's successes while glossing over its failures.

On March 4, 1943, the Mighty Eighth sent 238 B-17s on a bombing run over Berlin. The non-pressurized, unheated aircraft were developed in the 1930s (around the time Model "A" Fords were being manufactured). The gutsy raid did only minor damage in the end, but Cronkite's morale grew considerably. The ultimate objective of the Mighty Eighth, he understood, was to leave the Third Reich in ruins. The Mighty Eighth pilots were flying into the hornets' nest of the world's heaviest and most vicious concentration of antiaircraft guns. If not shot down in battle, these U.S. flyboys arrived back at Alconbury and Molesworth triumphant heroes (i.e., the new Billy Mitchells).

The RAF Berlin raid was also noteworthy to Cronkite because an embedded reporter had been allowed to fly on one of the warplanes. James MacDonald, a forty-seven-year-old Scotsman and World War I veteran, wrote on the front page of *The New York Times* about accompanying a Lancaster crew on its flight over the German capital. It was riveting stuff. "Royal Air Force bombers transformed a large area of Berlin into a particularly hot corner of hell last night," MacDonald wrote. "I know, because as a passenger aboard one of the planes making up the large force that battered the German capital I saw a great number of 4,000-pound high-explosive bombs and thousands of incendiaries blasting buildings right and left and starting widespread fires reminiscent of some of the big German raids we have gone through in London."

MacDonald's *Times* dispatch was spot-on regarding the impact of the air raid on the German capital, where Hitler resided. Emergency sirens echoed down Berlin's streets and back alleys. The Fuhrer was reported to be shocked by a bombardment that deep into the Third Reich. On the heels of the successful British strike, the Eighth Air Force prepared a follow-up bombardment. The joint Allied Command decided that the RAF would bomb Nazi-held territory at night, while the Eighth Air Force would make more dangerous daytime raids. With the air war about to accelerate, other news organizations were scrambling to catch up after *The*

New York Times's Berlin bombing raid scoop. For his part, Cronkite was pushing hard to be in the forefront of coverage of the air war for UP. "It was a question of befriending the right guys in the Eighth," Rooney recalled. "Walter was a charmer at that."

Just weeks after Cronkite arrived in London, the Eighth Air Force was set to join the RAF in the attack on the German homeland. And having weathered almost a year of impatient criticism, the Eighth Air Force had no intention of keeping its new initiative quiet. It embraced UP and other wire services with vigor, arranging access to the otherwise strictly guarded air bases, making crews available for interviews, and suggesting potential stories. Cronkite astutely befriended the public relations officers, whose trade was ideas—both giving them and helping to realize them. Around Molesworth air base, Cronkite became known for collecting all the spine-chilling, unnerving stories of the Mighty Eighth crews as they returned from their missions. He was the group's Ernie Pyle.

A master of small talk, Cronkite would often just shoot the breeze about BBC's popular radio program *It's That Man Again* or the latest pinup girl in *Yank*. A popular sport for the Mighty Eighth airmen was a contest to paint the sexiest gals possible on the sides of the B-17s and B-24s. Cronkite, who loved raunchy jokes, used to write the filthiest slogans imaginable to paint on the fuselage—they were too dirty to ever be used. To develop sources and earn trust, he would treat officers from the Eighth to dinner at Grosvenor House, whose restaurant reminded him of the Muehlebach Hotel grill room in Kansas City. He learned about how the bomber crews had been grappling with high-altitude flights, where they had to contend with the lack of oxygen and extreme cold. But he didn't just talk shop at these meals. It was important to befriend officers if he hoped to be invited on bomb runs. The U.S. Army Pictorial Service got quite a few shots of Cronkite and buddies clowning around like hooligans with soldiers from Poland, the Netherlands, New Zealand, Canada, and Norway. Cronkite called their booze-fueled confabs a "babble of tongues."

The Mighty Eighth pilots credited Cronkite for bringing Dixieland jazz into their lives. Walter could *swing*. Along with Herb Caen, the legendary *San Francisco Chronicle* reporter, Cronkite formed a band called the Latrios (because they practiced mainly in the latrines, where the acoustics were excellent). Cronkite could "play" bass fiddle with his voice. Caen was hot on the mouth trombone. Collie Small of *The Saturday Evening Post* had mastered "playing" the trumpet through his clasped hands. The musical trio memorized the Mills Brothers catalog, perfecting renditions of "Sweet Georgia Brown" and the "Bugle Call Rag."

One evening, the Latrios decided to perform around Piccadilly, starting with their version of "King Porter Stomp." Midsong, a large chamber pot full of water was dumped on their heads from above, followed by a loud . . . *Shut up!* The three correspondents raced into the building and up a stairwell to confront their attacker. A dozen or so GIs appeared to be sleeping with the lights out. Caen, in "Blood n' Guts" Patton-mode, barked, "Who threw the chamber pot?" A silence filled the room. "I'm counting to three," an angry Caen shouted, but no one confessed. The Latrios headed back down the stairs, deciding to let the matter rest. All they heard as they beat their retreat was a huge collective laugh from all of the GIs, at their expense. The Latrios disbanded not long after getting drenched.

On January 27, 1943, newspapers in the United States carried the first of many United Press dispatches written by Cronkite from Great Britain about the B-17 crews. It was bylined as both "A Flying Fortress Station, Somewhere in England" and "Beautiful Bombing, U.S. Flyers Boast." Cronkite was proud that it ran in the *New York World-Telegram*. It was a rah-rah dispatch on U.S. bombers ready to beat Germany to smithereens. "A Flying Fortress called 'Banshee,'" Cronkite wrote, "with a lad named Hennessy at the controls today drew the honor of being the first American plane to bomb Germany in this war." Cronkite recounted what it meant to fly at 25,000 feet—an altitude where temperatures often reached 50 degrees below zero. The United Press had just launched a massive ad campaign to promote UP correspondents such as Cronkite and other "shock troops of the press." It had even hired an illustrator to portray UP reporters as superheroes, using typewriters as weapons, as they stormed a fascist beach with the ferocity of Genghis Khan on a fiery steed. It was Cronkite's duty as UP's air war correspondent to explain all the mechanisms necessary to support a massive air force.

A warm relationship developed between Cronkite and many of the Eighth Air Force crews. He was constantly mobile, making regular rounds to the Eighth's logistic base, including supply and repair depots, air fields, living quarters, and mess halls. More than a mascot, Cronkite was their Boswell, the town crier of their heroism, the scribe who could make them famous back home in Texas and Ohio. When crews returned to Molesworth from a bombing raid on Germany, Cronkite would rush to interview them. A half-dozen crewmen Cronkite befriended were shot down by the Luftwaffe; a couple of them died. On each raid, Cronkite learned, the Eighth Air Force lost on average over 5 percent of its airmen. Cronkite would oftentimes commiserate with Andy Rooney, his best friend for life, over how ignoble it was to be boozehounds in London while crews were risking their lives over Germany. "After a while, we saw so many people we had gotten to know who were shot down, taken prisoner, or killed that we all began to feel guilty about covering this war the way we were," Rooney recalled. "It just seemed wrong to us."

Like the combat crews themselves, Cronkite learned his tasks "on the job." He would usually write up his dispatches directly from Cambridgeshire, under the surveillance of U.S. military censors. Once cleared, they would be forwarded to London for wire transmission to New York. Cronkite wrote great stories about how Mighty Eighth pilots were trained in the art of flying in tight formations and how radio operators learned Morse code. A fierce competition ensued between Cronkite of UP and Gladwin Hill of AP over who would log the best dispatch. "I would worry," Cronkite recalled. " 'Gosh, I wonder what Gladwin is going to write.' "

Two words in MacDonald's *New York Times* article of January 18, 1943—in which the fine reporter described flying in an RAF Lancaster bomber on a Berlin raid—haunted every war correspondent in metropolitan London, even as the bombing of German targets became front-page news stories. The two words were, "I saw." If only Cronkite would be allowed to go on a bombing mission with the Mighty Eighth over Germany, writing "I saw," he would become a hero at UP. Until green-lighted, Cronkite relied on post-raid interviews with flight crews. That was the best he could do. The challenge lay in the fact that the Mighty Eighth, in rapid deployment mode, had bases all over East Anglia, and the number was growing. Rushing to meet a huge story head-on, Cronkite took his cue from the Eighth's public relations officers at first. Playing the propagandist, he found the primary-source material for his stories by speaking to the Eighth Air Force pilots whom the army recommended.

In early February, that changed temporarily. "I don't know who decided to do it," Rooney recalled, "but we decided we'd better go on a bombing raid ourselves." Cronkite, Rooney, and a cadre of other reporters were invited to sidestep the crew interviews and actually embed themselves on a raid, one whose target, they learned later, was the ports and military facilities surrounding the German city of Bremen. Cronkite wanted to put *The New York Times* to shame with his matter-of-fact United Press prose from a B-17 or B-24 mission.

When General Eaker, who was now commander of the Eighth Air Force, made the decision to enhance the publicity surrounding the air war by allowing correspondents to accompany a bomber mission over Germany, the United Press received one seat. Cronkite campaigned hard to be UP's man in air combat. Harrison Salisbury, the esteemed reporter who was the able manager of the United Press London bureau, later reflected that "wild elephants couldn't have kept Cronkite from taking part in the mission." For a reporter to fly with the Eighth was extremely dangerous. But the potential for making front-page news back in the States was high. As Salisbury pointed out in his memoir, *A Journey for Our Times*, what Cronkite coveted was "to hold a ticket to a funeral . . . [his] own." Aware of the grave risk, Salisbury reluctantly agreed to allow Cronkite on the bombing run. "It was with great trepidation that I said OK," Salisbury recalled. "Walter came back all right. One reporter did not."

Before journalists would be allowed to fly bombing raids over Germany they had to take a short course in air survival. They would be flying under conditions that required an oxygen mask and electrically heated suits to ward off raging wind blasts and prevent oxygen deprivation. When Cronkite finished the training on February 6, he wrote Betsy a long, enthusiastic letter: "For the past week six other correspondents and I have been under full army regime going to school from seven thirty in the morning until ten thirty at night learning how to take our places as the tenth member of a Flying Fortress crew," he explained. "We've been assigned by our papers to the Eighth Air Force. We're going to live on the airdromes with them and, occasionally, when the story warrants, we're going along on their raids with them. The story involves a certain amount of risk but it's a terrific opportunity. . . . We're now called by the Air Corps boys, for no particular reason, the Writing Sixty-Ninth and we're just like a bunch of kids about the assignment."

There are a couple of versions of how the reporters got their name, the Writing Sixty-Ninth. One has sexual connotations, but according to the G-rated version, Hal Leyshon of the Eighth's public relations office created it, riffing off *The Fighting 69th*, a 1940 James Cagney movie about a World War I battalion. The name may have been manufactured for publicity purposes, but the intent was serious. The Writing Sixty-Ninth would help promote the Eighth Air Force in hopes of building stateside support for more air crews and equipment. "I don't know how that Writing Sixty-Ninth stuff got so big," Rooney recalled. "It was really a lot of hooey. We never really, in any serious way, actually referred to ourselves as that. But it stuck in history."

Besides Cronkite and Rooney, other Sixty-Niners were Paul Manning of CBS Radio, Denton Scott of the Army weekly *Yank*, Bob Post of *The New York Times*, Gladwin Hill of Associated Press, William Wade of the International News Service, and Homer Bigart of the *New York Herald-Tribune*. Cronkite fit in easily with the top-drawer assemblage and was nicknamed "The Major." Other airmen took to calling him "the Flying Typewriter." Everybody liked him; he was seen as both serious about his trade and entertaining at night. "Walter was really the class clown," Rooney recalled. "He made us all laugh. He was serious in believing we couldn't take ourselves too seriously."

A couple of bona fide celebrities were connected to the Writing Sixty-Ninth, including Hollywood director William Wyler, then a major in the army, whose 1942 film *Mrs. Miniver* told the noble story of an English family struggling to survive the Nazi Blitz. Wyler passed out 35mm cameras to flyboys so they could authentically capture the essence of a combat mission. Wyler, who would win six Academy Awards in his career, was in England making a War Department documentary about strategic bombing. He enrolled in the same gunnery school as Cronkite. One day Wyler

saw the B-17 *Memphis Belle* and said, "That's it"—
the plane his 1944 documentary would be based on.
Besides writing about Wyler's escapades to Betsy,
Cronkite also casually mentioned rubbing shoulders
with actor Clark Gable, *New York Times* publisher
Arthur Sulzberger, and future American ambassador
to the United Kingdom Jock Whitney.

On direct orders from General Jimmy Doolittle,
the Eighth Air Force taught the Writing Sixty-Ninth
how to perform the primary duties of the enlisted men
on a B-17 or B-24. The newsmen were exposed to a
curriculum that covered "first aid, the use of oxygen,
and high-altitude flights." Cronkite also took part in
target practice, high-altitude adjustment drills, emergency parachuting exercises, and enemy identification.
It was a lot of quick, life-or-death learning. There
wasn't much room for a reporter on a B-17 or B-24,
so Cronkite would have to earn his keep by knowing what to do in case of emergency or enemy attack.
Due to his gunnery training class, he could dismantle
a weapon blindfolded and distinguish a Focke-Wulf
from a British Hurricane. When Writing Sixty-Niners
passed their training, Denton Scott, speaking for them
all, shouted, "God help Hitler!"

If there was such a thing as a ringleader of the
Writing Sixty-Ninth, it was Bob Post of *The New York*

Times, the hardest-working journalist of the cabal. How many bombs were dropped and from what kind of plane were the kinds of facts that the hyper-diligent Post never failed to procure. "There are ten of us here now," Post said of the Writing Sixty-Ninth. "It kind of makes you think when you realize that according to the highest proportion of losses supposedly standable by the aircorps, which is ten percent, that one of us will not be here after the first mission." On bomb run day they numbered eight, not ten. One Writing Sixty-Ninth was ill (or so he said). "Listen, it happens," Rooney wrote of the no-show. "The thought crossed my mind that I didn't feel too well myself."

At dawn on February 26, 1943, the eight Writing Sixty-Ninth correspondents took off in B-17s and B-24s for the wild blue yonder. The plan was to drop bombs on the German port city of Wilhelmshaven on the North Sea and the industrial area around Bremen. Cronkite, embedded with the 303rd, left from Molesworth in a B-17 that had a mad-as-hell Bugs Bunny insignia near its Plexiglas nose; it was commanded by Major Glenn E. Hagenbuch. This was just the second Mighty Eighth bombing mission over Germany, but the first to carry correspondents. One of the planes carrying two reporters turned back because of mechanical problems. That left six reporters—Cronkite, Rooney, Wade, Bigart,

Post, and Hill—in the air. At first, Cronkite's flight was tedious. Then holy hell broke out. "It was terrible," Cronkite recalled in 1981. "Exciting, but terrible. We had no fighter escort. Just four groups of planes, B-17s and B-24s. We had the German Luftwaffe attacking us for 2½ hours, all the way to the target—Wilhelmshaven—and back till we got to the North Sea. And flak so thick you could walk on it."

One of the B-24s was hit by a Nazi fighter plane over Oldenberg, Germany, catching fire in midair. The crew and embedded reporter Bob Post parachuted out of the Liberator, but they drifted directly into enemy fire. Post and the entire flight crew were killed.

From seventeen thousand feet above Earth, Cronkite saw German FW-190 and ME-109 fighter planes approaching to attack his B-17. Under the circumstances, the crew gave Cronkite a job to do: manning the Flying Fortress's starboard gun. No one on the B-17 felt quite as vulnerable as Cronkite, but then, no one had as good a panoramic view. Cronkite's colorblindness didn't seem to matter an iota. "I fired at an awful lot of Focke Wulfs and Messerschmitts that day," Cronkite recalled, adding with battlefield humor, "I don't think I hit any, I may have hit a Liberator or two."

With adrenaline still coursing through their veins, Cronkite and the other Writing Sixty-Ninth correspondents returned to Molesworth from the Wilhelmshaven bomb run, stunned by the aerial violence. For nearly three hours they had bounced around the sky like cannonballs, and now, understandably, they wanted to decompress. But not for long. They were all on deadline to produce copy about the bravery of the Eighth airmen. The game plan had been for all of the Writing Sixty-Niners to congregate in a windowless room at the base, compare experiences, divvy up assignment angles for the sake of diversity, and then bang out their stories. When they finished writing, they would collectively get censor clearance and then transmit their stories to London, where they would be sent on to New York. But the only thing the five safe-and-sound reporters could talk about after they landed was that Post had not returned.

The winner of the most bloodcurdling Wilhelmshaven survivor story was undoubtedly Rooney. He had been cramped in the nose of a B-17 eighteen thousand feet over Germany when a piece of shrapnel from a Messerschmitt hit the plane, breaking off a hunk of the Plexiglas nose. The bombardier on board quickly tried to stuff a parachute into the hole as cold air rushed into the cabin. When the bombardier took his gloves off, his hands froze on the spot. A startled Rooney, trying to stay composed, noted that his navigator was slumped over his desk. "His oxygen tube," he recalled, "had been pierced."

Rooney, his life hanging in the balance, got on the intercom and asked the pilot what to do. "We have emergency air in oxygen bottles up behind me," the pilot replied. "Take some deep breaths and come back up behind me and get the oxygen bottle; bring it back down and hook him up to that." Although not sure he understood the instructions, Rooney did as he was told to save the navigator's life. "I took some deep breaths," he said. "I took my oxygen mask off, and went through this alleyway up behind the pilot. There I got an oxygen bottle and hooked up the navigator, who was a much more experienced flyer than the bombardier." The man regained consciousness and then attended to the bombardier, who was in severe pain due to his frozen hands. "So," Rooney wrote, "I had by far the best story to tell of all the [Sixty-Ninth] correspondents who went out that day."

Cronkite's lede for UP about the Wilhelmshaven raid was unlike that of any of the others. What made him proudest was that he trumped Bigart, the legendary *New York Herald Tribune* writer. Both Cronkite and Bigart felt lucky that February 27, for they were alive. The 303rd, their bomb group, suffered no losses. Exhausted from a long day's raid over Germany,

Cronkite, at the Molesworth base, read out loud to Bigart from his notebook. "Homer," Cronkite said, "I think I've got my lede." He then read to Bigart the following:

> American Flying Fortresses have just come back from an assignment to hell—a hell of 26,000 feet above the earth, a hell of burning tracer bullets and bursting gunfire, of crippled Fortresses and burning German fighter planes, of parachuting men and others not so lucky. I have just returned with a Flying Fortress crew from Wilhelmshaven.

Bigart had a pronounced stutter. When he heard Cronkite's histrionic text, he reportedly put his hand on Cronkite's arm and moaned, "Y-y-y-y-you wouldn't." Decades later Cronkite, usually modest, boasted about his recounting of the Wilhelmshaven mission. "I swept the boards with my story on that," he declared. "Particularly in the British press. Every British paper bannered my story."

UP president Hugh Baillie encouraged his reporters to write the kind of copy that would attract lots of attention to the UP brand, as Cronkite's Wilhelmshaven story did. In a cable sent to his European news manager, Baillie gave specific instructions for the type of writing he wanted to see from Cronkite and his peers: "Tell those guys out there to get the smell of warm blood into their copy. Tell them to quit writing like retired generals and military analysts, and to write about people killing each other."

Salisbury, the UP London editor, wasn't offended by the emotionalism of Cronkite's account. Salisbury, in fact, later claimed to have suggested the "hell" metaphor, when Cronkite was at a loss for words after the raid. "Bigart, Cronkite and Hill were badly shaken by their experience," Salisbury recalled. News that Bob Post was missing—and presumed dead—stunned them. Their nerves were raw with grief. Stricken with writer's block, still shaken from the mission, Cronkite couldn't get his story started properly. After typing a few lines, he'd rip the paper from his Smith-Corona, wad it into a ball, toss it away like a baseball, and start over. Salisbury recalled what happened next: "Finally, as his editor at U.P., I fed him a typical wire-service overline: 'I flew through hell today.' Walter eyed the words with some doubt, but finally modified the phrase and used it to lead his story."

Cronkite's dramatic Wilhelmshaven account may have been riddled with cliché images, but somehow it worked. Hundreds of newspapers used "Assignment from Hell" the first week and, remarkably, others were still running the Cronkite piece a month or more after the event. Nearly two decades later, the editor of the book *Masterpieces of War Reporting*, Louis Snyder, selected it over the other contenders as the best journalistic account of a World War II air mission.

The dispatch made Cronkite popular in America; it also brought him a new level of media accolades in Great Britain. The piece was neither beautifully written nor an incisive overview of a bombing mission, but for the first time, Cronkite allowed his readers to see inside him. "The impressions of a first bombing mission," he admitted midway through the article, "are a hodgepodge of disconnected scenes like a poorly edited home movie—bombs falling past you from the formation above, a crippled bomber with smoke pouring from one motor limping along thousands of feet below, a tiny speck in the sky that grows closer and finally becomes an enemy fighter, a Focke-Wulf peeling off above you somewhere and plummeting down, shooting its way through the formation; your bombardier pushing a button as calmly as if he were turning on a hall light, to send our bombs on the way."

Cronkite's UP story came closer to what Murrow was doing on CBS Radio than most other wire service reporters would dare do. It was edgy in a contemporary way. In fact, Murrow's unit immediately arranged with

United Press to bring Cronkite in for a radio report. The night after the mission, Cronkite sat in a London studio, numb with fatigue, waiting for the airwaves to clear so that he could read the report he'd prepared. Time and again Cronkite started broadcasting, only to be told that the signal had faded. With blocked airwaves, he never was able to make that Wilhelmshaven broadcast for CBS Radio, but the exercise brought him to the attention of Murrow, who liked his relaxed reading style. Cronkite, it seemed, had a voice tailor-made for radio. Murrow usually hired journalists *despite* their voices. Because Murrow so often argued with Paul White over reporters who were ace writers and weak readers, there was a suspicion that he purposely favored bad voices. Nothing was further from the truth. He had developed his own vocal ability through long hours of grueling practice. He certainly valued the reporter who could deliver in both respects.

After Cronkite logged his UP report on Wilhelmshaven, a dark cloud of depression descended on him. The stark reality sank in: Bob Post had not returned. For a while Cronkite fantasized that Post was okay, a prisoner of war, captured on the ground and being treated with decency in some Nazi POW camp. Other crews in Post's formation reported seeing the stricken plane going down near Wilhelmshaven, a wing missing. Others claimed they saw men parachuting out of the B-24 as it spiraled downward toward disaster. As a reporter, Cronkite worked hard to find out *exactly* what had happened, only to come up with contradictory facts. Such was the fog of war. What made Post's death even more difficult was that his wife had recently arrived in London, ready for two days of R&R with her husband.

Once Cronkite submitted his United Press story, he composed a prose elegy for Bob Post that was imbued with a Fitzgeraldian sense of lost innocence. He tried to sound upbeat about his press colleague, letting the world know what a great bloke he was, but his typewriter kept hitting gloomy keys. "This is the story of Bob Post of the *New York Times*—the story he cannot write today," Cronkite wrote in a United Press tribute. "It's the story of a big lumbering bespectacled Harvard graduate who looked about as much like an intrepid airman as Oliver Hardy, but whose heart beat the same do-or-die cadence as the pilots and crew of the American bomber which he accompanied to doom somewhere over Wilhelmshaven."

Unfortunately Cronkite's tribute to Post didn't get play in American newspapers. The U.S. government was hungry for morale-boosting, we-bombed-the-bejesus-out-of-Germany stories. Nothing about Post's death worked as a morale-building Uncle Sam recruit-ment poster for the Mighty Eighth. In August 1943, *The New York Times* officially declared Post dead, based on information obtained by the International Red Cross. Rooney, in retrospect, believed the whole push to embed with the Eighth was contrived and idiotic. Looking back on photos of the Writing Sixty-Niners in heavy fur-lined jackets, pants, flying overalls, fur-lined caps, goggles, and oxygen masks made him shake his head in disbelief. "I was scared to death of those missions," he admitted. "Going up like that was a foolish thing to do. Reporters like to be close to the action. But what did we accomplish, really? Nothing. On those bomb raids over Germany all we did was take up space."

Most of Cronkite's post-Wilhelmshaven dispatches of 1943 recited facts in an organized way aimed at cre-ating "personal heroism stories." His first question to an airman was always "Where do you hail from?" What surprised Cronkite was how easily he abandoned all the rules of objective journalism he had learned in Mr. Birney's class at San Jacinto High School and from Vann Kennedy at INS. All Cronkite stories now had one aim: spit in the eyes of the Nazis. "The Yanks are here, all right, and Adolf Hitler has good reason to worry about it," he crowed in a May 15 UP article on the Mighty Eighth buildup. "One can't go near an American base without catching the spirit of 'we've got the stuff now.'"

PR officers were interested in exactly that sort of morale-boosting piece—something to encourage the army airmen as well as the we-are-all-in-this-together civilians back home. Most correspondents supplied the puffery only as necessary, to remain on good terms with the PR officers. Cronkite eagerly wrote propaganda for the good of the Allied cause. He was a reporter for Democracy. "We were all on the same side," Cronkite later said, "and most of us newsmen abandoned any thought of impartiality as we reported on the heroism of our boys and the bestiality of the hated Nazis."

No matter what Cronkite now wrote—even patriotic pablum—it was eagerly printed in U.S. newspapers. In New York, Hugh Baillie was extremely happy with his suddenly star reporter. It was as if Cronkite had a gold-starred passport after the Wilhelmshaven raid. As 1943 closed, he had achieved a bit of journalistic glory. His November 19 dispatch ("Nazi Air Force Seen Beaten at Every Turn") ran in *The New York World-Telegram* and was circulated among the flyboys. But, missing Betsy terribly, he grew despondent after receiving a memo from UP's New York bureau manager, Earl Johnson: "We do not have the least idea how many years this war will last, but we would be less than smart if we did not prepare for a long war."

The eventual successes of the Mighty Eighth, which Cronkite documented at a time when the air war was hanging in the balance, had expedited the time frame of the Operation Overlord (D-day) invasion plan of Supreme Allied Commander Dwight D. Eisenhower. The Third Reich was losing planes at an alarming rate. Hitler was forced to pull his Luftwaffe from northern France to defend the German homeland. When *Playboy* magazine asked Cronkite about his Mighty Eighth experiences in 1973, the then–*CBS Evening News* anchorman responded, "I'm embarrassed when I'm introduced for speeches and somebody takes a CBS handout and reads that part of it because it makes me sound like some sort of hero." Compared to Bob Post or Andy Rooney, Cronkite felt like an "overweening coward of the year" who was "scared to death" all the time. His rule was "to avoid getting into combat."

7.

Dean of the Air War

SHADOW OF MURROW—SAVILE CLUB INCIDENT—
FAVORITE WAR STORY—ORCHESTRATED HELL—THE
AMAZING 303RD—A TOUCH OF FAME—HAVE I BEEN
SIDELINED?—D-DAY AT LAST—FLYING IN A B-17—
PEA SOUP FOG—WAS THAT OMAHA BEACH?—
REFLECTIONS WITH EISENHOWER—THE BIRTH OF TV
JOURNALISM

After the Wilhelmshaven mission, as Cronkite reported the burgeoning air war for UP, CBS News occasionally asked him to deliver radio reports about flyboys. It was mainly the morale-boosting stuff—reports of Eighth Air Force baseball games and seeing Clark Gable in the flesh. United Press was more than willing to lend Cronkite out, on the theory that the CBS broadcasts broadened his, and UP's, audience share. Cronkite even played the role of a fictionalized Walter Cronkite on three episodes of the action-adventure radio show *Soldiers of the Press*. Instead of G-men as heroes, World War II reporters were given the Superman treatment. The show was UP's way to do PR, offer wartime propaganda, and let Americans know that wire service reporters were risking their lives for democracy. "It expressed the jargon and explained the processes of covering combat in a time when communication technology made live battlefield reporting impossible," Cronkite later told NPR. "Dramatizations like these were a kind of reporting, sort of journalism once removed."

With his firm, clear, and penetrative voice, Cronkite sounded distinguished on radio. He had a genius for accentuating syllables in a compelling way. In the fall of 1943, Murrow, a gifted talent scout, asked Cronkite to lunch at the Savile Club in London, a rarefied gentlemen's institution that had counted Kipling and Darwin as members. For Cronkite, getting to dine with Murrow was the high point of his time in London. He found the chain-smoking broadcaster extremely erudite, exhibiting his broad range of knowledge brilliantly in conversation. He was a natural newsman, larger and looser than Cronkite had expected. After some good-natured casual chat, Murrow offered Cronkite employment at CBS. According to Murrow, Cronkite's first posting would be a prominent one—Stalingrad—and his base pay would be $125 per week, more than twice the $57.50 he received from United Press. It was a heady offer.

The former UP night-shift deskman from Kansas City—Walter Cronkite of St. Joseph along the Missouri River—was being courted by Edward R. Murrow at the prestigious Savile Club in London. Imagine that! The spirit of Horatio Alger was still alive and well in America. Murrow had assembled the stellar group of war correspondents for CBS that came to be known as the Murrow Boys. This collection of acolytes was a genuine phenomenon from 1939 on. Focused and brimming with confidence, the Murrow Boys moved stealthily and quickly in pursuit of a story. Although the typical journalist of the era was more slovenly and sardonic, the Murrow Boys were dapper and knew how to make a great martini. This group—which included Cecil Brown, Winston Burdett, Charles Collingwood, William Downs, Thomas Grandin, Richard Hottelet, Larry LeSueur, Eric Sevareid, Howard K. Smith, and (the lone woman) Mary Marvin Breckenridge—constituted the cream of the crop of wartime radio journalism. Cronkite didn't waste much time accepting Murrow's generous offer to become CBS Radio's eyes, ears, and voice in Stalingrad. Cronkite and Murrow shook hands on the new job. "I guess he was looking for cannon fodder more than broadcaster," Cronkite later joked about getting the Stalingrad beat. "But I accepted."

Cronkite immediately zipped over to the UP office and told his boss, Harrison Salisbury, about the exciting CBS Radio offer, adding, with a degree of breast-beating, that he intended to seize the life-changing opportunity to work with Murrow. When Salisbury heard the details of CBS's lucrative (by journalism's meager standards) offer, he suddenly remembered a telegram that (so he claimed) had been sitting on his desk for three days. The message was from UP president Hugh Baillie; it increased Cronkite's salary by 25 percent. Cronkite was flattered. Describing Baillie's feelings toward Cronkite as paternal, Salisbury handled his reporter with finesse, saying he *knew* Cronkite wasn't the sort of low-rent cad to abandon his Unipresser "family" for CBS in the middle of World War II. Wasn't he a team player? "Well, he drove a stake right in my heart," Cronkite recalled, "because I loved the U.P., I really did." Nonetheless, Cronkite left

Salisbury's office reiterating that he had already agreed to CBS's handsome offer.

The same evening, the telephone rang in Cronkite's shabby London hotel room. His roommate, Jim McGlincy, a fellow UP reporter, fielded the call. It was Baillie—their boss—on the other end of the line. Somehow Baillie had placed a call from New York to this London flophouse, which was by itself a difficult feat in wartime. Once he and Cronkite established that they could hear each other clearly, Baillie, through a backbeat of static, went to work. "He gave me a sales pitch like you never heard in your life before," Cronkite recalled. "And he said, 'I'm going to raise you $20 a week just to show my good faith. You're going to be president of the United Press before you're 30.'" Cronkite was overwhelmed. Yet even when Walter was overwhelmed, he tended to his interests where money was concerned. "I said," Cronkite recounted, "'Does that include the $17.50 that Salisbury just told me already?' There was kind of a long pause, and he said, 'No, no, no, this is on top of all that,' which meant I was going up to $95 a week, a huge amount for United Press." Flattered and happy to stay in London with the boys of the Mighty Eighth, Cronkite reversed his Murrow decision and told Baillie that he would indeed remain a proud Unipresser.

Had Cronkite's decision been based only on money, he'd have jumped to CBS without a backward glance, but other root factors were also at play. In the first place, he had yet to be truly convinced that broadcast radio was a moneymaking vocation. Although Murrow was all the rage, his own experience announcing Oklahoma football games had left him cold. On a more personal level, he was less than eager to become one of the Murrow Boys like Sevareid and Smith, trying to ride the Great One's coattails to fame. As sterling a career opportunity as the CBS gig might have been, it would have entailed abandoning print journalism and the Eighth Air Force, whose flyboys were like family to him. And, it should be added, he *definitely* preferred living in wartime London than wartime Stalingrad.

Cronkite scheduled an appointment to see Murrow immediately. They met again at the Savile Club. Cronkite knew the legend deserved to hear of his reconsideration man-to-man. Unlike on previous occasions, Cronkite now noticed how deeply penetrating the CBS broadcaster's eyes were as he stared at him. Sheepishly Cronkite reported that he would be staying at United Press after all. Murrow was incensed at the about-face. From Murrow's perspective, Cronkite was reneging not just on a CBS job offer but on a Savile Club handshake, a matter of honor: an agreement between gentlemen.

Murrow was wounded by Cronkite's reversal but was too diplomatic to chide Cronkite for his decision to stay at UP. They shook hands as they parted. "I don't think it cost him any prestige," Cronkite guessed, "because it all happened within twenty-four hours."

Murrow was eight years older than Cronkite—not a great gap, but one that saw Murrow in a secure career as of 1943, when he was thirty-four. The underling Cronkite, at twenty-seven, was still—as Andy Rooney of *Stars and Stripes* had put it—"scrambling." Later in life Murrow, as was his wont, claimed he didn't recall the Savile Club incident. But according to Cronkite, Murrow intimated that Cronkite had parlayed the CBS offer into a higher salary from Baillie. That was, Murrow believed, low-road behavior. Cronkite didn't quite see it that way. Although he and Murrow would work professionally together at CBS, their personalities never meshed; permanent friction existed between them. "Murrow couldn't believe it," Stanley Cloud and Lynn Olson explained in *The Murrow Boys*. "How could Cronkite prefer the formulaic writing and anonymous existence of a U.P. reporter to life as a CBS correspondent?"

As *The Wall Street Journal* aptly put it, "a certain chill" pervaded Cronkite's relationship with the Murrow Boys "for the rest of his career." After turning down the CBS offer, Cronkite was too busy covering the Eighth Air Force beat to worry about his Q factor with Murrow, who had won the Peabody Award for his broadcasts from a besieged London. After nearly a year covering the air war for United Press, Cronkite continued to draw publicity of his own. His byline, as part of a deliberate campaign by UP to tout its own correspondents, had earned a certain cachet. Cronkite was made available for radio interviews and was the subject of discussion throughout the United States in newsrooms. In November 1943, *Look* magazine featured an article by Cronkite reliving the flight over Wilhelmshaven as "My Favorite War Story." And Murrow never blacklisted Cronkite from reporting on CBS Radio. "Despite my turning down Ed's offer, CBS kept inviting me to do pieces on the air," Cronkite recalled. "They kind of used me as an air war correspondent. . . . And, later, sometime in 1945, I was on CBS's weekly roundup of war news. I did a piece for them. So I had a connection with CBS through that whole period."

United Press was paying Cronkite what it considered an enormous salary and it wanted to turn him into a household name. Celebrity reporters were good for business. In January 1944 the wire service released a story about Cronkite, anointing him in the headline as the "Dean of the Air-War Writers" for his heroic interviews with bombardiers, flight engineers, and radar technicians based at Molesworth. In terms of the American air assault from British bases, it was true: he had helped UP come in first with scoops on the broadening extent of bombing during 1943. By the end of that year, the Eighth Air Force comprised two hundred thousand military personnel. It was capable of sending more than two thousand Flying Fortresses (B-17s) and Liberators (B-24s) into the air on a single day. But the death of Bob Post meant that journalists were now rarely allowed to go along on a bombing run. Murrow campaigned heavily to do so and was repeatedly turned down, until December 1943, when he was taken on a bombing mission to Berlin with the RAF. His vivid account was a major news story, easily eclipsing anything by UP's "Dean of the Air-War Writers." Murrow, to Cronkite's amazement, called the Berlin bombing "a kind of orchestrated hell." Cronkite childishly thought Murrow had stolen his Wilhelmshaven "hell" metaphor.

No reporter spent more time hanging around the Molesworth Boys and drinking at the Cross Keys tavern than Cronkite. When the men of the 303rd Bomber Group came back from missions, Cronkite, their chronicler, would dutifully record their harrowing recollections. Most of his prose sketches never made it into UP articles, but the flyboys liked thinking that if they were killed in action, then at least Cronkite would be able to let America know how brave they had been. In February 1944, Cronkite boarded *Shoo Shoo Baby*—named after a song by the Andrews Sisters and famously plastered with a towering image of Bugs Bunny—and fastened his flak jacket. By now, he had learned how to write about the plane's two waist-gun emplacements and top-turret gunner's perch like a pro. He considered himself a veteran war correspondent.

On this bombing mission, he sat between bombardier F. E. Umphress Jr. and navigator Kenneth Olsen. But he later joked that he had turned his life over to Captain Bob Sheets, known as one of the best U.S. pilots in England, a man who hated Nazis more than the clap. Cronkite knew from interviewing Sheets after previous missions that he wasn't afraid of Focke-Wulf 190s or Messerschmitt 109s. The gutsy Sheets actually liked going after the Luftwaffe. He thought dueling with the Nazi pilots over the North Sea was exhilarating for a singular reason: he always won.

Still, even with a ballsy pilot like Sheets, the risk that February was very real. The B-17 Cronkite had flown on in an earlier mission, for example, a plane called *S-for-Sugar*, had been shot down while dropping five-hundred-pound demolition bombs on an aircraft assembly plant in Oschersleben, Germany. All of the men on board perished. So Cronkite's gallows humor before the mission was actually a camouflage for fear. Years later, when writing about the 303rd in his memoir, *A Reporter's Life*, Cronkite signed a photograph to his old B-17 pilot that read: "For Captain Bob Sheets—with a lifetime of gratitude for getting us back."

By late March 1944, Cronkite, while not privy to classified information, knew that the Allied invasion of France was approaching. Betting on the exact day, place, and time of the invasion had become a parlor game for Molesworth beat journalists. The waiting game kept Cronkite on high alert. But as Cronkite's fourth wedding anniversary approached—March 30, 1944—he also grew lovesick for Betsy. "I just sent you a cable . . . saying the only thing I seem to be able to think," Cronkite wrote his wife. "That the first two years seemed to go so quickly, and the last two have dragged so horribly. Two whole years out of our lives. It makes this war with Hitler a pretty personal matter."

A glitch occurred that almost prevented Cronkite from covering D-day. For some reason, Cronkite wasn't selected to be the UP reporter covering the Normandy invasion. The decision made that May was that Jim McGlincy would be one of the five hundred correspondents chosen for the invasion across the Channel. The snub stung. He was mystified as to why he was being benched. In a letter to Betsy he conveyed how "broken hearted" he was at not being chosen. But he did, in the end, play a minor role in the D-day landings.

At 1:30 a.m. on June 6, 1944, he was shaken awake in his London hotel room by a friend, Major Hal Leyshon, the PR man from the Eighth Air Force, madly pounding on his door. A breathless Leyshon told Cronkite, "We've gotten a new mission with the Eighth Air Force. And it's going to be a highly dangerous operation, very dangerous, something we've never done before." Leyshon told Cronkite he would have the *first* and *best* story of the cross-Channel assault. "There's a pretty big story breaking," Leyshon concluded. "I think you better come with us." Cronkite quickly changed clothes and grabbed his bag. Once they were in Leyshon's sedan, driving through the dark, Cronkite received a full explanation. "The invasion is about to start," Leyshon said. "We're sending a B-17 bomber group over the coast at low altitude as a spearhead."

"It struck me," Cronkite wrote decades later, "that this was D-Day and I was going to be there." As the car rumbled down a back road headed to the airstrip, Cronkite understood that D-day was the make-or-break moment for the Allies. How strange that living in such a grand moment felt so routine. Leyshon claimed that historians would someday think of June 6 as another Gettysburg or Waterloo. Cronkite knew he was probably right. "You have the greatest story of the war because you're going to get back before any other stories will be released," Leyshon told Cronkite when they reached the airfield at 3:00 a.m. "You will be back in your office ready when the story of D-day starts hitting the wires. You'll be able to write, 'I've just returned from flying over the beaches.'"

Cronkite remembered thinking, "Jesus Christ, that's the greatest."

After a full year of round-the-clock reporting, Cronkite was excited to think that he would be a part of D-day, flying in a tight formation of B-17s, witnessing the beginning of the liberation of Europe. Leyshon warned Cronkite that the flight would be at a very low altitude because of the lousy weather. Once at the Molesworth base, Cronkite sat through a series of fast and furious intelligence briefings. A huge map of Normandy was unveiled that showed arrows and estimates. For the first time, Cronkite grasped the enormity of the Normandy invasion. Every aspect of D-day amazed him. He didn't know the Allies had over four thousand vessels in their armada.

Off Cronkite went into the sky on a B-17 in a V-formation of nine planes. Instead of flying at seventeen thousand feet (as he had during the Wilhelmshaven raid), Cronkite was now cruising only a few hundred feet above the ground in a thick fog. "And then the order came to arm the bombs—remove the safety pins so they would explode on contact," he wrote. "If we collided, the bomber would probably go, and the 303rd could go up in one terrible series of blasts."

Cronkite's flight over the North Sea didn't accomplish its mission of dropping bombs on German defensive positions. The fog made that impossible. Nor did Cronkite, craning his neck in vain, have a genuine view of the beachhead. The greatest invasion fleet in world history was below him—battleships, cruisers, destroyers, large transports, and a phalanx of lesser vessels—but he couldn't see them because of cloud cover. He did get a few glimpses of the Allied armada crossing the Channel, which he deemed an "unbelievable sight." There were so many vessels, he wrote, that there "didn't seem to be room for any more" in the Channel.

His own reporting that morning was understated. With perhaps too much humility, he didn't even mention that he'd been on board a B-17 bomber during the early going with the Mighty Eighth. Unlike Murrow for CBS Radio or Hemingway for *Collier's* (on Omaha

Beach), Cronkite didn't really have much of a story. The first part of Cronkite's UP report was a succinct account of the all-night bombing strikes on German positions along the French coast. Then Cronkite gave some idea of the sights and sounds of D-day's first air battle. "Many of the German gun nests were blanketed by thick cloud formations, but the British bombers sent their blockbusters crashing down dead on the targets through flare rings dropped by their pathfinder planes," he wrote. "Throughout the night the skies over the channel reverberated to the ceaseless beat of Allied planes and the roar of exploding bombs rolled back to the British coast."

The most riveting journalism report of June 6, 1944, came from George Hicks for ABC. He stood near the bridge of the American command ship U.S.S. *Ancon* (a sophisticated communications ship) as it lay off Omaha Beach on D-day just after 6:00 a.m., in the midst of the Normandy invasion, which included more than five thousand Allied ships and thirteen thousand Allied aircraft. A stunned Hicks described the magnificent flotilla as it deposited soldiers on the beach. There was no air battle on D-day; the decimated Luftwaffe didn't show up in force, as feared. Hicks stayed where he was and continued recording for more than ten minutes. The present tense was radio's strength, and rarely had

it been quite so effective as with a man and a microphone at the core of battle, in this case, Hicks for ABC:

> *The planes come over closer* (sound of plane)...
> *Smoke... brilliant fire down low toward the
> French coast a couple of miles. I don't know
> whether it's on the shore or is a ship. Here's very
> heavy ack-ack now.* (Heavy ack-ack.) *The plane
> seems to be coming directly overhead.* . . . (Sound
> of plane and machine-gun fire and ack-ack.)
> *Well, that's the first time we've shot our guns* . . .

Hicks stole the show. "After that," said CBS News
director Paul White, referring to Hicks's report,
"everything was anti-climax." White was in New York,
choosing reports from the pool for broadcast over the
network. A workhorse with CBS since 1930, he believed
radio had covered the invasion brilliantly, though others
pointed to technical problems that reduced the number
of reports available. The newspaper coverage was more
complete, as papers all over America put out "extra"
editions to cover the unfolding story. Virgil Pinkley,
UP European manager and one of Cronkite's immediate bosses, assumed the job of amalgamating the many
reports into UP's lead story on the day's events, which
ran under banner type on the front page of hundreds of

newspapers. Cronkite's account of the early-morning bombing was buried in the back pages of the few U.S. papers that ran it.

What Cronkite took from D-day was that radio broadcasting was still *the* medium of World War II. When Murrow had first come to Europe in 1937, he tried to join the American Foreign Correspondents Association; he was turned down because he was a broadcaster, not a print reporter. After the Normandy invasion, Murrow was anointed president of the London-based organization. That honorific said it all in an overwhelmingly easy-to-comprehend way. Radio was the new print. Murrow by 1945 had grown accustomed to wearing garlands as neckties.

Once all the D-day activity had settled down, Cronkite wrote a long and tangled letter home on June 12. "It turned out that I did fly the morning of the invasion after all but the Eighth Air Force public relations people who thought they were doing me a favor and handing me a scoop on a silver platter managed to botch things up," he wrote to Betsy. "We were above a solid cloud bank all the way over the Channel and back, and although I was over the invasion beaches shortly after zero hour and inland over Caen and Carentan, I did not see a single thing. I never was so disgusted in my life. Why, we didn't even get shot at. A dozen bursts of flak and that was my invasion experience. It was like taking only one drink on New Year's Eve."

When asked decades later whether he had flown over Utah or Omaha Beach, Cronkite nonchalantly shrugged. "I think it was Omaha," he said. "We didn't know about those names then, of course; all I knew was it was the beach. I didn't even know how extensive the landings were." What Cronkite *did* know was that Eisenhower was the true man of the hour, the architect of Operation Overlord. In 1964, Cronkite got the opportunity to interview Eisenhower on Omaha Beach for a *CBS News Special Report* called "D-Day Plus Twenty Years." Staring out at the English Channel, Eisenhower turned philosophical. "You see these people out here swimming and sailing their little pleasure boats and taking advantage of the nice weather and the lovely beach, Walter, and it is almost unreal to look at it today and remember what it was," Eisenhower told Cronkite. "But it's a wonderful thing to remember what those fellows twenty years ago were fighting for and sacrificing for, what they did to preserve our way of life. Not to conquer any territory, not for any ambitions of our own. But to make sure that Hitler could not destroy freedom in the world."

Cronkite nodded along in agreement, remembering his own D-day experience in the fog, a non-eyewitness to the turning point in the liberation of Europe. "To think of the lives that were given for that principle," Eisenhower said to Cronkite, "paying a terrible price on this beach alone, on that one day, 2,000 casualties. But they did it so that the world could be free. It just shows what free men will do rather than be slaves."

In the aftermath of D-day, Cronkite knew the tide had indeed turned for the Allies. "I suppose I actually have been just as busy since D-day as I was before, but the work is more tedious," he wrote his mother on August 15. "I no longer am handling the top story of the day: the air war has been relegated to second, third, or even fourth place, by the French fighting, the Russian Front and inner German politics. So, although scarcely two years ago I would have been thrilled to handle any big story, now I find myself getting just a little bored if it is not [a] number one story every day."

A month later, in the 263rd week of World War II, Cronkite would no longer find himself bored. But Cronkite's Eighth Air Force reportorial beat wasn't *the* story. The liberations of Paris and Brussels dominated headlines. Cronkite told his mother he'd ask Virgil Pinkley, the general manager of United Press, about finagling a quick two-week leave-trip home. He missed Betsy terribly. Even during war, keeping a foreign correspondent away from his wife for too long was cruel. No superior at the UP provided Cronkite much encouragement on the "break" front. "Hugh Baillie is coming over for a few weeks and Virgil thinks that, since I probably will be one of our post-war European bureau managers, I ought to be on hand when the president is here," Cronkite wrote. "I agree with him to that extent, and also want a chance to see a little of the action before the show is over. But I also would like a couple of weeks with you all again."

While Cronkite manned the UP desk in London and worried that his rising career might be on the post-D-day downswing, a group of men and women in New York were doing work of far greater import to his future. The four American radio networks—CBS, NBC, ABC, and Mutual—knew television would be the new trend in broadcasting once the war was over. The medium had been around since the 1920s, but now its long infancy was coming to a close. Almost no one had a television set yet, and the networks had voluntarily suspended TV broadcasting for the two last years because of the war. But around D-day, CBS renewed its TV broadcasting efforts. Paul White, director of news, took a strong interest in transferring the expertise of the Murrow Boys into the new television medium.

By the mid-1940s, while radio news was sleekly produced and as respected in terms of integrity as its print counterpart, television was just plain clumsy. White wrote with sturdy self-assertion, "There's no question that television has tremendous possibilities, especially in the fields of news and special events. The news broadcaster, assisted by maps, charts, films, animation devices and photographs, should be able to give the news a dimension not possible when it is heard only by the ear and not seen by the eye."

White's CBS division, overflowing with futuristic optimism, started producing an experimental TV broadcast twice a week. Hosted by an "anchor," this fifteen-minute news show was innovative in the use of illustrations, and it impressed even Marty Schrader, the stern critic at *Billboard* magazine. He roundly disdained the rest of CBS's TV programming but thought that the news show was equal in quality to anything on the radio. Since the other radio networks had yet to return to television, CBS and its news department now had a head start on the new medium. As White observed, the public was much more curious about television than about any of the innovations on the horizon for radio. But with the Second World War still in full swing, television would have to wait its turn until victory over both Germany and Japan could be declared.

8.

Gliding to V-E Day

THE WAR GRINDS ON—PINING FOR NORMALCY—TV
HOLDS ITS OWN (BARELY)—WHAT AN AIRBORNE
OPERATION!—OUTHUSTLED BY MURROW REDUX—
FEAR AND LONELINESS IN BRUSSELS—ARDENNES
FOREST TALES—HELL'S HIGHWAY WITH BILL
DOWNS—THESE ARE THE GOOD OLD DAYS—TULIP
JUBILEE—V-E DAY AT LAST—REPORTING ON THE
RUBBLE—OPENING UP BENELUX BUREAUS—
REFUSING TO THROW IN THE TOWEL—WELCOME TO
THE ATOMIC AGE

The Waco CG-4 was the most widely used U.S. troop and cargo glider in World War II. Cronkite suddenly found himself strapped inside one like a sardine in a can. It was September 17, 1944, and he was participating in Operation Market Garden (the combined armored/airborne attack through Holland north from the Belgian/Dutch border that aimed to cross the lower Rhine River and outflank the Siegfried Line to break into Germany's back door). It seemed odd to Cronkite, as the lead C-47's tow rope was cut and his glider headed toward the Dutch farmlands below, that this flying coffin had been made by the Wicks Aircraft Company's factory in Kansas City.

Of all the books written about World War II, Cronkite's favorite was Cornelius Ryan's *A Bridge Too Far*. Not only did he cooperate with Ryan about his own role as the UP reporter attached to the 101st Airborne's assault on the Germans along the border of Belgium and the Netherlands, but he also recommended Ryan's book to everybody because it portrayed the bravery of both the Allied soldiers and the Dutch resistance fighters determined to defeat the Nazis following the liberation of Brussels. "Market" was the code name for the airborne assault Cronkite found himself a part of that day, while "Garden" denoted the name given to the armored forces. "I was unceremoniously crash-landed in a troop-carrying glider," Cronkite told Ryan. "The German Army welcomed us with machine-gun fire."

Cronkite was dropped into the largest airborne operation of World War II, in which over twenty thousand men rode in 478 white-striped gliders and 1,544 transport planes to help rid Holland of the Germans. His partner on his jarring descent in the glider was Brigadier General Anthony Clement McAuliffe; with them was a group of 101st Airborne staff officers. A flurry of antiaircraft fire rocked the sky as the Cronkite-McAuliffe team tried to engineer a smooth landing. The martial noise was deafening. As Cronkite's glider thumped hard on the ground, almost knocking him unconscious, he thought of how idiotic he had been for believing a glider was like a kite—no "roaring engine," simply a "silent glide into eternity." For a few seconds, Cronkite thought he had died. In a conversation with historian Don Carleton, Cronkite joked, "if you have to go to war, don't go by glider!"

The 101st Airborne glider Cronkite was riding in landed near the Dutch village of Zon and the Wilhelmina Canal. The objective of Market Garden was to capture eight bridges that spanned the network of canals and rivers on the Dutch-German border—a feat that would require British and American troops to fly behind enemy lines. Cronkite was surprised immediately by the heavy volume of artillery fire left in the Third Reich's arsenal. "I thought the wheels of the glider were for landing," Cronkite told Ryan. "Imagine my surprise when we skidded along the ground and the wheels came up through the floor. I got another shock. Our helmets, which we all swore were hooked, came flying off on impact and seemed more dangerous than the incoming shells. After landing I grabbed the first helmet I saw, my trusty musette bag with the Smith-Corona typewriter inside and began crawling toward the [Wilhelmina] canal, which was the rendezvous point. When I looked back I found a half dozen guys crawling after me. It seems that I had grabbed the wrong helmet. The one I wore had two neat stripes down the back indicating that I was lieutenant."

The eight-day objective of Market Garden, authored by the usually cautious Field Marshal Bernard Law Montgomery, commander of the British forces in Europe, was to hasten Allied victory by outflanking the Siegfried Line, a stretch of defensive forts along the western border of Germany. The astonishing Allied success of the D-day landings in France had become mired in the languid and costly advance through the Normandy glades and hedgerows, which the Germans defended with dexterity and resolve.

Market Garden was largely unsuccessful in creating a back door into Germany for the Allied forces. That, of course, didn't mean that Cronkite didn't sell

Market Garden as a victory to his American readership. "Thousands of Allied parachutists and glider troops landed behind the German lines in the Netherlands today, liberated village after village from enemy troops who fled in panic before them, and, as I write, are pushing to their first big objective, which they expected to reach by nightfall," Cronkite reported. "I landed with the glider troops in this greatest airborne operation in all history—an invasion in which most of the intrepid men engaged are Americans seasoned in the Normandy invasion."

With Hitler's prized Panzer units offering the Allies stiff resistance, Cronkite's glider had turned upside down and was cracked in two like an eggshell. Ironically, Cronkite didn't want to write about his near-death experience. His assignment was to write about the heroism of others. Cronkite's upbeat Market Garden stories ran in an unusually high number of newspapers, including *The New York Times*, which normally gave Associated Press reporting precedence over United Press. In rah-rah fashion, Cronkite reported that Montgomery's monumental push aimed at having the Allied troops and tanks go through Nazi-occupied Holland and then across the Rhine into Germany proper was a game changer. Outside of Zon, Cronkite had difficulties in transmitting his UP stories to Allied headquarters.

Nothing went well for Cronkite—the Zon bridge over the Wilhelmina Canal had been blown up, leaving him stranded for thirty-six hours before repairs could be made. And Cronkite—who later called his stories from Holland "lame"—wasn't the star reporter of Market Garden. The ubiquitous Murrow rode a C-47 carrying paratroopers to the drop zone and recorded a spectacular commentary for CBS Radio:

Bob Masell of the Blue Network is sitting here working on the recording gear just as calm and cool as any of the paratroopers, but perhaps both of us should be because they're going to jump and we aren't. . . . There's a burst of flak. . . . It's coming from the port side, just across the nose, but a little bit low. . . . Nine ships ahead of us have just dropped and you can see the men swinging down.

Murrow continued to build drama for CBS listeners:

I can see their chutes going down now, every man clear. They're dropping just beside a little windmill near a church, hanging there . . . They seem to be completely relaxed, like nothing so much as khaki dolls hanging beneath a green lampshade. . . . The whole sky is filled.

Murrow ended his report from the airborne C-47 with a line that stuck with Cronkite: "That's the way it was." As Edward Bliss Jr. pointed out in *Now the News: The Story of Broadcast Journalism*, Murrow's "That's the way it was" antedated, by nineteen long years, Cronkite's signature TV signoff, "And that's the way it is." Cronkite never gave Murrow proper credit for this.

What Cronkite didn't tell readers—couldn't for propaganda reasons—was that Market Garden was plagued with logistical failures. Instead, he focused on the liberation of Eindhoven. And he rightly reported that except for a single engagement at Neunen, the American troops hurled the Germans back at every point. The armored column Cronkite was embedded with passed through the center of the operation controlled by the 82nd. Eventually, Cronkite made his way to Brussels and, using it as his base city for a few days, covered Montgomery's Second Army regrouping and Belgian politics. Sometimes he camped outside or lived in a cramped, bug-infested hotel. He also reported on the battles to liberate the Low Countries. Many of his dispatches from Eindhoven were propagandist, claiming that the U.S. paratroopers had routed the Germans when they hadn't. Arnhem stayed in German hands no matter how Cronkite spun it. Sometime in November, he saw a German V-2 rocket being launched toward England. "It looked like a gigantic skyrocket that disappeared into the stratosphere but never went off," he wrote. "There was only a speck of glow, but there was what must have been a huge column of creamy white smoke clearly visible to the naked eye more than 100 miles away."

A number of Cronkite's great war stories came from Market Garden. His sidekick in the flat Dutch countryside was frequently Bill Downs of CBS, a former Unipresser and Cronkite's closest friend among the Murrow Boys. With Downs as his constant companion, Cronkite maneuvered around the shifting battlefields of rural Belgium and the Netherlands that month. Downs, who had been attached to the British Second Army, and Cronkite were in rural Belgium when a merciless Luftwaffe strafing occurred. They sprinted together to the nearby forest for cover. Soon they were separated. Cronkite called out to Downs, but to no avail. He feared for his friend's life. For hours Cronkite shouted for Downs until he was hoarse. Once back in Brussels, he told friends that poor Downs was missing in action. Then one evening, Cronkite headed over to the Hotel Metropole for a cocktail. To his astonishment, there was Downs, sitting at the bar with friends, having a gay old time.

A wave of anger swept over Cronkite as he headed to Downs's table.

"I thought you'd been killed," he said. "I went through the woods calling your name."

An embarrassed Downs had an alibi. "I couldn't go around calling *your* name," he said. "They'd think I was shouting German."

By December 1944 Cronkite had spent two years in Europe. He was much skinnier and had less hair than when Betsy had last seen him in New York. Covering the war without a break aged a man. Few correspondents had shown the kind of stamina that Cronkite had displayed during the war. Even Murrow visited the United States quite frequently while he was posted in London. Cronkite, who had, ironically, been turned down for military service on a medical deferment, was indestructible, always wanting to be in the middle of the soldier story. Not the battle itself. Ensconced behind his Smith-Corona typewriter in Brussels, feeling hot and irritable, he complained loudly about wanting a break, needing to go home. But a few minutes later he was hatching plans about how to cover the demise of the Third Reich for UP.

In early December 1944, Cronkite was pleased to be filing stories on political developments in recently liberated Belgium; it constituted the type of daily-life reporting that he hoped to do after the war. On December 16, just as the Allied line in Western Europe seemed to solidify, the Germans swept against its weakest section, precipitating the Battle of the Bulge. "I was back in Brussels the night that Field Marshal Von Rundstedt started pounding through the Ardennes," Cronkite recalled. "I got a call from U.P. in Paris that something had happened." There were reports of action in the Ardennes, the forested plateau about seventy miles to the south.

Cronkite had barely put the phone receiver down when he heard a rap on his door. It was a breathless John Fleischer, a fellow Unipresser with the First Army. "This goddamn thing is real," Fleischer said of the Bulge. "We have a headlong retreat." For the next half hour, Cronkite interrogated Fleischer on everything he knew about the Bulge. He got the story out of his colleague and then drove as fast as he could—against the onslaught of retreating troops—to be near the battle line. Fleischer returned to the Bulge battlefield; soon thereafter he was killed by a bomb. When Cronkite got the news of Fleischer's death he broke down crying. But he also had the presence of mind to get Fleischer's last story out over the UP wire.

The fact that Cronkite managed to book a room at the Cravat Hotel in Luxembourg City, the HQ of General

Omar Bradley, located only miles from the front, made his efforts no less valiant. It only demonstrated that he was a newspaper reporter willing to seize hotel comfort when available. The southern shoulder of the German breakthrough was north of Luxembourg. Cronkite followed General Bradley, who had lost communication with his units to the north as the invasion swept by. Eisenhower was alarmed that Bradley had no way to communicate with the Third Army and Ninth Army of 300,000 men. From the Cravat Hotel, he could only contact the First Army on the south side. There was a sense of general peace and safety in Luxembourg. The German thrust was eighty miles wide and forty miles deep, from Monshau to the north, to Eckternacht in the south. Ike suggested that Bradley move his HQ to the apex of the Bulge so he could communicate down both shoulders, but Bradley balked, telling Cronkite that it would look bad for the men to see a general retreating. Ike didn't care for appearances and wanted communications established. Since Bradley could not and would not retreat, Eisenhower turned over two-thirds of Bradley's command to Montgomery, who had no problem doing so, on the north shoulder. Cronkite, marooned with Bradley, didn't have much of a story. "During the early days of the Bulge," Cronkite later said, "there was little to do but watch. A complete news blackout on all ground activity was added to normal censorship."

Reporters were lucky to send back snippets from the front, to be compiled into articles by desk editors. Censorship wasn't eased until after Christmas, which was a turning point for the Allies in the Bulge. (The battle lasted until January 25.) Starting in late December, Cronkite could file stories pertaining to British and American troops, yet he wrote little about them compared to his previous postings from Eindhoven. That didn't make him recall these incidents any less vividly years later. "The heroic events of that Christmas," he said about the Bulge in an essay for National Public Radio in 2004, "still mingle in my memory with the frigid air, the crunching snow, makeshift trees and carols echoing from tinny loudspeakers. . . . Memory often plays games when facts and emotion collide. But if the sound of Christmas music seems to lend a false sentimentality to the savagery of a horrible battle, it's not because either the sentimentality or the savagery is dishonest or untrue. It was all wrapped up in a genuinely heroic story that Christmas of 1944."

Although Christmas 1944 was a turning point for the Allies, there was still great suffering and death during the first two weeks of January. After the Battle of the Bulge ended on January 25, 1945, Cronkite returned to

London and spent much of the next few months there. As a war correspondent, Cronkite's unintentional problem in 1944 and 1945 was that he was always just on the outskirts of the action area. But he was the UP authority on the Netherlands, Luxembourg, and Belgium. That counted for a lot. The filings from London, as Allied forces pushed into Germany, kept him busy at the United Press bureau, but he was occasionally sent back to the Low Countries to report from the field. Like most U.S. reporters, he didn't care much for Montgomery, perhaps as a result of attending too many of his briefings. "He really didn't deserve the credit he got," Cronkite insisted. "In Europe he sat on the Rhine intolerably long." While stuck in Luxembourg, Cronkite befriended General Bradley. The only problem was that the gripping news was coming out of Bastogne, not the Cravat Hotel.

What Cronkite did gain from the Second World War was the ability to say he'd been a war correspondent. Murrow, Collingwood, Sevareid, Liebling, and, yes, Cronkite had become famous names. Unlike Murrow and his CBS Boys, Cronkite hadn't pioneered the use of recordings from a C-47 flying over Holland or captured the gunfire ratchet of house-to-house combat in Aachen, Germany. However, he had gone on a combat bombing mission over Germany and been through

D-day, Operation Market Garden, and the Battle of the Bulge (largely from the remove of Luxembourg). That was a damn impressive résumé.

During the Second World War (and the early cold war years that followed) the Charles Street Club in London was a favorite hangout for international newsmen. Everybody raved about how well the martinis were shaken and served. Don Hewitt, destined to become one of the most successful producers in television history, was hanging out there one afternoon, minding his own olives, when the United Press bureau chief walked up to the crowded bar. Suddenly everybody was whispering in awe. "Before you knew it, you could hear people saying, 'You know who that is? That's Walter Cronkite,'" Hewitt recalled in his memoir, *Tell Me a Story.* "Today, fifty years later, people still say, 'You know who that is? That's Walter Cronkite.'"

To his credit, Cronkite didn't try to milk his World War II experiences for personal glorification. In fact, he liked to tell the story of the day in September 1944 when he and Bill Downs, after participating in the Market Garden glider landings in the Netherlands, were riding in a Jeep down Highway 69 (dubbed "Hell's Highway") and sharing a wild kind of momentary euphoria when they ran into serious crossfire. Ack-ack gunfire echoed all around them. A mortar exploded

within yards of their Jeep, sending the two correspondents scrambling for cover in a nearby drainage ditch.
Cronkite and Downs kept their heads down, helmets
firmly fastened, just as General Patton insisted, but
the outcome was uncertain, to say the least. The flak
seemed endless. They were terrified that death was
upon them. "Downs, lying behind me, began tugging
at my pants leg," Cronkite recalled. "I figured he had
some scheme for getting us out of there, and I twisted
my neck around to look back at him. He was yelling to
me: 'Hey, just remember, Cronkite. These are the good
old days.'"

On May 5, 1945, at the hamlet of Wageningen,
near Arnhem and Nijmegen, German generals signed
the protocols of capitulation surrendering Denmark
and the Netherlands. V-E ("Victory in Europe")
Day had almost arrived, and rumors of an armistice
were announced on the UP wire. Cronkite borrowed
a U.S. Army command car to ride from Brussels to
Amsterdam to witness the liberation celebration at Dam
Square. The landscape he traversed was geographically
low lying, with vast swaths of land below sea level.
Since Nazi Germany had invaded the Netherlands five
years earlier, in May 1940, the Dutch people had lived
in terror daily. Their response to their liberators was
ecstatic. "They pelted us with tulips until our car was

fender deep in them," Cronkite recalled. "Tulips are heavy flowers. In bundles they are dangerous. The only blood I spilled in the war was that day—hit by a bunch of tulips tied together with a piece of wire."

Wearing his government-issue correspondent's uniform, cuffs hemmed so high you could see his socks, Cronkite joined in the Amsterdam revelry on May 7, V-E Day in Holland (determined to stay sober, he limited his libations there). "I got a lot of garlands and heard a lot of welcoming speeches," he later explained to *Time* magazine. "The Canadians were not amused." (It was the Canadian Army and the Royal Canadian Air Force that had liberated the country.) This was the greatest day in Cronkite's life, except for the day he married Betsy. An irrepressible joyousness, a downright rapture, swept over him at the realization that the Yanks had won, that Hitler was dead, that the people of the Netherlands had been liberated. Walter Cronkite, he gloated to himself, had been part of the historic liberation of Dutch soil. He was proud to be among the brave Dutch people, to whom he felt a bloodline connection. Wild yelps of jubilation echoed up and down the canals along Dam Square. Honking car horns created an almost single rumbling symphonic effect. Traffic was at a standstill. "The sound of Allied aircraft was the one sound of war the Dutch welcomed,"

Cronkite recalled. "The Royal Air-Force came at night and the Americans during the day."

On May 8, 1945, Germany surrendered to the rest of Europe. History was happening fast. Urgent UP stories needed to be filed from The Hague, Utrecht, Maastricht, Bruges, Antwerp, Luxembourg City, and Brussels. While Amsterdam was rip-roaringly festive, Cronkite headed south to The Hague, the capital of the Netherlands, to reclaim what had been the UP bureau before the Nazi occupation. To his utter amazement, he discovered that three former Dutch UP staffers had already reestablished the office and were waiting for a correspondent to appear. Cronkite had been able to save about a quarter of his income and now used his money to help his UP staff get proper food and clothing. "Through their tears of joy they couldn't wait to tell me that they had a teleprinter available, that we could put the U.P. back in business," he recalled. "With incredible courage, they had disassembled one of our teletypes before the Germans entered Amsterdam. Each of them had taken a third of the parts to hide in their homes. If they had been caught, they would have faced certain execution."

Cronkite realized that the Dutch celebrations belied the simple, ineradicable truth of Europe in May 1945. Death and loss were looming everywhere. Reports came over the UP wire that were shocking. When Soviet troops liberated Auschwitz in Poland, ghastly new confirmation of the Holocaust was produced. A race for eyewitness accounts and photographs was on. The UP wanted copy about the dire fever of the immediate postwar situation: concentration camps, stolen art, dangerous dikes, flooded lands, widespread disease, and the devastation caused by the Soviet army. The list was long. "There were a number of great stories from the Netherlands," Cronkite recalled, "but I didn't get to print any of them because of the German surrender."

While Cronkite was celebrating V-E week in The Hague, Murrow broadcast in a somber mood for CBS Radio from among the throngs massed in Trafalgar Square in London, unwilling to sound a trumpet. He had seen too much carnage to be unreservedly happy. He had been to the newly liberated Buchenwald camp in Germany that April. When Murrow took to the CBS Radio airwaves, he prayed for the Jewish people who had been victims of the most horrendous atrocities known to humanity. Compared with Murrow in London, covering top-level meetings going on in Whitehall and Westminster, Cronkite's UP articles about the rebuilding of Dutch canal towns seemed bush league.

The United Press was still having Cronkite write uplifting boilerplate pieces about the victorious U.S. Army in Europe, morale-boosting copy aimed at producing Allied propaganda heroes because of the continued fighting in the Pacific. In fact, an argument could be made that Cronkite was flacking for the army under the guise of UP reporting. If his V-E journalism for UP was edited into an omnibus it could be labeled as nonfiction propaganda. "You can't write horror stories every day," Cronkite said in defense of hired-gun writers, "because nobody would read it, for one thing. It's repetitious."

As Cronkite intuited, once the euphoria of V-E Day passed, life in Europe was only a little less disturbing than it had been during the war, and the future no less uncertain. Throughout the Netherlands, war refugees roamed highways on foot, pushing wooden carts loaded with all they had. Displaced Dutch families were looking for relatives, retribution, or just a safe place to start life over. The Nazis had starved and beaten the Dutch, but had never defeated them. Vast tracts of blighted cities across the continent lay in rubble. More than 80 percent of Nuremberg, the Nazis' showcase city in Germany, had been bombed out. There were shortages of nearly every commodity. For a reporter, the situation on the ground was overwhelming because the devilment of war could be churned up on every block. Throughout defeated Germany, everything looked wrecked as though by earthquake or eruption. Although not quite a pacifist with a capital *P*, Cronkite thought the Second World War taught that the age-old ways of militarism couldn't continue in the second half of the twentieth century. No matter the circumstance in 1945, he declined to carry a pistol as he traveled dicey European neighborhoods where crime and chaos still reigned. He was strictly an observer of the destruction, not a participant.

On May 20, Cronkite wrote home from Utrecht about the abominable, inhumane conditions he encountered among the starved Dutch people. Tulips were being cooked into stews and soups. Eggs and milk were rare commodities. Medicine was not readily available. Adults looked like children because they were so gaunt from habitual malnourishment. Once-prosperous streets now looked like vales of poverty. "There is absolutely no food in this part of Holland," a distraught Cronkite wrote. "It is impossible to tell you how bad things are. I have seen several persons faint in the streets from hunger. A prominent newspaper publisher whom I invited to meet me downtown said he could come but he couldn't bring his wife. 'Her feet are swollen too badly,' he said, 'no food, you know.'

The people are walking skeletons. Their eyes bulge from shrinking sockets and their skins are bleached of natural color. I find it sickening to sit across a desk and talk business with many of them." For his part, Cronkite survived on the army rations he received as a member of the press that late spring of 1945. His government-issue uniform was always a ticket to special treatment.

For the rest of his life, Cronkite kept in contact with Dutch friends he made around V-E Day when he was setting up UP bureaus. When nobody else at UP (or later CBS) thought news from the Netherlands interesting enough for an American audience, Cronkite anchored pieces on how the Dutch dug massive drainage projects, built monumental dikes, and even found the wreckage of Allied and German planes from the war so bodies could be sent home. Whenever the opportunity came, Cronkite bragged that he was a Dutchman. The fact that President Franklin D. Roosevelt—of Dutch ancestry himself—was credited with winning the Second World War only made Cronkite prouder of his heritage. "It would serve America well to listen to Dutch thought and opinion regarding their continent," Cronkite believed. "Our friends in the Netherlands are in a unique position to help us interpret European moods and directions."

Cronkite's pace didn't slacken with the defeat of the Axis powers, but his role changed for a time. He helped UP rebuild its presence in Europe, and with the widespread destruction, there was plenty to write about. Besides scooping Associated Press, his UP directive was to rebuild the technological side of his company's business in the Low Countries. United Press leased telegraph wires between European cities, but then had to find the equipment to send and receive messages. A veritable scavenger hunt was staged by Cronkite (even in Germany) to procure hard-to-find communications equipment.

Recognizing that Cronkite was an excellent manager of The Hague bureau, UP asked him to establish one in Brussels; the AP had just set up shop in Amsterdam. Working with Sam Hales, a UP salesman, Cronkite was able to procure a couple of Teletype machines from the Siemens electric plant in Germany. Spreading Belgian francs around like seed, Cronkite was able to buy wire on the Brussels black market to establish a transmission link with Paris. Not only did he reestablish United Press bureaus in Belgium, Luxembourg, and Holland after the war, he also opened one in Germany. In New York, the UP bosses recognized Cronkite's managerial competence—an unusual quality for a roaming reporter. It was the beginning of Cronkite's lifelong reputation for being a "company man" at heart. His understanding of the money-making aspects of news delivery would serve him well in the coming decades.

Because Cronkite had such interesting Eighth Air Force bomb run stories, he could have returned to the United States to write a history of General Eaker's celebrated flyboys, marketing himself as the "Dean of the Air War." His UP clippings from London between 1942 and 1945 would have been good bait for a publishing contract. A few of his foreign correspondent colleagues indeed went that route. A book deal for Harper and Row or Random House would have meant more money for Cronkite than the meager pay and migraine headaches associated with opening UP bureaus without much capital outlay. Or he could have returned to America to look for a radio job, as United Press's David Brinkley did, starting as a news writer at the NBC affiliate in Washington, D.C., and moving into radio announcing by war's end.

As the consummate print reporter, Cronkite didn't think NBC Radio was a step up from being a UP bureau chief in the Low Countries. Jokingly, he boasted that he was part of the informal "Murrow-Ain't-God Club," which promoted print reporting over radio news. As of 1945 he had an uphill battle in making that case. Murrow remained in London after

V-E Day, preparing to return to New York for good, and working to protect the jobs of his "Boys." A few, exhausted by all that they'd done and seen during the war, entered other fields by their own choice. Charles Collingwood of CBS, for instance, married the actress Louise Allbritton and moved to the Hollywood Hills for a while. Eric Sevareid, locking himself in a secluded cottage on the Monterey Peninsula, remained with CBS, but after seven years as a correspondent, he was spent and struggling just to recognize his old self. "I had a curious feeling of age," Sevareid wrote, "as though I had lived through a lifetime, not merely through my youth."

Cronkite, by contrast, was not given to the introspection of Sevareid or the joie de vivre of Collingwood. The ultimate anti-Proust, he was opposed to navel-gazing. By choice, he kept doing the job at hand for United Press in war-torn Brussels, refusing to retreat to the United States. He wasn't looking for transcendent truths or existential epiphanies; his guiding lights were bylines and paychecks. Even as other reporters thought of themselves as intellectuals, Cronkite, the Longhorn dropout, prided himself on being a tradesman. He was trained to report, so he did. His primary concern was finding the best vantage point, just out of harm's way, from which to write a story. After all, the

United States was still fighting the Japanese. Rest and relaxation were premature. World War II wasn't over by a long shot.

When the United States dropped an atomic bomb on Hiroshima that August 6, to the surprise of everyone, Sevareid and Collingwood read the historic news in California newspapers. As Sevareid wrote, he was "in a kind of mental coma for days." For Cronkite, learning about Hiroshima made him feel that America was invincible. Putting his military aviation know-how to work, he wrote about what the *Enola Gay* drop—of an atomic bomb containing sixty kilograms of uranium-235—meant from the limited perspective of war-weary refugees in Holland and Belgium.

The end of World War II came on August 15, after a second atomic bomb was dropped on the Japanese city of Nagasaki six days earlier. Six years of miserable war had left 70 million dead. Civilian casualties had outpaced military deaths by a three-to-two margin. A new wave of investigative journalism was needed to take historical stock of the global war. Cronkite, now a veteran of foreign wars, was in the profession for the long haul; he wasn't ready to return to the U.S. mainland, even though Betsy was waiting for him with arms open wide. History was being made in devastated Europe, where millions were without homes, not in Kansas

City's Chamber of Commerce meetings. No returning to the normalcy of hamburger cookouts, Clark
Gable matinées, and the Andrews Sisters for Cronkite.
Having been assured that he was on track for a managerial position at UP, he remained in Europe to await
assignment to one of the war-torn capitals that would
showcase his vital reportorial abilities and sharpen his
geopolitical understanding.

Even though Cronkite was living in Brussels, his
best UP stories came out of defeated Germany. He
was able to score a number of key interviews with
Nazi collaborators being rounded up for trial. After
General Patton was mortally wounded in an automobile accident that December 1945, Cronkite attended
his funeral in Luxembourg. Then, in late 1945, he was
assigned to a UP team to cover the war crimes trials at
Nuremberg, Germany. Every news organization sent
first-string reporters to watch the Nazi war criminals
being administered justice, including Drew Middleton
for *The New York Times*, Marguerite Higgins for the
New York Herald-Tribune, Louis Lochner for AP,
and Howard K. Smith and William Shirer for CBS.
Novelist John Dos Passos, author of the masterful
U.S.A. Trilogy, was even there with notebook in hand
for *Life*. *The New Yorker* had sent Janet Flanner and
Rebecca West.

The courtroom was an old German theater, and Cronkite, along with the correspondents from twenty-three countries, competed for the best tip-up maroon seats in the press gallery. The courtroom was flooded with bright lights for the newsreel cameras. Cronkite thought he was at Grauman's Chinese Theatre in Hollywood, not in a city that had been bombed to rubble.

9.

From the Nuremberg Trials to Russia

COVERING THE NUREMBERG TRIALS—MOVING TO
MOSCOW—DATELINE KREMLIN—CLOSED SOVIET
SOCIETY—DOWN WITH *PRAVDA*—FEELING
OPPRESSED—THE 1948 POLITICAL CONVENTIONS—
MURROW AND TV—ANCHORMAN WANTED—
DREAMING OF TV AMERICA

Filing UP stories from Nuremberg in late 1945 and early 1946 was a difficult task. All day long, Cronkite wore heavy headphones to listen to the English translation of the war crime trials. Wiring a daily story with staff research help, he explained the intricacies of the international military tribunal—mankind's first attempt to establish legal standards of responsibility for wartime atrocities—to his readers. He also tried scooping the other news organizations from sunrise to sunset. This was a double burden. Exclusives weren't easy to get. All the correspondents were cloistered together, hearing the same testimony. Differentiating copy was mostly a matter of detail and style.

But there was keen courtroom drama for Cronkite to write about as twenty-one of the most heinous captured Nazis—some wearing dark sunglasses as protection from the bright lights—faced the bench for crimes against humanity. (Three Third Reich architects— Adolf Hitler, head of the SS Heinrich Himmler, and minister of propaganda Joseph Goebbels—had committed suicide rather than be captured.) "Sitting there for the first time and seeing these twenty-one men who had caused such horror in the world I actually felt sick," Cronkite later explained in a documentary for PBS's *American Experience* series. "They had come into the dock as if this was not a fair proceeding, as if they knew they were going to hang already, why go through the whole thing."

As chief UP correspondent for the trials, Cronkite was able to arrange for Betsy to come live with him in Nuremberg. Decent quarters were tough to come by, but the resourceful Cronkite managed to co-opt a private guesthouse about five hundred feet from Faber

Castle, where most of the other journalists resided. The privacy allowed Betsy and him to enjoy themselves almost perversely as the trials went on. "We'd get drunk around the bar and debate the value of the trial and whether there should be *ex post facto* justice," Cronkite recalled. "We discussed all the arguments."

The fact-gathering assistance of his UP colleague Ann Stringer was key to Cronkite's ability to break news from Nuremberg. A salty Texan whose journalist husband, Bill Stringer, had been killed covering D-day for Reuters, Ann had previously scooped the first meeting of Russian and American troops along the Elbe River. According to Cronkite, his wife was just as intent at Nuremberg to outreport the press boys. "The real skill," he recalled of her, "was in getting tipped off to documents that were in the files before they were brought into trial and to get access to them. Ann Stringer worked the prosecution staff pretty well on these documents." Everybody knew the Nazis being charged were guilty, that the Third Reich had violated the Kellogg-Briand Pact of 1928 (which renounced all war), the Geneva Conventions (which created the Red Cross and dictated terms for the treatment of prisoners of war), and The Hague Conventions (which established common rules of military engagement). To break news in Nuremberg, you needed inside information about how the Nazi prisoners were being treated in the courtroom. "We got a lot of damn good front page stories," Cronkite recalled, "revealing the depths of the depravity of Nazi Germany."

All the correspondents filed the same boilerplate accounts of the trials. While most reporters focused on architect and armaments minister Albert Speer—the notorious "Nazi Who Said Sorry"—Cronkite was more fascinated that president of the Reichstag and commander of the Luftwaffe, Hermann Göring, the unrepentant war criminal, wanted to die waving the bloody swastika. Cronkite managed to scoop the competition by procuring "new information" given to Allied investigators: that Göring's financial fortune had been built on bribes from relatives of concentration camp inmates. For nine days Cronkite watched Göring get cross-examined. "On trial for his life," Cronkite recalled, "Göring displayed on the stand all the arrogance with which he had set out to rule the world."

What disturbed Cronkite the most at Nuremberg, what gave him nightmares for the rest of his life, were the films showing the Dachau death camps. According to Nazi criminals at Nuremberg, the prison was for political dissenters, habitual criminals, and religious fanatics. Cronkite practically vomited after seeing the "showers" (gas vents) in which cyanide powder was used to kill Jews. "As soon as the defendants saw the pictures, the film of the concentration camps, they began to whiten," Cronkite recalled. "As a matter of fact, several of them cried. They weren't crying, I don't think, for the Jewish people who were lost. They were crying because they knew that, when those pictures were seen in the world, they had no way to escape execution."

Cronkite was deeply impressed by the professionalism of the American prosecutors at Nuremberg like Robert Jackson (U.S.) and Roman Andreyevich Rudenko (USSR). The amount of research they did in preparation for the trials was impressive by any standard. "There has been much criticism over the years that the trials were the imposition of ex post facto justice on a beaten enemy," Cronkite told *Rolling Stone* in 1981. "But I've always felt they represented an effort to establish a judicial precedent for a system of world order before the outbreak of another war—after which, clearly it would be too late."

In the late spring of 1946, UP allowed Cronkite to return to Missouri for a spell. With Betsy at his side, he was confronted by all their family and friends wanting to hear about the historic Nuremberg trials. Somehow Cronkite had acquired a tiny palm-size camera at Nuremberg and secretly photographed the trials of deputy führer Rudolf Hess, Göring, Reich

Main Security Office director Ernst Kaltenbrunner, and others. It was against the rules, so he didn't brag about his smuggling act to anybody in Europe. But he had souvenir postcard pictures of the greatest trial in world history. "I have a vivid memory of Walter coming to visit us in St. Joe," his cousin Kay Barnes recalled. "His camera was amazing. It was just tiny. I couldn't believe that Walter took pictures of the trials with something that small."

Cronkite was no longer reporting the Nuremberg story at the time the verdicts were handed down that fall by the International Military Tribunal. In the summer of 1946, he was transferred to Moscow. He would now be stationed just blocks from the Kremlin. Having rejected Stalingrad when Murrow made the CBS offer in 1943, he took over UP's crucial Moscow post three years later. There was also the good news that Betsy could remain with him in Russia. Cronkite's primary job for UP in Moscow would be to interpret "Soviet Communists for the American public." He and Betsy made hurried preparations, barely knowing what to pack for an extended stay in a Communist nation, where goods could be scarce. Cronkite later laughed that Betsy brought an abundance of golf balls—a game neither played at the time and one that the Soviets considered unabashedly bourgeois. "I was chief correspondent,"

Cronkite later joked, "because I was the only corre-spondent of the United Press in Moscow at the time."

Upon arriving in the Soviet capital, the Cronkites slept on the office sofa of Richard C. Hottelet, one of the original Murrow Boys, who'd been a POW of the Gestapo. Their imposition on Hottelet lasted for ten days. They had eighteen pieces of luggage with them but had lost the keys for the locks. Nothing was going well. Betsy Cronkite soon went to work for Voice of America to help make ends meet; she also smuggled out a lot of contraband food from the VOA offices at the U.S. embassy for her husband to eat at night. Betsy's primary duty was to write what daughter Kathy would call "women's journalism"—self-help stuff about how to be a military wife in the cold war (the popular phrase used to describe U.S.-Soviet postwar tensions).

Life was hard in Moscow, but Cronkite found it deeply educational. For the first time he read Tolstoy and Gogol. The Soviets had lost at least 26 million people during World War II and many families were still in mourning. Once the Cronkites procured a modest apartment, they discovered they didn't even have a refrigerator; they left the milk bottles outside to stay cold. The electricity was hit or miss and the floorboards were rotting. At night, by stark contrast, the Cronkites were often invited to embassy functions where men dressed in white dinner jackets and caviar was served as an *amuse-bouche*. Moscow was to Betsy Cronkite "a last bastion of empire." Even though the couple couldn't afford a radio, they drank expensive French Merlot and Cabernet. Such aristocratic poverty was surreal. "They lived a dual existence, rich and poor," Kathy Cronkite recalled. "The deprivations of Moscow wore them thin."

The only Russian words Cronkite knew were "hello" (*privyet*) and "good-bye" (*do svidaniya*). The UP office was a short walk from the Kremlin and the American embassy. It consisted of a single room at the Hotel Metropol, a low-amenities art nouveau building that housed most of the English-language correspondents in Moscow. As Harrison Salisbury of *The New York Times* recalled, "Life at the Metropol was a little like living in a prison run by the Mad Hatter. We had adjoining rooms, we ate together, travelled together, drank together, we suffered together and fought together, we knew who slept with whom and who didn't and when the partners changed."

Cronkite initially suffered from a bad case of "Ain't Life Grand" intoxication in Moscow, a common malady for foreign correspondents living behind the Iron Curtain. He turned native, eating blini for breakfast and drinking vodka at night. With Betsy at his side he visited sights such as Lenin's mausoleum, the Bolshoi Theatre, and St. Basil's Cathedral, feeling the riptide of Russian history on every street corner. With UP picking up the tab, the Cronkites spent a long weekend in Leningrad and took a memorable cruise down the Volga. Right out of the gate, Cronkite wrote a colorful piece, full of lighthearted affection, about the differences between Russia and the United States. Datelined Moscow, the article ran in American newspapers on October 24, 1946: "Sprawled in a snowbank this morning I heard for the first time a guffawing belly-laugh by a Russian," Cronkite began. "A heels-over-breakfast tumble, like a funny paper character who steps on a banana peel, is just as uproarious in Moscow as it is in New York or Mooselookmeguntic, Maine."

If Cronkite's initial UP articles from Moscow read like goofy travelogues or cornpone jokes, they at least catered to growing American curiosity about Soviet society, which had been painted as bleak and colorless throughout the Stalin era, particularly during the unyielding defense of the homeland during World War II. Cronkite's articles showed that Muscovites were regular people who laughed, cheered, and flirted just like Americans. They were also the kind of pieces the Soviet press censors wanted foreign correspondents to write. The Soviet Union was a deeply totalitarian, closed society. To be a Western journalist in the USSR during the years right after the war was an exercise in frustration. Conflicting attitudes between the foreign correspondents and their Soviet hosts were coalescing, with a totalitarian government shielding its society from view. Cronkite responded to the handcuffed world of Moscow journalism by writing frequently on the subject of Soviet censorship—articles that he amazingly managed to file through the New York bureau.

Even as he failed to produce a single breaking news story during two years in Moscow, he became an operative in the snowballing American-Soviet cold war. At the time Walter and Betsy arrived, the USSR and the United States were still allies—wary ones to be sure, but joined in the afterglow of victory. Cronkite's early articles reflected the friendly curiosity of Americans regarding Soviets. By 1947, with the Truman Doctrine (which stated that the United States would provide aid to Greece and Turkey to counter the encroaching Soviet influence) and the Marshall Plan (which offered American economic support to rebuild the economies of Europe during the postwar years) in place, the Kremlin treated reporters such as Cronkite as if they were OSS or newfangled CIA spies. One of Cronkite's UP articles that drifted entirely away from hard news described his reportorial work in Moscow to the newspaper public in America, allowing them to understand the process by which news was gathered in the closed-door Soviet Union: "The foreign correspondent in Moscow is a blood cousin of a digest magazine editor," Cronkite explained. "Ninety-five percent of the news he files from Moscow is gleaned from newspapers, magazines, or other periodicals."

Soviet newspapers such as *Pravda*, the house organ of the Communist Party, obviously would not be trust-worthy sources of facts, but Cronkite did archly quote a Soviet TASS news commentator asserting that President Harry Truman "wants to be the ruler of the universe and use England as his lackey." Cleverly, he decided to cover *Pravda*—the censors couldn't find a problem with that. There was much to catch the eye of the American reader as both amusing and frightening: "After the smashing of the German source of international reaction and criminal aggression, another such source was formed, no less dangerous. It is in the United States, its headquarters are on Wall Street. Its heads are Truman and [Secretary of State George] Marshall, its agents all over the world are American generals and diplomats, its hunting dogs are American capitalist papers."

Cronkite cited that quotation in a UP article on the average Soviet's conviction that the United States was planning an imminent attack on Russia. He, and the brand of journalism that he was allowed by both sides to practice, now focused on the widening cold war gulf between the two nations. In a small way, he contributed to the anti-Soviet attitude developing in America by quoting the most outrageous demagoguery of Russian leaders. By the time he approached the end of his Moscow hitch in September 1948, the world's democracies no longer wanted to hear about the delightful way those melancholy Muscovites laughed when the winter weather played a trick.

There were various reasons for Cronkite's departure from Moscow after exactly two years. Betsy was expecting their first child and had left for the United States early in the summer of 1948, via West Berlin. She later bragged that she was part of the historic Berlin Airlift. Cronkite naturally wanted to go home to Kansas City to be near Betsy, to share in the joyous excitement of pregnancy. As he pointed out in *A Reporter's Life*, as an expecting father, he was increasingly nervous about being arrested on one pretext or another by the Soviet authorities. He wanted to leave Russia as soon as possible.

Everything about living in the Soviet Union now felt overtly oppressive to Cronkite. Whatever veneer of excitement that had glossed over him in 1946 had been wholly stripped away by 1948. Under Stalin the Kremlin was ending its policy of "limited friendship to brotherly Western correspondents," revoking even "marginal privileges." He was impatient, too, with the church-mouse penury of UP, tired of its penny-ante ways while NBC and CBS were growing. UP was always steadily downsizing, whittling down its greatness, cutting corners only until the sawdust was left.

Cronkite liked to tell his own story about his relationship with UP circa 1948. Leonard Lyons, a gossip columnist for the *New York Post*, met him on his return to America and the result was an anecdote about the Cronkites' life in Moscow. One day, they returned home to find that someone had painted a dollar sign on the door of their apartment. It was meant as an anti-capitalist gesture. Betsy, known for her verbal zingers, made an off-the-cuff comment about how godawful poor journalists were. According to Lyons's column, however, it was Walter who made the quotable remark. "If they had known I worked for the United Press instead of the Associated Press," he said, "they would have put a cents sign on the door." (Cronkite ever afterward insisted—not wanting to mock UP publicly—that the quote should have been "If they had known we were newspaper people, they would have put a cents sign on the door.")

In New York, on a quick stopover on his way to see Betsy in Kansas City, Cronkite learned that he would not be receiving an expected pay raise—and that if he accepted UP's offer of a posting in London, he would not receive any expense money. For Cronkite, one of the company's highest-paid foreign correspondents, this was the equivalent of a pay cut, not a minor trespass on his integrity. His entire reportorial life had been consecrated to UP, his allegiance to the wire service sincere. But UP's niggling for dollars caused him to break ranks. In truth, he might have already been tired of all that UP reminded him of: the grueling war coverage; the nomadic lifestyle of a foreign correspondent; the constant company of other heavy-drinking reporters, some of them friends, all of them competitors; the time zone distances from Kansas City.

By October 1948, Cronkite was feeling the urge to lead a normal life. Missing out on the GI Bill, which would have paid for him to finally get his college degree, he was light-years behind Murrow Boys in his industry such as Collingwood (class of '39 at Cornell) or Sevareid (class of '35 at Minnesota). Not having worked in America since the first year of the war, he didn't know much about the country in the present postwar tense. He had not taken a serious vacation since he'd left Missouri for New York back in 1941; that was seven years on the front line in Europe and Russia. With a child on the way, Cronkite relished being back in the Midwest, in Kansas City, where the trolleys still ran on time and no one was a spy.

In 1948, although he didn't know it yet, his life would soon change significantly. That year, for the first time, CBS televised the Democratic and Republican national conventions (both held in Philadelphia). There was a whiff of new technology about the TV coverage that was intoxicating to those with a nose for the future. Jack Gould, distinguished radio and television critic for *The New York Times*, wrote an article that summer about the significant role TV was playing in the presidential election. While he admitted that a lot of the proceedings of the conventions were an "arduous grind" to watch, there was no escaping the hard, futuristic fact that TV's influence on electing politicians was "going to be great indeed." When Truman arrived in Philadelphia he was dressed to the nines, like a riverboat gambler at a wedding, wearing a white suit and dark tie that was "the best masculine garb for the video camera."

What Gould saw missing from the 1948 TV convention coverage was a network master of ceremonies, a clever ringleader who could ad-lib when the marathon oratory got dull. Just as TV was going to place a premium on personality in politics, and being telegenic became almost a prerequisite for seeking national office, the networks needed to have a happy-go-lucky "anchorman"—a vague TV term not used regularly until 1952 and then specifically for Cronkite—to hold all the disparate parts together. In 1948 the seasoned CBS trio of Ed Murrow, Quincy Howe, and Douglas Edwards distinguished themselves from NBC by a long shot. The CBSers came off as good-natured, detached, and quick-witted. "In a town overrun with eager beavers," Gould wrote in the *Times*, "the Messrs. Murrow, Howe and Edwards acted as relaxed and seasoned reporters."

Murrow, it turns out, didn't like the notion of being an anchorman for CBS TV. His past experiences at national conventions had left him cold; such events tended to degrade reporters' professionalism, turning them into cheerleaders and spectators, clapping like silly sycophants at prewritten political speeches. Being obedient and rote was not the Murrow way. So there was a job opening at CBS. Although it wasn't posted until four years later, for the 1952 conventions, CBS executives had an ad in mind: "Anchorman Wanted."

Meanwhile, all across the United States, television affiliates for NBC and CBS were prospering. TV was incrementally becoming the communications medium of the future, and Cronkite wasn't yet in the game, his sepulchral voice yet to be truly discovered.

PART III

Cold War Broadcaster

10.
Infancy of TV News

BABY BOOM FATHER—TRUMAN'S MISSOURI—GOING TO WASHINGTON, D.C., VIA KMBC—THE TV PIONEER—DOUGLAS EDWARDS—KOREAN WAR BEGGING—GROWING FAMILY—TV NEWS AT WTOP— WORKING WITH SHADEL—ONE-TAKE WALTER— TRUMAN GIVES CRONKITE A WHITE HOUSE TOUR—GETTING THE 1952 CONVENTION GIG—FACE TIME RULES

Dutiful and determined to be a hands-on father, Walter Cronkite was in Kansas City on November 8, 1948, when Betsy gave birth to their first child, Nancy, at St. Luke's Hospital. He took a brief home leave from the United Press. While Walter was in Russia working, a pregnant Betsy had returned to Kansas City to live with Arthur and Eva Maxwell, her parents, at 3220 Agnes Avenue. "I raced half way around the world from Moscow to be present for the event," Cronkite was fond of saying, "only to find my presence was not required."

The Cronkites were participating in what became known as the Baby Boom, a phenomenon in the postwar years between 1946 and 1960 marked by a large increase in American births. Still a roving reporter, all he got to do was kiss newborn Nancy (the first of the Cronkites' three children) before heading out on the road again for UP. "That's the way it was in those days," Nancy said. "The wife took care of the kids while the husband traveled for business." What Cronkite realized upon his return to Missouri was that the United States—where baby items such as diapers, baby food, and infant clothes were easy to come by—was ideal for raising a family. Before Cronkite left for New York (and then back to Moscow), he had lunch at the Kansas City Club with Karl Koerper, vice president and general manager of KMBC, the CBS affiliate in Kansas City. Looking for career headway and anxious to move back to America, Cronkite suggested to Koerper that KMBC needed an able Washington-based correspondent. The pitch was that Cronkite would move to the District of Columbia on behalf of KMBC. The *Kansas City Journal-Post* was defunct and Cronkite theorized he could pick up the slack with radio broadcasts from Washington aimed at a Midwest—particularly Missouri and Kansas—audience. "It was a very fine, responsible radio station," Cronkite recalled of KMBC, "the sixth station Bill Paley had put together of the original CBS network."

Koerper, hoping to scoop up a talent like Cronkite, had KMBC hire Cronkite. Eventually ten radio stations across the Midwest would air Cronkite's syndicated radio reports. In a glass-half-empty sense, Cronkite's KMBC job was a demotion; he was reaching only a regional audience, not a national one. It was a step up, though, in the entrepreneurial aspect of running his own broadcasting operation, with clients but no bosses. In addition, the KMBC syndicate offered twice the salary he'd been receiving at UP in Moscow. What new father wouldn't like that? While his bosses at UP were unhappy about his departure, they understood what double the salary meant to a family man. Truth be told, any news organization—even *The New York Times*— would have been lucky to employ Cronkite. What one columnist at the New York *Daily News* wrote about Cronkite in 1965 was already his reputation in journalism in 1948: "Solid as a mountain," and "As reliable as the sunrise."

In the 1930s, Cronkite had bounced back and forth many times between his first love, newspapers, and the new medium of broadcast radio. With his move to Washington in December 1948, though, his newspaper-reporting days were finished. Electronic broadcasting was still young and had yet to tap its full potential. The same was true of Cronkite, the newest voice in radio news at KMBC. "When Walter got into radio everybody was trying to sound like Ed Murrow," veteran CBS correspondent Bob Schieffer recalled. "I mean even Charles Kuralt tried to sound like Murrow. Not Walter. He had his own, very distinctive way of talking. I don't know where it came from. He came from Kansas City and grew up in Texas and lived a lot overseas. What ended up happening was that by the 1960s everybody at CBS Radio started sounding like Cronkite, not Murrow. He had taken over the cadence of the network."

A columnist for the Kansas City *Atchison Daily Globe*, Jim Carson, ballyhooed Cronkite's new KMBC assignment as a regional boon. "Cronkite is in Washington to establish headquarters," Carson wrote on January 9, 1949, "and will begin his reporting about the first of February. Plans call for Cronkite to provide a daily news spot for each of the stations from our Nation's capital. . . . Localized news, as it affects Missourians and Kansans, will be scheduled on a quarter-hour program each week." The scuttlebutt in Kansas City, encouraged by Cronkite, was that his being a Missouri boy would open up access to President Truman himself. But in truth, the White House was new turf to Cronkite, a mystery mansion akin to mammoth caves. He had no "in" with Truman.

The Cronkites rented a little Georgian-style house across from Rock Creek Park and struggled a little to make ends meet, even though his new salary of over $15,000 a year lifted them into the upper middle class. It was more money than fellow Writing Sixty-Niners Andy Rooney or William Wade were making. He represented five states for KMBC: Missouri, Iowa, Nebraska, Kansas, and Oklahoma. Furthermore, following a newsman's primary instinct, he'd gotten to where the sizzling news of 1949 was: official Washington. Truman had defeated New Yorker Thomas Dewey in the 1948 election and was promising a Fair Deal to the American people. This meant the role of the U.S. government was going to grow. Because Cronkite was broadcasting for the Midwest, the Department of Agriculture was a mandatory part of his beat. Murrow was a semi-regular guest at the White House (joining Truman to dine with the likes of Charles de Gaulle and Winston Churchill). Cronkite, by contrast, was hanging out with wheat surplus traders and stockyard operators from Des Moines and Fargo.

One of the stories Cronkite covered in Washington for KMBC was the rise of Senator Joseph R. McCarthy, a Wisconsin Republican, and his determined hunt for Communists employed by the federal government. Speaking out against McCarthy was a dangerous idea for a radio or television reporter. The senator was at the forefront of a popular movement that portrayed communism as a threat as despicable as Nazism and even more insidious. To denigrate McCarthy was to appear, in many people's eyes, disloyal to American democracy. More pointedly, McCarthy indignantly investigated those who were at odds with him and freely substituted innuendo—even rank falsehoods—for hard facts. Very few broadcasters had either the bedrock courage or unassailable reputation—let alone job security—to withstand implication by McCarthy. But Cronkite did. In May 1950, he was asked to speak to the Rotary Club in Cedar Rapids, Iowa, a city whose WMT radio carried his District of Columbia reports. He might have chosen a safe topic, but instead he bluntly branded McCarthy a fearmonger—earning the respect of the White House. According to the Cedar Rapids *Gazette*, Cronkite said that McCarthy "has contradicted himself and proved little in his investigation of alleged Communists." No recording of Cronkite's Rotary Club speech exists today, but he insisted he didn't cower before his audience that day. "I couldn't believe that anybody was going to take McCarthy seriously," Cronkite recalled. "I thought he represented a kind of fringe fanaticism and personal ambition that wouldn't be followed by anyone of import."

In Washington, Cronkite had access to the CBS office at the National Press Club. His able assistant Eileen Shanahan, who went on to become a reporter for *The New York Times*, was tasked with mining daily White House and USDA news releases for valuable radio nuggets that would interest a Great Plains audience. Although Cronkite was good at ad-libbing, he had trouble finishing his reports on time. Working for the UP had been far different from his new job at the Midwest radio syndicate. Timing was now key to his position. It was also essential for him to cultivate Washington insider sources. Using connections first developed at *The Daily Texan*, Cronkite was able to fall in with the Texas delegation on Capitol Hill. "Walter being Walter, he got to know [Speaker of the House] Sam Rayburn pretty well," Andy Rooney recalled. "When I saw him in Georgetown one afternoon, he one-upped me by drinking bourbon with Rayburn."

While Cronkite was adjusting to the demands of radio, Ed Murrow was facing the challenges of television. He wasn't happy about being a bifurcated CBS reporter. "I wish television," he said in 1949, "would go to hell." Perhaps TV was Satan's tool, Cronkite felt like telling Murrow, but the medium wasn't going to be granted an exit visa anytime soon. Radio news had taken twenty years and a world war to learn to take full advantage of its inherent strength. At its best, in the hands of someone like Murrow, radio news had become a public art, a partnership between reporter and the listener. Television, on the other hand, was far from an art form in the late 1940s. Its newscasts looked like filmed radio, resulting in little more than spoken wire reports emitted to the viewer. "The people who say TV will destroy radio are as wrong as those who, twenty-five years ago, said that radio would kill the newspapers," Murrow told Ben Gross of the New York *Daily News*. "I sincerely believe that radio news will become more and more important."

Even as late as 1949, the potential of television news had yet to be seriously explored. "In the beginning," said Sig Mickelson, the first director of CBS Television news, "the Murrows, Collingwoods, Sevareids wouldn't deign to be caught in television. Television was for *Howdy Doody* and *Romper Room*. Radio was for adults." In the early years of television, in fact, producers didn't even know where to look for the potential. The priority, indeed, was the perfection of the on-air reading. Murrow, along with the producer Fred Friendly, had been doing a radio segment, *Hear It Now*, that was carried on 173 stations and won Peabody Awards. They were masters at script reading.

Douglas Edwards of CBS, the original face of TV news, ran his eyes over any script on the desk before him and then looked up into the camera to talk. He was smooth, but the bobbing of his head was regarded as a terrible distraction during his dinner-hour segment, *Douglas Edwards with the News*. In the truest sense of the word, Edwards was a journalism pioneer. Born in Ada, Oklahoma, in 1917, Edwards began his radio career as a teenager, working as a "junior" announcer at a 100-watt station, before cutting his teeth profession-ally at WKYZ in Detriot during the Great Depression. He didn't have much in the way of star power, but he pushed on during a time when television news faced a bias vis-à-vis radio broadcasting. There were two main reasons for this: "First it was *television*," Mike Conway explained in *The Origins of Television News in America*; "second it was *news* on television."

Edwards's fifteen-minute show on CBS was the only nightly news broadcast in early 1949. Later that year, NBC started its own competing TV news program, with John Cameron Swayze as host. Swayze, whom Cronkite had befriended when both were newspapermen in Kansas City, memorized the scripts for NBC's nightly *Camel News Caravan*. In fact, Swayze had made his first TV appearance in 1933 by reading the newspaper out loud at an experimental facility in Kansas City. It was transmitted live from the building's top floor and beamed into the lobby, where it could be watched on prototype sets. Arriving at NBC's studios on East 106th Street in Manhattan at about three in the afternoon, the forty-three-year-old Swayze would sift through reports from United Press or NBC radio correspondents. After writing the script for his fifteen-minute show, he would read it out loud three or four times, and with that, commit it to memory. Swayze could ad-lib a bit, but his talent was delivering his program with straight-ahead verve.

When Swayze immediately captured the larger part of the available audience, CBS executives strongly encouraged Edwards to memorize his scripts. He couldn't, and he didn't think it was a good idea anyway. Although Edwards had started as a velvet-voiced announcer, he had struggled to establish credentials as a newsman and he didn't want to devote too much of his time to learning words by rote.

The producer of *Douglas Edwards with the News* was a twenty-six-year-old maverick named Don Hewitt. Energetic, unafraid, and insistent, Hewitt, a native New Yorker, wasn't comfortable until he had his way. A former photo editor for Acme Newspictures, he had joined CBS in 1949, and worked on *Douglas Edwards with the News* since its conception. If Hewitt had a pet peeve, it was Edwards's on-air stiffness. Hell, he used to carp, Woodrow Wilson had been looser than Edwards. Long before the term *telegenic* was in vogue, Hewitt intuited that it was the key to a successful TV broadcasting career. Determined to loosen his guy up, Hewitt looked for a way to get Edwards to stop looking down at his script, even suggesting that he learn Braille. Based in New York, Hewitt and his CBS team experimented with cue cards and then settled on writing the script in large letters on a scroll, which turned just above the camera.

While Edwards and Hewitt were trying to jump-start CBS television in New York, Cronkite was in Washington, wondering whether he had dead-ended on KMBC radio. He missed the United Press. Few of the Midwest affiliate stations were properly using his reports from Washington. "Most of the news directors back at the local stations," Cronkite recalled, "didn't know how to query me for information."

When the Korean War erupted in the summer of 1950, Cronkite itched to cover the action. It saddened him to read UP stories from Asia by colleagues while he was stuck reciting wheat and soybean prices over the radio for a localized Midwest syndicate. With Betsy's okay, he wired Wells Church, the CBS news manager in New York, to volunteer his reportorial services in the Korean conflict. To Cronkite's surprise, he got a call from Edward R. Murrow instead of Church. "Ed said that not many guys get a second chance, but would you like to join CBS and go to Korea?" Cronkite recalled. "I said, you're darn right yes." Murrow green-lighted the hiring of Cronkite. He buried whatever residual animosity existed as a hangover from the Savile Club incident, when Cronkite had accepted, then reneged on, a CBS News job offer.

The cold war conflict started on June 25, 1950, when ninety thousand North Korean troops invaded South Korea. UP was the first news service to break the story. Before long, terms such as *limited war* and *military engagement* were bandied about as if the world were playing semantic roulette. The Korean confrontation played out not only in defined battles but also in a nameless kind of jousting at flash points in the spartan hills and mountains of the Korean Peninsula. Cronkite was bored with his KMBC job, though he *did* want to stay in radio. Cronkite believed he was good in the medium, but his midwestern syndicate didn't offer the opportunity to become better. That July, in his *Atchison Daily Globe* column, Jim Carson reported about Cronkite's doings, saying the "KMBC-KFRM Washington Correspondent has taken an indefinite leave of absence, and has joined the Columbia Broadcasting System Washington News staff. Cronkite, a former United Press War Correspondent, is subject to re-assignment at any time, and possibly will be sent overseas for the network."

What Carson failed to report was that Cronkite had ironed out a deal with Murrow wherein his Korean War reports would get aired first on KMBC; only then could other CBS affiliates air them. Betsy was pregnant with Kathy, the Cronkites' second child, and while Walter's going to Korea would indeed be risky, it also meant more money for the expanding family. Cronkite rationalized that Korea would be a short war, but the resulting exposure from reporting at the 38th parallel would launch his career as a major league CBS broadcaster. Cronkite's first task at CBS was to familiarize himself with Korean War minutiae. As he awaited posting to Asia, two days after getting vaccinated, his job situation suddenly changed.

CBS had acquired a local TV affiliate in Washington, D.C., from the FCC, and Cronkite was asked by Dr. Frank Stanton to broadcast a daily briefing on the Korean War on WTOP-TV. Stanton served as president of CBS between 1946 and 1971. A native of Michigan, he attended high school in Dayton, Ohio, and went on to earn a degree at Ohio Wesleyan University in Delaware, Ohio. Bookish, aloof, but not without humor, he earned his PhD in psychology at the Ohio State University in 1935. Stern and demanding, excellent at running with intellectual hounds, Stanton joined the CBS news division as its big brain. During World War II, he worked with the Office of War Information, regularly offering propaganda advice for the armed forces while serving as vice president of CBS. Generals and admirals never intimidated Stanton. Neither did lawyers. His steely schoolmaster resolve even made Bill Paley obedient. While Paley received all the kudos and big dollars for founding CBS, Stanton was the provost type, keeping things afloat, insisting that television indeed had a public affairs responsibility.

It was Stanton who gave Cronkite his crack at television news. The WTOP-TV news studios were located in residential northwest Washington, at Fortieth and Brandywine streets. Nothing about the operation— run by Ted Koop, head of the CBS Washington bureau—was fancy. But the network's TV operations were growing. "CBS asked me to go on the air and do the Korean War story, which was the big story at the time," Cronkite later recalled in a *Detroit News Magazine* profile. "They simply said, 'Go out and do five minutes on the evening news.' They asked what I needed, and I said, 'Just give me a blackboard with an outline of Korea with the 38th parallel marked on it.' "

Originally Cronkite hosted WTOP-TV's fifteen-minute late Sunday newscast *Up to the Minute* (which followed *What's My Line?* at 11:00 p.m. EST). On air, he drew arrows on the map to highlight troop movements on the Korean Peninsula. Washingtonians took notice. Cronkite might have had no experience on TV, but he was the ablest newsman CBS had available for duty. Cronkite excelled. Koop then asked him to take over the entire fifteen-minute 6:00 p.m. television newscast. "I said sure," Cronkite recalled, "because this was all fun and experimental stuff. We were still trying to figure out how to do news on television."

Cronkite, now thirty-three years old, soon exhibited the mysterious quality that Hewitt had called "telegenic" appeal. Others called it "camera charisma" or "star quality." The baffling art of connecting with an audience had long been studied in the theater (and more recently in film schools). But the only reliable conclusion, the great scholars decided, was that some folks had star quality and others flat-out didn't. In television, the on-air performer was in effect being invited into the viewer's home (at a distance equivalent to that of actual guests in living rooms). These visits were almost endlessly repetitive: a theatergoer might see the magnetic Richard Burton once a year on Broadway or the charismatic Edward G. Robinson at the movies twice a year, but Cronkite was going to be on five nights a week.

On September 15, 1950, the day of the Inchon landings, Walter and Betsy's second daughter, Mary Kathleen ("Kathy") Cronkite, was born. It no longer made sense for Cronkite, the father of two children, to become a foreign correspondent in Korea. Living in Truman's Washington, doing television, was the ideal billet for him. What really impressed Bill Paley and Dr. Frank Stanton in New York was that Cronkite even attracted a commercial sponsor: Hechinger, a local lumber and hardware company. So quickly did Cronkite establish himself as CBS's premier television newscaster that by Election Night that November of 1950, his was the only name CBS would promote in its television coverage. All the top CBS journalists—including Edward R. Murrow, Bill Downs, Eric Sevareid, Joe Wershba, Bill Shadel, Griffin Bancroft, and Alexander Kendrick—were working in radio. Although Cronkite's audience at WTOP-TV was local, his broadcast career had taken off, due to the twitching little box. Stanton advised Cronkite to stick with TV news, for it was soon to be a booming industry.

Working with Cronkite at the Washington station was Bill Shadel, a correspondent during World War II for *American Rifleman*, the NRA house organ. Shadel was impressed by Cronkite's Steady Eddy appearance and ability to ad-lib on TV as if he were born for the job. "Within six months he was the talk of the town," Shadel recalled of Cronkite. "He seemed to be the first to sense the necessary techniques for this new medium. His voice immediately was the voice of authority. His presence filled the screen. He realized that his audience was that camera and he chose to address that camera despite his script."

The TV studio at WTOP was very small, not much bigger than a mansion closet. Cronkite was to begin the broadcast delivering the headline news and then introduce Joe Wershba, who would interview in the studio someone who was profiled in that day's edition of *The Washington Post*. At the back end of the fifteen-minute broadcast was a sports and business roundup. It was all live. Cronkite didn't even have a script, just index cards that he studied before going on air. "How do you do the news so perfectly without a script?" Wershba's wife, Shirley, once asked Cronkite. "Nobody understands." Cronkite replied. "Every day at U.P. an editor would call me into his office and say 'What is the news today?' I'd have to tick all of the stories off in a precise and condensed way. That's all I'm doing at WTOP."

Cronkite did something else that was novel beyond covering the Korean War: he used charts, diagrams, and maps as props for other news stories. Sometimes he would even hold up photographs of the person he was talking about, things you couldn't use on radio. Cronkite and Shadel became pioneers in TV news and close friends. "[Shadel] came every Wednesday night to sit beside me and I put the broadcast together at a desk in the basement of the station," Cronkite recalled in 2000. "By one of those strange coincidences, the Hecht Department Store on Wednesday night did an on-air fashion show (perhaps the nation's first) immediately preceding the news. The models performed their rapid changes of costume behind a makeshift canvas curtain a few feet from my desk. Sometimes the view was, well, distracting."

Cronkite's performance covering the 1950 midterm elections drew accolades from Dr. Stanton in New York, not because he was so dynamic but because he didn't screw up and satisfied his two commercial sponsors:

Esso at 6:00 p.m. and Hechinger at 11:00 p.m. While the Murrow Boys looked down on TV and dismissed Cronkite as not good enough for radio, his career had caught fire. Joe Wershba, a colleague at CBS, tried to counteract that perception by writing a piece for *The Washington Post* praising Cronkite's prowess in the hot new medium of television. "Walter Winchell drops a line to the effect that television news reporters really read their lines off the cameras—and that's why they look and sound so smooth," Wershba said. "Walter is being unfair to CBS's own Walter—Walter Cronkite. Cronkite . . . works all day on his television news report, uses the old college instructor's technique of a few notes, and talks the news right at his audience. He does it so smoothly, people won't believe he isn't reading it 'off the camera.' No sense explaining it here: people still won't believe it. We who work with Cronkite can hardly believe it either."

Besides hosting the national Sunday-evening newscast of *Up to the Minute*, every Sunday afternoon he served as co-host of the WTOP-TV show *The Week's News* (with the chief of *Newsweek*'s Washington bureau, Ernest K. Lindley). The public affairs program started with heavy news and ended with a soft feature piece. On June 24, 1951, for instance, Cronkite and Lindley aired new combat footage from the Korean

War, followed by a discussion of nuclear weapons with Congressman Felix Edward Hébert and a "pretty golfers" segment featuring Patty Berg and Babe Didrikson.

There was another ingredient to Cronkite's TV magic: he had an innate understanding of the medium. The fact that he didn't even own a TV until his first broadcast made him something of a prodigy. No one at WTOP told him how to shape a broadcast, and while Edwards was a model for many new TV newsmen, Cronkite had his own ideas from the start. "I had a gut feeling that television news delivery ought to be as informal as possible," he explained in his memoir. "I imagined the newspaper editor running down a list of the day's big stories when asked at home: 'What happened today?'" Handed his own fifteen minutes of airtime for the news, Cronkite remained relaxed, determined to play the straight man. In fact, he outdid John Cameron Swayze in the unflappable department. Whereas Swayze memorized his script, Cronkite never had one: he memorized the content, from the broad issues to the pertinent facts. "I went on and I did the news," he recalled. "I ad-libbed it."

Cronkite's UP training of boiling down the essence of a story in bites served him well in TV news. He labored for accuracy and clarity, but not necessarily bright originality, memorable phrasing, nuance, or implication. Unlike most fine writers, he wasn't in love with his own words. Hence, he didn't feel compelled to memorize them. Abbreviation of complex issues came naturally to him. The extemporaneous newscast was no compromise for Cronkite; he could achieve the same accuracy and clarity without the perfect wording.

By contrast, Edward R. Murrow worked hard on his scripts, weighing the phrases like a jeweler. Murrow was always keyed up before a TV broadcast, as nervous as a newcomer. Even though he typically read every word off his script, he was still physically uncomfortable on the air. He smoked continuously to calm his nerves while he was in the studio, sweating profusely and often twisting his hands around under the table. Well aware that he would make a rather pathetic sight if he were filmed on a bad day, Murrow shied away from television, publicly criticizing it, yet making just enough appearances to convince himself and others that he could master the medium if and when he wanted.

In the autumn of 1951, though the thought of becoming a TV newsman gave him heartburn and spine-chill, Murrow was ready for television. He had been influenced by the immediacy of certain live programming, notably the broadcasts earlier that year of the Senate's Kefauver Committee investigation into organized crime. That riveting broadcast, which had

30 million viewers, brought Americans closer to the workings of their government than most had ever been before and made a media star of Tennessee Democrat Estes Kefauver, the chair of the committee. Other politicians duly took note of the power of TV. Murrow couldn't help being impressed by the visual spectacle of the images of actual thugs under verbal fire. "The television performance," he admitted about the Kefauver investigations, "has been fascinating." He was also influenced by his working partnership with producer Fred Friendly, a gregarious Rhode Islander who found ways to translate Murrow's style to the new television medium.

Starting on November 18, Murrow and Friendly collaborated on a half-hour documentary series called *See It Now*, covering various topics in the news. "Good evening," Murrow said on the debut show. "This is an old team trying to learn a new trade." Early on, Bill Downs made a pest of himself (a role very much in his nature), demanding that Murrow use his new pulpit to expose the destructiveness of Senator McCarthy's Red Scare investigations. Murrow demurred for the time being, but *See It Now* gained a reputation for confronting controversial subjects.

Much further down the CBS broadcasting ladder, Cronkite continued to hone his local shows in

Washington, D.C. He became the voice that warned WTOP viewers that a test pattern, a break in regular network programming, was under way. On other occasions, he interrupted entertainment shows for breaking news. His voice inflections always seemed reassuring. Cronkite also covered national stories for the network, garnering a desirable assignment as one of three hosts (the other two being Frank Bourgholtzer of NBC News and Bryson Rash of ABC News) of the first televised tour of the White House, where a renovation had just been completed. His May 4, 1952, interview with President Truman at the White House, while largely constrained to a chat about the mansion's antique furnishings, marked his first public interaction with a president. John Crosby of *The Washington Post* nailed the whole White House tour as being "a real slick job." A better phrase would have been "contrived beyond belief." Cronkite was embarrassingly awkward and nervous. "Do the clocks run, Mr. President?" asked Cronkite with excruciating deference. "Yes, they all run," Truman responded. "We have a special man to wind all of the clocks every Friday."

From that broadcast onward, Cronkite's friendship with Truman became ironclad because of the Missouri connection. Two months after the White House tour, Cronkite got another big break. Sig Mickelson, the head of CBS News in New York, summoned him from Washington to anchor the network's coverage of the national political conventions. Mickelson had approached others, including Murrow, but found no one willing to carry a broadcast through hours of ad-libbing. According to Don Hewitt, Stanton, the dour and formal president of CBS, "saw Cronkite as Douglas Edwards' successor as the front man of CBS News." Cronkite didn't hesitate to accept Mickelson's offer, but the network's announcement was low-key. "Walter Cronkite was not one of the Murrow Boys," David Halberstam explained in *The Powers That Be*. And other CBSers rolled their eyes in belittling envy. "Cronkite in 1952 was perhaps the one rising star within the company who was outside the Murrow clique."

If Cronkite found himself in a conundrum in the early 1950s it was about how to be a serious CBS News reporter when the money in television was in game shows. Mark Goodson and Bill Todman, producers of such popular quiz shows as *Winner Take All* (1948–1950) and *What's My Line?* (1950–1967), were the hottest acts at CBS, and they offered Cronkite a job as substitute host for the game show *It's News to Me*, which ran on CBS from 1951 to 1954. Cronkite could have refused to cooperate with Goodson-Todman Productions, taken a Murrow-esque stance that such

mindless drivel was beneath the dignity of a true journalist. But the quiz shows were so wildly popular that
he couldn't resist. He took the job—and the extra pay.
The show was a thirty-minute bluffing game in which
contestants tried to discern whether an answer was true
or false. The mildly popular series was originally hosted
by John Daly, but Cronkite, the substitute, became the
host in 1954 for its final three-month run.

11.

Election Night and UNIVAC

MICKELSON CUTS A DEAL—ANCHORMAN AS NOUN—
CRONKITE SCHOOL FOR POLITICIANS—CHICAGO GOES
HOLLYWOOD—CONVENTION EVE PARTY—BUGGING
THE CREDENTIALS COMMITTEE—SELLING OF THE
CANDIDATE—PALEY DREAMS OF 35 MILLION TV
SETS—GETTING DRUNK WITH CRONKITE—
EISENHOWER V. STEVENSON—THE BRAVE NEW
WORLD OF UNIVAC—BONDING WITH THOMAS,
STRUGGLING WITH MURROW—ERNIE LEISER TO THE
RESCUE—THE CORONATION OF QUEEN ELIZABETH
II—THE UBIQUITOUS WALTER CRONKITE—CBS VIPER
NEST—TOO STRONG FOR SECOND FIDDLE

The rise of Cronkite as America's first TV anchor-man had started in 1951 under Sig Mickelson, the first president of CBS News. It was Mickelson, an even-keeled Minnesotan approaching his forties and considered a pioneer in early television, who negotiated an agreement on behalf of all three networks for the 1952 political conventions to be covered live. The specter of television cameras on the convention floors left print reporters cold. Both CBS and NBC had experimentally televised parts of the 1948 conventions, but nothing remotely like the grand gavel-to-gavel production planned for 1952. Once Mickelson successfully negotiated on behalf of all the networks, he went about figuring out how CBS could do the best job. "It seemed then that a revolution with far-reaching implications had begun, that politics would never be the same again," Mickelson explained, "that the television camera would dominate the action and the television tube the voter response."

When he first befriended Cronkite in 1940, Mickelson was teaching at the University of Kansas in Lawrence, and Cronkite was at the UP bureau in Kansas City. Whenever Mickelson found himself in Kaycee, which was often, he'd invite Cronkite out for brisket and baked beans. But they lost contact with each other until Cronkite was hired by CBS. "I used to see him fairly frequently when he was doing the 11 o'clock news for WTOP television in Washington, D.C.," recalled Mickelson of being an early booster of Cronkite's career at CBS. "I would go down to

Washington often and watch the show and sometimes have a drink with him afterwards. He was not under my jurisdiction until 1954 when I became head of news for both radio and television. Until then he remained on the radio payroll, but all he did was television. Actually, he worked for me, but technically, he was not on my payroll."

Every broadcast communications student eventually becomes acquainted with the life and legend of Mickelson, who during World War II was news director at WCOO Minneapolis (the farm club for CBS News in New York). His two memoirs about television news gathering—*From Whistle Stop to Sound Bite* and *The Electric Mirror*—are often an integral part of Journalism 101 curricula. In his CBS years, from 1949 to 1961, Mickelson was the person most responsible for morphing CBS Radio and CBS TV into what became CBS News. When Mickelson, serving as Cronkite's rabbi, tried to get his old friend the CBS anchorman gig for the 1952 political conventions, he was met with stiff resistance from Hubbell Robinson, a program vice president. Robinson wanted dependable Bob Trout, a CBS radio legend like Lowell Thomas, whom he deemed a far more enduring, essential, and telegenic reporter. Murrow feigned interest in taking a few steps in the TV convention direction, then held back. Refusing to cross the threshold, he grumpily removed himself from the competition; stoking the egos of politicians just wasn't his stew. An argument ensued. "We had several conversations about it and I held to my [pro-Cronkite] position," Mickelson recalled. "I do not remember whether it got to the Stanton/Paley level before it was finally decided, but I held firm for a month or six weeks and finally Cronkite got the job."

Within the TV context, a running debate ensued over who coined the term *anchorman*. Sig Mickelson and Don Hewitt both made claims. But, in truth, the label had been applied to other, less successful news presenters before being famously applied to Walter Cronkite. Mickelson had indeed thought about using the term when Cronkite was CBS's host for the 1951 San Francisco conference that yielded the Treaty of Peace with Japan. But the dynamic didn't feel right. "I am not sure if that term was ever used in radio," Mickelson recalled. "But the concept was definitely in place. The way it got some notice was when the press information department at CBS asked 'what's Walter Cronkite going to do?' I said he is going to 'anchor for us.' Then they started thinking about it and started describing him as an anchorman and that seems to be where the idea really took off."

Murrow found the noun *anchorman* repugnant, but he also thought *televised conventions* were a horror show where no hard news was made. To Murrow, television was all part of a public relations game, and CBS's coverage of the 1952 conventions was essentially free advertising for the Democratic and Republican parties, not true journalism. His invective against CBS televising political carnivals became legendary in broadcasting circles ("political shell-game . . . rigged, traded, bought and bargained for. . . . There is more freedom of choice . . . at a track, where the horses run"). To Murrow's point, the Republican Party chairman, Guy Gabrielson, had offered to purchase the broadcast rights; the idea was nixed as an illegal corporate contribution. "I had little contact with Edward R. Murrow," recalled Mickelson. "To him I was a representative of management, and management was absolute anathema to Murrow, except for Paley."

Mickelson understood well how to drum-roll CBS News' personnel leading into the 1952 conventions. To promote the coming summer convention coverage, CBS News set up a "school" to teach politicians how to behave on the Tube. With Cronkite as the teacher, the how-to-look-good-on-TV school attracted media publicity and at least a few politicians, who learned what to wear (the color blue showed up well), how to speak (briefly, whenever possible), and what not to do (pound the table). Both Speaker of the House Sam Rayburn and Congressman John F. Kennedy enrolled as Cronkite's pupils to learn the art of TV makeup, dress, and diction; Cronkite taught them that "getting across" on television was "all in the eyes." The 1940, 1944, and 1948 conventions had been seen by a very limited audience, but as Mickelson said, that was "horse-and-buggy" television. The 1952 coverage of both Chicago political conventions—as Rayburn and Kennedy understood—would open the era properly, with a combined workforce of two thousand people for all the networks and at a cost of $7 million.

CBS News pulled out all the stops to turn the 1952 conventions into programming showcases. Paley was able to pressure Westinghouse to pay $3 million to sponsor the coast-to-coast coverage of the political events. According to Don Hewitt, the volcanic TV news pioneer who tended to monopolize conversations with his strange combination of bug-eyed humor and the backhand, the Chicago conventions transformed television almost overnight, making the medium more popular than radio. "TV had been radio's little brother," Hewitt recalled. "Radio could go anywhere. TV was stuck in a studio. Then we said, hey, let's cover a convention. We can stake it out like a football game.

We know when it's going to be played, we know where
the rostrum is, we know where the delegates are going
to sit. For the first time television could flex its muscles
and say, 'We can do anything radio can do, and we can
do it better.' "

Leaving no promotional opportunity unexploited,
Mickelson scheduled a "Convention Eve Party" on
the night before the Republicans convened. Cronkite
was to interview the major candidates as they arrived
for dinner. Unfortunately, both the dinner and the
candidates were still a long way off when the show
began. Cronkite was facing his first potential disaster
and the convention had yet to begin: a gaping half
hour of airtime to fill. He was ready. He interviewed
Howard K. Smith, one of the CBS roving correspondents covering the convention, as though it had been
planned from the start. "Those 1952 conventions were
not only the first but also the last time the American
public would have an opportunity to see our neat
political conclaves in pure, undiluted form," Cronkite
recalled. "By 1956 the parties had begun to sanitize
their proceedings."

The key to CBS News' success at the 1952 conventions in Chicago proved to be a combination of logistics
melding with weighty analysis. Hewitt and Robinson
had rented out both the sixth and eleventh floors of the

Conrad Hilton (extra camera crews were ensconced at the Blackstone and Congress hotels). Seventeen cameras were installed on the convention floors. An additional five pool cameras were used. A team was also assigned to Washington, D.C., to get the reaction to both conventions from President Truman, who wasn't running for reelection. The print media, however, didn't like the growing perception that the Big Three networks were glorifying the stresses and strifes of the Chicago conventions. *The New York Times* and *The Wall Street Journal* alike were up in arms about it. CBS told them all to stick it. "We were young," Mickelson recalled, "and aggressive."

Unlike its rivals, CBS News anticipated barren stretches during the conventions and placed much of the burden of filling them on Cronkite's shoulders. He coordinated reports from correspondents on the floor, and when there were no reports, he simply talked to the viewers. He had done his research in advance and had a lot to say. Still, he constantly worried about the precise level of his discourse. For a while, CBS planned to find a "common man" and seat him in front of a monitor during the convention broadcasts. Whenever the rube didn't understand something, Cronkite would be notified. The plan fell apart, though, when CBS recognized that it didn't know where to find a common man. But the network had clearly found the right anchorman in Cronkite.

Amid all the slow stretches, there were a number of exciting TV moments for Cronkite to cover at both Chicago conventions. The Democrats nominated Adlai Stevenson, governor of Illinois, a home-state favorite, on the third ballot; the hoopla was deafening. The 1952 Democratic Convention is remembered in the annals of U.S. political history as being the last brokered convention and the last to have more than one roll call. The GOP Convention, however, had a lot more TV appeal, especially with General Douglas MacArthur, commander of the U.S. Army Forces in the Far East during World War II, delivering the impassioned keynote address. And there was a kingdaddy fight between former general Dwight Eisenhower and Senator Robert Taft for the Republican nomination. It got so fierce that the credentials committee, overseen by Taft, tried to ban TV cameras from covering the proceedings. The Eisenhower team took the opposite approach, as NBC News' Reuven Frank recalled, "proclaiming that they favored television, they loved it, they wanted it, and barring it was an outrage, a denial of the American way."

Just how hungry Cronkite was to excel in CBS's coverage of the conventions became readily apparent when he orchestrated the secret tape recording of the Republicans' credentials committee meeting. Long before the Nixon administration bugged the Democratic National Committee office at the Watergate in 1972, Cronkite, after much deliberation, had a CBS technician wire the committee room under the shady rationale that the covert act was good for democracy. "He ran a wire," Cronkite recalled, "up the outside of the hotel and into a broom closet several floors above. There one of our newspeople listened through earphones and rushed notes . . . to me downstairs. The sources of these reports baffled both the Republicans and my broadcast opposition."

While Cronkite later told the story with folksy charm, his act was a dastardly invasion of privacy that could have landed CBS in serious legal trouble. But it was Sig Mickelson who approved the bugging, so Cronkite wasn't in jeopardy of being fired for the crime. "At this early period in television history," Mickelson said in shrugging explanation, "ethical considerations did not deeply disturb us." Cronkite and Mickelson pulled off the bugging with the consummate skill of veteran safecrackers. They embarrassed Taft's credentials committee into allowing the Republican Convention to be televised "gavel to gavel." The exclusion of cameras—which the print media wanted—was averted. The cameras played perfectly into the Eisenhower-as-folk-hero scenario. TV viewers liked Ike, not the pinch-faced Robert Taft of Ohio, hoping to ride to power on the gold-plated family name. Cronkite had, in a brazen way, helped Eisenhower, one of Paley's close friends, obtain the nomination. It was the beginning of a mutually beneficial friendship between Walter and Ike.

The response to Cronkite's hours of on-air work at the conventions was overwhelmingly positive on the part of critics, viewers, and CBS executives. CBS's convention coverage ran for 13.9 hours, with Cronkite as star. John Crosby, a syndicated television columnist known for snark, was an instant fan of the tough, warm-hearted, fact-hungry anchorman. "Walter Cronkite," he wrote, "the slot man for CBS, has done a magnificent job—providing commentary for as long as seven hours at a stretch." And the longer Cronkite was on the air, the more time there was to run Westinghouse commercials. "Television," David Halberstam wrote of early 1950s journalism, "was about to alter the nature and balance of American merchandising."

What concerned Cronkite about his convention performance was viewer mail accusing him first of partisanship for Eisenhower and then the same for Stevenson. "Then I came to a marvelous revelation," he wrote his friend Don Michel of WRAJ-AM (Anna,

Illinois) in 1968. "They were about equally divided between those who thought I favored the Democrats and those who believed I favored the Republicans! Since then, this has been my rule of thumb: If the charges stay in reasonable balance, I consider that I am succeeding in maintaining objectivity."

After the convention, Cronkite and Mickelson went on a drinking binge to drown the unending strain of the past month. CBS had done a bang-up job at both Chicago conventions, proving that television was a gargantuan new tool of mass communication. The emphasis at CBS regarding live news coverage shifted from radio to TV. It was, Cronkite believed, good for democracy. The TV camera would end up exposing disingenuous U.S. politicians as flimflam artists and charlatans. More Americans would end up voting that November for either Eisenhower or Stevenson, Cronkite believed, because CBS's coverage had turned politics into the biggest theatrical drama of all time. "We thought," Mickelson recalled, "we had really pulled off a revolution."

The 1952 conventions proved that watching special events on the Tube in your own living room was indeed the new postwar rage. Most Americans had never been to a political convention; now they were watching one in their own *homes*. Just as Murrow had linked Great

Britain to America with his voice during the Second World War, Cronkite brought the Chicago conventions into the living rooms of America. The power of TV was truly astonishing. Besides Eisenhower himself, the two real celebrities of the 1952 conventions were Cronkite and Betty Furness, then a Westinghouse spokeswoman and *What's My Line?* panelist. Hewitt, a Douglas Edwards loyalist, recalled that post-Chicago, Cronkite had become "not just 'an anchorman,' but '*the* anchorman.'" "Well, Walter," Mickelson said after the broadcasts, "you're famous now. And you are going to want a lot more money. You better get an agent." (At the time, Cronkite was making less than $200 a week; down the road he would become a million-dollar-a-year man.)

Cronkite didn't realize, as he relocated from Washington, D.C., to New York, that the goldfish bowl was also a shark tank. The word around CBS was that Murrow was dismissive of Cronkite's quick ascendancy at the network. "On the air Murrow treated Cronkite with collegiality," radio broadcaster Bob Edwards explained, "but off the air, with condescension."

Following up on Chicago, CBS News was determined to slaughter NBC News in its 1952 Election Night coverage. When Mickelson asked Cronkite to anchor CBS News' Eisenhower-versus-Stevenson contest coverage on November 4, 1952, the answer was:

"y-e-s, s-i-r!!" On September 25, CBS News issued a press release naming him "anchor-man." There was only one catch. UNIVAC, a computer manufactured in Philadelphia that was deemed the "electronic brains" of CBS, would be a principal sidekick.

The decision to team Cronkite up with a computer was made in the early fall of 1952. Mickelson, looking to make a bigger splash on Election Night, had found a futuristic gimmick: UNIVAC, the smartest machine in the world, able to project election results from returns better than humans. "The novelty value of using UNIVAC," Mickelson recalled, "was certain to attract attention from both viewers and the print media."

In the weeks before November 4, CBS heavily promoted its forthcoming Election Night coverage, featuring UNIVAC prominently. UNIVAC was portrayed as an electronic giant straight from *Buck Rogers*. To counter UNIVAC, NBC ended up getting its own computer, named Monrobot. This left ABC news director John Madigan to lampoon the new electronic gadget as a "gimmick," telling *Time* magazine that his network preferred its sterling *human* contributors, such as Elmer Davis and John Daly. Cronkite agreed, but wasn't in a position to squawk. And he wasn't going to be left alone with UNIVAC. Cronkite's posse included Murrow, Collingwood, Edwards, and Lowell Thomas.

Hewitt would be the Election Night director. What privately concerned Cronkite was the man-versus-machine narrative that CBS was trying to spin. To Cronkite, the eight-foot-long "mechanical brain" was an expensive experiment costing the network $600,000 that could have been spent covering the Korean War. As November 4 neared, Cronkite bought himself some distance from UNIVAC. "Actually we're not depending too much on this machine," he said. "It may turn out to be just a sideshow."

On Election Night, CBS began its coverage at 8:00 p.m. EST, a full hour before NBC. Cronkite anchored the special event from Grand Central Terminal in New York. As the cameras panned around the cavernous studio, correspondents, tabulators, and engineers buzzed around what Cronkite called a "teeming beehive." Teletype machines hummed in the background. Cronkite was trying to gin up excitement, having assistants hand him copy, bells ringing in the background. According to early reports, 61 million voters had gone to the polls to choose between Eisenhower and Stevenson.

CBS had pegged up popular and electoral vote count boards. Some states were declared early for Eisenhower and others for Stevenson. But Cronkite warned, as would become a network news tradition, that these were very preliminary results. Hedging bets, in fact, became a Cronkite trademark—reporting news laden with qualifiers. Just as he had positioned himself as both a supporter and critic of UNIVAC, Cronkite now tried to break news while leaving himself an out if it proved wrong. Around 8:40 p.m., the Jolly Electronic Giant, as some CBS technicians called UNIVAC, made its first much-ballyhooed appearance.

Collingwood was standing with UNIVAC behind him, describing how his computer friend was "one of a family of electronic brains." Both Cronkite and Collingwood were pathetically following Mickelson's order to "humanize" UNIVAC, to "treat it gently and semi-humorously but at the same time give full attention to the data it would produce." Cronkite and Collingwood were instructed to spoonfeed the data provided by UNIVAC to the American public because viewers weren't ready for "overly rich doses of high technology." By treating UNIVAC as human, Cronkite dumbed down the broadcast. Only his cutaways to Murrow and Thomas that evening prevented him from being a national laughingstock. And Collingwood didn't fare as well. Was this the same Collingwood who, during World War II, bravely broadcast from North Africa? "Can you say something, UNIVAC?" Collingwood asked like a horse's ass. "Have you got anything to say to the television audience?"

UNIVAC, ignoring its big cue, stayed embarrassingly silent. "You're a very impolite machine, I must say" was all a ruffled Collingwood could muster.

After a few minutes of blather, Collingwood handed the broadcast back to Cronkite, who didn't acknowledge the awkward minutes that had just passed. He simply hung Collingwood out to dry and continued to be anchorman. With a touch of irritation, he moved on to talk about South Carolina ballots and New England weather. No mention of UNIVAC at all. Like a puff of smoke from a genie's bottle, Cronkite had Lowell Thomas, his all-seasons hero since circa 1934 Houston, at his side. Thomas praised CBS News' television studio in New York, showing the audience the Teletype machines, revolving cameras, and switchboard operations. The net effect was to make Cronkite, not UNIVAC, the star of the evening.

With Thomas backing his action, Cronkite blazed like a meteor. Brushing off a technical glitch, he interviewed former GOP presidential candidate Harold Stassen, tossed out poll numbers, and offered a series of projections stating that Eisenhower was leading in twenty-two states. He was in the zone. The momentum he was establishing as a performer was almost tangible.

When forced to turn to Collingwood again, Cronkite did so with reluctance. Once again, Collingwood was awful. When Cronkite regained the broadcast again, he turned to Murrow for analysis of the election. The legendary radio broadcaster came across as agitated; he had been reduced to the role of Cronkite's roving correspondent, and he subtly let it be known. "As Walter Cronkite just suggested," Murrow archly started, "it may be possible for men and machines to draw some sweeping conclusions from the returns so far, but I am not able to do it."

Cronkite suffered through Murrow's self-serving analysis, then offered some fine state-by-state analysis of his own. In actuality, by 9:00 p.m., he was leading listeners to believe that Eisenhower would win. Newspapers such as *The Baltimore Sun* and *The Boston Post*, Cronkite told viewers, had already announced victory by Ike. Just after 10:00 p.m., Cronkite, with as much cheer as he could muster, turned to Collingwood for a third time. "Well," Collingwood said, "as a great believer in the machine, I hesitate to say that we're having a little bit of trouble . . . with UNIVAC. It seems that he's rebelling against the human element." Behind Collingwood were a bunch of Keystone Kops repairmen trying to get UNIVAC to cough out election data. Collingwood eventually extracted an electoral vote prediction from UNIVAC: Eisenhower 314 to Stevenson 217.

If Cronkite had been more powerful at CBS, he simply would have cut UNIVAC off for the rest of the evening. But Hewitt and Mickelson had spent a lot of Mr. Paley's money on the computer and they insisted that Cronkite check in with Collingwood from time to time. Hard as it was to imagine, UNIVAC only grew into worse and worse television. Trying to sound authoritative, Collingwood read a UNIVAC printout suggesting that Stevenson had the popular vote lead. This was patently false and in contradiction to what Cronkite had been correctly telling his CBS audience for the past two hours: Eisenhower was far ahead. This was embarrassing television. Cronkite knew the jig was up.

It was one thing for Collingwood to bomb, but Cronkite wasn't going to be challenged by a malfunctioning robot. "Charlie, very interesting indeed on the UNIVAC prediction," Cronkite said, shaking his head in disbelief, smirking so the viewers knew he wasn't part of the Brave New World boondoggle. "We who are only human and have to operate with flesh and blood instead of electronic gadgets still think this thing looks like it's pretty much on the Eisenhower side at the moment." All night long Cronkite had given accurate reports for a singular reason: he relied on UP wire service reports. As anchorman, he had expertly managed to keep UNIVAC somehow apart from his core broadcast. By constantly putting qualifiers on the election returns, Cronkite quashed the opportunity to be the big honcho who broke the news definitively for CBS. He was, in fact, outfoxed in this regard by Murrow. After UNIVAC malfunctioned, Cronkite turned to Murrow for analysis, and he stole the night from the anchorman. "I think it is reasonably certain that the election is over," Murrow said. "Traditionally, the Democratic strength comes from big cities and they have failed to deliver in this election."

Cronkite's face hardened, almost as though someone had doused him in quick-setting cement. Cronkite had been big-footed; Murrow beat Cronkite in announcing the night's victor. It was a comeuppance he'd never forget. Caution had its limits. A true TV broadcaster had to develop the innate instinct about when to call the match. Somehow at the end of Election Night, Murrow was left holding up journalism's gut instinct in the silly age of UNIVAC.

By Christmas 1952, Cronkite had proven to his CBS bosses that he was perfectly suited to become a national television impresario. On radio interviews, as if selling a product, he had the nerve to promote the virtues of TV news as an enhancer of American democracy. He also wrote an overly optimistic essay for *Theatre Arts* magazine about how TV would weed out the self-serving phonies from the public arena for the benefit of mankind. "Television has an X-ray quality," he wrote. "Television can detect insincerity as a more orthodox X-ray can detect a broken bone. Television can X-ray the soul; therefore, the future breed of politicians is going to be a much higher, not lower type than we have known in the past."

As CBS TV grew in popularity, new production talent was hired to beef up the news department, including the erudite, hard-knocks reporter Ernie Leiser. Born on February 26, 1921, in Philadelphia, Leiser made his mark as a journalist during the Second World War, covering D-day and the Bulge. While Ernie Pyle was the best prose writer at *Stars and Stripes*, Leiser had the best geopolitical sense of any print reporter working the Europe beat. From the very moment he was hired by CBS News, he bonded with Cronkite. Leiser soon became CBS's detective extraordinaire, finding dirt related to the Soviet Union's iron-fisted Communist rule. When the Hungarian Revolution occurred in October 1956, Leiser went into Budapest and shot the only footage of the anti-Soviet revolt, risking life and limb to get the dramatic film.

With Leiser on hand as producer, Cronkite's next special-event opportunity occurred seven months after Election Day 1952, when CBS covered the coronation of Queen Elizabeth II at Westminster Abbey. At issue was how quickly world events could be brought to an American audience in the pre-satellite age. The Cronkite-Leiser goal was to whipstitch a film account of the British royal ceremonies together. But CBS's race against the clock was thought to be miraculous. Once Leiser and Cronkite had developed the film of the royal pomp—a sea of well-groomed aristocrats draped in jeweled, pleated, furred, and embossed clothes—CBS used BBC facilities (a makeshift studio at Westminster Abbey) to prepare a special report for its American audience complete with B-roll footage of the procession and eyewitness raves. Cronkite and Leiser then raced to Heathrow Airport, got on a chartered plane, and flew to Boston. Speed was the governing ethos. On TV, Cronkite seemed to bask in the British gallantry of the crowning and enthronement. Off the air, chain-smoking cigarettes with Leiser, Cronkite was gleeful that CBS had "gutted" NBC by beating it to air by a full hour.

Unblinking as a fish when the camera was on, without a trace of showiness, Cronkite was becoming America's trusted anchorman. TV viewers, however, couldn't associate Cronkite with a particular CBS show outside of convention coverage on the network. Filling in for every coworker who was sick or on vacation, Cronkite seized every assignment he could. A broadcastography of Cronkite from 1950 to 1953 has him hosting *Walter Cronkite and the News*, *The News with Walter Cronkite*, *Walter Cronkite's Esso News Show*, *News of the Night*, *Saturday News and Weather*, and *Your World in Review* (taking over from Edward P. Morgan). One of the keys to success was *never* to turn down face time. He even narrated an episode of the 1953 CBS-TV drama *Suspense* about the death of a newspaper editor in Mussolini's Italy.

Cronkite was being groomed by Stanton and Paley as Murrow's TV successor. That was one reason Cronkite and Murrow eyed each other from separate corners in the 1950s, even as they found their own distinctive niches in televised news. A silent competition for being top dog ensued. CBS News was turning into a viper's nest. There was a labyrinth of different fiefdoms that didn't congeal. The network's headquarters on Madison Avenue and the TV studio, then located inside the Grand Central Terminal complex on Vanderbilt Avenue, were only a few blocks away but seemed like miles apart. A huge barrier had been erected between CBS Radio (Murrow) and CBS TV (Cronkite). The challenge for Cronkite was to figure out how to straddle both camps. "Cronkite and Murrow didn't work well as a team," Hewitt recalled. "Each of them was too strong to play second fiddle."

12.

Mr. CBS Utility Man

YOU ARE THERE—BACKING BLACKLISTED WRITERS—
EXPLOSION IN YUCCA FLATS—MICKELSON RUNS THE
TABLE—MURROW TAKES ON MCCARTHY—KEEP FAS-
CISTS OFF THE AIRWAVES—THE MORNING SHOW
BLUES—CRONKITE EMBRACES CHARLEMAGNE—JACK
OF ALL TRADES—SPEED RACER—COMPETING WITH
JACK PAAR—MINNESOTA CALLING—WATCH OUT FOR
HUNTLEY-BRINKLEY

Dressed in a standard dark suit, Walter Cronkite, a thoroughly modern man, looked out of place interviewing a Benedict Arnold reenactor in a powdered wig or a Louis Pasteur impersonator in a white laboratory coat. But that's precisely what he did on the popular weekly CBS TV show *You Are There.* Each half-hour episode—which aired at 6:30 p.m. on Sundays from 1953 to 1957—began with time lines and charts explaining a key moment or person in world history. Then Cronkite would calmly set the stage for the upcoming reenactment. Pick the topic—the Boston Tea Party, Battle of Waterloo, or Lincoln at Gettysburg— Cronkite served as lantern-carrier. No historical topic was out of bounds in the series, which re-created seminal moments of the past and reported on them as if they had just happened. No period costume detail was overlooked by the wardrobe department. Following the Cronkite send-off, in a jarring fashion, an announcer would almost shout out, "You are there!" as if grabbing the viewer by the collar.

Charles Russell, the show's ambitious producer, boasted that every line uttered in the kitschy *You Are There* was historically accurate. And so it was. CBS fact-checkers for radio shows met the very highest *New Yorker* standard. Russell, refusing "dramatic license" in re-creating the past, had started the CBS program on radio and now moved the teleplay to TV with Cronkite as host and Sidney Lumet, the future Academy Award–winning Hollywood filmmaker, as director. Lumet chose Cronkite because "the premise of the series was so silly, so outrageous, that we needed somebody with the most American, homespun, warm ease about him." When asked why Cronkite was chosen to host *You Are There*, the show's executive producer, William Dozier, explained the CBS management rationale. "He's good," Dozier said, "he's effective, and since the national political conventions, he's a household name." It seemed like an odd fit at first. But Cronkite's "serious demeanor and unpretentious style" made even interviews with figures such as Sigmund Freud and George Washington believable.

You Are There was strange live television for cold war America. Cronkite would play himself, a modern CBS News anchorman, hands clasped behind his back, full of intriguing questions. While Cronkite was under no illusion that the *You Are There* gig would help his journalism career, he hoped the program would raise awareness of his personal brand. Some teachers and educators took to dubbing Cronkite "the history teacher" of America. "I was brought on as an actor to trade in on my newly acquired fame and authority as a convention anchor," he explained to NPR in 2003. He later bragged to *American Heritage* magazine about all the great "players" *You Are There* showcased, including Paul Newman, Joanne Woodward, Kim Stanley, Yul Brynner, Canada Lee, Martin Gabel, Shepperd Strudwick, and E. G. Marshall. "We called them," Cronkite recalled, "Sidney Lumet's stock company."

Besides being a buoyant way to pique interest in history, *You Are There* served as a useful disinfecting agent for Cronkite in the age of McCarthyism; only a dyed-in-the-wool patriot, it was presumed, a real flag waver, could possibly host this kind of ma-and-apple-pie schmaltz devoid of contemporary controversy. What McCarthyites didn't know, however, was that Cronkite's *You Are There* producer, Charlie Russell, had surreptitiously hired three talented blacklisted New York writers—Walter Bernstein, Arnold Manoff, and Abraham Polonsky—to write the *You Are There* teleplays. At CBS script meetings, Russell hired "fronts" to fill in for the real troika, to protect their identities. As Cronkite explained to NPR in 2003, Russell wasn't willing to "play the blacklist game" just to placate CBS censors. Russell's writers cleverly produced *You Are There* sketches illuminating the tribulations of Joan of Arc, the Salem witch trials, the death of Socrates, and the Dreyfus Affair to draw subconscious parallels to the malevolence of McCarthyism. It was Cronkite's own kind of small-*p* political statement. "History," Cronkite noted, "offered no shortage of ways to deal obliquely with matters of deception and intellectual freedom." By 1955, the original blacklisted *You Are*

There writers had been replaced. The show shuttered for good in 1957.

Approving of *You Are There*, influential TV critic John Crosby called Cronkite CBS News' "man of all work." One day Cronkite was interviewing Paul Revere or Confucius and the next he was in Yucca Flats, Nevada (for real), where the U.S. Army had invited the press to witness an atomic bomb detonation. Instead of scrambling to the front of the pack on March 17, 1953, Cronkite and Morgan Beatty (for ABC News) cautiously positioned themselves about seven miles away from ground zero. There were limits, Cronkite believed, to earning a scoop—contracting radiation sickness from a multimegaton thermonuclear detonation was one of them. Chet Huntley of NBC News was one of two journalists who braved the Yucca Flats explosion from a closer proximity, unafraid of fallout. About 5:20 a.m. Pacific time, the bomb detonated into a raging ball of fire. Television viewers didn't see the ghastly flash on their screens because the camera lens was momentarily covered to protect it from heat-warp. But they *did* see the mushroom cloud form in the aftermath. A fiery gloom streaked across the dry desert basin. Cronkite did a masterful job of explaining everything to viewers about the atomic age, from fallout shelters to emergency duck-and-cover drills to radio warning sirens.

In the fall of 1953, CBS News beat NBC News in overall audience share on television. Cronkite and Murrow were major reasons why. By 1956, CBS's *Douglas Edwards with the News* sailed ahead of NBC's fifteen-minute *Camel News Caravan*, which meant a lot more advertising dollars for the "Tiffany Network" (a reference to the high-quality shine of the company's news product). Besides having an R. J. Reynolds cigarette product actually sponsor a news show, *The Camel News Caravan* broke other ground. Its host, John Cameron Swayze—always a suave dandy—created signature sign-off lines such as "A good good-evening to you," or "Hopscotching the globe" or "Glad we could be together." Long ago, back in Kaycee, Cronkite had taken notice of the well-groomed Swayze-style wardrobe, realizing that appearance mattered when communicating truths. Nobody wanted to be told about the Soviets testing a hydrogen bomb or China invading a country by Freedie the Freeloader.

When in early 1954 Sig Mickelson became CBS News vice president, Cronkite was comforted. Mickelson, a one-man organizing vortex, didn't get along with Ed Murrow (or producer Fred Friendly, for that matter), so he was always looking to give Cronkite breaks. As CBS correspondent Daniel Schorr noted, Murrow simply wasn't Mickelson's "cup of tea." Cronkite, on the other hand, was exactly what Mickelson thought TV news needed. If Friendly was Murrow's alter ego in the 1940s and '50s, then Mickelson was Cronkite's sponsor in the 1950s and early '60s. Whenever the opportunity arose, Mickelson, sounding like Colonel Parker promoting Elvis Presley, rattled off Cronkite's impressive résumé, from the New London, Texas, fire of 1937 (covered for UP) to the Yucca Flats, Nevada, blast of 1953 (covered for CBS News).

What differentiated Cronkite from the pack, Mickelson believed, was that he was preternaturally encyclopedic about U.S. political history. Who else had been at both the Houston and Kansas City nominating conventions back in 1928? Yet Murrow was the one regarded as a hero by New Deal liberals in New York media circles. While Cronkite was re-creating history on *You Are There*, Murrow had undeniably *made* history with his "Report on Senator Joseph McCarthy," which harshly criticized the senator's alarmist methods, for *See It Now*. The public only had a hint of the keen insight Cronkite had accumulated about how the Electoral College functioned. "The name which most viewers immediately identify with political coverage," Mickelson insisted, "is that of Walter Cronkite."

What worried Cronkite was that if television news could be used for good (as with *See It Now*), then it could also be used to further malicious ends—and who was to judge the difference? World War II was less than ten years distant, and the memory of the Third Reich's infamous radio and newspaper propaganda machine was fresh in the minds of many. Murrow might be trusted with the potential to turn news into opinion at CBS, and he was. But the disturbing thought to Cronkite was that an American-fried Joseph Goebbels type—somebody even worse than McCarthy—might take to the U.S. airwaves espousing hatred. To Cronkite, journalism had a mandate to challenge totalitarianism in any guise *everywhere* in the world. "I think newsmen are inclined to side with humanity rather than with authority and institutions," he explained to *Playboy*. "And this sort of pushes them to the left. But I don't think there are many who are far left."

Cronkite had liberal opinions like Murrow's regarding politics and trends in American society. But he didn't believe his preference for Adlai Stevenson over Dwight Eisenhower for president should be public knowledge. "I thought he'd gotten the nomination simply because of the hero worship of World War II," Cronkite explained of Eisenhower, "not by his ability to be president. Ike's association with a lot of the right-wing Republicans bothered me a great deal."

But Cronkite also knew that objectivity had its limits. Although he privately toasted the news of Soviet premier Joseph Stalin's death on March 1, 1953, he didn't editorialize. When on May 17, 1954, the U.S. Supreme Court unanimously ruled in *Brown v. Topeka Board of Education* that racial segregation was illegal, Cronkite again rejoiced. But he also knew that the South might soon become a tinderbox as the U.S. Department of Justice tried to enforce the landmark ruling. During World War II Cronkite's UP dispatches lacked objectivity because the Nazis were so heinous. Post-*Brown*, he hoped CBS News would do the same in covering the civil rights movement as it fought for the implementation of the Supreme Court opinion. "CBS executives sensed a more immediate concern," Cronkite recalled. "Their job was to gather an audience and sell it to advertisers. . . . In the 1950s, CBS chairman William Paley didn't want to alienate his Southern affiliates whose defection could weaken CBS ratings and revenues. Those of us who would do the reporting would feel caught in a rare dilemma between commerce and journalism."

Later in life, Cronkite skirted questions about why he didn't decry Joe McCarthy in the 1950s with tomahawk in hand or become a public advocate for the *Brown* decision like Howard K. Smith and Eric Sevareid. The honest answer was that such audacity would have been a career killer for Cronkite. He was hired by Mr. Paley to be a TV broadcaster, not a crusader. But by working with blacklisted writers on *You Are There*, he nevertheless earned street cred in the broadcasting industry for standing up, by proxy, to the Red Scare.

The same month that Murrow's "Report on Senator Joseph McCarthy" aired on CBS's *See It Now*, Cronkite started a new gig, one that the network regarded as paramount. He was to be the network's morning man, in counterpoint to Dave Garroway on the fabulously popular *Today* show on NBC. CBS longed for an a.m. ratings winner—that is, a reliable morning show of its own. And that was the title Cronkite's program received: *The Morning Show*, which he hosted for much of 1954 and 1955. Critics noticed a certain similarity between the NBC and CBS shows. They were, in fact, almost identical, combining a gently witty host with a gregarious weathercaster, a sober news announcer, and a nonhuman cohort. Garroway had a chimpanzee (J. Fred Muggs) to chat with, and Cronkite had Charlemagne, a lion puppet manipulated by Bill Baird. "A puppet," Cronkite said in defense of his cohost, "can render opinions on people and things that a human commentator would not feel free to utter. It was one of the highlights of the show."

Oddly, Cronkite was the perfect straight man for Charlemagne. While Murrow Boys such as Sevareid and Collingwood belittled Cronkite for goofing around with a puppet on *The Morning Show*, CBS was right to take advantage of how Cronkite combined, as one syndicated columnist put it, a "whimsical and frequently off-beat sense of humor." Cronkite, in person, had a delightful sense of humor and was extremely good with little kids. His mother, Helen, was bitingly funny, a lively conversationalist and sometime late-night card player, and so was her son. Walter was sprung of people, and an era, that valued parlor room wit and canned laughter. Instead of seeming like a doofus for being a serious newsman with a puppet, Cronkite came off—as critic John Crosby wrote—as nerdy *cool*. He just didn't look cool; therein lay the comic element.

At first *The Morning Show* aired Monday to Friday from 7:00 to 9:00 a.m. But David Garroway, host of NBC's *Today*, kept trouncing Dick Van Dyke and Cronkite in the ratings. As an interviewer, Cronkite was solid but didn't sparkle in that chipper, wake-up-everybody-it's-a-brand-new-day format. Before long, Paley cut *The Morning Show* in half, giving the second hour to *Captain Kangaroo*. Mickelson pulled Cronkite for a few weeks from *The Morning Show*, but ultimately put him back into the mix. But the verdict was in. Cronkite, even with the ace assistance of Barbara Walters (writer), Dick Van Dyke (slapstick), and Merv Griffin (music), simply wasn't well suited for the breakfast spot. There was a knifepoint to Cronkite's banter with guests that was more Drew Pearson or Walter Winchell than Captain Kangaroo.

At an afternoon meeting, Sig Mickelson told Cronkite he seemed overextended with substituting for Douglas Edwards on the *Evening News* and serving as impresario of *You Are There*. He was fired permanently from *The Morning Show*. His replacement was Jack Paar, a rising Ohio comic who set the mold for Johnny Carson, host of *The Tonight Show* from 1962 to 1992. While Cronkite spoke in a halting way, Paar had a quick-mind comic delivery that had the same stimulating effect as coffee. Many CBSers believed that Paar's success meant the reversal of Cronkite's upward trajectory at the Tiffany Network. Getting a lot of face time on a merry-go-round of CBS News shows was great, but for some reason Cronkite couldn't carry a major broadcast on his shoulders. Perhaps he was destined to be a CBS utility player. Maybe he had reached his peak at the 1952 Chicago conventions.

At CBS News in late 1954, Mickelson—still trying to find the right time slot for Cronkite—had him host, off and on, such shows as *Eyewitness* and *The Twentieth*

Century. He also considered having Cronkite moderate a new Sunday-at-noon show, *Face the Nation,* which premiered on November 7, 1954. Mickelson envisioned the show as probing U.S. government officials and world leaders. It was partially conceived as the CBS counterpart to NBC's *Meet the Press* and, later, ABC's *Issues and Answers.* Tellingly, however, even Mickelson thought that Cronkite wouldn't be tough enough as an interviewer to carry the Sunday show. He was too nice. The gig went to Bill Shadel, the brave CBS Radio correspondent who had reported from D-day in June 1944 and accompanied Murrow to Buchenwald in April 1945. It was humiliating to Cronkite, who practically blew a gasket at the news, because Shadel had worked *for* him at WTOP in Washington, D.C., and now was deemed by CBS management as a more "serious broadcaster."

There was a flaw in Cronkite's character that resulted from being the child of an alcoholic father: he couldn't handle shame. His chipper attitude camouflaged a deep hurt. Feigning relief at being scrubbed from *The Morning Show,* Cronkite told *The New York Herald Tribune* that dawn held zero appeal for him. "I don't like the challenge of getting up that early," he explained. "I am basically a creature of the night." His stubborn ego wouldn't admit he had bombed on

The Morning Show and was blackballed from *Face the Nation*. Denial was easier. Cronkite truly believed that he had outperformed Jack Paar, his replacement, on *The Morning Show*. The unflappable Paar ended up hosting NBC's *Tonight* from 1957 to 1962, a comic turn for which the quick-witted raconteur was well suited. One of Paar's more famous quips pertained to his old *Morning Show* rival at CBS: "I'm not a religious man," Paar said. "But I do believe in Walter Cronkite."

When off-duty from CBS, Cronkite could often be found racing cars or tinkering with old radios like a *Popular Mechanics* devotee. One day in 1955, he was passing a car dealership in New Jersey and impulsively bought a flashy sports car for $1,700. That British model, a Triumph TR-3, was soon replaced by an Austin-Healey that Cronkite drove only for weekend pleasure around Westchester County. Then he and Betsy began to compete with the Austin-Healey at road rallies. Helmets in place, they worked together—pilot and navigator—to negotiate road courses precisely as event organizers dictated. They were hoping to win trophies. Soon the Cronkites were invited to join a team at the "Twelve Hours of Sebring" race in 1959. The tabloids loved showing Cronkite in racing clothes, looking like a hybrid of the Red Baron and auto racing pioneer Barney Oldfield, explaining how liberated he became when the speedometer hit one hundred miles per hour. All of life's tension evaporated. But in 1961 Cronkite, while competing in an international rally, skidded off a road in the Big Smokies of Tennessee. The car flipped over an embankment, almost killing Cronkite (whose Austin-Healey landed in a lake one hundred feet away). "Cronkite," *The Saturday Evening Post* reported, "emerged wet but unhurt."

Life was good for the Cronkites. They owned a home at 519 East Eighty-fourth Street. They now had three children: Nancy, the eldest; Kathy; and a son, Walter Leland Cronkite III (known as Chip).Walter, in the CBS tradition, was seen about town dining at the trendiest lunch spots with Lowell Thomas and enjoying musical events at the Rainbow Room with variety show host Ed Sullivan.

Aside from his gruff, newspaper editor demeanor while at the CBS office, Cronkite was often described in profiles as a down-to-earth guy. The CBS affiliates found him a refreshing face, a voice from the heartland. But Cronkite felt underappreciated by Paley. He fantasized about becoming a local TV anchorman in the Midwest (where raising a family was cheaper). CBS's best-run affiliate in the 1950s was WCCO (channel 4 on TV) in Minneapolis; its 50,000-watt clear channel on radio could be heard as far south as

New Orleans. Frustrated over *The Morning Show* experience, Cronkite accepted an offer to become the anchorman of WCCO. When Mickelson learned of Cronkite's rash decision to move to Minnesota, he put his foot down. "You're our next Douglas Edwards," he scolded Cronkite. "You're staying put in New York." Unbeknownst to Cronkite at the time, CBS News executives had plans for him to anchor the 1956 nominating conventions.

What Mickelson was trying to convey to Cronkite was that CBS News was in flux. Paley announced that for the first time, in 1956, CBS radio operations had lost money while television was becoming a real breadwinner. Everybody was on the hunt for TV talent. As Reuven Frank, then the president of the NBC news division, recalled, some producers wanted to give a chance to a rangy, handsome newsman from Los Angeles, Chet Huntley. He was appearing on an NBC show called *Outlook*—a half-hour Sunday news and features segment—but neither the program, nor Huntley was well known by TV watchers. Scratching around for an alternative, a few executives promoted David Brinkley, but he was considered to be relatively unknown and quirky. With the 1956 conventions drawing closer, Frank recalled the panic that was starting to set in as NBC executives debated the merits of each of the two leading candidates: "And then, one of the great compromisers said, 'Let's put *those* two together,' meaning Huntley and Brinkley. It was like the light bulb going on over somebody's head in the comics."

Chet Huntley and David Brinkley arrived as a breath of fresh air for NBC News, something entirely new to American broadcasting in the mid-1950s. To CBS News diehards, Huntley and Brinkley were nothing more than Kukla, Fran, and Ollie fortified by Associated Press news flashes. Cronkite himself analyzed the NBC duo's on-air chemistry from a first-person perspective. "They received the critical attention," he explained. "I was the old hand."

13.

The Huntley and
Brinkley Challenge

DULL TIMES AT THE 1956 CONVENTIONS—MURROW'S
COMPLAINTS—BLAMING COLLEAGUES—THE HUNT-
LEY-BRINKLEY CHEMISTRY—AVOIDING MURROW—NO
DO-OVERS—CRONKITE AS SIMPLETON—MUDD IN THE
WINGS—PICKING THE WINNERS—EISENHOWER BEATS
STEVENSON—HOMAGE TO LOWELL THOMAS—
"ANSWER PLEASE!"—I'M NOT A STAR—COULD SPACE
BE THE NEW POLITICAL CONVENTIONS?—SPACE
RACING—THE TWENTIETH-CENTURY MAN—THE
AMAZING BUD BENJAMIN—LOOKING TOWARD THE
GALAXY—GRAPPLING WITH SPUTNIK—FLORIDA AND
THE NASA BEAT—CLIMBING TO THE TOP RUNG

The rap against Walter Cronkite at the 1956 political conventions was that he was a reliable dull-
ard on the airwaves. The man was only in his late

thirties, but he was already viewed as a TV veteran. Few Americans knew that the producers were the real innovators of television, that all an anchorman did was take election feeds from guys such as Sig Mickelson and Don Hewitt. Because the 1956 presidential election was sedate—the incumbent, Dwight Eisenhower, against the same old Adlai Stevenson of 1952—there wasn't much drama in the Chicago (Democratic) and the San Francisco (Republican) conventions. So the public demanded that CBS spice up the proceedings with fiber optics, new camera angles, upped voltage— anything cutting-edge to justify the preemption of popular prime-time shows such as *Lassie*, *The Red Skelton Show*, and *I Love Lucy*. Cronkite didn't deliver any unexpected sparks that summer. Instead, critic Jack Gould of *The New York Times*, who had once worked for CBS News as an "information adviser" (whatever that was), derided his live broadcasts at the conventions as painfully "dead pan," adding insult by asking Cronkite to cheer up.

Gould's words stung Cronkite tremendously. He was irritated now, as well as hungry for scapegoats. The problem at the 1956 conventions could not have been *him*. He was rock solid. Instead of letting Cronkite fly solo, Mickelson and Hewitt had saddled their anchorman with "outside" political commentators—Elmo Roper, the opinion polling pioneer; and Samuel Lubell, a writer good at picking political winners—both of whom proved lethally boring when the cameras rolled. Cronkite would have preferred giving Sevareid and Murrow more airtime than have those two hapless wonks compete in a snooze fest. An internal debate ensued at CBS News in the fall of 1956 to figure out what had gone wrong. "The low CBS morale," Sevareid wrote Mickelson in a memorandum, "was caused by too much executive tension, general uncertainty, and nervousness."

To Murrow, no fan of Cronkite, the problem with CBS News' 1956 convention coverage was executive producer Mickelson's overproduction and quasi-religious vulgarity in pleasing corporate sponsors. Murrow thought CBS's coverage was an orgy of distraction, false news, and propaganda. Everything was too staged in Chicago and San Francisco. The stodgy Cronkite unscripted, he argued, was better than the owlish Roper tethered to a desk, rattling off political factoids learned at some number-crunching camp. And there were other Mickelson mistakes that irritated Murrow considerably. Overly worried about being pro-Stevenson, Mickelson prohibited the showing of *In Pursuit of Happiness* (a triumphant Democratic National Committee short documentary) to the blistering consternation of DNC chairman Paul Butler. Why censor the most thoughtful bit of the whole confetti-crazed convention? Murrow didn't overly mind Cronkite's emphasis on ad-libbing analysis, but he thought Robert Trout, who broadcast the conventions for CBS Radio News, was better at it. Murrow came up with an idea. Why not have Trout become the anchorman of special events instead of Cronkite?

What infuriated Cronkite even more than the CBS boycott of *In Pursuit of Happiness* or UNIVAC, he wrote Mickelson in October 1956, was the unnerving commotion in the control booth. His beef was that while broadcasting to millions of Americans, he heard CBS staff chortling off-camera. It was beyond disruptive. A suspicious Cronkite even intimated that perhaps the Murrowites in Chicago and San Francisco had sabotaged his performance on purpose. Absolute "Q-U-I-E-T" was what he told Mickelson he needed in the booth. All Mickelson could do was stare at him in disbelief.

Self-consciously pointing fingers at the Murrow clique was perhaps convenient for Cronkite, but it was bull. The *real* problem CBS faced at the 1956 conventions was the stellar on-air chemistry of David Brinkley and Chet Huntley at NBC News. They, as Gould said in the *Times*, naturally "clicked." Paired for NBC's coverage of the conventions, these competent newsmen provided accurate and economic commentary. The NBC duo—with Huntley as straight man and Brinkley the dry wit—offered a chemistry that was pioneering to television news (or even radio news before it). If something quirky happened in Chicago or San Francisco, Huntley and Brinkley laughed. Cronkite, by contrast, *reported* that something funny had happened. Maintaining a journalistic remove had its limits. The nation, in one of its cultural whims, was starting to believe that two NBC anchormen were more profitable than one self-effacing Cronkite. It was like the double-dipped ice-cream cone or buy-one-get-one-free cheeseburger rages. "While past attempts at using two anchormen had mixed results," historian Michael A. Russo noted about the 1956 conventions, "Huntley and Brinkley brought to the task greater editorial skills, a closer coordination of ideas with visual illustrations, and a sense of humor which TV audiences liked."

Moreover, Huntley (based in New York) and Brinkley (in Washington, D.C.) could themselves be humorous when the moment cried out for lighthearted informality. Huntley had a Westerner's laconic sense of irony. And Brinkley was the undisputed master of the droll aside. It wasn't that Chet and David were clowning around or trying to score cheeky points. They just allowed themselves the flexibility to make succinct journalistic observations in a relaxed give-and-take style. With their unique toss-back-and-forth approach, Huntley and Brinkley were not merely broadcasters; they could momentarily become part of the audience as well, commenting to each other as the audience surely did at home with fellow family members in the living room staring at the Tube.

Unlike Cronkite, the press wizards didn't think the 1956 conventions required much on-the-run reporting. With a couple of shoo-ins in the incumbent Republican president (Eisenhower) and the second-time Democratic nominee (Stevenson), there was precious little breaking news to cover. Only Stevenson's vice presidential choice—would it be Estes Kefauver of Tennessee or John F. Kennedy of Massachusetts?—held dramatic possibility. "It was a situation made to order for Huntley and Brinkley," Mickelson explained. "Brinkley's sardonic wit enlivened the proceedings and created an attitude of mild amusement among viewers. CBS continued to view the proceedings as a serious news story long after there was no news remaining."

As a ploy to beef up CBS News' ratings at the 1956 Democratic Convention in Chicago, Cronkite—along with Douglas Edwards, Charles Collingwood, Eric Sevareid, and Robert Trout—went on the network's beloved game show *What's My Line?* It wasn't unusual in the 1950s for broadcasters to do commercials and host game shows: journalists such as Mike Wallace, Douglas Edwards, and John Cameron Swayze did it all the time. But *What's My Line?* was weird. The show's premise was that four celebrities guessed the occupation of a mystery person. Cronkite sat in the guest chair alongside host John Daly, while the other four CBS correspondents stood behind him like suited-up crows on a wire about to cackle. When Cronkite answered questions from the blindfolded columnist Dorothy Kilgallen, he altered his voice to sound like the Mickey Mouse of *Karnival Kid.* He spoke spasmodically, in blurt-outs with long pauses between words. Eventually, after a lot of canned laughs, Cronkite and his CBS convention team were outed. (Cronkite's *What's My Line?* appearance has become a must-watch YouTube clip; the kitsch factor remained quite high into the twenty-first century.)

What's My Line? didn't help. The CBS news division with Cronkite at the helm came out of the summer with a chink in its armor. Huntley and Brinkley were the new undisputed TV darlings. They owned the buzz. The newsmagazines *Time* and *Newsweek* pronounced the NBC reporters truly worthy of the intelligent viewer's time. Jack Gould poured on the praise in an August 1956 Chicago analysis. "Mr. Brinkley's extraordinary accomplishment has been not to talk too much," Gould wrote, not even mentioning Cronkite in his *New York Times* piece. "He has a knack for the succinct phrase that sums up the situation. . . . It is Mr. Brinkley's humor, however, that is attracting audiences. It is on the dry side and rooted in a sense of relaxed detachment from all the political and electronic turmoil around him."

A few critics rallied to Cronkite's defense by saying, "We like the straight-news simplicity of Cronkite." It was intended as a compliment for the Unipresser, but amid the general delight over Huntley and Brinkley, it was faint praise. Cronkite continued to broadcast with directness, but in the aftermath of the national conventions, "straight-news simplicity" was under siege. Entertainment was seeping into the TV news ship through the portholes of Huntley and Brinkley. Throughout the rest of Eisenhower's presidency, it would remain so, and from two directions: inside CBS (by correspondents blending a point of view into their factual reports) and outside (by NBC, which made no-nonsense straight news passé). When Mickelson asked Cronkite to critique his broadcasts of the 1956 conventions to get the kinks out for 1960, Cronkite refused. Throughout his career he followed an ironclad rule—a superstition, really—that helped him survive in the business: he never watched himself. "Walter thought that there were no do-overs," NBC News anchorman Brian Williams recalled. "Watching your own flubs set the ego back too many notches."

By early fall of 1956, with the political convention floors barely swept, John Cameron Swayze was fired as anchor of the evening news at NBC. To no one's surprise, Huntley and Brinkley replaced him, the former broadcasting from New York and the latter from Washington in a unique bi-city format that showcased their obvious chemistry. *The Camel News Caravan* was renamed *The Huntley-Brinkley Report.* While NBC News had yet to assemble a roster of ace correspondents to match those of CBS, Robert Kintner, president of NBC News, increased his division's budgets and recruited new talent, including the likes of Edwin Newman, Sander Vanocur, and John Chancellor. And the production quality of *The Huntley-Brinkley Report* was even more impressive than it had been at the 1956 conventions. NBC's ratings didn't skyrocket, but suddenly it was something that well-informed people *had* to see and fashionable people *wanted* to see. The suppertime evening news broadcast was on its way to becoming an American ritual. Where CBS News continued to excel was in documentaries and special reports (the Murrow tradition). Most important of all—in financial terms—CBS was also making tremendous inroads into NBC's traditional stronghold: entertainment programming. Its killer lineup of situation comedies, led by *I Love Lucy*, gave the company banner years during the 1950s. Inevitably, NBC retaliated. It signed its own big stars, including comedian Bob Hope.

That fall, Cronkite went into fighting overdrive,with a CBS News prime-time special called *Pick the Winner*, which ran right up to Election Night. Dr. Frank Stanton spared no expense in buying CBS News ads in *The New York Times* and *The Washington Post* to promote Cronkite's prime-time interviews (and sometimes debates) with a cast that included Governor Averell Harriman (D-N.Y.) and U.S. senators William Knowland (R-Calif.), Hubert Humphrey (D-Minn.), and Karl E. Mundt (R-S.D.). The *Pick the Winner* series ran for eight weeks on Wednesday nights. It paid off. On Election Night, November 5, as Eisenhower beat Stevenson by a whopping 457 to 73 electoral votes, CBS whipped the competition with a 25.3 rating, compared with NBC (13.8) and ABC (13.1).

Cronkite's fine Election Night performances guaranteed he'd remain CBS News' first-string anchor for live-events coverage. He nevertheless felt like second fiddle. With the political season over, he looked for a special-events angle that could grab him some precious prime-time real estate. He needed a hit show like Murrow had in *Person to Person* (which aired from 1953 to 1961 and consisted largely of the legend interviewing public figures in casual settings). "In the fall of 1957," Cronkite complained, "my presence on CBS was confined mostly to reruns of a waning series called *You Are There* and one newscast a week, the *Sunday News Special*."

He inventoried his options, making an honest appraisal of the threat Huntley and Brinkley posed. He thought about loosening up more on air. He might easily have tried to meet Brinkley head-on, giving his news copy piquant turns of phrase and his on-air banter the humor of *Poor Richard's Almanac*. Yes, Cronkite had ideas about changing news broadcasting, but they didn't run toward aping someone else's style. His fascination with broadcast journalism wasn't with the delivery so much as the selection and organization of the news. By 1958, CBS News had restructured into two major operating divisions: the CBS TV network (with 243 affiliates) and the CBS TV stations (with five CBS-owned stations). The business of the medium was in boom mode. All Cronkite wanted, in the end, was to help shareholders win a fair share of the pie.

It wasn't just Huntley and Brinkley whom Cronkite had to keep his eyes on in 1957. The up-and-coming

Roger Mudd was already creating a lot of noise at CBS headquarters. Although Mudd's primary job in Washington was doing the 6:00 a.m. radio newscast and the local news inserts on the TV morning show *Potomac Panorama*, his star kept rising. Before long, Mudd—a native Washingtonian who had begun his career as a reporter for *The Richmond News Leader*— was hosting a 6:00 p.m. newscast on WTOP that he wrote himself (including a weekly commentary piece). By May 1962, Mudd had joined the CBS News Washington bureau as a congressional correspondent. Whenever Cronkite had a lackluster performance on some special—which wasn't often—rumors circulated among CBS employees that newbie Mudd (the network's future) would take over the plow.

Somewhat ironically, Mudd developed an easy friendship with Cronkite. The Murrow Boys were attracted to Europe and New York. Cronkite and Mudd, political junkies, liked the official Washington beat. In his fine memoir, *The Place to Be*, Mudd told how the younger men at CBS News used to scoff at how awful Cronkite's pop culture knowledge was. Mudd laughed when Walter confessed that he didn't know who balladeer Woody Guthrie was (when hosting an episode of *The Twentieth Century* called "The Dust Bowl"). "Although we all snorted about his gaffes behind his back," Mudd explained, "what mattered to us was that Cronkite believed that almost everything that happened in Washington was important."

What Cronkite and Mudd had—since they both came out of the print media world—was an always-rigid determination of what constituted *real* news. But they weren't in charge. In 1957, CBS Entertainment division was rather inexplicably given the right to decide what was news. To Cronkite, this power was an abasement of sorts. Yet Cronkite played along. On October 17, CBS broadcast remotely from Madison Square Garden a party thrown by Hollywood producer Mike Todd for eighteen thousand guests. Cronkite was assigned to report on Todd's promotional extravaganza—choreographed to celebrate the one-year anniversary of the release of his Academy Award–winning film *Around the World in Eighty Days*—for CBS's *Playhouse 90*. The promo literature claimed that music from Boston Pops conductor Arthur Fielder and a procession of one hundred elephants (there were only ten elephants deceptively re-costumed and marched out again to the unsuspecting crowd) would launch the party-to-end-all-parties.

On air Cronkite gamely commented on the excess and inanity for the full ninety minutes, holding CBS's lame coverage together. Todd's wife was actress

Elizabeth Taylor, and she played the grand dame hostess at the party; Cronkite suffered from star-struck distraction. He later felt he had "breached the shallow wall" between entertainment and news, and squandered "a bit of journalistic authority" for the sake of Mike Todd. It can't be said that Cronkite lent the occasion any dignity—that would be asking too much of any mortal. True to the job description of reporter, though, he spouted off statistics and the names of products in what he later recalled as the world's first and most well disguised ninety-minute infomercial. It was *Entertainment Tonight* meeting reality TV before the advent of either. "Even the smooth-as-silk Walter Cronkite," wrote critic Fred Brooks, "lost his aplomb. Halfway through the show, he sensibly gave up trying to describe the hodgepodge."

Cronkite might have wriggled free of such silly *Playhouse 90* assignments, even without going so far as to refuse them—although that would also have been understandable. He didn't refuse, though. As if in explanation, he was later quick to point out that just one week after Todd's garish stunt, CBS News broadcast the first episode of *The Twentieth Century*, a program of modern history narrated by Cronkite that replaced *You Are There. The Twentieth Century*—which aired from October 1957 to May 1961 and was sponsored by the Prudential Insurance Company of America—concentrated on recent topics and presented them in a straight documentary format. The first show, airing on October 20 and titled "Man of the Century," was a video biography of Sir Winston Churchill that had a heavy emphasis on his World War II leadership. After that success the episodes immediately took a turn toward the futuristic. *The Twentieth Century*, produced by Burton Benjamin, became a kind of primer on cold war technology. The next six shows after "Man of the Century" were "Guided Missile" (the development of Nazi Germany's V-1s and V-2s at Peenemunde during the 1930s and 1940s), "The Story of the FBI" (law enforcement under J. Edgar Hoover), "The Flight of the X-2" (rocket technology), "Mach Busters" (the air force's supersonic pilots), "Brainwashing," and "Vertijets" (experimental aircraft). During its first three years on the air, *The Twentieth Century* was the *sole* regularly scheduled fifty-two-weeks-a-year news and public affairs documentary on network television (twenty-six weeks of new shows, twenty-six weeks of reruns of the previous season).

The narrow focus of *The Twentieth Century*'s early broadcasts wasn't an accident. On the contrary, the show's content was a direct response to the opening of the space age with the Soviet Union's *Sputnik 1* launch on October 4, 1957. With this successful satellite mission, the Soviets appeared to have an edge in missile technology over the United States. How did the Kremlin pull off such a feat? *The Twentieth Century* was determined to provide answers to post-*Sputnik* angst. Cronkite later called *Sputnik 1* "a surprise attack against something believed invulnerable: American confidence. . . . We had lost the space race before we knew we were in it," he reflected years later. "It hurt badly." *The Twentieth Century*—which was sold in twenty foreign markets by 1960—was almost an infomercial for the U.S. Air Force, the CIA, and the National Aeronautics and Space Administration (NASA).

There was about the Cronkite of *The Twentieth Century* a lot of Lowell Thomas–style reporting. The TV viewer never knew which exotic location Cronkite would visit next. In the 1959–1960 Emmy Award–winning season, for example, Cronkite and Benjamin journeyed down the Atlantic Shooting Range to Ascension Island, reporting at a handful of the Caribbean tracking stations en route, for the episode "Down Range." For the first shoot of "Minuteman at Cape Canaveral," Cronkite was on hand with breathless space reporting that predated his historic Mercury, Gemini, and Apollo broadcasts. Taken collectively, *The Twentieth Century* was like a novel, showcasing the newest weaponry the United States had contracted from Boeing and McDonnell Douglas to *win* the cold war. Although *You Are There* ended up being remembered as Cronkite's signature show of the 1950s, *The Twentieth Century* really represented his best work. What *The Twentieth Century* did was remind people that Cronkite, no matter what the goofy Huntley-Brinkley boys were doing, was winning every award imaginable (including Emmys and Peabodys) and becoming, along with Murrow, one of the premier action journalists and eyewitnesses of modern times. Considered the finest half hour in television, the series foreshadowed the plethora of weekly compilation documentaries that would eventually populate both network and cable TV.

Cronkite discovered clever ways to stay ahead of NBC News on space and missile technology. A space nut, he started collecting missile information in a CIA-like fashion from U.S. government sources. It was easier than it sounded. He would neatly type out a request to the Martin Company or McDonnell Aircraft or the Department of Defense, usually to someone in public relations, and a week later reams of information would arrive. He also frequently went to Cape Canaveral on reconnaissance missions. Space exploration combined Cronkite's love of military aviation with cold war politics. It also gave him a rare chance to distinguish himself at CBS. Frequenting the Gotham Book Mart on Forty-seventh Street, he purchased the visionary science fiction novels of Isaac Asimov and Arthur C. Clarke. In early 1958 he journeyed to Los Angeles to cover the unveiling of the X-15, an aircraft that was part plane and part missile. Having read an astounding amount of technical jargon about ICBMs, he was knowledgeable about the stunning capabilities of America's cold war defense system. "From the beginning [Wernher] von Braun's team dreamed of sending men into space," Cronkite recalled, "I began to dream with them."

The key to *The Twentieth Century* was producer Bud Benjamin, who became Cronkite's Svengali. An Ohio native with movie star looks and a sense of adventure, Benjamin earned a BA at the University of Michigan in 1939. Like an arrow, he was ready to make his mark on journalism. Calm, always organized and methodical, never known to curse or lose his temper, Benjamin started in journalism at United Press's Cleveland bureau. A lot of UP reporters knew how to gather solid facts for a story, but Benjamin was the quickest story *closer* Cronkite had ever encountered. He joined the U.S. Coast Guard during World War II, rising to the rank of lieutenant. After the war, he joined TV news because it paid more than radio. To Benjamin, classic television documentaries like *The Plow That Broke the Plains* (1939) and *A Diary for Timothy* (1945) were high-art endeavors as valuable as the realist photography of Walker Evans and Dorothea Lange. Cronkite, who later wrote a foreword to Benjamin's self-effacing memoir, *Fair Play*, considered his *The Twentieth Century* producer the "finest" documentarian he was "ever privileged to work" with.

Besides being a real gentleman, Benjamin also had a good sense of TV news as business. If he hadn't joined CBS News, one could have easily imagined him as CEO of a medium-sized company in Ann Arbor or president of a small New England college. He knew how to spend money, but he also knew how to raise it. *The Twentieth Century* wasn't a moneymaker for CBS per se, but it was brilliant educational television of an unprecedented kind. Benjamin found ways—international rights, classroom distribution, movie house showings—to make the show profitable. It was Benjamin who helped Cronkite realize that his armchair appreciation of aerospace technology could become a huge asset.

What made *The Twentieth Century* such important television was the commingling of rare film footage and amazing scripting. Cronkite and Benjamin hired a knot of brilliant writers, including Hanson Baldwin (military editor of *The New York Times*), Emmet John Hughes (chief of foreign correspondents and editor for *Time*), Merriman Smith (former United Nations correspondent), and John Toland (historian) among them. Benjamin's assistants—particularly Bob Asman and Isaac Kleinerman—were like safecrackers when it came to unearthing rare, previously unseen historical footage of everyone from Buffalo Bill to Hitler to Gandhi.

Cronkite wasn't the only newsman hoping to dominate the TV space franchise. Two days after *Sputnik 1* was launched, Douglas Edwards hosted a half-hour special (produced by Don Hewitt): *Sputnik One: The Soviet Space Satellite*. The CBS documentary included commentary from Howard K. Smith in Washington, D.C., Daniel Schorr in Moscow, Alexander Kendrick in London, and Richard C. Hottelet in New York City's Hayden Planetarium at the American Museum of Natural History. But no Cronkite. Just two months later, the U.S. Air Force scheduled the launching of the *Vanguard* satellite from Cape Canaveral, and CBS gave the plum assignment of covering it to Harry Reasoner. Cronkite was miffed. "In those days . . . I was temporarily one of the chief CBS authorities on the space program," Reasoner wrote in *Before the Colors Fade*. "We worked out an elaborate plan to ensure that, while

Russia may have beaten the United States, no one was going to beat CBS News."

Usually distinguished-looking, with a calm voice, Reasoner blared out, "There she goes!" at the *Vanguard* liftoff on December 6, 1957. Cronkite took notice of his informal style. Then the rocket blew up into tens of thousands of pieces of fiery debris. If the Vanguard hadn't exploded on takeoff, it's reasonable to surmise that Reasoner would have become CBS News' go-to space reporter; it wouldn't have been Cronkite's beat. In the late 1950s the U.S. government was very secretive about launches, but Reasoner—like Cronkite—had been embraced by the government as a trustworthy correspondent. From a ratings point of view, along with technical production, CBS was beating ABC and NBC. But the Vanguard flop caused CBS to time-delay its coverage of *Explorer 1* (the first successful U.S. satellite) a few months later. "It's difficult to remember now how impossibly dangerous space flight seemed," Cronkite recalled to *Newsweek* in a 1998 cover story. "The stakes couldn't have been higher, nor the risks greater; we were in a Cold War space race, we thought then, for the heavens."

One of the most beneficial things about *Sputnik 1*, from Cronkite's perspective, was that it motivated Democrats like Senators John F. Kennedy and Stuart

Symington to warn against a missile gap with the Soviets. By the late 1950s, Cronkite had become an anti-Soviet cheerleader, helping lead a national charge to win the space race. In January 1958 he hosted a ninety-minute edition of *The Twentieth Century* devoted to explaining exactly the situation vis-à-vis the Soviet Union, "Where We Stand," comparing the military might of the United States with that of its main cold war opponent. The Soviets had argued convincingly that *Sputnik* was a scientific program, not a military one. Cronkite rejected that stand and warned Americans not to be naïve.

Cronkite's outstanding work on "Where We Stand" was a far cry from his *Playhouse 90* gig describing the melee of Mike Todd's Madison Square Garden party four months prior. This stark contrast became known as High Cronkite and Low Cronkite. He not only liked the role of space reporter, he also needed it. Whether it was almost crashing in a Curtiss-Wright plane with his father in the 1920s, breaking the "Lochinvar of the Air" story in the 1930s, or embedding with the Eighth Air Force in the 1940s, aviation was Cronkite's bailiwick. His relationship with military aviation was a comfortable beat, the one that came most naturally to him. As the once-forlorn Cape Canaveral was being developed as a rocket launch center, "Walter saw *The*

Twentieth Century as a sly way to build the best space Rolodex in the business," Andy Rooney recalled. "He simply out glad-handed Harry Reasoner at the Cape to keep the space beat away from him."

The space program and the U.S.-Soviet technological competition related to it were appealing for another reason, one more sinister and more serious. Cronkite needed to find a safe perch in the cold war. CBS was putting pressure, directly and indirectly, on its staff to take a stand against communism. In 1950, employees were forced to sign a loyalty oath disclosing any affiliation with communist or fascist organizations. CBS employees were investigated officially and unofficially in the early 1950s. That was true for people in a variety of industries, but broadcasting was under special scrutiny, for the simple reason that it wielded the astonishing power to reach millions of people and perhaps influence them. In those pre-1957 NASA days, the U.S. Air Force was running the space program, with all experiments kept top secret. Cronkite's security clearance, even with the air force, wouldn't allow him near a rocket launch. But by promoting the new U.S. military hardware on *The Twentieth Century*, Cronkite became a salesman for the Department of Defense, showing the American people what the Pentagon was doing for them in a futuristic infomercial-type way.

In various theaters—China, Korea, Hungary, the United Nations, and even the Olympic Games—the United States had transferred the ferocious passions of the Second World War to another us-versus-them mentality. For a long time, Cronkite was on the sidelines, missing out on the cold war intrigue as he chugged along with *You Are There* and *The Morning Show.* Avoiding controversial news topics might have been a brilliant career decision, but it wasn't brave. Too settled a family man to be a foreign war correspondent, not ideological enough to stir paranoia on the home front, Cronkite had used *You Are There* as his coy way of challenging McCarthyism. But that wasn't the same as owning an important news beat or making history. He now realized that his passion for rocket technology could easily be translated into episodes of *The Twentieth Century.* The early launches might have been at the outer edge of the cold war, but for Cronkite the space job was his opening to please *everybody* except the hard-left (sympathetic to communists) and hard-right (anti–federal government) factions.

Just as Cronkite did when he covered the U.S. air war in Europe against Germany, he established a rapport with officers and officials in the various agencies overseeing space and defense projects in the late 1950s. Emerging as CBS's space race correspondent, he was, once again, practically a member of the team in terms of his tacit enthusiasm for the work of his new friends. Cronkite did not often evince his own opinions; that was not his style. Yet he could become part of the mainstream when he believed in the goal and the means of achieving it, providing coverage that was predictably supportive. Cronkite believed that the growth of technology was crucial to defense in the cold war, and he was all for it. The heavy truth about him in the late 1950s was that he had signed up to promote the U.S. Air Force, seeing space as a beat he could own.

NASA was founded on July 29, 1958, courtesy of the National Aeronautics and Space Act. Cronkite, from day one, was a huge cheerleader for NASA, always promoting America's technological prowess. For CBS, he visited NASA research laboratories such as Langley Aeronautical, Ames Aeronautical, and Lewis Flight Propulsion. From the early Project Mercury launches through the groundbreaking Gemini missions to the subsequent Apollo moon walk of Neil Armstrong and the space shuttle program, Cronkite was an avid believer in what he called the "conquest of space."

He got to enter the space race fun for CBS News in earnest on August 17, 1958, when the U.S. Army attempted to launch a scientific satellite from central Florida. However, the launch rocket exploded after being airborne for only seventy-seven seconds. CBS ran two reports of the rocket failure that afternoon—Cronkite broadcast the second one.

Throughout his career, Cronkite was far more outspoken off camera than he was on television. In the many lecture circuit speeches he delivered in the Midwest, he could be surprisingly opinionated about his desire to beat the Soviet Union in the cold war. For example, in the winter of 1959 he told an audience that in the critical new sciences associated with missile defense, the USSR was demonstrably superior. This Cronkite claim has been proved untrue. Meaning to deliver a wake-up call to the American public, Cronkite described the United States as a "second-rate nation" in its intercontinental missile (and space) capabilities. He intended the commentary as a form of prodding for increased U.S. efforts in those fields and to help pry loose more congressional appropriations for NASA research. It wasn't a particularly controversial stance in 1959. But the on-camera Cronkite wouldn't have been quite so blunt. There was too much risk involved. *Pravda* praised Cronkite as the man who called the United States a "second-rate nation." Publicity like that, Cronkite understood, he could do without.

One of Cronkite's heroes at CBS throughout the late 1950s remained the legendary radio broadcaster Lowell Thomas. Cronkite essentially studied under Thomas in the 1950s, learning how to be a reassuring voice instead of a sharp knife jab of hard truths. When he heard Thomas salute the nation every weekday with "Good evening, everybody," he knew that was the guy he wanted to be. There was a folksy, reassuring, sometimes bland aspect to Thomas's delivery of the news. But the listener trusted him. Maybe Thomas wasn't a crusader like Edward R. Murrow—he called himself a "news communicator." And that's what Cronkite strove to be.

Cronkite had first gotten hooked on Thomas while at San Jacinto High School in the 1930s. He modeled his public persona after his boyhood idol. It was an easy fit. What Cronkite wanted to emulate was sounding as confident, knowledgeable, and breezy as Thomas, an obviously serious man of good humor. Distinguished in an ordinary way, Thomas exuded the romantic aura of Hemingway minus the bloodlust. With a mop of curly brown hair, penetrating blue eyes, and a thin mustache, he was a dashing figure. Thomas didn't just *think* he was larger than life; he *was*. Somehow he persuaded leading figures from T. E. Lawrence to Mahatma Gandhi to Field Marshal Montgomery to grant him exclusive interviews. "His almost forty-six years of reporting the news nightly set a record for longevity," Cronkite later boasted about his evergreen idol. "His total audience was once estimated at 125 million people."

All this set Cronkite's wheels in motion. While everybody else at CBS News was trying to be the new Murrow, he would aim to be the new Thomas. Everything Cronkite did in the 1950s was aimed at someday grabbing the intrepid Thomas's crown. Cronkite used to read whatever Thomas wrote—and there were more than fifty books. His favorites were *With Lawrence of Arabia* (1924) and *Hungry Waters* (1937). On summer weekends the Cronkite family would vacation at Thomas's home in Pawling, New York, sitting on the porch to discuss world events as the children went swimming. "Everybody he met, as far as I know, he made a friend of," Cronkite said. "And he had a million of them around the world. . . . All walks of life. . . . If you spoke to Lowell Thomas, he spoke back, grabbed your hand and you were one of his followers from that point on."

By the late 1950s, Cronkite's career trajectory at CBS had hit a plateau. Pulling down a good salary, he had stayed out of trouble during the Red Scare, never getting attacked for working with blacklisted writers on *You Are There* and pioneering with *The Twentieth Century*. His radio show "Answer, Please!"—which involved responding to mail queries on the air—was extremely popular. The specific questions were easy to answer. But sometimes CBS radio listeners wanted Cronkite to display psychic powers.

"Will we ever have war again?" one letter read.

"Will we ever get ahead of Russia?" read another.

Cronkite eased out by answering, "If I knew, I'd be working for the Pentagon instead of CBS Radio."

Never before had America produced such a fast flood of media personalities as in the golden age of television. A lot of on-air reporters like Cronkite were now being asked for autographs, as if they knew the answers to war and peace. An appearance on CBS's *Face the Nation* or *The Twentieth Century* guaranteed an immediate rise in popularity, with average citizens simply wanting to shake the hand of a personality beamed into that little five-by-eight Philco or RCA box in their living rooms. When he entered a Manhatttan restaurant, it was like Moses parting the Red Sea. Before long, Cronkite befriended the intellectual pundits Benjamin booked on *The Twentieth Century*—Robert Shaplen and Sidney Hertzberg among them. Ad-libbing with such experts, Cronkite believed, was the essence of smart television. But for all the fame Cronkite accrued from being a CBS News broadcaster, the instant recognition by the man on the street, the job seemed superficial, at times even farcical. As Cronkite told a columnist friend in Iowa, "It's difficult for a celebrity to be a working newsman."

14.

Torch Is Passed

BEYOND UBIQUITOUS—VOICE OF THE OLYMPICS—
HIGH Q FACTOR—TOO MANY IMAGE MAKERS—THE
EDUCATION OF DAN RATHER—WHY NOT GO
CRONKITE?—LOCKING OUT MURROW—THE STEADY
DR. FRANK STANTON—KENNEDY COVETS POWER—
THE CHIPPER NIXON—PRESIDENTIAL COUNTDOWN—
STANDING UP TO KENNEDY—WHO WON THE
DEBATES?—KENNEDY WINS THE CLIFFHANGER—
CRONKITE HOLDS HIS OWN

The CBS "eye device" logo was first unveiled on television in the early 1950s. Designed by graphic artist William Golden after he studied Pennsylvania Dutch hexes and Shaker drawings, the eye device quickly became an iconic part of the television land-scape, serving as backdrop for entertainers such as Jack Benny, Lucille Ball, and Rod Serling. The "eyemark"—as Walter Cronkite called the black-and-white logo—was ubiquitous by 1960, known the world over, even serving as cufflinks for the old Unipresser's monogrammed WCL dress shirts. Logos hadn't mattered on radio, but for TV logos were visual brands that could make or break a network. "Walter was the ultimate company man," Andy Rooney recalled. "I regularly teased him that he should get the CBS Eye tattooed on his ass . . . he didn't find it funny."

If a television viewer turned the dial to CBS in 1960, there was a good chance that in addition to the eye device logo, Cronkite would be on the Tube. For *The Twentieth Century* series, Cronkite spent days in the Atlantic on aircraft carriers, destroyers, and submarines and then followed President Eisenhower around Ankara, Kabul, Tehran, and Delhi. CBS chartered a plane so Cronkite, producer Bud Benjamin, and seventeen technicians could bring what *The New York Times* called "unprecedented" TV coverage of a presidential foreign trip. Anytime there was breaking news, the public, it seemed, wanted to know what Cronkite thought. Whenever a foreign assignment came up, Cronkite, perhaps without much conscious involvement, reflexively said "Send me." "Between anchoring and narrating various TV series and doing a Sunday news broadcast," *The Washington Post* said about Cronkite's commitments, "he trots the globe in pursuit of current history."

Throughout the Eisenhower era, most newspapers offered only spotty coverage of the Winter Games; this changed in 1959, when CBS News purchased exclusive rights from the Olympic Committee for $50,000 to cover the eleven-day spectacle. When the marvelous CBS sports commentator Jim McKay suffered a nervous breakdown in early January 1960, Cronkite replaced him at the Olympic Winter Games, which were held in Squaw Valley, located along the California-Nevada border. Cronkite, filling in for McKay, quickly became the TV master of the global sports spectacular.

Downhill skiing, ice hockey, bobsledding—Cronkite boned up on sports in preparation for his Squaw Valley broadcasts. Doing homework was one of his strong points. It fascinated him that for the first time—he was obsessive about firsts—speed skating, figure skating, and ice hockey would be held on artificial ice at an Olympics. And he studied up on the competitors from thirty-three nations, memorizing factoids from more than six hundred capsule biographies of athletes. Somehow Cronkite made the CBS viewer feel that he was a former gold medalist himself, enjoying the abundant snowfall while explaining the Nordic combined competition. He talked knowledgeably about downhill plunges, challenging pistes, frostbite, and snowcat climbs. Wearing blocklike boots, a fur-hooded parka, and mittens that made it awkward to hold his hot-chocolate mug, Cronkite looked like a rejected model auditioning for an L. L. Bean catalog. But nobody held it against him. Playing the man of all seasons, he metamorphosed into a hybrid athlete, reporter, spectator, cheerleader, humorist, worrywart, and good-time Charlie. While he served as anchorman for the Winter Games, his on-air color men included former Olympic stars Dick Button and Art Devlin and sports reporters Chris Schenkel and Bud Palmer.

The CBS ad campaign promoting the multisport Winter Games was bold. A Madison Avenue firm had designed an edgy-looking display ad with a downhill skier floating in midair holding an Olympic torch with a giant CBS eye logo over his head. A quick look through the TV guide section of *The Washington Post* showed that Cronkite's name appeared right after the 7:30 p.m. time slot announcement. This was significant. CBS sports in 1960 was under the umbrella of CBS News. Sig Mickelson was building Cronkite up as the star broadcaster of special events, news, and sports.

Squaw Valley, the smallest locale in the world ever to host the Olympic Games, a one-stoplight hamlet high in the Sierra Nevadas, was an ideal stage set for Cronkite. The village environment worked in CBS's favor because camera crews didn't have to roam all over Placer County looking for remote shots; all the competitions were within a few miles of one another. Not only did Cronkite get wonderful reviews for his Olympic broadcasts, the first held in North America in twenty-eight years, but also the prime-time ratings were robust. Cronkite was accorded some historical credit for making the Winter Games a popular four-year TV ritual in America. And he was the quarter-back of a newfangled technology developed in Squaw Valley that forever changed sports broadcasting: In the men's slalom event, Olympic officials, unsure if an athlete had bypassed a gate, asked CBS to review its tape. That simple request gave CBS the pioneering idea of instant replays—a mainstay feature for nearly all subsequent televised sporting events.

Rewarded for the Squaw Valley success, Cronkite was assigned to anchor the Summer Olympics of 1960 (held in Rome from August 25 to September 11). Because there was no satellite transmission, CBS couldn't broadcast live. Instead, sitting in the broadcast center in New York, Cronkite served as the connective tissue for the Rome games, announcing that Cassius Clay had won the gold medal for light-heavyweight boxing and former polio patient Wilma Rudolph had won three gold medals in track and field.

What Cronkite did brilliantly was parlay his Squaw Valley–Rome work, which received glowing reviews in a dozen newspapers, into a larger win, setting himself up as the anchorman to tune into for the 1960 political conventions. Asked that June what his concept of an anchorman was, Cronkite said, "We think of him as the on-air editor and coordinator of an event which by its nature is in several parts. For the Olympic Games in Rome this summer I will stay in New York as the anchorman, tying together the segments. For the Olympics, it's almost a host job. For the conventions, it's an on-air editing job, keeping a running story going."

As he continued anchoring the overall coverage of special events throughout 1960, it became clear that Murrow and Edwards were being replaced by Cronkite. He was the new Lowell Thomas, the master juggler of egos, the number-two guy from Safe Corner, U.S.A., who always seemed right in the number-one person's broadcast chair even when dealing with astrophysics or pole vaulting. He had come to personify the CBS eye even more than Murrow, and was anointed by the TV viewers as America's most likable and professional eyewitness to the twentieth century. More than anything else, he wanted to be seen as a Horatio Alger type, a scrappy wire service reporter who had made it by dint of hard work and long hours—and who had done it on his own terms. "Of the great men of television," Theodore White, author of *The Making of the President, 1960*, observed, "only Walter Cronkite had not been moved forward by an assist from Murrow somewhere along the line."

Cronkite's hunch was that the 1960 presidential election would be a historic cliffhanger. Everyone would be tuning in. Advertisers, he intuited, liked being part of history; they salivated at being in sync with the zeitgeist. Everyone had known in 1952 and 1956 that Eisenhower was going to win. But in early 1960, the next president was anyone's guess. And no longer did the election season begin with the gavels of the summer conventions; the springtime primary and caucus systems were now important stepping-stones for presidential aspirants. Cronkite, as reportorial beneficiary, had a yearlong opening to break political news and get CBS News in the front-page mix.

There was a steep downside to the intertwining of campaign politics with television. As primaries and caucuses swelled in number, so too did the cost of running for the White House (for example, TV ads had to be purchased in dozens of local markets). The age of television caused presidential candidates to fund-raise nonstop so their campaigns could become Rockefeller rich. In 1948, President Truman needed to pass around a fedora to afford to move his "Whistle Stop" train out of an Oklahoma depot. By 2012, in the age of Obama, candidates for president would need to raise an astonishing $1 billion for a campaign to survive. But even by 1960, it seemed that raising money had become what politicians did more than legislating.

A few serious-minded journalists, following Murrow's lead, also worried that having electric wagons loaded with cameras, microphones, and other paraphernalia on political convention floors actually *discouraged* participatory democracy. But their protests soon got muted. Whenever the red light went on, the politician being filmed spoke in phony-baloney, overly cautious sound bites. A whole new breed of TV image makers was introduced to the conventions— media consultants, makeup artists, and public relations experts. TV cameras had made political conventions more superficial affairs. It was Cronkite's determination in 1960 that CBS—no matter what—would whip NBC in the ratings with historic special-events coverage of the Democratic Convention in Los Angeles (from

July 11 to July 15) and the GOP one in Chicago (from July 25 to July 28).

By 1960, presidential aspirants had learned how to use TV in their favor. (Vice President Richard Nixon had pioneered this eight years earlier, during his famous "Checkers" speech.) John F. Kennedy advanced the unsettling art of TV manipulation during his campaign for the presidency when he spoke to the Protestant Ministerial Council in Houston about his Catholicism; the event was televised only locally, in east Texas. Even so, the Kennedy campaign had cleverly procured a copy of the Houston tape and ran highlights as commercials all over America before the candidate arrived to speak. The Big Three networks themselves pushed the idea of presidential debates, which forever changed U.S. election politics. But before there could be televised debates in 1960, the two candidates first had to be chosen, still the job of the political conventions. And Cronkite needed to have his CBS team beat NBC in the convention ratings to prove his staying power as a special-events wizard.

There wasn't much inherent drama in Chicago in 1960 for Cronkite to capitalize on to earn another Teddy White callout. Vice President Nixon was guaranteed to win the GOP nomination, and it was fairly obvious that the blueblood Henry Cabot Lodge, the former Massachusetts senator and ambassador to the United Nations, would be Nixon's VP choice. Cronkite at least scored a major interview with Lodge; that was *something*. But the Democratic Convention in Los Angeles, by contrast, was thick with subplots and subterfuge. JFK didn't like Senator Lyndon Johnson, but many pundits believed the wheeler-dealer Texan had to be on the ticket as VP if Nixon was to be beaten. There was also the real possibility that Kennedy would choose Senator Stuart Symington of Missouri or Adlai Stevenson of Illinois over Johnson.

Every major CBS News affiliate in the nation sent a reporter to the convention to get baptized in the new era of TV journalism. Dan Rather, a twenty-nine-year-old Texan, arrived at the Los Angeles Memorial Sports Arena in July, excited just to be covering his first national political convention for the CBS station KHOU in Houston. It wasn't until 1954 that Rather had even seen a TV. "I remember the scene," he recalled. "We were on a shopping trip, ambling through the appliance section of a department store, and we were bowled over by a stunning sight. People were watching a ball game on a tiny screen." Now, as news director for KHOU-TV, Rather found himself covering Lyndon Johnson, the Senate majority leader who was challenging John F. Kennedy for the Democratic nomination as delegates gathered in downtown Los Angeles.

With the nomination still undecided, the convention promised the kind of drama that live television news thrived on. *The Huntley-Brinkley Report* had surpassed the ratings of CBS's *Evening News* show (hosted by Douglas Edwards) in 1958, and remained in front, with momentum at its back. It was not so much that *Huntley-Brinkley* had finally found its audience as that it had found its coast-to-coast affiliates, setting NBC up for a ratings showdown with CBS at the 1960 conventions. A lot of vengeful energy was circulating around William Paley's office on Madison Avenue; he hated being number two in anything. "This was supposed to be comeback time for CBS in convention coverage," Rather recalled. "Cronkite, having got a good start in '52, had been creamed in '56. Huntley-Brinkley were white hot."

The Democratic National Convention began on Monday, July 11. Team Cronkite was assigned a balsam-lined, air-conditioned little studio at the Los Angeles Memorial Sports Arena from which to broadcast. Sig Mickelson, the director of CBS News, immediately perceived that his crew was off its A-game, that it "didn't have the inner drive and enthusiasm" needed for riveting convention coverage. Viewers perceived the blandness, too. The overnight ratings gave the first day's honors to NBC. Cronkite groaned to colleagues like a soldier, anxious and peeved, feeling ambushed. A frustrated Mickelson attributed CBS's lackluster performance to a bloated corps of floor reporters, most of whom didn't know enough about the political world to recognize the backroom strategies suddenly at play. It was far too late to change the correspondents, yet something dramatic had to be done to ratchet the numbers upward toward the sterling White Sox–Dodgers ratings. Two days into the convention, and still lagging behind NBC, CBS was floundering. A radical change was implemented by Mickelson in record time.

Don Hewitt, the moxie-driven director of CBS News coverage, was fixated on the winning combination of co-anchors next door in the NBC booth at the Los Angeles arena. On Wednesday morning, as he recalled, "I panicked and went to Sig Mickelson and told him we had to team Cronkite with *someone*." Hewitt, unafraid to whip up a firestorm, was so desperate to return CBS to its familiar place on top of the ratings, he decided to resort to the network's magic bullet from the Second World War as Cronkite's co-anchor. "Hewitt, whose judgment was normally impeccable, approached me before the opening of the Wednesday session," wrote Mickelson, "and suggested that we try Murrow in the 'anchor studio' to work with Cronkite." For all their traditional antagonisms and obvious stylistic differences, Hewitt was convinced that Cronkite-Murrow was the winning ticket. It made sense.

When Brinkley and Huntley burst onto the national scene at the 1956 conventions, they were largely unknown broadcasters. When Cronkite and Murrow were paired in 1960, they were two of the most famous newsmen in America. Murrow, who had risen like a rocket in the late 1930s, was descending just as steeply twenty years later. At times, he was openly critical of CBS as a company, casting the same cold eye on it as he had on other institutions through the years. "One of the basic troubles with radio and television news is that both instruments have grown up as an incompatible combination of show business, advertising, and news," he scolded colleagues in his brilliant 1958 speech to the Radio and Television News Directors Association (RTNDA). "Each of the three is a rather bizarre and demanding profession. And when you get all three under one roof, the dust never settles. The top management of the networks, with a few notable exceptions, has been trained in advertising, research, sales or show business. By the nature of the corporate structure, they also make the final and crucial decisions having to do with news and public affairs."

Paley was no longer impressed with Murrow's high-handed opinions. They were the antithesis of TV populism in the extreme, where ratings mattered most. Through the long, lively years of their friendship, Paley had always been Murrow's boss—and he had never had to remind Murrow of that fact. But as the relationship unraveled, there was little left for Paley to do except make clear to Murrow who was in charge of CBS. "Murrow thought he was a larger historical personage than rich old Paley," Hewitt explained. "Paley had all the wealth and corporate power. But Murrow had the thoroughbred fame. They were both alpha males. But Paley was the hare while Murrow the tortoise. Ed knew he would win the history game." Cronkite, even though he wasn't a Murrow booster, thought his colleague's 1958 RTNDA speech was brave. "I applauded it wildly, like all of us did in the news department," Cronkite recalled. "I admired his courage for saying it. I said, oh boy, there's our leader. Glad it was done. I was obviously sorry it got him in trouble with Paley, but I didn't consider that entirely unexpected."

Not long after the RTNDA speech, Murrow left CBS for a one-year sabbatical, a year of global travel that would allow him to try life without the network, and vice versa. Murrow ended his sabbatical early and immediately received job offers from academia and nonprofit organizations, but instead returned to CBS, going to work as a regular reporter—not a producer—at the documentary program *CBS Reports*. The most notable Murrow documentary became "Harvest of Shame," a gut-wrenching, Peabody Award–winning look at the miasma of Mexican migrant farm labor in America.

Hoping once again to excel at CBS, Murrow was on the scene as a reporter at the Democratic Convention in 1960 when he was suddenly reassigned to co-anchor the coverage with Cronkite. That's where Rather encountered Murrow—his coming-of-age hero. Rather was an up-and-comer who had journalism in his blood. As such, he had been scheduled by the network to have a picture taken that morning with Murrow (his idol) and, rather indifferently, with Cronkite (a fellow Houstonian). "Walter was big," Rather said. "But Murrow was like a god."

If Rather was surprised to hear that Murrow was to start co-anchoring with Cronkite, he wasn't the only one. At the appointed morning hour for the photo session, well before the Democratic Convention went into session, Murrow and the network's publicists appeared in a smoky anteroom outside the CBS anchor booth. "Murrow came and sat," Rather said. "We waited a very long time and then Walter didn't come." The heavy atmosphere was flammable, and Rather half expected the grim-faced Murrow to throw a tantrum, the anger was so evident on his face. It was painful for Rather to see his hero being denigrated. Eventually, the photo session was canceled, and Murrow huffed out. "What had turned out," Rather said, "is that Walter had locked himself in the anchor booth. Walter didn't want to anchor with Murrow. He just locked himself in the booth and said, 'To hell with it.'"

Decades later, historian Don Carleton of the University of Texas at Austin interviewed Cronkite about his feud with Murrow at the Los Angeles convention, and Cronkite admitted that the two didn't really click. But he blamed much of the friction on CBS management's foolhardiness. "Who's supposed to do what?" Cronkite explained. "What's Murrow supposed to do? I don't think they said anything about him doing analysis. They just said that he was supposed to help me. They just wanted Murrow on camera to cash in on his popularity. . . . I think Murrow and I might have had chemistry that worked under different circumstances, but the management at the convention in 1960 was not one to create great chemistry."

For all the sleek corporate culture of CBS, for all the fast-cash TV boom profits, the network was essentially a herd, and in that respect, Murrow was a wounded animal. The younger bison were leaving him out to pasture. Paley and the other CBS executives in charge had hobbled Murrow, taking away his executive status and keeping him out of planning meetings. The Murrow Boys—including Collingwood, Schoenbrun, Sevareid, and Pierpoint—were still loyal to him, as far as their powers at CBS would allow. Youngsters such as Rather looked up to him with unadulterated reverence. But for Cronkite, never sycophantic toward Murrow, the situation was quite different. He didn't feel compelled to suddenly start kowtowing at the 1960 convention.

When Cronkite was abruptly informed that he would, indeed, not be an anchor but a co-anchor with Murrow in Los Angeles, he gasped. Cronkite believed that Murrow blossomed when he composed his on-air material carefully in advance. That was how Murrow had exposed McCarthy as being nothing more than a disingenuous paper tiger. Burrowing into mounds of documents, devouring information, Murrow liked to memorize his high-powered words or read them off a TelePrompTer. Cronkite was just the opposite. He crammed his mind with vetted facts about the cold war, inflation, government spending, the space race, sports, and integration, then let his preternatural ability to ad-lib take over the show. Cronkite and Murrow did not mesh professionally, possibly because they lacked a basic attribute of nearly any kind of professional partnership, especially one involving communication: neither appeared to care what the other was saying.

At times in Los Angeles, the rival CBS broadcasters didn't even seem to be *listening* to each other. Dan Rather recalled the teaming as the epitome of everything to be avoided in broadcasting: "long pauses, awkward things, battle for the microphone." Jack Gould, *The New York Times* television critic whose praise for Huntley and Brinkley continued to be generous, declared that "the pre-eminence of CBS in news coverage, which has been something of a tradition in broadcasting, no longer exists."

Don Hewitt, who paired them in the first place, admitted in retrospect that it had been "a terrible idea, a complete disaster." He recalled, "I mean, if there were two chemistries, two personalities, that didn't blend, it was Murrow and Cronkite."

For the network news departments, the political conventions arose every four years as a showcase, an Olympiad in gathering and delivering news. For CBS, the 1960 season was a turning point of the most disheartening kind. Not only did the network come in second that August, but it was a distant second, with NBC pulling 51 percent of viewers to CBS's 36 percent. The internal numbers showed, moreover, that over the course of the Republican convention, CBS lost viewers to ABC—then a flyweight in the bruising sport of televised politics. Everyone in CBS's news department was touched by the sense of failure afterward—or, nearly everyone. "Strangely," wrote CBS correspondent David Schoenbrun, "Cronkite was not blamed at all. Paley felt he had done his usual good job, but the chemistry in the CBS coverage was not good, and that must be the fault of the news director."

Stanton had wanted Cronkite to conduct breaking-news interviews with John F. Kennedy and Richard Nixon in the spring of 1960, giving CBS News momentum leading into the summer conventions. Kennedy was the presumptive nominee of the Democratic Party when Cronkite caused a ruckus. On the evening of the Wisconsin primary—on April 5—CBS persuaded Kennedy to appear as a commentator from Milwaukee. Unbeknownst to Cronkite, though, JFK's brother, Robert F. Kennedy, had cut a deal with some producer at CBS with the precondition that no discussion of Catholicism be allowed. Nobody informed Cronkite of this deal (if there really was one). "In the course of the interview [with JFK], I naturally asked his opinion of how the Catholic and non-Catholic vote was going," Cronkite recalled. "He was obviously upset by the question."

After the CBS broadcast a brouhaha ensued between the Kennedy campaign and CBS News. The sheer intensity of it was astonishing. Cronkite, for his part, grew indignant at JFK for insinuating he would ever play the quid pro quo game. There were rumors that Kennedy was going to denounce CBS publicly; instead, he called Stanton, full of fury at Cronkite's intransigence. What a hardball player Kennedy could be, Stanton realized, when he felt double-crossed. Feeling betrayed by CBS, the presumptive Democratic nominee reminded Stanton that if elected to the White House, he would be selecting leaders of the FCC, the governmental regulatory agency to which radio stations and television networks were beholden. "Dr. Stanton courageously stood up to the threat," Cronkite recalled of his brush-up with Kennedy, "as he did on so many other occasions in defending television's free press rights."

Not long after the Wisconsin primary, Don Hewitt bumped into JFK. "Walter Cronkite's a Republican, isn't he?" Kennedy asked. "No," Hewitt said, "I don't think so." Kennedy, not buying it, said, "He's a Republican. I know he's a Republican." Holding his ground, Hewitt again denied it. "He's always with Eisenhower," Kennedy insisted. "Always having his picture taken with Eisenhower and going somewhere with him."

Given the helter-skelter nature of broadcast news, Cronkite couldn't afford to hold a grudge against the Kennedys for too long (and vice versa). Following the summer conventions—with Kennedy and Nixon becoming the nominees—Cronkite hatched an idea that would involve both politicians. CBS News was promoting a thirteen-week series modeled on *Pick the Winner* titled *Presidential Countdown*, aimed at taking an in-depth look at the presidential and vice presidential candidates through interviews. *Presidential Countdown*'s first telecast would be on September 12. The program would run for nine weeks, in half-hour segments on Mondays at 10:30 p.m. EST, until October 31. While Cronkite had done this in 1952 and 1956 with *Pick the Winner*, the popularity of the show reformatted as *Presidential Countdown* grew with Kennedy and Nixon being in such a tight electoral race. "I came up with the idea that during these interviews I would ask questions deliberately aimed at bringing out their personalities—or that was the idea," Cronkite explained in the 1990s. "Up to that time, we'd been talking entirely about issues. That seems so strange today because we've gotten so far away from talking about issues. The concentration today is far too much about personalities. So I guess I have to admit to some complicity in helping that unfortunate development. But I wanted to find out what makes these people tick."

All Cronkite's formidable energies in the fall of 1960 centered on his political interview show catching fire. It would help erase his middling failure at the conventions. CBS had persuaded Westinghouse to be a sponsor of *Presidential Countdown*, which was a financial boon. Cronkite befriended campaign managers and pollsters. His programming vision was based on not leaking questions to the candidates in advance. It was to be a mano a mano exercise. For dramatic effect, Cronkite imagined he would confidently enter from one side of the room, and Kennedy, Nixon, Johnson, or Lodge, depending on the day, from the other side. They would meet in the middle, shake hands, sit down, and the no-holds-barred interview would begin. The candidate would do the Q&A cold turkey. No preparation. No handlers serving as pre-interview interlopers. While in principle Cronkite's *Presidential Countdown* program sounded good, all the top CBS brass (minus Stanton) scoffed at the idea that any candidate would allow himself to be so vulnerable; Cronkite rose to the challenge of proving management wrong.

To jump-start *Presidential Countdown*, Cronkite went to see JFK at his Senate office. Kennedy was still miffed that Cronkite kept being quoted in the press about the burden of Catholicism for a presidential candidate. Everyone knew that Kennedy was incredibly suave and comfortable around the press. As a young man, he had even longed to be a reporter for a spell after his service in the Navy in the Second World War. Furthermore, because of his youth and inexperience, he needed TV exposure more than a two-term vice president such as Nixon. But the Wisconsin primary incident had left him annoyed with Cronkite. "You must think I'm crazy," Kennedy told Cronkite when presented with the *Presidential Countdown* scheme. "I'm not going to do that. You can forget it."

"Well," Cronkite snapped, "if I got Vice President Nixon, you'd almost have to do it then, wouldn't you?"

Kennedy just stared fixedly at Cronkite with disdain. "You're not going to get him," he said dismissively. "That's not my problem."

Refusing to be flummoxed by Kennedy, Cronkite hunted down Nixon, who was at his campaign headquarters at Sixteenth and K streets. Nixon listened intently to Cronkite's pitch for the new CBS program. He kept nodding his head up and down at all the ground rules. "Sure. I think that's fine," Nixon said with good-natured warmth. "That's a great idea. I'd be glad to participate."

Cronkite claimed he was "dumbfounded" that Nixon had agreed to go along with the *Presidential Countdown* guidelines while Kennedy had balked. Go figure. Off Cronkite went, flagging down a taxi to shuttle him back to Kennedy's office at the Russell Senate Office Building. Suddenly he had a panicked thought: Who would go first? Whoever went last on the show had the strategic advantage of studying the interview format. Cronkite asked the taxi driver to swing back to K Street. Up the elevator he went, to be greeted again by a cheerful Nixon. To Cronkite's astonishment the former vice president was nonchalant about the pecking order. "I don't care," Nixon said. "I'll be glad to go first if it's any problem."

For the only time in his life Cronkite felt like kissing Nixon's ring. He now headed back to Kennedy's office. When told that Cronkite had gotten Nixon to sign up for the series without hesitation, Kennedy blanched. His eyes barely concealed his utter contempt for Cronkite. Kennedy now felt hemmed in. "I suppose if you've got Nixon," the senator snapped, "we'll have to do something. You talk to my campaign manager." That was a reluctant yes, but a yes nevertheless. Cronkite, his luck holding, headed over to CBS's Washington, D.C., bureau to gloat about his impending triumph.

Thus was born *Presidential Countdown.* Nixon, as promised, taped the special first. As choreographed, Cronkite and Nixon each marched into a studio from different doors and shook hands on the center mark. Then, following a few formalities, they were off to the races. Cronkite's first question was direct: "Mr. Vice President, you're a skilled politician," he began. "You certainly can't have missed what people say about you. Many of them say, 'I don't know what it is about the man, I just don't like him.' What do you think it is they just don't like about you?"

Instead of being rattled, Nixon wrapped himself around the question with self-evident glee, gazing fixedly at the CBS reporter's face. "Well, I think it's three things, Mr. Cronkite," Nixon said. "I think the first is my physiognomy. I have a rather heavy beard and a dark complexion and between those things, I just can't shave closely enough. I always look a little blue in the face, like I have a little growth of beard, and that's unfortunate. The second thing is those campaigns for election to the U.S. Senate against Helen Douglas and to the Congress against Jerry Voorhis, which I would probably do a little differently. I wouldn't take back any of the charges I made, because I think they were perfectly justified, but I would handle it a little differently with the experience I have now. And third is my leadership in the House Un-American Activities Committee. I'm not one bit ashamed of that, but that created a body of propaganda . . ." And on and on, Nixon answered with great skill. It was quite an acrobatic performance for the Californian known for robotic stiffness. Cronkite threw unexpected questions at Nixon about his Irish ancestry and Quaker background, and he in turn hit them over the fence. By Cronkite's closing question about Nixon's fitness for the White House, it was clear that, surprisingly, the *Presidential Countdown* format worked in the vice president's favor.

A week later, Cronkite interviewed Kennedy at his Federal-style Georgetown home at 3307 N Street NW. The house had been a gift from Kennedy to his wife, Jacqueline, after the birth of their daughter, Caroline, in 1957. Cronkite recalled the handsome Massachusetts senator being, at best, a "reluctant guest" on *Presidential Countdown*. Unlike Nixon, Kennedy blew the entire CBS interview. It was clear that he hadn't properly boned up for the program, confusing even his own résumé on film. Once the camera rolled, Kennedy was all hems and haws. Every other line was a clumsy "Well . . . uh . . . I think, well . . . I believe, I, well . . . uh . . ." Not only was he unfocused and dithering, but also, the entire hour, he seemed to be grasping at straws. If this had been his opening night on Broadway, he would have gotten the hook. "When it was over, we thanked him, and he was kind of mean about it," Cronkite recalled. "He gave me a rather perfunctory good-bye."

While Cronkite was watching Kennedy's botched interview in the CBS truck outside the candidate's house, the producer of *Presidential Countdown*, Warren Abrams, came barging in, clearly panicked.

"We've got to do the program over," Abrams said.

"What's the matter with it?" a perplexed Cronkite asked. "It's all right in here. I'm looking at it."

"Well, the senator says we have to do it over," Abrams said.

"But we don't do it over again," an incredulous Cronkite sputtered, his muscles taut. "That's part of the deal."

"Kennedy insists," Abrams shot back. "He won't let it be shown this way."

"Well," Cronkite fumed, "what right does he have?"

Abrams considered. "I don't know," he said. "His complaint is that we had him sitting in a big soft sofa, and he didn't look right."

"Oh come on," Cronkite scoffed. "We know better than that. It's because he blew that last question. Where is he?"

"Up in the bedroom," Abrams said.

"Well," Cronkite said, hurrying out of the truck, "I've got to talk to him."

Fueled by his righteous indignation, Cronkite stomped up the stairs of Kennedy's home to encounter a startled JFK lying on one twin bed and Ted Sorensen—his best friend, speechwriter, and special assistant—on the other. Sorensen recalled that Cronkite had frightened them by walking stealthily up the stairs, and that he hadn't knocked. Kennedy and Sorensen both saw "a fire in Walter's eyes that they didn't know he had." For his part, Cronkite was surprised at how young and petulant Kennedy and Sorensen looked, like a couple of graduating prep school kids sleeping off a hangover on a rainy Sunday. "They had their shoes off and their ties undone," Cronkite recalled. "There was this big Harvard banner up on the wall, and football pictures; it looked like a college dorm room. They were lying there, dangling their feet."

Suddenly Kennedy, looking straight at Cronkite and, clearing his throat ominously, said, "Tell me when you're ready."

"Senator," Cronkite replied. "I don't think we ought to do this again."

"I've already discussed it with your producer," Kennedy retorted. "We're going to do it."

Overwhelmed by the unremitting tension, filled with the desire to assert himself as the superior power, Cronkite tried a sly new angle. "But you know," he told Kennedy, "we're going to have to carry a disclaimer. We're going to say that Nixon's was unrehearsed but that you requested to do yours over."

"I can live with that," Kennedy said.

"I don't think you understand the impact of that disclaimer," Cronkite continued. "I don't think it's going to make you look very good."

"I'm not concerned about that," Kennedy said, holding his ground.

"All right, Senator," Cronkite said in disbelief. "We'll do it over. But I've got to tell you, I think it's the lousiest bit of sportsmanship I ever saw in my life."

Suddenly Kennedy turned gray with embarrassment. Cronkite, in a thespian gesture, turned around and started heading down the stairs.

"Wait a minute," Kennedy shouted, sitting up in bed with pronounced dislike on his face. "Let it run!"

Because Cronkite had bagged his big Kennedy and Nixon interviews that fall and a ratings bonanza for *Presidential Countdown*, his place as a CBS broadcaster was secure. That was important, because shake-ups were imminent at CBS, but not just because Jack Gould of *The New York Times* had publicly mocked the news division. NBC was now the established ratings leader: CBS had been running second to the Peacock Network in the evening news for more than two years. The convention ratings showed all too bluntly the same thing. And then, in the fall of 1960, NBC shed its former runner-up humility once and for all by launching an attack directed at the very heart of CBS News: investigative documentaries via the program *NBC White Paper*. Frank Stanton was genuinely shaken by NBC's forward-driving hubris. Five years before, NBC would have had neither the talent nor the budget to produce hard-hitting documentaries.

What worried CBS executives the most—why they had tried making Cronkite and Murrow compete with Huntley and Brinkley—was that NBC had a knack for creating successful new TV formats. After all, NBC had introduced the desk-and-sofa talk show (*Today*, *Tonight*), the TV special, the prime-time movie showcase, the made-for-TV movie, the Sunday press conference (*Meet the Press*), and, later, free-form comedy shows (*Rowan & Martin's Laugh-In* and *Saturday Night Live*). You couldn't blame Stanton for not wanting to be left in the dust by Huntley-Brinkley as Election Day approached.

CBS News had a special problem to face in the fall of 1960 as it tried to regain the top spot in broadcast news: the eminent Ed Murrow, the one employee who couldn't be fired. He was the news division's greatest asset, a tall, chain-smoking, handsome icon who still demanded the respect accorded a statesman or a war hero, both of which he had been. At the same time, Murrow was barely accommodated by CBS management, treated as an antiquated pariah figure best kept at arm's length. After the widespread protests from U.S. agribusiness over his program "Harvest of Shame," a documentary that showcased the dire situation of migrant workers in the United States, Murrow's dark brow seemed increasingly furrowed as he paced the halls of CBS. He was always fatigued and displayed teeth marred by nicotine stains. Paley often complained that he was sick and tired of controversial news shows such as those that Murrow regarded as worthwhile for *CBS Reports*. They literally made Paley sick to his stomach, already aggravated by ulcers, as he anticipated the viewer backlash that typically resulted. If Murrow were to be given any more leash, Paley fretted, CBS News would become a doomed sinkhole as corporate advertisers held a quiet boycott. "CBS is not the Ministry of Justice, not an avenging angel," Paley carped. "We are a big business and we are being hurt."

Paley's position was not based entirely on expediency. Trained as a financier, he had learned much of what he knew about journalism from Paul White, whom he had hired as CBS's first news director in 1935. At the time that White and Paley introduced serious journalism to radio, newspapers—the only other time-oriented news media—were mired in partisan viewpoints. Nearly every paper in the nation was understood by its readers to tilt in one political direction or another. (The major wire services were far more evenhanded, catering as they did to a variety of papers; United Press, Cronkite's alma mater, was regarded as the least slanted of them all.) White convinced Paley that for a number of economic reasons, CBS radio was in a position to start fresh and assert itself as a wholly objective news medium.

White convinced Paley that "honesty" (objectivity) was the element that could make or break journalism. Murrow had agreed wholeheartedly when he joined the network under White's aegis in the 1930s, but with his increasing stature during World War II, he added his own editorial viewpoint when he felt compelled to do so. White and Murrow clashed on that very issue. After the war, when their differences came to a head, Paley sided with his star and allowed White to be fired. Such was the power of Murrow.

A dozen years later, Murrow and the reporters he influenced at CBS worked under the theory—antithetical to White's philosophy—that the power of broadcasting increased with the addition of some point of view, carried in the words, the pictures, or the invisible hand of the editing. White would have argued that the impact increased temporarily, but that a steady diet of slanted reports would only train the viewer to think twice about every report, and to take none at face value. The Murrow legacy in TV news was the desire to counter the entertainment industry's effort to inject bottom-dollar values into the sacred world of fact.

By the end of the 1950s, Paley had returned to White's teachings. His motives were questioned, as some suspected that he was giving in to pressure from his GOP friends in government and Wall Street to make CBS News shallow and nonthreatening. Paley's reversal was crucial not only to CBS but also to broadcast news in general. The degree of "analysis," "commentary," and "editorialization" tolerated in news shows has been the subject of passionate debate ever since. The benchmark broadcast of Murrow's *See It Now* program on McCarthy has been looked on as a magnificent moment—and a Pandora's box. In that documentary's riptide, bad opinions and sensationalized commentaries have been able to masquerade as serious news shows. Paley, in trying to reduce the slant, probably raised the objectivity level of broadcast journalism overall as he backtracked from Murrow even as he stymied the ambitions of some excellent reporters at CBS News. Broadcast news was a rotten business in 1960, but the American public had a growing appetite for it—CBS aimed to please its consumers just like any other big business.

While Murrow had received garlands from intellectuals ("the Harvards," as Lyndon Johnson called them) for "Harvest of Shame," Cronkite was the ever-embraced anchorman of CBS by the general public. Although the privations and inhumane treatment of Mexican migrants were horrifying, the big story of September 1960 was the presidential election. TV was becoming a reflection of America itself, and Cronkite had emerged as the medium's most consistently trustworthy mirror. The hottest thing in television in 1960 was the coming Kennedy-Nixon debates. And it was Cronkite, not Murrow, who was chosen as one of four reporters—along with Frank Singiser (MBS), John Edwards (ABC), and John Chancellor (NBC)—to ask the candidates questions at the all-important October 21 fourth (and final) debate, which was moderated by Quincy Howe of ABC News. Knowing that foreign policy would be the subject du jour, Cronkite boned up on topics such as Cuba, Berlin, and NATO so he could make his mark on the broadcast. "The networks had insisted that the interrogators on programs one and four be selected exclusively from network news staffs," Sig Mickelson explained in *The Electric Mirror*, "and picked by the networks themselves." In the end Cronkite was so mild-mannered an inquisitor, handicapped (to be fair) by time restrictions, that he was an almost invisible presence in the square-off. But being part of the Kennedy-Nixon debates was, at the very least, an impressive résumé booster and a historical feather in his cap.

Besides the *Presidential Countdown* interviews and a Kennedy-Nixon debate, Cronkite served as host of a special on November 4 in anticipation of Election Day. All CBS News' contributing reporters summed up for host Cronkite what their gut told them with only four days left before voters went to the polls. Determined to outshine ABC's competing *Presidential Round Up*, CBS News spent a fortune taking out display ads in newspapers for the show, with Cronkite's name in boldface letters. Cronkite's guests included two-time Republican presidential nominee Thomas Dewey, Adlai Stevenson, Senator Eugene McCarthy (D-Minn.), and Henry Cabot Lodge. Cronkite's "Final Campaign Report" seemed to put Kennedy in a more favorable light than

Nixon. But Kennedy—still miffed at Cronkite—didn't think so. Convinced that Cronkite was an Eisenhower Republican, Kennedy thought the show pro-Nixon.

Before Election Night, November 8, 1960, CBS News took out ads promoting both Cronkite and Murrow as lead anchors. But pecking order matters, and Cronkite's name came first. He was the marquee player. CBS purchased full-page ads in *The Washington Post* and *The New York Times* showing Cronkite (not Murrow) surrounded by a sea of telephones, looking like he was the ringmaster of a Jerry Lewis–like telethon, the anchorman easily engaging citizens willing to dial a few numbers. Whom to watch on Election Night was obviously a matter of personal appeal and Cronkite was marketed as the Everyman. What were Huntley-Brinkley? The Everytwo? CBS News issued press releases boasting about the extraordinary job their boy Walter had done during that year's Olympic Games and the final Kennedy-Nixon debate. The seemingly avuncular Cronkite, the Midwesterner with a centrist disposition, was becoming the franchise.

15.

New Space Frontier on CBS

JITTERS AT THE JFK INAUGURATION—CBS MAKES
SPACE A PRIORITY—CRONKITE, WUSSLER, AND THE
ART OF SPECIAL EFFECTS—WITH EISENHOWER AT
GETTYSBURG—BACK AT THE BOOKIE JOINT—
BEATING THE COSMONAUTS—GUTS AND GRIT OF
ALAN SHEPARD—GO, GUS GRISSOM—INTERVIEWING
WALTER LIPPMANN—APRIL 16, 1962—OF NOAH'S
DOVES AND ARTIFICIAL SATELLITES—GODSPEED,
JOHN GLENN—NO-FRILLS WALTER

On the morning of Friday, January 20, 1961,
Washington, D.C., glittery as a glacier, was an
exhilarating place to be. John F. Kennedy was poised
to become the thirty-fifth president of the United

States. For the first time, a Catholic would occupy 1600 Pennsylvania Avenue. Although the city was dusted with snow, a freezing winter wind whipping around Capitol Hill and Georgetown alike, the CBS special-event crews kept warm with gloves, scarves, and hot chocolate in the bitter cold. They were part of a pool of cameras that would follow President-elect Kennedy from his Georgetown residence to the White House, where he was supposed to arrive at about 11:30 a.m. and give President Eisenhower a ride to Capitol Hill. Chief Justice Earl Warren was slated to administer the oath of office to Kennedy at noon. While Cronkite didn't consider himself a New Frontiersman (a Henry Wallace phrase circa 1948, applied to die-hard Kennedy supporters in 1961), he thought the Massachusetts senator's rise to power from Brookline to PT-109 to *Profiles in Courage* to beating Richard Nixon was an irresistible story.

What worried Cronkite about the Kennedy inauguration was the potential for technical glitches that could turn CBS' live broadcast into a TV white-noise static fest. Many of CBS News' top technicians were stuck in New York because of inclement weather. It had taken Betsy hours in a CBS car to get from National Airport to the Hay-Adams Hotel across from the White House. CBS News producers had laid cables down Pennsylvania

Avenue in preparation for the inaugural parade; these had short-circuited because of heavy water damage. "Our guys," Cronkite recalled, "were pulling cables all night."

Cronkite himself was doing last-minute homework just before the start of CBS's broadcast that Friday morning. Joining him for the broadcast were Howard K. Smith, Edward R. Murrow, Paul Niven, and George Herman—a marvelous cast of correspondents. But all the CBSers were grumpy because they'd been outplayed by NBC News, which garnered all the buzz for plans to televise the inaugural parade in color (a historic first). Meanwhile, CBS management in New York was nervous about cables, wires, and soundboards. During that same worrisome prebroadcast lull, the news division's Sig Mickelson pulled aside his special-events general assistant, Bobby Wussler. "Young man," Mickelson said to the twenty-two-year-old Wussler, "I've been watching you and I have a big job for you. What do you know about the space program?"

"Not much, sir," Wussler responded.

It was an odd question for Mickelson to ask Wussler when the CBS workforce was fretting over perfecting the impending Kennedy inauguration coverage. There were more newsy questions that needed to be answered. Did Sorensen write the inaugural speech? How many columns are on the podium? Are we *sure* JFK will be the youngest president in U.S. history? Not many minutes were left before the beginning of the telecast, but Sig was thinking about NASA.

Born in Newark, New Jersey, in 1936, Robert Wussler vividly remembered his family's first TV, a Crosley 9-420M, purchased when he turned twelve years old. He attended Seton Hall University in South Orange, New Jersey, majoring in communication arts. Graduating in 1957, he was determined to land a job at one of the Big Three networks, so he walked into CBS headquarters in New York and was hired as a mailroom clerk. His coworkers soon learned that Wussler was a visionary who thought the CBS News specials could be produced as high-octane drama with the help of electronic gizmos. Mickelson met him, appreciated his talent, and promoted him to the position of CBS News production assistant after only five weeks on the job. Wussler started helping Douglas Edwards with the *CBS Evening News* show, while Don Hewitt simultaneously took him under his wing. What Wussler had a better grasp of than the old CBS Radio News hands was the potential boon of using graphic art to make newscasting a more entertaining endeavor.

Wussler's big break came with the Winter Olympics of 1960, when he orchestrated pioneering TV graphics and production techniques. Cronkite called him the Plotter because he always sat in a corner devising ideas for special effects in a giant looseleaf journal. Cronkite, like Hewitt, fell under the spell of Wussler's technical talent in Squaw Valley, where the U.S. team won three gold medals. Thanks to the big ratings garnered by prime-time broadcasts, CBS Sports became a separate division within the CBS television network in 1961, and Wussler deserved a hunk of the credit for the new status it enjoyed. Besides graphics, on-location logistics were also a Wussler specialty. He ran the CBS News special-events unit almost like a SWAT team hungry for complicated assignments in far-off places.

"Men are going to fly in space—this year, throughout the Sixties," Mickelson told Wussler the morning of the inauguration. "We'll probably visit some other planets. And you're going to be in charge of our coverage. As a matter of fact, there's a monkey going up from Cape Canaveral in ten days, and you're going to go down there and find out all about this."

Wussler, like a good lieutenant, nodded his acquiescence. Then he went about overseeing CBS's broadcast of the Kennedy inaugural, trying to stay warm in the twenty-two-degree weather that felt like subzero because of the wind chill. Visions of space ships and rockets were swirling in his mind. Mickelson had jarred his sensibilities. Soon after the inauguration, Wussler started his research, devouring the science fiction books of Arthur C. Clarke, Isaac Asimov, and H. G. Wells for ideas. During the first half of 1961, CBS News was investigating numerous issues, such as Cuban prime minister Fidel Castro, U-2 spy flights over the Soviet Union, and missile technology. But when it came to space, carte blanche was given to Cronkite-Wussler by the president of CBS News himself.

Mickelson had been slightly off with his facts when he tapped Wussler. The United States was about to launch a *chimpanzee* (named "Ham"), not a monkey. The implication that space coverage was something new for CBS was also a bit off. As Mickelson knew full well, CBS had been deep in the world of rocketry since 1958. Cronkite himself had claimed that during the Second World War, he saw a German V-2 rocket launched by the Third Reich soaring over Holland; he had even written a UP column about it that ran in *The New York Times*. Nevertheless, Mickelson was prescient. Space *was* going to be the huge news story of 1961. Assigning Wussler to work the NASA beat with Cronkite was a masterstroke. The Cronkite-Wussler creative collaboration proved unbeatable. Besides being a great juggler, booker, technician, imagist, producer, and arranger, Wussler had youthful energy, that rare quality that the poet William Blake had called the hall-mark of genius.

The Murrow Boys became part of history during World War II, and the Cronkiters were going to do the same covering Project Mercury, the first concerted American effort to send humans to space. "It was a little bit like being along for Columbus or Magellan," Wussler recalled in a 2003 oral history interview. "It *was* a New Frontier. It *was* the Sixties. I had grown up as a Depression baby, a World War II kid, and in the slow days of the Eisenhower Fifties. And Kennedy—it *was* Camelot, as corny as it may sound. It was Camelot. And Camelot, and the Kennedy mystique, and the Space program, and the Magnificent Seven guys, the first astronaut class, all sort of came out of the same short period."

It's difficult to understand Cronkite's rise during the 1960s without understanding Wussler. Cronkite's engaging strengths were his original voice, work ethic, ability to edit scripts, nomadic nature, competitiveness, and eccentric curiosity that not even the most ambitious hotshot could match. Attracted to the dramatic news stories of the day, he nevertheless had a limited sense of the visual production of TV news. Wussler, on the other hand, always looked for new camera angles, fresh graphics, and ways to improve the sound quality of a CBS special, be it Vietnamese jungle gunfire or a Saturn V rocket engine revving for liftoff. He was an ideal partner for Cronkite. It was Wussler, a cyberkinetics junkie, who invented, for better or worse, the split screen of talking heads.

What CBS News had discovered by 1961, through a combination of luck and talent scouting, was the right special-events team. Don Hewitt, the third key member of the troika, had been with the news division since 1948 and had worked on special events with Cronkite since Queen Elizabeth's coronation in June 1953. Together Cronkite and Hewitt, world-trampers at heart, had spent more time in adjoining hotel rooms than any other duo in television. To Cronkite, CBS live events coverage was an "intoxicating endeavor"; the boundaries of TV news burst wide open in such unlikely places as Squaw Valley and Cocoa Beach and Hyannis Port.

Driven like a one-man Sousa band, Hewitt was innovative, almost maniacally so, and he had definite ideas about space coverage. For example, the modern viewer, he insisted, needed Disney-like visual models to comprehend the solar system. CBS installed in its studio a micro-planetarium, with all the planets and the Moon built to scale. Cecil B. De Mille had nothing on CBS News when it came to pageantry and re-creations. Just as Walt Disney had advanced animation with Mickey Mouse, the Hewitt-Wussler-Cronkite team developed a whole new generation of visual effects based on high-tech simulations. CBS News special events—like NASA itself—established a distinct personality: competitive, modern, and unstoppable for the space race against the Soviet Union.

As Cronkite was poised for important on-location assignments, Ed Murrow was in a strangely sequestered position at CBS News. The corporate chiefs were tired of his controversial let's-punish-the-bad-guys public service programs. And Murrow was tired of everything else about the TV age. Paley couldn't strong-arm Murrow into resigning without incurring a tidal wave of resentment from the nation, but he could stand by as the news division shifted Murrow to a smaller and yet smaller role at CBS. An intuitive Murrow sensed his diminution, and in early 1961 he let go of his hold on CBS, accepting an offer from President Kennedy to run the U.S. Information Agency. It was a matter of widespread CBS corridor gossip at the time that Dr. Frank Stanton, working behind the scenes at Paley's behest, had convinced the Kennedy gang to offer Murrow the USIA job as a "sneaky way" to get him to leave the company. The short-lived second act for Murrow at CBS was over.

Before Murrow's departure, Cronkite had been involved with a slew of CBS documentaries. Building on this unheralded aspect of his résumé, he now tried to inherit Murrow's mantle. When the Nazi mass murderer Adolf Eichmann went on trial in Israel in April 1961, Cronkite and producer Sandy Socolow were determined to cover the proceedings for the *Eyewitness* program, which Cronkite hosted every Friday evening at 10:30 p.m. starting in 1959. Full of Nuremberg déjà vu, Cronkite thought the Eichmann trial was going to be *huge* news. Stanton agreed. Not only did he dispatch Cronkite and Socolow to Israel, but he also sent a second CBS News crew to Argentina to re-create the Mossad's capture of the Nazi lieutenant colonel.

When the trial started on Wednesday, April 11, 1961, the Cronkite-Socolow plan was to shoot the opening day and quickly fly back to New York City for a Friday night *Eyewitness* broadcast, mostly pre-produced with a strategic hole to be filled by last-minute footage of the trial. At a refueling stop in Rome, Cronkite read a headline in *Il Messaggero* about Soviet cosmonaut Yuri Gagarin being the first human to orbit the Earth. An anxious Cronkite called Sig Mickelson in New York and was told to put the kibosh on the Eichmann broadcast. Instead, CBS wanted Cronkite and Socolow to get on the Gagarin story ASAP, to tap old UP Soviet contacts for scoops. Instead of the Eichmann story, there would be a "prime-time examination" of where NASA (the United States) stood in the space race vis-à-vis the Soviets now that Gagarin had shattered the power dynamic.

Gagarin was almost as big a news story as the Soviet *Sputnik* launch in October 1957. It didn't take Price Waterhouse to calculate that the Russians had the first satellite, the first dog in space, and now the first man in space. Not wanting to miss out on the cosmonaut juggernaut, Cronkite flew back to New York, determined to get the biggest slice of the Soviet space pie that CBS News was carving up for its reporters. With a dose of luck, Cronkite and Marvin Kalb interviewed Gagarin only two days after the Russian cosmonaut made history. "American prestige was jolted," Cronkite recalled years later on NPR, "as the world heard the quickened pulse of *Vostok 1* orbiting the Earth."

On the strength of Cronkite's work hosting *The Twentieth Century*, Stanton personally assigned him to cover the *Freedom 7* mission of Alan B. Shepard that May. "There was great pressure in the United States to get a man into space," Cronkite recalled. Amid fierce competition among air force pilots, Shepard had been selected by NASA as one of the original group of seven Mercury astronauts. A graduate of the U.S.

Naval Academy class of '44, Shepard had, as a cold war test pilot, logged more than 8,000 hours flying time (3,700 in jet aircraft). Cronkite, who befriended Shepard, deemed him the greatest "rocket jock" of all time. Although NASA was selling Shepard as the all-American boy, Cronkite knew better. Shepard, who cursed like a banshee and drank with lust, had to attend NASA "charm school" to learn, for example, how to say "darn" instead of "damn." The acquiescent Cronkite went along with the NASA charade of Shepard as wholesome American hero. Reporters in Florida covering the *Freedom 7* launch noticed that Cronkite had a behind-closed-doors alignment with NASA, as if he knew their secret handshake. There was some speculation that Cronkite worked for the CIA. "We were quite aware that the image that NASA was trying to project was not quite honest," Cronkite later admitted. "But at the same time, there was a recognition that the nation needed new heroes."

On May 5, 1961, Shepard suited up to be shot into space on a Redstone rocket. Unlike Gagarin, Shepard had some control over Freedom 7. All America was watching on television; the possibility of a fireball disaster was very real. The entire mission was a game of blind man's bluff. Shepard himself mumbled to the Lord to make sure he didn't "fuck up." According to fellow Mercury astronaut John Glenn, when reporters asked Shepard what he thought about while he was sitting on top of the Mercury Redstone rocket, waiting for liftoff, he had replied, "I wasn't scared, but I was up there looking around, and suddenly I realized I was sitting on top of a rocket built by the lowest bidder."

What worried Cronkite about the *Freedom 7* mission was that it seemed rushed. He felt that NASA (post-Gagarin) was hell-bent on launching Shepard ASAP, putting his life at unnecessary jeopardy, anything to avoid further embarrassment. "We feared that Shepard's flight was premature and that NASA was taking a terrible risk," Cronkite recalled. "I watched that launch with greater trepidation than any of the many space flights I would see in the years to come." Rocketry was so uncertain in 1961 that it wasn't an exaggeration to think that Shepard was going on a possible suicide mission. "We had been watching failure after failure—rockets blowing up on the pad, tumbling from the air a few hundred feet up," Cronkite explained to *The Christian Science Monitor.* "And now, suddenly, a man was going to sit on top of all the fireworks."

CBS News' studio consisted of Cronkite and Socolow in a station wagon parked in Cape Canaveral. Wussler was ensconced in a nearby control trailer. As launch day approached, adrenaline coursed through Cronkite.

Some competitors thought he must have been hopped up on amphetamines. When Shepard was blasted 116 miles up (in a flight that lasted only fifteen minutes) Cronkite, broadcasting from the car, was the aerospace version of Murrow reporting from an in-flight C-47 during World War II. By the time Shepard's capsule was recovered at sea, he was the national hero. Cronkite, full of aw-shucks expressions, was beside himself with patriotic joy, saying excitedly to CBS colleagues, "We did it! We did it!"

As was prearranged, Cronkite nabbed the big Shepard exclusive interview for *Eyewitness* later that very afternoon. Cronkite had trumped NBC, beaten them badly on all accounts. Overnight, Cronkite found his own name attached to Shepard's on wire service stories. One could argue that Shepard had made Cronkite a mega TV star. The Kennedy administration treated Shepard as the modern American paragon in the tradition of Audie Murphy, the highly decorated soldier-turned-actor of World War II. Besides a grand postflight ticker tape parade down Fifth Avenue in New York, Shepard actually accompanied Kennedy to the National Association of Broadcasters (NAB) meeting in Washington, D.C., just three days after splashdown and the day before FCC chairman Newton Minow delivered his excoriating critique of TV as a "vast wasteland" to the same NAB attendees. After ripping into TV executives for running pablum such as rigged game shows and idiotic comedies on the airwaves, Minow singled out the excellence of the Shepard coverage by CBS as the grand exception to the rule. When he praised the "depth of broadcast's contribution to public understanding" of the Mercury program, he was patting Cronkite on the back.

With the excitement of President Kennedy's pledge to put a man on the Moon by decade's end, Cronkite's next major CBS News assignment was the suborbital space flight of *Liberty Bell 7*, on Friday, July 21, 1961, with astronaut Virgil "Gus" Grissom aboard the MR-4 capsule. The flight's purpose was to acclimate man to each stage of a complete space flight and study human physiological reactions to flying in space. NASA wouldn't allow CBS to air live Grissom broadcasting from space. Instead, Cronkite set up shop at Cape Canaveral with a clear view of the Mercury-Redstone booster spacecraft. He was relegated to conversing on air with John "Shorty" Powers of NASA Command and Control. Cronkite didn't care. The important thing was that Stanton, as promised, had chosen him over Harry Reasoner to be the CBS voice of NASA's launch. Cronkite, a nervous wreck, sounded—for fifteen minutes and thirty-seven seconds that evening—like a play-by-play horserace announcer, describing moments with controlled angst.

Cronkite: You just saw the umbilical cord come away now.

Powers: Thirty seconds and counting.

Cronkite: That means that all ground contact with the capsule, with the rocket, has now ended.

Powers: Periscope has retracted—15 seconds and counting. 10, 9, 8, 7, 6, 5, 4, 3, 2, 1 . . . Ignition. Liftoff! Liftoff! Control by pilot.

Cronkite (joyfully): It looks good, it looks like a good launch! Go, baby, go! Straight as an arrow. Should be a little pitch over here, to go into the trajectory. It looks like a good launch!

Powers: Trajectory is A-OK. Flight surgeon reports the pilot is in excellent physical condition. Gus reports he is picking up a little bit of the noise and vibration. The fuel is GO. One and a half Gs. The cabin pressure has settled down to 5. Trajectory reported GO. Cabin pressure holding 5.5. Fuel is GO; two and a half Gs. Oxygen is GO. All systems are GO. And Gus Grissom sounds like a very confident test pilot today.

It's apparent that Powers was the real reporter that evening. Cronkite was only his rah-rah color man. But this arrangement turned out to work in Cronkite's favor. By letting Powers be the dominant voice Cronkite, with a three-dimensional map tracing the path of the space capsule as aid, became deeply trusted at NASA; he was uplifting, controllable, willingly submissive, part of the cold war team, the facile voice of a fellow player. Fate had made them allies. From the Shepard-Grissom missions forward, NASA brought Cronkite into the family fold, giving him national security information no one else received. He was Mr. Full Access Pass.

Cronkite, hitching his wagon to NASA astronauts, was undoubtedly rising in public stature. Space allowed him to reconfigure his career up from puppetry on *The Morning Show* with grace. Fashioning himself as elder statesman of World War II, he scored a coup in late 1961 with an eleven-hour oral history interview with Dwight Eisenhower at his farm in Gettysburg, Pennsylvania. Producer Ed Jones cut it down so CBS could run three hourlong *CBS Reports* prime-time shows. It was Eisenhower's first extended TV appearance since leaving the White House. Cronkite gave the ex-president a lead-in question and let him reminisce. In a *New York Times* review, Jack Gould wrote that Cronkite—and executive producer Fred Friendly, who had received a pro-Cronkite letter from Ike—had brilliantly "captured the phenomenon of Eisenhower like never before." Jack O'Brian of the *New York Journal American* likewise credited Cronkite with conducting a "brilliant historical interview."

Although the forty-six-year-old Cronkite was receiving kudos for his NASA reports and the Eisenhower interview, they were hardly serious investigative journalism. Getting spoon-fed press releases from the U.S. government wasn't Pulitzer-worthy stuff. So Cronkite organized a team at CBS News to look into the dark world of police corruption. Ever since he had worked as a bookie joint announcer in Austin to make extra cash as a University of Texas student, he'd been fascinated by police turning a blind eye to criminal activity. Were cops across America being bought off? How much money was being pocketed by police in collaboration with gambling rings?

Cronkite's CBS News team focused on Boston's police and infiltrated a bookmaking parlor undetected. CBS set up a hidden camera across the street from the joint and was able to show uniformed police officers coming and going but never shutting down the operation. One thousand Bostonians a day visited this illegal establishment. CBS producer Jay McMullen, under the direction of Friendly and Cronkite, smuggled an

8mm camera into the gambling den by concealing it in his lunch box. Hours of footage were shot of customers placing off-track bets. The *CBS Reports* segment, "Biography of a Bookie Joint," aired on November 30, 1961, with Cronkite as host-narrator. (The show was not broadcast in Boston because of pending prosecutions.) The CBS investigation threw the Boston police into disarray. As Cronkite noted to close the program, "At this point, you may be inclined to say, 'Well, those people in Boston certainly have their problems.' Don't deceive yourself. The chances are very great that you have the same problem in your community."

If there was a downside to Cronkite's busy schedule, it was that he was away from home a lot. In the fall of 1961, when the CBS season began, Cronkite's three children—Nancy, twelve; Kathy, eleven; and Chip, four—had to vie for Dad's time with the world of journalism. Betsy had learned that her husband would cancel dinner at the last minute because he needed to be in Scotland to report on a U.S. nuclear base at Holy Loch, or in Camp Century, Greenland, headed toward the North Pole. When at home, Cronkite—according to Lewis H. Lapham of *The Saturday Evening Post*—was competitive beyond belief; he was a "relentless adversary," even when playing Monopoly with the kids. And that was only if spare hours away from CBS could be found. "There's no physical exhaustion," Cronkite said, "because my adrenaline pumps faster the more I do."

Of all the interviews Cronkite conducted in 1961, the one he enjoyed most was a *CBS Reports* conversation with the seventy-two-year-old Walter Lippmann, who had won a Pulitzer Prize for his 1958 "Today and Tomorrow" columns. Cronkite had been an ardent reader of Lippmann since the 1930s. Appearing with Cronkite just days before Christmas, Lippmann assessed the Kennedy administration on foreign policy as identical to the Eisenhower administration, only "thirty years younger." The esteemed journalist–political philosopher, a luminary to Cronkite, embraced the European Common Market, denounced Fidel Castro as "a demented man," and cautioned that the radical right in the United States was becoming fanatically anti-communist. The show was marketed as "Walter Lippmann, Year End." Cronkite lapped up every minute of the exchange. After the frivolity of Mike Todd's elephants, pretending to interview Benedict Arnold on *You Are There*, having to hand off to UNIVAC on Election Night, and co-anchoring *The Morning Show* with Charlemane, Cronkite had earned the honor of getting to talk about the cold war with Mr. Lippmann.

Compared to a two-camera job like the Lippmann interview, covering human spaceflight for television was wildly dramatic and very expensive. But CBS seemed not to be worried about costs now: it had aired the Shepard and Grissom launches without commercials. Even when astronaut John Glenn's *Friendship 7* mission was scrubbed, or postponed, nearly ten times in early 1962, Cronkite and company didn't complain. They knew that when the ominous phrase "T-minus zero" was heard, all Americans would be glued to their TV sets.

CBS had pooled its resources at Cape Canaveral with those of the other networks to cover the Mercury program. For the Glenn mission, it had a team of four hundred correspondents, cameramen, producers, directors, and technicians to shoot Glenn from all angles. Cronkite knew that Glenn's orbit was going to be a hell of a story—especially for CBS, because it had assigned more resources to all-things-NASA than any other news source. When Glenn first met Cronkite in 1959 at Cape Canaveral, he was flabbergasted by how knowledgeable the broadcaster was about the intricacies of Project Mercury. "Space travel was so new that most people didn't know how to relate to it," Glenn recalled. "They understood an Indy driver because they knew how to turn a steering wheel right or left. Walter's gift was helping the public understand the science of space. He was a teacher. His CBS broadcasts were the main factor in the public understanding my mission."

After seven postponements and what seemed like a trillion difficulties, the big day finally arrived. The clouds cleared and the wind dropped, prompting Mercury Control to at last greenlight the Glenn mission. On February 20, 1962, with over 40 million American homes tuned in at 9:17 a.m. EST, and with Glenn aboard the highly complex, phone booth–sized *Friendship 7* capsule, the rocket lifted off like a heat-seeking missile. Excitement overcame Cronkite, who continued to broadcast for the next ten hours under the banner "Man in Orbit: The Flight of John Glenn." There weren't live cameras aboard any of the Mercury spacecraft (as there would be in later Apollo missions), so once the rocket blasted off, Cronkite engaged in what one CBS hand called "a glorified radio broadcast," appearing on air 140 times. He tied together CBS's coverage of the event beautifully. At the CBS News control center, only 8,800 feet away from the Mercury launchpad, was the indefatigable Cronkite. As Glenn circled Earth three times during his four-hour, fifty-five-minute, twenty-three-second flight, Cronkite became the voice of what *The New York Times* called the orbit that "united the nation and the world in a common sharing of the excitement, tension, and drama" created by TV's coverage.

During the marathon coverage, Cronkite alerted CBS viewers to the fact that the capsule's heat shield had come loose and adjustments would have to be made to the craft's trajectory on splashdown. When he landed, Glenn, a lieutenant colonel, the so-called Clean Marine, became the biggest exploration hero of the century since Charles Lindbergh in 1927. "The best moment," Cronkite wrote in a syndicated column, "was when Shorty Powers announced from Mercury Control: 'We have a hale and hearty astronaut.'"

The Glenn orbital flight and safe return was Cronkite's grandest moment yet in journalism. The broadcast set him free. Basking in the glory, Cronkite packed his pipe and puffed with contentment. Whether it was talking to members of the Glenn family from the astronaut's hometown of New Concord, Ohio, or to employees of the aircraft company in St. Louis where the capsule was built, Cronkite was a scoop machine. And Bob Wussler was always a step ahead of the press pack with graphics. At one point or another on that historic day, Cronkite spoke with correspondents in London, Paris, and Moscow. For the Glenn coverage, Cronkite was on CBS for nine hours and fifteen minutes. "When President Kennedy comes to pin a medal on the hero," an amazed Alistair Cooke wrote in *The Manchester Guardian*, "he might have a ribbon ready for Mr. Cronkite, who made engrossing sense of a miracle otherwise beyond the comprehension of the hundred million Americans who are watching."

Other "verbal journalists," as *Newsweek* called them, did a great job covering Glenn's three orbits. They have been insufficiently recognized. On CBS Radio, Dallas Townsend was exceptional. ABC's Jules Bergman, who had spent 1960 on a science fellowship at Columbia University, had a fine sense of the astrophysics involved with the *Friendship 7* launch. NBC's Peter Hackes and Roy Neal had done their NASA homework just as diligently as Cronkite. At CBS, Charles Von Fremd was solid on color commentary. But it was Cronkite whom *Newsweek* declared the "grand panjandrum" of "Glenn mania" for his prudent observations infused with glee. When the air force was running the space race, TV cameras were frowned upon. But the Glenn mission proved once and for all that George M. Low, the manager of the Apollo Spacecraft Program in Houston, was right: the more TV cameras trained on the launchpad, the better. CBS cameras were even ensconced on the aircraft carriers U.S.S. *Randolph* and U.S.S. *Forrestal*, hoping to catch the initial glimpse of *Friendship 7*'s billowing parachutes. "I think we have a lot more knowledge than the newspaper reporters," Cronkite said in defense of his ilk, "because we have to have it spontaneously—the newspaper guy has time to check it out."

Other CBS technical touches differentiated the Tiffany Network from ABC and NBC. Don Hewitt, for instance, had developed the brazen idea of erecting a giant twenty-by-thirty-foot Eidophor television screen on top of the central mezzanine in New York City's Grand Central Terminal so commuters could watch John Glenn on CBS. (This was the building from which most CBS News telecasts originated.) And the Hewitt scheme worked. There was Cronkite, Godzilla-sized, broadcasting from Cape Canaveral on the giant screen, with commuters enraptured by the Glenn mission, waiting until the very last second to board their trains to Westchester County, New York, or Fairfield County, Connecticut. Even John Wayne or Elizabeth Taylor on a drive-in movie screen wasn't much more outsized than Cronkite at Grand Central. CBS News had created a communal aspect during the Glenn mission that was then unprecedented in broadcasting. As NBC News veteran James Kitchell said, the big-screen stunt was "a one-up" on his network.

To Helen Cronkite, it was ironic; her son, who had failed physics at the University of Texas, was explaining Glenn's flight to millions of Americans live from the Cape. The college dropout was now teacher to the nation. During Glenn's reentry into Earth's atmosphere—those minutes when the NASA tracking stations lost contact with him—thousands of people watched the big screen in breathless anticipation. "The cheer that went up when I said that Glenn was safe and sound and back from space was deafening," Cronkite recalled. "It was just what I was after." Glenn had taken the country along on the happiest ride of the cold war, and CBS News milked the publicity for all it was worth. It ran a special titled *Man in Orbit* that covered Glenn speaking to a joint session of Congress live. The network even aired his New York City ticker tape parade, preempting soap operas. And *CBS News Extra* devoted three segments to the Glenn mission. Cronkite was an active participant in all of the hoopla. While on his way to the studio one afternoon, he was quoted telling a reporter, "Can you imagine how great it would be to say to an audience, 'Good evening, ladies and gentlemen, this is Walter Cronkite reporting for CBS direct from the surface of the Moon?'"

Call it a lingering U.S. Eighth Air Force complex, but Cronkite, the American booster, thought Shepard, Grissom, and Glenn were good for cold war America—and, it shouldn't be overlooked, they were helping to advance his career at CBS. By throwing away the script at key junctures during the Glenn mission, letting his enthusiasm bubble, Cronkite outshone the competition by a country mile. The frenzied ticker tape parade thrown for Glenn in New York nine days after the mission proved that America, too, saw the astronauts as its new heroes, that "instead of looking down despondently, we could look up at the stars."

Cecil Smith, writing in the *Los Angeles Times* about Cronkite as the voice of NASA, surmised that Glenn's three orbits were "quite possibly the finest excuse for television's existence that the little tube has ever offered." Looking fit and feisty, Cronkite soared to TV newsman fame on the exhaust of John Glenn's Redstone rocket. TV journalism as an art was almost virgin territory, for the simple reason that the medium was so new. Therefore Cronkite could claim to be a pioneer in his own right. "This is not just Cronkite the old reportorial warhorse fleeing the confinement of his New York headquarters," Smith wrote. "It's part of a major design to do more and more of the CBS newscasts from remote locations."

CBS grew so determined to showcase Cronkite as the media star of the Glenn mission that it published a colorful souvenir book titled *Seven Days*. Cronkite was treated as the new Murrow, the voice of space, the resplendent broadcaster John Glenn's mother wanted to meet. The trifecta of Shepard, Grissom, and Glenn had transformed Cronkite's career in dramatic ways. "At

NASA," Glenn recalled, "we all took to calling Walter 'Mr. Space.'"

What space exploration had going for it from a TV perspective wasn't astronauts squabbling, but rather the high-stakes drama of liftoff and recovery. Cronkite was a master at narrating those nail-biting moments with the right mixture of reverence, exclamatory judgments, and long pauses. CBS helped him out by using artists' animations and full-scale models. Cronkite, using his newfound gravitas, worked to persuade Low of NASA to allow astronauts to bring TV cameras into space. Seeing color photos of Earth from space was a breathtaking experience. All the networks benefited from Cronkite's pestering impatience when NASA ultimately ordered astronaut Gordon Cooper to send back live pictures from space during his May 1963 Mercury mission. Cooper orbited Earth twenty-two times and logged more time in space than all the previous space ventures combined (thirty-four hours, nineteen minutes, and forty-nine seconds, traveling an astounding 546,167 miles).

By 1963 there was a plethora of Project Mercury enthusiasts in America, but Cronkite was the first among equals. He publicly embraced Kennedy's moon pledge with the ardor of a convert. He often described space in grand historical and even biblical terms.

Understanding that the American people were keen to beat the Soviet Union in space, Cronkite, the veteran sports broadcaster, cloaked his reporting in almost jingoistic, high-octane nationalistic, anti-communist rhetoric. He was more NASA collaborator than reporter. Yet there was something wholesome and country-fried and urbane—all at once—about his ability to broadcast space travel. Cronkite, the tech-geek, knew before most that satellites would soon revolutionize the communications industry in astounding ways. "Just as Noah once sent out a dove to explore an unknown and dangerous landscape, man is now sending mechanical birds to feel out the perilous highway from here to the Moon," he said on *CBS Reports* with Glenn looking on. "What we are hearing now is the curious song of those birds. They're artificial satellites wandering through Space."

Walter Cronkite braving a Missouri snowstorm, circa 1918. While his father was in France serving in the Army during World War I, Walter and his mother lived with his maternal grandparents in Kansas City. *(Whitehurst Photos)*

Helen Cronkite with her son, Walter, circa 1921. *(Whitehurst Photos)*

A six-year-old Walter Cronkite riding in a goat-drawn carriage in 1922. *(Whitehurst Photos)*

Cronkite as a young man (undated). An only child, he was an undistinguished student, but a voracious reader. *(Whitehurst Photos)*

The Purple Pup student newspaper for April 24, 1929, featuring an article by Walter Cronkite, then twelve years old. *The Pup* was published at Lanier Middle School in Houston, Texas. *(Dolph Briscoe Center for American History, the University of Texas at Austin)*

A family outing to the seaside city of Galveston, Texas, in 1930. *Bottom row:* Walter sitting between his grandparents, Matilda and Edward C. Fritsche. *Top row:* Walter's parents, Helen and Walter Cronkite Sr. *(Whitehurst Photos)*

Cronkite on the day of his graduation from San Jacinto High School in Houston, Texas, 1933.
(Whitehurst Photos)

COMPLETE INTERNATIONAL NEWS WIRE SERVICE

THE DAILY TEXAN

The First College Daily in the South

AUSTIN, TEXAS, FRIDAY, MARCH 22, 1935   SIX PAGES TODAY

Miss Stein Not Out for Show, But Knows What She Knows

Editor's note: Gertrude Stein arrived in Austin unexpectedly last night. Because of the widespread controversy over the works of Miss Stein and the author herself.

By WALTER CRONKITE

A cow may be a cow a cow, but no writer that had interviewed Miss Gertrude Stein, that had chatted with her for any length of time over two minutes, would ever again write such an inane review of the works of one of the most publicized of modern writers.

She is genuine—the real thing in person. Her thinking is certainly straightforward; her speech is the same.

She enters wholeheartedly into any conversation. She is extremely modern. She enjoys to talk, and her enthusiasm is no private thing. It spreads to anyone with whom she comes in contact.

We imposed upon her at a late hour last night. She was cheerful and eager to answer our questions, to throw a little light on the person they call Stein. She did just that; perhaps a little more. Dressed in a mannish blouse, a tweed skirt, a peculiar but attractive vest affair, and comfortable looking shoes, Miss Stein appeared much more of the woman than do the pictures that currently circulate. She strokes her close cropped hair with a continuous back to front movement. Even this nervous gesture is easily accepted by her present company.

The conversation last night ranged from the Walter Winchell comment that the most beautiful girls in America are in Dallas, to the possibilities of another war.

"A writer isn't anything but contemporary. The trouble is that the people are living Twentieth Century and thinking Nineteenth Century," Miss Stein said in answering a query concerning the attitude of Americans toward her works.

"Why the fact was evident up at Hockaday (where she stayed in Dallas). The girls of from fourteen to seventeen understood perfectly, but their teachers did not," she continued. "You must represent in your work what I call the time-sense of your period."

Miss Stein was greatly interested in the Junior Prom idea.

Her principal remark was "isn't that peculiar." Her interest turned toward the psychological quirk that caused the establishment of the tradition.

Miss Stein attributed the depression to the psychology of the people. The depression is more moral than actual," she observed. "No longer the people think they are depressed, the depression is over."

Miss Alice B. Toklas, Miss Stein's traveling companion whose title is not "secretary," according to the author, was present. This lady who walked in on Miss Stein twenty-five years ago and has been with her ever since, has absorbed much of the charm possessed by the most famous of the pair.

This is Miss Stein's first trip to Texas, and she seems to like it very well. Her comment was that "this is a beautiful big State of yours." She liked Dallas, too, but was disappointed that they insisted on showing her oil wells.

"What are your observations on the war rumors in Europe?" she was asked.

"Before I left, those who know in France didn't believe that there would be a war," she answered. "But then war is just like anything else. When people get tired of peace they will have war and when they get tired of war they will have peace. Don't you, when you have been good for a long time, want to be bad?"

To her question there was no verbal answer.

"There are a great many adults who are now writing as I do. When 'Three Lives' was first published people said it was not understandable, but now I don't think there is anyone who couldn't read and understand every word of it," Miss Stein remarked in returning to the subject of her own works.

The author explained her reason for staying so long in France, and so long away from this country, by the simple statement that she lacks the initiative to do much moving around.

Miss Stein is to appear at Hogg Memorial Auditorium for a lecture tonight at 8:15 o'clock. Miss Toklas will be with her.

On March 22, 1935, *The Daily Texan*, the student newspaper at the University of Texas, led with a Cronkite scoop: his interview with literary figure Gertrude Stein, who was then visiting the campus. According to his article, he found her to be "genuine—the real thing in person. Her thinking is certainly straightforward; her speech is the same." (*Dolph Briscoe Center for American History, the University of Texas at Austin*)

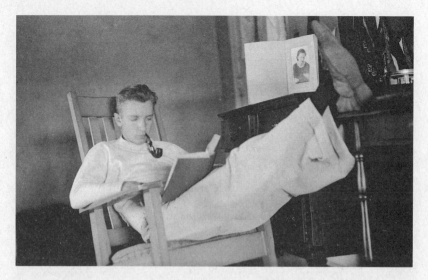

Cronkite at college, in a photograph taken for the *Cactus*, the yearbook of the University of Texas. The picture was probably taken in 1935, the year Cronkite left school. The young woman in the open photo book is Cronkite's high school girlfriend, Cornelia "Bit" Winter. *(Dolph Briscoe Center for American History, the University of Texas at Austin)*

"Walter Wilcox," better known as Walter Cronkite, preparing for a 1936 broadcast at KCMO, a Kansas City radio station. Cronkite was the sports director at the station, where a bright young woman named Betsy Maxwell soon started working as an advertising copywriter. They began dating and were married four years later. *(Whitehurst Photos)*

Cronkite during a 1937 radio interview with Beryl Clark, future star quarterback for the University of Oklahoma football team. Throughout the 1937 season, Cronkite broadcast Oklahoma football games for WKY, in Oklahoma City. (*Whitehurst Photos*)

Walter and Betsy Cronkite, shortly after their 1940 wedding. (*Dolph Briscoe Center for American History, the University of Texas at Austin*)

Cronkite at work for United Press during World War II while wearing the uniform authorized by the Army for credentialed correspondents. After the United States joined the Allies, the UP named Cronkite, then twenty-five, a war correspondent. Throughout the war, Cronkite sought assignments at the vanguard of the action. *(Whitehurst Photos)*

Cronkite *(right)*, ready for flight, with the crew of a B-26 bomber at an air base in England on February 9, 1944. Cronkite was then preparing to join another crew on a mission to destroy a German V-1 rocket base in France. *With Cronkite, from left to right:* Ceibert C. Bragg (flight engineer), Enrique Zepeda (tail gunner), Arthur W. Brand (radio operator), Norman M. Rosner (bombardier), and Jack W. Nye (pilot). *(Whitehurst Photos)*

Cronkite *(left)* with fellow United Press correspondents during the Nuremberg Trials. *(Dolph Briscoe Center for American History, the University of Texas at Austin)*

Poster depicting CBS television newscasters, circa 1950–1959. This picture, drawn by Joe Kaufman over the caption, "America's Most Celebrated Reporters," shows Cronkite in a white shirt at the lower left. *(Dolph Briscoe Center for American History, the University of Texas at Austin)*

President Harry Truman with Cronkite during a televised tour of the newly renovated White House on May 3, 1952, that all three major networks cooperated to broadcast. (*Whitehurst Photos*)

An advertisement for the CBS television series *You Are There*, hosted by Cronkite. The show staged re-creations of major events in world history, allowing Cronkite's correspondents to step into the action and "interview" famous personalities from Galileo to Benedict Arnold. It originally ran from 1953 to 1957. (*Dolph Briscoe Center for American History, the University of Texas at Austin*)

Walter Cronkite standing in front of a weather map while holding the *Farmers' Almanac* during a *Morning Show* broadcast on June 1, 1954. *(CBS Photo Archive)*

Walter Cronkite on CBS's *The Morning Show* with the puppet Charlemane, circa 1954. The lion puppet, created by Bill and Cora Baird, introduced musical numbers on the show and also discussed current events with Cronkite. *(Dolph Briscoe Center for American History, the University of Texas at Austin)*

Walter Cronkite at Washington's WTOP television studio in 1954. After trying to establish himself in radio during the late 1940s, Cronkite joined the staff of WTOP-TV, a CBS affiliate, in 1950. He would stay until 1954. (*Dolph Briscoe Center for American History, the University of Texas at Austin*)

CBS composite photo, highlighting Cronkite's coverage of the space program. He is shown with six members of *Mercury* 7 (undated). (*Dolph Briscoe Center for American History, the University of Texas at Austin*)

Doris Duke, heiress to a tobacco fortune, with Walter and Betsy Cronkite at a party. The Cronkites were active members of New York's social life (undated). *(Dolph Briscoe Center for American History, the University of Texas at Austin)*

Cronkite explaining the *Explorer 1* mission to CBS viewers in 1958. *Explorer 1* was a hastily constructed response to *Sputnik*, the Soviets' 1957 earth-orbiting satellite. Because nearly every concept surrounding *Explorer 1* was new to American viewers, Cronkite used models to clarify the principles of aerospace. *(CBS Photo Archive)*

From the left: Eric Sevareid, Walter Cronkite, and Edward R. Murrow at the news desk during CBS's election-night coverage on November 8, 1960. (*CBS Photo Archive*)

On May 4, 1961, Cronkite rehearsed in his station wagon for CBS's coverage of *Freedom 7*, which would be launched at Cape Canaveral, Florida, on May 5. *Freedom 7* would take Alan Shepard on America's first manned space flight: a fifteen-minute orbit of the earth. (*Whitehurst Photos*)

Cronkite covering the *Freedom 7* manned space flight on May 5, 1961. Viewers worried along with him that Shepard might not survive the return to earth. Ultimately, the flight was a success, giving America— and Cronkite—a future in space exploration. (*CBS Photo Archive*)

Cronkite's longhand notes on astronaut Gordon Cooper's space flight on the thirty-four-hour *Faith 7* mission, May 22–23, 1963. (*Dolph Briscoe Center for American History, the University of Texas at Austin*)

Cronkite interviewed President John F. Kennedy for the first thirty-minute broadcast of the *CBS Evening News* on September 3, 1963. Previously, the program had been fifteen minutes in length. *(Whitehurst Photos)*

Cronkite, in a moment of undisguised emotion, having just announced the death of President John F. Kennedy on November 22, 1963. Cronkite was dubbed "healer of the nation" in the wake of his exemplary coverage. *(CBS Photo Archive)*

Cronkite met former president Dwight D. Eisenhower in France in 1963 to film "D-Day Plus 20 Years: Eisenhower Returns to Normandy." The program aired on CBS in 1964 and was repeated on national television many times afterward to commemorate the D-day landings. Cronkite's softball interviewing style suited the occasion, turning the program into a special conversation with the former supreme Allied commander. (*Whitehurst Photos*)

Cronkite interviewing Barry Goldwater in 1964. A longtime Arizona senator, Goldwater was the Republican nominee for president; he ultimately lost by a wide margin to Lyndon Johnson. CBS News management warned Cronkite not to let his anti-Goldwater feelings seep into the *CBS Evening News*. (*Dolph Briscoe Center for American History, the University of Texas at Austin*)

PART IV

Anchorman

16.

Anchorman of Camelot

FREQUENT FLYING—KENNEDY MAGIC—THE AMERI-
CA'S CUP GOES NEWPORT—CAPTAIN CRONKITE—
WHO SPEAKS FOR BIRMINGHAM?—JOCKEY FOR
ANCHOR—BOTCHING THE CLOSE—WHIPPING NBC—
THE EDWARDS ERA ENDS—ENTER RICHARD
SALANT—CRONKITE TAKES THE HELM—DON
HEWITT TAKES CHARGE—APRIL 16, 1962—TELSTAR
REVOLUTION—BILL SMALL ARRIVES IN D.C.—VOICE
OF THE CUBAN MISSILE CRISIS—MARTIN LUTHER
KING'S DREAM—THE THIRTY-MINUTE EXPERIMENT—
INTERVIEWING JFK IN HYANNIS PORT—BIGFOOTING
ROBERT PIERPOINT—THAT'S THE WAY IT IS

To Cronkite, daring was the vital element of *being.*
Once, when he left New York for Cape Canaveral
to film a space-themed episode of *The Twentieth*

Century, he ended up instead on remote Ascension Island, located off the coast of Africa in the equatorial waters of the South Atlantic Ocean. When Cronkite got situated on the island, he called home and spoke to Betsy.

"Say," he said, "don't you realize where I am?"

"No," she said. "Where are you?"

"I'm in Ascension," he answered, pleased to show off his intrepid daring.

"Wonderful," the space-minded Betsy replied. "How many times have you been around?"

Cronkite wanted to be the go-to guy who orbited all things JFK. Working with CBS producer Les Midgley on *Eyewitness*, he understood that any Kennedy-tinged story generated excellent ratings for the network.* In the early 1960s, every verbal aside, press conference, camera zoom shot, and line of give-and-take dialogue that President Kennedy uttered was gobbled up by millions of curious TV viewers. Cronkite hoped his Friday show, which aired from 10:30 to 11:30 p.m. EST, could

---

* *Eyewitness* originally aired in 1959 as *Eyewitness to History*, with Charles Kuralt serving as host. Walter Cronkite took over the show in 1961, when the program's name was shortened to *Eyewitness*, and hosted it until 1962. Charles Collingwood acted as the show's emcee from 1962 until the end of its run in 1963.

showcase the Kennedy family. Not only was Robert F. Kennedy the U.S. attorney general, but Edward M. Kennedy had been chosen to fill his brother's vacated seat in the U.S. Senate. "Walter wanted to ride on the Kennedys' coattails," Andy Rooney recalled. "Every time Kennedy was on *Eyewitness*, the ratings went through the roof. If he did something on Alabama tenant farmers or Charles DeGaulle, nobody seemed to care."

David Halberstam, in *The Powers That Be*, rightly called Kennedy the "first television president." Kennedy's charismatic breakthrough in the 1960 presidential debates had made him an electronic superstar, one Cronkite planned to capitalize on. All White House galas, foreign trips, holiday parties, and yacht outings were shot by CBS News cameramen. Ever since NBC News broadcast the JFK inaugural parade in color, CBS News had grown determined to dominate the ongoing Kennedy story. Cronkite knew that if he wanted to eventually replace Douglas Edwards, whose position was tenuous as long as CBS News was second to NBC News, as anchorman, he would have to win the Kennedy scoop sweepstakes.

During the Kennedy years, not all U.S. viewers lived in a city with three network television stations. If you lived in Aroostook County in Maine or

Plaquemines Parish in Louisiana (or thousands of rural areas like them), you didn't *choose* CBS over NBC, for there was no choice available. You took what your rabbit-eared antenna could pull in, which, in the case of those two areas, was CBS. Advertisers wanted to sell hair products and first cars to the all important eighteen- to twenty-five-year-old demographic. But as TV reception improved, consumers could choose a network brand in the same way they chose a car model or soda. Young people, polls showed, liked Kennedy far better than stiff GOP types like Richard Nixon and Nelson Rockefeller. The CBS snag was that Cronkite, a network broadcaster since 1950, wasn't considered "Kennedy cool" in 1962; he was still Eisenhower plaid, seemingly believing that what was good for General Motors was good for America.

As Cronkite became a serious contender for the anchorman job of the proposed *CBS Evening News* in 1962—in competition with four or five others to replace Douglas Edwards—he retired from his long-time hobby, auto racing. CBS management didn't like having Cronkite, who had gotten in a car wreck in Tennessee, unable to even carry a life insurance policy. You couldn't build a TV franchise around a corpse. Paley might have tolerated Cronkite's speed racing hobby if it brought him White House access, but the blue-blooded Kennedys preferred yachting around Martha's Vineyard and Rhode Island Sound to the smell of diesel at the Daytona 500. With his physician telling him speed racing was bad for his heart, and possessing far too much energy for golf, the universally accepted pastime for upper-class white men, Cronkite needed to excel at a different sport. Maybe, he thought, his passion for sailing—first developed in Carmel, New York—could grow into the more challenging sport of yachting from Maine to Cape Cod to Newport on the Atlantic Ocean à la President Kennedy. His friends the William F. Buckleys and James Micheners and Bill Harbachs had already taken to mother ocean . . . why not the Cronkites?

Cronkite and Midgley understood that the Kennedys had turned Cape Cod into a lifestyles-of-the-rich-and-famous playground. Their challenge was finding a way for *Eyewitness* to capitalize on what became known as Camelot.

Born in Salt Lake City, Midgley was first hired by CBS News in the mid-1950s. A gangly Ichabod Crane–like character, Midgley, a Mormon, was a close friend of tycoon Howard Hughes—no one understood why. He championed the idea of the Kennedys becoming part of a proto-reality show. His thinking went as follows: President Kennedy and Jacqueline

Bouvier had been married in ultra-exclusive Newport, Rhode Island, and held their reception at Newport's Hammersmith Farm. In the fall of 1962, the America's Cup race was to be held off Newport. The challenger was *Gretel*, a twelve-meter sloop owned by Sir Frank Packer, an Australian media mogul. Its skipper was Jock Sturrock. The New York Yacht Club would defend the Cup with the *Weatherly*, captained by Bus Mosbacher. The America's Cup defenders in those days were all wooden twelve-meter sloops, about sixty feet long, built at the Minneford Boat Yard in City Island, New York.

Midgley decided that CBS, riding the wave of Cronkite's Squaw Valley and Rome Olympics coverage in 1960, could cover the America's Cup for *Eyewitness* by spicing it up with Kennedy magic. Together Cronkite and Midgley developed a concept for the Friday show that combined the America's Cup drama with the public's fascination with the Kennedy family, one that would look at picturesque Newport and its famous "400" families—including the Vanderbilts and the Astors—and their mansions. Because Midgley knew that Lew Wood—a former U.S. marine from Indiana who started broadcasting for WDZ radio (the third-oldest station in America) in Decatur, Illinois, after graduating from Purdue University—*loved* sailing, he got the assignment to work with Cronkite for the *Eyewitness* episode to air in September.

Wood, with ace cameraman Walter Dombrow in tow, traveled to Newport numerous times to do advance work on the race. If *Eyewitness* could turn the America's Cup into a sporting event as popular as the Kentucky Derby or Indianapolis 500 every year, CBS News would have an advertising cash cow on its hands. Dombrow and Wood chartered a Bertram Moppie powerboat and filmed B-roll shots of sleek yachts and sunsets. Back in 1962, there was no bridge between Jonestown and Newport, so it was necessary to take the ferry across. Having given up auto racing, Cronkite began to seriously eye sailing as a new recreational activity for him to master. "Once Cronkite came to Newport with his director Vinny Walters, he fell madly in love with the whole yachting life," Wood recalled. "I met them at the Newport side of the ferry, got them settled in our rooming house, and provided press passes for them for the next day to get on the Press Boat to watch the race."

Wood later boasted that he "turned Cronkite onto the yachting world"; that perception was true enough. Born with a profound appreciation of the sea, Cronkite told Wood that once he was financially sound, with $100,000 in his savings account, he was going to gallivant around Cape Cod like a Kennedy. Eventually, he would own one of the most handsome ketches on the Atlantic seaboard. For the time being, however, all he could afford was a twenty-two-foot Electra sloop to sail on Long Island Sound he named *Chipper*. He had purchased it at a New York Boat Show. Cronkite claimed that if he became CBS News anchorman—replacing Edwards—the pay raise would allow him to upgrade his modest vessel to a twenty-eight-foot Triton, then a mauve double-ender. And who knew? Maybe one day he could commission his own magnificent yacht, built to his personal specifications, and name it *Wyntje* (WIN-tee), in honor of a lovely Dutch ancestor and "all the women who've made Cronkite men happy in the New World—in whatever capacity."

CBS News producer-director Don Hewitt was hungry to have a post-Edwards anchorman with grit, one bloodthirsty for combat against the dreaded NBC News; the analogy he liked emanated from the rope-line tug-of-war where you put your biggest and baddest dude at the far end to anchor the defense. The soft-spoken Edwards didn't fit the billing. Having started out in radio broadcasting at age fifteen in Alabama, he rose to work side by side with Murrow in London from 1943 to 1945 and became the host of *Douglas Edwards with the News*. But in early 1962, his CBS superiors were ready with the hook. The big question at CBS News was not just who would replace Edwards at the city desk, but also Murrow on the freedom march.

A queue of talented broadcasters formed while Edwards logged his last weeks as anchor. Cronkite assumed that Howard K. Smith would get the nod. When President Kennedy summoned Murrow to run USIA, Smith was dispatched to Birmingham, Alabama, to work on a searing *CBS Reports* exposé about Jim Crow bigotry. While Cronkite had latched on to NASA, Smith was all about Montgomery, Birmingham, Little Rock, and the Freedom Rides. On May 18, 1961, Smith had seen Birmingham sheriff "Bull" Connor's police force pummel civil rights workers with clubs. An incensed Smith lashed out at the segregationist bullies responsible for the bloody melee. In late 1961, he replaced Murrow as host of the documentary *Who Speaks for Birmingham?*

There was nothing objective about Smith's excellent documentary of the white-black divide in Birmingham; he clearly championed civil rights activists over the Big Police. He had put his finger on many Southern boils, larded with hatred, and then lanced them. It was painful television. Smith, quoting British philosopher Edmund Burke, ended *Who Speaks for Birmingham?* by saying: "All that is necessary for the triumph of evil is for good men to do nothing."

CBS News president Frank Stanton, CBS News vice president Blair Clark, and other executives were livid over Smith's one-sided reporting. The provocative Burke line—a powerful documentary close—was deleted from the TV broadcast. An intransigent Smith, refusing to be bullied by Dr. Stanton and insisting that moral judgments were imperative in broadcasting news in a democracy, defiantly read his uncensored text on his CBS radio show. A confrontation with CBS management ensued. Who the hell did Smith think he was? Martin Luther King Jr.? The new Murrow?

Smith wrote a high-minded memo for CBS management about the need for subjective morality in journalism. It was the ultimate indictment of Paley as a money-driven millionaire. The finical Paley dismissed Smith's argument, saying, "I have heard all this junk before. If this is what you believe, you had better go somewhere else." When push came to shove, CBS News needed bigoted Southerners and fair-minded northern viewers alike. Paley, like any corporate owner with stockholders, didn't want to alienate either vast demographic. Objective journalism was about not pissing anyone off.

Smith's forced resignation from CBS News in late 1961 served notice to all of Paley's headstrong news employees that the high-and-mighty days of Murrow's

ACLU-infused mania were over. Getting Smith out of the way was, ironically, a tremendous career booster for Cronkite. A popular story that circulated around CBS News held that Cronkite once called in sick on an Election Night (midterm) with one of his colds. Howard K. Smith was chosen to take his place. "Within fifteen minutes," Smith wrote in his memoir *Events Leading Up to My Death*, "Walter was in the studio sucking on cough drops and sending me back to the Southern boards. Murrow told me that as author of his recovery I should send him a doctor's bill." Now Smith, his primary competitor in the race for the anchor job, had dropped like a fly.

With Smith gone, Eric Sevareid aimed for Edwards's job. Craving Murrow-like fame and the quantifiable ability to be heard and heeded, Sevareid undoubtedly had the stature for the post. The problem was that Sevareid—nicknamed "Eric the Red" by GOP conservatives—was star-crossed. No one went after Joe McCarthy on CBS Radio with the verve and vengeance of Sevareid. And career-wise, no media personality paid for it more. There was about Sevareid the aura of an elitist in a country that honored Lowell Thomas and Walt Disney, not fourth-estate hauteur. If Sevareid was perceived as a Minnesota know-it-all who read too much Camus and Dostoyevsky to be trusted in the

Edwards chair by conservative CBS affiliate owners, then Cronkite was the prototypical Middle American straight from the pages of Sinclair Lewis.

As the viable candidates for anchorman dwindled to a few, Charles Collingwood—the model for the Joel McCrea character in the 1944 Billy Wilder movie *Foreign Correspondent*—was also considered by Dr. Stanton to replace Edwards. The CBS foreign correspondent's wardrobe proved problematic, though. While Cronkite always dressed like a Missouri businessman who shopped at Harry Truman's favored off-the-rack Kansas City haberdashery, Collingwood usually dressed like the Gieves & Hawkes–tailored Prince of Wales. Some colleagues were quizzical about Collingwood's showboating style. Others were even rude—he clearly had never spent any time picking Iowa corn or working on a Detroit assembly line. Depending on how the stars were aligned, Collingwood would dress in eye-catching Vincent Price capes or gray kid gloves or even wear jazz age spats on his shoes. In a perfect world, it wouldn't matter if the TV anchorman were something of a Beau Brummell. But in Collingwood's case, his dapper clothes hinted toward his love of Russian caviar and French espionage. To an average CBS affiliate owner in Toledo or Topeka, he just was not relatable.

While the anchorman guessing game went on at CBS News that February, seismic shake-ups were afoot at the network. Paley fired Sig Mickelson (Cronkite's original CBS cheerleader) and his news director, John Day; it was a brutal double dismissal attributed to NBC News' clobbering of CBS News in the ratings at the 1960 conventions. All Cronkite could do was duck for cover as it rained pink slips. "Sig had begun at ground-zero and built a very good, worldwide television news organization," Howard K. Smith explained. "He had not yet been able to get Cronkite named anchorman on the evening news in place of Douglas Edwards, which would bring a new day at CBS, but he would later be credited as 'the man who invented Walter Cronkite.'"

The unlikely Richard "Dick" Salant was appointed by Paley to replace Mickelson. Sensing his neck was next in the noose, Cronkite was "shocked" and "alarmed" that Salant—a Harvard-trained corporate lawyer from New York City without any journalism experience—had been chosen over the hard-news veteran Mickelson. The mismatch was self-evident. "We were naturally terribly worried," Cronkite recalled years later of Salant. "A nonprofessional, a man who as far as we knew had never set foot in a newsroom."

During World War II, Salant had served in the navy as a lieutenant commander. Because he was a Harvard

Law School graduate (class of '38) with great promise, the prestigious Manhattan law firm Rosenman, Goldmark, Colin & Kaye hired him. CBS News was a client. Paley stole Salant away from the firm in 1952. A stickler for detail, allergic to controversy, and a fervent advocate of First Amendment rights, Salant, given the title of vice president of CBS News, was anti-glitz, the exterminator of hyperbole in reporting. For CBS on-air reporters such as Cronkite, Sevareid, and Collingwood, Salant was too legalistic, nitpicking adjectives out of scripts, always bare-knuckling down to basics. At a luncheon, the three broadcasting talents pleaded with Dr. Stanton not to empower Salant. The on-air talent insisted that the middle-aged lawyer was a legalist sponge who would drain all the journalistic drama from their broadcasts to avoid legal controversy. Stanton disregarded their concerns. "We were," Cronkite recalled, "all depressed."

With Salant as president, Cronkite feared that the Edwards post might be given to someone unexpected. Cronkite didn't know whether his paranoia proved his sanity or pointed to the edge of psychosis. The grapevine hinted that forty-three-year-old Mike Wallace, whose gritty experience as a newsman dated back to the 1940s, when he was a reporter for the *Chicago Sun*, would be Salant's Anointed One. Somehow Cronkite construed that Wallace's having been born in President Kennedy's hometown of Brookline, Massachusetts, was a feather in the cap with Salant for covering the New Frontier on CBS News. Utter nonsense. Otherwise, Wallace's résumé was loosely similar to Cronkite's own: a naval communications officer in World War II; a news reporter for WMAQ in Chicago; and an on-again, off-again broadcaster for CBS News since 1951. But Wallace was also the most aggressive newsman Cronkite had ever encountered. Only when Wallace got his own TV shows—*Night Beat* (1956–1957); *The Mike Wallace Interview* (1957–1959); and *PM East* (1961–1962)—did Cronkite realize how starkly opposite their core personalities were. Cronkite used the butter knife when conducting interviews with politicians, while Wallace had a penchant for wielding the double ax. If Cronkite was squeamish about blood, Wallace was a regular Count Dracula. Another plus for Wallace was that he had hosted a radio show in Detroit with Edwards in the 1940s. The program was sponsored by the Cunningham Drugstore, and the Wallace-Edwards team became fondly known as the "Cunningham Aces." A paranoid Cronkite thought Salant might try to spark an Aces reunion to butt heads with Huntley-Brinkley.

CBS News correspondent Charles Kuralt was also a contender of some dimension. He favorably reminded many people of Brinkley, a fellow Tar Heel whose life script had a Thomas Wolfe–esque follow-the-lonesome-train-to-New York halo about it. In 1948, at the age of fourteen, Kuralt was named one of four National Voice of Democracy winners. It had all been uphill for him ever since. In later years, Cronkite used to joke that if a folksy-a-thon were ever held, Kuralt would win hands down. Kuralt, ever the Tar Heel, even wrote a book titled *North Carolina Is My Home*. Blessed with a warm bass voice, Kuralt was a resonant figure with CBS affiliate owners. From an aural perspective, he was like lightning in a bottle for Salant. But CBS News correspondent David Schoenbrun explained why Kuralt was passed over: he was "bald and heavy, not the right image for an anchorman."

On March 15, 1962, CBS News finally announced that Cronkite—nicknamed "one-take Walter" by Salant—was Edwards's replacement as CBS's evening news anchor. The determining factor was Cronkite's universally celebrated coverage of John Glenn. Edwards, nursing his disappointment, asked to be released from his CBS contract, but Salant, who had recently endured Smith's defection to ABC News, refused to let his Peabody Award–winning on-air talent go. Edwards, ego in check, soon let the matter drop. He remained with CBS until 1988, quietly going about the job of delivering midmorning and other news reports. Kuralt was named CBS News' chief West Coast correspondent the following year. That spring Collingwood won the plum task of hosting the one-hour show *A Tour of the White House with Mrs. John F. Kennedy*, which was met with off-the-charts ratings of over 70 million viewers, and took over *Eyewitness* (though Cronkite got to keep the America's Cup story).

It was murmured that Paley himself had chosen Cronkite as the anchor, managing editor, and new face of the *CBS Evening News*. What management liked about Cronkite was his cogent character: the conjunction of hard work with an uncommon judicious sensibility of what constituted headline news. He promised a return to the mandates of Paul White (that is, news would have a point . . . but not a point of view). "We didn't pick Walter to anchor the *Evening News* because of his hairdo—he didn't have one," Salant joked at a Museum of Television and Radio dinner in 1988. "We didn't pick Walter because he was beautiful—he wasn't. We didn't pick Walter because a focus group, wired up to a machine, palpitated at the sight of him. They didn't have things like that in those prehistoric days, so we were on our own. We picked Walter for the only sound reason to pick an anchor: He was a real pro, a superb reporter—a newsman who always gave his audience an honest account, no matter what his personal beliefs. It was the right assignment."

At 6:30 p.m. (EST) on April 16, 1962, Cronkite anchored the *CBS Evening News with Walter Cronkite* for the first time.* It was an agile fifteen-minute recitation of facts distilled from the AP and UPI. No longer was he the utility player. Cronkite closed that broadcast with, "That's the news. Be sure to check your local newspapers tomorrow to get all of the details on the headlines we're delivering to you." Paley, who had just injected a couple million dollars into modernizing CBS's five-hundred-thousand-square-foot broadcast center on West Fifty-seventh Street, was watching, and fumed. Cronkite, he charged, was telling CBS News shoppers to go buy elsewhere. "The suits—as we used to call them—went crazy," Cronkite's longtime producer Sandy Socolow recalled. "From their perspective, Walter was sending people to read newspapers instead of watching the news. There was a storm."

David Brinkley, taking the high road, closed his April 16 edition of *The Huntley-Brinkley Report* by

---

* The *CBS Evening News with Walter Cronkite* was telecast at 6:30 p.m. (EST) from 1962 to 1981, though some affiliates elected to carry the broadcast at a later time (such as WCBS-TV in New York), until that practice was outlawed in the 1970s.

welcoming Cronkite and his footmen to the fast-paced world of evening news. If NBC News had been a little less secure or a little less confident, it undoubtedly would have been a lot less generous with its nemesis. As ratings kingpin, Brinkley could afford to be magnanimous. Just before signing off on the night of Cronkite's debut, Brinkley told viewers, "Over on CBS tonight Walter Cronkite takes over their nightly news program after some years of doing special weekly and other programs of various kinds and doing them well. We'd like to welcome him to the thin and battered ranks of news broadcasters who have to work every night."

Viewers who took Brinkley's cue and tuned in to see the revamped *CBS Evening News with Walter Cronkite* were not likely to be terribly impressed. Aside from a simplified set, the production quality of the Cronkite show looked about the same as before. And so did Cronkite, whose trustworthy face was known to anyone who owned a television set. Being the maestro of the political conventions since 1952, Cronkite earned an edge as an inside-the-Beltway guy because he had started at WTOP-TV. "He was the father figure of television journalists; he had no rival except for maybe Brinkley," *Washington Post* editor Ben Bradlee recalled. "But Cronkite had a kind of paternal quality that made him different from David, and that is what set him apart. He was a great-white-father type—not quite that, because that connotes doddering, which he never was—but he was the dean. He was the big cheese."

Cronkite's first assignment as anchorman, perhaps the only one, was to whip NBC News in the ratings. While not an impossible task, it would be an uphill climb. Although the transition had been abrupt, the dismissal of Edwards having ruffled some feathers, Paley was committed to the new Cronkite show. Spurred by NBC News into head-to-head competition, CBS News had money to burn because of the success of the network's entertainment division. In 1962, CBS's prime-time shows—led by the resounding successes of *The Andy Griffith Show*, *Candid Camera*, and *The Lucy Show*—topped the ratings all seven nights of the week. And CBS's daytime programming was such a powerhouse—especially *As the World Turns*, which ran time-slot supreme from 1956 to 2010—management chest-beat they invented daytime TV. In the early 1960s, CBS, in fact, had all top ten daytime programs. "Doug Edwards used to brag that he had the highest rated newscast in the business," CBS scriptwriter Merv Block recalled. "That was because it followed the wildly popular soap operas."

A Madison Avenue governing truth was that Fortune 500 companies purchased commercials on a *network* as much as on a *show*. Part of Cronkite's job was to encourage companies to choose the CBS eye over the NBC peacock and the ABC circle. In the days before remote control devices, viewers tended to leave their televisions on one channel all evening. Television was different from radio in that way. Listeners often sat right next to their radios, but viewers were at least six feet from their black-and-white TV sets. The Big Three networks fought hard to control that stretch of carpeting or hardwood in the American living room, anxious to keep viewers from breaching it. One program needed to lead seamlessly to the next so that viewers would not feel the compunction to channel-surf. CBS couldn't afford to be hobbled from the start of each evening at 7:00 p.m. by conceding a huge majority of the audience share to Huntley-Brinkley. Seventy-five U.S. cities aired the *CBS Evening News*; Cronkite was tasked with making it closer to one hundred. A bigger audience and more out-of-town bureaus meant commercial advertisers would come knocking at Mr. Paley's door. Public approval via high ratings translated directly into increased revenue for CBS. "Walter," said Fred Friendly, the superstar producer at the network, "knows the future of CBS news is riding on him."

Behind the scenes, Don Hewitt was the uncompromising puppeteer of the *Evening News*. He instituted news teasers before commercial breaks and the hyping of featured stories. He produced CBS's nightly news through the entire Edwards era. Just as he did for Cronkite in the 1952 and 1956 conventions, Hewitt masterminded major live events for CBS during the Kennedy era. Short, dark-haired, imbued with the idiosyncratic instincts of a Reno dice-roller, he could be uncouth without losing a certain likable Borscht Belt appeal. Full of threats and bluster, he worked the telephone at CBS News like some manic switchboard operator. No one was better at news gathering and news deciding than Hewitt; by the time he created *60 Minutes* in 1968, he was in a carny league all his own.

Having collaborated with the docile Edwards for fourteen years, Hewitt was wary of Cronkite and of the supposed influence he hoped to exert as "managing editor." Hewitt's central impulse was to be a lone wolf. What really separated Cronkite from Huntley and Brinkley was his insistence on continuing to work as a reporter on his own show. From Hewitt's perspective, on-camera personalities like Cronkite needed to focus exclusively on the off-camera prompters—not on the program's management. Hewitt saw himself as the arbiter of what constituted nightly news; he was merely continuing the Edwards tradition. This arrangement didn't last long. Cronkite, as managing editor, was contractually the boss, no matter what Hewitt thought. What Cronkite possessed that Hewitt didn't was a reliable instinct for the oncoming headlights of major news stories. Hewitt thought in terms of that day's programming; Cronkite was telepathic about next year's trend. Cronkite knew the Mercury Seven astronauts were bigger than Sinatra before CBS management and producers did. "Again and again," CBS News producer Ron Bonn recalled, "Cronkite would foresee the Next Big Story and gear us up for it."

That summer of 1962, while gearing up for the America's Cup, Cronkite participated in an unprecedented milestone moment in communications history. On a hot day in mid-July, at the NBC studios in Rockefeller Center, Cronkite took a seat at the anchor desk next to Chet Huntley of NBC and newly hired Howard K. Smith of ABC News. The twenty-minute occasion was the first live TV link-up relayed between the Big Three networks of the United States and Eurovision, the television branch of the European Broadcasting Union. As Cronkite saw moving pictures from Europe flooding his black-and-white monitors at the NBC facilities, courtesy of Telstar, the first active communications satellite (albeit just in low Earth orbit, not high geosynchronous orbit), he was in awe. BBC's Richard Dimbleby, in Brussels, appeared on the monitor and called out, "Hello, Walter Cronkite. Hello, United States." Keeping his wits about him, Cronkite spoke for posterity, "Good evening, Europe, this is North America Live, via ATT Telstar, July 23, 1962, 3 p.m. Eastern Standard Time in the East." During the Glenn mission, just four months earlier, the United States didn't have the technology to provide Europe with even intermittent live transatlantic pictures of *Friendship 7*; now the Kennedy administration did. Cronkite's profession had been revolutionized with the transmission of images to Europe that included the Statue of Liberty, a major league baseball game in Chicago, President Kennedy's news conference, buffalo roaming the Great Plains, and a boy admiring a Sioux chief in South Dakota. The American broadcasters were treated to such sights as the Eiffel Tower, Big Ben, and reindeer in the Arctic Circle, among other iconic images. "The reality of live telecasts to Europe seemed so unbelievable," Cronkite recalled, "it was as if we had to keep telling ourselves it was happening."

Regardless of the Telstar excitement, Cronkite's *Evening News* broadcast was still a work in progress, victim to the truest maxim in television: "In news an audience is slow to grow and fast to go." Cronkite was very good, very clear, very quick, and very second place. CBS had increased budgets, such that it topped the other networks in the number of reporters, producers, cameramen, and script writers, but not in the number of viewers tuning in. Cronkite managed to stop the *Evening News* from hemorrhaging viewers, but that wasn't enough of an accomplishment for Paley. CBS had to be first. The public knew Cronkite mainly as "Iron Pants" or "Mr. Space." To be successful, he would have to become "America's Anchor," quite a tall order. "He's nervous," Fred Friendly said, "No. Not just nervous. I think Walter is running scared. And that's good. That's healthy."

Just a couple of months after Cronkite became the *CBS Evening News* anchorman, William Small, a news director at WHAS-TV in Louisville, Kentucky, became the news director and bureau manager of CBS News in Washington, D.C., leapfrogging over a stable of more obvious candidates for the prestigious, high-octane job. Before moving from Louisville to Washington, Small spent an arduous couple of weekdays in New York City getting to know Cronkite and other bigwigs at CBS corporate headquarters. They got along splendidly from the get-go. Small learned a secret about Cronkite's modus operandi: if you were a brand-new hire he treated you like a prince. Grooming newbies at CBS, helping the rookies machete through the weird thicket of Mr. Paley's world, was de rigueur behavior for Cronkite. It was how you turned staff into your stable.

Hanging around Cronkite all day had made Small mistakenly think that CBS News was a genteel place. When Cronkite left the studio to use an electric razor, the abrasive Don Hewitt, chewing a cigar, banished Small from the high-tech studio. Dutifully following instructions, Small headed up to the glass booth overlooking CBS Studio 42 in Grand Central Terminal to watch the Cronkite telecast. The countdown had started. Usually the sequestered holding tank was reserved as a courtesy zone for corporate sponsors of the *CBS Evening News*. That night, Small was left alone with an elderly woman counting down the minutes before broadcast. When Hewitt entered the dugout in full cock-of-the-walk mode, he pointed to the granny in the booth sitting next to Small. "Who is that old bitch?" he blurted out. For a split second Small was mortified. After dropping such a word bomb, Hewitt then scurried back to his control room seat. It was Helen Cronkite, the anchorman's mother, whose tongue could be pretty raucous.

"Are you really going to run the Washington bureau?" Helen asked Small incredulously.

"Yes, ma'am," he replied.

"Well," she said, "you'll have a lot of influence."

"Suppose so," he answered.

"Well, look," she said. "When the press does pro-files on Walter they often mention my age—they make me feel undateable. You make sure they leave my age out of it. Okay?"

Small felt as if he had walked into the New York City version of the popular CBS show *The Beverly Hillbillies*—he was an outsider, for sure. "Turns out Helen was a swinger," Small recalled. "She dated retired naval admirals and the like. She wasn't kidding about her known age hindering her dating life."

The network relentlessly publicized Cronkite's unmatched Soviet-analyst experience in 1962 during the Cuban Missile Crisis that October, presenting him as the cold war anchorman to trust at a time of anxiety. For thirteen days, President Kennedy dueled with Soviet premier Nikita Khrushchev about Soviet missile launch sites in Cuba. And for thirteen days, Huntley-Brinkley beat Cronkite in the ratings. Instead of firing Cronkite, Paley doubled down. In December 1962, Salant proposed that the *CBS Evening News* be expanded to a half hour. (At the time, all network news shows were only fifteen minutes long, patterned after radio news.)

Cronkite loved the idea. In a half hour he could give TV viewers the front page, along with a bit of the editorial page, some of the features, a peek at the

business section, and even some sports, when warranted. Considering that by 1962 most other television programming was packaged and sold in minimum
half-hour increments, the idea would seem to have
been obvious. Looking for free publicity, CBS News
announced the expanded broadcast with fanfare on the
Fourth of July. "To listen to [CBS]," wrote John Horn,
TV critic for the *New York Herald-Tribune*, "the half-
hour news show was a communications creation second
only to the printing press."

The typical complaint about the *CBS Evening News*
time expansion was perplexing: Was there really that
much *news* to fill a half hour each weekday evening?
At best, TV news was merely a headline service that
read viewers the condensed AP and UP wire service
reports. Salant felt CBS News' well-received coverage
of the November 1962 midterm elections had generated a bit of critical momentum. This caused Paley to
choose December as the ideal time to declare that its
Evening News was more important—and needed to be
longer—than the shallow *Huntley-Brinkley Report*.

Some people remembered where they were when
they heard about the attack on Pearl Harbor or the
D-day landings. Reuven Frank, the former NBC News
producer of *The Huntley-Brinkley Report*, remembered precisely where he was when he heard about

the half-hour *CBS Evening News*. As Frank told it, he had just parked his car and was walking toward the NBC News offices at Rockefeller Center when he met a friend from the same network.

"What do you plan to do today?" he asked me.

"Sit in my office and wait for [NBC News president William] McAndrew to call."

"Why?"

"It was in today's *Times*."

"Haven't seen it yet."

"CBS is expanding Cronkite to a half hour."

As Frank suspected, he was called in by his NBC bosses. They all had catch-up work to do. The Peacock Network, hungry for parity with CBS, immediately announced that *The Huntley-Brinkley Report* would also be expanded to thirty minutes. ABC News would eventually follow suit in 1967. The changes at each show were scheduled for the late summer of 1963, as each hired yet more staff members. The expanded broadcasts came just in time to cover the Vietnam War, Project Mercury, civil rights, and the antiwar movement. Theodore White, the author of the classic *Making of the President* book series, properly believed that CBS's news expansion "revolutionized" the American political process.

After the time for commercial breaks was subtracted, *CBS Evening News*, in reality, was to be twenty-two minutes long. Such excellent reporters as Robert Pierpoint (White House), George Herman (State Department), Roger Mudd (Capitol Hill), and Charles von Fremd (Pentagon) girded their reports with both wire service news and original research. One of Salant's first decisions was to devote two minutes each night to a commentary, labeled as such, by the sagacious Eric Sevareid. Cronkite saw this as a handicap. He wasn't enthusiastic about ceding two of his precious minutes to a Murrowite like Sevareid, full of pompous ways, but he didn't have a vote in the matter. CBS assigned Sevareid—who had been host of a weekly CBS News show called *Conquest*—to the close spot and built the commentary around him, even down to ending each of his essays with a graphic of his signature, larger than John Hancock's on the Declaration of Independence.

During the first six months of 1963, CBS News staff grew excited about the start of the new thirty-minute experiment to be launched around Labor Day. Hewitt—at great pocketbook expense to Paley—had Cronkite tape a series of thirty-minute unaired broadcasts as a sort of dress rehearsal for the fall premiere. "Hewitt wanted to get all the kinks out of things," Socolow recalled. "Harry Reasoner did the fifteen-minute live news broadcasts over the summer, while Cronkite did thirty minutes as a trial-and-error exercise." It cost a fortune, but Paley green-lighted the shadow broadcast. Cronkite's new writer, Ron Bonn, recalled that when the CBS broadcast was only fifteen minutes, script makers would "rip stories off the half-dozen wire service Teletypes chattering away in the corner, rewrite them as stories to be read aloud, and then hand [them] to Douglas Edwards." Now, with Cronkite at the helm, and the broadcast thirty minutes long, CBS News changed from *disseminating* news to *gathering* news.

For Cronkite, the March on Washington for Jobs and Freedom, a large-scale political rally in support of civil rights for African Americans in August 1963, was uplifting. Having won a Peabody Award that spring for his nightly assignments on CBS, he hoped his coverage of the march would lead to repeat glory. He had no compunction about deeming Dr. Martin Luther King one of the great orators of the century. But Harry Reasoner was primary anchor for CBS's special-event summertime coverage as an army of journalists descended upon the National Mall to document the Dr. King–dominated spectacular. On Wednesday, August 28, the evening before the speechifying began, Cronkite hosted a one-hour *CBS News Special Report* on the state of the African American freedom struggle. By the luck of the draw, CBS had been chosen by lot to coordinate the pooled coverage for what was being billed as a "Jobs and Freedom" march.

Each of the Big Three networks had slated four hours of live telecast on August 29; only CBS stayed with the activities (including King's awe-inspiring "I Have a Dream" speech) to the culmination. The Chesapeake and Potomac Telephone Company provided nearly thirty television station pickups to enable CBS to beam the event worldwide. "They called it the March on Washington for jobs and freedom," Cronkite broadcast that evening. "They came from all over America, negroes and whites, housewives and Hollywood stars, Senators and a few beatniks, clergymen and probably a few communists. More than 200,000 of them came to Washington this morning in a kind of climax to a historic spring and summer in the struggle for equal rights."

That August, while King was the hot interview to procure in TV journalism, Hewitt and Cronkite kept their focus on President Kennedy. A deal was struck with the White House for Cronkite to interview JFK on September 2 (Memorial Day) for his inaugural thirty-minute *Evening News* broadcast. The Kennedy family summer home in Hyannis Port, Massachusetts, was the venue. Cronkite was deeply grateful to the president for the exclusive, oblivious to the possibility that the White

House was using him to float a new Vietnam policy initiative. Hewitt had cut a deal with Kennedy's press secretary, Pierre Salinger: give Cronkite the exclusive, and CBS News would be able to present U.S. involvement in Vietnam front and center in a beneficial way.

Not everybody at CBS News thought Cronkite's coming to Cape Cod was a good thing. The White House press corps felt that Cronkite wasn't being an objective journalist, that he was in cahoots with Kennedy. "As I drove up to the motel where the White House press corps stayed," Cronkite recalled, "our veteran correspondent was waiting at the steps. He lit into me in a show of daring disrespect for the anchorman."

CBS correspondent Robert Pierpoint—a native of southern California who had worked at CBS News since 1951 as one of the Murrow Boys—was livid. And for good reason. The Associated Press inferred that President Kennedy was indeed using the Cronkite show to make a public policy statement on South Vietnam. Cronkite, in order to garner the attention of critics and create buzz for his new half-hour format, the story said, was essentially allowing President Kennedy to manipulate the *Evening News*. But Pierpoint had yet another problem with it: Cronkite's bigfooting.

"Listen, if you're going to break a big story," Pierpoint fumed to Cronkite, "it seems like the least you could do is tell your own White House man about it."

"What big story?" a genuinely confused Cronkite asked.

"That the president is going to make a major statement on Vietnam on your broadcast tomorrow night. It's all over the AP."

Pierpoint's harangue unnerved Cronkite. The rumor sweeping through the White House press corps was that he had told Kennedy the questions in advance. Not only did this make Cronkite seem like a White House patsy, but it was also prohibited by CBS News guidelines. "I was getting a little fed up with the big-foot idea, that is, an anchorman like Cronkite jumping in on my beat," Pierpoint recalled. "Ed Murrow never would have done what Cronkite did. When Ed visited me in Korea, he said, 'You're going to do my broadcast tonight because you know the politics, terrain, and people better than I do.' It was a sign that Ed respected my work. So, yeah, I resented the fact that Walter came to Hyannis to bigfoot my beat. I was ticked."

A defensive Cronkite, wounded by the allegation that he was a conduit for Kennedy, suspected that Salinger was behind the misleading AP story. When Cronkite encountered Salinger, a supposed friend, at a Hyannis bar, he lit into him with a vengeance, driving his forefinger into Salinger's chest. Cronkite contended that his journalistic integrity had been compromised by Salinger's big mouth. "I promise you I'm not going to even bring up Vietnam when I talk to the President tomorrow," an agitated Cronkite threatened, red in the face. "I'm not even going to bring it up!"

"You'll be sorry, Walter," Salinger told him.

Once Cronkite arrived at the Kennedy compound on September 2, still bickering with Salinger, he had an epiphany. The problem, he decided, was that the president controlled the interview because he was able to talk about Vietnam if he pleased. A tactical change of plan was made by Cronkite: he would ask Kennedy about Vietnam late in the interview, as a ploy designed to torment Salinger. When Cronkite and the president got seated in their lawn chairs, waiting for the CBS News camera crew to set up, Cronkite chatted with Kennedy about Newport and Martha's Vineyard. He told him how covering the America's Cup for *Eyewitness* had transformed him into a yachtsman. Then it was camera-ready-action. A full ten minutes into the interview, Cronkite—following questions about the effect of civil rights on the 1964 election, unemployment, and the nuclear test ban treaty—indeed turned to South Vietnam. "It is their war," Kennedy told Cronkite. "They are the ones who have to win it or lose it. We can help them; we can give them equipment; we can send our men out there as advisors . . . but in the final analysis it is their people and their government who have to win this struggle. All we can do is help."

The entire CBS interview with JFK ran thirty minutes, but it was edited down to twelve minutes for the 6:30 p.m. broadcast. This proved to be a problem for the White House. Salinger complained vehemently to CBS News that the way Cronkite and Hewitt edited the video made Kennedy seem more dovish than the reality. But in truth, the blockbuster interview illuminated that the Kennedy administration was distancing U.S. policy from the South Vietnamese president, Ngo Dinh Diem.

Because Diem would be assassinated on November 2, 1963, the theory that JFK had thrown Diem overboard in the Cronkite interview gained credence. Salinger later published the book *With Kennedy*, in which he accused CBS News of "partial distortion." Cronkite was forced to admit that CBS had indeed edited out the JFK line "I admire what the president [Diem] has done." But Cronkite charged that Salinger was overstating the whole Hyannis episode to protect the New Frontier from seeming culpable in the assassination of Diem. "My assumption," Cronkite wrote in his own defense, "is that Salinger was preparing a preemptive defense should history, as it has since, uncover the American part in the anti-Diem coup."

Minus the controversial backstory and editing flap with Salinger, Cronkite's first thirty-minute *CBS Evening News* broadcast was a ratings winner by any standard. (It caused CBS to end the *Eyewitness* show so that more resources could be put into the Cronkite show.) The features unfolded like articles in a glossy magazine: the interview with President Kennedy; a report on racial violence in Louisiana; a tour of Saigon with Henry Cabot Lodge (then the U.S. ambassador to South Vietnam); and a segment on the musical *My Fair Lady*, as produced by a theater troupe in Japan. But the initial excitement over the thirty-minute news format died down in a hurry. Media critics were disappointed, though not surprised, to see that both CBS News and NBC News petered out of fresh ideas rather quickly. After the first few weeks, the shows didn't seem to offer anything more, in terms of substance, than the fifteen-minute editions had. However, the long-term impact of the expanded news shows would prove integral to the pace and texture of the rest of the 1960s and beyond. Segments about civil rights and Vietnam got much more airtime because of the extended broadcast.

Besides the Kennedy exclusive and a chrome-spangled newsroom set, Cronkite received a lot of hype for what became his signature sign-off statement at the end of the half-hour broadcast. Lowell Thomas had "So long until tomorrow," and Edward R. Murrow had "Good night and good luck." Cronkite thought it appropriate that he have a tagline as well. At the end of each thirty-minute broadcast, the *CBS Evening News* was now closing with what Cronkite called a "quirk of fate" segment. It could be as sad as a cancer death or as happy as spring wildflowers. Either way, Cronkite needed a sign-off, and one that, depending on inflection, could work for both circumstances. After a great deal of thought, he came up with "That's the way it is," a modified poach of Murrow's "That's the way it was," said during his famous C-47 bombing mission over Germany during World War II.

When Salant heard Cronkite deliver that line of schmaltz ending the first historic thirty-minute CBS broadcast—derived from an evergreen Murrowism, no less—he was ticked off. He immediately called Cronkite and told him that his sign-off was ridiculous. To the literal-minded Salant, it seemed as if Cronkite was bragging that CBS News never got stories wrong; they did, weekly. The next day at work, Salant pulled Cronkite aside, instructing him to come up with something more suitable. But as fate would have it, the critics loved "That's the way it is." The CBS switchboard was bombarded with supportive telephone calls. Within about forty-eight hours, Salant recognized that he was the odd man out; Cronkite had prevailed. As Cronkite later boasted in an Archive of American Television interview, his nightly catchphrase "caught on instantly."

17.

The Kennedy Assassination

STAR OF *NEWSWEEK*—EATING COTTAGE CHEESE AND PINEAPPLE—WIRE-REPORTING FROM DALLAS— MERRIMAN SMITH OF UPI—FLASH HORROR— STAYING CALM—NATIONAL PASTOR—IRON PANTS—BLOWING HIS COOL OFF THE AIR— FOLLOWING THE FUNERAL—THE BROADCASTING PERFORMANCE OF A LIFETIME—TRYING TO SOLVE THE MYSTERY—BACKING THE WARREN COMMISSION—PERHAPS IT WAS A CONSPIRACY— STILL NUMBER TWO

Walter Cronkite was at his desk in the CBS broad- cast newsroom at a little after 1:00 p.m. on November 22, 1963, eating a low-calorie cottage cheese and pineapple salad—a meal he never finished; Betsy had brown-bagged it for him. Most of his colleagues were enjoying the Friday Manhattan ritual of white-collar lunch at a decent restaurant to close a humdrum news week. Cronkite was in shirtsleeves with his tie loose, reading some incoming dispatches from Europe and Southeast Asia. Hewitt was floating around the building, plotting the 6:30 p.m. broadcast. Just down the hall from Cronkite's desk, the *CBS Evening News* news editor, Ed Bliss Jr., a *New York Herald Tribune* veteran, was at the Teletype machines, glancing through stories about President Kennedy speaking at a breakfast in Fort Worth, Texas. Afterward, Kennedy was due to fly to nearby Dallas in Air Force One before a downtown motorcade took him to the Trade Mart for an international affairs speech.

Piled high on Cronkite's desk were recent *Newsweek* issues, one with his photographic profile on the cover; the image conveyed reportorial suaveness and an all-encompassing decency. When, in 1961, the chairman of the FCC, Newton N. Minow, declared television a "vast wasteland," he clearly did not have this forty-six-year-old *Newsweek* cover star in mind. Cronkite's "Golden Throat" act, as *Newsweek* put it, carried a steadily growing heft as the year wound down. Americans liked rooting for the underdog. Cronkite was perfectly positioned: he was the suppertime staple on 169 TV stations across America; Huntley-Brinkley aired on 183. The photograph's accompanying cover line read, "The TV News Battle" (an allusion to the wildly competitive audience-share ratings dance between CBS and NBC). CBS News was poised to win the ratings war over NBC's *Huntley-Brinkley Report* (which Cronkite later called "H-B"). "Hell, yes, there's a battle," Cronkite was quoted as saying. "I don't feel at a disadvantage with two against one. Let 'em put up four in there if they want to. I've taken on two. I can take on four."

That Friday afternoon, everything was also calm at the Washington bureau on M Street. Bill Small had CBS News White House correspondent Robert Pierpoint following Kennedy on his November 21–23 swing through four Texas cities: Houston, San Antonio, Fort Worth, and Dallas. When Kennedy had hopscotched around Florida a few days earlier— making stops in Miami, Palm Beach, Tampa, and Cape Canaveral all in one day—Lew Wood of CBS News' southern bureau (based at WWL in New Orleans) found it impossible to keep up with the off-and-up Air Force One. Flummoxed by his Florida experience, Wood recommended to Bliss, who agreed, that for the Texas trip three CBS crews—those of Dan Rather, Nelson Benton, and himself—be dispatched. A fourth crew from Chicago was even added. "We were," Wood recalled, "loaded for bear."

With Rather, Pierpoint, Benton, and Wood broadcasting from Texas, CBS News had the president's whirlwind trip well covered. Pool reporting would also enhance the coverage. Wood was assigned to report on a Kennedy fund-raising dinner for a Texas congressman at Houston's Rice Hotel. As Air Force One whisked POTUS away to Fort Worth, the Wood crew drove the 250 prairie miles to catch up with him. Wood caught up with Kennedy on the morning of November 22 at the Texas Star Hotel in Fort Worth. As the president shook hands with his adoring fans, his wife, Jackie, was dressing in their oversized suite with original Picassos and Monets hanging in all five rooms. Wood then followed Kennedy to nearby Carswell Air Force Base, where the president worked an appreciative receiving line of military families before flying to Love Field in Dallas. "We drove back to Love Field for our next assignment after Kennedy's Dallas motorcade and speech at the Trade Mart," Wood recalled. "Dan Rather was downtown to cover the motorcade itself, and remained at KRLD, monitoring the event."

Wood now had a little time to kill, so he took the crew to lunch at the Ramada Inn at Love Field. It would be a while before Kennedy finished his Trade

Mart speech, so why not stop for a burger? With a little free time finally, Wood decided to check in with Rather at KRLD-TV, the Dallas CBS affiliate where he was stationed. Covering a presidential motorcade was tough for TV crews (and everyone else involved). The Kennedys had throngs of people goggling at them, full of cheers, questions, and the occasional boos. For Rather and Wood, fear that CBS wouldn't shoot the best motorcade film footage, that NBC or ABC would one-up them, fueled their aggressiveness.

While Wood chatted with Rather about the Texas Star Hotel, Carswell Air Force Base, and Love Field events, there was an abrupt intrusion. "Hold on, Lew . . . don't go away," Rather said. Within a minute or two, Rather was back on the phone and said, "The president's been shot . . . get to Parkland Memorial Hospital as fast as you can!" Hanging up, Wood rushed into the Ramada dining room, shouting *pronto* to his crew. CBS News cameraman Wendell Hoffman undoubtedly pestered Wood about what was happening. Wood whispered to him that Kennedy had been shot en route to the Trade Mart.

"WHAT, the president's been shot?" Hoffman blurted out in his Kansas farmer's voice.

Everyone in the Ramada dining room heard Hoffman's resounding disbelief. A waiter dropped the dishes he was carrying and a woman gasped. Word was that the Secret Service had removed the bubble top on the president's four-door 1961 Lincoln Continental convertible, which wasn't bulletproof or even bullet-resistant, so Kennedy could enjoy the fair weather and interact more with the crowds during the ten-mile motorcade into downtown Dallas. "We figured there might be some good footage for Walter to run of Kennedy glad-handing," Pierpoint recalled. "I thought we had a good chance of leading that Friday's news."

NBC News had sent a young reporter, Robert MacNeil, who started his career at ITV in London, to cover the presidential trip; he rode in one of the buses in the motorcade. Four cars behind Kennedy, ABC News' Bob Clark rode with the two wire service reporters, United Press International's congenial Merriman Smith and his hard-shelled Associated Press rival, Jack Bell. At fifty-one years of age, Smith was the chief Washington reporter for UPI, a job Cronkite himself had coveted after World War II. Clark and Bell were in the backseat of the limousine; "Smitty," as Cronkite called Smith, rode up front. AT&T had supplied the car in recognition of the large amount of business the news services transacted over the telephone wires. As AT&T property, it was equipped with a car phone in the front seat. This hotline was how the world first learned that Kennedy had been shot.

About 12:30 (1:30 p.m. EST), those reporters riding in the presidential motorcade, sweating in the seventy-six-degree heat, heard loud, sharp cracks cutting through the din of the procession. They were winding their way through downtown Dallas, about to turn on Elm Street in Dealey Plaza. They couldn't see what was happening at the front of the motorcade, but Smith was a gun collector and recognized the triple pops of a bolt-action weapon. He ignored the comments around him that a police motorcycle must have backfired. Picking up the car's telephone, Smith called the local UPI office. All the reporters in Dallas were now operating on reflex. They would need good instincts in the ensuing mayhem and mass confusion. Someone had indeed fired three shots from an upper floor of the redbrick Texas School Book Depository building. A mortal terror was in the air, a gnawing sense of disbelief as the motorcade sped up and raced to the Stemmons Freeway to get to Parkland Memorial Hospital. A Secret Service agent leapt into the rear of the presidential vehicle to prevent the First Lady, who had climbed out of the rear seat, from crawling onto the limo's trunk deck.

Those bullets Smith heard were very real. The first one missed its intended target. The second bullet hit the president high in his shoulder and exited from his throat—a survivable wound. But the final, third, bullet entered Kennedy's right ear, blowing out brain tissue and skull fragments. Texas governor John Connally, riding in the same car as Kennedy beside his wife, Nellie, was shot in the chest. The First Lady, Jacqueline Kennedy, screamed, "My God, they've killed Jack. . . . They've killed my husband, Jack, Jack!"

At 1:34 p.m. in the CBS newsroom in New York, Bliss, a veteran Murrow writer and editor who started his journalism career at the *Bucyrys Telegraph-Forum* in Ohio, was glancing through the Teletype rolls from the wire services when the bell on the UPI machine rang five times. A bell always attracted an editor's attention; five signaled an "urgent story." The only higher designation was a fifteen-bell "flash." Bliss studied the "BULLETIN" story as it was typed out on the machine ticker tape scroll:

UPI A7N DA
PRECEDE KENNEDY
DALLAS, NOV.22 (UPI)—THREE SHOTS WERE FIRED AT PRESIDENT KENNEDY'S MOTORCADE TODAY IN DOWNTOWN DALLAS.
JT1234PCS.

The UPI New York bureau immediately forbade other bureaus from filing stories and issued the highly unusual instruction: "DA IT YRS NY" ("Dallas, it's yours. New York"). Cronkite rushed to the UPI machine at the sound of the bells. He and Bliss together read Smith's convoluted dispatch, slightly dizzy with disbelief. For just two or three seconds Cronkite was numb with trepidation. "Got a shooting in Dallas!" he shouted authoritatively to the newsroom. Nothing further was coming over the other Teletypes. Had the gunfire been serious or not? Frenzy ensued as CBS News quickly tried to garner more information from Texas. When word of the shooting reached Dan Rather at KRLD-TV, he sprinted toward Dealey Plaza. At 1:36 p.m. EST, ABC News radio reported the shooting of Kennedy. Rather was trying to get the lay of the land. Although Rather's version of events has changed over the years, with an aim of placing himself nearer the site of the shooting, Lew Wood swears he was actually holed up inside KRLD-TV.

Workaday competition among the news outfits didn't melt away as the Dallas tragedy took its inevitable course. On the contrary, it intensified. Rather, a native Texan, wanted to own the story. Immediately, he ordered a search for home movies from someone in the crowd—wanting to document the president's visit—might have taken of the shooting. Dick Salant, up in New York, put together a special unit to investigate the crime ASAP. The AT&T "pool car" broke from the motorcade route, rushing instead to Parkland Memorial Hospital. UPI's Merriman Smith, dean of the White House correspondents, who had been an Eisenhower favorite, knew the story was only beginning to unfold and kept the car phone in his hands. Jack Bell demanded the phone so he could file a story to AP, but Smith mumbled that he had a bad connection. Bell knew this was a lie. With the car speeding through the Dallas streets at seventy miles an hour (and probably more), Bell pounded on Smith with both fists, determined to get the damn phone. As the car reached Parkland Memorial, Smith, having filed with the Dallas UPI office, finally tossed the phone to his rival and leapt out of the vehicle, sprinting inside the hospital.

The Kennedy assassination was two massive stories rolled into one: the shooting mystery and a larger question of whether the U.S. government was under siege. Smith of UPI, still pushing to outrun Bell of AP, spoke to a Secret Service agent at the hospital, who told him the president was dead. Smith chose not to report it without further confirmation. After hospital employees leaked more bleak information, Smith phoned another dispatch to his office. It was becoming more and more apparent that the president might be dead. Smith's clumsily written scoop went over the wire, and at 1:39 p.m. in New York, fifteen bells rang on the Teletype at CBS.

> *FLASH*
> *FLASH*
> *KENNEDY SERIOUSLY WOUNDED PER-*
> *HAPS SERIOUSLY PERHAPS FATALLY BY*
> *ASSASSINS BULLET*
> *JT1239PCS*

One UPI man (Smith) was passing the story on to another UP veteran (Cronkite). The wire service bells were ringing worldwide. Cronkite, who was managing editor in addition to being CBS's on-air anchorman, read Smith's dispatch and pounced. "Let's get on the air," he called out, unfazed. "Let's get on the air." The network was then broadcasting a popular soap opera, *As the World Turns.* Cronkite was already in the main studio, the CBS newsroom, but the cameras needed ten or fifteen minutes to warm up. The studio lights just weren't "hot" for broadcast. Refusing to be derailed by the lighting delay, Cronkite rushed to an empty radio studio adjacent to the TV studio. Hewitt called the network's master control and arranged for a patch into the television broadcast. *As the World Turns*—with a love-warped family Thanksgiving dinner plot—was replaced with a generic graphic slide reading, "CBS News Bulletin." Cronkite's clear and modulated voice, live from the radio booth, went out over the airwaves at 1:40 p.m. EST. Cronkite's words, "We interrupt this program," could be heard. But only the CBS eye logo was displayed on-screen:

Here is a bulletin from CBS News. In Dallas, Texas, three shots were fired at President Kennedy's motorcade in downtown Dallas. The first reports say that President Kennedy has been seriously wounded by this shooting.

There was an interlude of stillness, then CBS returned to *As the World Turns*, which was taking a commercial break for Nescafé coffee. Cronkite, using the UPI report, had beaten NBC in announcing the Dallas event on the air by nearly a minute. Even as Cronkite was making the announcement, slowly and emphatically filling out the terse phrasing of Smith's 1:39 p.m. EST report, a staffer slipped into the studio and handed him another wire service dispatch. He scanned it quickly. "More details just arrived," Cronkite said on-air with grim determination, clearly disturbed by the update. "These details, about the same as previously: President Kennedy shot today just as his motorcade left downtown Dallas. Mrs. Kennedy jumped up and grabbed Mr. Kennedy; she called, 'Oh, no!' The motorcade sped on." Cronkite returned to Smith's report. "The United Press says that the wounds for President Kennedy, perhaps, could be fatal. Repeating, a bulletin from CBS News: President Kennedy has been shot by a would-be assassin in Dallas, Texas. Stay tuned to CBS News for further details."

Cronkite was nothing if not rivalrous. Years later, he shamelessly bragged about CBS's scoop over NBC and ABC, a boast that, if written by anybody else, would have seemed ghoulish. ("We beat NBC onto the air by almost a minute," he proudly recalled in his memoir.) Taken without an understanding of the TV news industry, such statements were callous. But hypercompetitiveness, especially in the realm of historic breaking news like the JFK assassination, remains a powerful reality in the TV news world. In American journalism, being first, and right, has always brought the critics' accolades. After that, you *own* the story for days to come. Smith had beaten Bell by the luck of sitting near the pool car phone. It was also Smith who first used the term *grassy knoll* in a dispatch; the label has become part of the American lexicon when discussing the Kennedy assassination.

After returning to the soap opera broadcast, for about ten minutes CBS started regularly interrupting *As the World* turns with updates from Cronkite about President Kennedy and Governor Connally. By now some CBS staffer was handing him an update every minute. As the crisis deepened, Eddie Barker, news director of KRLD-TV, the CBS affiliate in Dallas, offered the best on-the-ground reporting, for he spoke directly to a Parkland Memorial Hospital doctor. A mass of ominous details, such as the arrival of two priests at the hospital, kept dribbling in from Dallas. As a commercial for Friskies puppy food ran, Cronkite assembled the puzzle of the Dallas story in the CBS radio studio. Friskies would be the last commercial CBS would run for many hours. When the broadcast returned, Cronkite again took over the microphone, and he was the CBS network incarnate from that point on for the next five hours. CBS News stayed on the air under direct instruction from Bill Paley. Cronkite wasn't allowed to return to regular programming, a decision that obviously pleased the anchor. "Because of Barker and Rather," Cronkite asserted, "we were on top of the story throughout."

Perhaps because Cronkite had spent time in the 1930s working out of Dallas's UP office, he felt ideally suited to discuss that city's downtown grid. He knew the bus lines. Because the Dallas tragedy came without a warning flare, the coverage of the Kennedy assassination on November 22 was entirely different from any major story that Cronkite, Hewitt, or even Bliss had ever grappled with. More than 175 million traumatized Americans tuned in to the three major networks for updates—the largest audience in TV history until then. CBS stayed live for fifty-five hours (with Cronkite carrying the bulk of the burden), ABC-TV for sixty hours, and NBC-TV for seventy-one hours and thirty-six minutes.

Like a trapeze artist without a net, Cronkite was on his own that November 22, anchoring only by his wit. He had the ability to smoothly amalgamate three or even more jobs at once with ease. He had a teacher's desire to share knowledge with an audience. Just like any other emergency worker, when a crisis occurred, "the adrenaline pumps," Cronkite said; a professional has a "job to do and you do the job." He was a sort of multidimensional synthesizer, spinning order out of chaos, doing his editing, producing, and announcing while on air that Friday. What the CBS audience heard was not a series of dispatches but a dramatic story of remarkable roundness and clarity unfolding in real time. He was communicating to viewers that they were now *witnesses*—secondary ones, for sure—but witnesses nevertheless to an epoch-defining event. "The details would come in and it would build up in me," Cronkite later reminisced. "I don't even recall the spots."

Cronkite had help from loyal lieutenants in Dallas, New York, and Washington, to be sure. CBS was the largest news organization in television, yet in the Kennedy assassination drama, Cronkite's raw ability to communicate would make or break the network's coverage. At first, he struggled to find the right words, as if cautiously making his way through a thicket of brambles. But before long, he had created a modulated rhythm for the broadcast that remained poignant for days. The grotesque surrealism of the Dallas chaos brought out his professional best. Never putting on his suit jacket, remaining in shirtsleeves for the duration of the epic broadcast, Cronkite brilliantly balanced his composure with skillful interludes of raw emotion. He was memorable without swamping the story. "Walter ate all of this up," Socolow recalled. "He loved the excitement of the Dallas story. Don't get me wrong, he didn't like the president being shot. But he loved the frenetic newsroom utility."

No one handled his TV duties during the Kennedy assassination ordeal with the high grace notes of

Cronkite. NBC was on the air as the local WNBC-TV (New York) anchorman, Bill Ryan, broadcast the Dallas news. He was soon joined by Chet Huntley and Frank McGee, that network's first-string anchor for live events (including space reporting). ABC started its coverage with reporter Jim Hagerty, former president Eisenhower's press secretary, who was then replaced by the regular anchor, Ron Cochran, and reporter Ed Silverman. Howard K. Smith, then on a jet returning from Europe, became a mainstay on ABC almost as soon as the plane landed in New York. All the networks reported details of the shooting as they came in, but the key was Kennedy's condition. Was he dead or alive? CBS News' Robert Pierpoint was at Parkland when he made a call to Barker of KRLD-TV, who had spoken to a doctor who knew (for sure) that Kennedy was dead. Barker announced the death on KRLD at 1:18 p.m. EST, before anyone else, later regretting he omitted the detail of Jackie Kennedy's pink Chanel suit being saturated with blood. "I was in shock," Barker said. A few well-intentioned people suggested that Jackie change out of the suit. "No," she replied, "let them see what they've done."

CBS Radio went with Barker's KRLD-TV story and announced nationally that the president was dead, but CBS Television wouldn't follow suit. Cronkite urged caution. He felt a "chill" when he heard Kennedy's death had been reported on CBS Radio. What if Kennedy weren't dead? What if Barker had reported bum information from a Dallas doctor?

At 12:40 p.m. CST, Merriman Smith sent a lede on the UPI wire that quoted a Secret Service agent confirming that the president was indeed deceased. A correspondent for KRLD-TV made reference to such reports while the affiliate was on a feed into CBS, but Cronkite still refrained from airing it. NBC was also cautious, awaiting firm confirmation from Parkland Memorial Hospital. No one was certain who had killed the president or whether it was part of a larger attack on America. A hell's stew of conspiracy theories would eventually bubble forth, blaming the murder on Fidel Castro, Lee Harvey Oswald, LBJ, the Mafia, the CIA, the Dallas Police Department, and the Kremlin. Television was the fastest way to deliver news—words and pictures—and likewise, the fastest way to spread mere conjecture. As the afternoon spun forward, even the most aggressive television veterans were daunted by the task at hand: making sure they didn't accidentally feed the conspiracy.

From CBS News headquarters in New York, Hewitt anxiously called Rather and Pierpoint down in Dallas. Who were Barker's sources for the report that Kennedy was dead? Rather told Hewitt about a priest and a doctor, but Cronkite wanted more specifics before he could break the news definitively. "Even if you are right (and God help you if you are wrong)," Rather later explained of Hewitt's wise hesitation, "you are not going to go with a story of that proportion as confidently on television as you would on radio. It's just the different intensity of the two mediums, the size of the audience, the weight of the news."

Hewitt handed his conversation notes with Rather to Cronkite, who was talking on the air. Although Cronkite had been more cautious regarding false starts and piecemeal reconstructions, he now chose to use the Rather ledes from Dallas. "We just have a report from our correspondent Dan Rather in Dallas," Cronkite said, "that he has confirmed that President Kennedy is dead. We still have no official confirmation of this, however. It's a report from our correspondent Dan Rather in Dallas, Texas." Cronkite's punctuated delivery was bracing. Covering his own back, Cronkite used Rather as his potential fall guy if the Barker report proved false. Cronkite wasn't yet ready to attach his own mint *Newsweek* cover name to a possibly untrue announcement of Kennedy's passing. Hesitation was his ally of the moment. Confirmation from Parkland—not Rather—was the ultimate best source from Cronkite's cautious perspective. If Kennedy had survived, then Rather would have gotten thrown under the bus.

On NBC, McGee took the lead, while Huntley and Ryan were on hand to add to the discussion. ABC's coverage was in the able hands of Cochran and Silverman, though ABC also used one or two feeds from Barker of KRLD-TV. However, even as Cochran emphasized that all reports regarding Kennedy's condition were unconfirmed, the president's name and "1917–1963" appeared on-screen. That tombstone-like R.I.P. graphic drove home the reality of Kennedy's death in a visually visceral way.

Missing from CBS News' coverage of the Kennedy assassination that November 22 was Edward R. Murrow. Rumor had it that Murrow, unhappy at USIA, might return to CBS in early 1963 to do documentaries. But in fact he had undergone emergency cancer surgery to remove his left lung. The three-hour operation left him weak and feeble, horizontal in bed throughout the autumn, mired in depression. The radiation he had endured discolored his chest to a coarse leathery brown shade. "Whoever said talk is cheap," Murrow quipped, "had two lungs." When Murrow's wife, Janet, told him Kennedy had been shot, he felt nauseous. He watched Cronkite's commentary that dark day, calling it one long, flawless note.

With his hair slightly tousled and black horn-rimmed glasses on, Cronkite actually looked supremely unpolished during his broadcast. A man somehow in need of a shave, eventually he had no whiskers. At least the air-conditioning system kept him from sweating under the hot lights. "I was really just a disreputable character up there on the air," he later said, "as far as my appearance went." That characterization was overdrawn, but Cronkite's unpowdered face and work-grunt attire indeed added to the urgency of the moment. As he described the unsettled atmosphere in Dallas during the weeks preceding the president's trip, setting the stage for JFK's visit, he was interrupted by someone off-camera handing him yet another piece of paper. He quickly absorbed the note's contents. His eyes became wells of sadness. Removing his glasses, fidgeting with them, he shot an intense look at the camera—at the viewer—as though to warn people to prepare themselves. He put his glasses back on and tried to speak. Pulling himself together, Cronkite read the newest dispatch with pained authority:

"From Dallas, Texas, the flash apparently official, President Kennedy died at 1 o'clock p.m. Central Standard Time, 2 o'clock, Eastern Standard Time, some thirty-eight minutes ago."

The wall clock now drew Cronkite's attention. Assuming the role of historian, he wanted to record the exact time of the momentous announcement. "We knew it was coming," Cronkite recalled of the death flash, "but still it was hard to say." With eyes affixed to the big-and-little-hands, Cronkite didn't talk for two or three seconds. He was mute, searching for meaning in a world turned absurd. He pursed his mouth, a recognition of shock and sorrow that nearly every viewer shared simultaneously. "It was touch and go there for a few seconds," he later explained, "before I could continue." Decades later, speaking to the Archive of American Television, Cronkite explained that "the psychological trauma didn't touch him" until he "hit that punch line that he's dead."

Unbeknownst to Cronkite, Vice President Johnson had been whisked by the Secret Service to Air Force One, parked at Love Field; he was hungry for accurate information about the extent of the assassination plot. Immediately Johnson ordered the shades drawn. The lack of air circulation made the 707 feel like a swamp. Johnson walked briskly down the aisle to Air Force One's little communications room where agents, wearing headsets, were actively gathering intelligence. Johnson, demanding answers more quickly, hurried to his private stateroom to watch Cronkite.

"Shhh . . . shhh," Johnson said with his finger to his mouth, hoping to learn new details about Dallas from CBS News. Cronkite—dispatching his roving detectives Rather, Wood, Benton, and Pierpoint—was already ahead of the FBI in finding out biographical information about the bizarre misfit named Lee Harvey Oswald.

To Cronkite's amazement, Oswald, the alleged assassin, had quietly walked away from the Texas School Book Depository after the shooting and ridden a public bus to the neighborhood where he shared a flat at 1026 North Beckley. There, he grabbed his loaded .38 caliber pistol and walked back out into the bright afternoon. When Dallas police officer James Tippit, who had heard a Wanted Man description of the assassin on the radio, stopped Oswald and asked for his identification, Kennedy's murderer pulled out his pistol and shot and killed him. Oswald then sought sanctuary in the nearby Texas Theatre without paying, prompting the terrified cashier to call the police. With *War Is Hell*, starring Tony Russel, playing on the big screen, the Dallas cops scuffled with Oswald briefly before arresting him.

The CBS News team grew determined to help Cronkite own the Kennedy assassination coverage. Rather, Pierpoint, Wood, and Benton would shuttle in and out of KRLD-TV all day, catching Cronkite between location shots. Wood went to Oswald's rooming house to interview his landlady and film its interior. From all over the world, so-called journalists streamed into Dallas to be part of the crime of the century. Everyone wanted a little exclusive about Oswald. Transmission of such information was difficult; back then there were no two-way radios, video cameras, or cell phones. "I think we just kind of intuitively knew what to do," Barker recalled. "You rise to the occasion."

Although Wood had all of this great visual material, Cronkite was nervous about airing it. His heart opened toward the Kennedy family. He became impresario of the American post-assassination mourning. CBS News became the meeting hall, the cathedral, the corner bar, and the town square—wherever people went when they wanted the healing comfort of a group. Television became the national grief center, with Cronkite, sipping strong tea throughout the weekend to soothe his sore throat, the philosopher of congruent counsel. Cronkite never pretended to process JFK's death—his broadcast was a lesson in humility. "When the news is bad, Walter hurts," explained Fred Friendly. "When the news embarrasses America, Walter is embarrassed. When the news is humorous, Walter smiles with understanding."

With straightforward reporting, never leapfrogging ahead of the unfolding narrative, Cronkite steadily held the air for four more hours after the shooting. Sensing that "Iron Pants," the nickname given to Cronkite by Unipressers and now being used at CBS, was showing strain and noticing that his anchorman's neck was stiff, Hewitt made the executive decision to bench Cronkite for a spell. Like a good coach, he saw his star pitcher needed relief help in the ninth inning. Dutifully and without complaint, Cronkite turned his chair over to Charles Collingwood. Away from the three cameras, Cronkite headed into his glass-walled office, only a few paces away, to commiserate with Betsy and his children on the phone. As a father, the shock of the JFK murder now made him angry. In what kind of America was he raising his children? But as Cronkite entered his office sanctum, hoping to decompress, his telephone rang incessantly. An annoyed Cronkite grabbed the receiver and barked out a cold "Hello." A thistleish Manhattan liberal was on the other end, full of double-distilled complaints from her Park Avenue penthouse.

"Is this CBS News?" she asked.

Cronkite confirmed it was.

"I just want to say," she snapped, "that this is the worst bad taste to have that Walter Cronkite on the air when everybody knows he hated the president."

"Madame," Cronkite said, "what is your name?"

"Mrs. Blank," the woman snapped.

"Mrs. Blank," Cronkite said, "this is Walter Cronkite, and you're a goddamn idiot."

Years later Cronkite recalled to interviewer Oriana Fallaci of *Look* how embarrassed he was that the Park Avenue shrew, whom he called Mrs. Blank, had caused him to lose his cool. How trivial his disputes with JFK about Catholicism and with Pierre Salinger over Vietnam on his first thirty-minute *CBS Evening News* broadcast seemed in hindsight. "Unfortunately, that Park Avenue lady drove me mad," Cronkite told Fallaci. "I am not proud to have invoked the Lord's name in losing my temper."

Both Wood and Pierpoint were at Parkland Memorial Hospital when White House press secretary Malcolm "Mac" Kilduff (filling in for Salinger, who was in midflight over the Pacific, accompanying Robert McNamara on a trip to Asia) informed the press that JFK had died of a severe gunshot wound to the head at 1:00 p.m. A senior surgeon soon offered more gruesome details. What Cronkite wanted to know from his roving CBS News southern bureau correspondents was, how the hell could Oswald have made the bull's-eye shot from the Book Depository window?

Rather, always brazen, came up with the novel idea that Wood borrow a rifle at a Dallas pawn shop (not difficult in Texas) and re-create the Oswald shooting for the *CBS Evening News.* You had to admire Rather for his gumption. Dutifully, Wood rented a Mannlicher-Carcano .30 (or 7.62) caliber rifle (a very similar model to the one Oswald used) from a nearby shop. He had it fixed with a four-power telescopic sight and "waltzed" into the Book Depository with it slung over his shoulder, film crew in tow. "We were not challenged," Wood recalled. "The Secret Service had not even sealed off the building, but they had scoured it after the shooting, discovering the discarded rifle and empty cartridge cases."

The assassin's window was still wide open. All the cartons of books that Oswald arranged to create a sniper's nest were still in place. "The target sight picture was a going-away target, not a crossing target, so while moving, it remained in the sights," Wood remembered. "The range was no more than 100 yards. The president's head (judging from other passenger cars that morning) must have appeared as big as a melon through the telescopic sight. Some have questioned how Oswald could have fired three shots in such a few seconds. Remember, one round was already in the chamber of the bolt-action rifle. Once he squeezed off the first shot, he only had to bolt twice more. Take my word for it. It was an easy shot."

Cronkite, Hewitt, and Bliss nixed Wood's stunning re-creation segment, believing it unfit for the *CBS Evening News*. They also refused to run Wood's footage of the bloody Parkland Memorial Hospital operating room where trauma surgeons Dr. Charles Carrico and Dr. Charles Baxter had worked on Kennedy. It was determined that airing those pieces would have been insensitive to the Kennedy family's feelings during their time of grief. But *CBS Evening News with Walter Cronkite* made history by airing a two-hour telecast that Friday, and a one-hour broadcast on Monday (both apparently network TV firsts).

For four straight days, until the body of President Kennedy, a World War II hero, was laid to rest at Arlington National Cemetery on Monday, November 25, all the networks ran largely uninterrupted coverage of the events surrounding the president's death. Donning his canonicals to reassure the world, Cronkite steadied the 70 million friends of CBS News, who almost felt his reassuring hand on their shoulders. On Sunday morning, though, CBS goofed: it didn't show live footage of Oswald being transferred from Dallas Police Headquarters to the sherriff's county jail. NBC News president Robert Kintner, watching from the array of monitors at his home, instinctively called the studio at 30 Rockefeller Center and told the director to switch coverage to Dallas. Moments later, NBC viewers watched as Jack Ruby killed Oswald with a pistol shot to the stomach.

CBS News *did* have a camera at the Dallas police department basement, but it wasn't airing the feed because Roger Mudd had gone live with a stand-up report from Washington, where Kennedy's coffin was being moved to the Capitol Rotunda to lie in state. After Jack Ruby shot Oswald, CBS News immediately cut to Dallas. ABC didn't broadcast Oswald's death because they didn't have a live camera present at the police headquarters. "One of the great misfortunes at CBS was that we were off the air when Ruby shot Oswald," Cronkite later recalled. "I watched it on one of the competing networks. We got on the air pretty quickly thereafter, but we missed the drama of that moment."

Tom Shales of *The Washington Post* declared that the JFK assassination coverage proved TV had become "the national hearth." One of America's worst hours ever had produced CBS News' finest moment. According to Nielsen, an astounding 93 percent of U.S. homes with televisions were tuned in to Big Three coverage. Over half of those viewers watched the drama

THE KENNEDY ASSASSINATION · 467

unfold for thirteen consecutive hours that November weekend. Viewers in twenty-three countries saw some segment of Cronkite's marathon coverage.

Every CBS News frame from Washington—the flag-draped coffin; 250,000 mourners paying their last respects; six gray-white horses; three riders pulling the caisson; world dignitaries such as President Charles de Gaulle of France, Chancellor Ludwig Erhard of West Germany, Queen Frederika of Greece, and Haile Selassie of Ethiopia weeping (a CBS cameraman had shouted into Cronkite's earpiece, "I've got a whole bunch of kings!"); and the final eulogy of Philip M. Hannan, auxiliary bishop of Washington—manifested what media theorist Marshall McLuhan called the power of TV "to involve an entire population in a ritual process."

Cronkite harnessed that power as he wrapped up his *CBS Evening News* broadcast on November 25, the day of President Kennedy's burial at Arlington National Cemetery:

It is said that the human mind has a greater capacity for remembering the pleasant than the unpleasant. But today was a day that will live in memory and in grief. Only history can write the importance of this day: Were these dark days the harbingers of even blacker ones to come, or like the black before the dawn shall they lead to some still as yet indiscernible sunrise of understanding among men, that violent words, no matter what their origin or motivation, can lead only to violent deeds? This is the larger question that will be answered, in part, in the manner that a shaken civilization seeks the answers to the immediate question: Who, and most importantly what, was Lee Harvey Oswald? The world's doubts must be put to rest. Tonight there will be few Americans who will go to bed without carrying with them the sense that somehow they have failed. If in the search of our conscience we find a new dedication to the American concepts that brook no political, sectional, religious or racial divisions, then maybe it may yet be possible to say that John Fitzgerald Kennedy did not die in vain. That's the way it is, Monday, November 25, 1963. This is Walter Cronkite, good night.

What to make of Cronkite's historic CBS broadcasts of November 22 to 25, 1963, when America turned to him for information and comfort? Was he the perspicacious communicator of news or an even-keeled pastor? Had he been wrong to not air Wood's re-creation from the assassin's perch? Ultimately, Cronkite was just a pro who wanted to whip NBC News in the ratings. "Walter was really in his element," remembered producer Sandy Socolow, who rushed to the broadcast center from Millbrook, New York. "He was like an actor in the middle of his performance of a lifetime. It's possible that the scene of him taking off his glasses was consciously staged. Any director would tell you that what Walter did with those glasses, the fidgeting, was a fine prop to convey both human emotion and an air of spontaneity. The performance worked. The proof is in the pudding—Walter's glasses are constantly being replayed. Everybody knows it."

Since the advent of real-time Web journalism in the early twenty-first century, breaking news is disseminated differently, with a different—and less unified—experience than that of the millions of Americans synchronistically watching as Cronkite announced Kennedy's death. Should there be such an event today, a huge population of citizens wouldn't turn to their TV sets. They'd go immediately to their Apple laptop or BlackBerry or iPhone. Real-time information can now be found on the Web *before* it makes its way to the news bureau. In the age of Twitter and five-hundred-channel cable TV, it's unlikely that any single anchorperson could pull Americans together the way Cronkite did in those dark days of 1963.

In the wake of Dallas, President Johnson created the President's Commission on the Assassination of President Kennedy (known as the Warren Commission after its chairman, Supreme Court Justice Earl Warren). On September 24, 1964, after ten months of investigation, the final 888-page Warren Commission report was handed to Johnson. Cronkite devoured every page. CBS News, in fact, had asked the commission to publicly release supporting documents and evidence. More than twenty-six volumes of testimony and depositions were released as part of the Warren Commission's conclusion that Oswald was the lone gunman. Lew Wood—who, after re-creating the Book Depository event, covered Jack Ruby's trial for CBS News in 1964—may have been right all along in his conjecture that Oswald acted alone.

After the Warren Commission Report was released to the public on September 27, CBS News received thousands of letters asking the network to further investigate the suspect claim that Oswald had acted alone. The pesky letters wouldn't cease. Cronkite, along with the man in charge of CBS News' prime-time coverage, Les Midgley, decided to make a four-part analysis of the Warren Report in 1966. Paley backed the Cronkite-Midgley film with a million-dollar budget— then an unprecedented amount of production money.

"What fed the conspiracy notion about the Kennedy assassination among many Americans was the sheer incongruity of the affair," Eric Sevareid recalled. "All that power and majesty wiped out in an instant by one skinny, weak-chinned, little character."

Following Cronkite's instructions, CBS reporters put the Warren Commission Report under intense scrutiny, reconstructing the ballistics and audio tests. They watched all the film footage taken in Dallas on November 22, 1963 (including the Zapruder footage, a twenty-six-second home movie shot by Dallas dressmaker Abraham Zapruder, that *Life* magazine purchased after outbidding CBS News). Around one hundred witnesses were interviewed for *CBS News Inquiry: The Warren Report.* Few stones were left unturned. After a thorough investigation, Cronkite, in this four-part series that aired from June 25 to June 28, 1967, dispelled the notion of an octopus-like conspiracy to get Kennedy. "We concluded," he said, "that nothing else could be proved beyond what the Warren Commission was able to establish. . . . It was perfectly possible with that particular rifle to get that kind of accuracy." Rick DuBrow, the UPI media critic, called CBS News' documentary, anchored by Cronkite (along with Rather and Sevareid), "a rare and important experience in television journalism."

Over time, Cronkite grew more skeptical about the Warren Commission Report. Many things about it just didn't smell right. Cronkite first raised his doubts that Oswald acted alone in a 1981 Q&A conducted for the *Columbia Journalism Review*. "I wonder how much has been hidden that we don't know?" he asked Osborn Elliott, then dean of the Columbia Graduate School of Journalism and editor in chief of *Newsweek* when Cronkite made the cover back in late 1963. "I do know that I interviewed the late President Johnson, and he said to me that he had some feeling that it might have been a conspiracy, and then he asked that that be stricken— and we did, under some duress, strike that. I've always thought that there was a second person involved in the thing, but not in the manner of a grand conspiracy. But I still don't believe, despite the House Committee's investigation, the multiple gun theory. . . . I wonder now, with the CIA plot to assassinate Castro, about the possibilities of setting up something of this kind for whatever international purpose. I'm not as happy as I once was with the Warren Commission Report."

Under Cronkite's leadership, CBS News continued to collect information on the assassination as a public service during the Nixon, Ford, and Carter years. In 1975 the network ran the special *The American Assassins*, which concentrated on Lee Harvey Oswald.

Relying on the newest technology, CBS News micro-analyzed the Zapruder film frame by frame and explored the topic of the CIA's relationship to Oswald and the Cuban connection. Credit for the George Foster Peabody Award–winning documentary went to producer Bernard Birnbaum and correspondent Dan Rather. But Cronkite gained by letting CBS News viewers know that the network never stopped investigating the Kennedy assassination. And the most estimable clip from *The American Assassins* was Cronkite revealing that LBJ had told him off the record that an "international" conspiracy was at play in the Kennedy assassination.

The CBS News mailroom in late November 1963 was awash in letters thanking Cronkite for his public service. A few missives implored him to run for the White House or U.S. Senate. Being a celebrity, which Cronkite undoubtedly was by 1964, meant people thought he could excel at anything. His face now appeared not just on magazine covers, but also on billboards and buses and benches. Executive producer Fred Friendly, who in March 1964 replaced Salant as president of CBS News, hoped to capitalize on Cronkite's post–JFK assassination fame. He told *Newsweek*, "A man lands on the moon. A president dies. Anything. If you can have *one* man in the world tell it to you, who do you turn on?" After a pause, Friendly then offered a one-word answer: "*Cronkite.*"

NBC News refused to play by the stricture of Friendly's question, continuing to insist that two, Huntley and Brinkley, were better than one. A cold fact remained. On the escalator ride of nightly news, CBS News was still in second place.

18.

Who's Afraid of the Nielsen Ratings?

LBJ, STANTON, AND THE FCC—CONNECTING WITH IKE—THE NIELSEN VIEWING BOX—CAN CRONKITE BE A HEAVYWEIGHT?—THE AUBREY FACTOR—CIVIL RIGHTS ACT OF 1964—CIVIL RIGHTS REALITY—MURDERS IN MISSISSIPPI—THE INTEGRATIONIST—CHARGING NORMANDY WITH IKE—STICKING BY UNCLE SAM IN THE GULF OF TONKIN—THE DOMINO EFFECT

Lyndon Johnson's wife, Lady Bird, had purchased KTBC (later KLBJ), the CBS radio affiliate in Austin, in 1943 (an often underplayed part of LBJ's rags-to-riches saga). A quid pro quo system was set up between the Federal Communications

Commission—which reviewed all broadcast license transfers—and the rising Texas political wunderkind from the get-go. When Lady Bird purchased KTBC, it was licensed to operate only in the daytime, and it shared bandwidth on 1150 kilocycles with another local station. But then LBJ did a little influence-peddling. Aiming to be a regional giant, KTBC received permission from the FCC to broadcast around the clock and move to 590 on the dial (the uncluttered end), where its broadcasts could be heard in well over thirty counties in Texas. By 1945, the FCC had granted the station the right to double its power, now airing in over sixty counties. At one juncture, LBJ visited Paley and point-blank asked him if KTBC could become a CBS affiliate. The request was quickly approved. One of LBJ's closest business allies was now Dr. Frank Stanton, president of CBS and Cronkite's ultimate boss. "Their deep friendship went back a long way," Johnson aide Harry Middleton explained. "Back to the early Senate days." Before long, Lyndon and Lady Bird were making millions from their CBS radio and television stations and using Austin as their business headquarters.

Lyndon Johnson's overwrought disposition always impressed Cronkite, even when it repulsed. Standing six foot two or three inches tall, always well groomed in contemporary ranch clothes or tailor-made dark suits, chain-smoking Camels, a reader of newspapers, regularly flirting with the nearest beauteous girl, Johnson was a Pecos Bill–style folk figure in Texas when Cronkite befriended him. What frustrated Cronkite about Johnson was that for all his loquaciousness, LBJ clammed up when speaking into a microphone. Whenever Cronkite visited Johnson at his 1,500-acre Pedernales River ranch near Austin, they had a fine time talking about CBS business, cattle prices, the effects of drought, and NASA excellence. (LBJ was influential in procuring $60 million for a space center outside Houston.) But when wired with electronics, Johnson—as senator, Senate minority leader, Senate majority leader, vice president, and president—became too self-conscious to spill the beans (the dread of any reporter covering politics).

Full of braggadocio and unparalleled parliamentary skill, Johnson was ill-disposed to most reporters, deeming them mischief-makers determined to sabotage ambitious politicians' great dreams. Like a hungry hawk circling a desert sink, LBJ was always ready to berate a Big Three network executive over bad press. Nevertheless, radio was his mistress and television part of his daily routine. No sooner did he move into the Oval Office than he had a three-television console installed, with giant rabbit-ear antennae placed on the

White House roof. Cronkite assumed that the FCC would force Johnson to sell his Texas broadcast properties, which had made him a fortune. Instead, Cohn and Marks, the president's law firm, concocted a way for him to put his Texas stations into a trusteeship. Hoping to exert control over CBS, LBJ would routinely call Stanton to grouse about both on-air content and the fees that his CBS stations had to pay for shows' syndication rights. Whenever LBJ went to New York, Stanton would fete him with limousines, private cocktails, and coffee with the liberal intelligentsia—anything to keep the Texas power broker happy. "LBJ and Frank Stanton were good friends," Tom Johnson, personal assistant to the president (no relation), recalled. "LBJ would complain about various CBS reporters, including Bob Pierpoint and Dan Rather. Frank spoke as the most respected network head on broadcast in TV matters in D.C."

What the president knew about Cronkite was that he was a real company man. CBS, which had gone public and ranked on the New York Stock Exchange as far back as 1937, was the "candy store" of Paley and Stanton. LBJ was part of the profit sharing as TV became the most lucrative advertising medium in the world. While that doesn't mean that Cronkite intentionally went easy on Johnson from 1963 to 1967, the

Evening News, except for a few tough Vietnam stories, rarely drew blood against the administration. The LBJ-Stanton relationship was so rock-solid that Cronkite, way down on the power totem pole, was careful not to be perceived as a broadcasting antagonist of the White House. Allergic to East Coast condescension, Cronkite knew that LBJ wasn't "Huckleberry Capone," as some reporters portrayed him, but was instead a brave champion of minorities and the downtrodden.

Sensing that hailing from Houston bred fraternity, LBJ from 1964 to 1967 treated Cronkite more like a second cousin than a fourth-estate adversary. Perhaps it was an intra-Texas thing—or a political thing inasmuch as Cronkite had an inordinate amount of power as CBS News' main voice. The fact that Cronkite publicly supported broad-minded Great Society policies aimed at helping the poor, elderly, and minority populations didn't hurt relations. The Longhorn dropout had also made Houston proud in his *CBS News Special Report* "109 Days to Venus" (about a *Mariner 2* spacecraft's first planetary flyby). "[Johnson] watched all the newscasts," Cronkite recalled. "He would call me right after my newscast and say, 'You got that one wrong. I want you to fix that at your next broadcast.'"

Johnson wasn't the only U.S. political giant who cultivated Cronkite as an obliging ally. In 1964 a story circulated in broadcasting circles concerning Dwight Eisenhower's unbridled respect for the CBS anchorman. What most impressed Eisenhower about "D-Day Plus 20 Years: Eisenhower Returns to Normandy" was that it had achieved rare "perfect clearance" status by airing on every CBS TV affiliate (even in Alaska, Hawaii, and Guam). Learning that Cronkite had been benched during that year's Democratic Convention in Atlantic City, the former president telephoned Paley to express his unhappiness. "Walter," Eisenhower purportedly said to Cronkite, "I called Bill Paley." Full of instant consternation, Cronkite grew uncomfortable, even queasy as Eisenhower continued his anecdote. "Bill said he didn't do it," Eisenhower told him. "According to him, it was some fellow in Chicago named Nielsen."

The story, perhaps apocryphal, was pervasive around the CBS, NBC, and ABC broadcast centers in the mid-1960s. Newsmen relished it. Not even a former five-star general such as Dwight Eisenhower or an FCC manipulator like Lyndon Johnson could hobble the power of the television ratings system.

Arthur Charles Nielsen Sr., a market analyst, started a television ratings service in 1950. His Chicago-based A. C. Nielsen Company gathered data on television viewing by selecting 1,100 households that represented a demographic sampling of the nation. Each received a free television with a locked box attached. The box recorded the viewing habits of the household—not what the residents might tell a survey-taker about Tube habits, but what they *actually* watched. In the mid-1960s, Nielsen and its competitor, Arbitron, could supply basic raw headcount statistics overnight, but Nielsen delivered more detailed profiles of national television viewing on a weekly, monthly, or biannual basis. Upper-level CBS executives occasionally ignored the ratings, but only at their own peril. Midlevel network executives never strayed from the numbers. Low ratings could ruin a career; conversely, high ones could instantly launch one.

What the Nielsen ratings showed in 1963–1964 was that CBS virtually owned prime time in America. The network also had a lock on daytime television. CBS, the largest advertising-based business in the world, took in twice as much from television operations as NBC, its second-place rival. Paley's company comprised seven divisions: Television, Radio, Records, News, Television Stations, Laboratories, and International. Television was by far the cash cow of the corporate enterprise. All the top ten daytime shows were on CBS. In the evening's prime time, CBS broadcast fourteen of the top fifteen shows. In the fall of 1964 CBS premiered *Gomer*

Pyle, U.S.M.C.; *Gilligan's Island*; and *The Munsters*—all three mega-hits.

CBS Television president James Aubrey was holding a hot hand, but *The CBS Evening News with Walter Cronkite*—which had begun its half-hour format in September 1963—was not among the winners. Throughout 1964, with Johnson in the White House, CBS continued to lag *The Huntley-Brinkley Report* in the evening news time slot. Cronkite, who was managing editor on the newscast, had closed the gap by a small margin, but that was to no real avail. Demographic data showed that his show was gaining in popularity with television viewers who were older and less affluent than those who watched NBC. That made for weak advertising revenue. Aubrey worried that Cronkite, who would talk to *anyone* and take *any* general assignment, would never beef up to become a Nielsen ratings heavyweight. Something about his sweet aw-shucks demeanor, Aubrey feared, shouted "back-up plan" or "fill-in." Defending Cronkite against Aubrey was Fred Friendly, who wasn't afraid to become verbally aggressive with Aubrey in defending CBS News programming.

Just as intimidating as LBJ in person, the six-foot-two Aubrey (known as the Smiling Cobra), who had become a CBS executive vice president on June 1,

1956, was considered abrasive, gladly telling a particular showbiz talent his or her performance reeked, or dictatorially demanding high Nielsen ratings for all his prime-time shows or face the ax. He was full of firing surprises. The threat of cancellation hovered above CBS stage sets like Damocles' sword. As CBS News anchorman, Cronkite, for the record, insisted that Aubrey never intimidated him and that he never sweated the Nielsen ratings. If that was true, it was equally true that Cronkite didn't need to study them. The mood in the executive offices reflected with crystal clarity the frustration caused by his middling numbers. One way or another, Cronkite knew exactly where the ratings put his show. "He is the most competitive person I ever met, always driving to win anything, from children's games to a yacht race to the television ratings contest," CBS producer Les Midgley noted about Cronkite. "What he wanted, for himself and the show, was to be first and best."

As a final twist, one that could have serious repercussions for his career, Cronkite was frustrated that his *Evening News* wasn't winning new viewers, the very reason he'd been given the anchor chair. CBS News division president Dick Salant later reflected on the corporation's frustration on the record: "Douglas Edwards had been replaced with Walter Cronkite; we had expanded the evening news to a half hour—but so far as the Nielsen ratings were concerned, nothing had happened." Not that Cronkite didn't try. Hoping to attract young people to the *CBS Evening News*, he made history and scored a big ratings coup by being the first TV journalist to interview the Beatles when they came to America—the interview was conducted before the Fab Four appeared on CBS's *Ed Sullivan Show* on February 9, 1964.

The Beatles were a one-night bump, not a salve. The thirty-minute evening TV news broadcast, the use of communications satellites, and the doubling (or tripling) of reporters and budgets were snowballing problems for the Big Three. The networks were all trying to convince themselves—as well as audiences and critics—that television news could make a greater public service contribution, something larger than newspapers, to American society. Something far bigger than radio, too, or even the town crier of bygone days. The Big Three executives couldn't quite define what that main contribution meant in historical terms. And so, as the critical excitement over the thirty-minute nightly broadcast waned (far more quickly than it had arrived), television news was still a dinnertime convenience that defined its pioneering identity in terms of on-air gimmicks. David Brinkley's sarcastic wit on

NBC, Eric Sevareid's piercing intellect on CBS, and other high points of news shows on the Tube were actually only parts of a greater entertainment program picture. None of the shrewd people like Stanton or Hewitt or Benjamin who had been drawn to the burgeoning television industry could see the picture in its entirety. Yet executives and reporters alike knew the nightly news was more important than thirty minutes of droning TV in which advertisers bought time. What they didn't know was that success in the industry had little to do with gimmicks or even technology. Even Cronkite, the veteran wire service reporter, was on the wrong track, trying to measure news broadcasts in terms of newspaper columns. He might as well have been using a yardstick to weigh a rock.

Radio had been in the same predicament in 1940, trying everything from canned laughter to serenades to crystalline wit, but still misunderstanding its own potential. Then Edward R. Murrow bravely stood with a microphone on a rooftop in London during German air raids, his voice one of authority and fire, epitomizing the power of broadcast radio with every syllable uttered. Between the courage in his voice and the screeching London sirens, listeners in the United States felt as if they were *there*, fending off Luftwaffe strikes from their living room sofas. Murrow's reporting for

CBS Radio meant that hardworking autoworkers in Detroit and apple farmers in the Willamette Valley alike viscerally felt Western civilization on the brink of collapse. They were brought directly into the historical moment by the hyper-engaged Murrow.

If television history had ended in 1963 when Cronkite interviewed the Beatles, it also would have left rich accomplishments in comedy (*The Lucy Show*), drama (*Perry Mason*), and, of course, in news documentaries (*See It Now*). All these programs were genuine artistic high points to applaud for the ages. And Aubrey was their master puppeteer. But Paley fired him all the same, tossed him into the street in 1965 like a wino for "unmanageable insubordination." *Life* magazine published a tribute to the suddenly unemployed Aubrey, treating him as a TV revolutionary. "In the long history of human communications, from tom-tom to Telstar, no one man ever had a lock on such enormous audiences as James Thomas Aubrey, Jr. during his five-year tenure as the head of the Columbia Broadcasting System's television network," the *Life* reporters wrote. "He was the World's No. 1 purveyor of entertainment."

TV, Cronkite understood, was a cutthroat business. Millions of Americans in 1963 were grateful to him for gracefully announcing Kennedy's death to the world. But Paley saw the deficiencies in Cronkite's act: young people, an all-important demographic, thought he was too starchy. Nielsen said so. At the beginning of the 1964 election year, the pressure for high ratings was intensifying at CBS. The company had poured money into the broadcast center studio set and hiring new personnel. The dictates of business now demanded results from Cronkite, Hewitt, Salant, and the rest of the news division gang. For a decade CBS had been—and would remain for years to come—the biggest advertising medium in the world, employing over 13,500 people. Its boom was comparable to General Motors or General Electric. If Cronkite had purchased one hundred shares of CBS stock in 1929 and kept them through 1964, through stock dividends and splits he would own thirteen thousand shares, worth $520,000.

The key question was how to spike the *CBS Evening News* ratings share upward. What Cronkite, Stanton, and Paley all understood was that presidential elections boosted public interest in political news. Over the first three decades of television, the importance of the Democratic and Republican conventions cannot be overestimated. When NBC newsman David Brinkley published his memoir in 1995, he organized chapters by conventions, not elections. That was the way television journalists looked at the political world: in terms of two conventions, on-screen epics neatly scheduled a month apart every four years. A network's coverage, as Jack Gould pointed out in *The New York Times*, set the tone "of its public relations image for the four years that follow." With the Republican primary in New Hampshire approaching on March 10, 1964, the process was set to begin. Then, on the very eve of the '64 season, CBS suffered a crisis of confidence. The team, it was determined, had to be made stronger. Paley's ax was drawn and someone had to go.

On March 2, Dick Salant was removed as head of CBS News by his boss and friend, Frank Stanton. (He was "promoted" to special assistant to the president of CBS and vice president of Corporate Affairs.) Stanton claimed full responsibility, only much later acknowledging that Paley, who regarded dominance in the news as a "CBS birthright," had dictated the move. Everyone knew that the true culprit was, in fact, a numbers-obsessed Illinois market analyst named Nielsen. The *Newsweek* cover publicity of September 1963 and the JFK assassination coverage hadn't translated into increased viewership for the *CBS Evening News*. Salant had to pay the price. "If Paley could fire Aubrey and demote Salant with the snap of a finger," Andy Rooney recalled, "Walter was only a bad ratings week away from the unemployment row."

Fred Friendly was named the new president of CBS News. Friendly, whose specialty was news documentary production, made few changes to the Cronkite show at first, instead asserting that "getting Ed back here is my first order of business." Friendly had partnered with Murrow for the launch of *See It Now* and also worked with him on its replacement, *CBS Reports.* Contrary to his name, Friendly was not especially popular around CBS. A workhorse whose red-rimmed eyes betrayed his long hours burning the midnight oil, he was resented for the viciousness of his tantrums, but no one doubted his integrity or the high standard of the programs he produced. Nonetheless, when his champion, Ed Murrow, left CBS in 1961 to assume the USIA directorship, the assumption was that Friendly, too, would soon be gone. Defying expectations, he remained as the executive producer of *CBS Reports*, a prestigious documentary program that aired Sundays at 7:00 p.m., but one that drew light audiences. According to the prevailing theory, the size of the audience didn't matter, since the program was so well respected with the Emmy Award folks. Not that everyone at CBS agreed with that type of thinking. Even on slow-mo Sundays.

Murrow, the Babe Ruth of broadcasting, had been separated, if not exiled, from the company for three years. Friendly believed that bringing back the home run king from USIA would be a grand gesture. Sadly, though, because of his cancer, Murrow couldn't return to broadcasting. He didn't want to, anyway. The Murrow era was over, but the next time frame at CBS was just lurching forward—without a name. It could not rightly be called the "Cronkite Era," not with his mediocre Nielsen ratings. The verdict was still out on Cronkite. The news division desperately needed a whoppingly successful ratings season over NBC. Then it would recognize its next in-house broadcasting hero.

Friendly began almost immediately to meet with Cronkite in early 1964 to plan convention coverage. The first idea in the new Friendly regime to affect the *CBS Evening News* was a good one. Friendly, seizing a suggestion from Bill Small, talent-tapped one of the younger CBS correspondents on the company roster, Roger Mudd, based in the Washington bureau. Mudd had gotten his journalism start working for *The Richmond News Leader* in the 1950s. His sponsor at CBS had been Howard K. Smith. "Friendly proposed that I cover every day of the coming Senate filibuster on an omnibus civil rights bill not only on the *Evening News with Walter Cronkite* but also on each of the network's four other TV newscasts and on seven of the network's hourly radio newscasts," Mudd recalled. "No story had ever gotten such coverage."

Mudd was aware that Cronkite protected every one of his twenty-two minutes (minus the Sevareid commentary) on the *CBS Evening News* and he suspected Cronkite would be wary of committing to a nightly segment on a Senate filibuster, which is by definition a stalling tactic designed to bore and frustrate the opposition into compromise. It oughtn't to have been good television. Senators such as James Eastland of Mississippi and Richard Russell of Georgia, old-school segregationists who opposed the landmark Civil Rights Act of 1964, babbled their way through more than two months—fifty-seven congressional working days.

But Mudd reported it as if from ringside, standing on the steps of the Capitol in all weather and updating viewers on the action (or lack of it) as if he were describing a fifty-seven-round boxing match. It got hard to imagine Mudd without a CBS microphone clutched in his hand, standing on the Capitol steps. Friendly had learned from the McCarthy era that the longer a politician spoke, the more rope there was with which to hang him. He unleashed Mudd on the bigoted Washington, D.C., politicians as surely as Bull Connor had loosed police attack dogs upon peaceful civil rights marchers in Birmingham. "We're going to cover this civil rights story every day," Friendly told Mudd. "Yes, sir," was Mudd's pleased response, "yes sir."

An enthusiastic Cronkite, as managing editor of the *CBS Evening News*, directed Mudd to provide short profiles of such filibustering senators as Strom Thurmond and Robert C. Byrd. Mudd complied, and the story grew dramatically to one with its own narrative drive. From March 30 to June 19, Mudd delivered an astounding 867 reports on various CBS outlets, television and radio. The word *ubiquitous* doesn't do his act justice. Americans were intrinsically interested in the fate of the civil rights bill, but with the CBS coverage, they became riveted by the deliberations on it as well. Friendly even considered having Mudd grow a beard to emphasize the length of the filibuster; both Small and Cronkite thought such a stunt was too much hokum. As the filibuster continued into June, public protests encouraged the Senate majority to end the filibuster through the use of cloture (the first time a cloture vote had ever prevailed in a civil rights debate). Soon afterward, Congress passed a version of the bill that was closer to the original than political veterans might ever have predicted. The long filibuster had failed—on television and to some extent *by* television. "Friendly deserved a lot of credit," Mudd recalled. "He was a volcanic man of great enthusiasms. You couldn't help but get to work on his ideas. Covering the filibusters was novel. And, from a news perspective it worked. Friendly next wanted me to go to Vietnam. I had a family and said 'NO.' "

In Friendly's schema, the civil rights struggle was a chance for Cronkite's *CBS Evening News* to beat *Huntley-Brinkley* in the Nielsen ratings. CBS had the technical and financial resources to dispatch corre-spondents to follow the gallant Martin Luther King Jr. on every protest march, from Montgomery to Selma to Memphis. Like NASA's space race with the Soviets, it was a reliable story full of drama. Dan Rather contin-ued to work the Deep South beat for CBS with verve and commitment. Southern CBS affiliates were livid at the way Cronkite, Mudd, Rather, and Co. were back-ing the "negro action." South of the Mason-Dixon Line, CBS was mocked as the "Colored Broadcasting System." The insular CBS affiliates in New Orleans and Atlanta threatened Paley to cool his jets, to stop giving the National Association for the Advancement of Colored People (NAACP), the Student Nonviolent Coordinating Committee (SNCC), the Congress of Racial Equality (CORE), and the Southern Christian Leadership Conference (SCLC) so much free nightly news time for their radical street antics. "But we never felt that pressure on the news desk itself," Cronkite recalled. "We had a marvelous management that kept it off our backs on the *Evening News.*"

At Stanton's suggestion, correspondent Bill Plante started working for Cronkite in June 1964 as the junior guy on CBS's New York City assignment desk. Just two weeks later Plante found himself in the kudzu land of Mississippi covering Freedom Summer. A Chicagoan with a strong Irish-Catholic sense of social justice, Plante had never been farther south than St. Louis. To his virgin eyes, the whole state of Mississippi seemed a war zone with blacks and whites pitted against each other. Federal-versus-states'-rights battles were taking place in Jackson, Oxford, Clarksdale, Hattiesburg, and along the Gulf Coast. "It was like the dark side of the moon," Plante recalled. "*Terra incognita.* It didn't take me long to see that these white southerners thought they were defending a way of life. Generally speaking, we were fair at CBS in covering all sides of the freedom struggle. But I knew, back in New York, Don Hewitt and Walter Cronkite were aghast at Jim Crow, wanted to see it smashed."

On July 1, 1964, Cronkite served as host of the *CBS News Special Report* "The Summer Ahead." The tease for the prime-time show was "Will passage of the Civil Rights Bill help to avoid what some have predicted will be a summer of violence?" Cronkite worked with a seven-man reporting team on various aspects of the civil rights unrest in Mississippi, Alabama, Georgia, and Florida. The protest marches covered weren't intended as entertainment, but that is what they became. On Cronkite's *CBS Evening News*, Bull Connor–like villains with barking dogs and water hoses were pitted against the Nobel Peace Prize winner Martin Luther King Jr. and unarmed men, women, and children.

With or without television, the Civil Rights Act—signed by President Johnson on July 2, 1964—was destined to be a big story. In focusing on the filibuster, though, CBS News had demonstrated that special-events coverage could be sustained over the course of weeks or months, perhaps years. Mudd's excellent broadcasts proved that some viewers craved the sausage-factory reality of congressional legislation.

The next chapter of the civil rights story, as covered by CBS News, offered none of the humor of Strom Thurmond or John Stennis reading the Yellow Pages to kill time. It carried the burden of too much stark reality. Three civil rights volunteers, fresh from a course on registering voters held at the Western College for Women in Oxford, Ohio (later part of the Miami University of Ohio), were missing—and presumed dead—in Mississippi. James Chaney, Andrew Goodman, and Michael Schwerner were part of the

Freedom Summer protests and were in the Mississippi Delta to register African American voters. Their burned-out station wagon was discovered at the edge of the Bogue Chitto Swamp, near Philadelphia, Mississippi. "The Senate action came just before 8 p.m. on a Friday," Cronkite explained to NPR in 2005. "It still might have been our top story on Monday. But late Sunday night, something happened in the swamps of Mississippi."

Cronkite led with the somber story of the Mississippi disappearances on Monday night's edition of the *CBS Evening News*, June 22, 1964. Horror engulfed his face. "Good evening," he began. "Three young civil rights workers disappeared in Mississippi on Sunday night near the central Mississippi town of Philadelphia, about fifty miles northeast of Jackson. The last report on the trio came from Philadelphia police, who said they were picked up for speeding on Sunday, fined $20, then released." The circumstances were deeply disturbing. The vanishing of Chaney, Goodman, and Schwerner, Cronkite believed, was a microcosm of the ongoing southern brutality toward blacks. "Where I grew up, in my household in black Sacramento, after the way Walter Cronkite covered the Mississippi murders, we knew he was on our side," activist Cornel West, a Princeton University professor, recalled. "We appreciated that Cronkite was willing to reveal the anti-democratic hypocrisy of Jim Crow."

Cronkite called the South in 1964 "a deeply isolated civilization that hadn't changed its mind in 200 years. You had to live in the South to understand how deeply separate it was, as I had when my family moved to Texas when I was 10. I quickly learned that the Civil War was the 'War Between the States' and the Confederate flag could still inspire patriotic fervor. Now, in the 1960s, the time capsule that had been the Old South and had been left alone for so long was being pried open like a rusty tomb. During that week in June, the country would be shocked by the skeletons it began to find." Of all the American warts, the curious calculation of racism caused Cronkite to flinch with the most anger. Just like his father, who walked out of his boss's Jim Crow house in Houston during the Great Depression, Cronkite was someone for whom prejudice of any kind was anathema. To Cronkite, segregationist politicians such as George Wallace of Alabama and Lester Maddox of Georgia were thugs. But the CBS corporate mandate insisted on network objectivity. Cronkite often circumvented this rule, not in direct commentary but rather in the airtime accorded to Dr. King's movement. As managing editor of the *CBS Evening News*, he believed in fair reporting. And he didn't want to overtly tick off the CBS affiliates in Atlanta, Dallas, and Nashville. But he couldn't be "objective" about innocents like Chaney, Goodman, and Schwerner being murdered in Mississippi by Dixiefied bigots.

In the early part of the Freedom Summer of 1964, many in the South continued to complain that the coverage on the *CBS Evening News* was skewed in favor of the civil rights movement. All the networks heard the same criticism. They were frequently accused of staging protests for their conflict-hungry cameras or happily playing the stooge for civil rights leaders like Hosea Williams or John L. Lewis, who supposedly staged protests for cinematic effect. At the very least, CBS rewarded civil unrest with *Evening News* coverage. Just as Murrow had crusaded against McCarthyism, Cronkite was now doing the same, albeit in a behind-the-scenes way, against neo-Confederate hatemongers. "I always considered CBS News an ally," civil rights leader Julian Bond recalled. "Not that Cronkite was an activist. Far from it. But his show—and NBC's—following in the tradition of Murrow, let the cameras roll and gave us airtime. It was TV that caused many Americans to denounce bigotry in the 1960s."

In a CBS News program that aired in June 1964, Cronkite focused on a less controversial subject than Jim Crow: a "we're-all-in-this-together" retrospective

of World War II, including his place in it as a UP correspondent. U.S. Army generals were still de facto heroes
in 1964, none more so than Dwight Eisenhower, with
whom Cronkite returned to the beaches of Normandy
in honor of the twentieth anniversary of the D-day
landings. Where Eisenhower was concerned, according
to executive Bill Leonard, CBS "had the edge on other
networks because of his friendship with Bill Paley." The
special, "D-Day Plus 20 Years: Eisenhower Returns
to Normandy," was filmed in August 1963 but broadcast in early June 1964 on *CBS Reports*, with excerpts
shown on the *Evening News*. "He only made two visits
back to Normandy since the war," Cronkite boasted of
his Eisenhower exclusive, "and both were ceremonial.
This was his first chance to fly in a helicopter over the
area, to drive a jeep, to walk along the beach. Our one
problem was that of selection [of scenes to use in the
final cut]. No matter where we stopped, at any road-
side, he would have stories to tell."

Cronkite had met Eisenhower early in 1944, in the
course of his war reportage, for a glancing handshake.
Nothing more. His opinion of the Eisenhower presidency wasn't noticeably high until he had the opportunity to interview the former president in 1961, at his
home in Gettysburg, Pennsylvania, an envious Sevareid
hovering nearby off-camera. With Friendly as producer

and Cronkite as interviewer, Eisenhower talked to CBS for a whopping thirteen hours, the ex-president's intelligence flowing naturally through each topic raised. For five straight days, two to three hours a day, Cronkite and Eisenhower conducted what amounted to one of the seminal oral histories of the century. It was boiled down to a three-hour special, "Eisenhower on the Presidency," which aired in December 1961 to rave reviews.

While Cronkite wasn't a superstitious man, he came to think of Eisenhower as a combined four-leaf clover and rabbit's foot. Following the success of "Eisenhower on the Presidency," the "D-Day Plus 20 Years" program was even more well received. *The New York Times* featured a front-page article on June 6, praising the "simple eloquence" of Eisenhower's Normandy recollections. In the broadcast, Cronkite was respectful and slightly stiff, but in that, as in so much of his work, he delineated the attitude of most of his viewers. Americans didn't want a scoop or a chance to see Eisenhower trapped into an unpleasant revelation. They wanted to remain in awe of the Supreme Allied Commander who had made Operation Overlord a colossal success. As Eisenhower reminisced, he and Cronkite watched swimmers cavorting at Omaha Beach, greeted nuns leading schoolchildren across the once-bloodied sands, and gazed through the German gun casements on the chalky cliffs of Pointe du Hoc. CBS News' publicity department circulated a photo of Cronkite driving Ike around in a Jeep; both UPI and AP picked it up. When they visited the American cemetery near Saint-Laurent-sur-Mer and walked past some of the more than nine thousand graves there, Eisenhower fell silent. He had signed the death certificates of many of those buried soldiers. Looking back on the day in 2004, Cronkite said of his meeting with Eisenhower at Normandy, "It may have been the most solemn moment of my career."

Cronkite harbored a similarly respectful attitude—on a lower frequency—toward the American engagement in South Vietnam in 1964. He accepted intelligence updates on the war from the Johnson administration and military leaders without feeling compelled to question them. When Secretary of Defense Robert McNamara fed him raw information, he believed the data. Later admitting to swallowing the Pentagon's battlefield distortions for too long, Cronkite pointed out that he had adopted the space race, civil rights, and the Great Society as his turf, causing him to only haphazardly grapple with Vietnam. Looking back, he further admitted that other ongoing stories—notably U.S.-Soviet relations and the cold war in

Europe—also pushed Vietnam to the back of his consciousness. "Over the years," wrote CBS producer Les Midgley, speaking of the mid-1960s, "Cronkite personally tended to be on the side of those who believed the U.S. should be involved in Vietnam."

In April 1964, CBS aired a far-searching documentary often overlooked by scholars, *Vietnam: The Deadly Decision*, hosted by Charles Collingwood. It aired to anemic ratings. Later that year, Collingwood would write and host an overview of U.S. involvement in Vietnam since the 1950s for *CBS Reports* titled "Can We Get Out?" Those pioneering documentaries reached only a modest share in the Nielsen ratings. On the *CBS Evening News*, Cronkite, Friendly, and Hewitt duly aired excerpts and reported news of Vietnam, but a full commitment was lacking. The pictures and the words, often prophetic, had yet to outrage the general public or the anchor and managing editor of the *CBS Evening News*.

Two months after the broadcast of "D-Day Plus 20 Years," on Tuesday, August 4, 1964, Cronkite was by chance in the CBS newsroom when word came over the UPI and AP wires of a supposed attack on a U.S. destroyer in the Gulf of Tonkin off the coast of Vietnam. It was the second report in three days of an act of aggression against a navy ship. Frustrated with military activity emanating from North Vietnam, Johnson prepared his response to the Gulf of Tonkin incident, a speech later that evening calling for military action in retaliation. This event triggered preplanned American bombing raids on North Vietnam. That same day, the bodies of Schwerner, Chaney, and Goodman were finally found in Mississippi. Two of the major stories of the year had broken on the same day. Cronkite led the *CBS Evening News* with a headline regarding the alleged Tonkin attack, but he turned immediately to a full report on the case in Mississippi.

Just after 11:30 that night, President Johnson went on the air to give the American people a disturbing description of the Gulf of Tonkin incident as a justification for "military action." He rushed the Gulf of Tonkin Resolution through Congress the next day in what Cronkite later denigrated as a "nimbus of patriotic fervor." Some Washington observers had already cast doubt on the story's veracity and bemoaned the rush to retaliate. Cronkite was not among them. He acknowledged "supporting" Johnson's decision. Usually obsessive about checking facts before they were aired, Cronkite accepted Johnson's version of events without question.

In *The Powers That Be,* reporter David Halberstam recounted an interview with Fred Friendly, who admitted that he'd received a phone call from Murrow on the night of Johnson's Tonkin speech. Ailing but intense as ever, Murrow was infuriated by CBS's complacency. The facts regarding the attack by North Vietnam were murky and uncertain. "What do we really know about what happened out there?" Murrow fumed. "Why did it happen? How could you not have Rather and the boys do some sort of special analysis?"

In that early period of the Vietnam War, though, Cronkite was in effect still the UP man attached to the Mighty Eighth in England, circa 1943. "I was still living with my old feeling of sympathy for the original commitment," he said, "in line with Kennedy's promise that 'we shall support any friend to assure the success of liberty.'" As a Main Street patriot, he had also been born and bred to believe the U.S. president during international flare-ups such as the Tonkin incident. So had the vast majority of the American viewers to whom he delivered the news at night. Somehow Cronkite couldn't swallow the premise that the U.S. military establishment was lying to Johnson for breakfast, lunch, and dinner. Call it naïveté or brainwashing or wishful thinking. Although Cronkite later cringed at the allegation, he was in fact behaving in 1964 like a rubber-stamp sycophant for LBJ—and, it should be added, as a reliable spokesman for NASA, with top-security clearance credentials, and as an ardent foe of the Soviet Union since being based in Moscow under Stalin for the United Press, with a myopic cold war worldview.

Cronkite's "private feeling" after the Gulf of Tonkin incident was that the United States needed to stop the domino effect that would have Southeast Asia topple into Communist hands. He tried to maintain objectivity in keeping with the CBS credo (and his own conviction) that the news anchorman should not comment or editorialize upon Vietnam. "I won't say he was hawkish," CBS News reporter Morley Safer recalled of Cronkite. "But I would say he was in World War II frame of mind. We were the good guys, and the North Vietnamese were the bad guys. Vietnam wasn't like that."

19.

Paley's Attempted Smackdown

HEIL GOLDWATER—AVUNCULAR FACTOR—HARD NEWS-MAN—EMPEROR OF CBS—LAUGHING TO SUCCESS—CARE AND FEEDING OF CRONKITE CLUB— NANCY CRONKITE IS FOR LBJ—CHEERS FOR TEDDY WHITE—COW PALACE DEBACLE—WHAT THE HELL HAPPENED TO WALTER?—WORM'S-EYE VIEW— ATLANTIC CITY HUBRIS—SURVIVING THE END GAME—BARTLEBY THE CRONKITE

Every day in the early summer of 1964, Cronkite grew worried that the Arizona senator, Barry Goldwater, could actually capture the presidential nomination of the party of Abraham Lincoln and Theodore Roosevelt. Like Walter Lippmann, whom Cronkite admired, the CBS anchorman thought Goldwater's appeal was covertly racist, a coded rallying cry of "white resistance" to Martin Luther King Jr.'s nonviolent movement.

The bad blood between Cronkite and Goldwater started during the JFK assassination trauma. Goldwater had been in Muncie, Indiana, attending the funeral of his mother-in-law that fateful day when Cronkite was handed a note from a CBS staffer while on air. Nodding his head in thinly veiled contempt, Cronkite reported that Goldwater, when asked about the Kennedy assassination, had callously said, "No comment." The implication was clear to Cronkite: the Dallas tragedy didn't bother the deeply insensitive Barry much.

Goldwater was rightfully mortified by Cronkite's snide interpretation, calling such liberal claptrap "a dad-burned dirty lie." A rewatching of Cronkite's CBS News broadcasts from April to August 1964 confirms that Goldwater was often treated as a kind of neo-Nazi freak by the network, the horn-rimmed face of the John Birch Society, a sagebrush reactionary even more unfit for White House command than Joe McCarthy. To the Goldwater campaign staff, Cronkite was a relentless liberal crusader like Murrow, constantly wanting to break stories, slinging arrows at conservatives, rifling through his gold-star Rolodex to hunt down a lead that would embarrass the Arizona senator. Most of this was overdrawn by the Goldwater campaign, but there were elements of truth in it. "They haven't even the decency to apologize," Goldwater complained to KOOL-TV in Phoenix about a series of CBS News insults. "Now I have no respect for people like that. I don't think these people should be allowed to broadcast."

Feeling unfairly picked on by Cronkite, Goldwater complained to Bill Small (Washington, D.C., bureau chief for CBS, and later NBC News president) that the CBS anchorman didn't even know how to pronounce *Republican* properly on air. "No, Barry," Small said to Goldwater. "It's *February* that he can't say." (At CBS, Cronkite's "February problem" was very real; he'd pronounce it "Feb-yoo-ary." Every last week in January, producers forced Cronkite to rehearse *February* over and over again. "And it would work," Sandy Socolow recalled, "for a day or two, but then there was a relapse.")

As the July 1964 GOP Convention in San Francisco approached, the *CBS Evening News* continued to portray Goldwater as harboring fascistic views. A deeply perturbed Cronkite, worried that Goldwater would use low-yield atomic weapons against North Vietnam if elected president, thought he had an obligation to expose the senator's right-wing extremism. "Goldwater was a fervent hawk who believed that nuclear weapons would help bring victory in Vietnam," Cronkite explained years later. "If that sounds extreme today, it sounded extreme then, too. But he said it."

As managing editor of the *CBS Evening News*, Cronkite seemed to relish pricking Goldwater from time to time for sport. In late July, he introduced a report from CBS correspondent Daniel Schorr, a hard-and-fast liberal working from Munich. With an almost tongue-in-cheek smile, Cronkite said, "Whether or not Senator Goldwater wins the nomination, he *is* going places, the first place being Germany." Schorr then went on a tear, saying, "It looks as though Senator Goldwater, if nominated, will be starting his campaign in Bavaria, the center of Germany's right wing." The backstory was merely that Goldwater had accepted an invitation from Lieutenant General William Quinn for a quick holiday at Berchtesgaden, a U.S. Army recreational center in Germany. But Schorr made the takeaway point that Berchtesgaden was once "Hitler's stomping ground." Goldwater, trying to show off his NATO bona fides, had granted an interview with *Der Spiegel* in which he mentioned a possible trip to Germany soon. Some Democratic opposition researcher floated the idea that Goldwater was infatuated with the Nazis. It was ugly stuff. What was even uglier was the way Cronkite and

Schorr elevated the story to *CBS Evening News* status. Cronkite, clearly disgusted with Goldwater's German stunt, next introduced a report about an African American church burning in Mississippi, smack on the heels of the Berchtesgaden revelation. "The Germany story," historian Rick Perlstein explained in *Before the Storm*, "hit San Francisco like a freight train."

When Paley learned that Cronkite and Schorr had double-teamed Goldwater, he hit the roof. Paley had financially backed Governor William Scranton of Pennsylvania to be the Republican nominee and didn't want the Goldwater campaign to attack him for conflict of interest. This was no simple matter. Paley ordered Cronkite and Schorr to repudiate . . . *pronto* . . . to make it clear that Goldwater hadn't spoken to *Der Spiegel* about Berchtesgaden to "appeal to right-wing elements." Paley became so irate about the way Cronkite and Schorr had behaved in using the *CBS Evening News* to take digs at Goldwater that he decided to go to San Francisco himself to see what the hell was going on. "A lot of people at CBS blew a gasket about the Goldwater-is-Nazi thing," Dan Rather recalled. "That was Schorr's report. Cronkite, however, was the conveyor belt. Walter was sore at Schorr. But Cronkite became the target of CBS management."

None of this controversy helped Goldwater. The DNC photocopied the Cronkite-Schorr broadcast transcript and disseminated it in San Francisco to the gathering press pool and to people on the street. Cronkite's dear friend from wartime London, Herb Caen, the popular *San Francisco Examiner* columnist, had a field day linking Goldwater to Hitler. "You can say what you want about Goldwater's conservatism and right-wing views," Caen joked, "but personally, I find him as American as apple strudel."

While the Goldwater campaign viewed Cronkite as a Lyndon Johnson reelection stalking horse, the public relations department at CBS News marketed Cronkite as a *Father Knows Best* type, making $150,000 a year, married for a quarter century, with three cookie-cutter-perfect children. When *Cosmopolitan* (pre–Gloria Steinem) decided to profile Betsy Cronkite, she uncharacteristically played dutiful Scarsdale wife whose hero was Mamie Eisenhower. Instead of Betsy's trademark sarcasm, the reader of *Cosmo* got saccharine pap worthy of a former Hallmark publicist. In an "At Home with . . . Mrs. Walter Cronkite" story in the *New York Post* published a few years after the *Cosmo* piece, Betsy told how her bibles were the *Better Homes and Gardens Cook Book* and the *Joy of Cooking* (Walter's favorite dish was veal stew). Life had treated Betsy well; her only beefs were that Walter didn't have enough time to build model airplanes, run electric trains, downhill-ski, and sail his recently purchased twenty-two-foot Electrica around Long Island Sound. "Everybody including the trash man calls him Walter," she told the reporter. "He likes that. He's always been famous for knowing everybody. There isn't a remote corner of the world where Walter doesn't know somebody."

Around the shop, at CBS, Cronkite kept to a narrow path, that of a serious fact-stickler whose stock-in-trade was breaking news nightly. That was how deferential correspondents such as Dan Rather, Harry Reasoner, and Bob Schieffer saw him. Sig Mickelson, whom Murrow disdained, had sold Cronkite to the CBS affiliates as a what-constitutes-news expert, a field marshal, an asset to the company, and, aside from that, a rising star like Ed Sullivan, Lucille Ball, and Lassie. With blind faith, Mickelson believed that what differentiated Cronkite from other broadcasters was his tyrannical demand for answers. Other colleagues of Cronkite agreed. "He had this great curiosity," Schieffer explained. "If there was a car wreck and Walter saw it, it would be like the first car wreck he'd ever seen in his life. He'd want to know all about it."

A major "Walter Want" that staff religiously adhered to was letting the anchorman read his viewer mail, which was delivered regularly to his office. No pre-screening. He liked keeping his ear to the ground. As producer Les Midgley and vice president of CBS News Blair Clark both noted, Cronkite, unlike most TV performers, liked his praise and criticism straight-up. What Cronkite adored about producer Sandy Socolow was that, unlike either the CBS correspondent pool or the corporate executives, he delivered rotten news without a candy-coated veneer. When employees got shy about approaching Cronkite with an idea or problem, they used Socolow as a sounding board. Out of the thousands of letters Cronkite received daily, he picked favorites to answer. The front runner was from two little girls in Atchison, Kansas, around the time of John Glenn's epic orbit: "Dear Mr. Cronkite, What do the astronauts do when they gotta use the bathroom? Yours truly, Pam and Margy."

Whenever Cronkite thought a *CBS Evening News* viewer made a salient critical point, even if it meant admitting error on behalf of CBS, he replied. When the *CBS Evening News* accidentally misrepresented a comment that Governor George W. Romney of Michigan made regarding the Black Power movement, Cronkite quickly ate crow. "Your complaint was justified and our handling of the story was not," Cronkite wrote to Romney's press spokesman. "It is neither justification nor rationale but only by way of explanation that the news service copy which carried the Governor's statement buried the full text of the pertinent remark and our writer and editor missed it. I hope we made amends by seeking an interview with Governor Romney, which was used yesterday with the full text of his observation."

Because President Johnson was a shoo-in to be the nominee at the Democrats' Atlantic City convention, to be held August 24–27, all eyes were fixed on the GOP Convention in San Francisco, which was scheduled for the previous month, on July 13–16. The Goldwater-versus-Rockefeller drama was being promoted by CBS, NBC, and ABC as a club fight for the heart and soul of the party. Still furious about the Berchtesgaden story, the Goldwater campaign refused Cronkite any access to the candidate. If possible, Goldwater's lawyer would have gotten a court-issued restraining order against the CBS News anchorman. It was reminiscent of the way Cronkite and Hewitt had angered Taft (the conservative) in 1952 by giving Eisenhower (the moderate) preferential treatment.

Bill Leonard, a friend of Cronkite's since 1952 who had served in the U.S. Navy during World War II before being hired by CBS as the radio anchorman of *This Is New York*, was the head of the special Elections Unit, formed by Fred Friendly in the aftermath of

CBS's disappointing convention coverage in 1960. Cronkite was delighted when he heard that Leonard would be overseeing 1964's conventions. Leonard felt much the same way; he regarded Cronkite as his closest friend on the news-gathering side of the network. They had worked well together on various *CBS Reports*. But that was before the two were thrown together into the cauldron of the 1964 convention mayhem. For starters, Goldwater was the big interview catch in San Francisco, but that bridge had been burned for CBS. "By the time the Republican Convention rolled around," Leonard wrote in his memoir *In the Storm of the Eye*, "Bill Eames, Bobby Wussler and I were charter members of the CAFOC—Care and Feeding of Cronkite—Club. We met daily, sometimes late at night. The trick was to get Walter to do what we wanted him to do and thought was good for the broadcast or the news division—and to keep him reasonably happy in the process. *His* trick was generally to resist suggestions that involved change—Walter was, by nature, a tad superstitious, skeptical of people who professed to do things for his own good, particularly if it might alter his role in the proceedings and even more particularly if it threatened to reduce his role."

Brushing Goldwater off as a weird aberration who would get crushed by LBJ come Election Day, Cronkite didn't bother to rev up for San Francisco. In his mind, Goldwater lived on some far-right-wing side of the planet that he never cared to visit. If he got blacklisted by Goldwater, it would only endear him to President Johnson at the Democratic Convention in Atlantic City. And once Johnson got elected in November, which polls suggested was likely, he would have the best access to the White House. He was set to preside over CBS's extensive convention coverage, to wear his two hats simultaneously, anchoring and newsroom managing. He saw himself as being the star quarterback and coach combined: one part of his brain could carry on talking, even as another part sorted through the possibilities for the next segment. Executive producer Don Hewitt and others certainly had input into arranging those possibilities on the fly, but Cronkite had the system arranged so that he made the final decisions on the air. With his well-trained (and fast-writing) assistants holding signs out of camera range to update him on unfolding events, his earphone keeping him abreast of the audio from the dais, and an array of monitors at his side showing him the "feeds," Cronkite didn't have to fret. He was at the top of his game.

But he had a Day-Glo problem. His animosity toward Goldwater had brought him unwelcome scrutiny by the gossip columnists. He had become part of the story. There was tabloid gold in trying to document Cronkite's bias for LBJ. The powerful Drew Pearson wrote a troublemaking item in his *Merry-Go-Round* column about Nancy Cronkite, the anchorman's fifteen-year-old daughter, and her covertly infiltrating a Goldwater hospitality suite to put up "Scranton for President" signs. Pearson also intimated that Nancy was flirting with Michael Goldwater, the Arizona senator's son. Joining Pearson in the let's-out-Cronkite-as-a-liberal game was the always-probing Walter Winchell.

"I saw your daughter Nancy," Walter Winchell said to Cronkite.

"Where?"

"Carrying a Scranton sign with a Goldwater page," Winchell said. "She tells me she isn't for Scranton. Her heart belongs to LBJ."

It was already believed within journalism circles that Cronkite was pro-Johnson in 1964. But it was also understood that his personal bias wouldn't affect CBS News's convention coverage. Cronkite knew how to play it down the center. The CBS executives planning the convention coverage selected twenty-two newsmen for the reportorial team, among them the company's hungriest reporters to cover the floor. These included Dan Rather, Roger Mudd, Mike Wallace, and Martin

Agronsky. The durable Robert Trout, who had been broadcasting political conventions since FDR-Landon in 1936 on CBS Radio, would preside over radio coverage and appear with Cronkite occasionally on TV. Harry Reasoner would be on hand to keep the anchor chair warm when "Iron Pants" needed a quick break. The plan also called for Theodore White, writing *The Making of a President 1964*, to offer punditry. "All of us have been the beneficiaries of a new form of political journalism that Teddy White brought to us," Cronkite believed. "He was the one who began digging into the mechanics of campaigning."

White had been living on the campaign trail for months in early 1964, attending the same fund-raisers and county fairs as the candidates. Politics was a serious business to him. This didn't mean, however, that he was dull. Both on TV and in print he brought a novelist's flair for the arcane world of the electoral college with insouciance and wit. Cronkite had immense respect for White's print journalism background; he had cut his chops at Henry R. Luce's *Time-Life* empire. He was not only a true double-source reporter but also one with a historian's big-picture sense of what mattered in the long run. Whenever Cronkite sat in on CBS convention coverage meetings from 1960 to 1980, he always had one request: for Teddy White to be his sidekick, for both on- and off-air advice.

By the time the San Francisco conventions rolled around, Cronkite had filled his binders with election 1964 research material. He had five volumes bulging with statistics, newspaper clippings, and succinct anecdotes. Because it was summer, Cronkite had Betsy and the kids accompany him on the trip to tourist-friendly San Francisco. Cronkite hoped to take his family to Fisherman's Wharf, Chinatown, Muir Woods, Seal Rock, and other Bay Area tourist sights. It was yet another sign of his hubris—this attitude that the covering of the GOP Convention at the Cow Palace was a slam-dunk. After the Kennedy assassination coverage, watching Goldwater, Rockefeller, and Scranton in action would be a yawn to Cronkite, easier than tying his wingtips—or so he thought.

The GOP Convention was expected to be a no-holds-barred clash among Republican Party factions. The party had been around for about a hundred and ten years and had been actively in search of an identity for the last fifty. Eisenhower had served as something of a placeholder in the debate from 1952 to 1960 because he was not, at heart, an ideological politician. Nixon, his vice president, had won the party endorsement in 1960 and ran a losing campaign. In 1964 the

Republicans were more than ready for their long-awaited new era to begin. The driving movement of the campaign had been the ultraconservative juggernaut led by Goldwater. Rockefeller represented a more progressive approach. Scranton was the moderate, hoping to lead the party back to the centrist days of Wendell Willkie and Thomas Dewey. Going into the convention, the nominee-apparent Goldwater had a substantial lead in the primary vote, but a tough floor fight was expected. Any convention would be exciting enough for network news divisions, but the Cow Palace gathering was going to be one for the history books, and everybody knew it.

On July 10, Cronkite arrived at San Francisco International Airport with his family in tow. As Betsy took the kids to the Mark Hopkins Hotel, Walter met Fred Friendly to share a taxi to the Cow Palace. They were going to reconnoiter the CBS facilities specially constructed for the coming coverage. What seemed like a pleasant chore turned into a nightmare. Cronkite was "appalled" at the primitive plywood treehouse-like facilities. Far from being a command center, the setup looked like a gutted Mojave Desert motel room with a single phone. Where were the desks for his staff? Where was the fantastic maze of phone lines? The radical diminution of the anchorman's role had not been presented to Cronkite according to CAFOC protocol. Mickelson hadn't told Cronkite of the new roving-correspondent system in advance. "Walter exploded," Bill Leonard recalled. According to the plan, Cronkite was supposed to have less to say, so that the weight of the coverage would be spread among more commentators and reporters. He negotiated small concessions, such as one regarding the physical proximity of the seating for himself and Sevareid, but as the convention began on July 13, Cronkite was wounded and angry, his volcanic emotions close to the surface. In a rare flare-up of envy, he thought Huntley-Brinkley had better digs.

When Cronkite learned that Sevareid would be getting a fair share of face time, he kicked the floor in disgust and let out a long, low moan. He felt that Sevareid, prone to break out in hives from nervousness when the red camera light went on, was ill suited to live convention television. To Cronkite, Sevareid was an albatross around his neck. Paley and Stanton didn't agree. That November Friendly named Sevareid a national correspondent based in Washington, D.C., who would appear on the *CBS Evening News* nightly (instead of two or three times a week). Friendly went so far as to say that Sevareid—not Cronkite—was the James Reston or Walter Lippmann figure at the network. "The only time Walter was difficult was in dealing with Sevareid, whom he didn't care for," Small recalled. "Walter wasn't happy about Sevareid getting to do a minute commentary at the back end of the *Evening News*. Eric was supposed to be used sparingly. When, for some breaking-news reason, Sevareid was bumped, Walter would say, 'Good.'"

The major producing decisions about the convention coverage were slated to be made in the control booth, where Fred Friendly and Bill Leonard followed developments on the floor and then fed cues to Cronkite through an earphone. Paley didn't often appear at conventions, but the 1964 coverage was crucially important to his network. Looming over the Cow Palace like Godzilla, Paley inevitably added to the tension for CBS staffers. A lot of concerned RNC bigwigs questioned Paley—a Republican—about Cronkite's disdain for Goldwater. All Paley could say was that nobody did "story-line" coverage with the skill of Cronkite. He was the gold standard.

The CBS News protocol went as follows. When one of the floor reporters, such as Mudd, garnered a piece of breaking news or captured a key figure for an interview, he would tell the control booth. Hewitt would then cue Cronkite to turn and introduce the reporter. If it was a news spot, Cronkite would typically question the reporter to bring out certain points in view of other developments. Cronkite was adamant about doing the same with interviews. At the hub of news in the anchor booth, he often knew things that a reporter wouldn't. For that reason, one of Cronkite's techniques was to tell the reporter, on live television, to hand his earphones to the interviewee. Cronkite would then conduct the interview while the reporter stood aside holding the microphone and feeling stupid. It didn't endear Cronkite to the team. Once, he directed Hughes Rudd, whom he brought to CBS News from UP in 1959, to surrender the earphones on the convention floor. "If the old son of a bitch does that to me one more time," Rudd carped, "I'm going right up to the anchor booth and put the earphones on him and tell him to interview himself!"

Rudd's comment reflected the rap against Cronkite within the CBS family following the JFK assassination: he was an air hog. Cronkite—"Iron Pants"—could stay on the air until the cows came home. He didn't need or seem to want anyone else. In the glory days of radio, CBS's Bob Trout had demonstrated the same ability to wax eloquent by the hour or the whole day. Cronkite, too, considered himself a storyteller as much as a newsman, pacing the presentation of the events. Empty distractions and dead-end digressions were as annoying to him as they presumably were to the viewer. At times, though, in San Francisco, he took this vestige of his former anchor chair discretion one step further. Even as Hewitt cued him to introduce one correspondent or another for a floor report, Cronkite ignored the cue until, for one reason or another, it was too late for the report. He had done the same thing at other conventions, but then he was accorded the power to make decisions over content. At the Cow Palace, he was not. Needless to say, squabbles erupted during commercial breaks, an unprecedented occurrence on a Cronkite broadcast.

With Cronkite usurping interviews, refusing to encourage Sevareid, and rejecting some floor reports, he began, as Roger Mudd recalled, "swallowing up great chunks of air time for himself." Being an air hog might not have been bad if Cronkite had been at his broadcasting best. He wasn't. Momentum proved elusive to him. "Our convention coverage was the shambles I expected it to be," Cronkite admitted in *A Reporter's Life*, "and I certainly contributed to it by sinking into a slough of hopelessness as the week developed." Like a circus juggler unable to catch his pins, Cronkite was a regular fumbling machine that July. It was awful to see a broadcaster of Cronkite's pedigree tumble down a drainpipe in front of forty million viewers. "I was one of the correspondents who came to San Francisco wanting to beat NBC," Rather recalled. "None of us did well from the convention floor. We got clobbered. To watch our old tapes of that convention is painful."

Cronkite had other problems at the Cow Palace besides GOP leaders in San Francisco demonizing the press, especially the television news, to memorable effect. Angered by what they perceived as a biased media, taking cues from Goldwater, the convention-eers were openly antagonistic to correspondents. Lapel buttons critical of Huntley and Brinkley as well as Cronkite ("Stop Cronkite") were hawked on the side-walks outside the Cow Palace. A chorus of young men and women wandered around loudly singing a song with the refrain "The hell with Walter Cronkite." NRA gun owners, bank presidents, small-town councilmen, churchgoers, corporate executives, John Birchers, military heroes, engineers, and oilmen all cried foul against CBS News (and other outfits). The bile of the right-wing movement was directed toward CBS News; the animosity grew out of Murrow's going after McCarthy and Cronkite's dissing Goldwater. It grew out of the standoff in the Deep South, where segrega-tionists resented the New York City–based networks for using the power of television to reveal the ugly Jim Crow side of race relations. When Goldwater said at the convention, "Extremism in the defense of liberty is no vice," a few conservatives turned toward the CBS booth and flashed Cronkite the middle finger.

But Cronkite wasn't alone in getting heckled. In San Francisco, David Brinkley and Chet Huntley were routinely threatened by a curious assortment of GOPers as they journeyed from their hotel to the Cow Palace, and took to speaking in loud tones about an omnipotent (if nonexistent) security detail awaiting them nearby. The NBC News duo almost needed it when Eisenhower—at the time a credentialed and highly paid commentator for ABC—uncharacteristically vilified "sensation-seeking columnists and commentators" from the podium. The phrase from Ike transformed the delegates into an angry mob, hollering in what Brinkley called "a deep, hoarse roar of hatred." It was unlike anything he—or nearly anyone else since Marie Antoinette—had ever seen. "The delegates," Brinkley wrote, "left their chairs and rushed over to the edge of the convention floor just below where Huntley and I and the other networks' news people were working high up in glass booths over the floor, several of them in their anger and haste stumbling past the chairs, shouting at us and waving their fists. . . . I don't know what they would have accomplished had they been able to get to us, but they were furious enough to do anything."

Chris Wallace, the son of then–*CBS Morning Show* host Mike Wallace who would go on to host a highly successful Sunday-morning talk show for the Fox News Channel in 2003, was an eyewitness to the anti-media furor. Cronkite had hired Chris as his personal assistant. Besides having Mike Wallace as his dad, Chris Wallace had Bill Leonard, head of CBS News' Election Unit, and Cronkite's direct boss, as his stepfather. Only sixteen years old at the time, Chris worked diligently at the San Francisco convention. It was a perfect fit. Cronkite had known Chris since he was a little kid interested in his Triumph TR-3 races at road rallies in Westchester County. The Wallaces and Cronkites also sailed together around Long Island Sound. Adding to the familial element, Chris Wallace was dating Nancy Cronkite. "She was my first girlfriend," he recalled. "You know, those were the days when everyone used to bring their families to these events. So I got my first convention job with Walter while dating his daughter."

Wallace was the gofer for Cronkite's CBS booth at the Cow Palace, getting coffee and sharpening pencils for the famed anchorman. But nothing seemed to go well for Cronkite. Wallace recalled being in the CBS booth when Eisenhower denounced sensation-seeking columnists and commentators and all the Republicans started stomping the floor and shaking their fists at the anchor booths. Eric Sevareid, sitting in the CBS booth, was the target of epithets hurled from the conservative crowd. Making matters even worse, Wallace felt he was stuck in the middle of a feud between his stepfather and Cronkite. "Walter would just ignore directions and keep talking," Wallace recalled. "He was kind of infamous for that anyway—I mean he was a great correspondent and a great journalist, but he was something of an air hog. And there was quite a power struggle between my stepfather and Cronkite about this. In any case, the convention ended and the ratings were poor."

The convention was indeed a ratings disappointment for CBS News. Some sadistic NBC executive scotch-taped CBS News' paltry Nielsen ratings to Cronkite's convention booth door. Cronkite found no humor in the gesture. The Tiffany Network was an embarrassing distant second to NBC. Nevertheless, the presumption was that the same CBS lineup would go to Atlantic City, where the Democrats would hold their convention in mid-August, to fight a new match. Trying to cheer everybody up, Cronkite said that with flashier graphics and a better workstation, CBS could beat NBC the next round. President Johnson would surely give Cronkite preferential treatment. The CAFOC crew of Leonard and his assistants would work assiduously with Cronkite in the intervening weeks to iron out all the kinks.

All of that might have happened, except that the problems at San Francisco were serious enough to concern the chairman of the corporation. Paley was out of patience with CBS News' second-place position in convention coverage and appalled by Cronkite's boorish behavior. Why had Cronkite brought his family to San Francisco, as if the convention were a Disneyland vacation? Couldn't his anchorman have tried to make peace with Goldwater over the German flap? Why had Eisenhower—his ultimate hero—seemingly turned sour on CBS? Paley called Friendly and Leonard to a meeting in late July, back in New York City. Frank Stanton asked the first question, as Leonard recalled in *In the Storm of the Eye*:

> "*What the hell happened to Walter?*"
>
> "*Walter wasn't quite himself,*" Friendly offered weakly.
>
> "*Why not?*" snapped Paley. "*Was he sick?*"
>
> "*No,*" I said, "*I don't think so.*"
>
> "*Well,*" said the chairman, "*I thought the idea was that Walter was going to do a little less, and you were going to spread the load around, so the pace would pick up. Wasn't that the idea, didn't you tell me that's what you all had in mind, Fred?*"
>
> Fred looked at me, as if to say, You tell 'em.

"Well, sir, that was the idea, but Walter sort
of . . . I guess you could say . . . resisted it."

"What does that mean?"

Leonard described how Cronkite would sometimes
ignore instructions to go to a floor report from Mudd
or Rather. He continued, in his recollection of the
conversation:

The chairman's voice rose perilously. "You mean
he would get what amounted to an order and he
wouldn't obey it?! Is that what would happen? Did
you actually give him orders and he wouldn't carry
them out?"

I realized we were sinking fast.

"I wouldn't put it quite that way," Fred inter-
posed. "You know, Walter is Walter."

"I don't know anything about 'Walter is
Walter,'" snapped the chairman. "It sounds to me
as if Walter wouldn't do what he was told and you
weren't able to do anything about it!" Paley had hit
the nail on the head.

Friendly and I fell silent, praying that his outburst might put an end to the matter.

It was just the beginning.

"Who do you think could replace Walter?"
Paley asked a few minutes later.

Paley, brooding angrily, knew about media stars and their egotistical conviction that they had a unique understanding of the TV audience and thus had to have their own way. In the recent past, Paley had tangled with Jackie Gleason, Arthur Godfrey, Lucille Ball, and Jack Benny—and while he would have liked to win every time, he often had to capitulate to their diva demands. The difference was that each of those stars had top-rated shows; Cronkite didn't. The tooth-and-claw dictates of television therefore made Cronkite expendable. Paley didn't want to hear about what a great job Cronkite had done during the JFK assassination drama. That was eight months ago. He'd blown San Francisco. "One trouble with this business is it's like Hollywood," Cronkite grumbled to Peter Benchley of *Newsweek* a day after the news broke that he was being dropped as the CBS anchorman for the Democratic National Convention in Atlantic City. "No one tells you—you can't get an exact reading of what's going on."

Fred Friendly and Bill Leonard flew out to the San Diego yacht basin, where Cronkite was vacationing with his family at Hotel Del Coronado. They had come all the way from New York to inform him of his demotion from the approaching Atlantic City convention, and of the promotion of Bob Trout and Roger Mudd as co-anchors. Cronkite was devastated. Reporter Tom

Wolfe, in a *New York Herald Tribune* article, wrote that Friendly and Leonard had "expressions on their faces like the college-liberal doctors at the cancer clinic who believe every patient is owed the simple human dignity of being told the truth." Cronkite also found out from a mole that CBS's ad agency, Batten, Barton, Durstine, & Osborn, was told to pull his name from the print ad campaign that fall season. A gutting was taking place, and he was the fish. He couldn't believe that Paley had the audacity to sideline him. All Cronkite was offered by Fred Friendly for Atlantic City were a few interviews with a random U.S. senator or housewife from Peoria; he rejected that humiliating toss of a bone. Cronkite tried to stand up straight when Friendly told him the news, but inside of him everything was painted black. *Newsweek* ran a comical photo of the ascendant Trout with Cronkite next to him under the caption: "The anchorman was hoisted." When Benchley asked Cronkite if he was going to fulfill his recent nine-year commitment to CBS, Cronkite responded affirmatively, but with the arch qualifier that "any contract is breakable."

The news that Paley had deposed Cronkite from Atlantic City blew up into a major news story itself. Newspapers across the country carried long pieces full of trenchant commentary and analysis. No one wrote about the incident more succinctly than Wolfe, exclaiming, "Walter Cronkite—demoted!" Adding insult to injury, Friendly told *The New York Times* that Sevareid and Reasoner would also play larger roles in Atlantic City while Cronkite stewed in the doghouse. The common assumption was that if Trout and Mudd were a hit, Cronkite would next lose his job on the *CBS Evening News*. In fact, Friendly feared that Cronkite would move first and quit the network altogether.

During the last week of July, Cronkite was inundated with interview requests. Though in low spirits, he held his emotions in check. "We took a clobbering in San Francisco," he told Robert J. Williams of *The Philadelphia Evening Bulletin* with appealing frankness, "and it seems perfectly reasonable that management at CBS would like to try something else to regain the audience." Privately, Cronkite was far more irate. The *Times* ran a leaked story saying that Cronkite might not be allowed to anchor Election Night in November and that Paley was thinking about firing him. Americans had revered Cronkite in the wake of the Kennedy assassination and now he was headed toward obscurity like Douglas Edwards. What saved Cronkite was his loyal viewership. Letters came pouring into CBS headquarters by the thousands, saying *Don't you dare fire Walter.* A Cronkite counterinsurgency was underfoot. Doing damage control, Friendly spun an old cliché for public consumption: "We've got a team here—the best team in electronic journalism. We just change the batting order from time to time."

Cronkite recognized that, in those terms, he was still batting cleanup: anchoring the *CBS Evening News* and hosting *The Twentieth Century*. He astutely saw that he had an opportunity to solidify his power if he moved his *CBS Evening News* to Atlantic City during the convention, so he and Hewitt could broadcast their regular 6:30 p.m. EST show there. Retreat was not an option. CBS producer Ernest Leiser had the temerity to tell a *New York Times* reporter that Cronkite, like Bartleby the Scrivener in Herman Melville's short story, had decided he *preferred* to broadcast from Atlantic City instead of New York. Talk about hubris. "I'm not bitter yet," Cronkite said. "But I might be later."

When Paley heard about the Cronkite plan to broadcast the half-hour *CBS Evening News* from Atlantic City, he grew choleric. While Leonard tried to defend Cronkite, Paley would have none of it. When Leonard threatened to quit CBS, Paley said, "Well you can quit or not quit, but I want Cronkite out of the anchor booth in Atlantic City." Leonard tried to tell Cronkite to go zen, not Bartleby. Cronkite rejected the advice. Chris Wallace was horrified: if Cronkite squared off against

Leonard, his stepfather, and Paley, Chris couldn't keep making romantic progress with Cronkite's daughter. "From my worm's-eye view of history," Wallace later joked, "I kept thinking this is really going to screw up my relationship with Nancy."

Murrow used to tell his Boys that any self-respecting journalist who vigorously investigated stories and challenged bosses should always be willing to clear his or her desk in twenty minutes flat. To Cronkite, who had three children to support, that notion was arrogant bravado. The key to broadcast journalism, he believed, was survival. His strategy was public contrition followed by the stubborn refusal to play a minor role in New Jersey. Cronkite admitted to having been too hard on Goldwater. And then he bore down to stick it out like Bartleby the Scrivener, to weather the storm. Instead of clearing his anchor desk, Cronkite set up in Atlantic City and proceeded to deliver the *CBS Evening News* in martyrdom even though he had lost the convention assignment to Paley's underlings, Mudd and Trout. Taking aim at both Huntley-Brinkley and Trout-Mudd, Cronkite opined that a "two-man team is less efficient than one." He also admitted that he had "fifth person feelers" headhunting a new job for him away from CBS.

When Gould of *The New York Times* praised CBS for shelving Cronkite even before the Mudd-Trout debut,

Paley smiled. Cronkite was about to be left behind like an old junker, encrusted in the old-style UP wire journalism and solo-flight anchoring to which he clung out of habit. The assumption was that he would soon be replaced on the *Evening News* by the surging duo of Trout-Mudd. At best, Cronkite would revert to hosting *The Twentieth Century* and covering space launches, which no one could take away from him post-Shepard, Grissom, and Glenn. Paley now envisioned his news division with Cronkite gone: Trout-Mudd would be carried by the critical momentum of the Atlantic City convention to ratings victory on the *Evening News.*

Right before the Atlantic City convention began on August 24, Don Hewitt, in an act of solidarity with Cronkite, asked to be relieved of his duties helping Trout and Mudd. He would instead work only with Cronkite, whom Lady Bird Johnson had agreed to do a *Person to Person*–style exclusive interview at the Texas ranch (she willingly shared personal details of her First Family life like never before, creating buzz). Dick West of UPI helped the Cronkite cause by lambasting the Mudd and Trout performance on day one of the convention. West detected on-air jockeying for supremacy between the CBS co-anchors, something he'd never seen with ABC's duo of Howard K. Smith and Edward P. Morgan. Nor did Trout-Mudd pull off the warmth of Walter Cronkite flying solo. "Once after Mudd had given the viewers some information," related West, "Trout responded with some contradictory tidbit of his own, which he described as 'the exception that proves the rule.' " Critic Richard Martin of *The Salt Lake Tribune* likewise thought that Mudd's "rather desperate attempts at being funny were contrived. . . . This preoccupation with showmanship, I feel, tends to cloud, rather than clarify convention proceedings." A whole line of critics, in fact, countered Gould's view that Trout-Mudd had "stylish punch": Cronkite had anchored seven previous presidential nominating conventions and three presidential elections and there was no good reason to sideline the still-blooming legend in 1964.

With the power of the dial, TV audiences had a similar reaction. According to results provided by Arbitron, CBS garnered its highest share in the first half-hour of the first night's coverage. That figure dropped as the evening and the week wore on. Overall, NBC walked away with its highest convention ratings *ever.* CBS's woeful numbers were even lower than they had been in San Francisco with Cronkite as helmsman. Paley, in retreat, not wanting Cronkite and Hewitt to defect, quietly dissolved the team of Trout and Mudd. He had buyer's remorse. Friendly, Leonard,

and Midgley later claimed that they had been reluctant participants in Cronkite's 1964 unseating. These
were ahistorical claims of convenience, a distancing
from a failed coup. Feeling hung out to dry, Mudd
considered a career change, perhaps teaching journalism at a university. While he served as scapegoat for
the "Cronkite loyalists," of whom there were suddenly
many, the blame actually rested on Bill Paley's shoulders. Brooks Atkinson, critic-at-large for *The New
York Times*, wrote a column ten days after the Atlantic
City convention, castigating CBS for its lousy treatment of Cronkite. "By brutally dumping and publicly
humiliating its ablest newsman," he wrote, "it equated
[political] conventions with the box office."

Paley, in his 1979 memoir *As It Happened*, didn't
mention the abrupt change in convention anchors,
but he did pay tribute to Cronkite as "the stalwart
kingpin," choosing to forget how he neutered his star
anchorman in 1964. "Walter is so objective, careful,
and fair in his presentation of news," Paley said, "that
he has been characterized—if not immortalized—with
the oft-heard line: 'If Walter says it, it must be so.'"
Paley's change of opinion was understandable; by 1979,
Cronkite was his North Star, blazing a way through
a galaxy of lesser lights. Yet other news anchors contemporary with him were just as objective and as fair.

Others shared the qualities Paley praised in Cronkite, his "sheer hard work, attention to detail, and a sense of journalistic honesty, integrity and fairness."

It took some kind of magic to get eighty-sixed by Paley only to become a broadcasting folk hero because the public missed your mug and the First Lady rallied in support of your cause. The Cronkite game plan was to outlast all the Mudd-Trout commotion, in a defiant act of refusal, then massacre his in-house rivals when they weren't looking. He believed that for all of the spectacle and entertainment in TV news, there was still a flickering hunger for Main Street authenticity. "Walter said, 'I'm a newsman and I'm going to cover the story,'" Chris Wallace recalled. "This was a masterstroke. Because the scuttlebutt was that Cronkite, in truth, was a serious print newsman at heart. His defiance in Atlantic City, his refusal to throw in the towel as a newsman covering a story, endeared him to all the print reporters who still saw TV as a playing field for pretty boys."

20.
Civil Rights and Project Gemini

COLOR TV—RAISKY'S TOUCH—THE GOLDEN HOUR—
TRUST OF SOCOLOW—PALEY WANTS RESULTS—
COVERING CIVIL RIGHTS—EQUAL RIGHTS AT
CBS—TAKING ON BULL CONNOR AND SHERIFF
CLARK—GIVE AIRTIME TO MLK—HUGHES RUDD
GOES SOUTH—ONWARD TO CAPE KENNEDY—LOVING
GEMINI—THE GEE-WHIZ FACTOR—DEATH AND DE-
STRUCTION AND *APOLLO II*—BOMBINGHAM—DEATH
OF MURROW—BEFRIENDING VON BRAUN—RATTLING
AND ROLLING AT CAPE KENNEDY

The *CBS Evening News with Walter Cronkite* ran its first color broadcast on August 19, 1965, and switched to color permanently on January 31, 1966.

"No one has a larger stake in going into color than I have," Cronkite told a New York *Daily News* media critic with a smile. "I'm much slenderer in tints than in black and white."

A huge effort was undertaken at CBS News to make the Cronkite set appealing to the viewer for both special events and the *Evening News*. The talented set designer Hugh Raisky, who started out in the mailroom in the late 1950s, was hired to give CBS's space coverage a "solar system" look. He even took astronomy courses that taught him how to pioneer in space art. More than any other person, Raisky was the visual guru at CBS who gave Cronkite the modern set design that proved so durable and fetching. "A lot of New York designers steered clear of the newsrooms," Raisky recalled. "But I had wanted to be a political cartoonist, so getting to be in the Cronkite newsroom, designing sets for everything from the 1964 political conventions to the 1992 debates, became my calling."

All day long Cronkite's *Evening News* team careened around him like moths to a flame. Whatever Cronkite's top five stories were, right down the pecking order, become America's top five stories of each and every weekday. "There are no back pages," Cronkite explained to *Time* magazine, "for our type of journalism." And there was zero tolerance for error. The young *Twentieth Century* series writer Jon Wilkman recalled what a grueling taskmaster Cronkite could be. He'd make Wilkman cough up his research, making him *prove* that Atlanta was in Georgia and Rome was in Italy. "You better have it right," Cronkite snapped one afternoon, "because it's my face hanging out there."

The CBS workplace was notably small—the newsroom just paces away from Cronkite's own glassed-in, venetian-blind-covered cubicle. The pipe-puffing Cronkite liked feeling in control of the news organization, typing copy, scribbling notes, working the phones, cracking lighthearted jokes through a haze of smoke. As the day advanced, the tension became palpable, and a NASA-like countdown ensued. Moments before airtime, Cronkite would take a quick glance in a handheld mirror, making sure his hair was slicked back properly. While getting a dab of powder on his face, he slipped on his suit jacket with just ten seconds left on the clock. Order miraculously emerged from broadcast center chaos. A lockdown now occurred. Nobody would make a peep. Cronkite would move his chair an inch, sit up straight, and glance down at his notes. At first gander, he looked like a well-intentioned midwestern newspaper editor preparing to inform out-of-town visitors about that day's local happenings. The camera zeroed in on him.

"Good evening," Cronkite said, and the broadcast began.

Along with Cronkite and Hewitt, the other essential facilitator of the *Evening News* was thirty-five-year-old Sandy Socolow, who knew the anchorman's likes and dislikes better than anybody at CBS. The buoyant, round-faced Socolow, who was raised in rural Connecticut but spent his teenage years in New York City, was an odd mix of small-town reporter and big-city editor. While attending the City College of New York and editing *The Campus* student newspaper, Socolow moonlighted as a copy boy at *The New York Times*, alongside soon-to-be legendary journalist extraordinaire Gay Talese. Drafted into the U.S. Army during the Korean War, Socolow ended up serving with the Voice of the UN Command, working to dissuade Asian listeners from the lures of Communist totalitarianism. "We tried beaming propaganda into North Korea and China from Tokyo," Socolow recalled.

After the war, he worked all over the Far East for the International News Service (the Hearst wire service that later became the "I" in UPI). Then, in 1957, his résumé impressed CBS, and the network hired him as a stringer. It was while working as a studio producer with Cronkite on the 11:00 p.m. *Sunday News Special* that their lifelong friendship blossomed. By 1962, Socolow (or "Soc" as his nickname went) was Cronkite's all-purpose alter ego. He would remain Cronkite's right-hand man until 1974, when he took over CBS News' Washington bureau.

On November 3, 1964, Cronkite shelled out state-by-state projections that proved to be accurate. (He had pollster Lou Harris to thank.) *The Huntley-Brinkley Report*, on the other hand, that beloved Laurel-and-Hardy news act, fumbled over the importance of the many different election numbers they were being fed over the wires. The predominant call, that Johnson would be victorious over Goldwater, was one of the easiest to make in U.S. history (the eventual electoral vote count was 486 to 52), but CBS, at 9:01 p.m. EST, was first to say it on television. In fact, it was the first to announce most of the important races during the evening. Cronkite, adrenaline racing, told a CBS reporter at the Election Night scene in Austin, Texas—where LBJ had voted and was now following the results—to hand his earphones to the president-elect. Lyndon Johnson gladly took the earphones when he was told, "Walter Cronkite wants to say hello."

Although Johnson's KCBS-Austin was in trustee-ship, Cronkite knew that the president would rather give the big "I won" interview to the Tiffany Network than to either NBC or ABC. Johnson and Cronkite spoke casually with each other, like a couple of ranch hands leaning against a fence. Cronkite's LBJ interview was a coup for CBS News and an indication that Cronkite, a reporter central to his times, was back full strength. Gossip columnist Walter Winchell, a longstanding Cronkite fan, beamed, "LBJ's phone chat with CBS News star newsman Walter Cronkite (from Austin) certified the respect Americans have for the commentator." The headline for Jack Gould's review of Election Night coverage in *The New York Times* was music to Cronkite's ears: "CBS by a Landslide: Network's Coverage of the Election Is Called Far Superior to Its Rival."

Not all journalists were impressed with Cronkite's ability to score exclusive interviews with powerful players such as President Johnson by "hale yeah, fine fellow" tactics and various quaint ways. Many CBS reporters—especially Alexander Kendrick in London and Daniel Schorr in Berlin—resented Cronkite's bigfooting anchorman routine. Robert Pierpoint remained suspicious of his cozy relationship with the Kennedys and the Johnsons. Whenever a colleague intimated that Cronkite was behaving like a sycophant of those in power, the anchorman stared back in surprise. He insisted that his interview style with everyone was the same: "fair play." If CBS News thought it needed a knockout smear artist to anchor the news, then he'd quit the network. "We used to call Walter 'Mr. Softball,'" Pierpoint explained. "If you were a president or a general, Walter turned submissive."

Following the LBJ exclusive, the unanimous conclusion in the media world was that Cronkite wasn't the problem with the *CBS Evening News*. Paley concurred. During the last months of 1964, the always-insistent Don Hewitt was replaced by Ernest Leiser as executive producer–director of the program. Hewitt moved to a newly created position—as executive producer of "developing and innovating a new kind of news broadcast—the 'live documentary.'" In 1968 this "live documentary" premiered as the phenomenally successful *60 Minutes* (airing Sunday evenings). Leiser, who began his career with *Stars and Stripes* during World War II, was a former correspondent with *Collier's Weekly* and the Overseas News Agency and a longtime executive with CBS. And he was a Cronkite crony. While Dan Rather thought Leiser had a blunt, Broderick Crawford–like manner, Cronkite treasured him as the ultimate foxhole companion with more than twenty years' experience as a foreign correspondent, editor, and producer.

In the aftermath of the 1964 convention experimentation by Friendly, Leiser was, if anything, anti–show business regarding the *CBS Evening News*. He tended to share Cronkite's core philosophy that the first obligation of the dinnertime news was to produce a crystal-clear communiqué, neither sanctimonious nor sluggish, more courtly than anything else, ensuring that viewers were aware of the day's events. Leiser considered Cronkite's great strength his tone: rigorously unpretentious. Cronkite viewers wanted an unslanted broadcast. "I never pretended that we could do anything more than be a headline service," he explained. "I felt that the headlines, that is 15 or 20 seconds of information on all the news of the day, were more important than covering some of the news of the day and then an in-depth look at one or another of the story of the day. And that created a tension. This dialogue went on constantly."

The tension existed because the 1960s, more than other decades, presented bullet-holed news stories that couldn't be explained in a couple of fast paragraphs or even in a couple of minutes. Southeast Asia, most pointedly, was more than a series of military actions that could be defined by battles, casualty counts, and the give-and-take of territory. What to do in Vietnam, which was then covered by Bernard Kalb of CBS in Tokyo, led to confrontations throughout American society—including the Cronkite home. Kathy and Nancy, in their late teens, became involved with the antiwar youth movement, protesting escalating U.S. involvement in Vietnam and lashing out at their parents' indifference. Cronkite, as CBS's leading newsman, cautious and watchful, was tardy both at CBS and in his own household in recognizing the depth of the Vietnam story as a reflection of American values and the government's cohesion with the citizens it served. "Having survived the 1964 convention brush-up, Walter was in the throes of a long, hard slog to overtake Huntley-Brinkley," Rather recalled. "Because CBS did well with the Kennedy assassination and space—special events—they wanted Cronkite to *own* big stories, to flood the zone with them; that would be our franchise. Only when the Vietnam War became a CBS franchise did Cronkite pay keen attention to the happenings in Southeast Asia."

As news, the civil rights movement circa 1964 was ideal drama for CBS News to be following raptly. Ernie Leiser had set up CBS bureaus in Dallas, Atlanta, and New Orleans primarily to cover the freedom struggle. For a decade, starting in 1954, television had led the way in presenting the problems of race in the United States and, as Cronkite saw it, in unlocking the closed society of the Old Confederacy. Once the *CBS Evening News with Walter Cronkite* and *The Huntley-Brinkley Report* on NBC went to a half hour in the fall of 1963, television covered the civil rights movement with greater intensity. Throughout the segregated South, CBS in particular was denounced by white supremacists, who labeled the network communist. A defiant CBS wanted to *own* the civil rights franchise, to scoop the great NBC reporter John Chancellor, who was on the beat with stories from Georgia, Mississippi, and Alabama. The CBS affiliate in Atlanta, WAGA, stoutly refused to feed civil rights stories to New York. Leiser had assigned the strong-willed Rather, to run the southern bureau in New Orleans, twenty-three states (plus Mexico and Central America). A sense of awe welled up in Rather over everything Dr. King did. Rather, serving as a friend to the movement, helped King understand which nonviolent protest stunts would make the *CBS Evening News* broadcast and which wouldn't; Cronkite never knew about this. "I couldn't do feeds from Dallas to Atlanta," Rather explained about the tension. "New Orleans was the only dependable city. WWL took our civil rights feeds. It was owned by the Catholic Church, and they were sympathetic to us."

The net effect of CBS News—both radio and TV—on the freedom struggle proved immeasurable. Dr. King had a genius for setting up foils such as the brutal Sheriff James G. Clark Jr. of Dallas County, Alabama, who used cattle prods, bullwhips, and clubs on protesters.

Ditto for Bull Connor, commissioner of public safety in Birmingham. "If anyone got manipulated by King," reporter Jack Bass noted, "it wasn't the media—it was Bull Connor and Sheriff Clark." CBS News became a powerful agent in conveying to the world the horrors of the Jim Crow South. These CBS segments were excruciating theater, the high drama of frenzied dogs, tear gas, and billy clubs causing viewers to wince in shame and disbelief. To Dr. King, the CBS eye represented the cavalry coming to the rescue. He staged marches, sit-ins, and demonstrations timed to get maximum television coverage. "To the movement," Julian Bond recalled, "Cronkite was the voice of God on TV. Murrow, Howard K. Smith, Rather, Rudd, Cronkite, and Sevareid helped wake America up to the problems in the South."

To Bond's point, John Hendricks, the future founder of the Discovery Channel, grew up in Huntsville, Alabama (a.k.a. Rocket City), in the 1960s. Having hailed from West Virginia, a United Mine Workers stronghold (and where President Kennedy was warmly embraced as the new FDR), Hendricks was startled to encounter a neo-Confederate culture fueled with bigotry toward blacks. His solace from all the local hate-mongering he experienced at school was to watch the enlightened *CBS Evening News with Walter Cronkite*. "My father was very much a liberal in his thinking,"

Hendricks recalled. "We felt totally out of sync with the racism in Alabama. Television was our way to connect with a large national community who clearly knew [that] what George Wallace was doing in Alabama was repugnant. Because of Walter Cronkite, I didn't feel isolated. Every night, we watched Cronkite, including when he turned to the thirty-minute news format, to follow the civil rights struggle in our own state."

Just how much power Cronkite had to sway public opinion became self-evident when the Sixteenth Street Baptist Church in Birmingham was firebombed on September 15, 1963. Four young black girls were murdered. Eugene Patterson, the editor of *The Atlanta Journal-Constitution* editorial page, wrote a heart-rending column that lambasted the "sick criminals" and "politicians who beat the kettle of heat" and "little men who have their nigger jokes." Cronkite thought Patterson had written an evergreen column for the ages and directed a CBS crew to film him reading it aloud as a camera scanned the church rubble. Patterson thought that the *CBS Evening News* might run a five- or ten-second sound bite of him. But Cronkite went to town on his telecast, giving Patterson full say:

I tuned it in and, sure enough, Cronkite had given up a huge chunk of his time for me, just sitting at my desk [reading] the column from beginning to end. That was the beginning of my education as to the impact of television. Within a week or two I received close to two thousand letters, telegrams, or phone calls from all over the nation. When a newspaper editor gets 20 letters he usually feels he has scored big with a column. The magnified reach that television brought to this piece bewildered me. For every one who felt moved to communicate there must have been a hundred or a thousand who responded [in spirit] but stayed silent.

The CBS reporter whom Cronkite tapped into most on civil rights issues was Hughes Rudd, a native of Waco, Texas. Cronkite hired the thirty-eight-year-old Rudd away from UP in 1959 to be his writer. Rudd had attended the University of Missouri from 1938 to 1941 before enlisting in the U.S. Army during World War II. Cronkite was awed by Rudd's bravery in flying Piper Cubs as an artillery spotter in Africa and Europe. He was awarded a Silver Star, a Purple Heart, and six Air Medals. After the war, Rudd wrote for *The Kansas City Star* and *The Minneapolis Star*; that's when Cronkite poached him from print journalism. Sardonic and a marvelous raconteur, Rudd was tasked by Cronkite with serving abroad in Moscow, Bonn, Berlin, and

Vietnam. At Cronkite's suggestion, the gravelly voiced Rudd also opened CBS News' southern bureau in Atlanta, spearheading coverage of protest marches and sit-ins. "Back then you were really on your own," Rudd recalled of CBS in the early 1960s. "You told New York what you were gonna do. You didn't have to run all over hell because somebody in New York got up in the morning with a bright idea. You didn't have any of this nonsense with 'bureau managers.' You just had a reporter . . . and a camera crew."

Without question, Cronkite belonged in the pantheon of pro–civil rights reporters who made a historic difference in ending institutionalized racial discrimination in the South. Cronkite's *CBS Evening News* stage manager was African American vaudevillian Jimmy Wall, who eventually became known to schoolchildren of the era as Mr. Baxter on CBS's *Captain Kangaroo*. Wall joined *Captain Kangaroo* as a stage manager in 1962, and from then on he worked as the stage manager on several other CBS shows, including the *Evening News*, for nearly fifty years. Cronkite depended on Wall to count down the minutes to airtime in his rich baritone voice five nights each week. "TWO MINUTES TO AIR," he would shout out, all the way down to "IN FIVE." Wall, in essence, was the eyes and ears of Cronkite's director. A natural-born storyteller, Wall regaled Cronkite over the years with stories of bootlegger stills during Prohibition, USO shows in Europe, and hanging out with Jackie Robinson in Brooklyn. They were almost the same age and shared a long and prosperous history at the Tiffany Network.

Nobody thought Cronkite harbored prejudice. Although Cronkite was an ally of Dr. King, some liberals were irritated by how the term *negro* was used on the network. This came to a head in 1966, when CBS correspondent Steve Rowan reported on "negroes" in Vietnam and then generically referred to them as "men," rather than giving their surnames, as was done with white soldiers. One of Cronkite's assistants flagged the Rowan report as discriminatory. Cronkite, embarrassed by the accusation, blanched as he read an irate letter from Mrs. Allie F. B. Stanford in Willingboro, New Jersey: "The CBS Evening News on this date [August 3, 1966] is not yet over as a matter of fact, not half of it is over and I am sick, sick, sick! I am so infuriated that I am even nauseated," she wrote Cronkite. "The report by Steve Rowan from Andrews AFB, MD referred to the *Negro* wounded only four (4) days ago as 'this man.' When two others—whites—were interviewed with their names and hometowns on screen. 'This man' happens to have been coming from the same place, wounded for the same purpose and in the same damn way as the whites were!"

The CBS Evening News was being accused of treating blacks, specifically Vietnam servicemen, as distinctly second-class citizens. A concerned Dick Salant ordered an overview of all CBS News broadcasts to make sure they were being, as the 1980s phrase puts it, "politically correct." Mrs. Stanford had scored a policy change. (While Cronkite supported the major equal rights movements of the day—for women, gays, Native Americans, Hispanics, et al.—the idea of political correctness seemed to him a kind of language-police fascism.) CBS correspondent Ed Bradley, first hired to WCBS Radio in 1967, believed that Cronkite and Rudd were the "least bigoted guys in media." And it wasn't just because Cronkite aired broadcasts helpful to the NAACP, SNCC, and CORE. Or that he was an early promoter of Martin Luther King Jr. Day as a national holiday. "Black people can detect prejudice in a person," Bradley explained. "We've got radar. When I ate lunch with Walter and Rudd, which wasn't often enough, they didn't think of me as a black correspondent. I was their friend and colleague, Ed. It was that simple."

Anytime Cronkite did a pro–civil rights segment in the 1960s or 1970s, the CBS switchboard would light up with angry callers. Cronkite's chief manager was a tough Brooklyn Jewish woman named Hinda Glasser. "You didn't want to mess with Hinda," CBS writer Ron Bonn recalled. "She'd peel off a couple layers of your skin if she got mad at you." But when she took anti-black calls from the Deep South, a different Glasser emerged. "The content of the calls, invariably, was 'nigger,' 'nigger,' 'nigger,' with a couple of 'kikes' thrown in for good measure," Bonn explained. "And Hinda, all sweetness, would tell the caller, 'I'm sure Mr. Cronkite would like to hear your opinion in person; do you mind if I put you on hold until he can come to the phone?' Well, no, the caller never minded." The Bell System office phones had five buttons for different lines. From 7:00 to 7:30 p.m., Bonn, Socolow, Benjamin, and others would sit in the fishbowl watching the buttons from all those angry racist callers blinking, as they waited for their chance to tell Walter Cronkite off. "When we left to go home at 7:30," Bonn later laughed, "most of those lights were still flashing."

By 1965, Cronkite's favorite beat, space, was satisfying in all the ways that other stories of the day, such as Vietnam and civil rights, were confusing. The Gemini program, the follow-up to Mercury, marked the return of manned space flight after Alan Shepard's historic suborbital flight in 1961 and Glenn's orbits in

1962. Gemini would test a wide variety of technological feats in anticipation of the first moon shot. The program began with unmanned flights in April 1964 and January 1965, hitting full stride in March 1965 when Gus Grissom and John Young went up in *Gemini 3*; there were four others that year. Five Gemini launches went ahead in 1966. Each shot was different from the one before, presenting its own engineering marvels and risks. Gemini had four primary and newsworthy goals that served as stepping-stones to the Moon: subjecting two men to a long-duration flight, working out the rendezvous and docking (linkup) technique, practicing "space walks," and perfecting reentry from orbit and landing at predicted target areas.

Cronkite would be at Cape Kennedy for all the Gemini flights. This was not just news, it was history presented on a schedule so a CBS news crew could be camera-ready for liftoff. It was possible to prepare for Gemini missions. In the 1950s, when Cronkite had been the host of *You Are There*, he pretended to be a newsman on the scene at the high points of history. Now, in 1965, he was on a historic scene, this time a real one, as the rockets blasted off from Florida. With each liftoff, another chapter in space exploration began. Fuel sources, new docking, navigation, and propulsion systems were all initiated and mastered, as was long-term "station-keeping." The most exciting flight was that of *Gemini 4.* On June 3, 1965, Edward White became the first American to walk in space, leaving the confines of the space capsule for a twenty-one-minute walk in the infinite void. (The first person to walk in space was a Russian cosmonaut, Alexey Arkhipovich Leonov, on March 18 of that year.) "Jules Bergman of ABC and Walter Cronkite of CBS were the iron men of the day in television," Jack Gould of *The New York Times* wrote, "carrying the burden of running the report practically by themselves."

Critics praised Cronkite's relaxed cadence during the Gemini missions. He didn't saturate the air with extraneous babble. He spoke only when his voice added to the outer space imagery. As he had learned in convention coverage since 1952, it wasn't necessary to underscore what the viewer was seeing. The governing atmosphere during blastoffs on CBS was mostly pro-longed silence. Then the stolid Cronkite would calmly pick up the storyline of the nerve-racking event. "One minute into the flight; she seems to be going well—very well," he emphasized quietly on June 3. At times, he might have been providing hushed commentary on a golf match. "There's the contrail that sets in at a given altitude. . . . It's approaching Max-Q—that's maximum dynamic pressure. Coming right now. Going through it right now. . . . Seems to be safely through." Cronkite relaxed noticeably with that observation and brightened, though his tone was still muted. "Safely through the first dangerous point after liftoff and it looks like this baby's going . . ."

Always exposing a vein of optimism, he was television's best physics explainer, with an amateur's grasp of the concepts and the terminology combined with a perfect understanding of the science deficit of the Tube-watching public. He knew when to be vague—"There's the contrail that sets in at a given altitude"—so as not to dizzy the viewer with statistics or unnecessary detail. Viewers could see the muscles relax on Cronkite's face when all the protocol necessary for a successful launch proceeded without a hitch. Before the first Gemini launch of 1965, *The Chicago Daily News* asked Cronkite how he prepared. "I don't attempt to commit anything to memory, but somehow it gets there," he said. "I learn by doing; I don't learn by reading. I've been to the basic sources and tried to talk to people involved in the project. I've been to McDonnell Aircraft in St. Louis, where the capsule was made; to Houston, where the astronauts live; to the Martin Company near Baltimore, where the booster was built; to the Goddard Space Center. And I've been at Cape Kennedy for this week—talking, taking notes, reading. Then I sit down and write page after page of notes for my background material, organizing it chronologically—pre-launch, launch, orbit, etc. And then what happens is that after I've done all that, it's all there in my mind. I haven't consciously attempted to memorize anything. In fact, I have a lousy memory and a week later I can't even remember the names of the astronauts. But I cram it in for the assignment, use it. After the job, it all flees."

Cronkite thought that NBC News' Huntley, Brinkley, and McGee were too dry when they bantered about space exploration. They were afraid of the gee-whiz factor (that is, they refused to say something like "Go, baby, go!" when a manned rocket was rising above the Cape). *The Huntley-Brinkley Report* team, in turn, thought Cronkite was pandering when he called rockets "baby"—like a patron encouraging a stripper at some Tenderloin District burlesque house. From a distance, the two networks might have seemed to be delivering much the same news in almost the same way. Up close, though, within the sausage factory of TV news, minor differences were meaningful. Just as Murrow owned the McCarthy era, Cronkite was the space age interpreter—nobody came in even a close second. In reality, he had more power than Murrow could have dreamed of, for in 1950, only 9 percent of

U.S. homes had TVs. By 1970, that number was 96 percent. On TV he had defeated ABC's Jules Bergman and NBC's Frank McGee and Roy Neal for the heavyweight title of "Dean of Space."

On April 29, 1965, Murrow lost his battle with lung cancer. Cronkite devoted much of that evening's broadcast to recalling Murrow's spirit of inquiry, repeating a large segment of the *See It Now* program of March 1954, which dealt with Senator Joseph McCarthy. Dr. Stanton lamented that "the first golden age of broadcast journalism" was now over. Eric Sevareid provided heartfelt commentary on the *CBS Evening News*, calling his mentor "incandescent." There is no record or remembrance of how Cronkite felt. "He just didn't say a word about the death," Socolow recalled. "It was like it didn't happen."

Perhaps because of his feud with Murrow, Cronkite seemed to lean on other CBS reporters to frame their mentor's life on air. But Cronkite himself choked up when at the end of that *CBS Evening News* broadcast, he ran a clip of Murrow signing off: "Good night— and good luck." Four days later, Cronkite and Charles Collingwood cohosted a special-events broadcast, "An Hour with Ed Murrow."

Cronkite, who attended Murrow's funeral in Manhattan, understood that by doing documentaries

such as "Harvest of Shame," Murrow had alienated
segments of the viewing public. Likewise, civil rights
and Vietnam were polarizing topics. But almost everybody was cheering on the Gemini astronauts. Year in
and year out, the NASA program dictated Cronkite's
schedule. He never missed a launch—for the sake of
illness, vacation, or another assignment—during his
entire career. "We all knew Walter owned Gemini,"
Roger Mudd recalled, "It was his turf."

CBS News vice president Gordon Manning, in
charge of all hard-news stories, thought Cronkite was
dead right about the moon race being as historically big
as the Vietnam War. Bob Wussler, the executive producer of CBS's space coverage, recalled that the successful *Gemini 3* mission of 1965 had been the turning
point for CBS. Corporate resources were now devoted
to whipping NBC and ABC on all things moon-related.
But before the glory of *Apollo 11*, the first lunar landing, Cronkite had to deal with the ghastly tragedy of
Apollo 1. Its crew was Virgil I. "Gus" Grissom, Edward
H. White, and Roger B. Chaffee. On January 27, 1967,
while they were sitting in the command service module
atop a Saturn 1B rocket, a flash fire occurred. All three
astronauts were asphyxiated within a few seconds. This
was during a countdown for a simulated launch. "It was
a great shock to Cronkite," Robert Pierpoint recalled.

"Walter had befriended the crew. His real worry was that this would cause NASA to delay the push for the moon."

The *Apollo 1* mission hadn't been scheduled for launch until February 21, so Cronkite wasn't on the scene to report on the fire. In fact, he couldn't be found the night it happened. He was dining at the Stork Club, but CBS didn't know that. CBS ran *Special Reports* bulletins with Bill Martin and Mike Wallace anchoring. Whiz kid Bob Wussler went on the air for the first time ever with NASA models to educate the public visually about what had happened on *Apollo 1*. Eventually, Cronkite made his way to the West Fifty-seventh Street broadcast center and went on the air. Already two CBS employees—producer Joan F. Richman and correspondent David Schumacher—were on their way to Florida to set up remote interviews about the tragedy.

That evening, back at his Manhattan home, Cronkite wept as never before. He had befriended Grissom, White, and Chaffee, considering them the white knights of an America being torn apart by Vietnam and civil rights unrest, and now they were gone.

CBS News called the fatal fire the "Cape Kennedy Disaster" and ran regular *Special Reports*, even showing photos of the burned-out "white room" where the astronauts had perished. On January 30, 1967, Cronkite anchored a half-hour *Special Report* of the astronauts' flag-draped coffins leaving Cape Kennedy. It was gut-wrenching television. But Cronkite, full of what the British call phlegm, assumed the job of telling America to keep its chin up. From that disaster onward, Cronkite became an oracle of space exploration, describing NASA as the "glue" holding America together "at a time when we seemed to be coming apart."

The disaster temporarily dampened the morale of NASA and much of the public alike. The space program was in flux. Was it really worth taxpayer dollars to go to the Moon? Was it too high-risk a venture? A tidal wave of self-doubt swept the country. The "Cape Kennedy Disaster" only made Cronkite more of a bull-horn promoting the Apollo program. While NASA called a twenty-month halt on U.S. human space flights, putting the Apollo program on hold, CBS—at Cronkite's urging—ran a documentary titled *To the Moon.* The documentary's resident expert was Isaac Asimov, author of dozens of science fiction books, of which Cronkite was a huge fan. What Cronkite drove home on the broadcast was that going to the Moon required a huge amount of cooperation between whole industries and economies.

For the *CBS News Special Report*, Cronkite went to Huntsville, Alabama, to interview the German rocket pioneer Wernher von Braun, who became a pliant collaborator. What made *To the Moon* such a vintage Cronkite special was the way space exploration was treated with a kind of *You Are There* aura. Journeys were made to Langley Field, Virginia, to experience firsthand the gravity of the Moon in a simulator. Of America's space commentators, only Cronkite incessantly compared the Apollo astronauts to Christopher Columbus, Ferdinand Magellan, and Ponce de Leon. "From the Moon we will truly step out into space," Cronkite said, "launching first instruments and then men to land on the other planets of the solar system."

To observers, Cronkite was so filled with adrenaline about the challenge of going to the Moon that he seemed to be having his second childhood. At dinner parties, he'd recount standing in the snake-infested weeds of central Florida to watch Alan Shepard's fifteen-minute up-and-down suborbital on a Redstone rocket, explaining that it was only one-fifth the size of the escape rocket carried on the nose of an Apollo spacecraft. He would describe tasting the prepacked nutrition bars the Gemini astronauts ate in zero gravity. It was clear in 1968 that Cronkite didn't want to cover space as much as he wanted to *be* a NASA astronaut.

Cronkite framed NASA's Gemini and Apollo missions in terms of old-fashioned American triumphalism.

Astronauts like L. Gordon Cooper and Frank Borman seemed to have jumped out of a starry sky fairy tale. The Apollo program was the biggest peacetime project the U.S. government had ever undertaken (depending on how you analyze the cost of the Eisenhower interstate highway system) and perhaps the most ambitious technical endeavor in world history. Ever since President Kennedy had delivered his "Special Message to the Congress on Urgent National Needs" on May 25, 1961, arguing that America would put a man on the Moon before the decade was over, CBS and Cronkite had been on board for duty. Lynn Sherr of ABC carped that Cronkite had become "much more of a cheerleader than a reporter." During the Gemini years, as NASA developed and tested the Saturn 1B launch vehicle and then the giant Saturn 5 (the launch vehicle used for the moon missions), Cronkite enthused, with a snatch of prayer for good measure, that the history of mankind was about to change. "We proved we could do it," Cronkite boasted to *American Heritage* about the American space effort of the 1960s. "We timed it dramatically. We set the pattern for man escaping his earthly environment."

To Cronkite the most frightening space mission was *Apollo 4*, in 1967, the first (unmanned) test flight of the powerful Saturn V launch vehicle—the largest ever to fly. It was designed by von Braun in Huntsville. Liftoff took place at 7:00 a.m. EST on November 9. The rocket blast jolted the CBS Broadcast Center, with Cronkite and producer Jeff Gralnick in it, to its foundation. Desperately, Cronkite tried to hold the big glass window—which looked out at Launch Complex 39—to keep it from shattering. Ceiling tiles came tumbling down. Everything was vibrating madly. But Cronkite, broadcasting, sounded like a thrilled kid at an amusement park. He was Murrow in London during the blitz, unafraid to allow a little emotion to enter his TV broadcast. "My God, our building's shaking here," Cronkite told viewers. "Our building's shaking! The roar is terrific! The building's shaking! This big glass window is shaking. We're holding it with our hands! Look at that rocket go! Into the clouds at 3,000 feet! The roar is terrific! Look at it going! You can see it. Part of our roof has come in here."

21.

What to Do About Vietnam?

AT ODDS WITH HIS KIDS—U.S. INVOLVEMENT IN
VIETNAM THICKENS—SMILE OF THE COBRA?—
VIETNAM TREK OF 1965—STUCK IN THE MIDDLE—
MORLEY SAFER AT CAM NE—THE LIVING ROOM
WAR—FRIENDLY BRINKSMANSHIP—TOO MUCH BAD
NEWS—AFTRA STRIKE—ZENKER FILLS IN—CHET
HUNTLEY AS SCAB—A MEGA-CELEBRITY—MIDGLEY
GRAPPLES WITH VIETNAM—SALANT SAYS SPEND
WHATEVER IT TAKES—ON THE ROAD WITH
KURALT—VIETNAM WOES—GEARING UP FOR THE
1968 ELECTION

Nancy Cronkite remembered a fierce argument with her father one Thanksgiving in the mid-1960s, over the Johnson administration's Vietnam

War policy. Her cousin, Douglas Caldwell, a U.S. Army engineer assigned to plant land mines around the demilitarized zone (DMZ)—the border between North and South Vietnam—was visiting for the holiday. A seventeen-year-old with liberal instincts, Nancy challenged Douglas at the Thanksgiving table over the ethics of the Johnson administration's war policy. "Boy, did I get it from Dad," she recalled, as if still feeling his gaze. "We kids were radicalized against Vietnam. Dad wasn't. For all his liberalism, he was a traditionalist. He defended Doug as doing noble work. . . . I had gotten him really mad."

In the early morning of February 7, 1965, Vietcong guerrillas attacked the U.S. Army helicopter base known as Camp Holloway in Pleiku, killing 8 American soldiers and wounding 126. The Johnson administration quickly retaliated, commencing another cycle of lightning reprisals and military escalations. Suddenly U.S. "advisors" in Vietnam were recognized as combat troops; twenty-three thousand U.S. personnel grew to nearly two hundred thousand by the year's end. On March 8, CBS News broadcast an hourlong showdown between pro-war Senator Gale McGee (D-Wyo.) and antiwar Senator George McGovern (D-S.Dak.). "Vietnam: the Hawks and the Doves," hosted by Charles Collingwood, became a divide as symbolic as the DMZ as many Americans chose sides. Cronkite didn't—or couldn't—choose publicly. Like a majority of Americans, he supported Johnson administration policies in Southeast Asia after the Gulf of Tonkin incident and championed America's maintaining a huge military presence around the world. "Our foreign policy, simply stated, is to preserve and foster an environment in which free societies may exist and flourish," Cronkite said in a major 1965 speech to editors. "We cannot commit ourselves to less—and to achieve these goals patently requires not less involvement, as the weak of heart now urge, but great involvement and renewed destruction."

Cronkite thought the U.S. military could defeat the North Vietnamese Army (NVA) and the Vietcong (the communist military group committed to fighting the American and South Vietnamese governments) and then turn military operations over to the Army of the Republic of Vietnam (ARVN; the South Vietnamese army). Remembering how the whole "limited" war gambit on the Korean Peninsula had cost Harry Truman his presidency ("We are trying to prevent a Third World War"), Cronkite hoped the Pentagon would find a quick victory formula in Vietnam and get out. He wasn't interested in criticizing President

Johnson, whom he regarded as a "master politician" surrounded by cut-rate political pygmies. During the 1964 presidential election, Johnson had ridiculed Goldwater's "trigger happy" desire to send U.S. troops to South Vietnam ("We are not about to send American boys nine or ten thousand miles away from home to do what Asian boys ought to be doing to protect themselves"). Given such rhetoric, Cronkite didn't suspect that Americans would get mired down in Southeast Asia for long.

"Cronkite gave great coverage and support to us," Joseph Califano, the president's deputy for domestic affairs, recalled. "We saw Cronkite as an invaluable partner in promoting civil rights. As for Vietnam? In 1964, 1965, and 1966 CBS News didn't question the president's policies much, if at all."

The Vietnam conflict began with widespread public support, but became ever more controversial as the war sucked up larger numbers of troops and materiel. For U.S. soldiers, it meant vicious combat—in impenetrable jungles, rice paddies, built-up areas, hillsides, and fortified positions—as brutal as any in the history of warfare. For antiwar protesters, particularly on college campuses, it reeked of imperialism and warmongering. For most American conservatives and many Americans of moderate political beliefs, it represented a crucial battlefield in the cold war confrontation with the Soviet Union and China. For blacks, Hispanics, American Indians, and poor whites, it stood for class hypocrisy as their children were sent to Southeast Asia while many rich youths received special deferments or cushy stateside assignments in the National Guard. For Cronkite, it meant catching up with NBC News, which started airing "Vietnam Weekly Review" (a series dedicated solely to Johnson's war).

Almost a month after the Vietcong attack at Pleiku, a small city in the central highlands, National Security Advisor McGeorge Bundy recommended a three-stage escalation of the bombing in North Vietnam. The U.S. Air Force began Operation Rolling Thunder to strike targets in North Vietnam and interdict supply flows to the south. A few days later, the first American combat troops landed on the ground in Vietnam. By April President Johnson had authorized the use of U.S. ground combat troops for offensive operations in South Vietnam. This escalation triggered a Students for a Democratic Society (SDS) antiwar rally in Washington that Cronkite covered on the *CBS Evening News*. Cronkite was so consumed with Project Gemini and Winston Churchill's death that he barely had time to think about Vietnam. But a *New York Times* article quoting Secretary of Defense Robert McNamara saying that he thought the war effort would cost U.S. taxpayers about $1.5 billion caught his attention. Cronkite wanted to know whether Vietnam was worth the steep price tag. That July, curious about U.S. strategic goals in Vietnam, he plotted a research trip to Southeast Asia. He was encouraged to go by Gordon Manning, the former *Newsweek* editor and CBS News executive in charge of Southeast Asia coverage.

Having just finished narrating "Abortion and the Law" for *CBS Reports*, a pioneering program that grappled with the taboo subject of a woman's right to choose, Cronkite started preparing for his first trip to Southeast Asia. He read Joseph Buttinger's *The Smaller Dragon*. He also met Homer Bigart, his colleague from the Writing Sixty-Ninth who already had a tour of Vietnam under his belt, for dinner to get a briefing. What astonished Cronkite from the briefing books he read in New York was the geographical smallness of Vietnam. With a total land area of 127,207 square miles, Vietnam— North and South combined—was smaller than East and West Germany. Cronkite, at Bud Benjamin's suggestion, decided to film a report about the helicopter pararescue teams who recovered downed pilots in the dense jungles and rice paddies of Vietnam.

With Cronkite on the trip were producer Ron Bonn, cameraman Walter Dombrow, and a sound engineer.

The basic field equipment was the Mitchell 16-mm movie camera—with a film magazine on top that looked something like Mickey Mouse's ears—which held a four-hundred-foot-long roll of sound film (ten minutes' worth). The Mitchell was adapted from a Hollywood 35-mm production camera; it was big and bulky, weighing over forty pounds. "It was a bitch in the field," Bonn recalled. "Because of those two 'ears,' a cameraman had to make himself visible in order to get a shot. And being visible frequently meant being shot at."

Cronkite first comprehended how surreal Vietnam was when he boarded a Vietnamese airliner in Hong Kong. The stewardess was a "beauty" with the smile of an angel. She brought Cronkite a beer and a copy of Saigon's English-language newspaper, the *Daily News*. Cronkite was in heaven. The interior of the plane was white and clean. He had a pipe packed for a relaxing smoke. Wasn't it wonderful not to think about the Congo, taxation, Mao, Castro, and de Gaulle while settling into a flight? But then he read the stark headline in the paper: "Air Vietnam Stewardess Held in Airplane Bombing." An uneasiness swept over him. He wondered, "Was my stewardess's smile the smile of the cobra?" At that minute, no longer relaxed, Cronkite learned the fundamental truth about Vietnam in the

1960s: "One could not depend on things being what they seemed to be."

The CBSers arrived at the U.S. air base at Da Nang in early July. This coastal city was the headquarters for the South Vietnamese army's I Corps and its Third Division. Cronkite was in awe of the twelve-thousand-foot concrete runway and brand-new airstrips, which relegated the ones at Chicago's O'Hare to second-class status. Although Cronkite knew that Da Nang—the scene of the first landing of Marines in 1965—was an important port for U.S. troops, he was surprised to land on such a jet-capable airfield. Both sides of the runway were lined with blastproof revetments, and inside each stood an expensive spit-polish-new warplane. Eisenhower's military-industrial complex at work; Cronkite, long familiar with military aviation, was delighted when he saw the F-102, F-106, B-57, F-4, F-104, and F-105 bombers lined up in Willow Run assembly line fashion. "I remember turning to Walter somewhat stunned," Ron Bonn recalled, "and saying, 'How can we lose?'"

Cronkite and crew spent three weeks touring the Vietnamese countryside, where they were treated to a velvet-trimmed version of the war, with private briefings and excellent seafood meals. They were filming segments for the *CBS Evening News, The Twentieth*

Century, and *Face the Nation.* Cronkite got to fire an M-16, the lightweight rifle that became standard issue to U.S. troops. He met privately with U.S. Army officers and grunts alike to take their pulse on the war. They called the Vietcong enemy "Charlie," while Cronkite, to Dombrow's amusement, insisted on "Mr. Charlie." Because of his long familiarity with air combat, Cronkite was invited to accompany fixed-wing aircraft on bombing sorties. The French cameraman Alex Brauer, one of the best combat shooters who had "balls of steel," took Cronkite into the boondocks, where artillery fire could be heard. On July 18, Cronkite scored an exclusive interview with South Vietnam's new premier, Air Vice Marshal Nguyen Cao Ky. At first he found Ky charismatic. But then, with a peculiar look on his face, the premier started praising Adolf Hitler's greatness as an air power strategist. "Then I kind of lost the thread," Cronkite recalled. Speaking in English to Cronkite, Ky said, "If really a U.S. Government wants to help us or give us everything we need, and if really in the next few months or in the future we have a good, frank coordination between the two Governments, U.S. and Vietnam, and without intervention of Red China or North Vietnam, I think within one year the situation will be better." But Cronkite, pushing for more, got Ky to admit that to rid

South Vietnam of the Vietcong guerrillas, there was still a "long, long, way yet to go—three, four years." The edited version of the important Cronkite-Ky interview aired on *Face the Nation*.

Cronkite, Bonn, and Dombrow—eager to outhustle NBC News—chatted with taxi drivers, street vendors, and waiters as if they were conducting mini Gallup polls on whether U.S. military intervention was a good thing. They also went to Bien Hoa, about an hour south of Saigon, to visit the U.S. Army 173rd Airborne Brigade. Using his trusty Mitchell camera, Dombrow—a loud, funny, roly-poly, and extremely talented documentary cameraman—had set up an interview in a moving Jeep between Cronkite and a brigadier general. In the era before handheld movie cameras, Cronkite's interview, filmed brilliantly by Dombrow as they traveled down a bumpy dirt road, was cutting-edge TV work—take that, NBC News' "Vietnam Week in Review." When Cronkite raised the subject of the Vietcong as a fierce fighting force, the general growled, "They're cowards!" How so? asked Cronkite "They're cowards!" he continued. "They won't come out and fight. Cowards!"

Cowards . . . cowards . . . cowards . . . the word rang in Cronkite's ears for the rest of the day. That night Cronkite, Bonn, and Dombrow discussed the hotheaded general over beer. If the Vietcong and/or the

North Vietnamese army were to "come out and fight," as the general suggested, all those U.S. warplanes in Bien Hoa and Da Nang would annihilate them. In a pitched battle, the well-armed 173rd Airborne Brigade would probably whip the Vietcong. But Ho Chi Minh's guerrilla fighters could definitely score points by hovering just inside the tree line and killing U.S. troops with sniper fire, one man at a time. And that's what Cronkite—and Ky—saw the enemy doing all over South Vietnam. "Walter, with his World War II experience, understood that," Bonn recalled. "So that night we all agreed: [that] was the dumbest general any of us had ever encountered. Yes, Walter was still gung-ho in '65. But the dumbest general really shook him."

Morley Safer of CBS News, a Canadian reporter who had been working the Vietnam beat for a few months, was among those who closely interacted with Cronkite on that 1965 trip. He had joined CBS News as a London-based correspondent in 1964, but after Pleiku he was told to open the CBS News bureau in Saigon. Cronkite also consulted former Unipresser Peter Kalischer, who, after winning an Overseas Press Club Award for his 1963 CBS coverage of the overthrow of South Vietnam's president Ngo Dinh Diem, killed in a coup, was working out of CBS News' bare-bones Saigon operation. "Walter was too skeptical, too savvy and had too sensitive a shit-detector to be taken in, but Walter could be diverted by machinery, by things with wheels and wings, and especially by things that float, and the military saw to it that he had a chance to see and use everything, go on air strikes, be made to feel an insider," Safer perceptively explained . "His itinerary was designed to keep him away, as much as possible, from correspondents and others permanently based in Vietnam who were considered to be naysayers."

Indeed, the Department of Defense and the State Department rolled out the red carpet for Cronkite in South Vietnam that July. The junket was hardly a baptism by fire. The U.S. Army let him shoot guns, fly planes, detonate mines, and throw grenades; they would do the same thing for novelist John Steinbeck in 1967 (the Nobel laureate ended up not only supporting Johnson's war, but also writing a series of pro-serviceman columns for *Newsday* as a result of his trip). All of the soldiers Cronkite met at USARV (U.S. Army Vietnam) headquarters in Long Binh (near Saigon) were impressive. A couple of GIs he met from Fort Riley, Kansas, regularly wrote him at the *CBS Evening News*; they became pen pals.

Toward the end of Cronkite's handshaking tour, Safer and an army officer—perhaps John Paul Vann, the infamous U.S. military source for *New York Times* reporters David Halberstam and Neil Sheehan— buttonholed the anchorman and gave him a "grunt's- eye view of the world" that was "completely different" from what the general had told him. In his memoir, *Flashbacks*, Safer stated that he set up at least a few meetings for Cronkite to learn the unvarnished truth about America's failures in Vietnam, to counter all the "lies and bogus optimism" that were being pitchforked his way. Nothing over the top, nothing intentionally antiwar. Just the Big Truths.

Sharing cocktails on the rooftop garden of the Caravelle Hotel in Saigon, which housed the CBS bureau on the third floor, Safer dumped in Cronkite's lap the Big Truth about the Pentagon propaganda offense. He was genuinely pessimistic. No one was telling the American people the tonnage of U.S. mis- siles and bombs being dropped on South Vietnamese, Laotian, and Cambodian villages by Operation Rolling Thunder. Safer told Cronkite that at least a certain per- centage of the fresh-faced GIs they had met—like the Fort Riley soldiers—would get killed if Johnson didn't rethink his policy. It was hard for Cronkite to digest the disturbing notion that McNamara regularly lied, that General William Westmoreland, who was commanding America's armed forces in combat in Vietnam, was as foolishly jingoistic as the ranting general. To Cronkite, smart reporters such as Safer and Kalischer, both of whom he personally admired, needed to help the American military win the war, as he had done during World War II with United Press. It bothered Cronkite that many of the young hotshot reporters and cameramen he encountered in Vietnam were flippant, calling the U.S. military press briefings "the five o'clock follies"; that was deeply disrespectful. "The truths I told him didn't come as a complete shock," Safer recalled. "But it was just difficult for him not to be supportive of the American troops in the field."

In early August 1965, Safer accompanied U.S. Marines on a search-and-destroy mission to the Vietnamese hamlet of Cam Ne. After they took sniper fire from the hamlet, the Marines systematically burned the thatch homes of Cam Ne to cinders. The Marines used everything from flame throwers to Zippo lighters. Safer was appalled: U.S. troops were supposed to be "winning hearts and minds." Residents, who had been instructed to stand aside by the Marines, pleaded for mercy. Their agonizing cries were ignored. Safer had his South Vietnamese cameraman—Ha Thuc Can—film the destruction and shipped it off to Russ Bensley to edit in New York.

On August 5, 1965, the Safer report of the torching of Cam Ne aired on the *CBS Evening News*. It caused a fierce reaction in Washington—the State Department, the Pentagon, the Marine Corps, and the White House all demanded that CBS replace Safer. The footage slammed home the uncomfortable fact that the destruction of Cam Ne by Marines had been unnecessary. Cronkite joined CBS News president Fred Friendly in defending the thirty-four-year-old correspondent. But the blowback was like a bazooka shot to the gut. "Some of the reporting I did pained Walter," Safer recalled. "But when the heat was on me about Cam Ne, when viewers wanted my head on a stick, and I was called to New York in the autumn of 1965 for reassignment, he threw a dinner party for me at his home. Anchormen don't usually give a shit about the reporter in the field. But Walter did. I was the new kid at CBS at the time. The White House wanted me fired. That prick Bill Moyers [White House press secretary to Lyndon Johnson] pilloried me. Hate mail came pouring in. The heat was on for me to get fired. And what did Walter do? He threw me a dinner party in New York. That was the kind of man he was."

Safer's edgy reporting from South Vietnam, in which Marines committed atrocities of ghastly proportions, pained President Johnson far more than it did Cronkite. Dr. Frank Stanton got a vicious, threatening call from the hot-under-the-collar White House that rattled his bones.

"Frank," Johnson said, waking the slumbering president of CBS.

"Who is this?" said the half-asleep Stanton.

"Frank, this is your president, and yesterday your boys shat on the American flag."

Johnson insisted that Safer was a communist. He just had to be. Upon finding out vis-à-vis a security check that Safer was Canadian, the president gloated. "Well, I knew he wasn't an American." The Pentagon chief spokesman, Arthur Sylvester, complained to Fred Friendly that Safer was a "Canadian Communist homosexual"; CBS News issued a memo saying the network had the "highest confidence" in Safer. CBS had Safer cover the Battle of Ia Drang Valley in November of 1965. While trying to do a story one afternoon, his chopper was shot down. No one was seriously injured. Safer recuperated for a few days, got airlifted to Saigon, and then flew to New York with footage in hand to prepare the CBS News *Special Report* "The Battle of Ia Drang Valley," which aired on a Friday evening in mid-November with an introduction by Cronkite. "It was after that broadcast that Friendly asked me to take a break from Vietnam and go back to London as bureau chief," Safer recalled. "Rather, who had replaced me in London, was sent to replace me in Saigon."

Cronkite felt horrible that Safer, who had done such gutsy work in Cam Ne, had been exiled. But besides throwing him a dinner party, he couldn't save Safer from getting pulled. President Johnson now believed that "Cronkite was out to get me!" Starting in early 1966, Cronkite frequently visited Safer in Great Britain to discuss Vietnam. Both Cronkite and Safer believed General Westmoreland was clueless about what made the Vietcong tick. "We knew in 1966 and 1967," Safer recalled, "that the only guys who knew Vietnam was a lost cause were CIA."

Even after the Cam Ne incident, Cronkite remained a cautious hawk. He thought the Americans would, in the end, win over the hearts and minds of the Vietnamese people. While Safer's sobering analysis and the brigadier general's "cowards" rant stuck with him, they didn't radically alter his thinking. On September 29, 1965, Cronkite offered remarks about the Johnson administration's foreign policy at the Associated Press Managing Editors Convention in Buffalo, New York. The speech was an odd and amazing window into how Cronkite processed his recent trip to Southeast Asia. On the dove side, he called the U.S. intervention in Vietnam a "bottomless pit" and a seemingly "insolvable quandary." By seeing firsthand how huge the U.S. construction projects around Da Nang were, Cronkite knew that President Johnson was downplaying the U.S. government's commitment to South Vietnam's nation-building effort.

Yet Cronkite didn't think America should retreat from the cold war chess game, just bury its head in the sand like Uncle Sam Ostrich. South Vietnam . . . Egypt . . . Cyprus . . . Indonesia . . . Cambodia . . . Af rica. Name the place and Cronkite thought increased U.S. aid and American military hardware were needed there. "Our foreign policy goal of preserving this environment for free societies brings us into the morass of Vietnam," Cronkite said to the AP editors. "If we were to be faithful to that goal, our aid to South Vietnam was not only justified, but required, and we cannot now grow faint of heart because of the almost unbearable frustration, but must endure and redouble our effort to find the means of victory."

That same fall of 1965, Cronkite lunched with R. W. Apple and David Halberstam, both *New York Times* reporters focusing on Vietnam, to better understand the Battle of Ia Drang Valley. Considered the first conventional battle of the Vietnam War, it was fought between one brigade of the U.S. Army's First Cavalry Division (Airmobile) and three regiments of the North Vietnamese Army. Cronkite was far more optimistic than the *Times* reporters. On October 13, Cronkite interviewed Secretary of State Dean Rusk for a "Man of the Month" feature on *The Twentieth Century* series. A few sparks flew over what the media's role was in covering foreign policy crises like the Dominican intervention and the Vietnam War. "You're interested in the drama of the news," Rusk upbraided Cronkite. "What we are working for is the repose of solutions and peace."

Around Thanksgiving, Cronkite had a map of Vietnam hung up in the CBS Broadcast Center, with pushpins that were used to help producers and writers locate exotic places such as Dien Bien Phu, Pleiku, Kon Tum, and Qui Nhon. It was an updated Rand McNally version of his map of the Korean Peninsula that he'd drawn on a chalkboard in 1950 for WTOP-TV. CBS News was now treating Asia, for the first time, as a major theater. "I returned from that first trip to Vietnam," Cronkite recalled, "with the feeling that the evidence in the field seemed to support the contention of the high command and the administration in Washington that we were making progress." Sounding like Westmoreland, Cronkite praised Johnson's "courageous decision that communism's advance must be stopped in Asia and that guerrilla war as a means to a political end must be finally discouraged."

But Cronkite also felt that CBS News needed to cover the North Vietnamese side of the war as well. On December 6, Cronkite, in an extremely controversial decision spurred on by Friendly, aired a taped interview that British journalist Felix Greene had conducted with President Ho Chi Minh of North Vietnam. "American imperialism is the aggressor," Minh said. "It must stop air attacks on North Vietnam. It must put an end to its aggression in the South, withdraw its troops from South Vietnam, and let the Vietnamese settle for themselves their own affairs as provided for in the Geneva agreements."

When Pocket Books published *Vietnam Perspective*, a collection of CBS broadcast transcripts, in time for Christmas 1965, Cronkite wrote in the introduction, "This is the meaning of our commitment in Southeast Asia—a commitment not for this year or next year but, more likely, for a generation. This is the way it must be if we are to fulfill our pledge to ourselves and to others to stop communist aggression wherever it raises its head." That was hawkish. But allowing Ho Chi Minh on his *CBS Evening News* broadcast, raising the ire of President Johnson, was definitely dovish. This strange dichotomy, this being pro-war while your correspondents on the ground in Vietnam were more skeptical, wore on Cronkite. He tried to stay UP-neutral, adhering to rule number one in journalism, objectivity: "If the World Goes to Hell in a Handbasket It's the Reporter's Job to Be There and Tell What Color the Handbasket Is."

Cronkite was caught in a mid-1960s conundrum: whether to believe Robert McNamara (hawk) or Morley Safer (dove), who thought the Vietnam War was America's Waterloo. There was one constant in Cronkite's thinking: be objective. Everyone, hawks and doves alike, Cronkite thought, was acting squirrelly. Upstanding U.S. government officials had fibbed their way into a major war; unorthodox peaceniks answered to no one and yet pretended to be more knowledgeable about Far East Asian affairs than Secretary of State Dean Rusk. It was confusing to Cronkite. But the New Left's claim that Johnson was dead wrong about the Vietnam enterprise left him stone cold. Trying to soothe everyone, Cronkite skirted around that central foreign policy question in 1966. Erring on the side of "promotion of democracy" was always a good thing, in his view.

Along with Harry Reasoner, Alexander Kendrick, Marvin Kalb, Peter Kalischer, and Richard C. Hottelet, Cronkite contributed to "Vietnam Perspective," a four-part *CBS News Special Report*. While it was edifying for Cronkite to ask General Maxwell Taylor and UN

Ambassador Arthur Goldberg questions, Cronkite showed no real enthusiasm for this string of CBS News *Special Reports* about B-52s bombing North Vietnam to disrupt movement along the Mu Gia Pass or the Congress of Racial Equality claiming that the military draft was discriminatory against blacks. He had Project Gemini to focus on. His great achievement was getting President Johnson to read a January 21, 1966, speech announcing the resuming of the Rolling Thunder bombing campaign against North Vietnam—whose army was the fifth largest in the world—on CBS News for color film cameras. What Cronkite didn't tell his CBS viewers was that Rolling Thunder was a half-assed bombing campaign, constantly hamstrung by Johnson's crippling fits and starts, bombing pauses, and stand-downs.

The U.S. military had divided South Vietnam into four military corps areas—from I Corps up against the DMZ to IV Corps in the far south: Cronkite wanted to travel to all of them. "As field correspondents," CBS News correspondent Bill Plante recalled, "we knew a lot of bang-bang combat action [footage] would get our stories on the *Evening News.*" Plante had developed strong ties with the Marines in Da Nang. When Harrison Salisbury, Cronkite's old UP boss, now with *The New York Times*, visited Hanoi at the end of 1966,

Cronkite worried that CBS was perhaps being too timid, covering only the situation in South Vietnam. An effort was made to get Cronkite a visa to North Vietnam. "CBS thought better of sending Cronkite, fearing it would appear that he was somehow antiwar, so they switched his application with Collingwood's—with me as a back-up if that fell through," Safer recalled. "In the end, Charles Collingwood was given the visa and he sent back a series of reports from North Vietnam."

Bill Moyers claimed in hindsight that if Cronkite had been more courageous, like Murrow, and criticized the U.S. buildup in Vietnam in 1965, Johnson might have deescalated the conflict. This was ass-covering bullshit: every time the *CBS Evening News* ran a segment even slightly critical of Johnson policy, Moyers pounced with a White House threat. Cronkite thought that Moyers, a former reporter for Johnson's radio-TV stations in Austin, was a phony, acting like he was one of the press boys when in reality he was an LBJ stalking horse. "Moyers had a very nasty streak," Safer recalled. "Decades later at the Emmy Awards, he apologized to me for the way he pilloried CBS back then." When historian Don Carleton raised Moyers's point to Cronkite in the early 1990s, the anchorman bristled. "I just don't believe it," he snapped. "No. Johnson was riding high, wide, and handsome in 1965. I would have been a mosquito bite on Johnson's rear end; he would have flicked me off like an insect. I'm surprised Moyers said that."

While Cronkite was slow to seize the idea of a credibility gap between the Pentagon version of events in Southeast Asia and that of CBS News' Saigon bureau reporters, he was unafraid to show gruesome war images on the *Evening News* as troop levels topped two hundred thousand. Burning villages . . . mortar rounds . . . bomb craters . . . poisonous defoliants . . . screaming children . . . desecrated wetlands . . . wounded soldiers . . . casualties. The sheer barbarity of it all was beamed into Main Street America, giving the Vietnam conflict the nickname "the living room war." Color television only made the violence more memorable (and horrible). A three- to six-month rotation was implemented so that CBS News correspondents could serve a tour of duty in the Saigon bureau without being away from their homes for too long. Almost everyone went. There was an unspoken awareness that if you refused assignment to Saigon—as Roger Mudd did for family reasons—it would cost you career-wise with Dr. Stanton down the road. Others who refused to go were Terry Drinkwater (whose wife threatened to divorce him if he went), Robert Pierpoint (who had covered enough combat in Korea), and Eric

Sevareid (who said he had seen enough of war during World War II in the 1940s and in 1965 in the Dominican Republic).

Unlike his NASA boosterism, as a golden rule, Cronkite never glamorized war in a broadcast. CBS News executive producer Russ Bensley used to spend hours every day in a screening room dedicated to putting together Vietnam segments using raw footage shipped to New York from Saigon via Los Angeles or San Francisco. (Satellite hookups didn't become available until late 1967.) Both Cronkite and Bensley were careful not to show the most sordid war atrocities on the air (such as cutting the ears off enemy corpses). Still, both men believed TV viewers needed to see the harsh reality of war in their living rooms. It wasn't ethical to play ostrich as American soldiers died overseas. "In a war situation," Cronkite insisted, "every American ought to suffer as much as the guy on the front lines. We ought to see this. We ought to be *forced* to see it."

Throughout late 1965 and early 1966, the *CBS Evening News* ran stories about Operation Rolling Thunder pounding North Vietnam and antiwar rallies taking place in U.S. cities alike. CBS News president Fred Friendly also planned a series of debates to continue the "Vietnam Perspective" broadcasts under the new heading "Congress and the War." On

February 15, 1966, John Schneider, vice president of broadcast activities, decided that Friendly was broadcasting too many hours of the Senate Foreign Relations Committee's hearings on the escalating U.S. commitment in Vietnam during the advertising-rich afternoons. It wasn't good for the soap opera business. Schneider suspended CBS's special coverage of the hearings, reverting to *I Love Lucy* reruns and other standard daytime fare. While NBC continued its live coverage, Schneider decided that CBS would be best served by distilling the Senate committee testimony on Cronkite's *CBS Evening News.*

A livid Friendly deemed the Schneider move a "blackout" in favor of crapola programming that made a "mockery" of TV's aspirations as a news medium. It sickened Friendly that something as important as George Kennan, the father of cold war containment policy, dissenting about U.S. intervention in Vietnam was nixed by Schneider for the sake of a couple of quick advertising bucks. In the fracas that followed, most true reporters sided with Friendly—renowned as co-editor (with Murrow) of the *See It Now* documentaries—against Schneider, who became an opportune symbol of corporate greed.

Friendly threatened to quit. Actually, he was often enraged and frequently threatened to defect from commercial TV. But this time he followed through. Dick Salant, former president of CBS News from February 1961 to March 1964, was tapped by Paley to replace him. Friendly's resignation vexed the correspondent corps at CBS. Not Cronkite. While he admired Friendly, and appreciated that under his aegis the *CBS Evening News* ratings had grown, he didn't lose sleep over the tussle. He encouraged CBS writers and producers to sign a petition demanding Friendly's reinstatement, but he didn't sign it himself. Perhaps remembering what had happened when he warred with Paley back in 1964, Cronkite stayed publicly mum. From Cronkite's perspective, the Friendly-Schneider argument took place on CBS's daytime program stopwatch. It had nothing to do with his *Evening News* broadcast. (Cronkite, knowing his loyalties would be scrutinized by *The New York Times*, did eventually release a careful statement praising Friendly's "brilliant, imaginative, and hard-hitting guidance," without criticizing Stanton.)

Schneider, who remained a corporate force at CBS until 1978, held firm, resenting the print media's complimentary portrayal of Friendly while the rest of CBS executives were cast as "money changers in the temple." *The New York Times* even ran Friendly's resignation letter in full. Although Cronkite would never have admitted it, the Friendly resignation liberated him. Until 1966, he felt he was living in the House of Murrow. After Murrow died in 1965 and Friendly quit in 1966 for employment at Columbia University, where William Paley was a lifetime trustee, and the Ford Foundation, where McGeorge Bundy was sponsor, CBS News became a decidedly Cronkite enterprise. Although he didn't mention it much in *A Reporter's Life*, Cronkite usually got along well with corporate executive types. He was a company man. He wasn't sycophantic, but he valued the reasoned analysis of Stanton more than the showstopping histrionics of Fred Friendly, who was always waving his arms around and perspiring over a programming issue.

During his sixteen years at CBS News, Friendly had done a lot of things right. There wasn't much to be ashamed of. It was impossible to discuss *See It Now*, *CBS News Reports*, or the pioneering Vietnam War and civil rights coverage on the network without invoking his name. He was an industry legend. But Friendly was always the boss man in the newsroom, intimidating even Cronkite by his kinetic presence. Now he was gone. Former president Dwight Eisenhower telephoned Friendly from Indio, California, to find out what had happened, saying he was "shocked" and "distressed." Upon hanging up, Eisenhower wrote

Friendly a letter of support. "I have been partial to CBS because of my friendship with Bill Paley and later with Frank Stanton," Eisenhower said. "Then when I came to know, and work with, you and Walter Cronkite my partiality became truly pronounced. For a long time you have known that I found my association with you and Walter to be particularly pleasant; so much so that I almost lost all interest in any working arrangements with another. Now I have to review my own situation. But this is nothing compared to my feeling of regret that you felt it necessary to resign from CBS."

Cronkite welcomed Salant's steady manner after enduring that of the turbulent Friendly. Many media observers, especially those outside CBS News, were concerned that Salant, a lawyer and nonjournalist, would lock the newsroom into a conservative corporate environment. No more controversial Morley Safer at Cam Ne reporting on Zippo lighters or Nelson Benton in Birmingham, Alabama, bemoaning barking dogs. Those inside CBS like Cronkite knew better. Referring to the one quality Friendly and Salant had in common, Bill Leonard recalled that "serious journalism," as practiced by CBS News at its best, "ranked with God and Country in their scheme of things." At any rate, Salant didn't add pressure to an industry already soaked in it. "Salant," Les Midgley recalled, "always preached that the news department was interested only in facts, not ratings."

After "A CBS News Inquiry: The Warren Report" aired in June 1967, with Cronkite reporting front and center, Ernie Leiser retired as executive producer of the *CBS Evening News*. The pressures of TV were too much. His replacement was the soft-spoken Leslie Midgley. Under Midgley's auspices, CBS News carried Vietnam stories nightly. Midgley, executive producer of the *Evening News* from 1967 to 1972, was himself an old newspaperman of *Tribune* vintage. It was Midgley who understood that Cronkite was hell-bent on outpacing NBC on all things Southeast Asia. "If he saw some story on NBC which he deemed superior to the CBS version," Midgley recalled about Vietnam coverage, "he was quick to conclude that we were falling down on the job. 'Let's do it better—and beat them!' he would cry."

Before long, Les Midgley, tired of playing it down the middle, regularly tried to get Russ Bensley to edit segments of the *Evening News* to make the Johnson administration's Southeast Asia policies look bad. CBS News vice president Blair Clark, a confirmed liberal, found the U.S. military intervention in Southeast Asia morally repugnant. Like Midgley, he couldn't play the objectivity game. By 1964, Clark's pronounced antiwar views had led him to quit CBS News. He ended up as editor of *The Nation* and campaign manager to Eugene McCarthy in his unsuccessful bid for the 1968 Democratic presidential nomination. "Walter thought that Clark was too antiwar," Andy Rooney recalled. "We were pure World War II guys. It was unseemly to not be 100 percent behind the troops. Walter thought Clark was a boob for going into politics . . . still, he *liked* him."

Conflict seemed to always engulf CBS News in 1967 under Midgley's leadership. Cronkite tried to referee. But that changed in the last days of March 1967, as news viewers tuned in not knowing who would be sitting in the anchor chairs at CBS, NBC, and ABC. It certainly wouldn't be Walter Cronkite or David Brinkley, or the twenty-eight-year-old Toronto native Peter Jennings on ABC. All three were on strike as card-carrying members of the American Federation of Television and Radio Artists (AFTRA). The union represented about eighteen thousand performers, all of whom walked out in support of local news reporters, whose pay was considered by the union to be unfair. Entertainers such as Lucille Ball, Danny Kaye, and the Smothers Brothers were also on strike to help the cause. Television was a central part of many Americans' daily lives, serving as news source, babysitter, and mindless entertainer. So the strike was of genuine national concern. Soap operas such as *As the World Turns* and *Guiding Light* closed down production. Network entertainment shows that hadn't scrambled to finish episodes already in the pipeline simply replayed old ones. In the news divisions, management was recruited to read the text, and comedians had a field day with the results.

At CBS News, Cronkite's replacement was Arnold Zenker, a twenty-eight-year-old low-level TV manager with thick-framed glasses and some experience as a broadcast announcer. Rough and undoubtedly green, Zenker was just good enough to hold the broadcast together for Cronkite loyalists. But as the AFTRA strike continued into April, a person could spike just about any conversation with Zenker's name and be assured of a hearty laugh. It's a mystery why Zenker, of all people, was tapped to replace Cronkite for thirteen days; his specialty was soft-news features, and he had never even met Cronkite. "I still have no idea why they selected me," Zenker told *The New York Times* in 2006. "No one even offered to buy me a blue shirt."

An overwhelmed Zenker, nerves jangled, found himself competing for ratings with two network heavyweights as he vigorously tried to keep Cronkite's millions of nightly viewers from turning the dial. During the strike, Cronkite grew uncomfortable with Zenker's gleefully talking to the press about sitting in the CBS anchor chair. Cronkite complained nightly about him to Dick Salant. "I was shocked when Salant told me not to do any more interviews," Zenker recalled. "I couldn't believe that Cronkite was so insecure. But he was." (Years later, when Cronkite discussed Zenker in an oral history, he said dismissively, "I did not go to work. And CBS pulled in this guy, Adolf Hitler, or whatever his name was, Adolf Zinger or something . . . .")

At NBC News no one missed Chet Huntley because he was one of the few broadcasters who stayed on the job, taking a libertarian stance. Another was Huntley's NBC colleague, Frank McGee. Both expressed outrage that serious journalists were in the same union with entertainers and pointed out that they had been forced to join AFTRA as a condition of employment. Neither felt any obligation to the union. David Brinkley, for his part, was philosophically opposed to the strike, but he stayed away from work anyway, unwilling to break ranks with colleagues and friends in the industry.

Even though Cronkite had a wicked cold, chewing on Halls Mentho-Lyptus cough drops from morning to night, he walked the picket line outside CBS News headquarters in New York City. It was a sight to see: the celebrated anchorman pacing back and forth, a sandwich board draped over his shoulders like an all-one-big-union Wobbly in a Woody Guthrie song. The newspapers loved showing Cronkite on the pavement, contrasting him with Huntley, who went so far as to denounce the strike as nothing but "18,000 singers, dancers and jugglers." Cronkite told reporters he remembered how hard it was to make ends meet back in the Great Depression while working at *The Houston Press.* The message was clear: Cronkite hadn't forgotten his working-class roots.

Cronkite stayed out even though the *CBS Evening News* was losing ground in the ratings. Arbitron numbers for the initial days of the strike showed CBS losing about a quarter of its audience, while NBC was expanding viewership by the same percentage. CBS was poised to lose millions of dollars in advertising revenue. But then the worm turned. As the strike continued, Huntley began to be seen as antilabor and elitist, concerned only with how much jack he made. "Chet Huntley Slaps at TV Strike" ran the banner headline across the front page of the *El Paso Herald-Post.* Newspapers across the country carried the same story. Unions boycotted NBC News because of Huntley's corporate toadyism or Rocky Mountain libertarianism (depending on how you looked at the half-filled glass). The thirteen-day strike resulted in a slightly improved contract for the local correspondents. In the long run, the greatest impact might have been the taint Huntley left on NBC. Blue-collar, nine-to-five Americans now had reconfirmed their hunch that Cronkite was a stand-up guy. Huntley was portrayed as a scab. Only a cabal of John Birch types considered Huntley brave in taking on the unions in such an in-your-face way.

Cronkite gracefully ended his hiatus from CBS. Taking back his old position at the anchor desk, he looked into the camera with a little grin and said, "Good evening, this is Walter Cronkite, filling in for Arnold Zenker. It's good to be back." With a twinkle in his eye and a sandwich board on his back, Cronkite had played the strike the right way. Zenker received more than three thousand fan letters, with one faction marketing "Bring Back Zenker" buttons, but everyone knew Cronkite was safe in the chair.

At NBC, the situation was the opposite. After Brinkley returned, longtime observers sensed something was amiss. Not that the co-anchors held any animosity toward each other—they didn't—but audiences were less comfortable with the partnership. And CBS was in a good position to take advantage of the chink in the National Biscuit Company's armor.

CBS News began relentlessly promoting Cronkite in print advertising, to the extent that Eric Sevareid complained, reminding the company that he was a bona fide star, too. But Cronkite was *the* star at CBS News, and that was the way the network wanted it. Somehow he had succeeded in being both au courant and old school simultaneously. He might not have been the new Murrow, but he had the respect of reporters everywhere. Plus, Cronkite filled another role for his employer: he was a consummate ambassador for the company, making regular appearances at meetings large and small across the country, either to speak or simply to be present. At the annual convention for CBS affiliates in New York City in 1967, the network introduced its lineup of familiar faces. Audience members were surprised when Cronkite received louder, longer applause than Ed Sullivan, veteran star of a top entertainment show.

Cronkite, Huntley, Brinkley, Reasoner, Howard K. Smith, and a few others were at the forefront during the ascendancy of the TV news anchor into celebrity. Even while producers, correspondents, and writers worked hard to gather and communicate the news, polls found that TV viewers mainly judged network news by whether they liked, understood, and respected the anchor. Star quality was what counted. In the fickle world of TV journalism, only Cronkite was able to lure viewers to fix on his every word. If Cronkite made a little smile or half-raised an eyebrow, viewers noticed.

"It's not as though Walter were a movie star," Betsy Cronkite explained of her husband's allure. "People watch him when they are in pajamas in their bedrooms. They feel they know him."

David Brinkley drew headlines when he decried celebrity newscasters. "It must be all right for a program like Danny Kaye's or Lucille Ball's to have stars—famous personalities who are discussed and admired in fan magazines and asked for autographs, but when this system is carried over into television coverage of news, as it is, it is absurd," Brinkley complained. "It is also irrelevant and inappropriate." James Reston, writing in *The New York Times*, noted that David Brinkley railing against star anchormen "was a little like Lyndon Johnson attacking Texas." To Cronkite's secret amusement, he was more comfortable with star status than Brinkley, but he was as adamant as anyone that anchors be *journalists*, trained in investigating, reporting, editing, and writing, before ever uttering a word for the microphone. He had come of age in the 1920s, when great reporters such as Lowell Thomas had a rough-and-ready glamour akin to Arctic explorers or aviation pioneers. Cronkite also admitted that he enjoyed walking into any New York restaurant, anywhere, anytime—such as La Côte Basque and Le Cirque—and receiving a good table with A-plus service. If he wasn't recognized, he grew depressed.

In June 1967, Salant decided to amp up CBS News' coverage of the Vietnam War. No heavy speculation or long-range analysis. Just more GI grunts from Ohio and Texas shown carrying M-16s on the *CBS Evening News*. Ed Fouhy, a former U.S. Marine who started working the civil rights beat out of New Orleans and Atlanta for Mike Wallace's *CBS Morning News*, was named the new bureau chief in Saigon. Fouhy had a meeting with Cronkite at the broadcast center before his departure. "It was really a pep talk," Fouhy recalled. "Walter was a very competitive guy. He was worried that NBC was starting to outperform us in Vietnam. He didn't ask any foreign policy questions. It was about beating our rivals."

Fouhy arrived at the Caravelle Hotel in Saigon, where CBS News had taken over the third floor. His stable of reporters—Nelson Benton, Bill Plante, Don Webster, and Bert Quint among them—were told that Cronkite wanted more breaking-news coverage. The custom at both CBS and NBC was that correspondents served in Vietnam for three to six months, the majority of it in Saigon or Da Nang, with time off every six weeks for out-of-country R&R. Truth be told, the CBS correspondents did not often leave the comforts of

Saigon and go into the field to cover the troops (as Safer had done). Most reporters spent nights in a Saigon bed with clean sheets, not stuck in the jungle with American soldiers flushing out Vietcong guerrillas. The excuse back then was that the technology necessary to film at night had not yet been developed. Why, therefore, go to the great discomfort of carrying a sleeping bag, poncho, and liner, not to mention all that extra water and film stock, when you could be warm, dry, and snug in your own bed in Saigon or Da Nang? "This practice changed in 1967," correspondent John "Jack" Laurence recalled, "as a few correspondents discovered the rewards of getting to know the troops and winning their respect by living with them for days at a time and reporting what they had to say."

Salant wrote a highly confidential memo in the late summer of 1967 instructing correspondents to explain what their stories from Vietnam meant in the larger context of the war. *Tell us what it all means*, Salant implored. This, it seemed to Laurence, was an order to draw conclusions from what he witnessed in the war, to provide personal impressions at the end of his reports, to do commentary for the first time. The extent to which this memo from Salant to man- ager of news Ralph Paskman was circulated, however, remains unclear. Perhaps few others besides Cronkite,

Midgley, and Manning saw it. But by then everyone at CBS News knew that Marvin Kalb, the CBS News diplomatic correspondent who covered the 1964 Senate debate of the Gulf of Tonkin resolution, had found out that "contingent drafts" of the Tonkin Resolution were drafted long before the incident supposedly occurred.

But just before Laurence left for Saigon in August 1967 (his second tour), Paskman called his foreign correspondent into the office and closed the door. He told Laurence the meeting was confidential, not to be repeated to anyone. "I agreed," Laurence recalled. "Then he took the memo out of the drawer in his desk and showed it to me. He allowed me to read it briefly, as if it were secret, and then took it away and put it back in the drawer and closed it." Paskman reiterated not to mention the memo to *anybody*. Once again Laurence reassured him that mum was the word. "His expression was one of worry," Laurence recalled, "as if he were opening the door to an unknown, possibly dangerous new policy."

When Fouhy had visited with Salant just before leaving New York, he had one question: What is our Vietnam budget? "Spend," Salant snapped, "whatever it takes." The bureau grew to more than thirty-five employees (some of them South Vietnamese). The bureau chief, cameramen, and correspondents were

American, French, Japanese, German, and Australian (the exception was Safer's photographer at Cam Ne, Ha Thuc Can). Duong Van Ri, a Vietnamese sound-man, got promoted to camera work in 1968. "We all knew," Plante recalled, "that Salant and Cronkite, by 1967, didn't think the war was going to end well." WCBS-AM in New York, the second CBS radio station to adopt an all-news format, regularly ran cutting-edge reports from South Vietnam that differed wildly from what the Johnson administration claimed had taken place. Cronkite was its most devoted listener.

All this Vietnam angst had some CBS News folks going buggy. Midgley wanted to balance the grim news from the Saigon bureau with some relief for *Evening News* viewers. In 1967, Charles Kuralt, a CBS correspondent originally from Wilmington, North Carolina, who had been considered for the anchor position in 1962, suggested a new Americana feature for the show. He was tired of covering wars and revolutions in South America and Vietnam. Midgley was not at first receptive. The thirty-minute program needed, if anything, more news spots. He was reluctant to hand two or three minutes over to anyone—and to Kuralt in particular.

Slightly overweight, prematurely balding, with eyes that seemed to case every room he entered, Kuralt didn't look like a Nielsen ratings winner. He looked

like an innocuous man—a dead ringer for the hot dog–
vending Ignatius J. Reilly from John Kennedy Toole's
novel *A Confederacy of Dunces*—who was easy to
lose in a crowd. Furthermore, everyone at CBS knew
that Cronkite bristled at the very word *feature*. And
Kuralt's travelogue idea was at the opposite end of the
spectrum from hard-hitting news, for which Cronkite
and CBS were known. It involved no investigation, no
battlefield bravura, no blunt reporting on the injustices
of American society. Kuralt wanted to take a camera
and find stories about everyday Americans. Cronkite
was adamantly opposed. He couldn't bear the thought
of filling the *Evening News*—his *Evening News*—with
anything soft, fluffy, or deserving of the worst insult
of the 1960s: irrelevant. But this was a rare instance
in which he failed to have the last say on the *Evening
News*' content; he lost the battle. Midgley agreed to a
compromise by which Kuralt's "On the Road" feature
would run on a trial basis for three months, starting in
October 1967.

Building on a following he had developed as the
first anchor of *CBS News Sunday Magazine*, Kuralt
reported good news about big accomplishments in the
small worlds of innovative Americans around the country. Starting with a segment on New England autumnal
leaf color-changing, Kuralt soon profiled an old black

man in Winston-Salem, North Carolina, who made bricks; a train engineer who maintained working steam locomotives in Wisconsin; a Vermonter who marketed a nineteenth-century treatment for chapped cow udders; and a Southerner who fixed bicycles so that no child in the neighborhood would be without one. Kuralt's homespun two-minute stories were not the stuff normally regarded as national news. *Time* magazine succinctly described Kuralt's "On the Road" features as "two-minute cease-fires" from the tumultuous era. The gentle-hearted segments, for which Kuralt won two Peabody Awards and an Emmy, proved essential to the *Evening News*, allowing it to cover troubled times in stark terms by also celebrating the basic values upon which even a splintered country could agree: American generosity, humor, nonconformity, and dignity. As Midgley noted, Kuralt liked to talk with "oldsters," as if they were the only rational voices left in an America obsessed with Vietnam.

Cronkite soon came around to embrace the value of "On the Road" on the *Evening News*, ultimately befriending its host. Just as Murrow had developed a tag team of smart guys in the 1940s and 1950s, Cronkite was doing the same in the late 1960s. Kuralt became one of his favorite sidekicks. Together they toyed with the idea of buying a string of radio stations, with Kuralt eventually acquiring WELY in Ely, Minnesota.

At the end of 1967, the *CBS Evening News with Walter Cronkite* finally passed *The Huntley-Brinkley Report* in the ratings. Kuralt was a winning factor. It had been a tough slog since 1962. The excellence of the Vietnam correspondent corps was a major part of the broadcast's success. The likable Kuralt and the lofty Sevareid contributed to the appeal of the mannered Cronkite broadcast. The network's unceasing promotion of Cronkite as the *best* anchor helped, too.

It was becoming clear by Christmas 1967 that the Vietnam War was going to be *the* big issue in the 1968 presidential election. The entire *CBS Evening News* program was now in technicolor: the blood of Vietnam was now deep red in people's living rooms. President Johnson no longer trusted Cronkite and his CBS ilk. At a March 1967 dinner party, he told reporters that CBS and NBC were "controlled by the Vietcong."

Cronkite tried to differentiate Johnson's policy from the grunts who were fighting in Vietnam, young draftees whose main objective was to survive. None of the officers Cronkite interviewed in Vietnam below the rank of lieutenant colonel said they were fighting for the flag; they were fighting to protect their band of brothers. By 1967, Johnson's entire Vietnam enterprise was falling apart. Heroin use by troops was steadily increasing, as was NSU (non-specific urethritis, what the military called gonorrhea). There was a rash of "fragging"—tossing grenades into the tents and barracks of unpopular officers and NCOs. "No one had a clear idea of why they were fighting this war," recalled Safer.

With the promise of a close election in 1968, Cronkite knew in late 1967 that CBS News was in for a tumultuous year. President Johnson, with his overworked Texas mannerisms, was by now so roundly distrusted regarding Vietnam that Democrats were breaking ranks. As early as 1966, Salant expected Senator Robert Kennedy of New York to challenge Johnson for the Democratic nomination, and CBS News began covering him closely. Cronkite used to joke that his two newest hobbies were "bird and Bobby watching." At just forty years of age, Robert, the brother of John F. Kennedy, had written a book in 1967—*To Make a Newer World*—calling for the U.S. to withdraw from Vietnam. Eugene McCarthy, Minnesota's poet-intellectual senator, a dove on Vietnam, declared his candidacy in November 1967 as the antiwar choice; former CBS News vice president Blair Clark served as his campaign manager. Realizing that the Vietnam War was growing more and more unpopular, that November General

Westmoreland delivered a speech at the National Press Club in Washington, claiming U.S. troops had reached a point "where the end begins to come into view."

On the Republican side, Richard Nixon was back in politics, having lost the presidential race in 1960. He, too, distrusted CBS News. In 1968, he would be part of a field that included three GOP governors who were either declared or presumed candidates: Nelson Rockefeller (New York), George Romney (Michigan), and Ronald Reagan (California). George Wallace, the Democratic governor of Alabama, was rumored to be gearing up for a third-party run as a segregationist. Cronkite worried that the deteriorating situation in Southeast Asia had become more than President Johnson could handle. "LBJ, just bypassing Stanton, would telephone Cronkite directly to grouse about *CBS Evening News* war coverage," Charles Osgood recalled. "Vietnam was more than he could take, really."

22.

The Tet Offensive

WHAT THE HELL IS GOING ON?—THERE IS NO LIGHT!—
STILL THE RED MENACE—HEADING TO SAIGON—
WESTMORELAND LIES—OLD-STYLE REPORTER—HIS
FRIEND GENERAL ABRAMS—COCKTAILS ON THE CAR-
AVELLE ROOF—JOHN LAURENCE'S ADVICE—BARELY
ESCAPING—THE CRONKITE MOMENT—THE GREAT
STALEMATE—MARCH TO FOLLY—PRODUCER BENSLEY
GETS SHOT IN NAM—LBJ WON'T RUN—MYTHS OVER
THE SPECIAL REPORT—THE FAIRNESS DOCTRINE—AN
EVENING WITH TIM O'BRIEN

Walter Cronkite was sitting in his cluttered CBS
News office at the broadcast center on West
Fifty-seventh Street on January 31, 1968, when he

heard a clattering over the wire service machines in the *Evening News* newsroom. He meandered down the corridor to read the Associated Press dispatch from South Vietnam about a string of surprise North Vietnamese and Vietcong attacks on Saigon, Hué, and numerous other sites (soon to be known collectively as the Tet Offensive). Assault teams had even attacked the U.S. embassy, the South Vietnamese General Staff headquarters, Bien Hoa Air Base, and the U.S. Army base at Long Binh. The wire made Cronkite uneasy. Wasn't Saigon supposed to be a U.S. stronghold? His frustration made him determined to report the U.S. setback as thoroughly as he would a U.S. victory. Heading over to producer Sandy Socolow's adjacent office, where Ernest Leiser and producer Stanhope Gould were discussing that night's program, Cronkite waved the dispatch in their faces. "What the hell is going on?" he asked, full of consternation. "I thought we were winning the war!"

The CBS News bureau in Saigon had reported to New York that the U.S. and South Vietnamese army forces had been surprised and were suffering heavy casualties. Many reporters throughout 1967 had believed that the Johnson administration was lying about imminent U.S. victory in South Vietnam. The AP dispatch of the Tet Offensive was proof that the end of the war was nowhere in sight. When Cronkite read it, his first thought was that R. W. Apple of *The New York Times* was right: the war was indeed a stalemate. Cronkite, remaining pro–U.S. troops, had become frustrated by Johnson's "light at the end of the tunnel" drivel. "We spoke just after Tet," Andy Rooney recalled. "And he felt miserable that he hadn't taken Apple and, for that matter, David Halberstam, more seriously. He now knew they were spot-on."

At the *CBS Evening News* the grisly specter of the Tet Offensive dominated coverage for days. When Cronkite tried to wedge in long-form stories about a California physician performing the first heart transplant in the United States, and Japan becoming the world's second-strongest superpower, they got bumped for a Tet exclusive. When Pearl Harbor was bombed on December 7, 1941, there were at most ten thousand operating TV sets in the United States. In January 1968, sixteen out of every seventeen U.S. homes had a TV set. According to the Nielsen ratings, *CBS Evening News with Walter Cronkite* and NBC's *Huntley-Brinkley Report* were seen in more than a hundred million homes during the first week of the Tet Offensive. "Vietnam was America's first television war," *Washington Post* journalist Don Oberdorfer wrote, "and the Tet Offensive was America's first television superbattle."

When Cronkite was a United Press reporter, he learned an important lesson: be your own eyewitness. Worried about the proliferation of unsubstantiated rumors and deliberate misinformation streaming out of Saigon, he believed it was essential to now take in the Vietnamese situation for himself with "mind wide open." The UP and AP offered chunks of the story, but, as was to be expected, analysis was scant. The first statistics coming out of Tet were dire: two thousand U.S. dead and twice that number of South Vietnamese soldiers; around ten thousand civilians killed. Yet the initial CBS reports were overdrawn: the North Vietnamese Army and especially the Vietcong suffered a tactical disaster during Tet. Confusion reigned over whether Tet was a win or a loss for the United States. "I said," he recalled, "well, I need to go because I thought we needed this documentary about Tet. We were getting daily reports, but we didn't know where it was going at that time; we may lose the war; if we're going to lose the war, I should be there, that was one thing. If the Tet Offensive was successful in the end, it meant that we were going to be fleeing, as we did eventually anyway, but I wanted to be there for the clash."

Cronkite went to see CBS News president Dick Salant about broadcasting on Tet from Saigon. Cronkite decided before he even pitched Salant that he wanted to "try and present an assessment of the situation as one who had not previously taken a public position on the war." No longer would he be impartial. The time had come to weigh in. From a TV ratings perspective it was a calculated risk; he might end up driving the hawks away from the *Evening News* for good. According to Phil Scheffler, CBS News executive producer of special events at the time, Salant approved the idea of the South Vietnamese trip but wanted Cronkite to make his bold statement as a commentator at the end of a *CBS Evening News* broadcast. "Walter said he couldn't possibly do an editorial on the *CBS Evening News*," Scheffler recalled, "which he considered sacrosanct."

Salant listened attentively to Cronkite. At first, he was dismayed at his anchorman's insistence on flying to South Vietnam *immediately* to report on Tet. He couldn't afford for his star anchorman to get killed in a plane crash or ambushed by the Vietcong on a back highway. Each time Cronkite mentioned the Pentagon's exaggerations, Salant cringed as if his star reporter were throwing stones in the blades of a huge floor fan. He had never before seen Cronkite so animated. His response was that he was overreacting to Tet. "If you need to be there, if you are demanding to go, I'm not going to stop you," Salant said, "but I think it's foolish to risk your life in a situation like this, risk the life of our anchorman, and I've got to think about it."

That was Salant's typical way of saying no: *thinking about it*. To Cronkite's pleasant surprise, Salant then threw out a lifeline. "But if you are going to go," he said, "I think you ought to do a documentary about going, about why you went, and maybe you are going to have to say something about where the war ought to go at that point."

The ironclad rule at CBS News was that editorializing by a journalist was verboten. If Salant detected a single verb or adjective that lurched toward editorializing on the *CBS Evening News*, the reporter would automatically be taken to the woodshed. The brand of CBS News was impartiality. Now Salant, to Cronkite's utter astonishment, was willing to break the network's golden rule. He didn't have to press his argument further, because Salant was already on the same page. "You have established a reputation, and thanks to you and through us, we at CBS have established a reputation for honesty and factual reporting and being in the middle of the road," Salant told Cronkite. "You yourself have talked about the fact that we get shot at from both sides, you yourself have said that we get about as many letters saying that we are damned conservatives as saying that we are damned liberals. We support the war. We're against the war. You yourself say that if we weigh the letters, they weigh about the same. We figure we are about middle of the road. So if we've got that reputation, maybe it would be helpful, if people trust us that much, trust you that much, for you to say what you think. Tell them what it looks like, from you being on the ground, what is your opinion."

"You're getting pretty heavy," Cronkite said to Salant.

Salant and Cronkite settled on doing a prime-time *CBS News Special Report* that would be called "Report from Vietnam: Who, What, When, Where, and Why?" (Long after the Vietnam War had ended, Cronkite would fume whenever someone misrepresented his Tet commentary as part of the *CBS Evening News* when it was, in truth, a prime-time *Special Report*.) Bags packed, immunized, Cronkite was headed west into the Vietnam war zone. The Battle of Hué was being fought as ARVN and U.S. Marine elements counterattacked to expel enemy forces from the city, and Cronkite wanted to see the action firsthand. "It was an Orwellian trip," David Halberstam wrote. "Orwell had written of a Ministry of Truth in Charge of Lying and a Ministry of Peace in Charge of War—and here was Cronkite flying to Saigon, where the American military command was surrounded by defeat and calling it a victory."

The risks for Cronkite professionally were high. If he became known as a dove, his reputation for journalistic objectivity would be downgraded from that of "Sphinx to pundit."

On February 6, 1968, Cronkite flew from New York to San Francisco, then on to Honolulu and Tokyo. His mission was concise: to "see for himself what's happened in South Vietnam." On February 11, after major delays at the Tokyo airport, Cronkite, accompanied by producers Ernie Leiser and Jeff Gralnick and a combat-experienced camera crew, arrived in Saigon. From the beginning, the CBSers felt like sitting ducks on the tarmac. Bombs were bursting, whooshing, and screaming around the outskirts of the city and downtown alike. Long-range artillery fire could be heard in the distance. The faces of the Vietnamese street children they saw, terrified by self-propelled rockets and recoilless rifles and mortars, were wrought with fear. After World War II, Cronkite had encountered the same hollowed look in the eyes of displaced persons in Belgium and the Netherlands, a fright that spoke of hunger, panic, and confusion. The formerly elegant city of Saigon was a combat zone. Things had deteriorated since his 1965 visit.

Wearing a flak jacket and army helmet, Cronkite traveled all over the Vietnamese countryside south of the DMZ that February, keeping detailed notes, recording observations on Tet in the war-ravaged nation. A surreal picture made the wire services: the CBS anchorman wearing dark sunglasses with a gentleman's pipe jutting out of his mouth, like Douglas MacArthur headed back to the Philippines. This was quite a sensational return to being a war correspondent. Doubtless an adrenaline rush was coursing through Cronkite as his Jeep rumbled past soldiers and peasants alike. He gave a thumbs-up to every fellow correspondent he encountered. Members of the press tend to ignore one another on the job (even in a war zone) because they're always competing for the same story. Contrary to the norm, all the Vietnam hands in the press swarmed around Cronkite like bees, determined to tell the CBS anchorman about the *real* ground game in Hué and Khe Sanh. Cronkite's Tet notebook—today housed in the archives of the University of Texas at Austin's Briscoe Center for American History—is loaded with scribbled observations about the on-the-ground conditions he encountered that February in South Vietnam, as well as commentary from other journalists.

To make the *CBS News Special Report* work, Cronkite and Leiser knew they needed to interview soldiers at U.S. Army outposts throughout the South Vietnamese countryside and avoid clustering around official press conferences. Cronkite had made that mistake during his first trip to Vietnam, in 1965. The CBS team instead headed for the U.S. Marine Corps base in the hilly countryside of Khe Sanh. This was a very dangerous spot for any reporter to visit. The fighting around the city of ten thousand was so fierce that the CBS team couldn't get into the American garrison. Shifting plans, Cronkite and his team now headed to Hué. Quickly Cronkite saw that in all three places—Saigon, Khe Sanh, and Hué—anarchy appeared to be off the charts.

Only a few hours on the ground, Cronkite hustled up an interview with General William Westmoreland, commander of U.S. forces in the war. It didn't go well. Westmoreland was brusque and dismissive, with a predatory bearing. To Cronkite's amazement, the general claimed that Tet was an American victory, that the North Vietnamese had failed in their military objectives. That was true, but the strength of the enemy force, and its resolve, was far greater than the general and his staff were willing to concede to Cronkite. This was the twelfth day since the Tet Offensive began, and while the United States was indeed winning back territory, almost two thousand Americans had perished trying to thwart the Vietcong surprise attack. Westmoreland mildly reprimanded Cronkite to do his homework properly. The Vietcong laid siege to Saigon during the Tet Offensive, Westmoreland admitted, but didn't capture the city. Therefore, it was clear as day that, to Westmoreland, the Department of Defense was winning the Vietnam War. With one caveat: two hundred thousand more troops were needed.

The upbeat Westmoreland had told Cronkite, in no uncertain terms, that the ARVN and three U.S. Marine Corps battalions had defeated more than ten thousand entrenched People's Army of Vietnam (PAVN) and Vietcong at Hué. As Cronkite and company headed up Highway 1 (the main north–south road of Vietnam, running the length of the country from the Chinese border to the Mekong Delta) to Hué, they realized Westmoreland had lied. The Marines were still trying to retake the city. Explosions were going off everywhere. "The battle was still on in Hué when I got up there," Cronkite recalled. "It lasted twenty-seven days."

Reporters working for AP, *The New York Times*, UP, and Reuters were surprised to see the renowned Cronkite walking through the bombed-out streets of Hué, gunfire erupting in the vicinity, with the poise of a combat veteran. Like the younger correspondents, he slept on the bare floor of a Vietnamese doctor's house that had been turned into a pressroom. He ate C rations and used the overflowing latrine. No one thought he acted like a bigwig or was bigfooting. Cronkite operating in Hué was a sight to behold. Like a prosecuting attorney gathering facts, he interviewed everyone, from orphans to traumatized U.S. soldiers. He went on a marine patrol to survey the perimeter roads around Hué. According to him, he was only operating on a Journalism 101 principle learned in high school: the more information, the better the story. Besides interviewing Vietnamese, Cronkite managed face time with South Vietnamese president Nguyen Van Thieu, loyal opposition leader Xuan Oanh, and U.S. lieutenant general Robert Cushman.

For Cronkite that February, the "real" meaning of Tet was coming into focus: the South Vietnamese government had lost its credibility and was thus condemned to negotiating a quick peace accord. Touring Vietnam, Cronkite grew increasingly bitter toward the Pentagon. The credibility gap between the reality of Hué and Westmoreland's spin was blatant. What sickened Cronkite was that his own network from 1965 to now had largely bought into Westmoreland's military propaganda. He pleaded guilty. Along with NBC and ABC, CBS had not wrongly reported Hué as an utter U.S. defeat. Cronkite was determined to rectify the situation on his *CBS Reports* special. (Hué was, in the end, described as a U.S. victory, but only after a long, bloody battle.)

Cronkite, Leiser, and Gralnick left Hué on a transport chopper; their flight companions were a dozen dead Marines in rubber body bags: killed in action. "It was quiet," Gralnick later told *The Wall Street Journal.* "Nobody said anything. It was an instant understanding for everybody in that helicopter of the cost of the war." Hadn't Westmoreland told Cronkite that Hué had been pacified? The general's lie wasn't abstract now to the CBSer. It hung inside the craft as a desecration of the lives of the Marine corpses in rubber sacks. On the flight, Cronkite grieved for the thousands of American vets who had gotten their arms and legs and balls blown off. And then there were the hundreds of thousands of Vietnamese, Cambodians, and Laotians killed in an impossible and unnecessary war.

Determined to get to the bottom of the Pentagon's lies about Hué, Cronkite traveled to Phu Bai, twelve miles south, to learn more about Tet. He had arranged to interview General Creighton Abrams, deputy commander of the U.S. troops in Vietnam. Cronkite's best source in Vietnam was Abrams, whom he had befriended during the Bulge in 1944, when Abrams was one of Patton's squadron commanders. Sitting around a fireplace with Abrams and his staff in Phu Bai, Cronkite expected to get the lowdown. He found Abrams to be only slightly more candid than his boss, Westmoreland. While Cronkite respected Abrams, he thought his rationale for LBJ sending 200,000 more soldiers to Vietnam was ludicrous. "It was sickening to me," Cronkite recalled. "They were talking strategy and tactics with no consideration of the bigger job of pacifying and restoring the country. This had come to be total war, not a counterinsurgency or an effort to get the North Vietnamese out so we could support the indigenous effort."

Cronkite respectfully listened to Abrams and respectfully disagreed with the general's questionable assessment that with more reinforcements, the United States could "finish the job." He had seen too much evidence to the contrary to believe Abrams. But Abrams also let Cronkite know that the current U.S. military strategy wasn't working—the South Vietnamese needed to shoulder more of the burden.

"My decision was not difficult to reach," Cronkite recalled in *A Reporter's Life*. "It had been taking shape, I realized, since Cam Ranh Bay. There was no way that this war would be justified any longer—a war whose purpose had never been adequately explained to the American people."

Cronkite stood on the roof of the ten-story Caravelle Hotel in Saigon, watching as U.S. Air Force C-47s shot flares in and around the perimeter of Saigon followed by rounds of heavy artillery fire. He was tired and disheartened. He understood the impossibility of it all. Off in the distance he could hear the sounds of war: AK fire, helicopter rotors turning, and Claymore antipersonnel mines exploding. It was dusk, and the streets below were filled with Vietnamese riding bicycles and carrying baskets, seemingly oblivious that war was thundering at their doorsteps. Somebody handed Cronkite a drink and he just stared out at Saigon in utter disbelief. Reconciled to the fact that he was going to call the war a "stalemate" (at best) in his "Report from Vietnam," he went inside to keep a dinner engagement. He was ashamed that LBJ had strung him along, conned him really, for four bloody years about American victory being in sight. Besides serving fine French cuisine, the legendary hotel was home to the Australian and New Zealand embassies, along with CBS's Saigon bureau. Cronkite's dinner companions were three of the network's respected Vietnam War correspondents, John Laurence, Peter Kalischer, and Robert Schakne. "Walter said he wanted to know what was really going on," Laurence recalled of the debriefing. "He let us tell him whatever we knew in an open and honest way."

The central point of what Laurence told Cronkite (explained in great detail in his CBS memoir, *The Cat from Hué*, a book Cronkite later called "a masterpiece of war reporting") was that Washington and Saigon held to "the logic of past wars," that the U.S. Army would win the war because "its soldiers were killing more of the enemy than they were losing themselves." Some analysts even believed that the kill ratio was approximately ten to one. However, Laurence argued, the North Vietnamese weren't going to give up, no matter what their losses were. They had been fighting for the independence of their country since the 1930s and their leaders were prepared to accept enormous casualties, even ten to one. The U.S. was destroying the countryside and massacring its people with military might, often indiscriminately, killing innocent civilians by the thousands with air strikes and artillery. At the same time, Laurence argued, thousands of outstanding American soldiers were being killed in an asinine war that was unwinnable. Laurence was so animated in his antiwar argument that Schakne kicked him in the shin under the table in an attempt to get him to cool his jets.

After dinner, Cronkite excused himself to look out over the city again. "At night from the roof of the Caravelle Hotel correspondents' headquarters," he later wrote to editor Robert Manning of *The Atlantic*

Monthly, "I watched the helicopter gunships circling the city, unloading their hail of death on suspected enemy hot spots scarcely blocks away. And at the bar below I heard angry, frustrated American civilians and officers who had been in charge of pacification of the villages and had a few days before claimed we were winning the hearts and minds of the people, report with bitter cynicism that their villages apparently had welcomed the returning Viet Cong."

Gralnick, Cronkite's field producer on the Vietnam trip and close associate for many years, couldn't predict how his boss was going to play the *CBS News Special Report* once they got back to New York to edit. They had spent an unforgettable time together in Hué, Khe Sanh, and Saigon, seen a lot of collateral damage, and met scores of soldiers and reporters. But Cronkite continued to be contemplative. "He held his cards close": this is how Gralnick described his boss's attitude. All humor had left him. While Cronkite avoided saying that America was "losing" the war, Gralnick *did* notice that on four or five occasions "stalemate" came out of his lips quite easily.

Cronkite, Gralnick, Leiser, and the CBS camera crew barely got out of Vietnam alive. To avoid mortar fire, Cronkite's Jeep driver took a circuitous route to the Saigon airport. There the CBS trio hooked up with two other CBS employees, who were working for *Face the Nation*: director Bob Vitarelli and sound engineer Dick Sedia. Boarding a DC-9 operated by Vietnam Airways for Pan Am, Cronkite sounded calm but removed about his work in-country. The conditions around the airport were dangerous. Takeoff was going to be a spin of the roulette wheel. The CBSers were happy to get out quickly, heading for Hong Kong. "You know, Walter was Mr. Unflappable," Vitarelli recalled. "But I was quite worried that we would get shot down."

Upon takeoff, the pilot flew the plane almost straight up like a rocket, determined to avoid enemy ground fire. Vitarelli, who had worked at CBS since 1953, had flown all over the world with Cronkite, from India to France to China. In the old days, before the satellite revolution of the sixties, Cronkite and Vitarelli would make crazed efforts to send film shot in Europe or Asia ASAP to CBS headquarters in New York for airing. Through all their peripatetic travels, they had never experienced such a gnarly departure as the one in post-Tet Vietnam. "I said, 'He's gonna stall this thing,'" Vitarelli recalled about the pilot's rocket-like stunt. "Walter kept saying it would be all right. Nothing anxious about his body language at all. His calmness was eerie."

Back in New York, working closely with Salant, Socolow, and Leiser, Cronkite mined his satchel of diaries, photos, notes, press releases, clippings, pro-paganda, and hunches into a "Report from Vietnam" script. Leiser helped Cronkite compose his powerful commentary, to be delivered at the end of the show. What Cronkite planned to say was a closely guarded secret at CBS. "It was Walter's writing," Gralnick explained. "We just helped frame the argument, keep the language harnessed. It was Walter who insisted on using 'stalemate' to describe Vietnam." Leiser, how-ever, told veteran CBS News correspondent Murray Fromson (based in Bangkok in 1968) that he wrote "every word" of Cronkite's "Report from Vietnam." That was also Dan Rather's understanding. What nobody disputes is that Cronkite, as managing editor, approved the blunt language.

Content with the meticulous Leiser-Gralnick draft, angry about the lies of the Johnson administration, and embarrassed that he had believed them from the Gulf of Tonkin to Tet, Cronkite was a man on a mission. He took to the airwaves on February 27, 1968, at 10:00 p.m. EST, to confront the Pentagon's spin machine. In his half-hour "Report from Vietnam," he calmly and objectively presented the hard facts, showing every-thing from U.S. air raids to Vietnamese villages in ruin. Millions of Americans tuned in. In the course of the prime-time show, Cronkite made a powerful case that

President Johnson was misleading the American public about the dire situation in South Vietnam. Victory wasn't even a blip on the horizon.

Most of "Report from Vietnam" was a kind of illustrated briefing. To Cronkite, one major point needed to be conveyed to his viewing audience: from a U.S. military perspective, the Southeast Asian war was unwinnable. "Report from Vietnam" ably conveyed that main point in a very sharp, authoritative fashion.

After the last commercial break, Cronkite turned to speak personally to the viewers, looking straight into the camera from behind his New York desk. According to Diane Sawyer—a longtime CBS correspondent who in 2009 became an anchor for ABC News—Cronkite faced a personal crossroads in Vietnam, just as Murrow did when he went after Joe McCarthy in the mid-1950s on *See It Now*, and he didn't flinch. His closing words became known by millions of Americans and signaled a major shift in the public's view of the war. Those words have been included in the Library of America's handsome *Best Journalism of the Vietnam War*:

> *Tonight, back in more familiar surroundings in New York, we'd like to sum up our findings in Vietnam, an analysis that must be speculative, personal, subjective. Who won and who lost in the*

great Tet offensive against the cities? I'm not sure. The Vietcong did not win by a knockout, but neither did we. The referees of history may make it a draw. Another standoff may be coming in the big battles expected south of the De-militarized Zone. Khe Sanh could well fall, with a terrible loss in American lives, prestige, and morale, and this is a tragedy of our stubbornness there; but the bastion no longer is a key to the rest of the regions, and it is doubtful that the American forces can be defeated across the breadth of the DMZ with any substantial loss of ground. Another standoff. On the political front, past performance gives no confidence that the Vietnamese government can cope with its problems, now compounded by the attack on the cities. It may not fall, it may hold on, but it probably won't show the dynamic qualities demanded of this young nation. Another standoff.

We have been too often disappointed by the optimism of the American leaders, both in Vietnam and in Washington, to have faith any longer in the silver linings they find in the darkest clouds. They may be right, that Hanoi's winter-spring offensive has been forced by the Communist realization that they could not win the longer war of attrition, and that the Communists hope that any success in the offensive will improve their position for eventual negotiations. It would improve their position, and it would also require our realization, that we should have had all along, that any negotiations must be that—negotiations, not the dictations of peace terms. For it seems now more certain than ever that the bloody experience of Vietnam is to end in a stalemate. This summer's almost certain standoff will either end in real give-and-take negotiations or terrible escalation; and for every means we have to escalate, the enemy can match us, and that applies to the invasion of the North, the use of nuclear weapons, or the mere commitment of one hundred, two hundred, or three hundred thousand more American troops to the battle. And with each escalation, the world comes closer to the brink of cosmic disaster.

To say that we are closer to victory today is to believe in the face of the evidence the optimists who have been wrong in the past. To suggest we are on the edge of defeat is to yield to unreasonable pessimism. To say that we are mired in stalemate seems the only realistic, yet unsatisfactory, conclusion. On the off chance that the military and political analysts are right, in the next few months, we must test the enemy's intentions, in case this is *indeed his last big gasp before negotiations. But it is increasingly clear to this reporter that the only rational way out then will be to negotiate, not as victors, but as an honorable people who lived up to their pledge to defend Democracy and did the best they could.*

This is Walter Cronkite. Good night.

Delivered in strong, reasoned tones, Cronkite's nutshell editorial wasn't radical. Calling the Vietnam War a "stalemate" was a middling position. Over the summer, the *New York Times* bureau chief, R. W. Apple, had written a long article bannered "The Making of a Stalemate," which influenced Cronkite mightily. Standing side by side in the "stalemate" camp with Apple, a dear friend, wasn't really radical post-Tet; it was orthodoxy in the press. But in the harshly polarized environment of early 1968, it placed Cronkite in the dove camp. Cronkite had lent his august name to the antiwar movement and thereby put it into the mainstream. Michael J. Arlen had written a brilliant article for *The New Yorker* in 1967 famously calling Vietnam "Television's War." According to Arlen, the public would turn against Johnson's war when the Big Three networks turned against it—Cronkite's moment had now happened. As Cronkite said in a 2002 essay for National Public Radio, "That short editorial helped make an honest skepticism not only respectable, but necessary and patriotic."

The aftershock of Cronkite's reports was seismic. His opinion was quoted in the press, and it opened the door for NBC News' Frank McGee to take a similar stand in a documentary on Vietnam that aired two weeks later. The gossip in the press rooms of America was that Cronkite had offed the president. Even the conservative *Wall Street Journal* editorial page said, "The whole Vietnam effort may be doomed." A wave of relief hit Cronkite for giving voice to his dissent. As a CBS News executive later joked, "When Walter said the Vietnam War was over, it was over." A lot of Johnson administration officials, including Walter Rostow and Dean Rusk, weren't amused. "I was very disgusted with the media, particularly CBS and Walter Cronkite," General Westmoreland complained in an oral history interview. "I think they deceived the American people."

As the CBS special aired that February 27, President Johnson was traveling to speak at the Gregory Gymnasium at the University of Texas at Austin. He took Air Force One to his home state to take part in a birthday party for Governor John B. Connally, a close friend. According to former White House press secretary George Christian, when Johnson heard about

Cronkite's flagrant antiwar commentary, he blurted out, disheartened, "If I've lost Cronkite, I've lost the country."

Just what President Johnson really said about the "Cronkite Moment," as it is known in the history books, has been mired in scholarly controversy. There are a few alternative versions of what LBJ supposedly said, the most prevalent being: (a) "If I've lost Cronkite, I've lost Middle America"; and (b) "If I've lost Cronkite, I've lost the war." It doesn't make any real difference. The important point is that Cronkite had grabbed America's attention about Vietnam in a way that would have been impossible for LBJ to have missed. Former White House press secretary George Christian later gave a fuller rendering to Bill Small of CBS News about how the administration received the February 27 Cronkite special. "Believe me, the shock waves rolled through government," Christian said. "When Walter returned from Vietnam, I think the reports disturbed a lot of people about the conduct of the war; pessimism breeds pessimism. I do think he gave an honest reporter's view. But he is a household name far more than other newsmen; he is the man millions rely on for their summary of the news every day; he is not indentified as an editorialist, but as a reporter of great objectivity."

With his honest commentary about the Vietnam War being honorably lost (or a "stalemate"), Cronkite became more significant than a mere Nielsen ratings winner on the nightly news merry-go-round. He entered the main-game annals of American history. With white streaks in his closely cropped hair and mustache, Cronkite had come to epitomize old-fashioned values in an era of rote lies. America asked for truth about Vietnam, and Cronkite dutifully delivered.

When Barbara W. Tuchman wrote her 1984 opus *The March of Folly: From Troy to Vietnam*, the eminent historian depicted Cronkite as a folk hero because of his "Report from Vietnam." Not only did Tuchman quote Cronkite on what he had encountered in the "burned, blasted and weary land" of South Vietnam, but she also gave credence to the possibly apocryphal LBJ saying, "If I've lost Cronkite, I've lost middle America." Tuchman argued that it was Cronkite's report that caused Senator William Fulbright to have the U.S. Senate reinvestigate the Gulf of Tonkin Resolution, which he now feared was "null and void." Tuchman believed that Cronkite had crashed the house of cards concerning U.S. military inervention in Southeast Asia.

There has been a cottage industry of books about Vietnam since 1968, and in most of them, Cronkite's

TV dissent can be found in the indexes. That single *CBS News Special Report* guaranteed his status as a legend. Dozens of other reporters denounced the Vietnam conflict long before Cronkite, but his turning against the war was above-the-fold stuff. By conventional TV standards, where the anchorman played objective journalism and war down the middle, Cronkite was a revolutionary. While Cronkite's words themselves weren't unique or incendiary, his stance was eye-opening. "Cronkite's step out of character," historian Todd Gitlin noted in *The New Republic*, "was a formidable symbol of broken legitimacy in an age that liked its symbolism straightforward."

New York Times reporter Neil Sheehan, who would write the Pulitzer Prize–winning book *A Bright Shining Lie* about the Vietnam War, was also a media historian and monitored Cronkite's shift from hawk to dove with great interest. "If you watched the *CBS Evening News*, Walter Cronkite sounds like a Pentagon spokesman in 1965 and 1966," Sheehan told Brian Lamb in a C-SPAN *Booknotes* interview. "I hope I'm not making Mr. Cronkite angry by saying this. But he's essentially repeating—in an enthusiastic way—what he's being told. It is only after 1968, after Tet '68—the communist Tet Offensive of '68, which disillusioned the public—that you find an antiwar bias coming into the news media in general. You find figures like Cronkite really questioning the war."

Just how incredibly dangerous Cronkite's fact-finding mission to Vietnam had been became abundantly clear just a week after "Report from Vietnam" aired. CBS News co-producer Russ Bensley (who edited Cronkite's news segments) and cameraman John Smith were seriously wounded at Khe Sanh. Bensley, who started his broadcasting career at WBBM in Chicago, was wounded by mortar fragments and taken to a hospital in Da Nang. That wasn't the end of his horrific ordeal. A Vietcong rocket attack blasted his hospital and he was wounded again. Surgeons were forced to remove his spleen and cut open his colon. This wasn't an isolated case. Since Cronkite's visit, fourteen U.S. correspondents and cameramen had been wounded in Vietnam. Two ABC News reporters—Bill Brannigan and Jim Deckard—had also been seriously wounded in Khe Sanh. CBS News Tokyo bureau chief Igor Oganesoff, who frequently shuttled to Saigon for fill-in duty, wired Leiser that he now refused to take combat assignments. It pained Cronkite to air a segment on the *CBS Evening News* showing Bensley getting wounded in Khe Sanh, but he did. "Nowhere in Vietnam was safe," Bensley recalled. "After Tet, all our guys were getting wounded. I turned antiwar."

Like General Westmoreland, pro–Vietnam War hawks thought "Report from Vietnam" bordered on treason, antiwar exhibitionism marketing itself as CBS triumphalism to get high Nielsen ratings. And a ratings success it proved to be. Because Cronkite was honest about what he saw in South Vietnam, the *CBS Evening News* took on a new edge in its war reporting. Ratings went up. Ironically, this marked the end of TV network news anchormen's never taking policy positions. Opinion sold. Worries about editorializing became a quaint public policy notion no longer religiously adhered to. Cronkite, by speaking the truth, had allowed the dam of objectivity to break. If he regretted any aspect of his Tet special, it was that he had opened the floodgate for the line between commentary and news to be blurred. Beginning in 1968, everybody—movie stars, disc jockeys, musicians, novelists, corporate CEOs—felt compelled to offer his opinion on civil rights, urban poverty, abortion, and, above all, Vietnam. Jack Gould, still the arch media critic of *The New York Times*, complained, "It is only a matter of time before Chet Huntley and David Brinkley will be donning fetching leotards for their nightly *pas de deux* and Clive Barnes [*Times* theater critic] will be reviewing the New Hampshire primary."

In coming years, some historians would claim that Cronkite's analysis of Tet was premature: the 1972 Easter Offensive, for example, proved that the South Vietnamese could thwart a North Vietnamese invasion. There was a feeling that he hadn't given the U.S. troops who had defended Saigon a fair shake. Hadn't the North Vietnamese *lost* the Tet Offensive from a purely military perspective? Wasn't Vietnam a battlefield that had to be fought in order to win the larger cold war against Sino-Soviet hegemony? What no one disputed was that "Report from Vietnam" pitted Cronkite against Johnson's war policies in Southeast Asia.

LBJ never mentioned the nasty riptide of the Cronkite Moment in his presidential memoir, *The Vantage Point*. Nobody in the Johnson family believed that the Cronkite commentary was startling to Johnson (he had been grappling with the post-Tet condition himself for weeks). But as a master politician, Johnson must have known that the Cronkite broadcast, while stating the obvious, was doing him glaring political damage. As Diane Sawyer noted, not since Murrow lifted Senator Joe McCarthy by the skunk tail for public scrutiny in 1954 had one TV broadcast reflected such a fateful climate change in public opinion. Cronkite's editorial was truly an irritant to LBJ. The president's real concern was that Senators Eugene McCarthy and

Robert Kennedy had both signaled their determination to challenge him for the Democratic nomination; passions over the Vietnam War threatened to disrupt national life. Still, there remains a lingering controversy over whether President Johnson ever blurted out the popular "If I've lost Cronkite . . ." line. The root of the confusion stems from an interview scholar David Culbert conducted with Christian, who seemed to hedge on the validity of his famous quotation:

> *Johnson did talk about Cronkite going to Vietnam and in effect turning against the war and it did worry him immensely that Cronkite had in effect become dovish, because he saw the impact was going to be tremendous on the country. Now whether or not Johnson saw that program at X time and that sort of thing, I don't know. He saw newscasts of other things, I'm sure that Johnson is bound to have seen the program. I remember being with Johnson when he saw a commentary from Cronkite. Now whether it was on the morning news. . . . I think it was probably on the CBS Morning News, where it might have been an excerpt out of the program or something. I saw the programs. . . . I either saw them at home or I saw the videotapes. I don't remember. . . . I don't know whether he saw*

them. I'm pretty sure he saw all the [recorded] programs in some manner although I don't remember precisely. I know we talked about the Cronkite program and he was very concerned about Cronkite coming home from Vietnam and portraying the "cause is lost" in effect, the impact it was going to have. Now when it was and where it was, I don't really have a clear recollection.

Almost everyone who worked for CBS News was awed by Cronkite's "Report from Vietnam" in the spring of 1968. It was refreshingly risky, unexpected, and spot-on. All the network's best Vietnam veterans—Morley Safer, John Laurence, Peter Kalischer, Bert Quint, and Robert Schakne among them—were flat-out stunned.* "We were held to such a rigid set of values," recalled Ed Fouhy, then the bureau chief in Los Angeles. "You just couldn't inject opinion into a story. We all knew the war was a stalemate. The surprise was that Cronkite called the game over on prime time." Cronkite himself wondered whether he had done the right thing. Had he betrayed the old United Press

---

* In the coming years at least four other CBS correspondents distinguished themselves with edgy Vietnam reports: Ed Bradley, Bob Simon, Richard Threlkeld, and Bruce Dunning.

honor code of reporting, not editorializing? "I did it because I thought it was the journalistically responsible thing to do at that moment," he reflected in 2002. "It was an egotistical thing for us to do . . . it was egotistical for me to do it and for CBS to permit me to do it."

Jack Shafer of *Slate* offered the best rationale as to why TV news anchors like Cronkite, Chancellor, and Reasoner were so trusted by viewers in the late 1960s and early '70s: they were governed by the FCC's Fairness Doctrine. "The doctrine required broadcast station licensees to address controversial issues of public importance but also to allow contrasting points of view to be included in the discussion," Shafer explained. "One way around the Fairness Doctrine was to tamp down controversy, which all three networks often did." Shafer sees Cronkite's Tet special as a sparkling exception to the Fairness Doctrine protocol.

Because liberal historians consider the Vietnam War to have been a ghastly mistake, Cronkite's dissent has become an epic in the groves of academe. The novelist Tim O'Brien, winner of the 1979 National Book Award for *Going After Cacciato* and a Vietnam War specialist, credited Cronkite with inspiring him to write fiction. Growing up in small-town Minnesota, O'Brien would regularly catch *You Are There* on CBS. "I remember watching one episode on the OK Corral," O'Brien recalled. "Those shows were fact-filled, vetted, mini–short stories. If it wasn't for *You Are There* I might not have become a novelist." Having served as an infantryman in Vietnam from 1969 to 1970, in the division that contained the unit guilty of the My Lai massacre, O'Brien was also grateful that Cronkite spoke out after Tet. By the mid-1990s, Cronkite had become an admirer of O'Brien's novels on Vietnam. One evening, after *In the Lake of the Woods* was published, O'Brien was lecturing at the Horace Mann School in New York and was surprised to see Cronkite sitting in the front row. After the talk, Cronkite went up to O'Brien and said, "I'm stone deaf, didn't hear a word you said. Can I take you out for dinner?"

O'Brien was flattered. Over their meal at an Upper West Side diner, Cronkite asked him a direct question: "Did I do the right thing in February '68?" O'Brien was astounded. Cronkite wasn't looking for validation per se, but he wanted to talk about whether his '68 post-Tet broadcast demoralized U.S. troops in Vietnam. A Tet revisionism claimed that CBS News manipulated the American public into erroneously believing the Vietcong's Tet Offensive had worked. Cronkite wanted O'Brien, a fighting soldier, to tell him the truth. "He asked me whether I had felt betrayed by him," O'Brien recalled. "He wanted to talk about his decision with a combat veteran like myself. I told him he had been right to recognize the impossibility of our position in Vietnam. We could have invested the entire GNP into Vietnam or built a Metrodome around Saigon and it wouldn't have made a difference. Cronkite had the reportorial wisdom to recognize that central reality. Ninety percent of the soldiers blamed the media for losing the war, but I didn't."

Reflecting on Cronkite's post-Tet dissent, Newsweek, echoing O'Brien, noted that it was as if Lincoln himself had ambled down from his white marble memorial seat and joined an anti–Vietnam War rally. Cronkite's "Report from Vietnam" only grew in stature as the decades progressed and increasingly began to be taught as the turning point at which the U.S. government lost the confidence of the American people. "It was the first time in American history," Halberstam wrote, "that a war had been declared over by a commentator." The war, however, wasn't over. It still had years of anguish, death, and tragedy in store.

PART V

Top Game

23.

Calm and Chaos of 1968

ASKING RFK TO RUN—SENATOR CRONKITE?—
PEACENIK PRESS—LBJ BAILS OUT—THE ASSASSINA-
TION OF MARTIN LUTHER KING JR.—WHERE ARE MY
CHILDREN?—RFK IS KILLED—GOOFING AT BUCK-
INGHAM PALACE—CRAZINESS IN CHICAGO—A BUNCH
OF THUGS—ANARCHY IN THE AIR—DALEY GETS A
CRONKITE HUG—NO INSTINCT FOR THE JUGULAR—
GROOVING WITH ABBIE HOFFMAN—HEALING WITH
THE MOON

Just days after Cronkite's "Report from Vietnam" aired, the CBS anchorman met privately with Robert Kennedy, the increasingly popular Democratic senator from New York. On March 12 Eugene McCarthy, a super dove, had scored a near-upset of Johnson in New Hampshire's Democratic primary. To McCarthy's die-hard supporters, this proved that the irascible Minnesota senator was a viable candidate. Political veterans, though, doubted McCarthy had the donors necessary to topple the Johnson reelection machine. Most of the speculation instead fixed on Kennedy. Frank Mankiewicz, RFK's press aide, described Cronkite's off-the-record meeting at Kennedy's Capitol Hill office in great detail decades later in both *The Washington Post* and on C-SPAN. According to Mankiewicz, Cronkite led the conversation at the Senate office. "You must announce your intention to run against Johnson," he urged Kennedy, "to show people there will be a way out of this terrible war." A wide-eyed RFK listened intently, asking Cronkite for his opinion of the situation in Saigon, Hué, and Khe Sanh."

Evoking lessons learned from his UP days in the Second World War, Cronkite told Kennedy the war couldn't be won, that a huge segment of the South Vietnamese population secretly supported the Vietcong. The American people, he believed, weren't being properly informed about their nation's expensive cold war commitment to South Vietnam. Kennedy asked whether Cronkite was a registered Democrat; the newsman replied he was an independent. "RFK," recalled

Mankiewicz, "listened thoughtfully and then, with the beginnings of a smile, said, 'Walter, I'll run for president if you'll agree to run for Senate from New York.'"

Kennedy thought a Cronkite candidacy was a sure-fire winner; the anchorman was the most beloved man in New York City (maybe in all of America). Kennedy's suggestion was playfully earnest, but the flattered Cronkite wasn't seriously interested in a Senate run. Cronkite forfeited electoral politics to protect the integrity of American journalism. He feared that if he threw his hat into the ring, all prominent newsmen would thenceforth fall under suspicion of making news judgments based on their own self-promotional, future political ambitions. RFK persisted in pressing Cronkite to try for his New York Senate seat if he himself challenged LBJ that spring for the Democratic nomination, but no amount of lobbying was going to persuade Cronkite to run for the Senate. His answer to RFK was no, with no wiggle room. An unrelenting Kennedy continued to consider a presidential run, conferring day-by-day with a cadre of stalwart advisors and family friends (including Ted Sorensen, Richard Goodwin, Pierre Salinger, and Kenneth O'Donnell). All had been loyal New Frontiersmen in the days of JFK's presidency. Brother Ted Kennedy and brother-in-law Stephen Smith were also members of the inner circle.

Hopes were high at the *CBS Evening News* on March 13 that Cronkite was about to earn the biggest scoop of his broadcast journalism career: getting RFK to announce his intention to run for president. The exclusive interview ended up being surprisingly flat. Cronkite led with a question to Kennedy on a potential run for the White House. Kennedy wasn't biting. But he did leave the door wide open—a minor scoop. At one point, he commented on Nelson Rockefeller's chances against GOP front-runner Richard Nixon. "I gather that Rockefeller will come into the primary in Oregon," he said, and added that by that time, it probably would be too late to stop Nixon. Sensing he might have a scoop, Cronkite went off script, trying to find an ulterior motive. "Senator," he said, " I might trap you in a little word game there. You said 'come into the Oregon primary' not 'go' into it. Are you already in Oregon?" An amused Kennedy, charmed by Cronkite's coyness, quashed the implication. But Cronkite was dutifully emphasizing for the audience what political experts already knew: RFK was indeed going to seek the White House. It now boiled down to a matter of timing.

A transcript of the RFK-Cronkite interview was reprinted in *The New York Times* the next day. The paper also printed a full transcript of Cronkite's subsequent *CBS Evening News* interview with Eugene McCarthy. In the news industry, the flow was typically from *The New York Times* to the broadcast networks. The scoops and the ideas were so easily picked from the pages of the *Times*, in fact, that its influence was a primary reason the network news broadcasts often ran the same stories in the same order. Their respective producers weren't in collusion; they just read the same Big City daily. In the Vietnam War era, network news shows took greater initiative, and Cronkite actively steered CBS into the lead for breaking news. His nightly broadcast at 6:30 p.m. EST was itself news in the making.

On March 16, RFK formally announced he was running for president. Instead of declaring it on the *CBS Evening News*, he did so in the Caucus Room of the Old Senate Office Building: the same place where his brother had announced his candidacy years before. All hell broke loose in the Democratic primary field. In the White House, the specter of Cronkite and his CBS Tet special seemed to have tamped out the fighting spirit of LBJ.

Less than two weeks later, on Sunday, March 31, President Johnson scheduled a televised message about limiting U.S. involvement in Vietnam by declaring a partial halt to bombing missions. Few thought the speech was going to be historic. The Oval Office was set up with cameras for the speech. As Johnson entered, he muttered to a CBS technician he recognized, "Cronkite isn't going to like this . . ." Millions of viewers tuned in, thinking LBJ was only going to give a report on Vietnam. As the telecast began, LBJ stared at the television camera, looked uneasily at the lens for a second or so, and then spoke with his Hill Country twang. As expected, the president began talking about the Vietnam War. But then, quite unexpectedly, he announced, "I shall not seek, and I will not accept the nomination of my party for another term as your president."

It was a shocking announcement. Cronkite, thinking the address would be nothing special, was not at the CBS broadcast center that night. Always wanting to be the voice of "breaking news" and ahead of the pack, he was embarrassed at being caught off-guard. Having been so focused on RFK that March, he hadn't worked his White House sources properly. A question that immediately made the press rounds was whether "Report from Vietnam" had contributed to Johnson's surprise decision to sideline himself. Johnson later insisted in a CBS News interview with Cronkite that he could have won a second full term in 1968, but that March he was a tired man, facing medical problems and a crisis of confidence across the country. Extricating the United States from the Vietnam quagmire would be a formidable job. His energies were needed at the White House, not for gallivanting around at Democratic fundraisers. So, with the encouragement of his devoted wife, Lady Bird, the president abruptly bowed out of the 1968 presidential contest.

"We had not expected," Cronkite wrote Bob Manning of *The Atlantic Monthly*, "that the president himself would react like he did. No one has claimed, and I certainly don't believe, that our broadcast changed his mind about anything. I do believe it may have been the back-breaking piece of straw that was heaped on the heavy load he was already carrying—doubts about the reports he had been getting on alleged military success in Vietnam, concern that the military was now asking for another considerable increase in troop strength to finish the job, increasing public outcry as the nation headed into a presidential election. I think that we may have given him the last push over the edge of a decision he was on the verge of making anyway."

CBS News was as unprepared as the other networks for the Johnson bombshell. No one could have predicted he wouldn't seek reelection. Roger Mudd, covering the Oval Office speech from Washington, later wrote that the announcement "left me shocked, disbelieving and babbling." Cronkite, relaxing with Betsy at home, had missed reporting the year's biggest nonviolent political headline. But his "Report from Vietnam" was immediately seen as a catalyst by pundits in the Monday newspapers. They divined a cause-and-effect scenario between CBS and the White House: Cronkite turned dove, and the hawk Johnson lost his talons. "I think that Johnson felt like most of the American people said at that point: 'Let's just get out of this,'" Cronkite recalled. "But the president couldn't get out himself. He was too deeply committed. So the thing to do was get out of the job."

The public response to LBJ's shocker was welcomed by supporters and opponents alike. The president's popularity as measured in polls rose dramatically. Eugene McCarthy believed it was his own incredible showing in the New Hampshire primary on March 12—losing by only 230 votes—that caused Johnson to throw in the towel. Some analysts believed that after Tet, regardless of Cronkite, the president reached his own conclusion that the war wasn't worth the United States spending $30 billion annually. Another factor was the *New York Times* story about LBJ wanting to increase the number of troops by 206,000. Most Democrats believed that was an awful idea. Somewhat surprisingly, Cronkite was saddened by Johnson's unexpected withdrawal—to a degree. When not anchoring the *CBS Evening News*, he had praised on CBS Radio Johnson's Great Society domestic policies, including Medicaid-Medicare, wilderness preservation, civil rights, and a hopper full of antipoverty measures. Cronkite actually thought LBJ was a good president; it was only on the Vietnam War that the record soured. "Daddy and Walter stayed close," Lynda Johnson Robb, daughter of the president, maintained. "There were strains. They never let the war get between them."

Many CBS viewers wrote to Paley demanding that Cronkite be fired in the wake of "Report from Vietnam," which supposedly led to Johnson's decision not to run for reelection. But the New Left now heralded Cronkite and Eugene McCarthy as the Establishment peace heroes. While not quite a guru to New Left intellectuals such as Herbert Marcuse or Frantz Fanon, Cronkite was cheered as an honest journalist with a deep sense of public morality. But, at least in 1968, he declined to take victory laps. He was quite stunned at how ferocious the antiwar protests became all over the world and recognized that CBS News was in part responsible. Many of the public protests were being held to attract TV cameras. It was a main lesson of Martin Luther King Jr.'s nonviolent movement: protests equal cameras equal Cronkite's *Evening News* broadcast. Like all the networks, CBS thought street demonstrations were excellent television. The lesson Cronkite learned anew from the connection between "Report from Vietnam" and LBJ's resignation was that TV didn't just report events in the 1960s; it also helped shape them.

Decades later, Lady Bird Johnson made gracious efforts to reassure Cronkite that her husband always understood that his Tet dissent on CBS News had been an inherently patriotic act. By February 1968 her husband knew in his heart of hearts that Vietnam had been a godawful mistake. Instead of bemoaning Cronkite's stalemate analysis, LBJ understood that he had lost the political center. Cronkite's views were already in sync with what polls were showing: that the country was losing faith in the pro-war rhetoric of Westmoreland and McNamara. LBJ wasn't angry at Cronkite. He feared that the "middle-of-the-road folks," who had bought into the Gulf of Tonkin Resolution in 1964, were having buyer's remorse about Vietnam.

Whenever Cronkite went to Austin in the coming decade, he'd socialize with Lady Bird and her personal assistant, Liz Carpenter. "You have been a great force for good in this country," Lady Bird wrote to Cronkite. "We love you so much. A stalwart with whom we've shared moments that touched depths of despair and the farthest reaches of space. We've mourned with you some of America's saddest days and soared as we celebrated some of mankind's highest aspirations and achievements. You've been an advocate for what is best in the United States, and we are better for it."

While CBS News did receive hate mail for Cronkite's perceived role in causing LBJ not to seek a second term, it wasn't much. Whenever Cronkite was in New York, people thanked him for his candor. The pro-war GOP hawks likewise thought LBJ needed to go. Folklore, however, snowballed into the questionable assumption that it was his "Report from Vietnam" that had caused LBJ not to seek reelection; it was impossible to put the brakes on the myth. "Walter went out of his way to avoid the cause-and-effect syndrome," Sandy Socolow recalled. "A lot of people were trying to connect Walter's Tet offensive report to Johnson's abrupt resignation. Walter completely shied away from that kind of specious claim. There were over six weeks between the events. To his mind, they shouldn't be linked in history."

Press secretary George Christian also rejected the Cronkite-is-the-reason theory years later in an oral history. "Well, I don't buy it," he said about the broadcast's influencing Johnson's decision. "It didn't quite happen that way." Marvin Kalb of CBS News explained the impact of Cronkite on LBJ best: "What Walter was saying about Vietnam wasn't all that dramatic," Kalb believed. "He just moved the story an inch or two forward. Cronkite was scrupulous in being objective, of keeping himself out of the news. In many ways, all he had done was report the obvious. But LBJ, it's fair to say, was enormously impressed by anything Cronkite said on CBS. He had a huge, huge audience. So Walter made a difference."

Over time, Cronkite was of two minds about being branded the cause of LBJ's decision to step down. On the one hand, it made him beloved by liberals. Yet it called his Mr. Objectivity persona into question. Depending on whom he was talking with, Cronkite would flip-flop on the question over whether he was in any way responsible for LBJ's surprise March announcement. His most succinct answer occurred in a Q&A with Richard Snow of *American Heritage*. "I don't feel that a journalist's influence is so great that you can change the course of human events by a single broadcast," he said. "Whether it's a president's decision to act or not act, it doesn't work that way. It's just one more straw."

What no one debated was that the spring of 1968 was a time of great upheaval. On April 4, just days after LBJ announced he wouldn't seek reelection, the Reverend Martin Luther King Jr. was assassinated in

Memphis, on the balcony of the Lorraine Motel. He was preparing to lead a peace march to quell the racial violence that had broken out in the Mississippi River city because of a sanitation workers' strike. Cronkite, broadcasting from CBS's Washington, D.C., studio, provided the bare details of the Memphis shooting at the end of the 6:30 p.m. news. During the commercials that followed, Dan Rather broke the news of Dr. King's death in a special report from New York City. Moments later, Cronkite broadcast the news of the assassination on the 7:00 p.m. feed of the *CBS Evening News*. In a verbal tone that was, if anything, far more forceful than usual, Cronkite, visibly upset and angry, called Dr. King "the apostle of the civil rights movement."

When Cronkite got off the air, he sobbed in shame. Cursing, his head a mess, he predicted riots across America to his colleagues at the CBS News bureau. "I'd hate to be up on U Street tonight [in Washington, D.C.]," he muttered to coworkers as he wandered out of the M Street studio in a trance. Once at the Hay-Adams Hotel, where he was staying, he called his three children to discuss the King murder: eleven-year-old Chip, a student at St. Bernard's School in New York; eighteen-year-old Kathy, at school in Vermont because the ski trails were awesome; and twenty-year-old

Nancy, a student at Syracuse University. Somehow he needed reassurance that the family was whole.

The year 1968 was turning out to be a brutal, appalling, harrowing one. Ever since the Montgomery bus boycott of 1955, CBS had prided itself on its King coverage. The thought that King had been murdered caused all the CBS reporters who covered civil rights— Cronkite included—to fear for the nation. Cronkite wanted to attend King's funeral in Atlanta, but the grueling Democratic primary schedule in March prohibited him from doing so. Joan F. Richman, who oversaw special events for CBS News, dispatched the reliable Charles Kuralt instead.

Less than two months later, on the night of June 4, Cronkite was in New York City anchoring CBS's one-hour prime-time special coverage of the California Democratic primary. Preliminary results showed Kennedy on his way to a crucial victory over Eugene McCarthy. CBS News had two correspondents, Roger Mudd and Terry Drinkwater, working the floor at the ballroom of the Ambassador Hotel in Los Angeles, where Kennedy supporters had gathered to await the results. Presuming the coverage would trail off after Kennedy's victory speech and comments by Mudd and Drinkwater, Cronkite went home for the night. It was just after nine o'clock in Los Angeles when Kennedy made his victory speech, one dotted with humor and filled with hope that the nation would be less sharply divided in the future. CBS cameras were rolling as Kennedy made his way out of the rollicking ballroom. The cameras focused on the confetti-filled atmosphere of the primary triumph because Cronkite wasn't around to provide his usual commentary.

Just as RFK's followers began to chant, "Kennedy, Kennedy, rah, rah, rah," screams broke out from a corner of the room, with terrible anguish replacing the victory smiles. Mudd's voice could be heard asking bystanders what had happened and telling the control room to "keep me plugged in." Mudd, a personal friend of Bobby and Ethel Kennedy's, dashed into the chaotic passageway leading to a hotel kitchen, where shots had just been fired. RFK had been shot with a .22-caliber revolver by Sirhan Sirhan, a Christian Arab from Jerusalem angry about the senator's pro-Israel stance.

Cronkite recalled on his *Cronkite Remembers* video memoir, released in 1996, how he himself heard the news about Bobby Kennedy. "I'd left our New York newsroom right after reporting that primary and the Kennedy speech," he said. "I'd gotten home barely twenty minutes later and I was just undressing when the telephone call came. Another Kennedy had been shot. Well, I ran for a cab, buttoning my shirt on the way. The driver had his radio on. We were both just listening, speechless, I guess. Listening to the turmoil in that hotel kitchen, we cried. That cabdriver and I cried. We cried. And we weren't ashamed."

Americans of all stripes were stricken by the Los Angeles shooting, the second assassination in two months, the second Kennedy brother murdered in four years. The death of Robert Kennedy in many ways shattered the American psyche. Americans wondered about the moral character of their beleaguered nation, and whether worthy candidates would come to the fore in the future if the specter of assassination hung over all American leadership. Cronkite provided brief comments during CBS News' fifteen-hour coverage of Kennedy's funeral, concluding, "Robert Kennedy was shot at 12:15 am Pacific Coast Time, the end of a brilliant political and public career. . . . At the age of 42, Robert Francis Kennedy was dead. . . . The people weep for the Kennedys. Perhaps they should weep, too, for themselves. . . . This is Walter Cronkite, reporting."

Not since the Civil War had a six-month span been so full of deadly tragedy at home as the first half of 1968. Cronkite, while continuing as the bearer of disturbing news, was again filling his other role as a steadying presence in frightening times. He was a national leader of a new sort: the healer in chief. He hadn't sought the post. He had no real agenda. Even those who disliked his liberal leanings accepted his irreplaceable presence at the center of American events in 1968. According to an informal poll, politicians of all stripes considered him the fairest of the national newsmen. Everyone of consequence, it seemed, thought Cronkite gave people an honest shake in interviews. He was also reassuringly permanent when so much was in flux. Even when he was announcing tragic news, he was himself a reminder that America would persevere. Jack Gould of *The New York Times*, who had pointedly refrained from praising Cronkite over the previous decade, found something to appreciate during 1968 in the anchorman's ability to communicate the nuances of complex circumstances. Gould called him "the master of subtle variations in intonation of speech and facial expression."

That Fourth of July, in need of a break, Walter and Betsy flew to London for a week to be with friends ahead of the conventions. To start his July Fourth celebration, Cronkite took Morley Safer out for a bout of heavy afternoon drinking. Safer had been in London when Cronkite delivered his "Report from Vietnam" and was elated that the CBS anchorman had turned dove. Earlier that evening, Safer had met Jane Fearer, a graduate student in anthropology at Oxford, and they went on a double date with Walter and Betsy that evening. After dinner and a lot of wine and laughs, they decided to go for a nightcap. "It was after midnight. . . . I had an old Bentley convertible with a rumble seat," Safer recalled. "The four of us piled in, Walter and Betsy in the rumble seat. As we made our way to a favorite pub, Walter suggested we go past The Mall to Buckingham Palace. As we arrived, Walter stood up and did a remarkably convincing impersonation of Queen Elizabeth II, complete with that loose-wristed wave she reserved for adoring throngs. He insisted I make a half-dozen circuits of the palace, clearly trying to get the guardsmen in their red coats and busbies, to crack a smile, or even shift an eyeball, all to no avail. They could have been made of stone. That was my first date with Jane. We got married in October '68."

After Cronkite's return to New York, he met with Salant to reconsider how CBS News would cover antiwar marches and riots that summer. After the JFK and MLK assassinations, they didn't want to encourage kooks to seize Oswald, Ray, or Sirhan Sirhan–style notoriety. The national conventions were a particular concern. To impress upon the news division the need to refrain from using sensational images of protesters, Stanton issued a three-page guide that July, saying that "the best coverage is not necessarily the one with the best pictures and the most dramatic action." To Cronkite and others, Salant and Stanton were imbued with "near paranoia" about possible unrest at the Republican convention in Miami and the Democratic one in Chicago. Major corporate sponsors of CBS were urging the network not to turn a ragtag band of street protesters into TV heroes.

CBS management didn't tell Cronkite how to behave at the 1968 conventions. All they told him was that a lot of money was at stake. Covering the entire 1968 election cost CBS $12.3 million. Black Rock didn't want sponsors to pull advertising because CBS cameras were giving antiwar protesters extensive TV exposure. Salant never put profit ahead of integrity, but he also couldn't afford to lose sponsors over Yippies, Black Panthers, and malcontents. "Avoid using lights when shooting pictures," Salant said in an August 20 meeting, "since lights only attract crowds."

NBC and CBS might have been virtually tied for viewership in the main event, evening news, but every four years the presidential race offered an arena for even keener competition. The summer political conventions of 1968 presented each network with a fine opportunity to lure new fans and whip its rivals. Conventions could be what Cronkite once described as "great, brawling sweatshops of American political history" (that is, great TV drama). But everything about 1968 had Paley, Stanton, Salant, and Cronkite wondering if their own journalistic instincts were starting to crack. "We anticipated trouble," Cronkite recalled. "Before we ever got to Chicago, the Grant Park encampment was taking place near Lake Michigan and the Hilton Hotel, which was the Democratic headquarters. That's where the Weathermen and SDS and hippie anti–Vietnam War people camped out."

Former vice president Richard Nixon, the presumptive GOP nominee, had used primaries and caucuses to win a commanding block of delegates, making the Republican Convention predictable from the outset. "I don't know whether the convention is arranged for TV or whether TV is arranged for the convention," Mudd pondered, decrying the public relations atmosphere. *The Washington Post* reviewed the coverage of the Republican convention under the blunt headline "Boring Convention Ignored by Viewers." NBC didn't do any better. Ultimately, American viewers preferred real drama (or comedy), with the result that only one-third of the nation's televisions were tuned into the convention coverage during prime time.

As the Democratic Convention began in Chicago on August 26, the protesters ran headlong into nightstick-wielding security forces assembled by Mayor Richard Daley, who intended to show that his city was under his tight control. The security forces he assembled, however, acted like goons, proving more disruptive than the demonstrators. In what an investigative report later termed "a police riot" and what contender Hubert Humphrey called "storm-trooper tactics," Daley's cops used violence in the streets and in the convention hall itself. Moreover, citywide strikes by telephone workers and taxi drivers hindered the free flow of communication and transportation. As the acrid smell of tear gas filled the air, television trucks weren't allowed to park near the convention hall and reporters were chased by police from the area. In an on-air commentary, Eric Sevareid compared the deteriorating situation in Chicago to the Soviet Union's violent suppression of Czechoslovakia's Prague Spring reform movement for political liberalization. The main difference, he said, was that in Prague, at least there were "tanks in which to travel from A to B."

CBS News correspondent Jack Laurence teamed up with producer Stanhope Gould to cover the fighting in Grant Park on the first night of the convention. It was radical and bloody beyond belief. They were under extraordinary deadline and technical pressure to get footage of the mayhem in time for Cronkite's broadcast.

Russ Bensley was the only one to check the reporting before it went on the air. "All the executive producers were busy at the convention hall," Laurence recalled. To put it mildly, Laurence's five- or six-minute segment did not make the Chicago Police Department look good. "No one from the news division or corporate headquarters criticized me to my face about the story, but they took me off the air for at least the next twenty-four hours. I just could not get a camera crew or producer to work with me, although there were stories to be covered everywhere you looked."

The battle that raged on Michigan Avenue in Chicago and on hundreds of college campuses around the country also echoed in the Cronkite home. The conversations throughout 1968 often turned ugly. The Cronkites' two daughters, Kathy and Nancy, were teenagers more in tune with the counterculture than with their parents. "We both went through a period of time," Kathy wrote in her book *On the Edge of the Spotlight*, "when we didn't get along with the parents." Chip, the youngest, was still a boy, old enough to play a good game of tennis with his father but too young to rebel. Both Kathy and Nancy chafed under parental rules intended to keep them on a straight and respectable path.

Strangers sometimes asked the Cronkite children whether their father was as genuinely nice in real life as he seemed on television. Kathy sometimes gave an unvarnished answer, feeling emotionally barricaded by being the child of somebody so highly visible; she could be livid with him for putting his work ahead of their family. "I was awful when I was growing up," Kathy admitted. "I'd go on and on about how I hated his guts and how he made me stay home and gave me a curfew. I'd just give them the whole rap about what a drag I thought he was. . . . People thought I was fucked up, I'm afraid."

The generational tension in his household distressed Cronkite until he realized that many families were divided along the same lines: the Greatest Generation versus the Baby Boomers. At least he was now in agreement with the counterculture on the Vietnam War: the troops needed to come home. What Cronkite objected to most was that the State Department, the CIA, and the Pentagon acted as though the Vietnam War was too complicated to explain properly to the general public—a stance that was not acceptable when young men were at Walter Reed General and Bethesda Naval hospitals without arms or legs or genitals or faces. Nonetheless, Cronkite didn't have much use for either the SDSers or the Yippies (Youth International Party)—despite Kathy and Nancy being, in appearance and outlook, very much sixties hippies. "I didn't like their attitude," he said of the hippies. "I didn't like their dress code. I didn't much like any of it."

Cronkite was what the young generation called *square*. He was part of the *establishment*, a dirty word in the hippie universe. He was fifty-two and rich (two more reasons for suspicion)—a yachtsman, no less, who enjoyed summer sailing with the conservative William F. Buckley in the Atlantic. (Historian Garry Wills noted in *Outside Looking In* that Buckley "admired Cronkite's mind," actively seeking his counsel from time to time.) The generation gap wasn't just a news story that Cronkite reported on; his family was its living embodiment. Yet his reaction to the protesters in Chicago, like his "Report from Vietnam," showed just how fairness-driven the anchorman could be. As Chicago police savaged demonstrators, Cronkite was in a CBS broadcast booth at the International Amphitheatre, a good five miles away. When he first heard about the rioting, his information was incomplete, and he blamed the peace activists. "The antiwar demonstrators," Cronkite reported, "have gotten particularly unruly and are even battling in the lobbies of the hotels with police, who sent for reinforcements." Yet while the Yippies in Chicago, led by Abbie Hoffman and Jerry Rubin, were undoubtedly there to cause a ruckus, the police response was downright criminal. Assault and battery became commonplace police procedures.

As Cronkite gazed down on the convention floor from his CBS anchor booth, he saw scuffling and fist-fights as unidentified security men and uniformed police next turned on the delegates. The intimidation infuriated Cronkite. Credentialed Democrats who dared demonstrate against the war were removed from the hall—an action entirely against convention rules. Cronkite, as usual, refused to wear an IFB (inter-rupted feedback ear device), so he relied on producers Jeff Gralnick, Stanhope Gould, and Ron Bonn to keep handing him updates on the air.

On the convention floor, Mike Wallace was roughed up and hit in the face. Dan Rather took a hard blow to the stomach from security guards trying to keep him from interviewing a Georgia delegate who was himself being ejected. Both Wallace and Rather were trying to gather information on the removal of indi-vidual delegates. Cronkite saw the unprovoked attack on Rather, sucker-punched to the floor, as a national disgrace. "I think we've got a bunch of thugs here," Cronkite told viewers with unmasked anger. Filled with fury, he suggested that the roughed-up report-ers and cameramen leave the floor. More gently, he advised Rather to go and get medical help if he needed it. (Rather, having risen from the floor, said he'd be all right.)

Cronkite, like all the CBS leadership, considered the brutalizing of Rather inexcusable. Writing about the Rather incident in *Air Time: The Inside Story of CBS News*, Gary Paul Gates posited that it was the "only time in his long career that Cronkite displayed such undisguised wrath on the air." Democratic Party leaders issued all sorts of apologies, but the film footage lived on. In one fell punch, Rather had become an icon of freedom of the press. Joining CBS in First Amendment complaints were top executives of *Time*, *Newsweek*, and five newspapers. "An investigation by the FBI is under way to ascertain whether this treatment of news personnel involved violation of federal law," a joint protest letter to Mayor Daley read. Many conservative Democrats applauded Daley for organizing the security detail that manhandled Rather. The Chicago congressman Roman Pucinski, from the Polish-American Eleventh District, called CBS's coddling of protesters "outrageous and unfair, the zenith of irresponsibility in American journalism." Joining the anti-CBS chorus was Congressman Ed Edmondson of Oklahoma's Second District. "Network media personnel such as Cronkite," he said, "have done violence to the truth by their unfair coverage at Chicago, and the public deserves better at the hands of this great industry."

Eventually, the Daley machine's worst nightmare became a reality as CBS motorcycle couriers managed to evade police and deliver film of the battle outside the convention hall. "We put it on the air," Cronkite proudly recalled. "Delegates watched, first in disbelief, then in rage." The images shocked Cronkite, too, and his commentary from that point on no longer blamed the Yippies for the Chicago unrest. Anger was exploding in all directions. CBS's coverage alternated between convention business—Hubert Humphrey's grand moment on the national stage—and strong-arm tactics on both the convention floor and on the streets of downtown Chicago. This was Daley's grotesque street show. As CBS broadcast the film across the country, the Democratic Party itself sustained a body blow. Because Humphrey didn't respond strongly to the clashes all around him, the violence consumed his campaign from its start. He looked like a liberal weakling afraid to confront Mayor Daley. If he couldn't control a Democratic mayor run amok, how could he possibly face up to bullies like Ho Chi Minh and Mao?

A hubristic Mayor Daley was outraged at CBS's portrayal of Chicago as a fascist city. In a speech at the convention, Senator Abraham Ribicoff of Connecticut called Daley out by name and condemned the "Gestapo tactics" of the Chicago police. Daley loyalists stepped up to defend the mayor. Frank Sullivan, director of public information for the Chicago Police Department, held his own news conference after the convention ended. "The intellectuals of America," he declared, "hate Richard J. Daley, because he was elected by the people—unlike Walter Cronkite." Sullivan claimed Cronkite and CBS were among the mayor's enemies in the media.

That August 29, just hours later, Daley gave Cronkite an exclusive interview for CBS. Every journalist wanted a chance to drill him down to a damaged bit. But because Eleanor Daley, the mayor's wife, loved the *CBS Evening News*, Cronkite won the exclusive. Cronkite was certain he could outfox the mayor by asking him simple questions and giving him plenty of room to hang himself with his own words. But with millions watching, Cronkite botched the interview by being overingratiating. "I can tell you this, Mr. Daley," Cronkite said, "that you have a lot of supporters around the country as well in Chicago." Daley claimed he possessed secret reports that named him and three other leading Democrats on an assassination hit list. The strong measures taken by the police, he told Cronkite, had been necessary. "You could tell that Cronkite had decided to be very courteous to Daley," recalled newsman Brit Hume, who had worked for UPI. "It wasn't in him to climb all over Daley. He seemed embarrassed for having used the word *thugs* on air."

Cronkite's exclusive interview with Daley was beyond lame. It constituted the low-water mark of his journalism career. Everyone at CBS News knew that Cronkite thought Daley was behaving like a mobster that week. Full of civic pride, disdainful of supposedly unpatriotic, filthy hippies filling Chicago's parks and streets, Daley had turned bully.

In Adam Cohen's and Elizabeth Taylor's biography of Daley, *American Pharaoh*, the authors criticize how Cronkite allowed the Chicago mayor to spin one untruth after another in the interview without properly challenging the assertions. Cronkite seemed intimidated by the mayor's bluster and raw power. Daley had entered the CBS anchor booth as the bane of American TV viewers and almost miraculously emerged as a public service champion. On air, Daley claimed that certain reporters had been beaten by his Chicago police force because they were, in essence, plants for the antiwar movement. Cronkite merely nodded, seemingly in acquiescence. One CBS News executive, embarrassed by Cronkite's kowtowing to Daley, said sadly when the interview was finished, "Daley took Cronkite like Grant took Richmond."

Once retired from CBS, Cronkite made a lot of fanciful excuses for having allowed Daley to dominate him in the big interview. (The gist was that the mayor had startled him by walking straight onto his set without knocking.) Producer Stanhope Gould was there at the time and felt contempt for Cronkite for the one and only time in his life. "He just didn't know how to interview Daley," Gould complained. "Just let him off the hook."

What Cronkite was trying to do in the interview was heal the rift between Daley and CBS by being conciliatory; it was the worst tactical approach imaginable. The tension between television news and politicians of both parties was probably inevitable. Mayor Daley had provided a particularly vivid example of the shift in dominance between the two. Film drove the transition. It made every TV viewer a potential witness to police brutality. Newsreels had existed before, but they weren't distributed into millions of homes in real time, and they lacked the authority that came with a journalistic enterprise such as CBS. If a police superintendent in pretelevision days had stated, "The force used was the force needed to repel the mob," as Chicago police superintendent James B. Conlisk Jr. did say after the Chicago unrest, citizens would never have known the truth. Some would have believed the reporters on the scene. But many more would have believed the superintendent. In 1968, by contrast, as CBS News president Richard Salant would write, "The pictures and sound of the Chicago police department in action speak for themselves."

Film had the power to expose politicians and police betraying public trust. Martin Luther King Jr. had learned this early on, in his nonviolent effort to reach the nation, when motion pictures of Bull Connor's men billy-clubbing well-behaved, churchgoing protesters in Birmingham, Alabama, came to light. President Johnson learned it, too, when film of children screaming in terror after U.S. bombing raids undermined both the troops and the very rationale for U.S. intervention in Vietnam. The power of truth itself belonged to cameramen as they chose their shots; it belonged to network news producers; and at CBS, it belonged to Cronkite in his role as managing editor. Viewers believed Cronkite in the 1960s for reasons of character but also because he had the truth-telling cameras on his side. In the Daley interview, it was Cronkite who came out as cowardly. When told that Gary Paul Gates in *Air Time* used the Daley bungle as Exhibit A of Cronkite's inability to go after the jugular like Mike Wallace, Cronkite cried foul. "I think he missed the point by a wide margin," he snarled. "My interview technique is not to have blood spurt from the open vein, but to have it drain slowly from the body until you see the white corpse sitting there."

The Justice Department would soon go after the "Chicago Eight," a tangentially connected cabal of antiwar activists charged with conspiring to cross state lines to incite violence at the Democratic National Convention: David Dellinger, Rennie Davis, Tom Hayden, Abbie Hoffman, Jerry Rubin, Lee Weiner, John Froines, and Bobby Seale. Yippie leader Hoffman and Cronkite actually became minor friends of a sort. Daring and a convivial genius at street theater, Hoffman made for good television. Not long after the Chicago convention, Hoffman, full of mischief, wrote Cronkite an unsolicited letter suggesting that he abandon horn-rimmed glasses in favor of contact lenses. Hoffman thought the glasses made Cronkite seem Goldwater-square when he really wasn't. Cronkite accepted Hoffman's suggestion. "I took your advice, you know," Cronkite told him over the phone. The odd couple liked each other. (Or was Cronkite only flattering a valuable new source?) Whatever the reason, the charismatic Hoffman was an exception for Cronkite. In-your-face protests, Yippies, and LSD-high hippies generally left him cold.

Cronkite looked back on the decade of his ascendancy at CBS and called it "the terrible sixties." The era was marked by more internecine anger than any other in the twentieth century. Daggers flashed everywhere. Tear gas and urban riots had become fairly commonplace. Assassinations were the recurring theme between 1963 and 1968—the Kennedys, King, Medgar Evers, Malcolm X. Something seriously bent showed within an American society rife with violence. Sickening and degrading news segments fouled the *Evening News*, with only Charles Kuralt offering an insular salute to the Norman Rockwell era, when sarsaparilla cost a nickel and we were fighting the "good wars" against totalitarianism.

Yet Cronkite kept looking for a way for CBS News to play a healing role. The opportunity presented itself with the Apollo program. Americans turned away from all the anarchy to unite with relief and pride behind the well-financed gambit of sending astronauts to the Moon. "This is something we've been aiming at for all of these years," said Cronkite, still NASA's biggest booster. "We've been building toward this. Only thing comparable to it was splitting the atom, but we couldn't cover that. It was done in secret."

24.

Mr. Moon Shot

NEW MOON RISING—WE ARE CHILDREN OF THE
SPACE AGE—ONWARD IN THE FACE OF DEATH—
DOWN PAT WITH THE NASA LINGO—THE CHRISTMAS
MAGIC OF *APOLLO 8*—HIGH TIMES AT THE HOLIDAY
INN—CBS'S SPACE GIZMOS—HIGHS WITH SCHIRRA
AND CLARKE—OH BOY REDUX—ONE GIANT LEAP—
DAY 1 IN THE YEAR 1—A RELIEF FROM EARTHLY
NEWS—DRILLING NEIL ARMSTRONG—ONWARD
WITH APOLLO—TOUCHING MOON DUST

While other CBS newsmen staked claims on
Castro's Cuba (Sevareid) or Ho Chi Minh's
North Vietnam (Collingwood), Cronkite's reportorial
beat was central Florida. At Fat Boy's, the Cocoa Beach

barbeque joint, there were eight photos blown up large hanging behind the cash register—the Mercury Seven astronauts and the indomitable Walter Cronkite. Nowhere was Cronkite happier, not even on a sailboat circling Martha's Vineyard on a golden summer day, than at Florida's Space Coast.

With almost everybody else at CBS News seemingly consumed with the Humphrey-Nixon-Wallace presidential race in the late summer and early fall of 1968, Cronkite kept one intense eye fixed on the *Apollo 7* flight scheduled for October 7. "Walter had grown very sick of the 1968 election," said the CBS News producer Jeff Gralnick. "All I remember was Walter going on and on about how having George Wallace on the CBS News was a waste of time. Cronkite was a Wally Schirra man. After the convention, I got the feeling that Walter just said, 'A pox on all of their political houses' and reintensified his commitment for CBS to cover space."

Apollo 7 was a smashing success for both NASA and CBS News. Even though the astronauts suffered horrible colds and assorted technical problems, the men splashed down safely. While Cronkite dutifully broadcast Election Day 1968 for CBS News from New York—with Nixon winning 301 electoral votes to 191 for Humphrey and 46 for Wallace—his enthusiasm was still with Cape Kennedy, where NASA was gearing up for the *Apollo 8* mission, billed as the first human voyage to the Moon.

For Cronkite, the Christmas season of 1968 was the most memorable of his life. Based at the hundred-room Holiday Inn in Cocoa Beach, he was on hand for the *Apollo 8* liftoff on December 21. The astronauts—Frank Borman, James A. Lovell, and William A. Anders—orbited the Moon ten times beginning on Christmas Eve. This yuletide space endeavor, a crucial circumlunar precursor to the *Apollo 11* lunar landing, was the most-watched TV event in history at that time. It was hard not to feel the healing and unifying effects of *Apollo 8,* when images of Earth (the first ever taken by humans of the whole planet) were shown on Christmas and the astronauts read the opening verses of Genesis. When atheist activist Madalyn Murray O'Hair claimed the Apollo crew, as U.S. government employees, were constitutionally prohibited from promoting religion on the taxpayer dollar, Cronkite shot her down like a clay pigeon.

In a year when the assassins James Earl Ray and Sirhan Sirhan received so much press attention, *Time* magazine inspiringly chose Borman, Lovell, and Anders as its "Men of the Year." Cronkite applauded *Time* managing editor Henry Grunwald for his inspired choices. "We are the lucky generation," Cronkite enthused. "Not only were our achievements in space important in restoring our self-respect, they enabled us as well to enter the history books."

Every new capability NASA introduced on a mission was more exhilarating than the last. When *Apollo 9* launched in March 1969, a spacewalk was televised live for the first time ever. Cronkite was at Cape Kennedy for the historic moment. CBS News was now devoting more and more resources to the impending moon mission. Cronkite spent most of his waking hours that summer preparing for the *Apollo 11* liftoff with the intensity of an attorney rehearsing for trial. His NBFs (new best friends) were meteorologists and aeronautical engineers. "Never before had I seen Dad with such thick binders," Chip Cronkite recalled. "We all knew he was studying like never before."

Whenever Cronkite was on his NASA space beat, he rented a convertible from Jacksonville or Tampa Airport and headed down the central Florida coast. Sometimes he'd take boat rides down the Banana and Indian rivers for relaxation. "Walter would have on a Hawaiian shirt, drinking some fruity drink poolside," author Norman Mailer recalled. "If you just arrived to Cape Canaveral, like I did from New York or Boston, feeling jet-lagged or perhaps hungover, the sight of the straitlaced CBS anchorman in full tan mode was jarring. But I admired his relaxed panache. . . . Walter was right. Why not take full advantage of the remote Florida lifestyle while the fools up East, the suits, even *I*, thought Houston or Cape Canaveral was hardship duty?"

There was a lot of speculation that NASA's public relations office and CBS News were in cahoots to make a big show of *Apollo 11*. Though NASA had declined to let Cronkite join astronauts on a survival exercise in the Mojave Desert, he was essentially accorded carte blanche treatment by the powers at NASA; information embargoes were often lifted for him. Cronkite, NASA believed, was the ideal conduit to reassure U.S. taxpayers that $25 billion of their money was being spent nobly. "We were given absolute freedom to report the story, and a great flow of information from NASA," Cronkite told *TV Guide*. "I would suggest that this freedom and the comparative reluctance of the Soviet Union to tell the facts until after the fact is an indication of the difference between an open and a closed society."

Just how close NASA and CBS News were during the Apollo program period has never been properly analyzed by scholars. The paper trail linking the two organizations is quite thin. Gentlemen's agreements, in the end, aren't easy to footnote, but in a thirty-day period around the time of the *Apollo 11* mission, other startling events occurred (Chappaquiddick, the Manson murders, and the Woodstock music festival among them). At CBS, all else took a backseat to coverage of the moon shot. Don Hewitt, producing CBS News' *60 Minutes*, came closest to explaining the Tiffany Network's collaboration in his memoir, *Tell Me a Story*. "Nobody ever said it because nobody had to say it," he wrote. "But I always figured that there was an understanding between television and NASA— never spelled out, never even whispered, never even hinted at, but they knew and we knew. If we continued to help the space agency get its appropriations from Congress, they would in turn give us, free of charge, the most spectacular television shows anyone had ever seen."

Cronkite understood that the *Apollo 11* mission would put American technology to the test in one tremendous, almost miraculous, public display. That a rocket—an invention made practical less than thirty years before—could go to the Moon had been demonstrated by two previous Apollo missions. Now the big moment was upon NASA. *Apollo 11* added several bold steps: a lunar module would detach from the mothership, navigate its way to the Moon's surface, find a suitable landing spot, and later lift off and then rendezvous with the main ship. Each step and a hundred in between offered moments of gripping drama. But the most stunning possibility of all was that so much of the mission could be captured on video and sent back to Earth live. Cronkite credited John F. Kennedy for declaring in a May 25, 1961, speech to Congress that America would put a man on the Moon "before the decade is out." To Cronkite, the fact that Kennedy insisted that the space program be conducted in the open was another testament to his greatness.

A space geek from Norfolk, Virginia, wrote Julian Scheer, NASA's assistant administrator for public affairs, at NASA Headquarters in Washington, D.C., about making Cronkite an honorary Apollo astronaut in the spring of 1969. "We do not have an official or unofficial 'honorary astronaut' title to bestow," Scheer informed her. "But I can assure you that many of us in the program—including all the astronauts, I'm certain—consider Mr. Cronkite an honorary astronaut, officially or unofficially. He is a most knowledgeable reporter with experience in the space effort that dates back to the days when we were firing 'big' rockets, which now seem to be mere 'firecrackers.'"

America was plagued with the Vietnam War quagmire, high inflation, campus upheavals, pollution, and race riots, but moon exploration lifted the national spirit in the summer of 1969. Three All-American *Apollo 11* astronauts—Neil Armstrong of Ohio, Buzz Aldrin of New Jersey, and Michael Collins of Oklahoma—were rewriting the Icarus myth and flying nearer the sun than anyone before them. Approximately one million people were in Cape Kennedy to witness the *Apollo 11* liftoff on July 16. Thousands of police officers tried to control the jam-up of cars and boats that kept arriving on Florida's Space Coast.

There were hippies in VW bugs, retirees on Social Security looking for reduced fares, Pontiac station wagons crammed with antsy kids, and 4-H Club buses that had driven down from the upper Midwest—all participating in the Fourth of July–like festivities. *Reader's Digest* had distributed an astonishing sixty-eight million American flag bumper stickers for the moon launch extravaganza, and they were everywhere to be seen on the cars in the parking lots around Cape Kennedy.

Apollo 11 was slated to blast off at 9:32 a.m. on July 16, its huge Saturn V rocket propelled by 7.6 million pounds of thrust. For three days and three nights it would travel through space toward the Moon. The lunar module *Eagle* would land on the Moon with Armstrong and Aldrin, who would spend little more than a day on its surface while Collins remained behind to man the spaceship *Columbia*. The Holy Grail moment would be on July 21, when Armstrong would start to climb down off the *Eagle* on a ladder (pulling a lanyard as he descended that activated a television camera) and then take his first steps on the Moon. Buzz Aldrin would join him in the next hour to collect rock and soil samples to bring back to Earth. After about twenty-one and a half hours on the Moon, the module would take off from the Sea of Tranquility to dock with *Columbia*. On July 24, the *Apollo 11* mission would end with the astronauts splashing down in the Pacific Ocean as citizens of the world cheered, having watched the feat on television and hearing it on the radio.

All three U.S. networks vied to produce the most informed blastoff-to-splashdown coverage. NBC slated readings by performers such as James Earl Jones and Julie Harris—they were to read poems about the Moon. ABC commissioned the jazz legend Duke Ellington to compose a new musical composition—titled "Moon Maiden"—inspired by the landing; he would also sing its lyrics while the astronauts made their lunar debut. CBS lined up Orson Welles to narrate science fiction material from London, including a remake of his own infamous 1938 radio drama, *War of the Worlds*, in a panoply of race-to-the-moon nostalgia. "Now the Moon has yielded, not merely to man's imagination,"

Welles said with his great voice of authority, "but to his actual presence."

Dick Salant of CBS News spoke for all the network presidents, in a sense, when he said *Apollo 11* presented some of the most "formidable challenges" in electronic history. The network's main asset was Cronkite, covering his twenty-first manned flight. CBS had arranged for models and simulations to demonstrate (in color) what was happening whenever NASA footage (which was black and white) was unavailable. Cronkite would need a lot of cutting-edge techniques to compete with NBC and ABC. And Paley, recognizing that this was history in the making, opened his pocketbook wide.

At the CBS News studio at Kennedy Space Center's press site, the preproduction team was chased away on Wednesday, July 16, as the *Apollo 11* countdown to lift-off grew closer and closer. Only Cronkite (attached to his Smith-Corona, like the editor in *The Front Page*) and former Mercury astronaut Wally Schirra, producer Joan Richman, stage manager David Fox, and a few cameramen and technicians were allowed to remain in CBS's tiny Cape Kennedy studio. "I don't suppose," Cronkite confided to Schirra, "we've been this nervous since back in the early days of *Mercury*."

There was a debate at CBS News over which veteran astronaut to have as Cronkite's color man for *Apollo*

11. If fame was the main criterion, then Alan Shepard or John Glenn was the obvious choice. But Cronkite had developed a special affinity for "Wally" Schirra since he had done a half-hour prime-time *Sigma 7* preview broadcast from Florida in September 1962. To get Salant to offer Schirra a handsome retainer for exclusivity, Cronkite spread the rumor that ABC was after him. That quickly seized Salant's attention. The Cronkite-Schirra chemistry worked so well that the duo broadcast together from *Apollo 11* all the way to *Apollo 17*, and became known in CBS display ads as "Walter to Walter" coverage.

When Mission Control in Houston said on the morning of July 16, "We are still a go with *Apollo 11* . . . 30 seconds and counting," the tension in the CBS booth was overwhelming. At liftoff, Cronkite was speechless. Those present worried that he was so transfixed by the rise that he'd forgotten he was on air. David Fox broke the ice by whispering to Cronkite, "There she goes! It's beautiful," and giving a thumbs-up. But the CBS anchorman stayed quiet a little longer. Cronkite knew, from experience, that no voice should ever interrupt a reverie.

The towering Saturn V was 111 meters (363 feet) tall, about the height of a thirty-six-story building and 18 meters (60 feet) taller than the Statue of Liberty. Fully fueled for liftoff, the Saturn V weighed the equivalent of four hundred elephants. Its five large engines produced 160 million horsepower and 7.6 million pounds of thrust, generating more power than eighty-five Hoover Dams. Once Cronkite realized that the rocket wasn't going to explode, he snapped out of his trance. "Oh boy, oh boy, it looks good, Wally," he said joyously. "Building shaking. We're getting the buffeting we've become used to. What a moment! Man on the way to the Moon! Beautiful."

At summer camp in Vermont, Kathy Cronkite, like so many other schoolchildren, was monitoring the historic launch on CBS. "The principal let me go into his office to watch Dad," she recalled. "It wasn't a big deal seeing him, but the Moon was a big deal. We grew up with the space program in our family, and this was our payoff."

Her sister, Nancy, only nineteen, was living in Hilo, Hawaii, with her husband. She opposed the space program. "I had deep reservations," she said. "I was almost anti-NASA. We had no TV. I was living back to nature. I thought we were just now bringing our own junk, golf balls, lunar module, to pollute the Moon."

At least one of the Cronkite kids, twelve-year-old Chip, was delirious about *Apollo 11*. His favorite childhood memories were of Cocoa Beach at Henri

Landwirth's motel talking space and collecting sea-shells. Along with his mother that day, Chip attended a viewing party in Connecticut with family friends. "My previous Apollo experience had been bone-rattling," he said. "I had been at Cape Canaveral, and I felt it right down the spine. So I was really pumped up for Armstrong, Aldrin, and Collins. What impressed me most was watching Dad broadcast at night. And when I woke up many hours later he was still on TV extempo-rizing. I was like wow . . . you go, Dad!"

Although Cronkite and Schirra were the only on-air talent in the CBS News studio at liftoff, they had a lot of technical help. Working in CBS's central room, beneath the studio, was producer Robert J. Wussler. Ever since that fateful moment at Kennedy's inaugu-ral when Sig Mickelson assigned him to cover space, Wussler had been preparing for the history-making event. He usually stayed at CBS News in New York during space missions, but not for this seminal launch. Now, quite comically, this TV wunderkind pulled out his own little personal camera during liftoff to snap a few photos that wouldn't belong to CBS. "I wanted to be able to say," Wussler later recalled, "that these were the pictures I took on the day man left for the Moon."

All the dignitaries around Cape Kennedy were hoping to be on CBS News with Cronkite. Vice

President Spiro Agnew, for example, arrived in the CBS News booth to talk with Cronkite. When former president Lyndon Johnson arrived at the CBS studio Cronkite turned deferential. Just fifteen months earlier, he had damaged Johnson considerably with his Tet prime-time special. "I was—how to put this," Cronkite's producer Joan Richman recalled, "not a big Lyndon Johnson fan." But LBJ seemed to hold no grudge against what he called "the Cronkites" at CBS. All present remembered just how warm Johnson was to Cronkite that afternoon. For a while it seemed that LBJ might replace Schirra as Cronkite's new astrobuddy; they got along that well. While all Cronkite's on-air friends spoke about *Apollo 11*, LBJ honed in on the Great Society. Cronkite nodded admiringly in agreement. "Our family never held a grudge against Walter for a second," Lynda Johnson Robb, daughter of the president, explained. "Both Mother and Father admired him."

Cronkite's most imaginative guest was Arthur C. Clarke, author of the novel *2001: A Space Odyssey* (1968). The British-born science fiction popularizer augmented the Cronkite broadcast perfectly. Clarke had first auditioned to be Cronkite's astrobuddy during *Apollo 10* in May 1969 and imagined the world of the twenty-first century. He comprehended the vastness of space. Unlike Aldous Huxley, who feared the "global village" in *Brave New World*, Clarke celebrated that all countries were tuned into the celestial spectacle. Cronkite had chosen Clarke over Isaac Asimov because he considered him something of a prophet. Back in 1956, in a letter to space law pioneer and expert Andrew G. Haley, Clarke had written with great pre-science about what would become Telstar, GPS, and satellite TV. What Clarke envisioned was the world of a thousand-channel cable TV systems providing "global TV service" that would make possible a "position-finding grid" whereby "anyone on earth could locate himself by means of a couple of dials on an instrument about the size of a watch."

The CBS Television network was in full swing for the *Apollo 11* mission, coast to coast and beyond. Cronkite could talk directly to stations in eight U.S. cities. A roving mobile unit drove all over Greater New York collecting the opinions of everyday people. Cronkite didn't want to hear anything negative about NASA on his broadcast. Bill Plante, for example, clashed with him over CBS's *Apollo 11* reaction coverage. Plante had been asked to conduct the man-on-the-street segment in New York City, and in Harlem and the Bronx he got a surprise: a lot of New York residents thought *Apollo 11* was a waste of money that would be better spent winning the war on poverty. There were many Nancy Cronkites in America who saw the Apollo program as a bad use of time and money for environmental reasons. "Walter had so bought into space," Plante recalled, "that any criticism of the moon launch in 1969 was anathema to him. But he let it air."

What differentiated Cronkite from Armstrong was the effusiveness with which he spoke about the Moon. To Armstrong—the Korean War fighter pilot of seventy-eight missions—the lunar walk was an assignment. Armstrong was repulsed by the efforts of journalists who insisted that fame could supercede true accomplishment. While Cronkite had to make *Apollo 11* seem romantic for television ratings, Armstrong demurred. When asked decades later in an interview whether he ever looked into space in the summer of 1969 and thought how beautiful the Moon was, a stony-faced Armstrong replied, "No, I never did that."

Although Cronkite stayed his on-stage avuncular self, he didn't respect critics of *Apollo 11*. Kurt Vonnegut, riding the wave of publicity generated by the recent publication of *Slaughterhouse-Five*, appeared on Cronkite's *Apollo 11* broadcast full of scorn toward all things NASA, even calling the astronauts "short-haired, white athletes" infatuated with pressure cookers. Cronkite was "bitter" toward Vonnegut, a friend, for being so cruel to the bravest Americans he knew. When Norman Mailer belittled the *Apollo 11* astronauts in his book *Of a Fire on the Moon*, deriding them with bohemian bravado as "three young executives announcing their corporation's newest subdivision," Cronkite cut ties with him for five or six years.

Amused by Cronkite's lunar devotion, Schirra decided to play a long-running "gotcha" gag on Cronkite when they were live and killing time during slow moments of the *Apollo 11* broadcast. "Walter," Schirra said, "you are a world-class journalist. You were a wire-service writer, a war correspondent, and you are respected by us in the military. Now, what I want to know, Walter, is this. What are you going to say when a man first steps on the moon? What are the words you will utter at this historic moment?"

Cronkite was tongue-tied, giving Schirra a scolding look that was priceless. Cronkite hemmed and hawed. And then he just moved onto a different subject. "This was the first—and last, for that matter—time that I ever saw him flustered," Schirra recalled. "I put it to him again shortly before lift-off. 'Walter, have you any great words in mind?' Cronkite can be terribly intense, and he's very serious about his broadcasts. He's not one for kidding around. But I had gotten hold of a bone, like a naughty puppy dog, and I wasn't going to let go."

Over the course of the coverage, Cronkite had on-air help from two hundred prerecorded film "bank pieces" he could draw upon (such as short biographies of the key scientists who had masterminded the mission). Also available to vary the mix: entertainment segments and remote feeds from a full-scale simulated lunar module. Cronkite, however, was the personality who held all the pieces and segments together. "Walter and his guests discussed the epochal events evolving a quarter of a million miles away," CBS science advisor Richard C. Hoagland recalled, referring to Cronkite's elevated chair as a "megalithic throne." The voices of Mission Control could always be heard clearly, staccato advisories under or next to the comments of Cronkite, Schirra, and Clarke.

By Thursday, July 17, Cronkite had left Cape Kennedy to broadcast from Studio 41 at West Fifty-seventh Street in New York. His desk had been raised twenty-four feet above the studio floor. An artist had created a mock Milky Way as a background. Serving as bookends for Cronkite were two globes, each six feet in diameter: a Rand McNally model of the Moon and a Plexiglas conception of what Earth would look like from the astronauts' perspective. A record-breaking sixteen CBS cameras were trained on Cronkite sitting at his anchor desk. Four additional "slave" cameras were locked on clocks offering countdown information for the various stages of the Apollo mission. To keep the coverage from feeling stilted, dolly cameras were used to seek out different angles.

Joel Banow—CBS News' go-to director for its space coverage from Mercury to Skylab—got an idea from MGM's adaptation of *2001: A Space Odyssey*: the talking computer, HAL. Much like UNIVAC back at the 1952 and 1956 political conventions, the hooky HAL was now hired to liven up the Cronkite broadcast by offering color commentary.

Frank Stanton knew that Cronkite was doing an inspired job as *Apollo 11* anchorman. All the key CBS reporters of the *Apollo 11* mission—Ike Pappas and Ed Rabel among them—were doing the best work of their careers. Cronkite was slated to be live for twenty-four and a half of the crucial thirty-one hours surrounding the moon landing. He had only one extended break, lasting six and a half hours. The UPI writer Dick West described what it was like to watch more than twenty-four hours of moon coverage—as millions of people did, all over the world. Halfway along, he wrote, he developed a condition "in which one's eyeballs become uncoordinated as a result of peering too long at Walter Cronkite." The sense of global togetherness was called Cronkititis. "His sustained presence and attractive self-confidence," Jack Gould wrote glowingly in *The New York Times*, "were nothing short of remarkable."

Through pooled TV coverage, the global audience on July 20 was glued to the Tube waiting for the *Eagle* to make its powered descent to the Moon's surface. After boning up on NASA trivia before going on air, Cronkite started his live broadcast at 10:00 a.m. EST, offering a five-minute progress report on the *Apollo 11* mission right off the bat. At 11:00, after a religious program called *Nearer to Thee*, on which theologians and artists talked about God in space, Charles Kuralt did an ethereal piece to open what CBS News called "Man on the Moon: The Epic Journey of *Apollo 11*." Using Genesis as his text—harking back to that poignant Christmas Eve of 1968—the virile-looking Kuralt spoke about the spiritual aspects of space travel, showing beautiful images of planet Earth taken by other NASA astronauts and satellites. Cronkite, combining ad-libbing and filler material, turned the nerve-racking journey of the *Eagle* to the Moon into high-suspense theater. The interplanetary drama began when Michael Collins, aboard *Apollo 11*, released the module *Eagle* carrying Armstrong and Aldrin to their destination.

Eagle: Roger, understand. Go for landing. 3000 feet. Second alarm.

Cronkite: 3000 feet. Um-hmmm.

Eagle: Roger. 1201 alarm. We're go. Hang tight. We're go. 2000 feet. 2000 feet, into the AGS. 47 degrees.

Cronkite: These are space communications, simply for readout purposes.

Capcom: Eagle looking great. You're go.

Houston: Altitude 1600. 1400 feet. Still looking very good.

Cronkite: They've got a good look at their site now. This is their time. They're going to make a decision.

Eagle: 35 degrees. 35 degrees. 750, coming down at 23. 700 feet, 21 down. 33 degrees.

Schirra: Oh, the data is coming in beautifully.

Eagle: 600 feet, down at 19. 540 feet down at 30— down at 15 . . . 400 feet, down at 9 . . . 8 forward . . . 350 feet down at 4 . . . 300 feet, down

3½ ... 47 forward ... 1½ down ... 70 ... got the shadow out there ... 50, down at 2½, 19 forward ... altitude-velocity lights ... 3½ down ... 220 feet ... 13 forward ... 11 forward, coming down nicely ... 200 feet, 4½ down ... 5½ down ... 160, 6½ down ... 5½ down, 9 forward ... 5 percent ... quantity light 75 feet. Things still looking good, down a half ... 6 forward ... lights   on ... down   2½ ... forward ... 40 feet, down 2½, kicking up some dust ... 30 feet, 2½ down ... faint shadow ... 4 forward ... 4 forward, drifting to the right a little ... 6 ... drifting right ...

Cronkite: Boy, what a day.

Capcom: 30 seconds.

Eagle: Contact light. O.K. engine stopped ... descent engine command override off ...

Schirra: We're home!

Cronkite: Man on the moon!

Eagle: Houston, Tranquility Base here. The *Eagle* has landed!

Capcom: Roger, Tranquility. We copy you on the ground. You've got a bunch of guys about to turn blue. We're breathing again. Thanks a lot.

Tranquility: Thank you.

Cronkite: Oh, boy!

Capcom: You're looking good here.

Cronkite: Whew! Boy!

Schirra: I've been saying them all under my breath. That is really something. I'd love to be aboard.

Cronkite: I know. We've been wondering what Neil Armstrong and Aldrin would say when they set foot on the moon, which comes a little bit later now. Just to hear them do it. Absolutely with dry mouths.

When Cronkite officially heard the words, "Houston, Tranquility Base here. The *Eagle* has landed," at 4:17 p.m. EST he became emotional. Tears filled his eyes. Also Schirra's. They were struck dumb with admiration for America. Clarke, sitting beside Cronkite and Schirra, later said it felt like "time had stopped in Studio 41." For a while, Cronkite kept the broadcast silent, glasses in hand, shaking his head from side to side in disbelief. Schirra, like millions of viewers, was anxious to hear what immortal words Cronkite would utter for the history books.

The previous day, the two had met for a quick dinner at the old Regency Hotel on Park Avenue to discuss the impact of the anchorman's words. Schirra had even gone through *Bartlett's Familiar Quotations* to offer Cronkite ideas from Aristotle and T. S. Eliot. Now that the time-frozen moment had arrived, Schirra looked at Cronkite with anticipation. "Wow," the great journalist said. "Oh, boy!"

No two words could have been more apropos than "Oh, boy!" There was cunning in the ring of honest human simplicity. Cronkite, lost in thought, was oblivious to the audience and he was speechless. Yet, in truth, "Oh, boy" was a successful trope he had used since the Project Mercury days. It worked again for *Apollo 11*.

For Cronkite's CBS team, the post-landing coverage was the hardest part of the marathon broadcasts. Cronkite and Schirra had a lot of time to kill, with only the static-infused voices of the Apollo astronauts as reliable guides to what was happening. At that point, the banter between Cronkite and Schirra mattered the most. They had to build the suspense back up in a reverential way, getting people ready for a moon walk that was six hours and thirty-nine minutes away. Cronkite filled that void with reams of fresh information provided by the Manned Spacecraft Center in Houston and friendly banter with Schirra and Clarke. Then the matchless moment began, the *Eagle* door opened, and Armstrong started his descent.

Cronkite: There he is. There's a foot coming down the steps.

Houston Voice: OK, Neil. We can see you coming down the ladder now.

Armstrong: OK. I just checked getting back up to that first step. It didn't collapse too far. It's adequate to get back up.

Houston Voice: Roger. We copy.

Armstrong: It's just a little jump.

Cronkite: So there's a foot on the Moon, stepping down on the Moon. If he's testing that first step, he must be stepping down on the Moon at this point.

A billion people were watching on TVs all around the globe. Not many seconds had elapsed since the hatch opened when Armstrong said: "One small step for man; one giant leap for mankind." Unfortunately, those perfect words, prepared by Armstrong himself, were partially indecipherable due to static. Cronkite worked his Houston contacts to get the phrase right. And it was Cronkite, more than any other TV personality, who made hay out of Armstrong's choosing to say *mankind*, not *America*. "The step on the Moon was an awesome achievement," CBS News president Richard Salant recalled, "so was its reporting on television, because it emphasized television's extraordinary ability to unify a disparate world through communicating with so many people, in so many places, and thus providing them with a common—and an extraordinarily satisfying—experience."

Before long, Aldrin joined Armstrong on the Moon to collect rock samples and plant Old Glory on its surface, to Cronkite's obvious delight. The hatch was open on the Moon for two hours, thirty-one minutes, and forty seconds. As Armstrong and Aldrin bounced around on the Moon, Cronkite told viewers the two men were "like colts" finding their footing. He had gotten a lead from the White House that President Nixon would soon talk by radio-telephone to the *Apollo 11* astronauts. Cronkite reported that fact first. Armstrong and Aldrin had moved the existing camera, which had been activated by Armstrong as he descended the ladder, to be mounted in a fixed position on the tripod so that the world could watch their moon exploration live. This had been Cronkite's hope since he promoted cameras back in 1963 with Gordon Cooper orbiting Earth on *Faith 7*, the last of the Mercury missions.

After hours of exulation over Armstrong and Aldrin's antics, Cronkite raised the specter of how the astronauts were going to get home. Once Armstrong and Aldrin reboarded the *Eagle*, what would happen if its rockets didn't fire? Would they die on the Moon? Could they return safely to the mothership, where Collins was waiting for them? The most pressure-packed moment of the mission was yet to come: the lift-off of the lunar module. Cronkite built up the tension for these next phases of the mission. When the *Eagle* module did reunite with the mothership, Cronkite once again expressed his relief in a slang colloquialism: "Hot diggety dog!"

NBC's Chet Huntley and David Brinkley were boring compared to Cronkite; their attitude was oddly blasé, treating the excitement as a so-so affair. At ABC both Frank Reynolds and Jules Bergman came off as too academic and lacking any chattering warmth. When Cronkite ended CBS's historic thirty-two-hour broadcast, he signed off with this observation: "Man has finally visited the Moon after all the ages of wait-ing and waiting. Two Americans with the allitera-tive names of Armstrong and Aldrin have spent just under a full Earth day on the Moon. They picked at it and sampled it, and they deployed experiments on it, and they packed away some of it to pack with them and bring home." Sounding like a child, he hoped someday to touch the lunar rocks and dust that the *Apollo 11* astronauts were bringing home with them.

Talk about Iron Pants. Cronkite had stayed live on CBS TV for seventeen and a half hours straight. After a brief nap, he went back on the Tube for another nine hours. He claimed he never noticed the "fatigue factor." *The New York Times* saluted him for his "seemingly effortless performance." It applauded Cronkite's having read Archibald MacLeish's original poem "Voyage to the Moon" as a broadcast wrap-up of "Man on the Moon." Like Carl Sagan—best known for making space and science accessible—Cronkite was able to break down aerospace concepts for the average American without dumbing them down. Wussler, the executive producer for CBS, had pulled off miraculous television, making the well-schooled Cronkite the broadcaster beneficiary. Cronkite agreed that *Apollo 11* was the high-water mark of television; he called it the new "Golden Age of American Greatness." With his raw, nationalistic pride, he was in stark contrast to Eric Sevareid, though, who, like Armstrong, publicly fretted that *Apollo 11* would lead to the militarization of space. "History has never proceeded by a rational plan," Cronkite said, "not even science knows what it is doing beyond the immediate experiment. It is possible that the divine spirit in Man will consume him in flames, that the big brain will prove our ultimate flaw, like the dinosaur's big body."

Cronkite fervently believed that out of all the momentous acts of the sixties—the Kennedy assassinations, the March on Washington, Freedom Summer, César Chávez's boycotts, Medicare and Medicaid, women's liberation, the Vietnam War debate, take your pick—the *Apollo 11* mission to Earth's moon was the most historically significant of all. Cronkite's bold claim was credible. An astonishing 94 percent of all American homes had elatedly tuned in for the historic moon walk of Neil Armstrong on July 20, 1969. "It was a wonderful story of achievement, and everybody at Cocoa Beach and the Space Center at Cape Canaveral was looking up," Cronkite recalled. "They were looking toward the stars rather than looking down with the depressed state of world affairs, civil rights and Vietnam going on at the same time. So this was a relief story to all of us."

Of the three *Apollo 11* astronauts, Aldrin paid Cronkite the highest compliment of all. In his memoir, *The Long Journey Home from the Moon*, Aldrin praised Cronkite as the voice of the moon shot. With humor, Aldrin used to say he sometimes wished he could have stayed home, eaten potato chips, and watched

CBS News' commanding marathon broadcast. "Odd as it might seem," he wrote, "I have always wished that I could have shared that exhilarating experience [of walking on the Moon] with everybody else on Earth as they watched the electrifying moments leading up to our touchdown. We missed sharing in the reaction, the emotion embodied by the sight of broadcaster Walter Cronkite wiping away his tears."

Other reviewers were not as impressed with the Cronkite marathon. "CBS," wrote *The Washington Post*'s Lawrence Laurent, "did overwork Walter Cronkite and in his weariness, Walter did tend to fall into a monotonous, sing-song kind of delivery." More people saw Cronkite and stayed with him, though, than saw the coverage on either of the other networks. CBS drew 45 percent of the audience, NBC drew 34 percent, and ABC drew 16 percent. Cronkite had attached himself to the *Apollo 11* event, an earnest effort that had started a dozen years before, when he staked out space coverage as his beat on *The Twentieth Century*. His dedication had its own rewards, but it was a good investment of his time as well. Cronkite, the anchorman, wasn't merely the messenger of bad news. He was Mr. Moon Shot. At a reception room in Houston for the contractors who helped build *Apollo 11*, a hostess was stationed at the door. "The tourists who look in are always asking for Walter Cronkite," she said, "and are disappointed that he's not here. He's more popular than the astronauts."

Without question, Neil Armstrong was a veritable hero, and on August 17, Cronkite interviewed him, along with Aldrin and Collins, on CBS News' *Face the Nation*. Normally, Cronkite shunned the Sunday show. But getting to interview the three *Apollo 11* astronauts at KHOU-TV in Houston—one of his two hometowns—was irresistible. Cronkite, declining to be a panelist, bigfooted out George E. Herman, the moderator, for the first time in fourteen years.

While ostensibly Cronkite was going to debrief Armstrong about his moon walk on *Face the Nation*, the journalist in him couldn't help addressing the widespread rumors that the celebrity astronaut was an atheist, a charge propagated by Madalyn Murray O'Hair. When Armstrong was a test pilot in southern California during the 1950s, he had applied to become a Boy Scout troop leader at a local Methodist church. On the application form, when asked his religion, Armstrong had written, "Deist."

Seemingly embarrassed to be cornering Armstrong on the deist question, Cronkite nevertheless pursued the point on *Face the Nation*. If he hadn't, his two press colleagues on the show—David Schoumacher of

CBS and Howard Benedict of the Associated Press— would have. "I don't really know what that has to do with your ability as a test pilot and as an astronaut, but since the matter is up," Cronkite asked, "would you like to answer that statement?"

"I don't know where Mrs. O'Hair gets her information," Armstrong said, "but she certainly didn't bother to inquire from me nor apparently the agency, but I am certainly not an atheist."

"Apparently," Cronkite followed up, "your [NASA astronaut] application just simply says 'no religious preference.'"

"That's agency nomenclature," a frustrated Armstrong explained, "which means that you didn't have an acknowledged identification or association with a particular church group at the time. I did not at that time."

Because Cronkite was known as Mr. Moon Shot, he was especially reluctant to be seen giving Armstrong a free pass. But after that program, Cronkite felt like a bum. Had it really been necessary to push Armstrong on religion? Cronkite wasn't alone in trying to get Armstrong to reveal his inner self that summer, but his inquisition on *Face the Nation* was painful to watch. "Walter told me that the biggest on-air mistake he'd ever made was holding Armstrong accountable for his religion on the *Face the Nation* show," the CBS correspondent Ed Bradley recalled. "He said, 'I did the lowest thing a man can do, Ed. I embarrassed him about his very private relationship with God. . . . It's not worth it in the long run. You'll get one day of glory and a lifetime of regret.'" (Armstrong didn't hold it against Cronkite—he appeared exclusively with him on CBS's fifth-anniversary special about the Moon landing.)

On November 14–24, 1969, the *Apollo 12* mission flew to the Moon and returned safely. But CBS's ratings weren't particularly good. None of the networks' audiences came close to those for *Apollo 11*. *Apollo 12* astronauts Pete Conrad, Dick Gordon, and Al Bean didn't elicit the excitement of Armstrong, Aldrin, and Collins. While Cronkite did a fine job discussing how the LEM landing was controlled remotely and how the astronauts were bringing home pieces of the *Surveyor 3* robot that had landed on the Moon in 1967, there just was no "one giant leap for mankind" moment. Still, Cronkite received fine reviews for his on-air repartee with Schirra, and all the astronauts' wives watched CBS's coverage because of the "fatherly" anchorman.

An unforgettable moment occurred for both Cronkite and Arthur C. Clarke during CBS's *Apollo 12* coverage. Scientist Paul Gast, who ranked high in

NASA leadership, had arrived in the green room at the CBS Broadcast Center in New York. Like a drug dealer going psst . . . psst . . . , he summoned Cronkite to inspect the contraband goods he had stashed in his suit coat pocket. "He had little vials of real, 3.8 billion-year-old lunar material with him." An awestruck Cronkite stood in a druid circle with Schirra, Clarke, and a few others in hushed silence. He held the moon soil in the palms of his hands. It had been brought back from the Moon just a few months before on *Apollo 11*.

All Cronkite could do was stare. Words of any kind would have been sacrilegious.

25.

Avatar of Earth Day

"EARTHRISE"—RON BONN RALLIES—GOOD-BYE
UNION CARBIDE—CAN WE SAVE THE PLANET?—
WHERE ARE THE WHALES?—TAKING ON DOW
CHEMICAL—IS HE ECO-MAD?—THE EARTH DAY
PHENOMENON—ANTI-NUKING WITH BARRY
COMMONER—THE DUBOS PHILOSOPHY—FOUR DEAD
IN OHIO—EYE ON THE WORLD—EMMY MAVEN—
EARTH AS LIFEBOAT

At Cronkite's New York office was a desk covered
with manuscripts, incoming and outgoing correspondence, pipes in a rack, and assorted nautical gear.
Ever since he learned to sail Sunfish at Lake Gleneida
in Carmel, New York, Cronkite had been an advocate

of the conservation of rivers, lakes, bays, and seas. The Atlantic Ocean whales—humpbacks, minkes, and North Atlantic right whales—had by 1969 become touchstone species for Cronkite. Disturbed by the globe's ecological woes, he kept a framed photo over his desk, the elegiac "Earthrise" (with the Moon in the foreground), taken by *Apollo 8* astronaut Bill Anders in late December 1968. That symbolic picture, in which no national boundary lines could be seen, shrank all the world's troubles down to One World size. Earth was so lovely and fragile floating out there in the vast universe. With something akin to a conversion experience, Cronkite committed himself to protecting the planet from nature abusers, despoilers, and polluters. Lamenting the deteriorating condition of Earth's ecosystems from human-induced causes, Cronkite believed a new global environmental standard needed to be adopted by the United Nations. The Apollo program, in Cronkite's opinion, had been designed only to visit the Moon, but in the end, the emotional impact of images of the blue-green planet from a quarter million miles away had put humanity in ethereal communion with the universe.

As former Johnson Space Center director George Abbey noted, Cronkite wasn't alone in being bowled over by "Earthrise." Dozens of NASA employees developed "a new environmental appreciation" because of the profound photo. Joseph Campbell, the great American comparative mythologist, chose "Earthrise" to end a revised edition of his classic *The Hero with a Thousand Faces*—an endorsement of Cronkite's view that the photo was a hallmark of modern times. "Earthrise," in Cronkite's opinion, raised questions of whether humans had a sacred obligation to protect the natural beauty of Earth. Weren't huge corporations destroying rain forests, killing wildlife, and poisoning the oceans and skies? It dawned on Cronkite that the cold war mentality of the race to the Moon, which he had ardently promoted on CBS from 1961 to 1969, was perhaps off-kilter. Space exploration wasn't about the United States versus the Soviet Union. Cronkite, influenced by Stewart Brand's *Whole Earth Catalog*, which combined counterculture sensibility with computer musings and futuristic graphics, believed that technology could be used to help stamp out the evils of pollution. Cronkite decided he could use his position of media power at CBS to help protect the planet. Consulting with top scientists worried about toxic chemical pollution, contamination of groundwater, and endangered marine species, he turned into a proto-Green advocate.

Throughout the first half of 1970, Cronkite sought ways to connect the Apollo program with the environmental movement in the public imagination. It was an intrinsically difficult proposition. The *Apollo 13* mission, which lasted from April 11 to 17, 1970, *did* generate good ratings for CBS News, but only because there was an explosion in the spacecraft *Odyssey's* service engine oxygen tank, forcing the mission to be aborted. Once Cronkite heard "Houston, we have a problem," the live CBS broadcast became the drama of bringing the astronauts Jim Lovell, Jack Swigert, and Fred Haise back to Earth alive. They survived the ordeal, but public interest in the Apollo program steadily waned. Cronkite broadcast *Apollos 14, 15, 16,* and *17*, but with fewer CBS resources. Congress got tired of funding the expensive NASA programs and ended up canceling *Apollos 18, 19,* and *20.*

Later in life, Cronkite claimed that when the Apollo program ended in 1972, something in him died. Getting to know all those brave astronauts was the high point of his broadcast career. His critics claimed that his NASA obsession was overblown. He thought such people were fools. "Of all humankind's achievements in the twentieth century and all our gargantuan peccadilloes as well, for that matter—the one event that will dominate the history books a half a millennium from now," he believed, "will be our escape from our earthly environment and landing on the moon."

While Cronkite continued to champion the Apollo program in early 1970, venturing down to Cocoa Beach and Houston as often as possible, his space passions now transitioned directly into the environmental movement. To him, pro-environment warriors such as photographer Ansel Adams, oceanographer Jacques Cousteau, biologist Barry Commoner, and Sierra Club executive director David Brower were, like the astronauts, heroes of the first order.

While *Apollo 11* dominated news coverage in 1969, Cronkite had *CBS Reports* investigate two environmental catastrophes that occurred that year: the blowout at a Union Oil offshore well near Santa Barbara on January 28, which dumped more than three million barrels of crude oil into the southern California waters; and the Cuyahoga River, Ohio, fire of June 22, in which oil-soaked debris ignited and torched a railroad bridge. It seemed to Cronkite that industrialization run amok spelled doom for mankind. "The North American continent seemed ringed by oil slicks," Cronkite lamented, "off Alaska, off Nova Scotia, off Florida, and most dramatically, in the Gulf Coast off Louisiana."

At the CBS Broadcast Center in New York, there was a post–*Silent Spring* belief that the Tiffany Network had an obligation to spread the gospel of the age of ecology. A *CBS Reports* segment in September

1962 had Eric Sevareid famously interviewing the literary biologist Rachel Carson about the perils of the insecticide DDT at her home in Silver Spring, Maryland. Cronkite, at the time, had been focused on the Earth-orbiting flight of the second Mercury launch. But now that Neil Armstrong had walked on the Moon, Cronkite sensed that ecology would soon replace space exploration as *the* national obsession. CBS News producer Ron Bonn recalled precisely when Cronkite put the network on the front line of the fight. "It was New Year's Day, 1970, and Walter walked into the Broadcast Center and said, 'God damn it, we've *got* to get on this environmental story,'" Bonn recalled. "When Walter said 'God damn it,' things happened."

Cronkite pulled Bonn from nearly all other CBS duties for eight weeks so he could investigate environmental degradation. He wanted a whole new regular series on the *CBS Evening News*—inspired by *Silent Spring*, the philosophy of René Dubos, and those amazing photos of Earth taken by the *Apollo 8* astronauts. The *CBS Evening News* segments were to be called "Can the World Be Saved?" "We wanted to grapple first with air pollution, the unbreathable air," Bonn recalled. "But then we wanted to deal with the primary underlying problem, which was overpopulation."

In January 1970, the promise of a new environmentalism brought about the end of *The Twenty-First Century* (which had succeeded *The Twentieth Century* in June 1967). No longer would Cronkite tolerate Union Carbide (a major polluter) as a sponsor. The Texas-based Fortune 500 company was the enemy of "Earthrise," he told Bonn. At Cronkite's insistence, CBS canceled *The Twenty-First Century* to coincide with the debut of the "Can the World Be Saved?" segments.

No one at any of the Big Three networks, with the exception of Charles Kuralt, cared about environmental issues with the passion of Cronkite. By assigning his science producer Bonn, a trusted ally since their trip to South Vietnam together in 1965, Cronkite was getting way ahead of the news curve on the environment. In the mid-1960s, Bonn had done a couple of landmark *CBS News Special Reports* on global warming and overpopulation. Together, Cronkite and Bonn decided to begin CBS's coverage of the environment with an eight-minute piece on April 20—two days before Earth Day. *CBS Evening News'* graphics department made a special bumper slide for the "Can the World Be Saved?" segment that consisted of Bonn's hand clutching Earth (a photograph taken by the *Apollo 8* crew). "Earth, you understand, wasn't in the palm of my hand," Bonn explained. "We were trying to show humanity squeezing the Earth to death." The image became synonymous with the *CBS Evening News*, essentially the show's visual calling card.

Cronkite and Bonn launched the "Can the World Be Saved?" segments in the spring of 1970. The segments constituted perhaps the most important, if unsung, part of Cronkite's CBS legacy. More than any other top-tier American newsman (although David Brinkley and Charles Kuralt were nature lovers too), Cronkite put environmentalism on the front burner of public discourse. No longer would pollution be treated in a back-of-the-book, reserved, or filler way. Stories treated as major news included the Lake Erie perch being mercury-poisoned; the U.S. government recklessly pouring twenty-two million tons of sulfur dioxide into the atmosphere; Dow Chemical's ghastly dumps into Lake St. Clair and the Detroit River; sewage-coated Florida beaches closed for business; bald eagles being killed by DDT; towering garbage dumps choking the land; and the Everglades dying. The Cronkite judgments fell like hard rain on polluters. On his office wall at CBS was posted a Pogo comic adopted by environment activists: "We have met the enemy and they are us."

Even though Cronkite's celebrity status as anchorman transcended journalism in many ways, he seldom operated without reportorial allies when grappling with environmental issues. Two *New York Times* reporters—Gladwin Hill (a fellow Writing Sixty-Niner during World War II) and Joseph Lelyveld (the longtime *Times* correspondent who became executive editor of the newspaper from 1994 to 2001)—were lending their considerable prestige to making ecology front-page news. Once again Cronkite was reading the zeitgeist. The Santa Barbara oil spill of 1969 had become a rallying point for a new environmental awareness sweeping the land. When Hill wrote that the "environmental crisis" was "eclipsing student discontent over the war in Vietnam" in "intensity," Cronkite paid attention. The time had come, he intuited, for CBS News to act.

The Nixon administration's top environmental lawyer, William Ruckelshaus, who in December 1970 became the Environmental Protection Agency's first administrator, believed that Cronkite's coverage was a key factor in getting Nixon to back a spate of environmental legislation in the early 1970s. "Once Cronkite got on the environment, everybody started talking about it, worrying that we were destroying America," Ruckelshaus said. "Back when Sevareid interviewed Carson, the environmental problem was in black and white. By 1970, with Cronkite's ongoing 'Can the World Be Saved?' series, the belching smog and landfills and burning rivers were in color. That's what grabbed the public's attention."

Sandy Socolow, along with many others at CBS News, thought that Cronkite had gone eco-mad. Riled up about polluters, Cronkite was, as Socolow put it, the "grizzly bear" at CBS who insisted that the ecologically charged "Can the World Be Saved?" be a prime feature on the *Evening News*. "Walter was almost a nutcase about the environment," Socolow recalled. "He was really, really bothered by big companies' pollution and the destruction of America's natural resources. Everybody bemoaned that their stories were getting crowded out due to Walter's need for a new environmental awareness. He was over the top, a real pioneer in getting the mass media to profile American landscapes being desecrated."

Many of the CBS News technicians and producers thought that Cronkite was going a little gaga with his "Can the World Be Saved?" obsession. Whenever Cronkite ran an ecology story, the "Earthrise" graphic would appear behind him, with Bonn's hand holding the planet. *CBS Evening News* director Ritchie Mutchler would regularly bark to his assistant, "We'll need the hand job tonight!" To CBS News correspondent Bob Schieffer, it was akin to "Quiet on the set!" Feeling that he was being mocked, Cronkite, usually unflappable, called Mutchler aside. "Uhmm, could we call that thing something else?" he asked. "Every time I hear you call it that, my mind sort of wanders."

At Cronkite's insistence, CBS News played a major role in publicizing the first Earth Day observed across the United States, on April 22, 1970 (it also happened to be his son Chip's birthday). Not only did Cronkite build up Earth Day on his nightly broadcast, but he anchored a *CBS News Special Report* from 10:00 to 11:00 p.m. EST on that historic day when twenty million Americans launched the Green movement. He began "Earth Day: A Question of Survival" with Commoner, a Washington University biology professor who in February had been dubbed "the Paul Revere of Ecology" by *Time* magazine. While Cronkite continued to use Walter Schirra as his astrobuddy for Apollo launches, starting in 1970 he recruited Commoner— who had just finished his seminal book *The Closing Circle: Nature, Man, and Technology*—as his eco-cohort (Cronkite didn't hold it against him that he was a critic of space exploration). "This planet is threatened with destruction and we who live on it with death," Commoner stated. "The heavens rock, the waters below are foul, children die in infancy, and we and the world which is our home live on the brink of nuclear annihilation. We are in a crisis of survival."

While Cronkite had been cognizant of Commoner as a serious antinuke scientist, it was the professor's 1966 book, *Science and Survival*, which he read to prep for Earth Day, that further startled him out of a stupor. Commoner was remonstrating against what happened when the industrial order spun madly out of control, when society so fully believed in technology that it arrogantly treated nature as its slave. "Science can reveal the depth of the crisis," Commoner concluded, "but only social action can resolve it."

Only after Commoner had laid out the crisis did Cronkite say, "Good evening." It was clear that Cronkite was riding on the side of the Earth Day organizers demanding ecological balance in the country. Earth Day was the nationwide "environmental awareness day" that Commoner had long called for. In cities all across America, millions of citizens took part in teach-ins protesting the poisoning of Mother Earth. In New York City much of Fifth Avenue and Fourteenth Street were closed to traffic. Cronkite wandered all around New York, watching Americans improvise Earth Day with Frisbee contests, folk music, and pure-oxygen breathing exercises. Union Square became a beehive for the environmentally aware to wave placards and chant "Save the Planet," creating what the *New York Times* called an "ecological carnival" for pedestrians. A leading organizer of Earth Day, Senator Gaylord Nelson (D-Wisc.), thanked Frank Stanton and Cronkite for "devoting extensive time and energy to the task of educating the nation on the problem."

It's hard to measure the precise impact Cronkite had on the first Earth Day. As a commentator, he was brilliantly colorful in describing Earth Day on air as the opening salvo in a battle to protect from destruction the blue-green planet photographed by the Apollo astronauts from the Moon. To hear him bemoan the "littered Earth" and "filthy waters," calling the desecration a "crime against humanity," certainly seized viewers' attention. Cronkite—along with executive producer Ernest Leiser and Ron Bonn—had helped legitimize Earth Day as the major news event of the spring. In his *CBS News Report* commentary, Cronkite perhaps overreported the day's arrests and police altercations and Earth Day's extreme activists, who looked more like disaffected hippies than up-and-coming biologists. But merely by taking a deeply personal interest in Earth Day and treating the grassroots event as serious news, he lent his credibility to the environmental cause. "Whenever he mentioned it on the air," Sam Love, an Earth Day organizer, noted, "I noticed that the mail increased. I always thought CBS and Cronkite helped make the events because they gave it validation."

On the heels of Cronkite's Earth Day broadcast came the Kent State University shootings. On May 4, the troops of the Ohio National Guard opened fire on five hundred college students, some of whom were protesting against the U.S. invasion of Cambodia, which bordered South Vietnam. Gunshots killed four students and wounded nine others. Cronkite was at Century City in Los Angeles that afternoon, to attend a meeting with the owners of CBS affiliates. That evening, he delivered the Kent State news in a disapproving way, which had the net effect of infuriating the affiliates' conservative station owners. "The affiliates went crazy on Walter," Socolow recalled. "They thought he had treated the Ohio National Guard as criminals, not law enforcement professionals. Dick Salant, a real hero, absorbed all of their complaints. Boy, it was nasty. They thought Walter had turned hippie."

As with many other American tragedies, it fell to Cronkite to break the news to viewers that evening. Thomas and Colette Grace had settled into their living room to listen to Cronkite as usual. When the anchorman started talking about bloodshed at Kent State, they sat straight up. Their son was a sophomore at the Ohio university. It turned out that he had been wounded. They found out about this from watching CBS News. The Graces weren't the only ones to learn from the

Cronkite broadcast about their sons or daughters being killed or maimed by the Ohio National Guard.

With Ike Pappas and Harry Reasoner assigned to the story by Leiser, Cronkite reported for the next week on the fallout from Kent State, which included more than one hundred college strikes and closures, spontaneous memorials for the dead, and criminal prosecution of the guardsmen. With sympathy and concern, he interviewed leftist critics of the National Guard such as pediatrician Benjamin Spock, civil rights icon Coretta Scott King, and folk singer Phil Ochs, all of whom demanded that Nixon be impeached.

Five days after the shootings, a hundred thousand people demonstrated in Washington, D.C. Cronkite covered the gathering like a cub reporter. On May 14, just ten days after the Kent State shooting, two students were killed by police at Jackson State University. Cronkite led the call for Nixon to establish the President's Commission on Campus Unrest at once; the administration heeded the advice. Although the semantic shift wasn't commented on by media critics, Cronkite, along with CBS reporter Ike Pappas, began referring to Kent State as a "massacre." It was clear he sided with the college students protesting both the Cambodian incursion and the Kent State killings. The anchor even went so far as to encourage his friend, the novelist James Michener, to get to the bottom of the Ohio National Guard story. According to Cronkite, the American public needed answers, and he didn't trust the Nixon administration to provide them. Michener, with Cronkite spurring him on, published *Kent State: What Happened and Why* in 1971.

Because of CBS News' coverage of Earth Day and the Kent State massacre, Cronkite became popular on college campuses. The World War II generation had long trusted him, but by the spring of 1970 so, too, did the Vietnam generation. He now helped define the youth zeitgeist of America. He had given it his imprimatur. Cronkite delivered the commencement address at the University of Missouri at Columbia, where Betsy had graduated. The anchorman shocked the board of trustees by defending antiwar and pro-environment youth movements. "We must not reject those among us who dissent," he intoned. "We must assist, not resist."

Cronkite was flying high with his *Apollo 11* and Earth Day coverage, and his accolades for journalistic integrity were stacking up. The National Academy of Arts and Sciences honored him for two years in a row: 1970 and 1971. His CBS News special "The Flight of *Apollo 13*"—about how the lunar module *Aquarius* "lifeboat-rescued" Jim Lovell, Jack Swigert, and Fred Haise—had earned him an Emmy Award.

In acceptance speeches, Cronkite credited NASA with preserving American can-do greatness at a time of widespread discontent. "The 1960s, when we first launched humans into space and went to the Moon, were in other ways a drain on our spirit," Cronkite said. "The civil rights battles, the frightening divisiveness of the Vietnam War, the horrible assassinations— they drained the American spirit. It's no exaggeration to say the space program saved us."

Just how fervent an environmentalist Cronkite had become was apparent when, on December 3, 1970, the Environmental Protection Agency (EPA) was founded. Cronkite stood in happy disbelief as President Nixon, the reluctant environmentalist, signed into law a whole host of legislation aimed at curbing air, water, and pesticide pollution and ocean dumping. The first EPA administrator, William Ruckelshaus, whom Nixon called Mr. Clean, was astounded that Cronkite visited him just a couple of days after assuming office. "I was surprised," Ruckelshaus recalled, "how deeply interested Walter was in the environment, that he prioritized it in such a public way."

Cronkite had a pantheistic philosophy about life that came straight out of the transcendentalists and was captured by "Earthrise": how can humans stop the violence and destruction of the planet? He told millions of

TV viewers that the ravaging and raping of the Earth had to end. If Americans turned their backs on the problems of radiation, air pollution, water pollution, bulldozing the wilderness, draining wetlands, killing estuaries, filling the skies with noise, there would be no tomorrow. The U.S. government needed to regulate polluting corporations and force them to prioritize environment over profit. That was the Cronkite view of Earth Day, and it placed him in the vanguard of the ecology movement. He embraced young people, most of them in the same generation as his three children, in promoting the essential idea that all citizens had to be good custodians of the Earth. "Can the world be saved?" Cronkite regularly asked CBS viewers. "That is not doomsday rhetoric; it is, rather, the central question of our epoch." A full-page photograph of the Statue of Liberty jutting out from a garbage dump, a discarded TV with a shattered screen on top of the refuse heap, was shown by Cronkite on both CBS News and in his book *Eye on the World*, published in May 1971.

Never before had Cronkite been so daring about promoting public policy as in *Eye on the World*. The book is a clumsily constructed omnibus of CBS News' reporting on the major trends and stories of 1970, with an emphasis on ecology. Cronkite edited it and provided analysis and commentary. He had been coached by Yale law professor Charles Reich, whose book *The Greening of America* advocated "choosing a new lifestyle" undergirded in a new ecological consciousness. This was a stark departure from NASA boosterism, and it positioned Cronkite as a man of the left. Republicans had always liked the idea that Cronkite, even if liberal leaning, was pulling for the United States to whip the Soviets in the space race. But Nixon was now in the White House, and Cronkite's promotion of the 1970s as the Decade of the Environment was a slap at petroleum companies, forest product industries, auto companies, and corporations seeking minerals. All his heroes in *Eye on the World*—Senator Ed Muskie (D-Maine), Dr. Barry Commoner, biologist Dr. Paul Ehrlich, and consumer activist Ralph Nader—were left-of-center political figures.

The Big Four villains of *Eye on the World* were Dow Chemical, the Florida Power & Light Company, Consolidated Edison, and Chevron Oil Company. It seemed that Union Carbide caught a break for sponsoring *The Twenty-First Century* for so long, as Cronkite took aim squarely at corporate polluters. With uncanny prescience, he scolded them for the damage carbon dioxide was causing the planet's health. Long before Al Gore made global warming household words in his 2006 Academy Award–winning documentary *An*

Inconvenient Truth, Cronkite sounded the alarm on *CBS Evening News* and in *Eye on the World.* "Every year American power plants pour more than 800 million tons of carbon dioxide into the skies," Cronkite warned. "Some scientists suspect that carbon dioxide can turn the planet into a kind of greenhouse, sealing in heat so that temperatures gradually rise until the polar icecaps melt and a new deluge covers the lands of the earth."

Cronkite became personally involved in two save-the-coast conservation initiatives in 1970 and 1971. When an oil slick marred the waters off Edgartown, he became engaged with the Martha's Vineyard Eco-Action and Catastrophe Committee. While Cronkite himself didn't carry a "Don't Oil Our Ducks" placard, he did run a picture of his young environmentally minded friends on the Vineyard and he helped them raise money. Furthermore, he lent his prestige to a grassroots effort to stop heavy industrial users—such as oil refineries and bulk shipping stations—from damaging coastal areas in Delaware and Maryland. Deeply involved with the nonprofit World Wildlife Fund, he grew determined to learn how to identify the numerous species of water fowl. On a couple of occasions, he claimed that Roger Tory Peterson's *Guide to the Birds,* which went through six editions, was his favorite book.

Whenever Cronkite went on his twice-annual trip to Austin to see his daughter, he brought with him Peterson's *Field Guide to Texas and Adjacent States*. In 1980 he would get to collaborate with Peterson on the book *Save the Birds*. Cronkite's message in the manifesto was that if the birds die, we all die.

CBS Evening News won an Emmy Award for its "Can the World Be Saved?" segments. After that, all CBS reporters were anxious for environmental assignments; the airing of occasional "Can the World Be Saved?" segments lasted until 1980. By the twenty-first century, Earth Day had grown into an unofficial calendar holiday almost like Valentine's Day or Mother's Day. To commemorate its twentieth anniversary, the René Dubos Center for Human Environment presented Cronkite with its prestigious Only One Earth Award; his citation touted his promotion of environmental literacy. It was an honor he treasured. At the New York Hilton gala, more than one thousand environmentally minded citizens stood up to toast the man who helped put Earth Day and the New Environmentalism on the TV media map.

For the rest of his life, Cronkite would cite "Earthrise," *Silent Spring*, and *The Closing Circle* with opening his mind to the planet's peril. But it was sailing on *Wyntje*, a galaxy of stars overhead, that led him to worship God as the master of the universe. "It's about your own relationship with Mother Nature," he said. "At sea you are in league with her. But she's watching you with that cocked eye." When a Texas teenager asked Cronkite in 2000 what was the most significant event of his lifetime, without hesitation he said, "The conquest of space," adding that he still dreamed of walking on the Moon for the cosmic experience of seeing Earth, "this little lifeboat floating out there in space."

26.

The Nixon-versus-CBS War

WARRING WITH PAT BUCHANAN—COLSON GONE
HATCHET—AGNEW UNLEASHED—FBI ON THE
TRAIL—NOT ON THE ENEMIES LIST—CHALLENGING
THE NIXON ADMINISTRATION FROM ST. JO—CBS
RADIO ATTACK DOG—THE IMPLIED THREAT OF HERB
KLEIN—THE SILENT MAJORITY TURNS ON CRONKITE
(A LITTLE BIT)—DEFENDER OF ELECTRONIC
JOURNALISM—"THE SELLING OF THE PENTAGON"—
YANKEES, BROADWAY, AND PAPEETE—DEFENDER OF
EARL CALDWELL—MAKING MURROW PROUD

On November 13, 1969, Cronkite became flabbergasted by Vice President Spiro Agnew's blistering tirade—"On the National Media"—to a group

of enthusiastic Republicans in Des Moines, Iowa. The ardent address, written by Patrick Buchanan (then a thirty-one-year-old White House staff writer for President Nixon), focused specifically on the liberal bias of TV network news programs, the dominant communications medium on the national front. Buchanan recalled being summoned to the Oval Office to discuss his writing of the overbearing first draft of the Agnew speech. President Nixon "was enjoying himself immensely," cackling out loud with glee over the hard-hitting prose. Unleashing Agnew on the Big Three in such an ad hominem way was a blood sport of great amusement to the boss. "Nixon had his glasses on and was editing it by hand," Buchanan revealed in a 2011 interview. " 'This will tear the scab off those bastards!' " Buchanan remembered Nixon saying. "Usually, White House speeches got watered down. But not this one. Nixon liked the sting of it all."

Practically waving a tomahawk as he spoke in Iowa, Agnew excoriated the Big Three networks ("this little group of men who not only enjoy a right of instant rebuttal to every Presidential address, but more importantly, wield a free hand in selecting, presenting and interpreting the great issues of the nation"). Agnew's indignation, vivid and surprising, was aimed at Cronkite's tribe, that "small group of men, numbering perhaps no more than a dozen 'anchormen,' commentators and executive producers [who] settle upon the 20 minutes or so of film and commentary that is to reach the public." The small elitist group, Agnew caustically charged, was based in New York and Washington and didn't represent *real* America. With a final deft, sharp stab, Agnew implied that programs like the *CBS Evening News* bolstered radical elements in society and were prejudiced against President Nixon. It was inferred that if the Vietnam War was indeed a *stalemate*, the blame rested on liberal reporters such as Safer, Schorr, Rather, and Laurence because they had steered public opinion leftward with their gruesome field reports from the jungles of Vietnam. "It is time," Agnew warned, "that the networks were made more responsive to the views of the nation and more responsible to the people they serve."

President Nixon wasn't the first president to feel persecuted by the fourth estate, and to fantasize about browbeating it into lapdog obedience. But he brought the president-versus-the-press friction to radioactive levels. John F. Kennedy, a media darling, had carped regularly about unfair coverage back in the 1960 presidential campaign, believing that Cronkite was a Republican. At the beginning of Nixon's first term, as Cronkite recalled, "This administration's antagonism had been about like the antagonism shown by previous administrations." Cronkite actually judged Democratic presidents more combative with the press than Republicans. But Nixon had brought his overweening anti-press baggage with him when he moved into 1600 Pennsylvania Avenue. Early in his first term, he wrote in a memo that the majority of journalists had a "negative attitude" toward him and that "their whole objective in life is to bring us down." It became a self-fulling prophecy.

A preview of the distrust that developed between the *CBS Evening News* and the White House first flared on May 6, 1969. Cronkite hosted a *CBS News Special* called "The Correspondents Report," to analyze Nixon's first one hundred days in office. Dan Rather gushed about the "great vigor" Nixon showed in overseeing an enlightened foreign policy. Just three days later, the press found out about the secret bombings of Cambodia (a display of raw presidential power that sickened Cronkite).

Although President Nixon had anger burning in his breast toward journalists, he didn't lash out at the media himself. But Agnew—who had ironically enjoyed an amicable relationship with the press—*could*. When the vice president delivered Buchanan's speech (which Cronkite said "dripped with vitriol"), the Big Three networks—in lockstep—carried the speech live from Des Moines. Agnew charged that these New York–based networks, elitist bastions, were in conspiracy with *The New York Times*' editorial page. This was untrue. What Agnew failed to mention was that the top CBS, NBC, and ABC anchors hailed from North Carolina, Montana, Indiana, Missouri, North Dakota, and Louisiana—and that they didn't take marching orders from the same management. "To people in broadcasting, the picture of Chet Huntley, Frank Reynolds, Walter Cronkite, and the rest 'talking constantly to one another,'" Ed Bliss Jr. of CBS wrote in *Now the News*, "was laughable."

On November 25, 1969, Cronkite countered the image created by Agnew of a parochial New York–Washington point of view in the networks by speaking before the Chamber of Commerce in St. Joseph, Missouri. The Midwest venue was just a couple of miles from the Grey Lying-In Hospital where he had been born in November 1916. Cronkite, enthusiastically embraced by his hometown audience, spoke for two hours and answered myriad questions about broadcast journalism (the first half hour of the St. Joseph event aired on *60 Minutes*). With an American flag as his backdrop, he called Agnew's Des Moines speech and chairman of the Federal Communications Commission

Dean Burch's vocal support of it "a clear effort at intimidation." One of the residents of St. Joseph, seemingly sympathetic, asked Cronkite if the networks weren't overreacting a tad bit. "Perhaps we didn't react enough," Cronkite replied. "We reacted to an implied threat to free speech, and when there is that, we must react tough, we must react hard."

Coinciding with Cronkite's inspired public forum in St. Joseph, CBS president Dr. Frank Stanton likewise vented his frustration with Agnew in a scathing letter to the White House, claiming the vice president's ugly Des Moines address had the "gravest implications" for American democracy. Cronkite and Stanton were willing to go toe-to-toe with the White House to defend the fourth estate.

A deeply offended Cronkite was vocal in decrying what he called the Nixon administration's "implied threat." To Cronkite, the vice president was playing a blackmail game "dangerous to democracy in America." This was open warfare.

The Nixon crew grossly miscalculated how protective Cronkite was of his profession. He wasn't really avuncular at all. You didn't lock Murrow out of the CBS anchor booth, as Cronkite did during the 1960 Democratic Convention in Los Angeles, if you weren't a rumbler. Instead of rolling over, Cronkite repeatedly

criticized the Nixon White House. To the consternation of Stanton, he even testified at a congressional
hearing, charging the White House with *conspiracy*
against the press. A pretty heavy accusation. "Some of
my colleagues, even those at CBS, thought I had gone
too far," Cronkite recalled. "They said I had no proof
that the campaign was centrally directed and was in
fact a conspiracy. I think I used the old duck theory: If
it swims, walks and quacks like a duck, it probably is a
duck."

Back on October 15, 1969, President Nixon fumed
over the way Cronkite enthused about Moratorium
Day, when two hundred thousand protesters arrived on
the Mall holding candles in vigil, pleading for the end
of the Vietnam War. Television coverage had given credence to the protest. Cronkite, after listening to Coretta
Scott King speak at the event, said in a *CBS Special
Report* that the protest was "historic in its scope" and
that "never before had so many demonstrated their
hope for peace." For that act, a clearly irked Nixon
wrote in the news summary next to Cronkite's name
the kind of snarky language expected from Holden
Caulfield: "A nothing!"

Coinciding with Agnew's frontal attack on the Big
Three, the FBI started investigating Cronkite. The
bureau long denied that it monitored him, but it changed

its story in 2006 to say his records had been destroyed. A Freedom of Information Act request nevertheless managed to uncover proof of the Nixon administration's surveillance of Cronkite. The FBI unearthed at least one informant who claimed that Cronkite was collaborating with anti–Vietnam War activists beginning in 1969. The documents, publicized in 2010 by Yahoo! News, attest that an FBI informant infiltrated a protest group known as Youth for New America. When Cronkite was at WKMG, the CBS affiliate in Orlando, he spoke with the informant for about forty-five minutes, full of sympathy for the antiwar cause.

The files suggest that Cronkite encouraged the informant to hold a "Moratorium to End the War in Vietnam" rally at Rollins College in Winter Park, Florida. Nixon would be in Florida on November 14, 1969, for the launch of *Apollo 12*, and the group wanted to embarrass POTUS by holding a rally near Cape Kennedy on November 13 and 14. On November 15 a huge antiwar march was scheduled for Washington. The FBI learned that Cronkite, the supposedly neutral newsman, had told the informant that if the Youth for New America held an anti-Nixon rally in Florida at Kelley Park, CBS News would rent a helicopter to transport Senator Ed Muskie of Maine in from a fundraiser to speak at the event. Cronkite allegedly promised that CBS News would then extensively cover the rally in Florida and the subsequent march in the District of Columbia. To Cronkite, getting Muskie—perhaps the leading antiwar senator—guaranteed that the protest would qualify as big-time news. Whether the informant was telling the truth will never be known.

That wasn't the only revelation coming out of Cronkite's seventy-two-page file. The FBI had also monitored Cronkite's work with civil rights activists in Mississippi and had kept surveillance files on environmentalists who participated in his CBS News forum on Earth Day. "There was a battle between the Nixon White House and CBS that developed," Buchanan recalled. "About two-thirds of the American public relied on the network news. We knew that going after CBS wasn't risk-free. Nobody was going to cover for us. We were entering a hostile environment. War. Nixon truly saw the press as the enemy."

During the last half of 1969, Buchanan coordinated a study of network news to quantify the perceived liberal bias. His opinions took shape in a White House travesty called "The Enemies List," a paranoid tabulation of Nixon's perceived political critics and opponents. Compiled by Special Counsel to the President Charles Colson, the list's purpose was to "screw" Nixon's political enemies via tax audits from the IRS and the denial of grants, visas, et cetera. CBS News correspondent Daniel Schorr found himself perched at number eighteen on Nixon's "screw" roster. "For reasons I never quite understood," NBC News' David Brinkley later wrote, of being named in the Agnew speech, "Nixon thought I was his number-one enemy. I never liked him much but never attacked him on the air."

History has vindicated Cronkite's belief that Nixon himself—not surrogates—wanted to destroy the Big Three. When the Watergate tapes were released in July 1974, there was President Nixon giving the marching order: "The press is the enemy." Throughout the Nixon tapes, Cronkite's name is mentioned on numerous occasions. The White House was indeed bent on intimidating reporters. "Was there a conspiracy, as Walter Cronkite of CBS once solemnly charged, on the part of the Nixon administration to discredit and malign the press?" former Nixon White House speechwriter and future *New York Times* columnist William Safire rhetorically asked. "Was this so-called 'anti-media campaign' encouraged, directed, and urged by the President himself? Did this alleged campaign to defame and intimidate Nixon-hating newsmen succeed, isolating and weakening them politically? The answer to all those questions is, sadly, yes."

Nixon's offensive unleashed a pent-up response from millions of what he called the "silent majority," conservatives and libertarians frustrated by what they perceived as the unpatriotic liberal tone of the evening news. All riled up by Agnew, they suddenly found themselves part of a chorus of pro–White House voices who wanted to burn the House of Cronkite down. The issue of television news bias became a Republican rallying cry and gave the divided country yet another issue for bitter argument. Both *Time* and *Newsweek* ran cover articles on the Big Three anchormen under siege by the White House, legitimizing the question of whether they had too much power. Agnew, a former Maryland governor, was transformed from an obscure vice president into the party's most popular fund-raiser. Wherever he was scheduled to speak, especially about the media, his appearances were certain sellouts. It was like a Coney Island freak show: Come hear Agnew whip on the press! Red meat guaranteed! Nobody knows where his tongue shall go! The networks received hundreds of thousands of letters, telegrams, and telephone calls denouncing them as un-American. CBS News reported in December 1969 that it had never received so much feedback on an issue, and that the messages were running five to one in favor of Agnew's position.

Under Colson's leadership the White House investigated Cronkite's public utterances, hoping to expose him as a Kennedy liberal masquerading as an objective journalist. When Colson analyzed Cronkite's *CBS Evening News* broadcasts, he struggled to strike gold. But when Colson read transcripts of Cronkite's CBS Radio News broadcasts, which he had started doing in the early 1960s, the anchorman lit up like a Christmas tree. President Johnson had once quipped that if Cronkite had the audacity to say on TV what he said on his radio program, "there would be revolution in the streets." Colson was on the hunt, his rifle scope aimed at Cronkite's back.

The most controversial transcript Colson read was Cronkite's CBS Radio News broadcast in December 1969 that criticized the U.S. government for the 1968 My Lai tragedy, in which hundreds of South Vietnamese civilians were brutally murdered by U.S. Army soldiers belonging to Charlie Company, Eleventh Brigade, Americal Division. Cronkite editorialized aloud why more Americans weren't livid with the U.S. Army for trying to cover up the massacre. Discontented with the narrow confines of the *CBS Evening News*, Cronkite sowed his wild oats, as Friendly had suggested back in 1966, on his radio broadcasts. It was sort of the five-minute broadcast version of I. F. Stone's newsletter.

Sensing that the *CBS Evening News* wasn't the place to praise reporter Seymour M. Hersh for breaking the news of My Lai, Cronkite could nevertheless lend support for his impeccable research on his radio soapbox.

Decades later, Cronkite admitted that Colson wasn't wrong to interpret his CBS radio commentary as profoundly antiwar analysis. "I was certainly always amazed by what I got by with on the radio and why it never caught up with me," Cronkite reflected, "because I lashed out on the radio." Not only was Cronkite liberal on his radio show, but he also attacked the Nixon administration with some regularity for abandoning the poor, race-baiting, and violating the U.S. Constitution—not lighthearted stuff. "I thought that some day the roof was going to fall in," Cronkite laughed years later. "Somebody was going to write a big piece in the newspaper or something. I don't know why to this day I got away with it! We just got deeper and deeper and went further and further testing the waters and I never got called on it."

The horror of Nixon's continuation of the Vietnam War obliged Cronkite to become a left-leaning CBS Radio editorializer, which raises the question: how *did* he get away with such over-the-top commentary full of pro-Democratic partisanship? The "fun part of it," Cronkite maintained, was taunting Nixon and Colson to come after him. They tried. But after reading a batch of Cronkite's radio broadcasts, it became obvious to Colson that the anchorman used generic qualifiers to protect himself from slander. Lines like "people feel that" or "it is believed by some people" were routinely used by Cronkite to provide plausible deniability.

The war between the White House and CBS News had deteriorated into litigation. CBS News reporter Daniel Schorr accused Pat Buchanan's brother, Henry, of laundering money on behalf of the Nixon administration. That was no small story. In May 1973, Cronkite ran this as the lead story on the *Evening News*. Henry Buchanan brought a libel suit against Cronkite. Following the money was complicated; there was never sufficient evidence against Buchanan to prove his guilt. CBS News assembled a hotshot legal team to flog the Buchanans in court and clung to *The New York Times Co. v. Sullivan* case (in which the Supreme Court held that libel or defamation could be proved only if a publisher had prior knowledge that printed information was false or otherwise acted with a reckless disregard for the truth) as its defense. Henry Buchanan was a de facto public figure, and therefore malice had to be proved for Cronkite and Schorr to be guilty of libel. The whole lawsuit ended in a stalemate. "The Cronkite-Schorr charge against my brother was false," a still-irate Pat Buchanan maintained over forty years after the case had disappeared. "History proves it was false."

In February 1970, the White House, newly incensed by a perceived slight by David Brinkley on TV in regard to the defense budget, returned to its original plan of maligning the Big Three. "Concentrate on NBC," White House chief of staff H. R. Haldeman ordered Jeb Magruder, working under the umbrella of Nixon, "and give some real thought as to how to handle the problem that they have created in their almost totally negative approach to everything the Administration does." It appeared Nixon was gaining the upper hand, but not on Cronkite. Many journalists were timid about not ruffling White House feathers. They didn't want to get slimed by Agnew. *The New Yorker* printed a rare, five-page editorial denouncing the new journalistic environment. "In hundreds of tiny ways," the esteemed magazine charged, "news coverage now seems to reflect an eagerness to please the people in power." In March 1970, Cronkite agreed in an on-air interview with *The New Yorker*'s premise. "I feel that perhaps subconsciously," he said, "things are happening, but I'm trying to rise above it. But I think the industry as a whole is intimidated. Yes, I think that was the intention and I think it worked."

Six months previously, the *CBS Evening News* had broadcast footage of a South Vietnamese soldier stabbing an unarmed Vietcong prisoner to death in the hamlet of Bau Me. It was powerful stuff, showing the soldier knifing the prisoner in the side, laboriously pulling the blade out and then stabbing the prisoner's stomach. Cronkite had made a real commitment to the story. In spring 1970 a sudden spate of newspaper columns charged that the incident was staged and that fakery was a common practice on the network news shows. Cronkite considered this "an undercover campaign to discredit CBS News." He suspected the Nixon administration was trying to build support for its latest commitment to the South Vietnamese army and had fed themes and half-truths to columnists. White House director of communications Herb Klein, a former reporter for *The San Diego Union-Tribune*, was the troublemaking culprit for CBS News.

Under Cronkite's marching orders, CBS News reinvestigated the Bau Me footage and located the South Vietnamese soldier who had killed the prisoner. The soldier admitted to knifing the Vietcong guerrilla but claimed it was an act of self-defense, as the man was reaching for a gun lying nearby. The CBS News film showed that another prisoner had been reaching for the weapon. The *Evening News* reran the original story.

Afterward, Cronkite did not try to disguise his attitude. "We broadcast the original story," he said starkly, "in the belief it told something about the nature of the war in Vietnam. What has happened since then tells something about the Government and its relations with news media which carry stories the Government finds disagreeable."

In late 1970, CBS president Frank Stanton received a letter from Senator J. William Fulbright (D-Ark.), who informed him that the Pentagon itself was guilty of the very artifice the White House had accused CBS News of: "fraudulent press practices." Fulbright described incidents staged by the Department of Defense to provide film supporting its war policies. Determined to embarrass Secretary of Defense Melvin Laird, Fulbright detailed his charges in his 1970 book *The Pentagon Propaganda Machine*. CBS News subsequently produced a *CBS Reports* documentary, titled "The Selling of the Pentagon," about the Defense Department's propaganda activities. Its investigation exposed how the Pentagon wasted huge sums of taxpayer money to promote what President Eisenhower had called the military-industrial complex. CBS News had acquired from DoD's public affairs office all the anti-communist propaganda films made by the department in the cold war.

One segment included a clip from a U.S. military film espousing a Red Scare ethos that smacked of McCarthyism (or so it seemed to the 1970s youth). Called *The Eagle's Talon*, the 1962 Pentagon propaganda film warned that "an aggressive Communist tide has spread in Europe and Asia to engulf its neighbors. Communist China even now has plans to dominate Asia by mass murder—destroying ancient civilizations." The narrator for *The Eagle's Talon* was none other than Walter Cronkite. His distinctive voice lent a measure of credibility to the harsh anti-communist opinions delivered in the DoD film. This uncomfortable fact was going to be highlighted in "The Selling of the Pentagon," narrated by Roger Mudd and scheduled to air on February 23, 1971.

With the documentary a lock, someone had to inform Cronkite that this old footage was going to be aired . . . and that he looked and sounded like an idiot in *The Eagle's Talon*. But no one jumped up to volunteer. The problem was discussed at some length, and finally Gordon Manning, vice president of the CBS news division, was assigned the task of telling Cronkite during a long overseas trip the two were taking. But somehow, Manning never found the right time to bring it up.

Dick Salant, CBS News president, then stepped up. He screened the *CBS Reports* documentary with

Cronkite and Peter Davis, its producer. "Fine job," Cronkite said to Davis afterward, as the lights were turned on. "All right," Cronkite then said to Salant, in self-defense, "get that piece out of there."

Recognizing the frangibility of CBS News' position, Salant replied that *The Eagle's Talon* clip had to stay in. Cronkite, to put it mildly, wasn't a happy camper. "It seemed to some," recalled Bill Leonard, "Walter included, that we were going out of our way to inflict damage on ourselves in public if we included a clip from that film in 'The Selling of the Pentagon.'" The reason Cronkite's 1962 flacking for anti-communism couldn't be excised, Salant maintained, was that the Nixon White House would come roaring back at them for hypocrisy. After all, the Pentagon had provided a print of *The Eagle's Talon* to CBS in its shipment of propaganda films. The die was cast. "You can be sure," Leonard wrote, "it would have been a part of the ammunition hurled at CBS if we had suppressed it."

Cronkite's narration, a patriotic gesture in 1962 when Kennedy's New Frontiersmen were in charge, nine years later reeked of Nixonian anti-communist propaganda. Everybody knew that Cronkite was partial to NASA. But had he also been in the tank with McNamara? Was he a Kennedy patsy? The documentary left that unfortunate impression. Cronkite had lent his coveted voice to all sorts of documentary projects in the early 1960s. Every museum imaginable had asked him to narrate multimedia exhibits. Residual fallout from "The Selling of the Pentagon," it seemed, was the price he paid for those lucrative Kennedy-era commissions. How Cronkite wished in 1971 that he could be edited out of the embarrassing documentary. "I felt that I was being singled out," Cronkite complained. "In fact, a lot of people had done those films. It was a popular thing to do in Washington. They made it appear as if I was the only one that did it, and I didn't think that was fair."

Cronkite held a long grudge against Mudd for agreeing to narrate "The Selling of the Pentagon." Andy Rooney thought it cost Mudd the *CBS Evening News* anchor chair when Cronkite retired. It was all beyond embarrassing to Cronkite. There he was, a civilian broadcaster, dressed in the full uniform of a U.S. Marine colonel, narrating gobbledy-gook about the "Red Threat." Not that he was averse to the documentary's central message: that responsible citizens should consider what the government tells them and, if warranted, take the trouble to question it. On a *CBS Evening News* broadcast, Cronkite delivered one of the shortest editorial commentaries on record, no doubt spontaneously. Jack Gould mockingly described it in *The New York Times*. "Walter Cronkite," he wrote, "one of the anchormen most careful in keeping himself out of the news personally, on Tuesday night reported the involved, convoluted language used by the military to explain American air strikes in Indochina. 'Oh,' Cronkite said, after a pregnant pause." One word shorter than his "Oh, boy" outburst when Armstrong walked on the Moon.

In a public lecture, Cronkite spoke of the widening of the Vietnam War into Laos to illustrate why TV news was an essential part of democracy. CBS News had reported on illegal U.S. military engagement in Laos. The Nixon administration, hoping these true accounts would fizzle out, denied them. Conservatives claimed that the *CBS Evening News* had fabricated the Laos story to embarrass the president, an accusation that left Cronkite incredulous. "There are a couple of hundred correspondents in Vietnam who have reported it," Cronkite said in a speech to the Economic Club of Detroit. "Now does anybody seriously think they're sitting in a back room in Vietnam somewhere . . . saying 'Listen, let's put Americans in Laos this week. That'll be a whale of a story. Let's do that.' . . . Does anybody believe the press can sit there and dream that up? And yet people say, 'Are we really in Laos? I mean because the administration hasn't said we're there.' Well, I think we better start believing the press again."

On five or six occasions, to soften his stock image as an Eastern establishment figure at odds with the Nixon administration, Cronkite opened his personal life to magazines and newspapers. Everyone, it seemed, wanted to spend time with Walter and Betsy. When cavorting with reporters, Cronkite preferred dining on loaded-up cheeseburgers at P.J. Clarke's to discuss the circus aspects of American political life. His two favorite interview venues were his CBS News office or The Slate, a popular CBS News hangout on the West Side with low ceilings, sawdust on the wooden floors, and a homestyle menu. Best of all, Seymour Rand, the proprietor, allowed Cronkite to run up a huge tab. At times he'd even tell Cronkite that drinks were on the house—music to the tight-walleted anchorman's ears.

Including Betsy in profiles, to prove that Cronkite was a family man, was the norm. But her quick wit didn't always help his cause. Betsy's barbs at First Lady Pat Nixon sometimes reappeared in the tabloids. One example: When a group of Republican women Betsy was with discussed Richard Nixon's defeat by Pat Brown for the California governorship in November 1962, a sympathetic female friend cooed, "I felt sorry for Pat Nixon last night." To which Betsy caustically responded, "I feel sorry for her every night." Defending Betsy's mouth, Cronkite called his wife's comment "the definitive observation on Dick Nixon."

The two—Walter and Betsy—saw a dull New York evening as a shared tragedy. The gregarious couple often took in shows at the Copacabana and dined at hotel restaurants such as the Café Carlyle and the Waldorf-Astoria. Elaine's on Second Avenue became one of their favorite spots. They sometimes arranged for all three of their kids—or just one of them—to swing by the CBS News studio to watch Dad's nightly broadcast live. If they made so much as a peep during taping, they would be quickly ushered away, barred from the studio for months as punishment. Some nights, the family would then go out to dinner at Gallagher's Steak House or the 21 Club or Sardi's post-broadcast. Broadway plays were also a great family night out, and after CBS bought 80 percent of the Yankees baseball team in 1964, Cronkite would take Chip on the subway to the stadium for the games.

Nancy, Cronkite's eldest child, had been a student at Syracuse University, but she left early to marry. Younger daughter Kathy was a sophomore at Prescott College in Arizona and married a fellow student there in June 1970. Chip, at thirteen, lived at home and attended private school in Manhattan. Perks came with having a famous father, but there were downsides, too. The three Cronkite kids often bemoaned the fact that their world-beat dad wasn't home enough. "When I was little, I always used to sit in front of the television and scream, 'Daddy, out of the box!' " Nancy Cronkite recalled. " 'Daddy, come home!' " One time, Cronkite sat little Nancy down to try to explain what CBS News did, how TV was a miracle of modern communication. "Dad explained to me all about how television works," she said. "I was just a little tot, and he went on and on about how the airwaves go out. I was nodding and agreeing, and at the end of this explanation, I asked him, 'But, Daddy, how do you get in the box?' "

During the early 1970s, Cronkite cut a deal with Pan Am airlines to fly the entire family to a series of international vacation spots. His friend Louis Player, a vice president at the airline, made the arrangements. Other families who went along were James and Mari Michener, Art and Ann Buchwald, and Bob and Millie Considine. Together they island-hopped the South Pacific, and Michener took them to Papeete (the region that inspired his Pulitzer Prize–winning *Tales of the South Pacific*). Michener was a Quaker and a pacifist; Cronkite saw himself heading down the same spiritual highway. On a different junket, The Group, as they called themselves, journeyed to Haiti. They were like a gigantic *National Geographic* field trip around the globe. "Dad loved to snorkel and swim," Chip recalled. "He had a Leica with him and took all sorts of family photos. Sometimes the adults would drink doubles of whatever they could find. Dad and Art liked playing chess. Michener and I played Frisbee together all the time. He wrote about it in his book *Sports in America*."

When Salant heard about the Pan Am junket, he was understandably upset. The trips were a conflict of interest. It was the first time Salant had seen Cronkite display bad ethical judgment. Cronkite defended himself, saying it had just been something between friends, but Salant wouldn't buy it. "Walter had broken a 'no, no, no' rule," Bill Small, Washington bureau chief, recalled. "He caught flak over it. But Walter was the eight-hundred-pound gorilla in the CBS room. You couldn't fire him."

Cronkite was earning about $250,000 a year in 1970 as anchorman of the *CBS Evening News*. The U.S. median income that year was $8,730. After he won the prestigious William Allen White Medal for Outstanding Journalistic Merit, honors continued to pour in, so much so that a competition ensued between Cronkite and the economist John Kenneth Galbraith and the historian Arthur Schlesinger Jr. over who could win the most honorary doctorates. And Cronkite didn't rest on his cascade of laurels. He continued to dig out stories and gossip by telephone with his old Washington sources, which were, most often, at the Cabinet and congressional committee chair level.

In the spring of 1970, Cronkite sparred with the Nixon administration yet again. The Justice Department had brought charges against *New York Times* reporter Earl Caldwell, who had refused to provide grand jury testimony on his reporting on the Black Panther Party. "Walter Cronkite was one of the first people to come forward," Caldwell recalled in 2002, "to issue a statement that we would take into court arguing why you can't [force journalists to reveal sources] and why it was wrong what the government was forcing me to do."

Once again, Cronkite had spoken out to defend journalism. With Brinkley under siege from the Nixon administration, Cronkite assumed Edward R. Murrow's mantle, worried that television was usurping newspaper readership. "In doing my work, I (and those who assist me) depend constantly on information, ideas, leads and opinions received in confidence," Cronkite wrote in a letter to the editor of *The New York Times*. "Without such materials, I would be able to do little more than broadcast press releases and public statements."

Cronkite's *Times* letter was repeatedly entered into the proceedings as the Caldwell case made its way through the courts. It served as a reference for all reporters in need of legal protection. It was Murrowism without Murrow. Moreover, in interviews, Cronkite, keeping his fingers crossed, swore that if he were ever in Caldwell's position, he would go to prison before he'd reveal confidential sources. His outspokenness lent solidarity to journalists and restated a standard, one that many reporters would act upon. The Supreme Court decided against Caldwell—that is, against the right of reporters to keep sources secret. Now the specter of prison did loom for investigative journalists. Cronkite lamented the court's retrograde radicalism. More than any other journalist of the early 1970s, Cronkite absorbed the Nixon administration's anti-journalism punches without getting a scratch. Long before the term was applied to Ronald Reagan, Cronkite was "Teflon."

In May 1971, Cronkite received the Broadcaster of the Year Award from the International Radio and Television Society at a Waldorf-Astoria Hotel ceremony. Hundreds of people from the upper echelon of the media world were in attendance. Cronkite graciously accepted the coveted award and then surprised his audience by eviscerating the Nixon administration's assault on TV journalism. Speaking as a private citizen, he accused the Nixon-Agnew cabal

THE NIXON-VERSUS-CBS WAR · 767

of being perpetrators of an unwarranted "anti-press policy . . . a grand conspiracy to destroy the credibility of the press." Cronkite was the Muhammad Ali of American journalism and every verbal punch he threw was greeted with hoots, hollers, and cheers. "Nor is there any way," he continued, "that President Nixon can escape responsibility for this campaign. He is the ultimate leader. He sets the tone and the attitude of his administration. By internal edict and public posture, he could reverse the anti-press policy of his administration if that were his desire. As long as the attacks, overt and subtle, continue, we must even at the risk of appearing to be self-serving, rise to defend ourselves against the charges by which the enemies of freedom seek to influence a divided and confused population." Murrow would have been proud.

At the 1972 Radio and TV Correspondents Dinner, Pat Buchanan was talking amiably to a friend over cocktails when he was unexpectedly introduced to Cronkite—an archenemy of the Nixon's administration. "Hello, Pat, how are you?" Cronkite asked, hand extended.

"Fine, Mr. Cronkite," Buchanan said with deference, "how are you, sir?"

For days, Buchanan was disgusted with himself for having kissed up to Cronkite. He treated the *CBS*

Evening News anchorman as if he were royalty. "I was beside myself for giving the appearance of having truckled," Buchanan recalled. "Both the 'Mr.' and the 'sir' had come out automatically, reflexively, because Walter Cronkite was an older man, and because of those years of indoctrination."

27.
Reportable Truth in
the Age of Nixon

CHANNELING MURROW—THE PENTAGON PAPERS—
TRACKING DOWN ELLSBERG—DR. STANTON GOES
BEFORE CONGRESS—MAGRUDER PLAYS DIRTY—THE
NEWS TWISTERS—COLSON STAKES NIXON—BUNDLING
UP—THE GREAT OPENING OF CHINA—TOURING WITH
BUCKLEY AND MICHENER—STIFFING BARBARA
WALTERS—TABLOID FODDER IN SAN FRANCISCO—
POLITICAL CONVENTIONS—MCGOVERN'S VP—THE
STANHOPE GOULD FACTOR—RUSSIAN WHEAT DEAL—
WATERGATE BRAVERY—THE MOST TRUSTED MAN IN
AMERICA—COLSON AGONISTES—DISSED FROM THE
ENEMIES LIST

Cronkite's verbal barrage at the Waldorf-Astoria
was merely opening day of the fourth estate's
hunting season on Nixon, a season in which almost

every big-city newsroom was loaded for bear. Nixon had failed to heed the oldest and truest cliché in journalism: never get into a pissing match with folks who buy ink by the barrel (or air hourlong special reports on prime-time TV). When Cronkite spoke out against Nixon's ham-fisted intimidation at the Waldorf-Astoria, it was as if the ghost of Murrow hurled a lightning bolt from the podium. It didn't hurt that Cronkite's close friends included Arthur Ochs Sulzberger, publisher of *The New York Times*, and Katharine Graham, publisher of *The Washington Post*. Nixon, of course, wasn't wrong about a liberal media elite disapproving of social conservatives. But unlike Eisenhower—who simply ignored his bad press—Nixon wanted blood. "Seventy-five percent of those group hate my guts," he confided to White House press secretary Ron Ziegler on Christmas Eve 1970, about the Big Three network reporters. "They don't like to be beaten."

Just how appreciative other journalists were that Cronkite stood up for his profession became apparent when he won the George C. Polk Award (named for a CBS correspondent killed during civil strife in Greece in 1948) for resisting White House attempts to discredit the *CBS Evening News* for its disclosure of the Bau Me atrocity. The Polk Award coincided with

Paley's announcement that CBS was bringing back *You Are There*, the dramatic historic reenactment series of the 1950s, as a Saturday morning children's show, with Cronkite once again serving as host. Not only was Cronkite winning over converts in his battle with the Nixon crowd, but he was now courting a future generation of children with the beloved Bugs Bunny as his lead-in. Sick of all things Cronkite, the White House kept looking for clever ways to undermine his sterling credibility with the public.

It was a document leak, in the end, that turned the White House attack on CBS News into trench warfare over journalism's enduring role in the American republic. In 1971, Daniel Ellsberg, a Harvard-educated military analyst with the Rand Corporation, absconded with a photocopy of a Pentagon report titled *United States–Vietnam Relations, 1945–1967: A Study Prepared by the Department of the Defense*. It was classified top secret, with only fifteen copies printed. Ellsberg described the Pentagon Papers, as the report became known to the public, as "seven thousand pages of documentary evidence of lying by four presidents and their administrations over twenty-three years, to conceal plans and actions of mass murder." The report charted decades of Department of Defense misinformation, focusing most on the mendacity of the Johnson administration, which dictated Pentagon policies at the time the report was written. "I decided I would stop concealing that myself," Ellsberg wrote. "I would get it out somehow."

After serving in the Marine Corps from 1954 to 1957, Ellsberg had received a doctorate in economics from Harvard in 1962 while working for the Rand Corporation. An authority on decision theory and behavioral economics, he began work in 1964 as special assistant in the Defense and State departments. He returned to Rand in 1967 to work on the top-secret Pentagon Papers. What Ellsberg learned was that the Vietcong weren't going to collapse soon, that they were stronger than ever. When the upbeat Johnson administration hawk Walter Rostow, LBJ's national security advisor, gave Ellsberg an insanely optimistic account of imminent victory in Vietnam, the strategist balked. "I don't want to hear it," Ellsberg scolded Rostow. "Victory is not near. Victory is very far away. I've come back from Vietnam. I've been there for two years. I don't want to talk about it. I don't want to see charts . . ."

"But, Dan, the charts are very good."

Ellsberg had first turned against U.S. policy in Vietnam in early 1967. Too many American troops were being slaughtered for a gargantuan Johnson administration policy mistake now being exacerbated by the Nixon crew. "A line kept repeating itself in my head," he recalled in his memoir, *Secrets*: "We are eating our young." Ellsberg was also galled that the Nixon White House, spinning a web of distortions, had manipulated decision making in Congress and among the American people. Offered a first look at the Pentagon Papers, *New York Times* reporter Neil Sheehan and his legendary editor Abe Rosenthal made the courageous decision to publish excerpts from them, beginning on June 13, 1971. If it meant the end of the Vietnam War, Ellsberg was ready to go to jail. He went into hiding to escape the long arm of the FBI. Cronkite thought Ellsberg brave; others concluded he was a little nuts. Charles Colson, special counsel to President Nixon, started spreading rumors that Ellsberg was a sexual pervert who shot children from helicopters in Vietnam for sport—real ugly stuff. "Colson is a liar," Ellsberg argued in his defense. "Years later, after he went to prison and wrote *Born Again*, he claimed to have apologized to me. That was a lie. I tried to reach him on four or five occasions. His secretary would take down my number. But he wouldn't get back to me."

Nixon was not implicated in the Pentagon Papers (which were written before he took office), but his administration struck back hard, obtaining a court order to force *The New York Times* to cease publication of the illegally obtained documents—the first time the U.S. government had gagged a newspaper in more than a hundred years. The classified documents contained shocking proof of deliberate government malfeasance. But there was a shrill disagreement over the ethics of Ellsberg's action; some argued that the leak potentially aided the enemy, but others that the First Amendment protected a free press. During the second half of June 1971, the Pentagon Papers became a lightning rod in an already charged and polarized America. *CBS Evening News* covered the story heavily, with Cronkite interviewing many people about the explosive government documentation of the Vietnam War.

The Pentagon Papers leak lacked the key elements of effective television news: action and clarity. The enticing fascination of the Department of Defense documents lay in their mountains of detail, in which academics, not TV viewers, revel. When Ellsberg offered NBC News and ABC News a chance to release a portion of the Pentagon Papers, both flat-out turned him down. The documents were radioactive. Disseminating the report would take a network into precarious legal territory as well as dangerously dull television. Another reason NBC said no was that its news division was in flux: Chet Huntley had retired in 1970 and David

Brinkley was in the process of retiring. Ellsberg went to CBS News, home of *60 Minutes*, hoping it would have the guts to air explosive revelations. If Cronkite deemed it okay to report the Pentagon Papers—secret government deliberations about the Vietnam War— then a pack of journalists would follow suit. "We'd done what we could with them on the air," Cronkite recalled. "We wanted to interview Daniel Ellsberg, but he was on the lam from the FBI."

Mid-June also saw CBS embroiled in its own First Amendment struggle. Longtime CBS president (and trustee of the Rand Corporation) Dr. Frank Stanton was facing serious legal consequences over "The Selling of the Pentagon." Right-wing politicos charged that the *CBS Reports* documentary had been deliberately unfair, even doctoring quotes to distort the story. A subcommittee of the House Committee on Interstate and Foreign Commerce subpoenaed Stanton and the CBS News Department, demanding that they turn over outtakes and extra footage. Stanton, in a heroic First Amendment stand, refused, personally accepting the consequences. He would be exonerated, but as of mid-June 1971, there was a very real possibility that CBS's president would go to jail for contempt of Congress.

Given Stanton's situation, CBS might well have been wary of interviewing Ellsberg. Contact with the outlaw could potentially put the network in further legal jeopardy. It would certainly anger the committee members charged with deciding Stanton's fate. Even so, the *CBS Evening News* couldn't resist the scoop: the first televised interview with Ellsberg. Gordon Manning, CBS's vice president for hard news, negotiated with Ellsberg on two occasions, a cloak-and-dagger process involving clandestine meetings and communication by code. Reading parts of the Pentagon Papers over the air, as Ellsberg wanted, was impossible, but Manning arranged an exclusive interview with the fugitive for CBS News.

Cronkite remembered the advance work differently, claiming in *A Reporter's Life* that he used a personal connection with Ellsberg's family to land the interview. Nobody in America circa 1971 had a better Rolodex than Cronkite. He was encyclopedic about the comings and goings of bluebloods, military officers, and corporate CEOs. He made it his habit to trade in career updates, summer vacation plans, and casual gossip with the rich and otherwise powerful in American life. While other journalists were trying to fathom the real Ellsberg, Cronkite already knew: the now former Rand analyst was married to Patricia Marx, the daughter of Louis Marx, who with his brother had founded Marx Toys in New York City in 1919. As the FBI launched

REPORTABLE TRUTH IN THE AGE OF NIXON · 777

an all-points-bulletin manhunt for Ellsberg, Cronkite simply called a Marx family member from Lake Placid, while on assignment. It was a warm exchange. An arrangement was made for Gordon Manning to have a secret rendezvous with Ellsberg, who kept changing locations, in Cambridge. Cronkite, once protocol was set, wanted to quietly slip into town, allow himself to be blindfolded, and be whisked away to a secret location.

The fifty-four-year-old Cronkite was acting like a cub wire service reporter for the United Press or Scripps-Howard, hungry for an edgy exclusive. That very evening, Manning received a telephone call. Speaking in the cryptic language of espionage, a "Mr. Boston" said a taped interview with Cronkite "might be possible." The Old Library building on Harvard's campus near midnight was chosen as a rendezvous spot. Manning met with Mr. Boston, a college-age antiwar leader, who drove him to a Cambridge cottage where the Pentagon Papers (wrapped in brown paper and tied with string) were hidden. Arrangements were made for Cronkite to interview Ellsberg—the White House's number one enemy—the next afternoon, at the Massachusetts hideaway. Dick Salant worried that CBS News would be accused of aiding and abetting a fugitive, but the network's lawyers reassured him not to worry.

"I was proud of Cronkite for his Vietnam stalemate report in February 1968," Ellsberg recalled. "I was in D.C. at the time working as staff for Secretary of Defense Clark Clifford. When I had come back from Vietnam in 1967 with hepatitis, I had one goal: to get people to understand that Vietnam was a *stalemate*. President Johnson had given a direct order never to say *stalemate*. It was taboo. When Cronkite said the word, it meant a lot. So I wanted Cronkite to do the Pentagon Papers interview because he was the most famous journalist in America."

Cronkite, like a character in a John le Carré novel, was directed to meet a contact for Ellsberg in the lobby of the Commander Hotel in Cambridge on June 23 (the very day Stanton appeared before the Senate subcommittee). The hotel manager immediately recognized the famous CBS anchor and tried to be helpful, interrupting Cronkite's attempt to case the lobby for his secret contact. Cronkite felt like he was on an undercover operation that was going to backfire. He talked with the manager about where he might make a telephone call. The pay phone was downstairs, next to the bathrooms. Cronkite, afraid that his waiting around could be interpreted as looking for a "homosexual pickup," was starting to second-guess himself. "There were many amateurish aspects to the plot," Cronkite later said, laughing, "but the most obvious never occurred to any of us. It turned out to be pretty difficult for the anchorperson of the most popular television news broadcast in America to go incognito."

A young man finally made eye contact with Cronkite, who instinctively followed him out to the street. The FBI couldn't find Ellsberg, but after a cloak-and-dagger rendezvous worthy of spy intrigue, Cronkite could; that made him chuckle. Now in a get-away car and in the hands of anti–Vietnam War radicals helping a fugitive, Cronkite was asked to keep his head down so he couldn't retrace the route for the FBI. The car stopped at a nondescript house, and Cronkite went inside to find Manning and two film crews—and the visibly stressed Ellsberg—already waiting. Carefully the two exchanged updates on all things Vietnam. Although Ellsberg had debated Nixon's Cambodia bombing with Senator Bob Dole (R-Kans.) for the TV show *The Advocates*, a public television production of KCET in Los Angeles, he wasn't camera-savvy. The former Defense Department analyst didn't want to speak solely about the Pentagon Papers or his own employment experience in the mid-1960s for President Johnson. Manning and Cronkite argued over how many documents would be read on the air. Determined to end the Vietnam War, Ellsberg wanted to "present at some length to a prime-time national television audience an understanding of Nixon's secret strategy."

Parts of the Cronkite-Ellsberg interview were broadcast on the *CBS Evening News* that day; a longer version was shown on a prime-time special the next evening, June 24. Ellsberg and Manning had collaborated to come up with the perfect CBS stock footage from Vietnam—shot since 1965—to accompany the commentary. Ellsberg's story was full of gaps, and he artfully avoided Cronkite's most probing questions. At times, Ellsberg went into monologue mode (as was his tendency). The CBS anchor didn't push much in the way of follow-ups. When he asked Ellsberg why, at the very moment that President Nixon was winding down the war, he chose to kick the hornet's nest, the fugitive's unsatisfactory answer was, "We are seeing 1964 all over again." What? Cronkite just let the Gulf of Tonkin reference hang. No real news came out of the interview except that Cronkite had tracked down the FBI's most wanted ex-Pentagon official. This was enough to send the White House reeling. Why didn't Cronkite or Manning make a citizen's arrest? Or set up a sting operation with the FBI? A better question was: how could Cronkite find Ellsberg between tennis matches and the FBI couldn't?

Media critics said Cronkite was too gentle interrogating Ellsberg. Pro-war Americans said far worse. The very fact that Cronkite had the temerity to treat Ellsberg as anything more than a traitor irritated thousands of viewers. They didn't give a damn what the treasonous weasel Ellsberg said; the thief should be shot. According to the *National Review*, the Ellsberg interview was part of a liberal plot to undermine the Nixon administration. "It is the anti-Nixon CBS-Establishmentarian Walter Cronkite who got the interview," it editorialized. Criticism from the GOP mounted. "The Columbia Broadcasting System, Inc., led by Walter Cronkite and Eric Sevareid, have almost destroyed this great country," wrote the Kingsport, Tennessee, mayor. "Never have I seen men so dedicated to demoralizing and tearing their country apart. This is due to blind hatred or prejudice of the President and Vice President and seemingly sanctioned by president Frank Stanton of CBS."

While Cronkite was beloved for his *Apollo 11* commentary, his cozy interview with Ellsberg infuriated many conservatives throughout the Midwest, the South, and the West. Owners of CBS affiliates threw conniptions. The hate mail that Black Rock received multiplied and became more vicious. In June 1971, *TV Guide* journalist Edith Efron, an Ayn Rand acolyte, published a book titled *The News Twisters.* Underwritten by the little-known Historical Research Foundation (which gave grants to authors with conservative themes), *The News Twisters* followed Nixon White House henchman Jeb Magruder's strategy to "arrange for an exposé" to be written by pro-Nixon scribes Earl Mazo or Victor Lasky. Published simultaneously in hardcover and paperback, *The News Twisters* became a bestseller, with a blurb from the president himself. Once on the *New York Times* bestseller list, Magruder believed, the book would find its own readership.

The News Twisters begins by excoriating Cronkite. Based on Efron's study of the three network evening news programs over a seven-week span in the fall of 1968, the book concluded that 31 percent of the material presented on the *CBS Evening News* was opinion. Efron found that NBC was slanted 18 percent of the time, and ABC, because it devoted more time to designated commentators, 48 percent. CBS countered *The News Twisters* by commissioning a study from a nominally independent organization (headed by former CBS director Ed Bliss Jr.) at American University. It examined the *Evening News* over the same span and found, not surprisingly, that the program was entirely objective. Cronkite, in other words, was given a clean bill of health when the study was released in 1974.

After the first round of confrontation over Ellsberg, the Nixon administration decided that CBS News, not NBC News, was the bigger threat. The White House now targeted Cronkite. The anchorman had gotten under Nixon's skin. In his Watergate memoir, *Witness to Power*, White House counsel for domestic affairs John Ehrlichman wrote of how the president was now obsessed with Cronkite. "I have watched Nixon spend a morning designing Walter Cronkite's lead story for that evening," he recalled, "then send it to Ron Ziegler, Kissinger or me, to send out to a press briefing to deliver it in such a way that Walter Cronkite simply could not ignore it."

Magruder and Colson were flummoxed over how best to take the avuncular Cronkite down a notch. On September 30, 1971, Cronkite testified before the Senate Subcommittee on Constitutional Rights, which, under Senator Sam J. Ervin Jr. (D-N.C.), was very supportive of the press. With unblinking directness, Cronkite lambasted the Nixon administration for curtailing First Amendment rights "by fiat, by assumption, and by intimidation and harassment." CBS News continued to hold its substantial lead over NBC News in the Nielsen ratings for evening news. Cronkite was quoted as saying "ratings didn't matter," but his attitude was different in the newsroom, where he could be heard to mutter darkly—or yell—when another network gained a point.

After Chet Huntley retired in 1970, *The Huntley-Brinkley Report* (renamed the *NBC Nightly News*) faltered. Still Cronkite's major competitor, the NBC news program had difficulty finding the right anchor replacement before eventually settling on John Chancellor, a former *Today* host and correspondent for *The Huntley-Brinkley Report*. Cronkite considered Chancellor, a fellow college dropout with whom he served as co-inquisitor for the fourth Kennedy-Nixon debate, merely a safe bet for NBC News, not a potential usurper of his ratings supremacy. On December 10, 1971, a confident Dick Salant, just in time for Christmas, promoted everyone at CBS News in a single memo: Bill Leonard and Gordon Manning (senior vice presidents), Sandy Socolow and Bill Small (vice presidents), Russ Bensley (executive producer of the *Evening News*), and John Lane and Ed Fouhy (producers for Cronkite). Instead of having CBS News on the run, the Nixon administration had pressboys ascending en masse up the ladder of success.

By January 1972, the Nixon White House seemed less interested in destroying Cronkite than in having his swarm of disciples at CBS News cool their jets. It was an election year, and Nixon understandably wanted less antagonism with the fourth estate. If a scorched-earth war with CBS News, or any other journalism organization, became a central campaign issue, he might be doomed in November. Better the press should focus on the president's surprise trip to the People's Republic of China. But on February 13, President Nixon had an Oval Office meeting with Charles Colson, his valet Manolo Sanchez, and scheduler Stephen B. Bull about how to keep CBS News from further attacking the administration's Southeast Asia policies. A recent *CBS Evening News* broadcast—echoing Cronkite's testimony before the Senate Subcommittee—had questioned the ethics of the White House's attempts to try to control the media.

Nixon: Cronkite is one of the worst offenders.

Colson: Oh that Cronkite interview, Mr. President . . . I sent you the transcript of that report before it got on the news. It will be somewhere in your reading material. It is the most incredible transcript I have ever read in my life. I mean, he describes the evil influence of this administration and he talks about how we're intimidating advertisers and how we're trying to get advertisers not to advertise with CBS.

Nixon: I saw that. Jesus . . .

Colson: Talk about saying "ghosts under the bed."

Nixon: Have we ever influenced CBS?

Colson: No. But, see that's just creating a complete red herring and that shows you how dishonest the man is. He is basically a dishonest person.

Cronkite knew that Nixon was a brilliant political strategist. He thought the president's decision to visit China in the spring of 1972 was a stroke of genius. But Cronkite also feared that Nixon had something pathologically wrong with him. As the White House organized its China trip, the role of TV news was pre-eminent for Nixon, who didn't want print reporters with a true understanding of Chinese politics accom-panying him. What he needed was to have Cronkite, Chancellor, and Reasoner singing his praises on TV. At all costs, Nixon believed, reporters needed to refrain from discussing the sharp cold war differ-ences between China and the United States. As Nixon was preparing to break bread with Mao Tse Tung, he didn't need Robert Elegant of *Newsweek*, a China hand, writing magazine cover stories about how the Chairman was responsible for killing sixty or seventy million of his own people.

White House spokesman Ron Ziegler announced that eighty-seven newsmen would accompany President Nixon on his trip to China. Cronkite topped the list, which included twenty-one newspaper writers, six news agency reporters, three columnists, and six magazine correspondents. All journalists gossiped about was the protocol of the White House selection process. When Nixon saw Stanley Karnow of *The Washington Post* on the Ziegler list, he penciled a line through his name, with the added notation "absolutely not." Speculation mounted over Nixon's rationale for choosing reporters. Why did William F. Buckley get a billet when his magazine, *National Review,* had criticized Nixon's China overtures? Who had decided that Joseph Kraft of *The New York Times,* whose telephone had been tapped by the government, was the best liberal columnist to meet Zhou Enlai? The Nixon trip became the inverse of the Enemies List. Which journalists did Nixon (in the parlance of the times) *dig*?

The Nixon administration allowed CBS News to send its A-team reporters to China: Cronkite, Sevareid, Rather, and Bernard Kalb. To prepare for the winter trip, Cronkite shopped at Macy's for a parka, thick socks, and thermal underwear. "I understand it gets bitter cold when the winds whistle down from the China steppes," Cronkite said in early February, justifying his Macy's shopping spree. "I've already bought myself an imitation fur hat with flaps to keep my ears warm." In his memoir *White House Years*, National Security Advisor Henry Kissinger offered a hilarious anecdote about sightseeing amid elegant birch trees by a beautiful still lake near Hangchow, a provincial capital in eastern China. "All was tranquility and repose," Kissinger wrote. "Suddenly, into the picture swaggered Walter Cronkite. He was a little worse for the wear, dressed in heavy furs more appropriate for a polar expedition and weighted down by a spectacular assortment of photographic gear around his neck. Fond as I am of Walter, the scene lost some of its serenity."

In preparation for China, Cronkite had his physician inject him with gamma globulin to boost his immune system and inoculate him against cholera, diphtheria, polio, and influenza. He telephoned the CBS cameramen who were going—Skip Brown, Izzy Bleckman, and Jime Kartes—to make sure they also got shots. Cronkite boarded the red-eye to China from Honolulu with the rest of the lucky reporters. A paranoid Nixon was worried that one of the news-gathering jackasses would queer the trip; it didn't happen. As President Nixon stepped off Air Force One on that cold morning in Beijing to shake hands with the Chinese prime minister, Zhou Enlai, Cronkite swelled with pride. History was being made. But China clearly wasn't paradise. In the coming days, he would assess China's industrialization to be on par with Stalin's Russia in the late 1940s.

An obliging Cronkite wanted to play by the rules established by the Nixon administration in China. It was a matter of living up to his word. "It was very much like landing on the moon," he recalled. "Westerners hadn't been there for years. We were a source of wonderment for the Chinese." Dan Rather, in contrast, ready to break with stricture, was eager to interview the everyday people of Beijing. He was being too much the renegade for Cronkite's taste. Some CBSers trace the beginning of Cronkite's disapproval of his then forty-one-year-old protégé to Rather's aggressive grandstanding in Beijing and Shanghai. China, Cronkite believed, wasn't the place to tick off the Nixon crowd. Nevertheless, Rather did the best stories of any TV journalist in China, stories in a class of their own.

Cronkite's job in China as anchorman was to set the scenes of Nixon's historic trip. The White House froze out all reporters—Cronkite included—from the more serious diplomatic meetings. Much of Cronkite's time was spent with Stanhope Gould, ensuring his broadcast script was constantly fresh and accurate. CBS's makeshift base of operations was the Minzu Hotel, near Tiananmen Square, and after morning meetings, the CBS correspondents fanned out to report from the square, the Forbidden City, or the Great Wall. Bernard Kalb's expertise on China was extraordinary, and Cronkite made great use of it. Whenever Cronkite had a free moment, he spent time with his literary friends James Michener and William F. Buckley. Weighed down with cameras, enjoying each other's company, they goofed around like tourists looking for a giant panda. A competition occurred to tell the worst Barbara Walters stories known to mankind.

The February weather was bitter, snow sometimes swirling about, and Cronkite caught a cold. Guzzling codeine-infused cough syrup, he regularly hit up Bleckman for batteries to keep his socks heated. After wandering along the Great Wall, taking notes in a daybook, Cronkite joked that the greatness of the 2,300-year-old ruin was self-evident: few structures could sustain such a barrage of shutter-happy, historically ignorant Western photographers. Although Cronkite had boned up on Communist China in advance of the trip, he was nevertheless surprised to see what a deity Mao Tse Tung had become, his face plastered on billboards around every bend. "Cronkite spent a lot of free time with Sevareid," CBS cameraman Izzy Bleckman recalled. "That was unusual, but they went together to see the Forbidden City."

CBS News coverage of the trip was solid. But Cronkite knew that Nixon had turned the entire China trip into a staged guided tour cum cocktail hour for the press. By keeping such ironclad control of the schedule, the White House got what it wanted: TV reporters doing soft-news segments on how to use chopsticks, the beauty of Mao jackets, and why bicycling was healthy exercise. Ironically, it had been Cronkite's night in San Francisco, before he flew to Hawaii, that grabbed tabloid attention. Away from Betsy's watchful eye, he had cut loose like a sailor on leave. The rumor mill claimed that he had gone out with a floozy he'd found at a Geary Street strip club. Columnist Herb Caen of the *San Francisco Chronicle* saw Cronkite's partying and wrote a comical dispatch on February 17, 1972. The news raised eyebrows at Black Rock. Cronkite's wild evening out with Manning chasing skirts wasn't great for the serious-news brand. Not only did he and Manning hang out at the Condor, an infamous topless bar, but Cronkite was also later spotted dining with a go-go dancer clad in a miniskirt and barely there crop-top. "I'm a very quiet fellow in New York," Cronkite said in response to the Caen report. "But something gets into me every time I come to San Francisco. It must be the water."

News about Cronkite, the night owl, started appearing in tabloids. Instead of trying to cover up his love of strip clubs, he played up his penchant. Robert F. Kennedy once said, "The wise man hangs a lantern on his problem," an adage that Cronkite understood completely. He already knew what Nixon would learn the hard way during Watergate: the cover-up is often worse than the crime. Half of all European business-men, Cronkite weakly offered in his defense, enjoyed strolling around Amsterdam's red-light district. To him, San Francisco's Condor was the Carnegie Hall of Sex—it didn't hurt to soak up the art once in a while.

To Manhattan socialites, Cronkite letting his hair down was old news. He drank with reporters at Elaine's on Second Avenue; table number six was often reserved for him. Whenever he entered a Manhattan bar, people cheered. Along with Salvador Dalí, Lauren Bacall, and Woody Allen, Cronkite was one of the most easily rec-ognized celebrities who didn't have a bodyguard with him at the Stork Club. But there was a backlash from feminists over Cronkite's San Francisco escapades. Was Uncle Walter a misogynist? While Betsy didn't mind her husband's cruising the Tenderloin district from time to time, Gloria Steinem did. *Boston Globe* columnist Ellen Goodman would claim a few years later that Cronkite didn't understand the vocabulary of feminism or even how to interview women properly. "On a sexism scale of one-to-ten," Goodman wrote,

"Cronkite is only a four or so. I would label him Not Malevolent But a Bit Confused."

Cronkite was in Martha's Vineyard on June 17, 1972, when five men were arrested for breaking into the office of the Democratic National Committee in Washington's Watergate office complex. The biggest political story of the era began inauspiciously. Who could have predicted, that June day, that it would lead to the resignation of a popular U.S. president? CBS News followed the Watergate story briefly, but found it impossible to keep up with Bob Woodward's and Carl Bernstein's aggressive coverage in *The Washington Post*. Cronkite left Watergate to CBS News' Washington bureau. Consumed by election-year politics, the Summer Olympics in Munich (at which eleven Israeli athletes were killed by Arab terrorists), and sailing *Wyntje* to Maine, he followed Watergate in only a low-grade way.

Working closely with CBS News Washington bureau chief Bill Small, Cronkite encouraged his stable of correspondents to follow the suspicious money trail at the Committee for the Re-Election of the President (CRP, or CREEP as it came to be known). George Herman of CBS News' *Face the Nation* deserves credit for airing a program on June 11, 1972 (six days before the burglary took place), questioning John Mitchell—who had resigned as U.S. attorney general to become chairman of CRP—about the undisclosed sources of the $10 million collected by the committee. Much of that money was later found to have been contributed illegally.

Cronkite urged Daniel Schorr (reporting from the Pentagon), Dan Rather (from the White House), and Lesley Stahl (the newbie) to aggressively track down the Nixon administration's role in Watergate. Cronkite was too consumed with half-hour 10:30 p.m. specials on the New Hampshire, Florida, Wisconsin, California, and Oregon primaries to take Watergate on as yet another extracurricular activity. Nevertheless, CBS News won an Emmy for its dramatic early coverage of the break-in. "We were pinching virtually everything from *The Washington Post*," Stanhope Gould recalled. "I became imbued with the spirit of the Watergate thing. I was in bed with *The Washington Post*."

With Watergate simmering in the background, the Big Three struggled to maintain their traditional gavel-to-gavel coverage of the 1972 political conventions, both held in Miami Beach. Political conventions were still Cronkite's favorite assignments after NASA; it was unbeatable exposure. But with the Republican Convention set to call on Nixon-Agnew for a second term, and the Democrats certain to nominate front-runner Senator George McGovern of South Dakota, the conventions didn't promise much suspense. CBS looked hard for subplots, forgoing speeches from the rostrum for possible drama from the floor. Cronkite presided over the events, untangling and explaining them. Critics complained that the 1972 conventions seemed to be mostly about Cronkite. "The program might well be called 'Cronkite and His Friends,'" said one reviewer. CBS News did have one good plot line at the Democratic Convention in Miami: the selection of a vice presidential candidate.

Many Democrats were promoting the notion of Cronkite's becoming McGovern's vice presidential nominee. Stickers and buttons to that effect were manufactured. There was a groundswell of "We Want Cronkite" grassroots lobbying. He was, after all, beloved, credited by liberals with challenging the war hawks LBJ and Nixon. "We had conversations about this," actor Warren Beatty recalled. "One night we had dinner at Frankie and Johnny's restaurant in New York. Our conversation centered on whether he could be in politics—perhaps run for senator of New York—if not vice president." McGovern's campaign director, Frank Mankiewicz, tried to get McGovern to seriously consider Cronkite as VP, but to no avail. "I didn't really give it serious thought at the time," McGovern recalled. "Frank kept saying, 'Don't you realize he is the most respected man in America?' But I just didn't think Walter would be interested in leaving CBS News. It was a nonstarter, an unrealistic fun ten-second thought."

McGovern ended up choosing Missouri senator Thomas Eagleton, but after the senator's past psychiatric problems hit the news cycle, McGovern dropped him two weeks later and replaced him with the former head of the Peace Corps, Sargent Shriver. "If we had picked Cronkite, I could have avoided the whole Eagleton snafu," McGovern later reflected ruefully. "I think Cronkite on the ticket would have made a *major* difference. I should have listened to Frank."

What Cronkite most admired about McGovern, why he would have at least considered being on the Democratic ticket, was his conviction that Nixon's mad B-52 strikes against Hanoi and Haiphong, which were killing tens of thousands of North Vietnamese civilians, were reprehensible. To Cronkite, Nixon's invasion of Cambodia in 1970 and Laos in 1971 would be judged terribly in the annals of history. While Cronkite was pleased that Henry Kissinger and North Vietnamese negotiator Le Duc Tho spent much of 1972 in peace talks, he was also concerned that this news had deepened public apathy.

In September 1972, Cronkite surreptitiously met with Ellsberg again at a private CBS News office. No blindfolding or hotel rendezvous. Ellsberg's gripe was that Cronkite's *Evening News* kept portraying the Nixon administration as getting the United States out of Vietnam, saying that casualties were down, as were the number of U.S. troops on tours of duty. This was a gross oversimplification of the situation. "You keep showing the wind-downs," Ellsberg said to Cronkite. "The two things that aren't going down are the bombing tonnage being dropped—a Nagasaki a week—and the number of refugees." Cronkite was intrigued. They were sitting on opposite sides of a desk with a telephone pushed off to the side.

"Do you have proof?" Cronkite asked.

"All you have to do," Ellsberg instructed, "is call the Pentagon's public affairs office and say you're a journalist who wants the weekly bombing tonnage."

With a glint in his eye, excited to be in Ellsberg's orbit again, Cronkite said *deal me in*. To Cronkite's delight, Ellsberg had the Pentagon public affairs office number on hand. "You call," a nervous Cronkite said. "I don't want to give my name. But I also don't want to pretend I'm somebody else." A bit of comedy ensued. Cronkite, in the end, convinced Ellsberg to call the Pentagon as he listened in. "The Pentagon office gave Cronkite the stats," Ellsberg recalled. He said, " 'That's fascinating.' Next I told him to call Ted Kennedy's office and get the refugee statistics."

Cronkite found Ellsberg to be right on both accounts. The *CBS Evening News* no longer reported only the Vietnam troops' wind-down statistics that the Nixon administration wanted conveyed. On a number of occasions, due directly to Ellsberg's prodding, the bomb tonnage and refugee numbers were also featured on the broadcast.

Cronkite found time for a new type of report in late September 1972, one that easily consumed half of the available minutes in a given *CBS Evening News* program. The innovative format was an in-depth overview of a complex story with detailed follow-up segments. The first to make an impact was a three-part investigative series about the Nixon administration's deal to allow the sale of American wheat to the Soviet Union. The worst drought since 1963 had sent Russian grain buyers to the United States, where they purchased 25 percent of the annual wheat crop in what became known as the U.S.-Soviet Wheat Deal. "Walter decided the Russian wheat deal was the Teapot Dome Scandal," Gould recalled. "I was doing a long profile of McGovern's wife, but Walter pulled me off it. He was all about wheat graft. I came in with a ten- or eleven-minute long-form piece, and he wanted to *add* to it. That much time for one story on the *Evening News* just didn't happen."

For three evenings—September 27 (Wednesday); September 29 (Friday); and October 6 (Friday)— Cronkite, in what *The New York Times* deemed "the most encouraging development in electronic journalism," got up from his anchor chair (for the first time since 1962) to explain charts and graphs that exposed the corrupt aspects of the deal. The segments were expertly produced by Stanhope Gould and Linda Mason. Encouraged by the positive response to the wheat-deal story, including compliments from both R. W. Apple and David Halberstam, he immediately planned another multipart report, this time on Watergate.

Besides the Vietnam woes, Cronkite had been upset that fall that *The Washington Post* (or Woodward and Bernstein) had been eating CBS News' lunch (and everyone else's) on the Watergate story. A few of Cronkite's reporters—notably Daniel Schorr and Lesley Stahl— would collect fresh clues, but Cronkite never got a big story, and for one reason: CBS News never found Deep Throat. In early September, Cronkite called an *Evening News* staff meeting to figure out how to upgrade the importance of the Watergate story. Present at the meeting was executive producer Paul Greenberg (having succeeded Midgley) and producers Ron Bonn and John Lane (who replaced Socolow and Bensley).

The Cronkite unit all agreed that Woodward and Bernstein had the story right; their reporting seemed impeccable. And so Cronkite decided that, rather than let the story die the death of a thousand cuts with fragmentary TV reports, the *CBS Evening News* would do a report about what Woodward and Bernstein had reported. It was a practical decision that Cronkite hated, but he made it because the Watergate story *had* to be told on television to take hold of the public imagination. And it never had been. Cronkite and the producers tentatively decided on two long segments—longer than anything *CBS Evening News* had ever done—to run on successive nights. "Everybody from Walter down wanted to make this look *different*," Bonn recalled, "look *important*—because it was."

As Ben Bradlee, editor of *The Washington Post*, recalled, his old friend Gordon Manning telephoned one day in the middle of October and announced, "I'm going to save your ass in this Watergate thing. Cronkite and I have gotten CBS to agree to do two back-to-back long pieces on the 'Evening News' about Watergate. We're going to make you famous."

Watergate, which would become a historic test of the American form of government, was generally misunderstood in the fall of 1972. Despite revelations of the Watergate break-in and other illegal skullduggery, nearly two-thirds of Americans polled by the Gallup organization that October considered the scandal "just politics." The story lacked cohesion. For CBS News, the trouble with the Watergate scandal was that it wasn't a visual story like the Vietnam War or Earth Day or the civil rights marches. *The Washington Post* was almost alone in investigating Watergate, taking greater risks with each passing day. Cronkite was aware that the *Post* was under increasing pressure from the White House to drop the story, with major advertisers threatening to pull out of the newspaper if it continued to pursue the investigation. (Back then, the FCC also mandated TV license renewals every three years. In January 1973, the FCC tried denying licenses to *Post*-owned stations in Florida.)

CBS News president Dick Salant was taking a huge risk in airing "The Watergate Affair," a two-part story, just eleven days before the election. All major Nixon administration figures had refused to be interviewed for the pieces. In introducing part one of the fourteen-minute CBS News reports on Friday, October 27, Cronkite presented the reportorial work of Woodward and Bernstein as accurate and thorough. Nixon acolytes Haldeman and Ziegler were given a few seconds for balance. "Most of what is known as the Watergate affair has emerged in puzzling bits and pieces, through digging by the nation's press and television newsmen," Cronkite told viewers. "Some of the material made public so far is factual, without dispute—those men caught in the act at Watergate, for instance. Some is still allegation, uncovered by the press but as yet legally unsubstantiated. We shall label our sources carefully as we go along. But with the facts and the allegations, we shall try tonight to pull together the threads of this amazing story, quite unlike any in our modern American history."

It was Woodward and Bernstein who broke the story wide open; Cronkite only lent high-octane credence to their investigation and introduced it to a wider audience. The CBS broadcast gave millions of viewers a frame of reference by which they could make sense of the "puzzling bits and pieces" they'd heard about in drip-drip fashion since the spring. Thanks to the Cronkite imprimatur, the Watergate cover-up became decisively important for a large segment of America's television audience. No mere break-in and not "just politics," the unfolding Watergate scandal was deemed worthy of 64 percent of the October 27 *CBS Evening News* broadcast. CBS's part two, on Nixon's money laundering via CREEP for political sabotage and intelligence gathering (aired on the following Tuesday, October 31), had the White House in jitters. On both days, CBS employees congregated in the Washington bureau, gleeful that they had Nixon on a gangplank.

"There was great excitement in the bureau," Lesley Stahl wrote in *Reporting Live*. "We all knew that allotting so much time to reporting the charges of wrongdoing would incite the wrath of the Nixon White House and campaign."

Bill Paley didn't like Watergate Part I and dreaded the very idea of part two. A supporter of Nixon's reelection bid, Paley deemed the work of Cronkite, Gould, Manning, and Mason "unfair, unbalanced, derivative, inaccurate, based on hearsay, and mingling rumor with editorial opinion"—but he didn't order part two killed. He maintained that he expected CBS, as a newsgathering organization, to be responsible for everything it presented. Because Cronkite was a friend, Paley's rage was aimed more at reporter Daniel Schorr. "The broadcast troubled me," Paley later wrote. "It just did not seem in keeping with Cronkite's usual objectivity." After harshly criticizing the October 27 report, Paley allowed that the decision as to what to do about Part II still belonged with news division president Salant. But on October 30—the day before it was due to air—Paley called an emergency meeting at Black Rock with Frank Stanton (CBS vice chairman), Arthur Taylor (president of CBS), Jack Schneider (the president of the CBS Broadcast Group), and Salant. Paley's ultimate message was that the White House heat was getting unbearable.

On a regular basis, Charles Colson, full of veiled innuendo and cause-and-effect threats, would call Paley
to harass him about the FCC not renewing affiliate
licenses. Colson went into action in Florida—at WPLG
(Miami) and WJXT (Jacksonville)—determined to
revoke their licenses because they were owned by *The
Washington Post.* "We'll bring you to your knees,"
Colson threatened, "in Wall Street."

Nixon aide Charles Colson confronted Paley face-to-
face the day after "Watergate: Part I" aired, infuriated
at the content of the report and the timing, so close to
Election Day. "I had called Paley on Nixon's behalf
and went to see him in his New York office," Colson
recalled. "We got along extremely well. I told him how
Stanton was on a crusade against the president, that
Cronkite's long 'Watergate' segment sounded like the
DNC had written it. Paley told me he was embarrassed
by the segment. The net effect was that Paley called
me a few days later, letting me know he got the second
Watergate report cut way down in size."

While Paley denied that he was influenced by
Colson's arm-twisting visit, devoting nine pages of his
1982 memoir to his defensive version of events, it is reasonable to surmise it had a huge impact. After the Black
Rock meeting, Salant heeded the disgruntled Paley
and decided that Part II of CBS's Watergate exposé

could be reduced in length. Conferring with Cronkite's executive producer, Sandy Socolow (and secret producers Gould and Mason), Salant didn't mention his tense meeting with Paley. Although Salant did somersaults in his memoir to deny it, he had succumbed to White House intimidation tactics. He should have resigned in protest. The CBS producers resented paring down Part II, but agreed to make the necessary revisions. "Walter Cronkite," Salant recalled, "did not participate. At least, so far as I was involved, he never took a position one way or another."

Paley's meeting with Salant constituted the one and only time that the CBS chief ever tried to influence specific content within the *Evening News* during Salant's twenty-five-year association with the program. (Paley had asked Cronkite and Schorr to tone down their mockery of Goldwater in 1964.) A righteous Salant, worried about being seen as a patsy, said later that if he had known about Colson's confrontation with Paley, he would have stood his ground on sheer First Amendment principles and refused to shorten the second part. "If I thought [Paley] was responding to White House pressure," Cronkite wrote, "he might not be able to control the eruption."

"Watergate: Part II," cut from fourteen minutes to seven minutes, was broadcast as planned on Tuesday,

October 31. Cronkite then added a disclaimer to finish the broadcast. "The Nixon administration calls these allegations false, in some cases, overblown, hearsay, and misleading in others," he said. "But apparently this segment of the press, and those disturbed at the possible injury done to the country's delicate election process, will not be satisfied with mere denials, will not put their suspicions to rest unless or until some impartial body examines the case and renders its verdict. And that's the way it is, Tuesday, October thirty-first, nineteen seventy-two."

Washington Post editor Ben Bradlee was ecstatic about Cronkite's Watergate segments. No longer was the *Post* alone in the trench warfare with the White House. "When Cronkite aired the Watergate bits, the sun came out for me," Bradlee recalled. "It was just like being blessed; if Cronkite was taking the Watergate story seriously, *everyone* in journalism would."

Just eight days after Part II aired, President Nixon defeated McGovern in the biggest presidential victory in U.S. history: 520 electoral votes to 17. Clearly, Cronkite's Watergate reports hadn't been a game changer with the electorate. Nixon—who had taken the United States off the gold standard, allowing the dollar to float on international currency markets—was riding a strong economy that relegated Watergate to a cat-burglar farce with doubtful legs. But the dark clouds of scandal thickened overhead, in part because Cronkite had treated the Watergate break-in as Big News. The controversial two-part report on the *CBS Evening News* was credited with keeping Watergate on the front burner, where it dramatically sizzled for the next twenty-two months. As Bradlee put it, "Somehow the Great White Father, Walter Cronkite, the most trusted man in America, had blessed the story by spending so much time on it."

Days after Nixon was reelected, Colson delivered a blistering speech to New England newspaper editors, with Bradlee as bull's-eye. "I think if Bradlee ever left the Georgetown cocktail circuit, where he and his pals dine on third-hand information and gossip and rumor," Colson jabbed, "he might discover out here a real America, and he might learn that all truth and all knowledge and all superior wisdom doesn't emanate exclusively from that small little clique in Georgetown, and that the rest of the country isn't just sitting out here waiting to be told what they're supposed to think."

While Colson easily lacerated Bradlee, getting at Cronkite was a more difficult proposition. No one saw Uncle Walter as an East Coast elite. His brand was a benign, not-so-tough interviewer. But Colson was insistent that Cronkite—the patron saint of the liberal media—had to be knocked down a peg. President

Nixon himself, as revealed in the White House tapes of November–December 1972, was irate at CBS News for aiding *The Washington Post*. On December 15, he spoke to Colson about hitting CBS News with buckshot until it cried uncle:

Colson: I talked to Paley yesterday, Mr. President. . . . I'm seeing him Monday at one o'clock.

Colson: I'll just say look, you guys are crazy. You can hire all the executives you want; that isn't going to solve your problem. You need to put somebody on the air who is . . . going to give balance to all the goddamn slamming that we've been taking from Rather and Pierpoint and Sevareid and Cronkite and Schorr. . . . I tell you, I'm going to make a real pitch out of it . . .

Nixon: Well, you do it.

Colson: I'll, I'll put the screws to him. . . . He'll be here Monday and I'll put the screws to him very hard.

Nixon: Say we want [Herb] Klein and he ought to put him in there. They ought to have balance in their show and Klein is a hell of a television personality . . . and that they ought to have a little balance in the goddamn thing.

From the long "U.S.-Soviet Wheat Deal" report onward, Nixon came to believe that NBC's John Chancellor and ABC's Howard K. Smith were more fair-minded than Cronkite. By 1973, in fact, the White House tapes reveal that Nixon pejoratively deemed "intellectual people" who were against him "Cronkites" in the way LBJ used to rail against "Harvards."

Somehow the president had to curtail Cronkite's growing stature. "When Nixon got in the White House it wasn't the most hospitable environment," Colson recalled. "CBS acted like the Nazis had taken over. Only Sevareid was seen as worse than Cronkite, whom Nixon developed a 'cordial dislike' of." With the exception of Howard K. Smith on ABC, Nixon thought all the TV reporters were flaming Ted Kennedy anti-war lefties. "I'm a conservative," Colson said in 2011 in his defense. "Nixon wasn't wrong about the liberal media."

Through the controversies of Nixon's White House tenure, Cronkite remained popular with the American public. For twenty-nine years, he had worked at the network as writer, producer, and executive—everybody knew it was Cronkite, in the end, who decided what flickered blue in the suppertime darkness across America. When he took time off around Thanksgiving 1972 to have a benign tumor removed from his throat at Lenox Hill Hospital, the get-well-soon cards came pouring into CBS.

After the 1972 presidential election, with CBS still the ratings leader, Cronkite's lawyer negotiated a major contractual clause. Cronkite would get three months off every summer—June through August—to enjoy sailing off Martha's Vineyard on his ketch, *Wyntje*. Only NASA launches, Cronkite said, would warrant his leaving Cape Cod. His colleagues knew he had it made: $250,000 a year with three months off every summer. And Cronkite, trying not to war with the entire Nixon administration, threw a lifeline to Henry Kissinger (who was never implicated in Watergate). "I was Cronkite and the media's alibi for their treatment of Nixon," Kissinger recalled. "Cronkite had made a turn on Vietnam under Johnson. When Nixon came in, he continued to have that bias. But he tried to be fair to me."

In 1972, the Oliver Quayle and Company opinion research firm surveyed people in eighteen states, asking which public figure they most trusted. Strangely, Cronkite was included with Richard Nixon, Hubert Humphrey, Ed Muskie, George McGovern, Edward Kennedy, and Spiro Agnew on the "trust index" ballot. Cronkite finished in the lead, with 73 percent, compared to Richard Nixon and Hubert Humphrey, who were both rated at 57 percent. CBS News' public relations office seized on Cronkite's poll victory with gusto. When asked about being the heroic "Most Trusted Man in America," Cronkite chuckled, pleased with the designation. "I'll be glad to wear the crown." The poll confirmed overnight what had long been apparent: Cronkite was the ultimate reliable source. "When Cronkite was on CBS during the Nixon years," future NBC anchorman Brian Williams noted, "it wasn't mere anchoring. It was addressing the nation."

Cronkite secured many exclusive interviews with key figures of the Watergate saga, including John Dean; Archibald Cox (shortly after he was fired from his post as special Watergate prosecutor); and Leon Jaworski (on the day he was appointed to succeed Cox). Nixon loathed all of them.

But Cronkite was excluded from Nixon's infamous Enemies List. Daniel Schorr and Dan Rather interpreted the omission of Cronkite as proof that he hadn't warred enough with the White House. Andy Rooney teased Cronkite mercilessly about the exclusion. "I was always offended by the fact that [Nixon] put out an Enemies List midway through his administration and that somehow or other I wasn't on it," Cronkite recalled. "It was a kind of a source of embarrassment among my colleagues that I didn't make it."

28.

Fan Clubs, Stalkers, and Political Good-byes

GROWING UP WITH CAPTAIN KANGAROO—BREAKING THE COLOR LINE WITH BERNARD SHAW IN HAWAII—CONNIE CHUNG HAS A ROLE MODEL—TOM BROKAW'S JOE DIMAGGIO—THE CRONKITE FAN CLUB—LBJ'S DEATH ON AIR—ANSWERING MAIL—BOY SCOUT MANNERS—JUMPING LIKE A JAGUAR—GAY PRIDE—GOING ROGUE ON *THE MARY TYLER MOORE SHOW*—A HOME IN THE VINEYARD—NIXON FLEES—OF LESLEY STAHL AND BARBARA WALTERS—DARWIN'S TOP DOG

N o one has yet written the definitive history of television as babysitter for millions of cold war–era children. But starting in the late 1950s, the phenomenon hit its stride. American kids grew up with programs such as CBS's *Captain Kangaroo* and Cronkite's *You Are There* as educational explainers and directors of life. Bernard Shaw, growing up on Chicago's South Side in the 1940s and '50s, was one of many nurtured on the Tube. Shaw's father had bought a twenty-one-inch Zenith and his son watched *You Are There* on a regular basis. Just as the young Cronkite in Houston had a newspaper route, Shaw grew up delivering four Chicago dailies: the *Tribune*, *Sun-Times*, *Herald-American*, and *Daily News*. "We had Cronkite on the set and four Chicago newspapers delivered to the house," Shaw recalled. "Plus two black papers, the *Pittsburgh Courier* and the *Chicago Defender*. My idol was Cronkite. I decided I wanted to be just like him at a very early age. I followed *everything* he did."

Without money for college, Shaw joined the Marines in 1959. During the early Kennedy years, Corporal Shaw was stationed at the Marine Corps Air Station in Kaneohe Bay, Hawaii. One afternoon he was sitting in Barracks Number 225, reading the local *Honolulu Advertiser*, when an item made him sit straight up with excitement. Walter and Betsy Cronkite had arrived in Hawaii. Shaw was determined to meet his TV hero in the flesh. The *Advertiser* noted that the Cronkites were staying at the exclusive Reef Hotel in Waikiki. Overcome with excitement, Shaw bombarded the hotel switchboard with telephone calls. Try as he might, Cronkite was unreachable, out in the jungle conducting an interview for *The Twentieth Century* with an intransigent Japanese soldier who refused to accept his country's surrender in 1945. "I felt," Shaw later chuckled, "like a stalker."

Eventually Cronkite returned Shaw's calls and they arranged to meet the next day for an amicable chat in the hotel lobby. Shaw, full of nervous anticipation, arrived early. "I was convinced he wouldn't show up," he said. "He was running a little late. But suddenly there he was, sticking out his hand with 'Gee, Sergeant, I hope I haven't been keeping you long.' He had purposefully given me a promotion up from corporal as a joke."

It felt like a dream come true: Shaw, in full tropical marine uniform, discussing world affairs with his CBS News idol, who looked tan and bearish in a brightly colored Hawaiian shirt. Betsy excused herself to dress for dinner, leaving the men to mull over world events. A twenty-minute meeting became forty-five minutes long. They had bonded instantly. Shaw, an African American, told Cronkite that institutional racism would never bring him down, that he was going to be a Big Three anchorman someday. Did Cronkite have any advice? "Read, read, read" was the answer.

He paternally explained that a TV journalist first had to become a general assignment reporter. That meant knowing something about international affairs, sports, gardening, architecture—everything. "I'm not going to let anything or anybody *DEE-ter* me from succeeding," Shaw said.

"No," Cronkite replied, smiling. "Don't let anything di-TUR you."

If Shaw was going to reach the major leagues, his pronunciation would have to be *Webster's Dictionary* precise. But Cronkite took the ambitious Shaw, full of passion and unrealized potential, seriously. He recognized that the Marine was a wonderful monologuist blessed with a rich bass-baritone voice, and they made a pact to stay in touch. In 1994, when Shaw received the Walter Cronkite Award for Excellence in Journalism at Arizona State University, he recalled that the face time with Cronkite in Hawaii was "pivotal . . . seminal . . . inspirational . . . educational." After Shaw completed his military service and began studies at the University of Illinois in Chicago, he corresponded consistently with Cronkite, who followed his career trajectory with sublime pleasure as Shaw rose from local news to White House correspondent for Westinghouse Broadcasting. "My goal was to be at CBS working with Cronkite by age thirty," Shaw said. "I missed the mark by one year. I was thirty-one when CBS executive Bill Small hired me in 1971."

Shaw was assigned to the CBS News Washington bureau. Cronkite, presiding over the entire CBS News enterprise from his New York perch, bragged about how he had discovered the young talent in Hawaii back in 1961. He was elated to have Shaw, an excellent extemporizer known for his perceptive vitality, on his team. Starting in the 1950s, CBS News had executive producers—Bud Benjamin, Russ Bensley, Ernie Leiser, Paul Greenberg, and Sandy Socolow among them—who were unabashed civil rights activists. By the early 1960s, CBS News also had a stable of correspondents whom Martin Luther King Jr. embraced as allies: John Hart, Charles Kuralt, Nelson Benton, Murray Fromson, Robert Schakne, Howard K. Smith, and Dan Rather. "I'll never forget the first story I did for Cronkite's *CBS Evening News*," Shaw recalled. "When introducing me, a smile curled on Walter's lips. He looked so happy and proud that I had made it, that my dream to be his colleague was real." Cronkite welcomed Shaw with a warm letter that included a friendly warning about CBS. "We are a long way from perfection," Cronkite wrote, "and I know that you are sophisticated enough not to let the petty annoyances dim your broader vision of the outfit. Our feet may not be of clay, but our little toe is suspect."

Another member of the CBS News class of '71 who considered herself a Cronkiter was Connie Chung (née Jung Yukwa), whose father was a Chinese diplomat. Growing up near Washington, D.C., Chung—honest, smart, and utterly telegenic—tried emulating Cronkite in hopes of pioneering in broadcast journalism and refused to let being an Asian American serve as a roadblock to her professional success. Chung got her first serious job covering Capitol Hill for a local station. Before long, CBS News' Washington bureau chief, Bill Small, searching for women broadcasters in the early 1970s, hired her. Considered just a "kid reporter," Chung had no desk or typewriter at the bureau and was forced to borrow equipment from a few Murrow-era veterans. A number of the CBS correspondents—Daniel Schorr, in particular—were chauvinistic about Chung joining the boys club, but Cronkite wasn't among them.

With Chung, Cronkite was paradoxically lenient and strict at the same time. Feeling that Chung was going to become a huge star, sensing she had that special *something*, he warned her to "never get a big head." There was also advice about simply waiting for an AP or UPI wire, not believing a second- or third-tier source just to break the news. *Survival . . .* that was the key to success in broadcast journalism. In 1993, Chung, to Cronkite's delight, was chosen to co-anchor the *CBS Evening News* with Dan Rather. Having half of Cronkite's old job made her giddy with disbelief. "I said I wanted a no-asshole staff," she recalled. "Cronkite had raised the bar not just on the air but also in how to be in a workplace environment. He was kind of fatherly to me, Uncle Walter. The way he carried himself around women was charming. When he called me from New York, the first thing he said was, 'That was a very, very good job.' I felt I had come of age. A double *very* from Uncle Walter!! I was floating in heaven."

Tom Brokaw of NBC News, in his early thirties, was based in Los Angeles when he first met Cronkite at a White House press event in 1971. There was Cronkite in the flesh, Brokaw's all-seasons hero, just another face in the crowd of reporters. Brokaw was in awe of Cronkite from head to toe. "It was like being a diehard Yankee fan for all your life," he recalled, "and suddenly you're on the grass in Yankee Stadium getting to chat with Joe DiMaggio. The moment was indelibly carved on my imagination." For his part, Cronkite could tell from their first conversation that Brokaw was a "particularly fine ad-libber" with a "marvelous extemporaneous style." Brokaw was named NBC

White House correspondent during the Watergate scandal, and Cronkite became a trusted friend. The shorthand between the two was immediate—they could almost read each other's minds. What strengthened their friendship was the fact that Brokaw's wife, Meredith, was enamored of Betsy Cronkite. "To Meredith," Brokaw recalled, "Betsy was proof that you could be in the crazy TV news business and still have a strong, strong family life. As a couple, they became our ideal."

Another die-hard Cronkite fan was the future NBC News anchorman Brian Williams. Although Williams was born in New Jersey, he grew up in a small, cream-colored ranch house in Elmira, New York. His two-bedroom home was the kind that defined middle-class life in the cold war era. Around the time of the JFK assassination, when Williams was only four, his working-class parents started religiously watching Cronkite anchor the *CBS Evening News* every Monday through Friday. "I was a Cronkite groupie by the age of six," Williams recalled. "At our household, dinner was hinged on Walter saying, 'And that's the way it is.' Only then could the meal get served. That was the mid-1960s, and I continued to travel with him from the age of polyester to the age of his ever-thickening sideburns and beyond."

Williams didn't mess around when it came to Cronkitiana. He might as well have opened up a Walter Cronkite Fan Club chapter in Elmira. Every time there was even a mention of Cronkite in *Time, Look*, or *Life*—the three publications his family subscribed to—he'd clip out the story. All Cronkite's CBS News special events dealing with the Apollo program were almost sacred happenings in the Williams home. As if preparing for a role as a body-double, Williams analyzed the way Cronkite spoke, his voice inflections and facial expressions, even the stylistic bravado of his wide-knot ties and two-toned dress shirts. "I grew up in a CBS household," Williams recalled, "and even though I'm paid by NBC, I won't deny it. The Cronkite team members were my superstars. What Lambeau Field is to a Packers fan, Cronkite's newsroom was to me. I eventually made my way to West Fifty-seventh Street, the broadcast center, just to touch Cronkite's U-shaped Formica desk and see his woodcut map of the world behind him. Call me a CBS News nerd if you want. I knew more about Ike Pappas than I care to admit."

Not all future TV journalists grew up in awe of Cronkite. Bill O'Reilly, host of Fox News' *The O'Reilly Factor*, was raised in a decidedly non–*CBS Evening News* home, although he occasionally caught Cronkite hosting *The Twentieth Century*. Part of

O'Reilly's dissociation with Cronkite was simply a matter of circumstance. Bill's father, William O'Reilly Sr., a corporate accountant for an oil company, wasn't home for suppertime. As O'Reilly made his way up the electronic journalism ladder, working at CBS News from 1982 to 1986, he saw Cronkite as "too retro" to be relevant. "My guys were Tom Snyder and Howard Cosell," O'Reilly recalled. "They were lively and jumped out at you. Walter was bland by comparison. And he was always too much of a liberal who traveled in Martha's Vineyard and Upper West Side circles. I was from Levittown. He was obviously good, but not on my wavelength."

Time magazine did a cover story of Cronkite in 1966 titled "The Electronic Front Page" that grappled with how the anchorman held a "kind of subliminal authority" over the American home unprecedented in communications history. Cronkite, the managing editor, decided what *you*—mothers and fathers in all fifty states—needed to know about the world at large. While newspapers transmitted facts, television was about shared experience in its rawest, most emotional form. Growing up, Shaw (in Chicago), Chung (in Washington, D.C.), Brokaw (in South Dakota), and Williams (in upstate New York) all read different papers, each chockablock full of local news, but the Cronkite broadcast brought shared historic pageantry—like the death of Kennedy and *Apollo 11*—into their lives. CBS News vice president Gordon Manning described the Cronkite phenomenon this way: "Pictures plus words plus personality equals believability."

Robert Feder of Skokie, Illinois, was Exhibit A for Manning's point. From the time he was six or seven, Feder believed in the societal importance of the Cronkite broadcast. While other kids made Neil Armstrong or the Beatles their heroes, Feder fell for Cronkite. When he turned fifteen in 1972, he wrote the CBS anchorman a fan letter telling him he had created a fan club in his honor. To Feder's surprise, Cronkite wrote him back. "I personally am appreciative of your loyalty, given the assumption that you in reality are paying tribute to the efforts of all of us at CBS News to deliver the news fairly and impartially without fear or favor. Please extend my very best wishes to all the members of the Club."

The official *Walter Cronkite Newsletter* was born with that missive. To Cronkite's surprise, the mimeo-graphed sheet had a fine tactile quality. Working out of his parents' home, Feder eventually recruited more than a thousand members. With intelligent assistance from die-hard *CBS Evening News* fans, the monthly newsletter was packed with biographical tidbits about the CBS anchor in chief. Correspondence continued between Cronkite and Feder, and a friendship blossomed.

Casting a wide net, Feder solicited his activist members to scan newspapers and periodicals for *any* information—even gossip—pertaining to Cronkite. The newsletter placed Cronkite in a pantheon, promoting him as a towering reportorial icon in the same vein as Lippmann and Murrow. In January 1975, Cronkite, with prankish solemnity, even gave an interview to the *Walter Cronkite Newsletter* about his amazing on-air stamina anchoring Election Night marathon broadcasts. "I don't take any pills," Cronkite said. "I don't go on a low-residue diet. I just don't feel fatigue. I think the interest factor keeps me revved up." In the same issue, Feder asked Cronkite if the rumor was true that sometimes he actually wore tennis shorts or cut-offs when broadcasting the *Evening News*. "No," Cronkite told his fan club, "but sometimes my pants don't match my jacket."

Cronkite had good reasons for embracing Feder's club. The mimeographed newsletter was an excellent way to build a loyal fan base in those pre-Internet days. It was like a Facebook page or a Twitter account before its time. It was one more confirmation that by 1972, Cronkite had become part of the popular culture. Comedian Robert Klein recorded a song called "Middle Class Educated Blues," in which he crooned, "I watch the Walter Cronkite news . . . I love Walter." A *New Yorker* cartoon by Ed Arno showed an average guy having an after-work cocktail slumped down in an armchair with CBS News on the telly. Its caption read, "OK, Cronkite! Lay it on me!" The ABC News affiliate in Baltimore hung a poster of Cronkite dressed like the pope above the words "What makes you think the power has gone to my head?" Pick your comic strip— *Peanuts, Lil' Abner, Dennis the Menace*—the cartoonists all used Cronkite as Father Time and wise-man fodder.

For Cronkite aficionados, an essential moment in the anchorman's career occurred when Lyndon Johnson died on January 22, 1973. When the *CBS Evening News* returned from its first station break that night, viewers were jarred. Cronkite was on the telephone, his head bent and his eyebrows gathered together, full of consternation. Devoted watchers of the *CBS Evening News* had never seen anything like it. With the handset to his ear, the half-knowing, half-bewildered Cronkite was listening without speaking at all. It was as if the television veteran had been caught ordering pizza or humoring a long-winded friend. Cronkite interrupted the person on the other end of the phone line and explained the situation to his CBS viewers. "I'm talking to Tom Johnson," he said, "the press secretary for Lyndon Johnson, who has reported that the thirty-sixth president of the United States died this afternoon . . ."

After hanging up the phone, Cronkite ad-libbed briefly about the former president's recent health and activities. He then returned to the scripts of the day, detailing battlefield news of Vietnam. "What always impressed me about that moment," the future *CBS Evening News* anchorman Scott Pelley recalled, "was Cronkite's lack of formality. I'll always remember how he did it. How he told Americans to hold on for a minute, I think I have a big story. The folks trusted him, myself included." Or, as Brian Williams surmised, "Walter loved the challenge of broadcasting Johnson's death without a net."

Tom Johnson had first alerted the Austin bureaus of AP and UPI to LBJ's death. Then he reached out to NBC News, who wanted to wait for the "flash bulletin" from the wire services. Then it was CBS News' turn. In a blink, the news of LBJ's death traveled fast from Tom Johnson in Austin to the CBS News operator, then to producer Sandy Socolow in the fishbowl, and then to live news. Cronkite, breaking his own rule, went with only one source on the story. "Cronkite had just been with LBJ at the ranch," Tom Johnson said. "He didn't need confirmation. He knew me and knew my voice. It surprised me, too, but he simply talked with me on air. I even heard somebody in the CBS control room say, 'It's coming over the wire now.' But Walter had beaten the AP and UPI in announcing the news. That was the first time that network news was ever interrupted like that. There was a risk involved. But Cronkite was merely pioneering what we started doing all the time at CNN a decade later."

Cronkite had been at the LBJ ranch only ten days earlier, preparing what would be the last installment of a multipart special "conversations" series with the ex-president produced by Burton Benjamin. While the five-part series wasn't dramatic TV, it was a wonderful historical document. Lyndon Johnson had finished his memoir *The Vantage Point* and the Cronkite interview had been arranged to sell books. As Cronkite and LBJ sat in a guest cottage conducting the taped interview, both in casual attire, the haggard former president suffered a debilitating bout of angina pectoris, a condition related to the heart disease that would soon kill him. He retreated outside and took a prescription pill. When LBJ returned, he waved aside a conspicuously reticent Cronkite's suggestion that they postpone the rest of his questions, which focused on civil rights.

Health scares aside, Cronkite and LBJ got along extremely well during the grueling ranch interviews. There was something bittersweet about seeing the codgers reminisce about Vietnam . . . Selma . . . "We shall overcome" . . . Glassboro . . . Medicaid . . . Medicare. But behind the scenes, a volcano was erupting. CBS News producer Bud Benjamin and John Shamick had poorly edited the Cronkite-LBJ talks. Showing zero respect for the former president, Benjamin spliced the film footage in unflattering ways very different from the actual as-delivered answers. "It was just awful," Bob Hardesty, LBJ acolyte and editor of *The Vantage Point*, recalled. "Johnson had expected more of Cronkite. He redid his facial expressions so when Johnson spoke about Vietnam, it looked as if Cronkite had raised his eyebrows in disgust or nodded his head. Johnson was mad as hell."

The CBS News rough cut was viewed by LBJ himself, who declared it "dirty pool." A score of Johnson aides were tasked with keeping the blasphemy off the air at all costs. "It burned the hell out of the president," LBJ aide Harry Middleton recalled. "It was a matter of great concern. It was unbelievable. Benjamin had re-shot Cronkite asking the questions in a completely different way, giving a raised eyebrow and making expressions he hadn't done at the ranch."

LBJ's lawyer, Arthur Krim, who was then chairman of United Artists, threw a fit with Frank Stanton about the misleading Benjamin-edited interview. It was a real black eye to Cronkite. Eventually, Krim prevailed and the Cronkite-LBJ conversation was unscrambled back to its actual, as-delivered Q&A format. "It was my very first experience with that 'technique,'" Tom Johnson, who served as president of CNN from 1990 to 2001, recalled. "It was reprehensible."

That January 22, when LBJ died, the ex-president was still bitter toward Cronkite, not for his Vietnam dissent of 1968 but for his dishonest collaboration with Benjamin on what would be the last big interview of his life. Lady Bird Johnson, however, didn't hold a grudge against Cronkite at all. It helped that Cronkite had treated President Johnson like a colossus in death, a political figure on a par with FDR or Kennedy. In coming years, Lady Bird would visit the Cronkites at Martha's Vineyard for sailing trips around Cape Cod.

The spontaneous announcement of Johnson's death reminded Cronkite's CBS colleagues yet again why their anchor was Top Gun. His instincts were beyond formidable. When Bill Felling—who would later become a national editor for CBS News—started working at the network around the time of Johnson's death as a desk assistant, his principal morning job was to roll the AP, Reuters, and UPI copy into fat scroll-like documents at the crack of dawn and deliver them to the bigwigs according to their status. The first wire machine printout had the darkest, easiest-to-read type. The last printout was faint; a magnifying glass was needed to decipher some of the quasi-disappeared letters. That one went to "the schmuck" (in Felling's jargon). "Walter got the first roll," Felling explained. "I'd ink his name on it and type it up so nobody could poach it from him. I'd put them all on his desk. In ritualistic fashion, he'd come in, put his feet on the desk, and read all the rolls religiously. He'd rip off stories that mattered and use a ruler to make the tear clean."

Felling soon observed, as only a newcomer can, that all day long Cronkite had his ear tilted toward the wire room. The machines were kept under noise-dampening lids, in a corridor just across from the main newsroom. But Cronkite seemed to hear them like a dog hears a high whistle. Others waited to get served the copy, but Cronkite, a wire addict, was always ready to pounce. "If the three bells would go off, that old man would pop up like a goddamn jaguar and head down the corridor," Felling said, laughing, years later. "He couldn't wait to get his paws on the raw news first. He had simply conditioned himself to be the UP guy."

Cronkite had zero tolerance for slackers in the newsroom. It was best to leave your eccentricities at home if you wanted to survive. Socolow recalled that at one point Cronkite wanted to put the squeeze on a scriptwriter for being dangerously unstable. "We've got to get rid of him," he told Socolow; "he's a drunk." He had residual anger about his father's alcoholism and simply wouldn't tolerate a boozehound in the newsroom. Socolow told Cronkite to chill out; he had secretly searched the suspect's office and found no bottles. "I'm telling you, he's a drunk," Cronkite reiterated. "Fire him." Socolow refused, on the grounds that the scriptwriter hadn't done anything wrong. "That was until the Hilton Hotel in Washington, D.C.," Socolow recalled. "There had been a minibar in the writer's room. The scriptwriter in question cleared it out. Drank it all. Walter had been right after all. I dismissed him."

In late summer 1973, Cronkite flew with producer Ernie Leiser to Laos and Vietnam to document the release of American POWs. It was the newsmen's first visit since February 1968, but the psychic scars remained. Tagging along with them was photographer David Hume Kennerly of *Time*. Cronkite hoped to score interviews with the released POWs, including John McCain, about their ordeals of torture, dysentery, solitary confinement, and beatings. Many of the POWs were near death, not unlike survivors of Auschwitz. "These POWs were dressed in striped pajamas and were getting released one by one," Kennerly recalled. "One of the prisoners said to me, after I gave him a pack of cigarettes, that he didn't believe we were going to get out of Vietnam until he saw Walter Cronkite waiting outside the gate. That, to him, represented freedom."

While Cronkite was in Vietnam, charges of financial misdeeds (income tax evasion) surfaced against Vice President Spiro Agnew. He claimed through his attorneys to be "a victim of a deliberate [media] campaign calculated . . . to drive him from office." On October 10, Agnew resigned as part of a plea bargain that kept him from going to trial. He pleaded nolo contendere to a felony charge of income tax evasion. The news was not unexpected and yet caught many people by surprise when it was announced as a *CBS News Special Report* at 2:35 p.m.

Cronkite's broadcast led with the resignation, but did so without glee. There was no victory in kicking a man when he was down—even his nemesis. Viewers respected that posture. Cronkite saved several minutes at the end of the October 10 program for a comment, expressing both regret and irony. "I first met Spiro Agnew in 1967 and I liked him," Cronkite said. "He was warm, friendly, witty, candid, open—qualities that a newsman appreciates in a news source. Then there came that November 1969 speech that opened officially the Nixon offensive against the news media. Some of us thought it was demagoguery at its worst and frankly, I was surprised that Agnew would lend himself to it. But he did and because of my beliefs that a free press must fight any attempt to intimidate it, we became ideological enemies. But we would not have wished even on Spiro Agnew the disgrace in which his reputation, his hopes and dreams are smothered tonight. As Americans, we all share his tragedy."

Agnew's resignation enhanced Cronkite's appeal. He had become a full-fledged celebrity dragon slayer. No longer was Cronkite safe walking the streets of New York. Everybody, it seemed, wanted something from him. Refusing to have a limousine driver because it was too expensive, Cronkite set himself up to be an easy target for autograph seekers, photo hounds, and full-fledged kooks. Back in those pre-9/11 days, television studios didn't have security guards. A complete stranger could wander into the Fifty-seventh Street building and take an elevator right up to Cronkite's fishbowl office. It took gall, but it happened fairly often.

The days of lax security at CBS News abruptly ended on December 11, 1973, when twenty-three-year-old Mark Allan Segal, a demonstrator from an organization called the Gay Raiders, with accomplice Harry Langhorne at his side, interrupted a Cronkite broadcast, causing the screen to go black for a few seconds. Cronkite was delivering a story about Henry Kissinger in the Middle East when, about fourteen minutes into the first "feed," Segal leapt in front of the camera carrying a yellow sign that read, "Gays Protest CBS Prejudice." More than sixty million Americans were watching. Segal had insinuated himself into the CBS newsroom by pretending to be a reporter from Camden State Community College in New Jersey. He had been granted permission to watch the broadcast live in the studio. "I sat on Cronkite's desk directly in front of him and held up the sign," Segal recalled. "The network went black while they took me out of the studio."

On the surface, Cronkite was unfazed by the disruption. Technicians tackled Segal, wrapped him in cable wire, and ushered him out of camera view. Once back on live TV, Cronkite matter-of-factly described what had happened without an iota of irritation. "Well," the anchorman said, "a rather interesting development in the studio here—a protest demonstration right in the middle of the CBS News studio." He told viewers, "The young man identified as a member of something called Gay Raiders, an organization protesting alleged defamation of homosexuals on entertainment programs."

Segal had a legitimate complaint. Television—both news and entertainment divisions—treated gay people as pariahs, lepers from Sodom and Gomorrah. It stereotyped them as suicidal nut jobs, flaming fairies, and psychopathic villains. Part of the Gay Raiders' strategy was to bring public attention to the Big Three networks' discrimination policies. What better way to garner publicity for the cause than waving a banner on the *CBS Evening News*? "So I did it," Segal recalled. "The police were called, and I was taken to a holding tank."

But both Segal and Langhorne were charged with second-degree criminal trespassing as a result of their disruption of the *CBS Evening News*. It turned out that Segal had previously raided *The Tonight Show*, the *Today* show, and *The Mike Douglas Show*. At Segal's trial on April 23, 1974, Cronkite, who had accepted a subpoena, took his place on the witness stand. CBS lawyers objected each time Segal's attorney asked the anchorman a question. When the court recessed to cue up a tape of Segal's disruption of the *Evening News*, Segal felt a tap on his back—it was Cronkite, holding a fresh pad of yellow lined paper, ready to take notes with a sharp pencil.

"Why," Cronkite asked the activist with genuine curiosity, "did you do that?"

"Your news program censors," Segal pleaded. "If I can prove it, would you do something to change it?" Segal went on to rattle off three specific examples of *CBS Evening News* censorship, including a CBS report on the second rejection of a New York City Council gay rights bill.

"Yes," Cronkite said. "I wrote that story myself."

"Well, why haven't you reported on the other twenty-three cities that have passed gay rights bills?" Segal asked. "Why do you cover five thousand women walking down Fifth Avenue in New York City when they proclaim International Women's Day on the network news, and you don't cover fifty thousand gays and lesbians walking down that same avenue proclaiming Gay Pride Day? That's censorship."

Segal's argument impressed Cronkite. The logic was difficult to deny. Why hadn't CBS News covered the Gay Pride parade? Was it indeed being homophobic? Why had the network largely avoided coverage of the Stonewall riots of 1969? At the end of the trial, Segal was fined $450, deeming the penalty "the happiest check I ever wrote." Not only did the activist receive considerable media attention, but Cronkite asked to meet privately with him to better understand how CBS might cover gay pride events. Cronkite, moreover, even went so far as to introduce Segal as a "constructive viewer" to top brass at CBS. It had a telling effect. "Walter Cronkite was my friend and mentor," Segal recalled. "After that incident, CBS News agreed to look into the 'possibility' that they were censoring or had a bias in reporting news. Walter showed a map on the *Evening News* of the U.S. and pointed out cities that had passed gay rights legislation. Network news was never the same after that."

Before long, Cronkite ran gay rights segments on the CBS News broadcast with almost drumbeat regularity. "Part of the new morality of the '60s and '70s is a new attitude toward homosexuality," he told his millions of viewers. "The homosexual men and women have organized to fight for acceptance and respectability. They've succeeded in winning equal rights under the law in many communities. But in the nation's biggest city, the fight goes on."

Not only did Cronkite speak out about gay rights, but he also became a reliable friend to the LGBTQ community. To gays, he was the counterweight to Anita Bryant, a leading gay rights opponent in the 1970s; he was a heterosexual willing to grant homosexuals their liberties. During the 1980s, Cronkite criticized the Reagan administration for its handling of the HIV/AIDS epidemic and later criticized President Clinton's "Don't Ask, Don't Tell" policy regarding gays in the military. When Cronkite did an eight-part TV documentary about his storied CBS career—*Cronkite Remembers*—he boasted about being a champion of LGBTQ issues. And he ended up hosting a huge AIDS benefit in Philadelphia organized by Segal, with singer Elton John as headliner.

As the Watergate investigations circled closer to President Nixon's cover-up activities, Cronkite lingered on each new revelation without taking a further hand in developing the story. When Nixon in December 1973 called the press "outrageous, vicious and distorted," Cronkite responded, but without his earlier vehemence. A reporter who spoke with him about Nixon's remark concluded that "if there is any criticism of President Nixon in Cronkite's conversation, it is almost completely by implication." CBS News correspondents, notably Dan Rather and Daniel Schorr, were aggressively pursuing Nixon and his inner circle on matters related to Watergate and other crimes. Cronkite, by contrast, didn't push the story hard. He stepped back when the noose tightened. The Cronkite view was that CBS News could report on *The Washington Post*'s coverage without taking sides. "Walter liked presidents," Rather explained. "He was, for example, of two minds about his famous Tet report. He liked making history, but he wasn't comfortable when people said that he had helped bring LBJ down. Cronkite never thought his Vietnam broadcast was a good thing for the institution of the presidency."

With Watergate consuming the nation, Cronkite's fans and admirers, private and corporate, would send him everything from family photos to restaurant discount coupons and free Knicks tickets. IBM started delivering new computer models for him to try out. If he looked weary on air, a fan invariably sent him holistic cures. If his mustache grew too long, somebody would write in recommending the best barbershop to get a trim. Cronkite most enjoyed receiving news clips from local papers—such as *The Denver Post* or the *Los Angeles Free Press*—that he missed while marooned on Manhattan Island. It didn't matter whether the letter was praiseworthy or critical; Cronkite craved feedback and would often respond. "The Lenny Bruce cult certainly was (is) a strong one and while I can't say we've received as many letters as we get from the Ku Klux Klan, Birch Society, National Rifle Association, Daughters of the American Revolution, SNCC, the CORE, Ascap and other organized groups," Cronkite wrote a fan insistent that the comedian's death warranted more than a five-second obit on CBS, "I have heard from several persons who took offense at the tone and brevity of the Bruce death notice. I regret that I offended them."

Everybody, it seemed, knew exactly what aspect of modernity CBS News was neglecting, and Cronkite was their Wailing Wall. By 1973, he had developed a stock answer: *Sorry, we don't have enough time to do that story.* He tried to answer—or have answered by his secretary, Carolyn Terry—all serious letters in a businesslike manner. Oftentimes getting a reply from the legendary anchorman put a gripe to rest. Media critics tagged Cronkite the "Most Trusted Man in America" as a result of the Quayle survey, but the truth was that he had become the "Most Powerful Man in Journalism." Both monikers became his seal of honor. "There's something in Walter's style," Chet Huntley believed, "his character, his very face and delivery that promotes sincerity."

Doug James, an Alabaman who wrote a book on Cronkite for JM Press, interviewed John Chancellor of NBC News about Cronkite's trustworthy box-office appeal. Sipping coffee and relighting his pipe from time to time, Chancellor discussed Cronkite with James in his Rockefeller Center office in New York.

"Why do you feel Mr. Cronkite has risen to the high position he has?" James asked.

"I hope that it would be years in service and the kind of experience that Walter has—and I say that because my experience is, to some degree, comparable," Chancellor answered. "I'm younger than Walter is, so I didn't land at Arnhem in a glider. I wish I had. But Walter had that experience with the U.P. in Moscow, which means he understands the basic tenets—I think I would call them the ethics of print journalism—fairly well. . . . I think, in Fred Friendly's phrase, 'Walter has paid his dues.' "

Having achieved his seniority meant that Cronkite could, from time to time, pursue personal larks. One of his decisions didn't go over well with his boss, CBS News president Richard Salant. Cronkite, unbeknownst to anyone at CBS News, did a favor for CBS Entertainment: he appeared on the wildly popular *Mary Tyler Moore Show*. For his cameo appearance, which aired on February 9, 1974, and was done in one take, he played himself in a scene, hamming it up with Lou Grant (the actor Ed Asner) and the dimwitted Ted Baxter (Ted Knight). The comedy's premise was that the local Minneapolis–St. Paul television anchor, Baxter, wanted to become Cronkite's new Eric Sevareid–like colleague. The episode was hysterical and a ratings knockout. Oddly enough, Cronkite used as precedent for his sitcom turn Dwight D. Eisenhower, who had appeared on *The Colgate Comedy Hour* in 1955.

But the cameo caused Cronkite a fair amount of grief. Was it proper for a *real* TV anchorman to appear on a comedy show? Was Cronkite, who denounced the blurring of news and entertainment, being a hypocrite? When a ticked-off Salant asked why he hadn't gotten permission to go on the popular sitcom, Cronkite's retort was that he knew the answer would have been no. As it turned out, Cronkite's own private opinion was sound. The television-watching public, not as dumb as Salant thought, lost no respect for him. His appearance on *Mary Tyler Moore* showed he had a sense of humor, and even signaled, with a nod and a wink, that he wasn't a male chauvinist. Future network anchors such as Brian Williams and Diane Sawyer took a page from the Cronkite-Moore collaboration, using it as justification for their appearances on comedy programs such as *The Daily Show* and *The Tonight Show*.

A few months after Cronkite taped *The Mary Tyler Moore Show*, he was in Chicago, where he met with Feder, his fan club's president. With a tape recorder running, Feder asked him why he had done the sitcom.

I love The Mary Tyler Moore Show. *I welcomed the opportunity to go out and pal around with those people I had been on The Mary Tyler Moore Show to find out if they're real. And it was a chance to go out to the coast for a weekend with all expenses paid and a Cadillac at the other end. And I'd weighed it very seriously, and I must say my bosses weighed it terribly seriously—far more than I did—and the final decision was that if it was a sort of a walk-on thing and wasn't any more serious than that, why we could do it.*

And I did it—I did it—for fun. With some acknowledgement on my own part, privately and secretly, that there was a little bit of wearing away of the stone perhaps of Old Stone Face, if you please. But I didn't care that much about it. And also, I don't mind people thinking occasionally that I'm human. Twenty-three or 24 minutes a day of giving all this solemn news doesn't give you much chance for self-expression, and it shouldn't, and I've always believed it shouldn't, and it doesn't, I believe on my broadcast. So that's one reason I did that.

By the mid-1970s, Cronkite had put together a crackerjack staff at CBS News, the envy of the other networks. One of his smartest hires was Linda Ann Mason in 1971; she helped produce the long Watergate pieces in October 1972. For all his open-mindedness about women's rights, though, Cronkite loved telling dirty jokes out of the earshot of female employees. He and his producer friends—Sandy Socolow, Ernie Leiser, Les Midgley, and Burton Benjamin—didn't edit their locker room banter at the broadcast center. They let the off-color jokes rip. As the pioneering first woman producer-scriptwriter at CBS News in New York, Mason ignored the stale males. She had grown up in Middletown, New York, revering Cronkite. His performance during the Kennedy assassination was a defining moment in her life. "You watched Cronkite on Kennedy's death," she recalled, "and you couldn't believe it happened. But Cronkite helped guide me through it all. That might sound hokey, but he really did."

Mason had the right stuff to make it in the brutish world of broadcast journalism. An international affairs graduate of Brown University, she started her reportorial career at the age of sixteen. Like Betsy Cronkite at the *Kansas City Journal-Post*, Mason began her professional career writing for the "Woman's Section" of Rhode Island's *Providence Journal.* What made her unusual for a woman in the mid-1960s was her steely determination to enter TV journalism. After a stint at PBS, WCBS-TV in New York City hired her. "I thought I had arrived," she recalled. "I just started working my way up the ladder." Around every bend, though, Mason encountered a purposeful workplace bias against women. At times it became degrading. "I had a choice to make," she recalled. "Sue or fight. I chose the latter."

Mason soon realized that beneath the surface chauvinism, at a deeper human level, Cronkite's team was really mensch-like. When Mason arrived for her first eggnog bash, the Cronkites' annual Christmas party, Walter was warm and funny toward her. He introduced her to Betsy as the gal who was making her way up the ranks at CBS (although he called her "Mary" by mistake). With alcohol flowing freely and a player piano hammering out "Good King Wenceslas" and "Deck the Halls," Mason finally felt a new camaraderie with her work colleagues. No longer did she worry about an old-boys' club or chauvinist exclusion. Her dream had come true: she was a producer-scriptwriter at the Tiffany Network. For God's sake, her boss was *the* Walter Cronkite. Why complain?

By all accounts, Cronkite was a happy man in 1974. He bought a summer house in Edgartown on Martha's Vineyard, a dream of his since he first covered the America's Cup for *Eyewitness*. The six-bedroom, four-and-a-half-bath waterfront colonial had an amazing pier for Cronkite to dock the new forty-two-foot yawl *Wyntje*, which had teak and mahogany decks.

Friends considered him a "lunatic sailor," always wanting to circumnavigate the globe like Magellan. The 4,330-square-foot home allowed Cronkite space for his personal library—primarily books about American history, sailing, space, popular music, and the environment. His literary hero was C. S. Forester's famous Captain Horatio Hornblower. The house, which had been built in 1929, was set on a hill and had a tall chimney. Every clear-weather summer day, Cronkite would personally hoist up Old Glory on the tallest pole in Edgartown; his flag became a fixture of the harborscape. All three Cronkite children got a kick out of the fact that director Steven Spielberg was making the movie *Jaws* that summer on the Vineyard—and Kathy was an extra in the blockbuster film.

The Vineyard was as much an ideal as a reality. A routine developed during that summer of 1974: breakfast in the large kitchen, followed by work for a few hours in the uncluttered attic study. Then it was out on the *Wyntje* to sail the Atlantic blue. Sometimes Cronkite would go over to the Readers Room—a men-only private club—for a bowl of clam chowder. By late afternoon, before cocktails, he often napped. But he also shed his beach clothes for a suit and left his summer vacation for work breaks. He covered President Nixon's Mideast tour that year and had an exclusive interview with Egyptian president Anwar Sadat, taped a series of radio reports titled "The American Challenge," and conducted a brilliant interview with the Soviet dissident author Alexander Solzhenitsyn.

In early summer 1974, Americans of all stripes were deeply concerned about American political affairs. While Cronkite was proud of the CBS News team for its Watergate coverage, he worried that America was coming unglued. When he was asked in Austin, Texas, if he planned on interviewing President Nixon in San Clemente, he quipped, "San Clemente or San Quentin?" When Chief Justice Earl Warren died on July 9, 1974, Cronkite felt great sorrow. He had first met Warren in 1956, and had occasionally called upon the chief justice as a source. He saw Warren as a judicial giant without tolerance for racial discrimination: a man like himself, getting more liberal with age. "The Chief Justice himself said he was simply following the dictates of the Constitution," Cronkite said. "He wanted his court to be remembered as the 'people's court.'"

A people's court is an apt way to describe what Cronkite thought of his *CBS Evening News* bully pulpit. Shuttling between Martha's Vineyard, New York City, and Washington, he managed to cover the House Judiciary Committee's hearings on the impeachment of President Nixon on July 25 and 29 and present special late-evening reports on July 24, 26, and 27. Even though Americans were losing faith in the White House, Cronkite encouraged his fellow citizens not to lose faith in their government and its ability to do great things. The public would need that reminder, for, on August 8, after the release of taped proof that he had lied about his involvement in the Watergate cover-up, President Nixon announced he would resign the presidency. The Watergate scandal, it seemed, was almost over. Nixon's vice president, the genial Gerald Ford of Michigan, who had served in Congress from 1949 to 1973, would take over the White House.

When President Nixon finished his grand farewell from the Oval Office, Cronkite—in the Washington studio with Sevareid, Rather, and Mudd to provide the "instant analysis" that Nixon deplored—was anything but critical of the departing president. As with Agnew's resignation, Cronkite refrained from any we-got-the-bastard gloating. He, Sevareid, and Rather were at moments downright laudatory that August day, referring to the "class" of Nixon's resignation speech, calling it "magnanimous."

Many liberals—in the public prints, at least—were perplexed, if not disgusted, by the respectful, even wistful, commentary of Cronkite. Longtime Washington insider Tom Braden, who worked for the CIA from

1950 to 1954 before working as a newspaper columnist in the 1970s, thought CBS News was engaged in the worst kind of pseudo-patriotic pandering. "Did they consort in advance to provide us with this charade?" Braden wondered. "Did they theorize that having been the bearers of bad news for so long, they must at the end address themselves to the 20 percent of Nixon hard-liners who always wanted to kill the messenger?" Cronkite disagreed. It wasn't the job of CBS News, he said, to rub Nixon's face in the mud.

Just weeks after Nixon's resignation, Cronkite won five Emmy Awards for his investigative journalism on the *CBS Evening News*. Print reporters—not least Woodward and Bernstein—saw Cronkite's performance on CBS News as Watergate unfolded between 1972 and 1974 as brave. Cronkite believed—as Woodward eventually did also—that Ford's pardoning of Nixon was in the long-term interest of the country. He also told his press colleagues to cut Ford some slack. "We should declare a honeymoon," Cronkite said, "on any vocal gaffes or errors of speech the new president should commit." Many reporters listened to Uncle Walter, whose rationale was that Nixon, the antihero, lurked in the dark side of politics, while Ford "talks from the heart."

Nothing slowed Cronkite that August after Nixon's farewell. Back in New York City in the fall, he started putting together his team for the November midterm elections. Lesley Stahl, a recent CBS hire who had desperately wanted to be part of Team Cronkite: she got her wish when CBS News president Salant assigned her to work directly with Cronkite on Election Night, covering the congressional races in the West. Salant gave her a personal tour of the West Fifty-seventh Street set. "It's quite cozy," he said. "All of you are in a friendly circle. Nothing to make you nervous." He started pointing out where everybody would be sitting. "This is where Walter sits," he said, pointing to a desk with a CRONKITE nameplate. "And here's Dan's seat." Sure enough, a nameplate said RATHER. Then came MUDD. "And here's yours," said Salant. Suddenly he blushed with embarrassment. All Stahl's nameplate said was, FEMALE.

As Election Day approached, Cronkite's secretary called Stahl to invite her to dinner at his East Side town house. "I turned cynical," Stahl recalled. "I thought he wanted to suck me dry of all my hard work in the West, will learn everything about Colorado and California from me and then use it on the air." She couldn't have been further off the mark. "We have a rule," Cronkite told her at the door. "Zero shoptalk." Stahl remembers a wild night as Cronkite—the vaudevillian—told ribald jokes about living in Russia in the 1940s and working with Charlemane the puppet in the 1950s. "He played all the roles in his stories, imitating women, Germans, Frenchmen, and people we even knew," Stahl remembered in her memoir, *Reporting Live.* "And his jokes were earthy." The Cronkites treated her as though she were family. Stahl also learned what a hoot Betsy Cronkite was. Stahl, a shrewd judge of character, found her both puckish and sophisticated.

Stahl realized that all Cronkite had plotted was conviviality before they worked together on air for Election Night 1974. This was part of his egalitarian strategy. He had built the best reportorial team in the history of U.S. television news by befriending talent. As an investigative team, they were sometimes competing with *The New York Times* and *The Washington Post.* Cronkite shepherded the egos, making sure his flock stayed united.

Truth be told, for all his mentoring qualities, Cronkite didn't tolerate competition. Being Mr. Nice Guy only went so far. By the time he became CBS News anchor in 1962, there were always hotshots wanting his job. He became very territorial with the Mudds and Rathers waiting in the wings at CBS News, eyeing his job. "He was very protective of his seat of power," Brokaw recalled. "This nicest-guy-in-the-world was more Darwinian than you could imagine when it came to being top dog."

Cronkite in a reduced-gravity environment in 1964. Cronkite was often regarded as a staid character, sitting behind an anchor desk, but in fact throughout his career he was an enthusiastic, participatory journalist. *(Whitehurst Photos)*

The Cronkite family: Betsy, Nancy, Chip, Walter, and Kathy, circa 1966. *(Whitehurst Photos)*

Cronkite *(right)* interviewing John Glenn for CBS News on February 8, 1967. He spoke with Cronkite in the aftermath of a fire at Cape Kennedy on January 27 that had claimed the lives of three astronauts. *(Whitehurst Photos)*

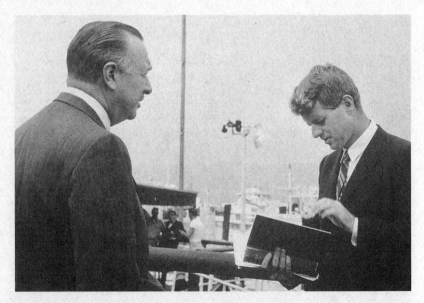

Walter Cronkite speaking with Robert F. Kennedy before a public event, circa 1967. Kennedy (D-NY) was considering a run for the presidency, a prospect about which Cronkite would voice an encouraging opinion in a private setting. *(Whitehurst Photos)*

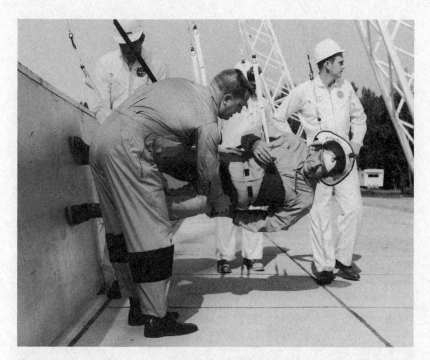

To better inform his space coverage in the late 1960s, Cronkite tried out a lunar reduced-gravity simulator at NASA's Langley Research Center in Virginia. *(Dolph Briscoe Center for American History, the University of Texas at Austin)*

A war correspondent again, Cronkite traveled through Vietnam in February 1968, at the end of the Viet Cong's Tet Offensive. Back home, Americans were being told by commanders, as well as President Johnson, that the United States was drawing steadily nearer to victory. Cronkite went to Vietnam to see for himself. *(Whitehurst Photos)*

February 1968: Cronkite at Hué in South Vietnam, the scene of grim, street-to-street fighting as U.S. forces, led by the Marines, sought to retake the city, which had been seized by the Viet Cong during the first phase of the Tet Offensive. Such heroism impressed Cronkite, but the overall strategies of the war did not. *(Dolph Briscoe Center for American History, the University of Texas at Austin)*

Cronkite interviews Richard M. Nixon on April 1, 1968, in Nixon's New York apartment. The former vice president led the race for the Republican presidential nomination, having recently vanquished George Romney of Michigan. Nelson Rockefeller of New York and Ronald Reagan of California would also fail to catch him. Nixon campaigned carefully and made little news in interviews, feeling that the nomination would be his if he avoided mistakes. He did, and won the White House in the November election. *(Whitehurst Photos)*

On July 21, 1969, the day after Neil Armstrong and Buzz Aldrin walked on the moon, Cronkite held up a copy of *The New York Times* while he was on the air. Trained as a newspaper reporter, Cronkite rejoiced anew when he saw the epoch-making story in print. (*Whitehurst Photos*)

Walter Cronkite talking with Lyndon Baines Johnson at his ranch in Texas in the early 1970s. Cronkite and Johnson engaged in a series of extensive interviews on Johnson's life and turbulent presidency. The last of their conversations occurred on January 12, 1973, just ten days before Johnson's death. (*Whitehurst Photos*)

Cronkite was an active amateur auto racer. He gave it up partly in deference to pressure from CBS, and soon took up sailing. (*Whitehurst Photos*)

Cronkite in 1970 with some of those directly responsible for the look and stature of the *CBS Evening News with Walter Cronkite*: Sandy Socolow (producer), Les Midgley (executive producer), and Richard Salant (news division president). (*Dolph Briscoe Center for American History, the University of Texas at Austin*)

Cronkite taking a break from sailing while on vacation near the Windward Islands in the Caribbean in 1971. *(Whitehurst Photos)*

Walter Cronkite in his office after a broadcast in 1971, shaving before a night out on the town. Cronkite's office, overstuffed with books, gadgets, awards, and memos, reflected the texture of his lifestyle. *(Whitehurst Photos)*

Cronkite and his son, Chip, clowning for a photographer from *Life* magazine in 1971. Cronkite was then forty-five and Chip was fourteen. Cronkite often broke into off-the-cuff numbers with only the slightest encouragement. *(Whitehurst Photos)*

Cronkite standing in front of the Great Wall during CBS News' coverage of Nixon's 1972 trip to China. *(Dolph Briscoe Center for American History, the University of Texas at Austin)*

Cronkite preps eight young people on the set of the CBS News special *What Ever Happened to '72?* Cronkite and the students, all from an Evanston, Illinois, junior high school, traded opinions on everything from the presidential election to the latest movies. (*Dolph Briscoe Center for American History, the University of Texas at Austin*)

"Ted Baxter Meets Walter Cronkite" was the title of the *Mary Tyler Moore Show* episode that aired on February 9, 1974. Ted Knight played Baxter, the news anchor at WJM, in a moment when he convinces himself that he is going to become Cronkite's co-anchor on the *CBS Evening News*. Cronkite made a cameo appearance on the program. (*Whitehurst Photos*)

Walter Cronkite interviewing Gerald and Betty Ford in the mid-1970s. Gerald Ford took office August 9, 1974, upon the resignation of Richard Nixon, but failed to win reelection in 1976. Betty Ford sometimes expressed opinions that contradicted those of her husband, making their joint interviews more unpredictable than those of most presidential couples. *(Whitehurst Photos)*

Israeli prime minister Menachem Begin and Egyptian president Anwar al-Sadat with Cronkite at the King David Hotel in Jerusalem, Israel, in November 1977. As a result of what was called "Cronkite diplomacy," Sadat flew to Israel for the historic and ultimately significant meeting. *(Dolph Briscoe Center for American History, the University of Texas at Austin)*

Cronkite speaks with Jimmy Carter. As president, Carter presented Cronkite with the Presidential Medal of Freedom on January 16, 1981, saying, "And when our nation has been in trouble or made mistakes and there was a danger that our public might react adversely or even panic on occasion, the calm and reassuring demeanor and voice and the inner character of Walter Cronkite has been reassuring to us all." *(Whitehurst Photos)*

Walter Cronkite stands aboard his beloved *Wyntje* shortly before the announcement of his retirement as anchor of the *CBS Evening News*. The *Wyntje*, a sixty-four-foot sailboat, was built for Cronkite and took him through American waters and those beyond. *(Dolph Briscoe Center for American History, the University of Texas at Austin)*

Walter Cronkite listening to Cuban president Fidel Castro on February 14, 1980, during a highly coveted interview. On the same day, Cronkite announced his plans for retirement from the anchor desk at the *CBS Evening News*. *(Whitehurst Photos)*

Cronkite in his office on March 6, 1981, his last day as anchorman of the *CBS Evening News*. *(CBS Photo Archive)*

The famous *All Laughing* photograph by Diana Walker. President Ronald Reagan, Walter Cronkite, Jim Brady, David Gergen, Ed Meese, Vice President George Bush, James Baker, and Bud Benjamin laughing at a 1981 White House party. *(Diana Walker)*

Cronkite on the set of *Walter Cronkite's Universe*, a summer series that premiered in 1980. Devoted to scientific topics, the prime-time show seemed to be a natural progression for Cronkite after he left the anchor chair. The program failed to find an audience, though, a situation Cronkite blamed on the network's lack of promotional support and its failure to keep the show in a single time slot. *(Whitehurst Photos)*

Walter and Betsy toast each other near Alaska's Mount McKinley during a break from filming *Universe* (undated). The couple traveled together extensively over the course of their sixty-five-year marriage. Betsy was known for her sense of irony, which helped them both maintain a sense of perspective as Walter's fame made them national celebrities. Betsy Cronkite died in 2005 after fighting cancer. *(Dolph Briscoe Center for American History, the University of Texas at Austin)*

Cronkite holding three kittens. A lifelong animal lover, he was incapable of hunting, or even killing insects that came into his house. *(Whitehurst Photos)*

CBS newsman Andy Rooney listening to Cronkite at Arizona State University in Phoenix on November 6, 2003. The two had been friends for sixty years, colleagues at CBS, and tennis partners for many of them. Rooney was set to receive the Walter Cronkite Award for Excellence in Journalism that day. *(AP)*

Broadcast journalists Brian Williams, Dan Rather, Walter Cronkite, and Tom Brokaw in New York City on March 16, 2004. *(Getty)*

Walter Cronkite
in 2004. *(Getty)*

A collage of photographs spanning Cronkite's career in journalism.
(Dolph Briscoe Center for American History, the University of Texas at Austin)

29.

A Time to Heal

SCHORR SCREAMS FOUL—CRONKITE THE GORILLA—
WILD FACTS—BRINGING BRADLEY INTO THE FOLD—
FORD PULLS OUT OF VIETNAM—DON'T BLAME THE
PRESS—AMERICA TURNS TWO HUNDRED—THE
GURU FOR LOCAL NEWS ANCHORS—BARBEQUE
TOURISM IN KAYCEE—FRIENDSHIP WITH NICK
CLOONEY—REAGAN CHALLENGES FORD—CARTER
AND THE SECRET SERVICE PLOY—I NEVER WORKED
FOR THE CIA—TOSSING ON ELECTION NIGHT—
GOOD-BYE, JERRY—MAD AS HELL FOR LUMET'S
NETWORK

Since Walter Cronkite was considered the "Most Trusted Man in America," the attack Daniel Schorr levied at him in a January 1975 speech at Duke

University stung. Schorr, who had won Emmys for reporting in each of the Watergate years of 1972, 1973, and 1974, accused Cronkite of kowtowing to the White House when former president Richard Nixon fled in disgrace to San Clemente, California, under threat of impeachment. Schorr was saying, in essence, that Cronkite was a whore for CBS management. At issue was Schorr's charge that network executives had forced Cronkite (along with Dan Rather and Eric Sevareid) to benignly report the historic news of Nixon's dramatic resignation. A disgusted Schorr believed that CBS had cut a deal with incoming President Ford—a quid pro quo—to "soft-pedal" an entire shopping list of Nixon's crimes and misdemeanors in order to establish a "general atmosphere of sweetness and light" under which America could bask. Brian Lamb, who later founded C-SPAN, was the publisher of the influential twice-monthly *Media Report* and reprinted Schorr's remarks verbatim.

By 1974, Cronkite had become disdainful of Schorr, whom he considered a phony-baloney I-Am-the-Reincarnation-of-Murrow grandstander. Cronkite joined Sevareid and Rather in writing an incensed joint rebuttal letter to *New York*, a popular liberal magazine that referenced Schorr's arch accusation. In a rare show of solidarity, the three newsmen denied "that executive orders at CBS News were handed down to 'go soft on Nixon' " or that "those of us who felt constrained from whipping an obviously beaten man behaved in response to such orders."

When Cronkite, who was on vacation, was asked by a reporter about Schorr's claims, hurled like a thunderbolt at his reputation, he said, "Oh, that the son of a bitch had done it again." From Cronkite's perspective, the arrogant Schorr had anointed himself as "one-man ombudsman" for CBS News. He thought Schorr was a terrific reporter but a lousy colleague. Cronkite believed the feud began when Schorr was excluded from CBS News' Nixon resignation speech analysis, which featured Cronkite, Rather, Mudd, and Sevareid. His Duke speech was payback.

After the frenzy surrounding the Duke University allegations settled, Cronkite treated Schorr as persona non grata in the CBS newsroom, refusing to put up with the field reporter's "strange wickets" anymore. Cronkite wanted Black Rock to quietly dismiss the fly-in-the-ointment reporter. "There was always a Schorr version," Cronkite groused, "and everybody else's version of almost everything that transpired." To Cronkite's way of thinking, the truth of the matter was simpler than that. "I think," he said in his own defense, "the circumstances required a sort of decency at that moment."

According to CBS News president Dick Salant, the joint letter to *New York* that Cronkite signed was less than truthful. CBS had planned to devote nearly five hours of coverage to the Nixon resignation speech on August 9, 1974. With hours of airtime to fill, Salant fretted that Cronkite, Sevareid, and Rather would have no real-time direction. That dead-air problem had plagued CBS News during takeoff delays in the Gemini and Apollo programs. "Our reporters would have to ad-lib all night except for the half-hour or so of the president's talk," Salant noted. "All that we in CBS News management could do was to try to set the general tone. So we telephoned the correspondents who would be covering the story that night to remind them that it was not a time, no matter how any of them felt and no matter what Nixon decided to do, for gloating remarks or for editorial attacks. Rather, we told the reporters, if, as appeared likely, Nixon was going to resign—the first presidential resignation in American history—it was a time for national unity and national healing so that the U.S. government and the nation could move forward."

Salant's posthumous memoir wasn't published by Columbia University Press until 1999, long after the

Cronkite-Schorr flap of 1975. It seemed to validate Schorr's charges, at least in part. The joint letter to the magazine, in which Cronkite participated, *had* been misleading. Executive orders at CBS News had indeed been handed down for Cronkite to treat Nixon (a beaten man) with kid gloves. That was not necessarily the wrong decision, and it had not been the result of a tit-for-tat agreement with the White House. But it was wrong for Cronkite to deny Schorr's charge unequivocally. To revert to Cronkite's template of the newspaper city desk, editors often told a reporter how to cover a story: from what angle and with what basic conclusion. It remains the prerogative of management in journalism, as in any business, to give direction. Problems arise when forces outside the newsroom— the advertising department, for instance, or the mayor or the publisher's tendentious spouse—begin nixing or assigning or editing stories. According to Salant's memoir, this didn't happen at CBS News on the night Nixon resigned. The gray area remained that CBSers *had* been presented as commentators, presumably independent commentators, which they apparently were not on that extraordinary broadcast. So each side of Schorr versus Cronkite-Rather-Sevareid was half correct. Schorr believed Cronkite's motivation (placating the conservative affiliates) was suspect and his conclusion (Nixon didn't deserve an exit drubbing) mistaken. Nixon had been an enemy of the fourth estate and Schorr wanted him to suffer accordingly. "It is as wrong [for the media] to take on the role of nation-healers as it is to take on the role of nation-wounders," Schorr argued. "That is the job of others, and we report it. . . . The media were accused of manipulation against Nixon, which was not true. We should also not engage in manipulation for him."

Like CBS News, *The Washington Post* also declined a victory lap in covering Nixon's fall from power, presenting the incoming Gerald Ford as the steadiest of public men, a football-playing Middle American at ease with himself and loyal to the republic. "Katharine Graham and Ben Bradlee issued a 'don't gloat' order that August eighth," Bob Woodward recalled. "Nixon's story, they believed, was in many ways a tragedy. Ben ran a picture of Nixon hugging his daughter on the front page. There was a sense of 'let's be humane' about it all."

Perhaps Cronkite didn't go comically soft on Nixon, but he was filled with human sympathy for the ex-president that late summer. Public humiliation made Cronkite uneasy. There was no thrill for him in having Nixon walk the plank just so reporters could throw tomatoes at him. From August 1974 to Nixon's death in 1994, Cronkite was surprisingly generous toward Nixon, praising his intellectual acumen as a global statesman and Sino-Soviet expert on many public occasions. Friends in the Vineyard recalled Cronkite's fury whenever it was intimated that the *CBS Evening News* was responsible for Nixon's flushing from the White House because of its edgy Watergate segments. It wasn't a mantle Cronkite embraced. He publicly rejected the "CBS got Nixon" allegation, praising the ex-president's "overtures in international politics" to China, the USSR, and Egypt in a *Denver Post* interview.

Schorr's accusation caused a permanent rift between him and the Cronkiters at CBS News. Sevareid repudiated him to the grave. Cronkite barely remained on handshaking terms with him. Nevertheless, when the crusading Schorr made public the contents of the classified Pike Committee report on illegal CIA and FBI activities in 1976, risking imprisonment by refusing to reveal his sources to Congress on First Amendment grounds, Cronkite wrote that he was "behind" Schorr "all the way." When CNN hired Schorr in 1979, Cronkite, perhaps with good riddance at heart, wrote him a generous good-luck note.

With only minor deviations, the *CBS Evening News* continued to hold a lead in the ratings race throughout Ford's presidency. Wags referred to the *CBS Evening*

News roster in the post-Watergate era as a kind of family, an oddball version of the popular show *The Waltons*, then running on CBS every Thursday night. Cronkite was a fan of the warmhearted hourlong drama set in the Blue Ridge Mountains, which celebrated familial strength in rural America during the Great Depression. The *CBS Evening News* edition of *The Waltons* included Papa (Cronkite), the wayward older son (Daniel Schorr), the cheeky little sister (Lesley Stahl), a prickly nephew (Dan Rather), the upstanding if distant brother (Roger Mudd), and, to be sure, the perspicacious grandfather (Eric Sevareid). The CBS News lineup was first-rate, perhaps even hitting a high mark in the mid-1970s with the inclusion of Richard C. Hottelet, Marvin Kalb, Charles Kuralt, Richard Threlkeld, Bruce Morton, Terry Drinkwater, Connie Chung, Phil Jones, and Ike Pappas. Some media critics credited the success of the *CBS Evening News* to the excellence of the roving correspondents rather than to the anchor. Yet it was Cronkite, always wearing his trademark CBS Eye cuff links, who was the personality. He was the hub, and all those talented correspondents— and perhaps the executives and producers—were the spokes. No one really thought of Leiser, Socolow, or Salant as Cronkite's bosses. "He knew," said Bill Leonard, "that his only boss was his wife, Betsy."

To his CBS News colleagues in New York City and Washington, Cronkite was seldom "Uncle Walter," the loving moniker used by viewers around the country. Like a gregarious friend, Cronkite, the public believed, was always in high spirits and at ease with breaking news, big debates, and famous people. The CBS employees, a close group, still called him "the eight-hundred-pound gorilla," who, Les Midgley explained, "gets anything he wants." One name that no one at CBS News dared call Cronkite was "Walt." Dan Rather, in *The Camera Never Blinks Twice*, the book he co-authored with Mickey Herskowitz while still working with Cronkite, poured on the adjectives to describe Cronkite circa 1974, including "assured," "unflappable," and "perfectly aimed." But he didn't dare call him "Walt."

No one understood Cronkite's Puritan work ethic better than his workhorse producer Sandy Socolow, who became like a second son. Everyone at CBS News knew the Cronkite-Benjamin-Socolow motto: "Get it first, but first get it right." He insisted that every broadcast be flawless. "God help us if NBC had a good story that we didn't, or handled a story better than we did," Bonn recalled. "Walter, flushed and furious, would come bursting into the fishbowl, and his first words would be, 'God damn it!' All of us were Type-A competitive to start with, and we *hated* to get beaten on a story. But Walter and his red-faced 'God damn it!' made us *really* hate to get beaten on a story, so it didn't happen very often."

Cronkite's defining quality remained competitiveness. After the nightly broadcast, the staff would frequently gather to watch the later broadcasts of the ABC and NBC news programs; Cronkite often joined in the group critique. CBS News correspondent Bob Schieffer, who had idolized Cronkite before joining CBS in 1969, thought the old Unipresser possessed more curiosity than any other individual in the media world. "Walter was the nicest guy in the world," Morley Safer recalled. "But as a managing editor, he was brutal." According to Roger Mudd, the CBS Washington correspondent bench was widely known, and got their phone calls answered, because the sources knew they could get their stories on the Cronkite newscast.

By and large, colleagues saw Cronkite as a tough old pro with the certain, decorous air of a sea captain. If a new hire was nervous in his presence, he told filthy jokes to put him at ease. He might not have been easygoing, but his mien was that of a serious professional; he didn't *overtly* play favorites inside the newsroom or as a reporter. But he was a master of graceful thank-you notes, condolence letters, and Christmas cards. Rigid ideology and political correctness bored him. Yet CBS News had an anti-Nixon slant from 1968 to 1974—no question about it. He publicly admitted that his stable of CBS reporters—himself included—were nondogmatic liberals; it came with the job description. "Most newsmen have spent some time covering the seamier side of the human endeavor; they cover police stations and courts and the infighting of politics," Cronkite told *Playboy.* "And I think they come to feel very little allegiance to the established order. I think they're inclined to side with humanity rather than with authority or institutions. And this sort of pushes them to the left. But I don't think there are many who are *far* left. I think a little left of center is probably correct."

In the days before the Internet, it wasn't easy to find information about an election in Algeria or an earthquake in Honduras at the snap of a finger—yet Cronkite demanded specifics about any and all subjects worth reporting on. One of his favorite phrases was "Find the Facts." To him, the effort to obtain and explain hard facts wasn't drudgery; quite the opposite. His demand for buttoned-down facts, those "Walter Wants," at CBS News was life-sustaining. "He took nothing for granted," remembered Don Hewitt in his memoir, *Tell Me a Story.* "He picked up the phone and checked with people he knew would give him a straight answer and, at the same time, throw in a couple of facts that made his reporting better than anyone else's. I can't think of anyone, including the president, who wouldn't take a phone call from Walter Cronkite."

During Ford's truncated 895-day presidency, it seemed as if Cronkite tried to help him out every chance he got. The atmosphere in Washington had improved a lot since Nixon left. After contributing to the downfall of Johnson (his Tet special) and Nixon (the Watergate reports), Cronkite was willing to grant Ford a year's worth of mulligans to grapple with the great politics of the day. During Ford's presidency, Cronkite anchored *CBS News Special Reports* on the historic *Apollo-Soyuz* rendezvous, the assassination attempts on Ford's life, and the accidental president's four-day trip to China. He helped Ford make a great TV epic out of ordering a U.S. military strike against Cambodia's meager forces for having seized the *Mayaguez*, an American merchant ship, in disputed waters.

CBS News correspondent Ed Bradley—who had been wounded in Phnom Penh covering the war in Cambodia, receiving shrapnel wounds in his back and arms—became Cronkite's go-to guy. With some conceit, Cronkite claimed he had *discovered* Bradley when the young reporter was on the CBS-owned New York radio station WCBS back in 1967. What Cronkite admired about Bradley was his tough interview style. "And at the same time," Cronkite recalled, "when the interview was over, when the subject had taken a pretty hard lashing by him—they left as friends. He was that kind of guy."

When on March 1, 1975, a fierce North Vietnamese offensive was unleashed in the central highlands of South Vietnam, Cronkite knew America's longest war (at that time) was over. Cronkite interviewed Ford from the Blue Room of the White House a few weeks earlier, along with colleagues Bob Schieffer and Eric Sevareid. Many South Vietnamese, Ford told them, were desperately seeking to leave the country before the Vietcong took over. In early April, Cronkite instructed Bradley to outperform NBC News and ABC News on the end of the U.S. military engagement in South Vietnam. Two days before the fall of Saigon, on April 30, President Ford, in a speech given at Tulane University, conceded that the United States' war in Vietnam was over: "Today, Americans can regain a sense of pride that existed before Vietnam. But it cannot be achieved by refighting a war that is finished. . . . These events, tragic as they are, portend neither the end of the world nor America's leadership in the world." Two U.S. Marines were killed in a rocket attack at Saigon's Tan Son Nhut airport on April 30; they were the last Americans to die in the war. Within hours, looters sacked the U.S. embassy and the North Vietnamese tanks rolled into Saigon.

CBS News scheduled a two-and-a-half-hour *Special Report* for the end of the Vietnam War. Cronkite was slated to anchor the special, but he was home in bed, racked with back pain, a condition that occasionally sidelined him. Stouthearted, he refused to take prescription painkillers or morphia, though he was barely able to move. Time and rest, his physicians advised, but Cronkite was a famously restless man. During the past fifteen years, almost a million Vietcong troops had been killed, a quarter of a million South Vietnamese soldiers had died, and fifty-seven thousand Americans had perished. Almost immobile, it behooved him to soldier through that night's *CBS Evening News*, even with excruciating back pain. "Nothing was going to stop him from doing this broadcast," Les Midgley recalled. "Nothing."

Cronkite called a doctor, who trussed his back tightly and accompanied him to the West Fifty-seventh Street studio. He went from wheelchair to anchor chair. At any moment, a jolt of shooting pain might cause him to flinch, but he started the April 30 *CBS Evening News* broadcast with a report about the People's Army of Vietnam capturing Saigon and made it to its end. The

Evening News footage of the chaos in war-torn Saigon as the last American helicopters rose from the U.S. embassy rooftop, desperate Vietnamese citizens clinging to their struts, was unforgettable. Cronkite now knew that the stalemate conclusion from his "Report from Vietnam" back in February 1968 stood up "rather well" in history. At the program's end, Cronkite had time to summarize the $150 billion war. "There is no way to capture the suffering and grief of our nation from the most decisive conflict since the Civil War," Cronkite said. "We embarked on this Vietnam journey with good intentions, I think. But once upon the path, we found ourselves having been misguided."

What worried Cronkite that evening, as he was put back in the wheelchair and taken home, was that the Pentagon was trying to blame the media for losing the war. " 'We could have won,' hawks insisted, if the press had not shown those pictures of naked, napalmed Vietnamese girls fleeing our bombing, of prisoners being shot in the head, of burning houses, of wounded G.I.s," Cronkite wrote in *A Reporter's Life*. "Television brought the war into our living rooms at home and destroyed our will to fight, the theory goes." In the coming decades Cronkite would be excoriated by General Westmoreland, President Nixon, and the *Military Review* (the official journal of the U.S. Army) for turning America's pro-war attitude of 1964 to the antiwar one of 1975. Cronkite knew that in the next war whoever was in the White House would try to say . . . *no television cameras!* In tribute to Cronkite's truth-telling about Vietnam from 1968 to 1975, *Esquire* put him on its cover as one of the "Great American Things," along with Marilyn Monroe, Jackie Robinson, and Lassie. Going with the praise, Cronkite boasted that his favorite album of 1975 was Paul Simon's *Still Crazy After All These Years*—an apt description for a wizened TV survivor like himself.

Cronkite's admiration of President Ford—another supposedly avuncular figure—grew considerably after the Vietnam War ended that spring of 1975, even though Bradley warned him that Cambodia's Khmer Rouge government was participating in a genocide the president was doing little to stop. While Bradley bonded with Cronkite over a shared appreciation of Ford, both Mudd and Schorr thought the anchorman was "too-much-the-toady" of the Ford White House. "Ford was probably the most personable, as far as just being a regular fellow, of any of the presidents," Cronkite recalled. "He was an old-shoe fellow, no presumption and no pretense. I don't think he was terribly bright in the presidential sense, but on the other hand, he didn't take on airs of being an intellectual, either."

For both Schorr and Mudd, Cronkite seemed too cozy with Ford. Cronkite believed that Ford's duty was to heal the nation of the Johnson-Nixon abuses of executive power. Cronkite felt Ford was doing a pretty good job of it.

Beginning on July 4, 1974, CBS News aired sixty-second "Bicentennial Minutes" for two straight years, construed as a healing gesture by the network. These popular segments won CBS News an Emmy for "Outstanding Program and Individual Achievement." On Independence Day 1976—the official bicentennial—Cronkite broadcast *In Celebration of US*. He anchored the festivities from Madison Square Garden from 6:00 a.m. to midnight, but he seemed to be at every crossroad town from Altoona to Yuma where there was a flagpole. Pretaped segments can have that effect. "It was," Cronkite said, "a glorious, spontaneous upwelling of enthusiasm for that special day in American history." During cosmic fireworks displays in Boston and New York City, he could be heard oohing and aahing like a little boy. Perhaps the most touching moment occurred when a massive choir from Washington, D.C., sang "America the Beautiful" and Cronkite, assuming his microphone was dead, proceeded to sing along loudly, as if he were standing in a baseball stadium, hand over heart. It was an endearing blunder. (Or was it staged, like the fidgeting with his glasses during the JFK assassination?)

Everyone at CBS, from correspondents to location scouts, excelled at Cronkite's eighteen-hour bicentennial coverage, with pickups from forty-two locations. Charles Kuralt reported from the parade of tall ships on the Hudson River, with Cronkite telling viewers how he envied that assignment. Dan Rather somehow managed to report a Battle of Gettysburg reenactment, a baseball game in Colorado, and a progressive-left protest in Washington, D.C. CBS News's Reid Collins was stationed at Battery Park in New York City, while Hughes Rudd delivered prerecorded *Jeopardy*-like did-you-know history pieces. CBS treated the Founding Fathers almost as national deities throughout the coverage—the longest CBS News broadcast since *Apollo 11*. (It would hold that distinction until the beginning of the first Gulf War in January 1991.) Segments were aired from a rodeo in Geeley, Colorado, and an Indian powow in Carnegie, Oklahoma. Cronkite was obsessed with a Freedom Train crisscrossing the country, displaying national oddments such as Dorothy's dress from *The Wizard of Oz*, Joe Frazier's boxing shorts, and Martin Luther King Jr.'s pulpit along with dozens of other pop culture thingamajigs and gewgaws. When Cronkite heard "Amazing Grace"—his favorite song—played on bagpipes that special Fourth of July from the Mall, he wept openly. This was the Great National Healing that Cronkite believed was exactly what America needed after Vietnam and Watergate. Cronkite used the bicentennial to tell Americans it was alright to be proud of their country again.

Brit Hume, an up-and-coming young reporter who reminded media executives of Roger Mudd, did a lot of the bicentennial remote work for ABC News. It was a grueling day of patriotic gore, with field reporters scattered all over the country broadcasting festivities. When an exhausted Hume got home around 10:30 that evening, he turned on CBS News and was flabbergasted to see Cronkite still doing live coverage. Holy cow! Talk about "Iron Pants" stamina! At 11:00 p.m., the local WCBS news came on and Hume naturally assumed that was the end of the Cronkite marathon. But to his utter astonishment, at 11:30 Cronkite was back on TV, live. "Walter came on the air and said, 'What a day! What a day! What a day it has been!'" Hume recalled. "I'll remember it forever. I thought . . . 'I'll be damned.' At that moment I understood why Cronkite was so good. He had that indisputable key quality for a long career in the business: enthusiasm. It was like he truly never wanted the bicentennial to end."

There were more fireworks yet to come that summer. Following the Independence Day celebrations were the political conventions of 1976. Bill Small recalled working with Cronkite at the Republican Convention, held August 16–19 in Kansas City. CBS had set up a booth at Kemper Arena, but Cronkite used the Muehlebach Hotel as his personal salon when off the air. At the Muehlebach, every bellman, waitress, and desk clerk treated him like a long-lost high school friend. While it wasn't quite Dorothy Parker at the Algonquin, Cronkite feted reporters from midsize Midwest newspapers such as the *Peoria Journal Star* and *The Topeka Daily Capital* with liquid meals. "Walter would endlessly talk with small-town newspapermen," Bill Small recalled. "He was a good party boy, a good mixer."

Cronkite made a fast friend with Nick Clooney, a reporter for WKRC-TV (Channel 12) in Cincinnati, the ABC affiliate. Clooney, whose son, George, would become a legendary actor in Hollywood, interviewed Cronkite about the advent of Barbara Walters co-anchoring with Harry Reasoner for ABC News nationally. The discussion turned into a heavy drinking bout where everything from Tom Brokaw becoming the new anchor of NBC's *Today* show to entrepreneur Ted Turner founding WTBS in Atlanta to Rupert Murdoch purchasing the *New York Post* was discussed. "Back then, Cronkite set the tone and tenor for all of us in local TV news," Clooney recalled. "Murrow was a radio guy. He had no influence, really, on local TV news. It was Cronkite who brought local TV anchors along with him in markets all over the country. His *Evening News* led the way in inventing the TV news format. He made us at WKRC feel that what we did was important, that TV news was a new American tradition."

Leslie Midgley seconded Clooney's claim in his memoir *How Many Words Do You Want?* Too often Murrow was cited as the role model for television broadcasting aspirants. But would KCTV in Kansas City or WREG in Memphis or WWCO in Minneapolis learn anything from Murrow's carefully produced and packaged *See It Now* or *Person to Person* or "Harvest of Shame"? Murrow was a mediocre broadcaster at live events like political conventions, election nights, and assassination tragedies. By contrast, Cronkite *loved* to ad-lib on the air and set a high standard for how to succeed at the art form. "Cronkite's picture should be hung in every local TV newsroom," Nick Clooney maintained. "He was our industry's George Washington."

Television had turned America into an indoor nation, delivering entertainment and news smack into viewers' living rooms. But Cronkite never abandoned the pavement, walking the streets of every city, adding two or four new cards a day to his Rolodex. CBS Washington bureau chief Bill Small discovered walking around a city block with Uncle Walter was an experience in friendly theatricality. Small was Cronkite's sidekick one afternoon in Kansas City, sampling the best barbeque Kaycee joints had to offer. Cronkite kept saying, "I have a friend at such-and-such place," and indeed he did. Folks would just drop free plates of ribs and chicken for Cronkite to eat, nourishing him to keep on keeping on, telling the truth about Washington power brokers. Cronkite might have risen up the ladder at CBS News in New York City, but he never stopped being the Kansas City kid willing to talk about how ABC's hot shows—*Happy Days, Charlie's Angels*, and *The Six Million Dollar Man*—were giving CBS's programs a run for their money. There was High Cronkite (anchorman) and Low Cronkite (storyteller); people loved both personas. This was a key to all the great TV newsmen's success: never forget your hometown folks. Cronkite's hometown just happened to be the whole damn United States of America. Holding court in various Kansas City bars, Cronkite willingly made a fool of himself by reciting the lyrics to C. W. McCall's hit song "Convoy" and spontaneously dancing when the Bay City Rollers' "Saturday Night" blared out of the speakers of a jukebox.

The big story in Kansas City in 1976 was the challenge made by California actor and former governor Ronald Reagan to incumbent Gerald Ford for the Republican nomination. Ford had won more primary delegates than Reagan but hadn't collected enough to secure the nomination. It looked like an old-fashioned floor fight might ensue. On the Democratic side, Senators Henry "Scoop" Jackson of Washington and Frank Church of Idaho were among those running against Governor Jerry Brown of California and Jimmy Carter, a former one-term Georgia governor. Both Democratic and Republican candidates were looking for ways to use television in the tight competition, and at least a few of the candidates were taking advantage of the medium through a significant tactical shift. Campaigning before the people was important, but appearing with Cronkite on the *Evening News* was essential for maintaining ballot-box appeal. "His persona became so prominent in American culture," Tom Shales recalled, "that he was credited with massive swings in public opinion."

Mudd had covered the California primaries in June, supplying the *CBS Evening News* with top-notch regular reports. He prepared a piece on the new attitude toward campaigning. Reagan, over a three-hour span, Mudd noted in the segment, talked "to no more than 2,000 people in the flesh. He took no new positions, he broke no new ground." But that night on Los Angeles's three local news shows, an audience of 1,071,000 people saw him for five minutes and fifty-one seconds. On the three network newscasts, thirty-seven million people watched Reagan for four minutes and four seconds. What Mudd understood was that television had turned campaign politics on its head.

Cronkite previewed Mudd's report when it arrived and, despite its fine quality, he rejected it. Always the watchdog, he didn't want to run a story that "cast television in a bad light by allowing itself to be manipulated." Mudd's report was important—something was new in political campaigning, an event we now know as the photo-op. Mudd was asking Cronkite to point out that television news was being used, or worse, that it was complicit in duping the public. The report was buried, aired on the *CBS Morning News* instead of the suppertime broadcast. Cronkite had been asked by Mudd to do something difficult, to look at his own world in the mirror that he held up for everyone else. And he had turned away.

During the Democratic presidential primaries that spring, Cronkite had realized that Carter might be able to win the Democratic nomination. What had alerted him was that the Georgia governor's security entourage was considerably larger than Scoop Jackson's or Ed

Muskie's. Based on this fact, Cronkite told a number of CBSers, Carter was at the front of the pack. "We investigated the security detail issue," CBS writer Sandy Polster recalled. "Walter had been impressed by it. It changed his impression of Carter as a small-timer. It was almost subliminal. Well, it turned out that Carter was paying for the visual of those guards. Cronkite, laughing, admitted that he had been duped. He fell for the perception-is-reality ploy."

Cronkite wasn't particularly excited about Carter at first; his trumpeted born-again Christianity on the campaign trail had troubled the anchorman. Cronkite's Episcopalianism was much more understated. While Cronkite still considered himself an FDR-Truman-Kennedy liberal—an Upper East Side and Martha's Vineyard one to boot—he nevertheless thought that having the first president from the Deep South since Zachary Taylor might be a good thing. And before long he found himself amazed by Carter's sharp mind. "I think," Cronkite said, "he's got one of the best brains of anybody I've known."

In 1976, Cronkite became involved in a minor scandal that left him livid. Television reporter Sam Jaffe of ABC News claimed he had seen Cronkite's name on a top-secret list of journalists who worked for the Central Intelligence Agency. Jaffe told a U.S. Senate committee that Cronkite regularly reported to the FBI when he had worked for CBS News. Jaffe also stated, correctly, that in 1959 Sig Mickelson had Cronkite (and other CBS reporters) receive a briefing from CIA director Allen Dulles. Dick Salant defended Cronkite, saying that once Mickelson left CBS in 1961 to become director of *Time-Life* broadcasting, he ended any CBS News cooperation with the CIA. But the damage to Cronkite's reputation was done. The Cronkite-CIA rumor spread like wildfire, and the anchorman sprang into damage control mode, traveling from New York City to Langley, Virginia, to confront CIA director George H. W. Bush about the bogus leak. Many competing TV journalists had long complained that Leiser, Benjamin, and Cronkite got preferential treatment from the National Security Council, the Department of Defense, NASA, the CIA, and other national security branches—this was one rumor Cronkite had to squash. "To remove the stain on him and on journalism, Cronkite demanded that Bush disclose the list of news people who actually had been CIA agents," Daniel Schorr recalled in *Clearing the Air.* Bush rightly refused to touch that request with a ten-foot pole.

A few weeks later, the CIA confirmed that two *former* CBS correspondents in the 1950s had worked for the agency. Names were never given. Hughes Rudd was suspected of being one of the agents. Speculation about a Cronkite connection tapered off. After looking into the matter, Cronkite wrote his fan club head, Robert Feder, to let him know what he'd discovered. "All of this is deplorable," Cronkite wrote the twenty-one-year-old, "and should be condemned, but as Sig Mickelson has pointed out, it did occur at a particular juncture in history when the horror of the relationship was blurred by what seemed to be a particular anti-Communist fervor."

By 1976 the Cronkite style of reporting election results to the American public had become the norm. There was an old habit that Cronkite had picked up at WTOP in 1950 that he wouldn't shed in 1976. Cronkite, unlike other reporters, refused to use an earpiece. Communication between him and the control board was done in the old-fashioned, circa-1952 way: anchor assistant Mark Harrington would place a card in front of the anchorman saying something like, "Toss to Stahl" or "Ford is about to appear." If something was really urgent, Harrington would crawl over to Cronkite, tap him on the knee, and hand him a piece of paper. Harrington worked at ground level, under the camera's frame. He called this the "foxhole."

On November 2, 1976, once again Cronkite proved a maestro on Election Night. Carter won 297 electoral votes compared to Ford's 240, the closest presidential election since 1916. Anybody watching CBS saw Cronkite at the top of his "And that's the way it is" game.

Just because the Watergate and Vietnam eras were over, and a Georgia peanut farmer and nuclear engineer had been elected U.S. president, didn't mean Cronkite felt good about political trends in America. What concerned him throughout the bicentennial year was the way corporations were influencing TV news as never before. The most talked-about Hollywood film of the year was *Network*, a black comedy written by Paddy Chayefsky and directed by Sidney Lumet (Cronkite's director at CBS back in the 1950s for *You Are There*). Cronkite never missed a Lumet-directed movie. To him, his friend Lumet outdid himself with *Network*, one of the best movies—maybe *the* best—he'd ever seen. The story of newscaster Howard Beale—who some said was modeled on a mad version of Cronkite— damned the news industry and the unbridled influence of corporate ownership. Kathy Cronkite, having previously made cameo appearances in *Jaws* and *The Trial of Billy Jack*, was cast as the Patty Hearst figure. The plot of *Network* centered on Howard Beale (Peter Finch), the longtime television anchorman of the *UBS Evening News* who is told by news division president

Max Schumacher (William Holden) he has only two more weeks left on the air because of sagging ratings. When Lumet gave Cronkite a private screening of *Network* in early 1976, Cronkite "howled with laughter," just "rolled over on the floor with the depiction of TV news," hoping someday he would have the courage of Beale to open up the window and shout "I'M MAD AS HELL, AND I'M NOT GOING TO TAKE THIS ANYMORE!"

After the laughs faded, Cronkite was left with a lot of haunting questions raised by *Network*. Lumet had hit close to home. Much about TV news gathering was a sham. To colleagues at CBS News, Cronkite compared the Academy Award–winning film to Aldous Huxley's *Brave New World*. "When Paddy Chayefsky brought out *Network*, in 1976, all of us thought it was a very funny satire—a wild exaggeration of reality," Ron Bonn of CBS recalled. "None of us realized that it was prophecy. But Cronkite thought the dystopian film might be prophecy."

30.
Live with Jimmy Carter

DROWNING IN HAPPY TALK—HIRING WOMEN WRITERS—RITA BRAVER AND THE CARTER INAUGURAL BALL—DIAL-A-PRESIDENT—THE VANOCUR SCOLD—REVOLTING AGAINST PANCAKE MAKEUP—BOYS' CLUB AT SEA—CRONKITE DIPLOMACY—QUITTING WHILE ON TOP (A CONSIDERATION)—THREE MILE ISLAND BLUES—HAMILTON JORDAN'S STUDIO 54 SNORT—REFUSING TO FORGET THE HOSTAGES IN IRAN—WHY NOT BE A U.S. SENATOR?—RATHER BEATS MUDD—THE OLD GOAT CONTINUES—JOHN ANDERSON'S NO. 2—UPSTAGING TED KENNEDY—DR. CRONKITE OF HARVARD UNIVERSITY—THE REAGAN-FORD CO-PRESIDENCY SCOOP—WHO'S AFRAID OF BARBARA WALTERS?—THE PRESIDENTIAL MEDAL OF FREEDOM

G iven Cronkite's mass audience, it was significant that he started championing the women's movement in the mid-1970s. Although he came to feminism late, once on board, he was an unhesitating public ally (even though he refused to apologize to feminists for doing a *Playboy* interview in 1973, noting that Albert Schweitzer set the precedent). On the rubber chicken circuit, he publicly supported the Equal Rights Amendment (ERA) for women and championed the historic 1973 *Roe v. Wade* decision legalizing abortion. Full of male swagger, Cronkite quipped that he "hoped all new CBS hires would be women"; it was a comment groaning with condescension. Feminist Gloria Steinem used to tell Cronkite, to his face, that he was a low-grade male chauvinist. He demurred. "I'd go to help her with her coat," Cronkite chuckled to friends, "and then I'd remember and pull back—and she'd [finger-wag] say, 'You seeeee?'"

Also complicating Cronkite's sudden pro-feminist attitude was the starburst ascendancy of Barbara Walters. Dubbed by *Time* the most influential woman in television, Walters had never been a print reporter. Having started her journalism career as a writer on CBS's *Morning Show* in the 1950s, she was hired by NBC's *Today* show in 1961 as a writer and researcher. She soon became a beloved on-air personality, attracting a loyal following of female viewers. In 1976, ABC News, hoping to compete with Cronkite, hired Walters to co-anchor its evening news show with Harry Reasoner.

It was reported that Walters would be paid a whopping $1 million a year. Scads of newspapers headlined the "Million-Dollar Baby." Roone Arledge, chairman of ABC News, desperate to beef up his news organization, had intentionally thrown that high-salary figure to the press, knowing it would generate a frenzy of attention. (What Arledge didn't stress was that Walters received that salary for anchoring and hosting four prime-time specials a year.)

The Big Three men in news—Cronkite at CBS, Chancellor at NBC, and Reasoner at ABC—each made around $400,000 annually. Was Walters worth that much more? Cronkite didn't think so. But he didn't want to be perceived as anti-Walters on the basis of gender, so he overcompensated with pro-ERA rhetoric, which gave him fig-leaf cover to regularly snipe at Walters for diluting real news with *People* magazine–style entertainment gossip. And Cronkite joked that ABC News was the schlock network, that if you wanted to end the Vietnam War, just put it on ABC and, like its programs, it would end very quickly. "Walter was very nasty about me," Walters recalled. "It was the old boys' club and I didn't fit in. I was a new generation. I started in TV, not the AP or UP. Walter didn't like any of this."

When ABC News announced that Walters was the industry's first million-dollar reporter, CBS management felt deeply embarrassed. Unblinkingly, they offered Cronkite the same salary. Cronkite—who thought Walters was too showbiz—feigned offense. "Not on your life," he told CBS News president Dick Salant. "Forget it. I'm not going to play the celebrity journalism game." It proved to be a hollow protest. A deal was struck for Cronkite to earn over $900,000 a year, with three consecutive summer months of vacation to enjoy sailing *Wyntje*. The network would also provide him with a town car and driver, memberships to private clubs, and corporate aviation to and from Martha's Vineyard. Not a bad deal. "Walter complained about me getting $1 million," Barbara Walters recalled. "But he soon was the great beneficiary. He didn't complain about making *a lot* more money a year, because I broke the mold, very loudly."

Most Americans in 1976 didn't distinguish fame from accomplishment. No one much cared about the personal life of syndicated columnist Andy Rooney until Hewitt hired him for a regular segment on *60 Minutes* (to deliver his signature curmudgeonly commentary on the pratfalls of American life). Suddenly Rooney, inundated with speaking requests, was all the must-get-to-know rage. If you were on TV, beamed into living rooms, the American public believed you were important. "A good journalist is worth more than a baseball player or a rock star, but I'm worried about where it's going," said Salant, following the Walters announcement. "A million dollars is a grotesque amount of money."

Unlike Salant, Cronkite had been careful not to snicker publicly about Walters getting paid more than double his CBS salary—for what he privately derided as "happy talk." When *Time* magazine asked him about Walters as his new competition, he had a ready high-road answer. "She has shown exceptional talent in interviewing," Cronkite said. "She's aggressive and studies her subject." Both Cronkite and Reasoner underestimated the talent of the irrepressible Walters by a long shot. As a tough interviewer, her only peer was Mike Wallace. (Cronkite used to say, "You don't know competition until you get in the ring with Mike Wallace.") The fast-rising tide of TV news changes that Walters heralded left Cronkite stone cold; he privately hoped she'd fail. "Back then, Walter was unbelievably competitive," Walters recalled. "Let's just say Uncle Walter wasn't Uncle Walter to me."

A female CBS News hire whom Cronkite adored was Rita Braver. Her first job in TV was writing copy at CBS affiliate WWL-TV in New Orleans. CBS's Washington bureau hired her in 1972. It was a propitious time for women to get into TV news. Before long, Braver was assigned to cover the Watergate story at CBS News' Washington bureau. "We all felt honored when Cronkite came to town," Braver recalled. "We got along extremely well because, as you know, Walter liked women! Not that he was overly flirtatious; he wasn't. He was courtly. It was as if he wished the entire newsroom were run by women."

Cronkite asked Braver to accompany him to the Carter Inaugural Ball on January 20, 1977, along with producer Bud Benjamin. Besides being a superb producer, Benjamin had been Cronkite's alter ego for a decade— each made the other one better. Betsy preferred to stay back in New York, so Braver ended up being Cronkite's escort. "Walter was all dressed in his tuxedo when we got in the limousine," Braver recalled. "He looked good. Suddenly he started frisking himself, looking for his inaugural ticket. There were no cell phones in those days, we were running late, and he didn't want to turn around and drive all the way back to the hotel. Bud kept laughing, saying, 'Relax Walter . . . I *promise* you they'll let you in the ball. You're Walter Cronkite.'"

Although Benjamin kept laughing hysterically, Braver saw that Cronkite was indeed deeply anguished over the embarrassing situation. He was mortified not to have a ticket. He didn't want to be perceived as a big shot, Mr. Red Carpet, a celebrity arrogantly thinking the inauguration rules didn't apply to him. "When we arrived," Braver recalled, "about four people were waiting to sweep Walter away so he could be with Jimmy and Rosalynn Carter."

On March 5, 1977, President Carter and Cronkite, hoping to capitalize on their strong chemistry, sat on Queen Anne chairs near a fireplace in the Oval Office and answered the public concerns of forty-two callers from twenty-six states. This was an unprecedented CBS radio call-in program: a cross section of Americans could dial into the White House and ask Carter questions, with Cronkite serving as moderator. *Newsweek* called the event "Dial-a-President." It was Carter's quirky gambit to field the type of questions "you never get in a press conference." To Cronkite's amazement, none of the 900-code long-distance calls was prescreened. AT&T, smelling a publicity boon, had established a people-to-president system in Bedminster, New Jersey, with a direct hookup to the White House, with only a three-second delay to censor obscenities.

That afternoon, Carter, grinning heavily, gave detailed, factual answers to questions about everything from the tax code to Ugandan politics to Castro's Cuba. "No matter how far out the question," Cronkite later wrote, "he had in his head a textbook of information about it." While there were no headline-caliber disclosures, Carter, the master of clarification, had handled the varied callers exceptionally well. But Cronkite's closing comment was met with surprising anger in journalism circles, a sign that Cronkite wasn't getting free passes anymore. "We [CBS] would be glad to sign you up again, Mr. President," Cronkite said. To which Carter responded, "Walter, I liked it. . . . My inclination would be to do this again."

Cronkite's performance stirred up envy and resentment from other press organizations. Cronkite, it seemed, was trying to corner the journalism market on the Carter White House. These carps were crystallized in a hard-hitting op-ed piece written by Sander Vanocur for *The Washington Post*, titled "The President Carter Show." Vanocur took Cronkite apart limb by limb for acting as White House master of ceremonies instead of as a journalist, for playing "Mr. Interlocutor to President Carter's Mr. Bones." White House press secretary Jody Powell didn't do Cronkite any favors when he said that Carter had personally selected Cronkite because "no one would be disrespectful" to him. NBC's *Saturday Night Live* did a hilarious spoof on the Oval Office and CBS call-a-thon, with Dan Aykroyd playing Carter and Bill Murray as Cronkite.

A lot of print reporters had taken to mocking Barbara Walters as the "Pope" and Cronkite as the "King" of TV news in 1977. Rejecting the weight of celebrity, Cronkite found solace aboard his double-ended *Wyntje* with friends like novelist James Michener. Cronkite even gave Michener the title of his memoir: *The World Is My Sea.* Together Cronkite and Michener would sail for days; the stormier the sea, the more their anxieties subsided. *Godspeed* had now become Cronkite's favorite directive. The cabin of his ketch was a sanctuary from the clatter of TV news. A deal was even struck for Cronkite to acquire a minority share in the *Waterway Guide*—founded in 1947—which contained yearly pertinent information for both the recreational and commercial boat owner. Cronkite's job was to decide which charts, anchorages, and tide tables to include for the scene from Maine to Key West to the Bahamas.

During the Carter years, Cronkite also began sailing, drinking, flying, and carousing with Mike Ashford, a well-known figure in Annapolis, Maryland, who was spearheading a revitalization of the waterfront city. Ashford (from Joliet, Illinois) and Cronkite saw

themselves as good-guy pirates straight from the foot-
loose lyrics of a Jimmy Buffett song. At yacht clubs all
over America, Cronkite was known as The Commodore.
The two rum-runners had met when Ashford, owner
of McGarvey's Saloon and Oyster Bar, held a "Save the
Bay" fund-raiser at his Annapolis home; Cronkite volunteered his services to the eco cause. "We hit it off
right out of the gate," Cronkite recalled. "I took him
out for a sail and we discussed books and nautical life."

After a carefree sailing summer with Ashford in
1977, Cronkite returned to the *CBS Evening News* desk
after Labor Day, covering in great depth Carter's signing of the Panama Canal treaties. The White House
was pleased. On the afternoon of November 11, a sleepy
Friday, a wire service report seized Cronkite's attention. Agence France-Presse matter-of-factly reported
that Egyptian president Anwar Sadat would be willing to visit Israel; this was huge news in the world of
Middle Eastern diplomacy. AFP reported that some
Canadian diplomats cited a rumor that Sadat told his
parliament in Cairo that he would be "willing to go to
Israel to talk peace."

Because Sadat had made similar statements before,
Cronkite felt that more information was needed to warrant broadcasting the report on the *CBS Evening News*
on Saturday (with Harry Reasoner hosting). Cronkite

decided to keep an eye on the AFP reports over the weekend. He instructed executive producer Bud Benjamin to begin setting up for a satellite interview with Sadat for Monday morning. Technology in the mid-1970s was laborious, and a hookup to Egypt would take time. Over the weekend, Cronkite, Benjamin, writer Sandor Polster, and others talked about what questions to ask Sadat. No one at the time thought to also line up an interview with Israeli prime minister Menachem Begin.

Cronkite interviewed Sadat on Monday, November 14, 1977, about his conditions for visiting Israel. In pro forma fashion, he spoke of Israeli withdrawal from the Sinai Peninsula and the Golan Heights. When pressed by Cronkite on the AFP report, Sadat matter-of-factly said, "I'm just waiting for the proper invitation" from Israel. An animated Cronkite, doing pantomime while Sadat spoke in his earpiece, turned and mouthed to Polster, "Get Begin!" Polster raced into the adjoining network newsroom to telex the CBS News bureau in Tel Aviv about the development. The AFP report was suddenly tangible to Cronkite, real breaking news. "Under my suggestive questioning," Cronkite recalled, "Sadat said he could go [to Israel] within a week, as soon as he had an official invitation. But we hadn't laid any lines to Begin for his response, so we had to scramble."

That evening, Cronkite began the *CBS Evening News* by reporting: "Not since the founding of the modern state of Israel—not as far as we know—has a leader of Israel met with a leader of Egypt. But now all obstacles appear to have been removed for peace discussions in Jerusalem between Egyptian President Sadat and Israeli Prime Minister Begin." The first two segments of that Monday broadcast were devoted to the separate interviews Cronkite had conducted that morning via satellite feed—first with Sadat from Cairo and then Begin from Tel Aviv. Each Middle East leader argued his side of the post–Yom Kippur War story. But Cronkite skillfully prodded them, for the first time, to agree to have face-to-face meetings with no preconditions. "It was later suggested by some critics that I had overstepped the bounds of journalistic propriety by trying to negotiate an Israeli-Egyptian détente," Cronkite recalled. "They did not know the full story— that my initial journalistic intention was to knock down the speculation over the visit."

Cronkite had become peace broker between Israel and Egypt. When *Time* magazine asked him about his diplomatic coup, he gloated. "There was a lot of desk-slapping and hot-diggity-damns around here." *Newsweek* called Cronkite's intervention the "most dramatic cross-coupling ever between mass media and the secret world of diplomacy." CBS executives wisely declined to boast. "It was a matter of a couple of good interviews coming at the right time," Bill Small, now senior vice president of CBS News, told *Newsweek*. "Both sides have a vested interest in the world knowing what they say." ABC's Roone Arledge tipped his hat to Cronkite. "CBS ought to be congratulated," he said. "It was dynamite TV." Peter Jennings of ABC News cabled Cronkite: "Walter, I'm sure Sadat would disagree, but dammit, I wish you'd retire. Congratulations again."

That November 1977, the world learned about the "Walter Wants" phenomenon. Walter wanted Begin and Sadat to come together—and they did. *New York Times* columnist William Safire, a conservative, called it "Cronkite Diplomacy," as a backhanded way to insult President Carter's lackadaisical approach to the Middle East peace process. "It took Walter Cronkite of CBS," Safire hyperbolically wrote, "placing an electronic hand on the backs of Israel and Egypt, to bring them together." Benjamin now realized that Cronkite had been the archetypal TV reporter for the ages. Like Murrow, his myth would never die. "We played Sadat and Begin off of each other and made history," enthused John Lane, a producer at the *CBS Evening News*. "It was a time when you thought '*damn* . . . we're making a difference.'"

On November 19, five days after his diplomatic foray, Cronkite flew from New York to Cairo so he could interview Sadat on his historic visit to Israel on a private plane. Both men had rich, distinctive voices layered with a quietly mischievous sense of humor. They were sitting together on the runway, chatting amiably, when suddenly, almost out of thin air, Barbara Walters appeared like a mirage on the tarmac. She had been in Israel interviewing Moshe Dayan when the announcement of the Sadat-Begin meeting became public fare. The always-resourceful Walters had managed to fly from Tel Aviv to Cairo—the first flight between those cities since the creation of Israel in 1948. To Cronkite's everlasting consternation, Sadat invited her to join them. His exclusive had been, in point, co-opted by his rival. A Gulliverian jealousy engulfed Cronkite to the point of burning his ears. "On the flight, I slipped Sadat a private note," Walters recalled. "I gave him interview options. He chose to speak with me alone."

For the next two years, every time Cronkite tried to wrangle a big exclusive interview—as he was used to doing—Walters seemed to beat him to the punch. The broad, a ticked-off Cronkite thought, was *everywhere*. The competition between them became tooth-and-claw fierce. A common refrain at CBS from 1977 to 1981 was Cronkite asking a producer, "Did Barbara get anything I didn't?" Before long, the rivalry almost became fun. "We became, over time, very fond of each other," Walters explained with an eye twinkle. "I was proud to be competing for interviews with *the* Walter Cronkite, a great, great newsman."

Marshall McLuhan's oft-repeated saying, "the medium is the message," has become cliché. But Cronkite's Middle East diplomacy proved the theory in a steroid-enhanced way. At one point Cronkite, interviewing Sadat, noted that the Egyptian president was "walking something of a tightrope here." A puzzled Sadat asked what Cronkite meant. "It's a very delicate matter for you, and how far you can go," Cronkite explained. "If you offend the Arab world by offering too much, you get in one position. If you don't come back with something, you're going to disappoint your own people. Can you successfully navigate those difficult waters?"

A bright-faced Sadat replied, "Marvelous Walter!" What impressed Sadat wasn't the mixed metaphor but Cronkite's strange ability to boil down the complexity of the Middle East peace process into a single sound bite. It was Cronkite's ability to be the editor and distiller of news that made him unique. A year later, Cronkite received the Anti-Pefamation League of B'nai B'rith's Hubert H. Humphrey Freedom Prize for his initial interviews, which the nonprofit said, "gave enormous impetus and thought to the peace process between Israel and Egypt."

Over the next two years, the diplomatic dance between Sadat and Begin proceeded, with starts and stops, in Cairo, Jerusalem, Camp David, and Washington. Cronkite interviewed Jordan's King Hussein, Syria's president Hafez al-Assad, and Israeli prime minister Golda Meir. It culminated with the establishment of diplomatic relations between Egypt and Israel on March 26, 1979 (the first by any Arab nation with the Jewish state). Cronkite called the signing of the historic Egypt-Israel peace treaty on the White House lawn one of the great moments in his life. "To see something like that blossom right in front of your eyes," he said, "my goodness, it was extraordinary—a heck of an experience."

Cronkite thought that, all humor aside, perhaps Peter Jennings was right. Why not quit CBS News while he was at the top of his game? The idea certainly had its merits. In 1977, Eric Sevareid retired from CBS News at the age of sixty-five. According to network policy, the retirement age was not, in fact, mandatory for on-air talent, but it was often used as an excuse to end careers. CBS News wasn't known for rewarding its most important newsmen once they turned too gray. Banished, they ended up living on Social Security checks in San Diego or Naples, Florida. Murrow was the most excruciating example. When Severeid's turn came to resign, he was promised appearances on CBS specials and news magazine broadcasts, but those invitations never came to pass. Collingwood, yet to turn sixty-five, was suffering a similar fate. One of the original Murrow Boys, he came to work every day only to sit in his office with nothing to do. He would formally retire in 1982, an embittered man. The network had proven its savvy in hiring smart, budding journalists, but in parting with them, it was graceless.

CBS News had an ego of its own. In the Paley hierarchy, stars were built. But as a corresponding corollary, this premise likewise rejected the notion that any on-air talent was bigger than the news division itself. Not Murrow, not Severeid, not Collingwood, not Cronkite—they all worked at the pleasure of CBS, not the other way around. So CBS News' reputation for cruel dismissals was well known in the industry, as was Cronkite's reputation as its biggest star. With the two certain to cross, speculation bubbled over just how long Cronkite would remain king of the broadcast center. To some CBS executives, Cronkite was becoming an aging dinosaur, stuck in old-style objective journalism, the kind that ignored entertainment glitz. "It'll be up to Walter to decide whether he wants to do more, or do less, or do nothing," Bill Leonard, who would replace Salant as CBS News president, said. "There is an awful lot of workhorse in Walter, and there are ways to keep him on despite mandatory retirement rules. No one took Lowell Thomas out and shot him on his 65th birthday."

Research showed that focus groups wanted more bells, whistles, and salacious gossip than Cronkite was offering. In a December 1977 interview with the *St. Louis Post-Dispatch*, Cronkite, uninterested in the fickle whims of viewers, continued his wholehearted assault on the desultory trends of tabloid entertainment-as-news. As Cronkite saw it, the nub of the problem was greedy shareholders demanding excessive profits without recognizing that they, as shareholders of a news-gathering organization, had a public responsibility. "What I rail against is the Action news, Eyewitness news," he said, "that consultant format that diminishes the importance of the story itself in favor of presentation."

Salant was constantly asked in 1978 about who would replace Cronkite. He developed the gag line that Ed Asner (who played the newsman Lou Grant on the CBS comedy *The Mary Tyler Moore Show*) was the leading candidate. That bought CBS some wait-and-see time to decide whether Cronkite—who won the Alfred I. duPont–Columbia University Award in Broadcast Journalism that year—should quit. Word on the street was that Roone Arledge was prepared to offer Dan Rather $1 million to jump ship to ABC News as anchorman. Talent agent Richard Leibner, who worked in spurts for Cronkite since 1964, was also Rather's hard-negotiating agent, responsible for getting ABC interested in Rather. Leibner met with Cronkite for lunch at Alfredo's, near Columbus Circle, to discuss his retirement date at CBS. Salant had anointed Roger Mudd as Cronkite's successor. But Cronkite pushed for Rather to be his successor because he was a terrific international correspondent. Mudd, by contrast, had just worked the D.C. beat. "People who blame Rather for pushing Cronkite out," Leibner said, "are peddling bullshit."

By the late 1970s it was fairly obvious to the big-time Opinion Makers that either Mudd or Rather would replace Cronkite within the next year to eighteen months. The decision showcased the congenital split personality of CBS News: it was sort of Salant (Mudd) versus Cronkite (Rather). Mudd had ably served as Cronkite's substitute for years. Rather, once vilified by right-wingers as "the president's archfoe," had, since 1975, become very popular as a host of Sunday evening's top-rated *60 Minutes*. The year 1979 came and went, though, with Cronkite still the paragon of TV news broadcasters. Yet Cronkite was indeed tired of the hectic rigmarole of managing the *CBS Evening News.* "Do you know what kind of a weight it is," he told incoming news division president Bill Leonard, "carrying this thing on your shoulders, week after week, month after month, year after year? It's getting to me. I need time. Time to sail. Time to relax. Time to . . . aw, hell . . . it's getting me down. I'd be a damn fool not to quit while I'm ahead."

Leonard staved off Cronkite's departure, telling him to stall until outgoing president Dick Salant retired. A prime directive to Leonard, as he took his new job in 1979, was to keep Cronkite from leaving the *CBS Evening News.* He managed to convince him to wait. But the let's-find-a-replacement strain was clearly starting to annoy Cronkite. "In the grimiest commercial terms, each rating point gained or lost by the *CBS Evening News* meant millions to the network," Leonard explained. "And year after year Walter Cronkite came through with a one- or two-rating-point lead over NBC, usually more over ABC. But that wasn't all. *Evening News* leadership meant . . . leadership in network news in the public mind, and that translates throughout the day. It helps deliver more viewers into the evening entertainment schedule. Prestige *and* money. And the wonderful goose that had been turning out those golden news eggs for so many years would lay no more."

While Black Rock festered out the new anchor situation, Cronkite continued to dominate TV news with smart exposés of China and Egypt. David Halberstam made Cronkite a veritable folk hero in *The Powers That Be*—published in 1979—illuminating the dramatic courage the CBS News anchorman exhibited after the Tet Offensive in 1968 by declaring the war a stalemate. That year both Cronkite and Halberstam agreed to lecture and lead seminars at Columbia University's Graduate School of Journalism. Hoping for one last Vietnam or Watergate or Begin-Sadat diplomatic foray before retirement Cronkite, long wary of nuclear power, got intensely involved with the partial meltdown at the Three Mile Island nuclear power plant near Harrisburg, Pennsylvania, in 1979. To Cronkite, the March 28 disaster was proof of the unacceptable risks both to humans and to the environment of this energy source.

The movie *The China Syndrome* was released shortly after the Three Mile Island nuclear accident. It seemed obvious to producer Sandy Socolow that the *Evening News* should do a feature piece showing the eerie similarity between *The China Syndrome* and Three Mile Island, and he mentioned it to Cronkite: "You know this is really uncanny that this movie should be so close to the bone," Socolow told Cronkite. "It's just stunning, a stunning coincidence, and I think we could make a story out of it." To which Cronkite, the anti–Barbara Walters, shot back, "I'm not in the goddamn business of selling movie tickets."

While Cronkite later took well-deserved credit for CBS News' deep investigation of Three Mile Island in 1979, he also blundered that year. White House chief of staff Hamilton Jordan, a handsome Georgia pol considered Carter's top confidant (besides his wife, Rosalynn), was charged with snorting cocaine at the Studio 54 nightclub in New York City. A special counsel was appointed to investigate the alleged narcotics use. Cronkite, to his everlasting regret, opened the *CBS Evening News* with a report about the incident. In 2001 he told Larry King on CNN that his airing of Jordan's cocaine problem was the "low point" of his career. "I think we did [Jordan] an injustice in reporting that," Cronkite admitted. "Not in reporting it so much as leading the broadcast with it as if it had great importance, and it had none really. Nothing important about it."

The *CBS News Special Report* "Showdown in Iran" (January 23), which grappled with the Islamic

Revolution (and included a Mike Wallace interview with the Shah of Iran) was extremely important television. Little did Cronkite realize that U.S. policy toward Iran—because of the hostage crisis—would become the foreign policy curse of the Carter administration by year's end. The shah of Iran had left his revolution-rippled nation in January 1979, coming to the United States to get medical treatment. In his absence, the Ayatollah Khomeini, an Islamist fundamentalist, tightened his grip on Iran. Within days of the Shah's arrival in New York, armed Iranian protesters sacked the U.S. embassy in Tehran and took fifty-two diplomats hostage. For the next 444 days—all that remained of his presidency—Carter struggled to have the captives released. "It was always gnawing away at your guts," Carter said. "No matter what else happened, it was always there."

The hostage crisis consumed President Carter in 1979 and 1980. Cronkite, worried that the media would abandon the story prematurely, made a bold decision, along with producer Ernie Leiser, that had far-reaching consequences. At the end of every *CBS Evening News* broadcast, Cronkite would sign off with the number of days the hostages had been held. CBS News started this count on Day 74. Cronkite's nightly in-your-face reminder of the hostages was a public relations disaster for the White House. It was as if, every day, Cronkite was chastising Carter, saying, "You still haven't brought our boys home, sir!"

Once again, Cronkite led the charge and the rest of the media followed suit. Before long, NBC News made updates from Khomeini's Tehran its feature story. ABC News launched the 11:30 p.m. *Nightline*, which focused for fifteen minutes almost exclusively on the Iranian hostage crisis—ABC would banner it "America Held Hostage." Former State Department undersecretary George Ball blamed Cronkite for starting a national TV soap opera. "Night after night, the television news dramatized the number of days the hostages had been held," First Lady Rosalynn Carter complained. "I tried to turn off the television quickly if we were watching CBS before Walter Cronkite could sign off with the daily count."

Despite his constant bluff about retiring, Cronkite was busier than ever at CBS News. But in a November 1979 interview with Michael Gorkin for the magazine *50 Plus*, Cronkite laid out his fantasy plan to retire and sail around the world, maybe get good enough to compete in the America's Cup. His wife, Betsy, knew the seafaring plan by heart. Whenever Cronkite grew depressed about the Iran hostage crisis, Three Mile Island, double-digit inflation, or long gas lines, his glorious dream lifted his spirits. "We'd do it slowly," he told Gorkin, "across the Atlantic to the Azores, then around Africa to the Persian Gulf, and so on . . ." He then closed his eyes, as if studying a nautical chart in his mind, smelling the spray of sea. "We could stop in various ports around the world, go ashore and spend time with friends, then sail on. It would be wonderful, absolutely fascinating. And really, could there be any better way for an old journalist to spend time after he's left his trade?"

Throughout the 1980 presidential election campaign, it was no secret that Cronkite's clock was running down at the *CBS Evening News*. That didn't mean his popularity was waning; to the contrary. With the exception of a couple of odd weeks, his *CBS Evening News* had topped the ratings ever since 1967. On the 1980 presidential campaign trail, Cronkite was a bigger celebrity than the politicians he interviewed (excepting Carter and Reagan). But he had grown overwhelmed by the workday grind of two jobs. He'd always been absentminded about keeping track of personal belongings, but now that tendency increased. Lost keys became almost a medical condition. He was also getting puffy under the eyes. When a friend from Houston visited the *Evening News* set, he was surprised to see how thick Cronkite's on-air makeup was. "I've spent thousands of dollars developing these bags under my eyes," Cronkite chuckled, "and CBS spends thousands of dollars trying to hide them."

Livid against exit polling, computer predictions, and "action news" as being "perfectly ridiculous," Cronkite criticizing news-as-entertainment became as predictable as the swallows returning to Capistrano. The gullibility of the American electorate worried him. "We need courses, beginning in junior high, on journalism for consumers," Cronkite said. "How to read a newspaper, how to listen to the radio, how to watch television. . . . People have got to be taught to be skeptical so that they won't become cynical about all news sources." Cronkite never grappled with the possibility that he—the biggest TV news star in U.S. history— was part of the cultural problem.

Duke University professor James David Barber accurately wrote that a revolution in presidential politics meant the new kingmakers weren't the Democratic or Republican parties, but Cronkite and other elite TV journalists. In April 1980, Barber published *The Pulse of Politics: Electing Presidents in the Media Age.* According to Barber, journalists could now make or break a candidate. If you were Reagan or Carter, kissing up to Cronkite was far more important than kissing babies on the campaign trail.

That spring, Hugh Sidey of *Time* covered a Chicago focus group evaluating voter trends in the coming Illinois primary and seconded the Barber thesis. "Their focus was not on a local luminary but on Walter Cronkite, who had come to the provinces and set up his majestic broadcast booth," Sidey wrote. "His noble gray head appeared at the bottom of the screen, a gigantic red, white, and blue map of the U.S. spread out behind him. Not since George C. Scott opened the movie *Patton* had such a dramatic entrance been filmed. There were quiet gasps among the appreciative Chicagoans."

On February 6, 1980, Cronkite gave *The Washington Post* the scoop: he would be leaving the *CBS Evening News* sometime in 1981. The announcement was big news across the country. A reporter for the *Atlanta Journal-Constitution* compared the retirement to ripping Linus's blanket away from an electronic America. Brushing aside rumors, Cronkite insisted that management hadn't forced him out. "I'd like to be able to step out right now," he said. He had adopted the get-out-while-you're-on-top strategy. But, he added, he would stay through the election season and probably leave on or around his birthday, in late November 1981.

With that, speculation about his replacement grew fervent. All America was guessing. On February 15,

The New York Times made it official: the darkly hand-some Rather would replace Cronkite as the *CBS Evening News* anchorman. The announcement, made by the new CBS News president Bill Leonard, was something of a shock. Mudd had been the Vegas bookies' favorite. The normally laconic Mudd, on the boil, cleared his desk immediately. He spent hours browsing the antiquarian shelves of novelist Larry McMurtry's Booked Up shop in Georgetown, pondering his plight. He would go to work for NBC News within the year. The rumor mill held that market researchers found Rather polled better than Mudd. Adding insult to injury, CBS News refused to let Mudd out of his contract early, knowing he would sign with ABC News or NBC News.

Cronkite played good soldier, telling the *Times* that Rather was extremely well qualified for the anchorman job. Whatever their personality differences, Cronkite knew that Rather was the relentless investigative gum-shoe reporter of the JFK assassination, civil rights, the Vietnam War, and Nixon woes; he was proud to call him his successor. But Cronkite also made it clear that *he* was in charge of CBS News' 1980 presidential election coverage. "I've covered every inauguration since Harry Truman's," he said, "and I want to do one more."

Just how dramatic the 1980 election would be became clear as Cronkite hosted a debate in Manchester, New

Hampshire, among seven Republican candidates—
Ronald Reagan, Howard Baker, Philip Crane, John
Connally, Bob Dole, Harold Stassen, and George H. W.
Bush. It was quite a playing field. Mark Harrington,
Cronkite's assistant producer, was once again his
human time prompter at knee level, flashing cards like
a railroad brakeman. As *The Washington Post* joked
regarding the debate, "Harrington tells Cronkite what
is happening. Harrington is Cronkite's reality; Cronkite
is ours."

Although Cronkite was a noncontroversial interviewer, he was a stopwatch stickler. Ronald Reagan
learned this the hard way. At one juncture, when Reagan
was on a roll, Cronkite interrupted and said time was up,
cutting Reagan off in midsentence. Reagan's campaign
team went ballistic after the broadcast. They believed
that Cronkite had tried to make his friend George H.
W. Bush look polished and Reagan the fool. Cronkite
wouldn't have any of it. Live TV was no place for rambling. Any good high school debater knew you couldn't
run over the clock time. It made the politician look
selfish, hogging the competition's allotted time. When
you entered the debate realm, Cronkite said, you played
by the rules. Reagan now understood, like Walters, that
despite all the off-camera avuncular charm, Cronkite,
like Reagan himself, was a tough customer.

Congressman John Anderson (R-Ill.) declared an Independent candidacy for president in 1980, eventually running in the November election against Ronald Reagan on the Republican side and President Carter on the Democratic ticket. At heart, Anderson was a Rockefeller Republican with an overweening Earth Day sensibility who had served admirably as a U.S. congressman from the Sixteenth District in Illinois. As a registered Independent, Cronkite, amazingly, was suggested as a vice presidential candidate for Anderson. The idea snowballed. Wherever Anderson went that month, he was dogged by reporters' questions about Cronkite as his running mate. At Georgia State University, Anderson fueled the rumor by ending his speech with Cronkite's trademark "And that, my friends, that's the way it is, April 29, 1980." The crowd went wild with applause.

On May 3, 1980, Morton Kondracke of *The New Republic* accurately reported that Cronkite, floating a trial balloon, told him "he'd be honored if asked" to join the Anderson ticket as vice president. A dispute erupted over whether the chat was supposed to be off the record or not. CBS News executives in New York got bombarded with media queries. Had Cronkite shed his objectivity yet again? Cronkite, unreachable for a few days, was off on *Wyntje*, away from radio contact.

Then the hullabaloo caught up with him. "Oh my God," Cronkite said in horror. "He totally misrepresented the spirit of our conversation."

In an op-ed for *The New York Times*, Cronkite defended being an Independent and quashed the Anderson rumor. "To be among the best reporters and analysts of government," he wrote, "does not in itself equip one to become a government leader, no more than being a good sportswriter equips one to play for the Dallas Cowboys." Senator Daniel Patrick Moynihan of New York, a political centrist, had also been bandied about as Anderson's vice presidential pick. He felt, in fact, that Anderson had offered the job to him. With devious humor, Moynihan wrote Cronkite that "knowing" the CBS News anchor's "devotion to TRUTH," he felt obliged to rip the curtain back on Oz. "The fact is," Moynihan told Cronkite, "that you were No. 2 for the No. 2 spot on the Anderson ticket."

Cronkite also found himself in a controversy over his urging President Carter to do something urgently dramatic to gain release of the U.S. hostages in Iran. On April 24, 1980, Carter's rescue attempt, code-named Operation Eagle Claw, proved disastrous. Two of eight U.S. helicopters were destroyed after colliding in midair, resulting in the deaths of eight American soldiers and a failed mission. James Reston wrote a

New York Times piece lambasting the president and his buddy "Ayatollah Cronkite," an "innocent villain," but in part responsible. "It seems slightly mad," Reston wrote, "but it happens to be true that the character in the White House really felt some pressure from Uncle Walter's announcing every night the number of days of captivity of the hostages."

Because people knew Cronkite would be retiring soon, the outpouring of emotion for him was torrential. One morning Cronkite joined Ted Kennedy, the liberal Massachusetts senator, on the campaign trail for a flight to Erie, Pennsylvania. As they left the aircraft together, the crowd went wild—for Cronkite, not Kennedy. "Walter!" they shouted. "It's Walter!" Cronkite was overshadowing the candidate. As Kennedy worked the crowd, everyone wanted to shake Cronkite's hand, not his. According to *The New York Times*, Cronkite was "seemingly embarrassed" by the commotion he had caused. He tried to get out of the way, maneuvering to a different part of the tarmac. But the crowd acted as if he were all four Beatles rolled into one and Kennedy was Pete Best. One woman shouted out, to cheers, "You ought to be running, Walter!"

On June 6, Cronkite earned an honorary doctorate of law from Harvard University. He was in a state of disbelief, for the first time seeing his career as truly historic in nature. At the commencement ceremony, he was praised for being the "preeminent figure" in contemporary journalism. No longer would he carry the stigma of being a college dropout. Now he was Dr. Cronkite, with "Harvard" affixed to his name. He embraced the advanced degree with awe and embarrassment. "You know, Anna Freud [daughter of Sigmund] got an honorary degree, Professor so-and-so who won a Nobel got one," a humbled Cronkite told Fred Friendly, with a trace of forced modesty, after the ceremony. "And yet, when I stood up, there was a standing ovation. What's it all about?"

"You know what that's about," Friendly snapped.

"You mean television?" Cronkite responded.

"No," Friendly said. "Not television. At a time when everybody was lying—fathers, mothers, teachers, presidents, governors, senators—you seemed to be telling them the truth night after night. They didn't like the truth, but they believed you at a time when they needed somebody to believe."

The Republican Convention—held in Detroit from July 14 to 17—had a spell of drama, with Cronkite acting as the catalyst. Reagan, the voice of conservatism, seemed likely to win the GOP nomination. The big unknown was who would run with him. A movement, somewhat unprecedented, was launched to have former president Gerald Ford be Reagan's running mate. Thirty-three-year-old David Kennerly had been White House photographer for the affable Ford. A great friendship—almost of the father-and-son variety—had developed between them. Ford invited Kennerly to tag along with him in Detroit, snapping a few photos and sharing some laughs. Barbara Walters of ABC News thought she had scooped Cronkite by getting an exclusive first interview with Ford. Cronkite found himself number two in the pecking order and wasn't happy. But while Walters got the first one-on-one, it was Cronkite who scored what Tom Shales of *The Washington Post* called the "scoop of scoops."

When Cronkite's turn arrived, he asked Ford about taking the vice presidential spot on the GOP ticket, "If Reagan chose you, wouldn't it be like a co-presidency?"

Ford, his wife Betty looking on, foolishly agreed. "I would not go to Washington," Ford told Cronkite, "and be a figurehead vice-president."

What a score for Cronkite. CBS News fanned the spark into a wildfire. Without time for Ford to swivel, the phrase *co-presidency* ricocheted all over America. Ford later said it best: "Cronkite had me in a pickle." Reagan would never accept a co-presidency. The disclosure squelched the novel idea of a Reagan-Ford ticket once and for all.

Meanwhile, Sandy Socolow received a hysterical phone call from Hinda Glasser, Cronkite's office manager. Barbara Walters was trying to bully her way into the CBS broadcast booth where Cronkite and Ford were still chatting. Socolow, arms crossed, acting like a bodyguard, rushed to Glasser's aid and prevented Walters from entering. "Barbara and I had an argument," Socolow recalled, "but I succeeded in excluding her. She didn't reach Ford until the Cronkite interview was over and Ford had exited our offices."

Cronkite, still the alpha newsmaker, now had an unexpected problem on his hands. Walters was high-heel-clicking mad and just outside the guarded booth. She was demanding a follow-up interview with Ford. "She had planted herself right outside the door," Kennerly, still amazed at her gall decades later, chuckled. "She was howling mad that Cronkite got the scoop, that the old-boys' club was in play."

Ford was afraid to exit the CBS booth. "Is she still there?" the former president timidly asked Kennerly.

"Yes," Kennerly said. "We've just got to walk past her."

That was easier said than done. Once Ford emerged from the booth, Walters pounced on him.

"You've got to give me the interview!" Walters raged. "You're making me look bad!"

"I'm busy here," Ford told her, walking swiftly away, desperate for escape, "I'm running late for an appointment."

Walters hadn't played her last card. "You've got to do it for Alan's sake," she implored, referring to her then-boyfriend, Alan Greenspan, who was chairman of the Council of Economic Advisers during Ford's presidency. Kennerly looked at the Walters spectacle with contempt. She was begging, pleading, arm-twisting, cajoling, like a spoiled child throwing a temper tantrum. But Walters got the follow-up interview. It was at that moment that Cronkite knew that Barbara Walters—his chief rival—was a real force of nature, one whose career would have longevity. "At a luncheon that both Barbara and I attended the next day, Ford told the group that he had a sore shoulder," Cronkite recalled, "suffered when Barbara twisted his arm to get him onto ABC."

A UPI reporter asked Socolow about the Walters incident, news of which had spread. He told a G-rated version of events, swear words left out. A little while later, Socolow fielded an irate call from Walters. She charged Socolow with betrayal. "Done what?" a perplexed Socolow responded. For four or five minutes, Walters ripped him a new one. "She said she was sorry," Socolow recalled. "That she had looked forward to someday, perhaps, working with me, and now I had made that impossible."

The Democratic Convention was held in New York City from August 11 to 14. As Rather predicted to Cronkite, the entire night was indeed "an entertaining brawl with elements of farce." President Carter easily defeated Ted Kennedy to win the party's nomination. But the most noteworthy moment of the night occurred when a seemingly inebriated Kennedy wouldn't shake Carter's hand onstage at Madison Square Garden. That night was Cronkite's last hurrah. When CBS threw Cronkite a surprise party at the Democratic National Convention, inviting reporters and producers from NBC and ABC to come, Cronkite was touched. "I am overwhelmed," he said. "I really am . . . even though I know that the free drink and free booze is a hell of a lure."

At the end of the convention, Cronkite's microphone was mounted like a trophy; its accompanying plaque thanked him for teaching "three generations of Americans the political process." Charles Kuralt, who had become a great pal of the anchorman, presented the memento to Cronkite as everybody held up a shot of Maker's Mark. A button in the back of the microphone played Cronkite's first CBS convention report from 1952, when the word *anchorman* was created for him.

That November 4, Cronkite broadcast his last Election Night for CBS News. Reagan easily trumped Carter by 489 electoral votes to 49. Cronkite sensed that the timing of his retirement was good, that before long the TV news standards he had spent decades establishing would recede into the land of folly. Though one can never trust statistics, a report had come out that November announcing that 27 percent of U.S. homes were wired for pay-cable, uninterrupted first-run movies, and specials. Within a year it would reach 38 percent. No amount of Maker's Mark or colleague assurance, mugs of beer at P.J. Clarke's, or fine wine on *Wyntje* could protect CBS News from the encroachment of the cable revolution. There would no longer be must-watch Cronkite personalities to offer headline news service to the 70 percent of the U.S. public that got most of its news from television. Depending on how you looked at the situation, cable TV was either the grand payoff for Telstar or Nixon's revenge. Cronkite saw it as both.

On January 16, 1981, just before leaving the White House, President Carter awarded Cronkite the Presidential Medal of Freedom. "For thousands of nights, the eyes of millions of Americans have been turned into the eyes and ears of Walter Cronkite," Carter said at the Washington ceremony. "He has reported and commented on the events of the last two decades with the skill and insight which stands out in the news world, in a way which had made the news of the world stand out for all of us. There is probably not a single American who doesn't know Walter Cronkite, and of those tens of millions who do know him, I don't believe there are any who distrust him."

PART VI

The Spokesperson

31.

Retirement Blues

THE LONG GOOD-BYE—NO SHAME IN CRYING—UPI
FOR SALE—RATHER IN THE HOT SEAT—RUSSIA,
REAGAN, AND REGRET—THE UNIVERSE—
GLOBETROTTING TO EXCESS—PALLING AROUND
WITH CHARLES OSGOOD—CABLE TV ROCKETS—OF
JOHN HENDRICKS AND THE DISCOVERY CHANNEL—
BANQUET SPEECHES AND SAILING—RECONNECTING
AS DAD—SADAT IS SHOT—DOWN WITH RATHER, UP
WITH KURALT—BETRAYED BY CBS—PRINTER INK IN
HIS VEINS—A PRISONER OF HIS CBS PAST—THE
JOURNALISM-CELEBRITY COMPLEX—FULL OF DISIL-
LUSIONMENT

Cronkite's last day anchoring the *CBS Evening News* was Friday, March 6, 1981. At the company's request, he had stayed through the February sweeps. There was a sense that Cronkite's leaving the broadcast was akin to his dying. A telegram from a Long Island woman reached Cronkite, begging him not to quit: "Keep it up, you're getting better." But Cronkite wasn't taking a hiatus; he was going out on top. A national magazine, in full mourning mode, contacted Cronkite with an offer for him to write his own obituary. Amazed at the letter's gall, Cronkite indeed mailed back a response: "Walter Cronkite, television and radio newsman, died today. He was smothered to death under a pile of ridiculous mail, which included a request to write his own obituary."

Upon stepping down, Cronkite, the preeminent television newsman of the twentieth century, insisted that he not be treated as a retired figurehead. Having negotiated a $1 million annual salary with CBS, he remained a vital part of the network. He would be regularly logging stories for the *Evening News* as special correspondent. Most of his time would be devoted to a weekly news magazine on science, space, and the environment called *Walter Cronkite's Universe* (with Bud Benjamin as producer). A progenitor to the Discovery Channel, the half-hour CBS pilot had first aired on June 27, 1979, to good prime-time ratings. In 1980, *Universe* ran four additional times, earning a Peabody Award. So it made sense that, in 1981, Cronkite would try, in thirteen summer episodes, to make *Universe* a hit show focusing on U.S. military affairs, NASA, oceanographic exploration, and ecology. But while still part of the company, he had left behind a leadership void at the *CBS Evening News.* "That little guffaw laugh of his wasn't around anymore," Connie Chung lamented. "No more of his warmhearted 'Attaboys' after doing a segment he liked in the hallway."

The forty-nine-year-old Rather was an aggressive newsman, to be sure: he even experimented with heroin for a story on drug addiction. No television correspondent had covered civil rights or went after Nixon with more doggedness. During Nixon's first trip to China in 1972, he pushed against White House rules and tried to interact with the common people of Beijing. The very year that Cronkite became CBS News anchor, Rather was a cub reporter at KHOU-TV in Houston, gaining superlative notice for his coverage of Hurricane Carla from Galveston Island. "We were impressed by his calm and physical courage during that hurricane," Cronkite said. "He was ass-deep in water moccasins."

But Rather also had his critics. Many felt he had been undignified in drawing President Nixon into a verbal clash at a Houston press conference in 1974. From that point on, Rather had trouble shedding the image of being a loose cannon. His deviating from protocol during Nixon's trip to China had rubbed Cronkite—a play-by-the-rules establishmentarian—the wrong way back in 1972; he considered it gauche. For all of Rather's intensity when he interviewed politicians, his questions tended to bleed into long digressions. Rather's style was quite different from Cronkite's down-home neighbor-next-door persona. Rather was folksy, but in a quirky way ("This is shakier than cafeteria Jell-O," "If a frog had side pockets he'd carry a hand gun," etc.) that Cronkite thought hokey and tedious. He sometimes came across as simultaneously loopy and wooden, edgy and insecure. One word often used to describe him was "enigmatic." Nobody at CBS ever mastered the riddling essence of his character. "I'm a different person than Walter Cronkite," he tried to explain, fearing unmet expectations, "and as time goes along, it will naturally be a different broadcast." Rather, for all of his great reportorial skills, was paranoid that Cronkite, after going on his global junket for *Universe*, would plot a return to the anchor chair.

What surprised Bob Schieffer of CBS News was how the Rather crowd purged the broadcast center on West Fifty-seventh Street of all remnants of the Cronkite regime. Cronkite's old beige set backdrop was repainted blue-gray, because Rather thought it enhanced his complexion. He even had the "Cronkite Newsroom" plaque taken off the wall. "I would have had the 'Cronkite Newsroom' sign plated in gold," a disgusted Schieffer scoffed. "I came to work that Saturday morning, March 7, after Cronkite quit. I was slated to do the *Evening News* that weekend night. And to my utter surprise Walter's anchor chair was gone from the set. 'Where's the chair?' I asked. I was told it had been moved to storage. 'Go get the damn chair,' I told a stagehand. This being CBS, it took them all day to find it. But I broadcast the news from Walter's chair."

Just how insecure Rather (whose salary was $6 million over a period of three years) was became apparent during his first appearance as anchorman on Monday, March 9, 1981. A direct order had been handed down from CBS executives that the set change from Cronkite to Rather was to be minimal, but Rather wanted to jazz things up a little bit. Among other things, a new desk and backdrop were frantically erected in the studio over the weekend to give things a Ratheresque aura. The new guard at CBS News wanted to make Rather's debut memorable. Cognizant that he had big shoes to fill, Rather himself indicated his broadcast needed a new tone and tenor.

Two minutes before airtime, Rather threw a fit over Cronkite's chair, which Schieffer had used for his weekend broadcasts. It was still behind the desk. He refused to sit in it. "I was in the fishbowl and got an emergency call from the film editing office that there was a problem with some footage of a segment," Socolow recalled. "I rushed out down the hall to take care of the problem. Then suddenly, over the loudspeaker, I heard director Richard Mutschler shout, 'Socolow, he's standing up! He's standing up!' "

The cameramen didn't know what to do. "It was a near-catastrophe that will not be soon forgotten all these years later," CBS writer Sandor Polster recalled, "by those who had worked so hard to make sure that his debut would be perfect." In a blog post titled "The Empty Throne" (posted on March 7, 2011), longtime *CBS Evening News* veteran Polster— one of the three news writers Rather inherited from Cronkite—detailed Rather's strange intransigence just before airtime that Monday. The drama began when stage manager Jimmy Wall barked, "Two minutes. Two minutes to air." Suddenly, Rather got up from Cronkite's old chair and pronounced, "I don't want to sit here," thereupon moving himself to a low table. Socolow lost his temper and cursed at Rather's selfish bad timing. "What an asshole thing to do," Socolow recalled. "It was so disrespectful to the crew; it makes me sick to my stomach."

The clock was ticking. Thirty seconds . . . ten . . . five . . . showtime. The newsroom floor hands, long-time professionals, scrambled to fix lights, re-angle the cameras, and make all sorts of instant lighting adjustments. "I still can see Dan Rather perched on that typewriter table," Polster recalled thirty years later, "looking a bit constipated, as if he were bracing for a hasty retreat." Schieffer put it more succinctly: "Quite frankly, Dan looked like he was going to the crapper."

Cronkite, working at home, was devastated by the way Rather treated his legacy on his first *CBS Evening News* broadcast. Why was he embarrassed to sit in his chair? It seemed to Cronkite rude and immature, like cooties in grade school. "It was goddamn crazy," Socolow recalled. "Dan's explanation to Cronkite and me was that he thought standing would be better than sitting. By the first commercial break he knew better and sat down."

To Connie Chung, who nicknamed Rather the "Stealth Bomber"—for his sneak character attacks— Rather had purposefully tried to humiliate Cronkite out of jealousy. Morley Safer, Cronkite's old drinking buddy at CBS News, a mainstay on *60 Minutes*, saw "Chairgate" as indicative of Rather's creepy personality. "Rather was determined to wipe out every vestige of Cronkite," Safer recalled. "It's that simple. That was the root of it. Rather was nasty toward Walter. The chair stunt was one of many slights. Dan's a liar and an unbelievably paranoid guy. He did his best to get rid of all the Cronkite people. Rather and Nixon, you might say, were strangely very much alike." When Jeff Fager was named executive producer of the *CBS Evening News with Dan Rather* in 1996, Rather was at first livid. "He told me he wasn't happy I got the job," Fager recalled. "This surprised me. I asked, 'Why?' He said, 'Because you're friends with Morley Safer who talks to Sandy Socolow who talks to Cronkite who talks to everybody.' "

Ratings dipped by 9 percent at *CBS Evening News* after Cronkite's departure, the largest number of defectors going to ABC's *World News Tonight*. Cronkite was not psychologically prepared for retirement. Just weeks after resigning as CBS News anchorman, he flew to the Soviet Union with producer Andrew Lack (who later went on to become NBC News president, Sony BMG chairman, and then head of Bloomberg LP multimedia operations) to report on the state of that nation. Cronkite's assigned point man in Moscow was Gordon F. Joseloff, who had been a UPI reporter there until CBS hired him in 1975 to write for the *Evening News*. Joseloff and Cronkite became fast friends. It was a UPI alumni thing. It always gave Joseloff a thrill to hear his own copy read on air at CBS by his boyhood idol. It was at the Cronkites' annual Christmas party in 1978 that Joseloff was asked to run CBS News' Moscow bureau. Salant thought that since Joseloff had once worked the Russian beat for UPI, he'd be ideal for the job. "Don't worry," Cronkite had told him. "We'll teach you what you need to know."

So Joseloff was thrilled to host a dinner for Cronkite on March 30 at his spacious Sadovo-Samotechnaya apartment, just a stone's throw from CBS operations. "Walter wasn't big on diplomacy," Joseloff recalled. "He got down and dirty, wanting to know *everything* going on in Moscow." Midcourse, somebody from Reuters banged on the apartment door to give Joseloff and Cronkite the grim news: President Reagan had been shot outside the Washington Hilton by a deranged John Hinckley. Videotape of the attempted assassination had just been shown on ABC. "I'll never forget Walter's reaction as he heard those words," Joseloff recalled. "He sat bolt upright, his face got red, he got to his feet, and he asked me to lead him to the Reuters office. A throng had already gathered around the incoming news wire. Walter pushed his way in. A couple of correspondents did double takes as they turned around to see that the older man breathing down their necks was none other than Walter Cronkite."

Here was the leaping jaguar that Bill Felling of CBS News had talked about. Reagan had been shot and Cronkite was ready for on-air action. NBC News pool footage was already being streamed to the Soviet Union. CBS in New York told Joseloff to get Cronkite, now all laser-focused on the Reagan tragedy, ready for a live interview, something more than a sound bite, even though it was almost midnight in Moscow. At first, all the Soviet satellite transmissions were tied up; state television was being uncooperative with CBS. But when they learned that it was *the* Walter Cronkite wanting a channel to New York, studio technicians were rushed to a state-run studio for an emergency broadcast.

Back in New York, Rather had been on the air for hours doing a fine job of explaining the circumstances of Reagan's near-assassination. When Secretary of State Alexander Haig stated incorrectly that he was constitutionally third in line of succession to the presidency, Rather correctly took issue, calling the remark "patronizing." A Soviet security vehicle came softly to the curb to pick Cronkite up and rush him to the camera. After a harrowing ride to a station located on Moscow's outskirts, Cronkite managed to get airtime. "America once again had Walter to watch at a time of national trauma," Gordon Joseloff recalled,

Not that Cronkite saw it that way. The Reagan assassination attempt put him in a deep funk. He didn't like
being sidelined. He felt marginalized almost into a state
of nonbeing at CBS. A bitterness swelled inside of him.
One CBS holdover from Cronkite to Rather was Linda
Mason. From her catbird perspective, Cronkite wasn't
merely disgruntled by Rather's trying to differentiate
himself from the former anchor on the air or by being
exiled in Russia for the attempted assassination story—
though those were factors. Cronkite, she believed, was
envious that Rather had gotten paid a $2 million annual
salary to replace him. Why hadn't Black Rock been as
generous to him? Meanwhile, the Ratherites simply
weren't impressed with the work Cronkite did from the
Soviet Union and Eastern Europe in 1981. That fall,
Cronkite went to Hungary for CBS News to cover the
twenty-fifth anniversary of the Soviet invasion of 1956.
Cronkite produced an ungainly ten-minute piece he
wanted Rather to air on the *Evening News*; it wasn't
very compelling. CBS News ran only an extremely
boiled-down, bottom-of-the-broadcast filler version
of it.

Wanting to make spot news, Cronkite and Benjamin
traveled to Poland to cover the Solidarity movement
(which emerged in 1980 as the first non-Communist
trade union in a Warsaw Pact nation). They hoped to

earn an exclusive U.S. broadcast interview with Lech Walesa, the movement's leader. Walesa, a humble shipyard electrician, fighting for workers' rights and organizing for democracy, was amassing the power to topple the Communist regime. It felt unsettling to Cronkite to be working as a far-flung cold war reporter in Poland for the pampered Rather, who was ensconced in his old New York studio. Could a five-star general of nearly two decades really become a corporal again? After a harrowing flight into Warsaw, having force-landed on a grass strip, Cronkite indeed scored an exclusive interview with the Polish freedom fighter. "Walesa and his whole retinue reminded me of Bobby Kennedy's 1968 campaign, with the young people surrounding him," Cronkite recalled. "He was constantly taking advice from them, conferring with them, deciding one thing one minute and then something the next. . . . And they all adored him. It was a damn good interview; I'm very proud of it."

Even though Cronkite scored big interviews with Lech Walesa and Wojciech Jaruzelski, Poland's last Communist prime minister, no one at Black Rock gave a damn about Poland. Apple Computer had introduced the first serious home computer, triggering a desktop revolution throughout the world, and CBS management was trying to see whether it would replace the wire service for instant news. Compounding Cronkite's difficulties in stepping down as CBS News anchorman was his boneheaded decision to join the Pan Am board. It proved to be a terrible mistake. The hitch was that he was still getting paid $1 million a year to be a CBS News special correspondent. Pan Am had a contractual relationship with NASA and the Pentagon. How could Cronkite cover the space beat for CBS while serving on the board of a company that profited from the program? It was a clear conflict of interest. Accused of breaching journalistic ethics, Cronkite quit Pan Am to save his reputation.

Cronkite was turning more and more bitter toward the Rather regime as the competition feasted on the opportunities left by his departure. ABC, led by news division chief Roone Arledge, regarded the end of the Cronkite era as a rare opening for the third-place network to excel. To Arledge, the CBS News lineup with Cronkite had been like "the Yankees when they had Murderers' Row." But with Cronkite, the cleanup hitter, gone, the lineup would start to unravel. ABC was determined to turn the perennial two-horse race between CBS and NBC into a three-way contest. Arledge steadily and strategically bolstered ABC's commitment to news, starting with its extensive coverage of the Americans held hostage in Tehran, from

November 1979 to January 1981. Much of his strategy anticipated Cronkite's eventual withdrawal from CBS. When March 6 arrived, said an ABC colleague, Arledge was "like a boxer who smells the kill and doesn't want to wait for the next round."

From March to October 1981 Cronkite promoted *Universe*. With an extra-high regard for scientists and professors, he visited the far reaches of the planet, trying to learn about the Islamic world, China, the South Pole, Alaska's Mount McKinley, and even chimpanzees along the Gambia River in Africa. It was Lowell Thomas–type fare. Cronkite also signed on as chairman of Satellite Education Service, a nonprofit company that produced the series *Why in the World* for the Los Angeles PBS station KCET. Between *Universe* and the KCET gig, Ed Bradley quipped, his friend Cronkite was acting like a "senior citizen" taking "crash courses at This-Is-the-World night school."

Universe was conceived as a half-hour newsmagazine with two stories each program, one story reported by Cronkite and one by staff reporter Charles Osgood, who had a literary style and bountiful good humor. The show—which aired at 8:00 p.m. EST on Tuesdays—was built around Cronkite's NASA, Israel-Egypt détente, and Earth Day accomplishments as CBS anchorman. "The basic idea was to take subjects that could have a strong impact on our world but were not getting attention from the evening news or daily newspapers," Osgood explained. "The environment was a major area we were interested in—also scientific exploration and the cutting edge of science."

For *Universe*, Cronkite retained members of his old *Evening News* team, from his loyal producer Bud Benjamin to his choice of researchers, writers, and off-camera assistants. During the spring of 1981, they completed thirteen episodes, to run during the summer. But Cronkite understood that building the *Universe* brand would be expensive; he worried that CBS was being chintzy on the promotional front. From June 14, 1981, to September 1982, Cronkite aired nine space-related segments on *Universe*, including programs on the search for extraterrestrial life; an advanced look at *Voyager 2*'s flyby of the ringed planet Saturn; Eta Carinae, a star one hundred times larger than our sun; an investigation of the aurora borealis and its effect on global communications and military surveillance; and a colorful look at Mars photographs taken by Viking spacecraft in the late 1970s. A few of the space segments fell flat (for example, a Camden, New Jersey, high school wanting to send ants into space), but for the most part, *Universe* was akin to PBS's *NOVA* before its time.

Cronkite's conceit was that he could become a public educator like Carl Sagan or Jacques Cousteau or Jane Goodall—at least in making environmental science entertaining to the masses. He visited a remote African village to compare its holistic medicine with that of the West. He spent time with field biologists in the Amazon. He studied photosynthesis and chemosynthesis. Playing a modern-day Robert Peary, he later flew low over the frozen Arctic Circle expanse. The world-famous Woods Hole Oceanographic Institution in Massachusetts allowed him to explore fissures on the seafloor with its top marine biologists. He rode in a small submarine to a depth of 8,700 feet off Cabo San Lucas, Mexico ("10 hours in a tin can," he called it). "I wouldn't go down that far," CBS cameraman Izzy Bleckman remembered of a submarine trip. "Walter essentially ran the camera on the *Alvin* himself. Adrenaline was racing through him. Sea life was everywhere."

Whatever it took: Cronkite simply *loved* reporting on the far corners of the Earth to the American TV viewer. No outdoor adventure was dismissed as being too dangerous. What didn't appear on air— the outtakes—would have made ideal programming three decades later as reality TV. A reviewer could be forgiven for thinking that the making of *Universe* was more interesting than the show itself. When the Cronkite-Bleckman team went to the Amazon, for example, they rented a motorized dugout canoe. The weather got incredibly hot, so Cronkite stripped down to his underwear and went for a river swim. Bleckman soon joined him. After only a few minutes in the water, they felt something nibbling at their legs; it was little four-inch piranhas. They quickly leaped out of the water. That evening they ate piranha cooked in olive oil at a little village restaurant. It tasted pretty good. "I asked the owner about the fish," Bleckman recalled. "He brought me to a little eddy where he kept the fish. For my benefit he dumped garbage in the pond. They all gobbled it up. We had just eaten garbage-fed fish."

Not all Cronkite's time filming *Universe* was spent in the bush. Charles Osgood recalled bumping into him by accident once in Paris, with Betsy at his side. They were headed to the Louvre to prepare a segment on Leonardo da Vinci. "I said, 'Walter, the Louvre is closed today,'" Osgood recalled. "I just got back from there."

"Great," Cronkite said. "Let's go drink at the Ritz Bar."

Universe was an expensive show to produce. Unlike *60 Minutes*, it was generally lacking in controversy, as was Cronkite himself, though the program was technically very sophisticated. The golden rule for *Universe* was that the science magazine didn't cross the line into entertainment. While noble, such old-school integrity hurt the ratings. In a stubborn display of archaism, Cronkite rejected using bells, whistles, drum bands, and colorful graphics to jazz the show up a bit (as cable networks like Animal Planet and the History Channel would do in the twenty-first century). To Cronkite, that would be akin to dumbing down learning. "Cronkite," wrote his friend Andy Rooney in a 1981 tribute, "is not a genius at anything except being straight, honest and normal."

Neil Postman, one of America's foremost communications theorists, challenged Cronkite's boast that he didn't pander to entertainment imperatives in his book *Amusing Ourselves to Death*. He mocked the fact that the official title of the CBS show was *Walter Cronkite's Universe* (not just *Universe*). "Television's strongest point is that it brings personalities into our hearts, not abstractions into our heads," Postman wrote. "One would think that the grandeur of the universe needs no assistance from Walter Cronkite. One would think wrong. CBS knows that Walter Cronkite plays better on television than the Milky Way." But the Cronkite of *Universe* was only magnetic to science buffs and environmentalists. Many TV viewers of the

1980s wanted to know about Michael Jackson's moon walk or Princess Diana's wedding or the behind-the-scenes gossip of ABC's *Dynasty*, not bioluminescent plants.

Working with Cronkite on *Universe* was his old writer-producer friend Dale Minor, formerly of *CBS Evening News*. One episode of the show was to be shot in wild Alaska, where high-tech digital mapping was being developed by the U.S. government. It was the pre-Google era, and Cronkite thought this technology could, in the end, be an amazing tool for TV broadcasters. Betsy had gone along for the Alaska junket to enjoy the grandeur of the Denali wilderness. As a surprise, Minor helicoptered in a card table, cooked turkey, and vintage wine so the Cronkites could have a high-altitude lunch with snowcapped Mount McKinley as the backdrop. "It was our way of telling Walter thank you," Minor recalled. "We made it this incredibly romantic lunch for them."

While *Universe* had a devoted following, the ratings were lukewarm. For one show, Cronkite flew out to Palo Alto, California, to interview the founder of a company called Failure Analysis. Although the company's business was aimed at teaching companies how to grow, Cronkite joked that *Universe* should be a client. Back in New York, one of the producers wore a Failure

Analysis ball cap, which generated a lot of laughs before *Universe* was canceled in 1982.

A veteran of forty-five years in journalism, Cronkite was now passé. Programs such as *Universe* just couldn't hack it in the Nielsen ratings sweepstakes of the Big Three networks; they belonged on PBS, where information was treated as something near-divine. "I suppose when *Universe* fell away, I could have said, 'let's have a Walter Cronkite piece once a week or once in a while,'" Dan Rather reflected in a 2011 interview. "But by the time *Universe* was finished, Socolow and Cronkite were just banging the tom-toms against me."

There was another door opening in 1981 where Cronkite might flourish. Cable television had been around for decades, but in the late seventies and early eighties it burgeoned into a new frontier of independent national channels. Turner Broadcasting launched the Cable News Network on June 1, 1980, a time when channels of all types sprang into existence. In 1981, when Cronkite reentered the TV journalism field, as a CBS personality on the prowl, he was competing with a far larger crowd and at a faster pace than would have been the case just five years before. What was new in television in the Reagan era was just about everything. Millions of new cable subscribers were exploring dozens of new channels such as C-SPAN, HBO, CNN, and WTBS, where formerly there were only three or four. The new world of television offered an exponential expansion on the old industry model, with hundreds of new shows and thousands of personalities. Cronkite had reentered the job market, so to speak, at an inopportune time for familiar faces. Viewers just then were delighting in unfamiliar ones.

The Big Three networks would continue to matter in the new cablecentric world, but they would be up against a lot more free-market competition from entertainment channels like ESPN, Disney, and Playboy. John Hendricks, founder of the Discovery Channel, surmised that one reason why Cronkite was so adaptable to the birth of cable television was that he was devoted to documentary films. Cronkite believed the new cable revolution would allow for a greater number of documentaries to be seen by larger audiences. And networks such as the Discovery Channel could feature more films produced in the United Kingdom, Canada, and Australia. The more international news programs America received via satellite, Cronkite firmly believed, the more informed the public would be. Already he was thinking about traveling to South Africa with director Ken Sable to expose the apartheid system for a CBS News documentary that would be titled

"Children of Apartheid." His anti-apartheid project aired on December 5, 1987, and won both an Emmy for "Outstanding Achievement in a Documentary" and the Overseas Press Club's Edward R. Murrow Award for "Outstanding Documentary." Someday, Cronkite hoped, South Africans would have their own CNN and C-SPAN, broadcasting political conditions truthfully from Johannesburg to Cape Town (two of his favorite cities) so the world could learn more about the extraordinary country.

Although Cronkite stayed amazingly busy, he was not prepared for his retirement from *CBS Evening News*. He had quit too soon. While he still cut an unforgettable figure wherever he went, he no longer exuded power. A void had now entered his life that all the trips to Timbuktu or the Amazon couldn't fill. He had never felt more hopeless. He had a partial interest in everything, without a sharp sense of mission about any one thing. When Bleckman visited the Cronkites at the Vineyard one summer, he recalled Walter holding court in the parlor, punctuating every sentence with anchorman-like authority, pontificating about world events, scarcely making a dent in his lunch. A hallmark of the Cronkites' successful marriage was that Betsy could cut Walter down to size—and he loved it. "Walter," Betsy sharply chided him at one juncture.

"You don't *have* to be the most trusted man in America anymore!"

In 1981, Kathy Cronkite published *On the Edge of the Spotlight,* a frank and well-rendered book on the difficulties associated with being the child of a celebrity. Fame in America was difficult enough, but being the child of an icon was a strange burden in need of understanding. Wherever Kathy went, people asked her questions, such as "What is it like to be Walter Cronkite's daughter?" or more specific ones aimed at procuring gossip, such as "What does your dad *really* think of Jimmy Carter?" Using her book as a forum to let the children of celebrities speak out—including the kids of William F. Buckley, Gerald Ford, and Zsa Zsa Gabor—Kathy Cronkite pulled few punches. She let readers know how people made her feel—like a "caterpillar in a jar."

When Cronkite first read *On the Edge of the Spotlight,* he didn't know how to feel. At a Manhattan dinner with Kathy, a couple of autograph seekers walked up to them mid-meal, thrusting pieces of paper at the CBS anchor; Kathy didn't seem to mind. Now, after having read her book, Cronkite knew better. Having a private meal out with Dad wasn't possible. In some ways he was annoyed by his daughter's complaints about being the child of a media star. But upon further reflection, he digested *On the Edge* as a guide for better parental behavior in general. It hurt him to look in the mirror and realize he had been an absentee parent. "There were moments when reading this book that I wanted to say of it: 'shocking,' 'appalling,'" he wrote in the foreword. "There were others, however, when I found my throat tightening and my eyes welling with the warm tears of overwhelming love."

Throughout the fall of 1981, Cronkite was determined to be relevant. Egyptian president Anwar Sadat—a Nobel Peace Prize winner because of his role in the Camp David accords with Menachem Begin of Israel—was watching a military exercise on October 6, 1981, when a vehicle stopped in front of the reviewing stand. Suddenly two men dressed in khaki army fatigues attacked the stand with explosives and gunfire. The fundamentalist cleric Omar Abdel-Rahman had issued a *fatwa* against Sadat that was carried out by soldiers loyal to a terror group called the Egyptian Islamic Jihad. Reports of the assassination attempt were heavily covered by all the networks.

Cronkite, a Sadat confidant, was invited to join Dan Rather on air at CBS. Seeking word of Sadat's condition, Rather secured an exclusive interview with former president Jimmy Carter, who said his Egyptian sources had confirmed that Sadat was all right. Rather was treating the Carter comment as a scoop, when Cronkite broke into the discussion. "I would caution against taking too literally these early reports from Cairo," he said. "We can be almost certain the regime is going to cover up what his real condition is." It was a wait-and-see situation.

CBS News senior producer Mark Harrington decided that if Sadat died, the network should have Cronkite travel to Cairo to broadcast. The thirty-one-year-old Alan Weisman, a producer, was tapped to accompany Cronkite to the Middle East. They had never been in the field together. "The Concorde leaves from Paris at two o'clock," Harrington told Weisman. "Walter will meet you in the lounge. Do *not* get on the plane unless Walter is with you. He's your responsibility. Never let him out of your sight."

A dutiful Weisman raced off to Kennedy Airport. While checking his baggage, news reached him that Sadat had died. Cronkite had been right to temper Rather's Carter exclusive. Pacing around like a caged animal, worried that Cronkite was nowhere in sight, Weisman kept obsessively checking his watch. Where was Cronkite? Weisman grew almost ill with nervousness. The plane's door was about to close. When Cronkite, at last, arrived with only two minutes to spare, Weisman sighed with relief. When he boarded, everyone on the plane was abuzz. Weisman, in an unpublished diary, wrote that he could *feel* the happy whispers. A mega-celebrity was traveling with *them*. Rifling through his carry-on bag, Cronkite turned grumpy.

"She forgot my socks," he said.

"What?" Weisman asked.

"Betsy forgot to pack my socks. I was in such a rush she just forgot. The only pair I've got I'm wearing," Cronkite said.

"We'll get socks in Paris," Weisman assured him.

"I'll need three pair. Blue or black," said Cronkite.

"I'll take care of it," Weisman replied.

It was an uneventful flight with lots of shut-eye and a few cocktails. Once Cronkite and Weisman landed at Paris-Charles de Gaulle Airport, they had a limo pick them up. On the way to the Paris hotel, Cronkite saw a red-light district, strip joints, and XXX video shops. "Boy," he said. "I sure would like to stop right here. But someone might recognize me."

Weisman surmised that Cronkite was a "dirty old man," but he was "too smart to let anyone see it." After a night in Paris, Cronkite and Weisman went airborne again, stopping to refuel on the island of Crete before heading to Cairo. Cronkite said he needed to visit the tiny airport newsstand to purchase pipe tobacco. "I watched from a distance as he walked up to the stand, bought his tobacco, slid over to the magazine rack, and after making sure no one had seen him, began thumbing through the girlie magazines. For me that was another smile. 'God bless you, Walter,' I thought. 'I've got your back. Knock yourself out.' "

The CBSers took a Caravelle jet—similar to the Lear jet—to Cairo. There were just the two pilots up front and Cronkite and Weisman in the back. The charter company had installed a wire service printer in the cabin, and Cronkite and Weisman spent the flight scanning rolled-up dispatches about the Sadat assassination and his successor, Hosni Mubarak, from around the world. But the big news was that President Reagan had dispatched three former U.S. presidents (Ford, Carter, and Nixon) to attend the memorial service, along with what seemed to be half of Reagan's State Department. As Cronkite stepped out of the plane and down the staircase onto the tarmac in Cairo, he surveyed the terrain and said, "I was here when Nasser died. There were thousands in the streets. Look at this. Nothing!"

The CBS News bureau in Cairo was dingy. Bureau chief Scotti Williston, a woman in her thirties with large black-framed glasses, had prepared briefing books for Cronkite. Everything he needed, except socks. Cronkite interrogated Williston about the lay of the land. Cronkite was interested in interviewing all three presidents *together*. But he was mostly hell-bent on getting an exclusive interview with Mubarak. With amazing speed, Cronkite managed to arrange a one-on-one with the new Egyptian president. How could Mubarak say no to Walter Cronkite?

Mubarak didn't know that Cronkite was *extremely* pro-Israel—many of his New York friends were borderline Zionists. Cronkite, full of consternation, was deeply worried that Mubarak wouldn't uphold Sadat's peace overtures to Israel. Before long Cronkite and Mubarak, who reeked of cologne, met for the interview. Cronkite was surprised to see Mubarak dressed in a pinstripe suit, looking more like a Russian gangster than an Egyptian statesman. Cronkite missed Sadat even more.

The interview began with Mubarak assuring Cronkite (and by extension the American people and the Israelis) that he would continue Sadat's foreign policy, that he would honor the Camp David accords. Cronkite later joked that Mubarak was trying to tell the American audience, "I am not one of the crazies . . . I'm a moderate . . . you'll have no trouble with me."

Not willing to be bought off that easily, Cronkite zeroed in on Mubarak's brutal oppression of dissidents, book burning, and other hard-line tactics used in Cairo in the wake of Sadat's death. "We must have discipline!" Mubarak said emphatically. "Discipline in the streets! Discipline in the factories! Discipline in the schools!" Cronkite had drawn Mubarak into expressing how he really felt. The CIA had a dearth of information about Mubarak, so what Cronkite was doing proved very helpful to Middle East watchers—which in September 1981 was the entire world.

After about forty-five minutes, the interview ended. Weisman scooped up six videocassettes from each camera, dropped them in a carry bag, and headed into the street with Cronkite, scrambling to find their car. Weisman, feeling victorious, grabbed the two-way radio to tell the bureau *mission accomplished*. "Put that down," Cronkite instructed. "You don't know who is listening. Let's keep this quiet until we're ready to go."

Because of the seven-hour time difference between Cairo and New York, Cronkite and Weisman were able to perfectly edit the piece for the *CBS Evening News*. But satellite technology was still hit-or-miss in 1981. Weisman concocted three different ways to relay the Cronkite-Mubarak interview to New York. The main facility in Cairo was ringed with troops and armored personnel carriers, standard procedure in a developing country when a leader was assassinated. Through grit and persistence, Weisman got the interview patched through. "The reaction in New York was ecstatic," Weisman recalled. Cronkite's exclusive led the broadcast and ran about five minutes, an eternity on an evening news program.

Having hit a home run with Mubarak, Cronkite and Weisman wanted to hit a triple—the exclusive interview with all three U.S. presidents.

"Weisman," Sandy Socolow said, "you deliver that and you get a week in Paris on our company."

"Deal," he replied.

When Cronkite and Weisman approached the Cairo hotel where all three former presidents were congregating, they were swamped by a mob of reporters and camera crews. Everything was cordoned off. Cronkite, puffing his pipe, told Weisman to follow along. Playing Moses, he walked determinedly straight ahead; the seas parted. The Secret Service, with earpieces and wires, smiled and stood at attention for Cronkite. "Good evening, Mr. Cronkite," one said. "So nice to see you again." Another asked, "How are you, Mr. Cronkite? We haven't seen you in a while." Cronkite replied, "Fine, just fine, fellas. Still climbing the stairs. Nice to see you too."

The Secret Service agents acted like little boys in awe of Cronkite—not the ex-presidents. Carter's former press secretary Jody Powell came racing up to Cronkite, clutching an "extra" edition of the English-language paper with the exclusive Mubarak interview bannered across the top. "You did it again!" Powell exclaimed.

Cronkite was easily able to get President Ford to agree to an interview. But he hit a snag when he broached the idea with President Carter. When Rosalynn Carter saw the anchor emeritus, she blanched. "It was a killer look," Weisman recalled, "one of utter disdain." She was still bitter about Cronkite's sign-off as anchorman during the Iran hostage crisis. President Carter reluctantly agreed to do a one-on-one interview with Cronkite, but *not* with Nixon and Ford. It saddened Cronkite a little that the Carters held a grudge against him.

To Cronkite's utter astonishment, he got the warmest reception from Richard and Pat Nixon. "Walter," the former president said with genuine warmth, "How are you?" Cronkite was amazed at how tanned, rested, and ready Nixon looked. "Walter!" he gushed. "Do you remember when you and I and President Sadat sailed down the Nile? Wasn't that a time!"

It was astounding. No bitterness over Watergate or differences of opinion about Cambodia, no bad blood after Agnew's venom and Colson's dirty tricks. Cronkite and Nixon bonded in Cairo. They were both veterans of American history, worn down a bit, but still gladiators who had struggled in what Teddy Roosevelt called "the arena," where men are "marred by dust and sweat and blood," but who nonetheless "strive valiantly" onward.

At the funeral dinner for the U.S. delegation, Cronkite was the only journalist present, seated at the head of the table along with Henry Kissinger, three former presidents, and their wives. After the program, Cronkite hopped in a car with Weisman to ride back to the Cairo bureau to do some work. That night, even a shot of Maker's Mark couldn't help him get to sleep. Worn out by his restlessness and the interminable memorial, Cronkite was anxious to fly back to France. This time Cronkite and Weisman arrived early and boarded their own private Caravelle. Cronkite was famished, having barely eaten since they'd arrived in Egypt, fearful that the food would make him sick. Suddenly, an Air France truck pulled up beside Cronkite's jet and the pilots produced a tray of smoked salmon and caviar along with several magnums of champagne. "Whoa!" Cronkite exclaimed, raising his famous eyebrows above his glasses. "Where are the dancing girls?"

Cronkite had done an incredible job for CBS News in Egypt. But assignments to contribute to Rather's *Evening News* dried up after Sadat's funeral. Even though Cronkite worked his Middle East sources, scoring the huge Mubarak interview, the Rather team cut the wire. The exemplary caution that Cronkite had displayed during CBS News' early Sadat assassination coverage now became his new calling card: Wise Man of TV Journalism. "It was very clear to me," Connie Chung recalled, "that Walter had grown bitter at Dan. He blamed CBS dissing him after the Sadat funeral on Dan. But Walter kept the aura of sage."

CBS News was undergoing major changes in personnel in late 1981 that would continue throughout the decade, presenting a stark comparison to the stability of Richard Salant's years as division president. In November, the president of CBS News, Bill Leonard, was replaced by a brash former executive at CBS Sports, Van Gordon Sauter, who wanted to make his own mark at the network. He had no particular use for Cronkite. On the corporate level, William Paley was fighting his own losing battle to maintain control of the company he'd founded.

Rather had his own troubles in late 1981. On air, he seemed a little stilted in the early days, not entirely comfortable in his own skin. Even worse was that CBS News had lost its comfortable front-runner lead, along with approximately 2.5 million viewers each night; this translated into about $20 million in annual revenue.

Rather was well aware of the rumor that if his ratings didn't improve quickly, he would be replaced by Charles Kuralt, whose Rockwellesque "On the Road" segments—that wonderful hybrid of prose and picture narrated by a deep, soak-it-up baritone voice—were beloved. Kuralt was bald, with a headful of interesting bumps and a wry whiskey smile. But he was a wonderful reporter and a real bon vivant to boot. Cronkite, furious at his post-Cairo treatment, promoted the notion that Kuralt should replace the interception-prone Rather as the quarterback of the *CBS Evening News*.

One way for Rather to bolster his audience share would have involved using Cronkite on a more regular basis. But Rather was not interested in that cotton-up approach. He was as vitally competitive as Cronkite had ever been. His team moved Cronkite out of the *CBS Evening News* office suites and the core of the news division as well. Given his druthers, Rather would have banned Cronkite from the broadcast center entirely. The story was as old as any transfer of power in any field. Cronkite knew it, understood it, and was utterly aghast when it was happening to him. Second-guessing his decision to leave the CBS anchor chair, he told historian Don Carleton in an oral history interview that his retirement in March 1981 had been premature. "I very much regretted it because it didn't work out as it was planned," he said in a volcanic display of disgruntlement. "Rather and company shut me out from doing anything. . . . [The thinking was] as long as I was on the broadcast, there would be unfavorable comparisons with Rather, and Rather couldn't establish himself as his own man. Well, I don't disagree with that too much. I can understand their coming to that . . . I think if I had been in the same place I would have had the same feeling about it. But, the thing is, it went on for ten years, it goes on to this day. And that's unconscionable, unreasonable."

In the fall of 1981, Cronkite invited Rather to lunch at a midtown Manhattan club. It didn't go well. "It was somewhere between awkward and a strain," recalled Rather, who went to the lunch merely to listen. "The comfort factor wasn't high. Walter was critical of me to my face. He told me I was 'too stiff' on the air." The takeaway from the lunch was that Cronkite wanted Rather to do the *Evening News* broadcast *his* way. Nothing else would be acceptable.

When Socolow visited with Van Gordon Sauter one afternoon, he suggested that Cronkite's desk be sent to the Smithsonian Institution for public display on the Mall in Washington. Sauter said that was a jolly idea, that he would take care of it. A few months later, after a little detective work, Socolow learned that the desk had been pulped during Rather's purge of all remnants of his predecessor. What a grave injustice, Socolow thought, what a vindictive, asshole thing to do. When told about this desk story, Rather shook his head. "Socolow," he said, "has been putting dirt on me for years."

Cronkite had contracted for a prominent role on the air as part of his CBS retirement agreement. But with *Universe* floundering, to put it mildly, he was reconsidering his options. He took a little solace in the fact that his conundrum wasn't unique. David Brinkley—fully in the shadow of John Chancellor—was going through much the same thing at NBC in 1981. One of Brinkley's problems was that his network had hired a cadre of former CBSers to manage the NBC news department. In fact, that was a problem both former anchors shared, inasmuch as men such as Richard Salant and Bill Small, supporters of Cronkite, had moved over to NBC, where they couldn't help Cronkite and didn't choose to help Brinkley. Forced into a smaller and smaller role, Brinkley found himself wishing he'd be fired. He daydreamed that he'd continue to receive his large salary and take an endless vacation in his native North Carolina. But NBC made it clear it wasn't going to fire him. So Brinkley quit.

Roone Arledge was ready to pounce. For Brinkley, the breakup with NBC News led to a fulfilling fifteen-year turn at ABC News, where he hosted the Sunday morning show *This Week*. Cronkite had much the same opportunity: to go to a new network, where his strengths would be assessed and then showcased. He had a standing offer from Arledge, as well as occasional feelers from NBC. CNN desperately wanted him to host an evening talk show. After weighing these options, Cronkite stayed at CBS News, a decision he later regretted. Sadly, he would never again be happy there. "I thought, well, the hell with them, if they want to pay me a million dollars a year not to work, that's all I ever need," he recalled. "But it sure was a mistake. I shouldn't have done that. I should have fought it. I should have quit with dignity."

The lucrative contract purchased Cronkite's affiliation, at least seven years of it, but not his blind loyalty. He deeply disagreed with the direction in which Sauter was leading the *CBS Evening News*, with drastically decreased emphasis on overseas reports and developments in Washington, D.C. Cronkite's resentment only intensified after Sauter canceled *Universe* during the 1982 summer season. The program had failed to find a sustainable audience. But Cronkite felt that management had willed the show's failure by not promoting its second season and by preempting it so often that even fans would forget to tune in, week after week.

"Howard Stringer [the executive producer of *CBS Evening News* after 1981] thought that Cronkite was a threat to Rather," longtime CBS News producer Bud Lamoreaux recalled. "Their strategy was to bury Walter. They didn't promote him at all at CBS. After 1981, the fix was in. Walter was bound to fail."

On February 22, 1982, *New York* magazine declared that "the Cronkite age is behind us, and TV news, which was the same for years, will change beyond recognition in the next five." CBS's news division was comfortably moving ahead without Cronkite. Before long Rather brought the *CBS Evening News* back to first place in the ratings. This didn't impress Cronkite. Full of despair, Cronkite was upset by Rather's superficial version of the *CBS Evening News* and didn't refrain from saying so in appearances throughout the country. In his time, Cronkite had worked himself into a frenzy, trying to shoehorn one more twenty-second news item into his allotted twenty-three minutes. He was convinced that turning away from that kind of passion for news and replacing it with feel-good features recommended by Research Analysis did the viewers a terrible disservice. "After leaving his anchor post," *New York Times* media reporter Peter Kaplan wisely noted, "Cronkite was always one step short of disillusionment."

32.

Struggling Elder Statesman

BIG BROTHER IS WATCHING—BACK TO NORMANDY—
BONDING WITH REAGAN—COSTELLO'S SALOON—NO
ROLE IN SAN FRANCISCO—THE ART OF NEWS
DOCUMENTARIES—CLOWNING AROUND WITH MIKE
ASHFORD—YELLOWSTONE—ALWAYS THE ROAST OF
THE PARTY—ROONEY AND BUCHWALD JABS—THE
MOUTH OF THE SOUTH—SUPPORTING BOB
SCHIEFFER—OLD AND IN THE WAY—BONDING WITH
FRIENDLY—OGN NEWS—PALEY PAYS CRONKITE
HOMAGE

E ver since Cronkite's "Report from Vietnam" in
1968, General William Westmoreland had become
persona non grata around CBS News. It didn't matter

whether you were part of the Cronkite cult or the Rather camp, everyone at CBS considered Westmoreland a congenital liar. While Cronkite took swipes at Westmoreland in many interviews about his famous "Report from Vietnam," his friend Mike Wallace, the toughest interviewer in CBS News history, got to go mano a mano with the former chief of staff of the U.S. Army. Wallace's interview of Westmoreland for the *CBS Reports* documentary "The Uncounted Enemy: A Vietnam Deception" (which aired on January 23, 1982) gave credence to the old Cronkite claim that the Army general who commanded American military operations at the peak of the Vietnam War had deliberately lied about Vietcong troop strength in 1967 to bolster morale, keep congressional appropriations flowing, and build civilian support back home. Cronkite had blown Westmoreland's deceit wide open in 1968, and Wallace stuck the knife in deeply in 1982. "I screened the broadcast," CBS News president Bill Leonard recalled, "and was very much impressed."

Shortly after "The Uncounted Enemy" aired, Westmoreland sued CBS News for $120 million. The charge was libel. Cronkite's producer for *Universe*, Bud Benjamin, was asked to conduct the network's internal inquiry into the controversial documentary. To Cronkite's surprise, Benjamin, who had worked for him as far back as 1957 (as executive producer of *The Twentieth Century*), ended up critiquing the documentary as deeply flawed and in violation of CBS News guidelines. The Benjamin Report, as Cronkite called it, didn't make much of a difference in the acrimonious *Westmoreland v. CBS* trial, because the burden was on Westmoreland to prove "actual malice." Westmoreland settled for accepting an apology from CBS, feeling he had, in part, cleared his name and restored his honor. The controversy petered out. While Cronkite had nothing to do with *Westmoreland v. CBS* per se, the general's disdain for the Eye dated back to "Report from Vietnam." In one oral history interview, Westmoreland charged that the *CBS Evening News with Walter Cronkite* had remorse about its own pro-Vietnam news segments from 1964 to 1967, and in 1982 had diabolically tried to put the "blame on my back."

All the media attention surrounding *Westmoreland v. CBS* galvanized Cronkite to make more TV documentaries destined to grab the public's attention. Abandoning the *Universe* formula, determined to follow in Murrow's esteemed footsteps, he rebelled against being the "definitive centrist American" and "everybody's uncle." Why not instead make a cutting-edge documentary on the order of "The Uncounted Enemy"? Cronkite didn't want to get sued but he wasn't ready to be neutered and put out to pasture. Don Hewitt convinced him that a *60 Minutes*–style documentary program was where the action at CBS News had moved to in the Rather era. With heart and soul, Cronkite went to work on the documentary "1984 Revisited" (a *CBS Reports* special that aired in prime time on June 7, 1983). Reading George Orwell's classic novel *1984*, published in 1949, had been a revelation for Cronkite. He was stunned by Orwell's raw insights into both Hitler's Germany and Stalin's Russia. To Cronkite, the dystopian *1984* was prescient in showing that America's civil liberties were being gutted by a right-wing agenda. To coincide with the *CBS Reports* documentary, Cronkite wrote a far-reaching opinion piece for *The New York Times*, warning about Orwell's Thought Police fast becoming the new American reality. "The total absence of privacy," he wrote, "the idea that the government is (or may be) always watching, means, most of us would agree, the ultimate loss of freedom."

As Cronkite imagined it, "1984 Revisited" would be a libertarian defense of the Fourth Amendment, which was under assault. Cronkite visited banks, supermarkets, and department stores to watch surveillance cameras spying on customers. The very fact that Miami Beach had cameras trained on street corners to monitor sidewalk activity, Cronkite believed, was Orwellian prophecy come true. To Cronkite, the fact that the U.S. government now had access to individuals' bank statements, medical files, and credit card records was a sign of creeping Big Brotherism.

What made "1984 Revisited" so difficult to film were the technical mishaps that trailed Cronkite's CBS crew around like a Murphy's Law dust cloud: everything that could go wrong did go wrong. "Walter blew his stack," writer-producer Dale Minor recalled of a trip to Spain. "His temper went into overdrive. It was clear for '1984 Revisited' that he wasn't getting A+ crews anymore. Semiretirement wasn't going well for Walter."

Having to suffer CBS cutbacks was one thing. But being assigned the C-crew by CBS News was more than Cronkite could tolerate. Then, compounding his frustration, the U.S. government blacklisted him while he was making the documentary. It was a scary new world indeed. *The Washington Post* reported in early 1984 that the U.S. Information Agency (USIA), the organization Murrow headed from 1961 to 1964, had put Cronkite on its blacklist for being "too liberal." Others on the USIA list included civil rights activist Coretta Scott King, *Washington Post* executive editor Ben Bradlee, consumer advocate Ralph Nader, and Harvard economist John Kenneth Galbraith. Congressional Democrats had a field day castigating Reagan's USIA for maligning such outstanding Americans as Cronkite, whose picture appeared in dozens of newspapers across the country accompanied by the blacklist story. To Cronkite, it was Nixon's Enemies List redux; he dealt with the ridiculous revelation with confident nonchalance. Reagan, who respected Cronkite, was embarrassed by the blacklist. Enemies lists weren't the Gipper's style. "The White House does not condone any blacklist," Reagan's spokesman, Larry Speakes, forcefully told reporters at a press conference in California. "We've communicated our displeasure to USIA."

On the heels of the USIA flap, *CBS Morning News* senior producer Missie Rennie scored for Cronkite a coveted exclusive with Reagan for the fortieth anniversary of D-day (June 6, 1984). The president was scheduled to deliver two speeches in Normandy: one at Pointe du Hoc (where the U.S. Army Rangers Second Division famously climbed the cliffs) and the other at Omaha Beach. Usually, when it came to exclusives, the *CBS Morning News* got outhustled by both NBC's *Today* show and ABC's *Good Morning America*; not this time around. Cronkite was incredibly popular with the World War II veterans and Reagan wanted atonement, so the CBS anchorman got to make the trip.

Long before Tom Brokaw's *The Greatest Generation*, Cronkite had asked America to start honoring every June 6, not December 7 (Pearl Harbor Day), as the formative anniversary of the Second World War. In Normandy, one by one, the vets told the CBS anchor emeritus about where they had been on D-day. "Everybody wanted to keep shaking Walter's hand," Rennie recalled. "They were moved to tears by the mere sight of the old anchorman returning to Pointe du Hoc." (After the D-day retrospective, World War II veterans started asking Cronkite to blurb small-press books about their firsthand combat experience in Saipan or Anzio or the Bulge. More often than not, he obliged.)

Surrounded by World War II veterans, with the English Channel serving as the dramatic backdrop, the Cronkite-Reagan interview was refreshingly candid from the get-go. Yet it could have been called the nostalgia hour. "Mr. President," Cronkite said after the Pointe du Hoc speech, "you know, this war—World War II, that is—was called a popular war, as opposed to the actions we've had recently—Vietnam, Lebanon, Grenada, I suppose. What are the conditions it takes for us to have a popular war, for heaven's sake?" Reagan answered with the same kind of softness toward Cronkite that he had exhibited in March 1981 when he called the anchorman the consummate "pro"; Reagan didn't mind the "for heaven's sake" coming from old Walter. Reagan told a story about a World War II soldier who used to say, "We all know, the shortest way home is through Tokyo." Cronkite seemed to agree. At the interview's end, Cronkite asked Reagan, in a corny way, what his "plan for D-Day" was against his Democratic rival—presumably Walter Mondale of Minnesota or Gary Hart of Colorado—in that year's presidential election. "Just tell them what we've done," Reagan said with humor on his face, "and what we're going to do and pretend they're not there."

After his Normandy coup, Cronkite felt certain that CBS News would have him co-anchor the 1984 political conventions and Election Night with Rather. Reagan was seeking a second White House term, heading the Republican ticket in 1984, while Walter Mondale— former vice president for Jimmy Carter from 1977 to 1981—was the Democratic front-runner and eventual nominee. Having Cronkite broadcast from the conventions on television had been an American tradition since 1952.

At the Democratic Convention in San Francisco (from July 16 to July 19)—the first up—there was rampant speculation about how much airtime Rather would allow Cronkite. "We're waiting to see if Dan talks to Walter with a 30-degree or 40-degree chill in his voice," became a standard joke at all CBS conventions in the 1980s. Rather, the grapevine maintained in 1984, was worried about being overshadowed by the most trusted man in America. It was said that having Cronkite and him together was like putting forty tons of dynamite next to a gas stove: combustion was likely. The convention pairing that garnered the most inside media attention at times wasn't Mondale and Geraldine Ferraro, but Cronkite and Rather. There was endless gossip about their feud.

Perhaps Cronkite's real power in 1984 was in educating print reporters from around the world about the hot-button political issues leading into convention season. Using Costello's saloon—which boasted James Thurber's original drawings on its walls—on East Forty-fourth Street as his New York think tank, Cronkite regularly hosted media powwows over scotch-and-waters, as if anchoring an inebriated version of *Meet the Press*. Journalists such as David Halberstam, Theodore White, R. W. Apple, Andy Rooney, Mike Wallace, and Morley Safer were regulars at these What-Walter-Thinks pub sessions. In keeping with his frugal nature, Cronkite drank for free at Costello's as long as his guests ran up a tab. One afternoon in July 1984, just before the Democratic Convention, Cronkite met with a group of British correspondents at Costello's to discuss what was shaping up to be a Reagan-Mondale presidential square-off. "Four years *is* too long," Cronkite told a New York *Daily News* reporter who had joined the happy hour. "But the British campaigning of six weeks is too short. There's not enough time to develop the issues. I'd like to see an American campaign of between two-and-a-half to three months."

On July 18, CBS aired "The Legacy of Harry S. Truman" in prime time. It was solid, but not great. Based on Cronkite's interviews with Truman's daughter, Margaret Truman Daniel, and former White House aides such as Clark Clifford, the documentary preempted CBS News coverage of the Democratic Convention. Much as he did in his interview with Reagan at Normandy, Cronkite seemed more like a cheerleader for American greatness than a hard-drilling journalist—a booster, in this case, for Truman's image to be chiseled into Mount Rushmore. "Walter was an excellent interviewer," Barbara Walters concluded after carefully watching the *CBS Evening News* for decades. "But he wasn't a tough one. As anchorman, there was nobody like him. But I was a much tougher interviewer."

Rather was angry that Cronkite had cut into his convention coverage with a triumphalist Truman fest. Cronkite was now in San Francisco, seemingly with all of Costello's saloon in tow, playing the fount of American political wisdom. Rather issued an edict: use Cronkite very sparingly. When Governor Mario Cuomo of New York gave his keynote address at the convention, Rather turned florid in trying to describe Cuomo's mesmerizing impact on the crowd at the Moscone Center. Cronkite, taking a talking-head turn, simply said on CBS, "The main thing was that this hall listened, and that's a major victory in any convention." It was classic Cronkite. "Nothing fancy about that kind of analysis," a *Syracuse Herald-Journal* critic noted, "but it got right to the heart of the situation."

Rather cut Cronkite, the critics' darling, off. He simply didn't want him around the CBS News broadcast booth. It was quite a stinging insult to Cronkite, who back in 1968 at the Democratic Convention in Chicago had denounced the "thugs" on the floor who had roughed up Rather. But it was eerily reminiscent of how Cronkite had treated Murrow at the Democratic Convention in Los Angeles back in 1960. The rivalry between Cronkite and Rather was dysfunctional and now on public display. David Brinkley, by contrast, had been asked to co-anchor ABC's convention coverage along with Peter Jennings; NBC had added John Chancellor into the convention mix with ease. Cronkite was barely given a cameo on CBS. So, for the first time in thirty-two years, Cronkite, getting jerked around on tedious waits for airtime, had at best a very marginal (almost nonexistent) role to play in San Francisco. "It was quite sad how CBS under Rather treated him that shabbily," Bob Schieffer recalled. "It didn't seem right."

Out of old journalistic habit, Cronkite now wandered around the streets of San Francisco, asking the man-on-the-street questions, not expecting much from the answers. People shouted out cheerful greetings, such as "Walter, you're the best!" or "We miss you, Uncle Walter." Others would stroll past Cronkite, hesitate, display a kind of is-it-or-isn't-it frown, then stop and ask if he was indeed the famous anchorman. When he would humbly reply in the affirmative, the inquirer would invariably say something to the effect of, "You're so much better than Dan Rather." All America wanted to see Cronkite on the Tube for old times' sake. As an added insult, CBS sequestered Cronkite on a completely different floor from Rather's at the Moscone Center, as if he were an irritant, not an asset. "It seems funny," Cronkite told Peter Kaplan of *The New York Times*, "that after all these years of having looked out through the big glass window over the convention hall, that all I'll have is a room with a monitor." Kaplan reported Cronkite's bitterness toward CBS in his *Times* article.

Roger Mudd recalled accidentally bumping into Cronkite in San Francisco and wondered why CBS had been cruel to his old rival and friend. Whatever tension Cronkite and Mudd had between them had largely vanished by 1984. Both men had come to see Black Rock as the home base of Mephistopheles. After losing out to Rather for the CBS anchorman job in 1981, the nimble Mudd had moved over to NBC News and would later move on to PBS and the History Channel. Much like Cronkite, he would always think of himself as a CBSer, even though neither was treated well by the Ratherites. All Rather could do in 1984 was process both Cronkite's and Mudd's attacks as sour grapes. "Being on the air five times a week [from 1962 to 1981] created egocentrism," Rather explained. "It led to narcissism that in Cronkite's case bordered on megalomania. Everybody who anchors is susceptible. Myself included. It is an occupational hazard, a disease."

Rather, clinging to his decision, made sure that Cronkite had virtually no role in the Republican Convention meeting in Dallas that August. Cronkite was used mainly as a dancing bear in Dallas, a meet-and-greet man at breakfasts for the CBS News affiliates. Throughout the fall, Rather nixed Cronkite from

all CBS's election coverage without the slightest under-
tone of human kindness. There were no entitlements
for living legends at CBS News. On November 6, Bruce
Morton was at Rather's side to provide cogent analysis
of Reagan's great victory over Walter Mondale—525
electoral votes to 13. It was the first time since 1952 that
Cronkite had been absent from CBS on Election Night.
Even Bill Moyers got a hit of airtime that evening. But
not Cronkite, who watched the election results on CNN
at home. A story was out that Rather had a head cold
and was taking throat lozenges, antibiotics, vitamin C,
and hot water to help see him through his first Election
Night as anchorman. When Peter Kaplan of the *Times*
telephoned, the lonely Cronkite broached the Rather
cold. "I would often come up with a cold before one
of those things, but my producer convinced me it was
psychosomatic," he said. "Maybe it is with Dan, or else
he decided he needed to copy me."

With the use of sophisticated poll projections,
Rather went on the air at 8:00 p.m. EST, and CBS
News named Reagan the winner within five minutes.
Although Cronkite got along well with Mondale, he
seemed genuinely excited about Reagan's landslide. To
him, it was a historic reelection, a confirmation that
Goldwater's conservative movement had indeed turned
mainstream. It was also well known that Reagan would

more likely green-light a Cronkite interview than one with Rather. A little while later, Martin Kaplan, Mondale's chief speechwriter, was asked who could have defeated Reagan in 1984. Without skipping a beat, he said, "Robert Redford. Maybe Walter Cronkite."

Cronkite, who still represented the ethics of broadcast journalism to most Americans, now hoped that a string of his *CBS Reports* documentaries scheduled to air in 1985 might bring him a new wave of acclaim. The first special was "Honor, Duty, and a War Called Vietnam," a reflection on the war and the lessons that were learned in Southeast Asia. It aired on April 25, to coincide with the tenth anniversary of the capture of Saigon by Communist forces. That February, Cronkite had returned to Vietnam for *CBS Reports* for the first time since 1968, with U.S. representative John McCain (R-Ariz.), a former bomber pilot and POW, at his side. McCain, on his 137th bombing mission into North Vietnam, had been shot down over Hanoi in 1967. Parachuting into a lake, he broke both arms and a leg. He then spent more than five years as a POW, many in solitary confinement. Now, with Cronkite at his side and a CBS News crew on their heels, McCain talked candidly about his POW ordeal. The sounds of M-16s firing in the distance and big Cobra helicopters roaring overhead could no longer be heard. On a pastoral afternoon, he led Cronkite to his prison cell, but wouldn't enter. "Not all of us can emulate John Wayne," he told Cronkite about the torture he had endured. "But I think the overwhelming majority of us did the best we could. There was a great deal of suffering, a great deal of loneliness." It was powerful television.

Following "Honor, Duty, and a War Called Vietnam," Cronkite hosted *CBS Reports* on such serious topics as terrorism, nuclear fallout, and education. All these documentaries were good in the old Murrow-Friendly tradition. None did well in the Nielsen ratings. After this tepid viewer response, the thought of additional Cronkite projects for 1986 seemed farfetched. Further complicating Cronkite's life as CBS News special correspondent was the requirement that producer Bud Benjamin clear Cronkite's paid speaking engagements in advance. Having to seek permission from CBS corporate brass—even a dear friend like Benjamin—bothered Cronkite to no end. To quell his legitimate squawks, CBS did allow the retired anchorman, still on its payroll, to collaborate with BBC and PBS on a space shuttle documentary. But to Cronkite, CBS News president Van Gordon Sauter treated him as an ill-defined hanger-on, a burr on the saddle of CBS's new horse, Dan Rather.

Constantly looking for a CBS prime-time news magazine to boost his sagging fortunes at the network, Cronkite gambled on *Walter Cronkite at Large*. The first program aired in September 1986, with two more following in March 1987 and June 1988. They were ratings flops. Cronkite, of course, blamed the network for not promoting the shows. Unhappy with his treatment by CBS News, bitter that he had retired too soon, he circulated at New York cocktail parties, a sacred ritual. Without the daily grind at CBS, he imbibed regularly. No matter how exhausted he was from international travel, he enjoyed closing the bar. "When he drank," his Texas friend Ben Barnes recalled, "he had an appetite for both history and political bullshit."

Entertaining of the sort Walter and Betsy did on both Martha's Vineyard and in New York City took money. Cronkite wasn't allergic to accepting handsome speaker fees during the Reagan years. He received a steady stream of lucrative gigs and traveled extensively, almost entirely on assignments for honoraria. At each of their homes, he and Betsy were very social and entertained often. All three Cronkite kids, in fact, have their best memories of Dad being carefree in Edgartown. The endless list of his prominent friends visiting them on the Vineyard became something of an

inside joke. On any given afternoon at the Cronkites',
you could find Lady Bird Johnson, John Lehman,
William F. Buckley, Jackie Kennedy Onassis, John
Kennedy Jr., or Joseph Heller. Bedecked in a colorful Hawaiian or Lacoste tennis shirt, Cronkite loved
taking visitors around the Vineyard by boat. Betsy
preferred the Upper East Side, jokingly calling the
Vineyard "Elba," the godforsaken isle she couldn't
escape.

Cronkite was once challenged to a name-dropping
contest; he boasted heavyweight credentials. His competitor was the harmonica virtuoso—and wit—Larry
Adler. Cronkite wheeled in as many Kennedys as he
could fit into one story. But Adler won by describing
a tennis match he played at Charlie Chaplin's house
against Greta Garbo and Salvador Dalí. "For Walter
and me it's like the Dr. Seuss story," explained Brian
Williams of NBC News. "Oh, the people you'll meet!"
Yet his favorite friends remained the ones from Texas
and Missouri. "A big part of his lovability," actress
Deborah Rush, who married Chip Cronkite in 1985,
recalled, "was that Kansas City—not New York or the
Vineyard—was always home."

Not all Cronkite's post–March 1981 gambits
involved news work. While in Martha's Vineyard,
he forged a business partnership with watercolorist

Ray Ellis. Cronkite was a fan of painter Thomas Hart Benton's Martha's Vineyard paintings. He thought Ellis was the next best at natural seascapes. They decided to collaborate on a trilogy of coffee-table books. In the early 1960s, John Steinbeck had traveled around America and wrote the marvelous memoir *Travels with Charley.* Ellis's idea was that they would sail all around the country—instead of journeying in a camper, as Steinbeck did. While Cronkite would write up the sailing experiences in vignettes, Ellis would paint the seascapes he saw. "A publisher had accepted my paintings for a book and wanted Pat Conroy or William F. Buckley to write the text," Ellis recalled. "I said, 'Why not Walter Cronkite? He's the most trusted man in America.' At first Walter said he was too busy. But I got him with the line, 'Wouldn't you like to be known as an old salt?' That was all it took."

What is remarkable about the Cronkite-Ellis collaboration was that they pulled off the trilogy, with Oxmoor House, a boutique publisher in Birmingham, Alabama. The books—*South by Southeast* (Chesapeake Bay to Key West), *North by Northeast* (New Jersey to Maine), and *Westwind* (Point Flattery, Washington, to San Diego, California)—were dedicated by Cronkite and Ellis to their grandchildren. Ellis became one of Cronkite's closest and most stable friends. They enjoyed sailing around Sandy Hook, "the hinge to America's front door" (and the approach to New York Harbor) and heading south to Cape May, New Jersey (a favorite anchorage). "He has the rapscallion look of a Welsh pirate—which he is by blood inheritance," Cronkite said of Ellis at a gallery opening. "A benign pirate, however. The hero rather than the villain of a children's book. He might terrify with a leer but restore utter confidence and affection with a hug."

The first Cronkite-Ellis volume was published in 1983, the last in 1990. Although Cronkite was a Cape Cod man at heart, he conceded that Puget Sound and the San Juan Islands of Washington state represented America's true nautical paradise. "Boating in the Pacific Northwest, in season," he would write in *Westwind*, "comes pretty close to perfection." As for the most beautiful town in the world, Cronkite chose Homer, Alaska, refusing to include the Kenai Peninsula seaport (the halibut capital of the world) in his writings, to give "the folks who live there hope to stave off as long as possible the pressure of development."

When each volume of the sea trilogy was published, Cronkite and Ellis hit the road together on a massive book-signing tour. Long lines of people would queue up for hours just to meet Cronkite. "I've been broad-casting for years," a gleeful Cronkite told Ellis at an independent book shop signing, "and this is the first time I met my audience. It's a treat for people to walk up and say, 'You've been in my bedroom every night for decades.'"

Eventually Cronkite, the proud father of three, would have four grandkids. Kathy lived in Austin with her husband, Bill Ikard, and hosted her own radio talk show. Chip was a film editor in New York City and was married to the beautiful actress Deborah Rush (best known for her roles in the Woody Allen films *Zelig* and *The Purple Rose of Cairo*). Nancy was a yoga teacher, living at alternate times in Hawaii, California, and New York City. In the mid-1970s she married Gifford Whitney in New York, a descendant of Cornelius Vanderbilt who also listed among his ancestors William C. Whitney, secretary of the navy under President Grover Cleveland.

Besides doting on his children and grandchildren, Cronkite tried to spend as much time as possible at sea. Ever since being turned on to yachting by Lew Wood back in 1962 during the America's Cup, Cronkite had incrementally upgraded his vessels until at last he had his dream boat. In lieu of book advance money, Cronkite had Oxmoor House sink his cash into financing a new, state-of-the-art sloop; it was a tax dodge. The upgraded *Wyntje* was a sixty-four-foot yacht (a Hinckley 64 built in 1979), equipped with the latest technology, including an electronic GPS-like navigator that served as an auto-pilot. When Cronkite told Betsy about it, he said that, in theory, he wouldn't have to touch the wheel of the ship all day long. "That is wonderful," Betsy replied. "Now we can just send the boat and we don't ever have to go!" Betsy often got seasick on the *Wyntje*, but she still regularly went with Walter on excursions. "Mom loved Dad *so* much," Kathy recalled. "She didn't want to be away from him for those sailing hours."

Cronkite's best friend in the 1980s, besides Betsy, was his sailing companion Mike Ashford. One summer afternoon Cronkite pulled up to Ashford's place in Martha's Vineyard and said, "Mike, I've got the best table at the Edgartown Yacht Club to see the Fourth of July fireworks. Do you want a date? I know a woman perfect for you." Because Ashford was recently divorced, he jumped at the opportunity. He was too much of a gentleman to crassly ask what the woman in question looked like. "I was imagining Lesley Stahl or some weatherwoman type," Ashford said. "That's not how it played out." At the appointed hour, Ashford found out that his date was Cronkite's over-one-hundred-year-old mother, Helen. Cronkite, in modern parlance, had punked him. "How far back do you remember?" Ashford recalled asking Cronkite's mom. Helen started storytelling about the days at Fort Leavenworth pre–World War I. She told in vivid detail of being chased around by a desirous sex hound named Douglas MacArthur.

Another new Cronkite sailing friend was singer Jimmy Buffett, whom he first met at the America's Cup in Perth, Australia, in 1987. Before long he became a Parrothead (the name given to Buffett's most devoted fans). Not only did Cronkite play Buffett's songs—"Son of a Son of Sailor," "Margaritaville," and "He Went to Paris"—when the *Wyntje* was docked, but he also enjoyed catching the guitar-strumming Alabaman's New York concerts. Like everybody Cronkite "let in," Buffett was amazed by the broadcaster's down-homeness. Oftentimes in New York, Ed Bradley joined Cronkite and Buffett for drinks at P.J. Clarke's. "I'd get up to Martha's Vineyard to sail and check up on Walter's view of the world," Buffett recalled. "I'd have him as my guest at Madison Square Garden. I knew how to make him happy. I sat him by the showgirls."

Besides Buffett and Ashord, the two old-time friends whom Cronkite enjoyed clowning around with in the 1980s were *Washington Post* columnist Art Buchwald and Andy Rooney. They made him laugh. In 1986, Rooney produced an entire column on the subject of savoring the wine of life with his pal Cronkite, who was occasionally a libertine but never a prig. "The greatest Old Master in the art of living that I know is Walter Cronkite," Rooney wrote. "Walter works and plays at full speed all day long. He watches whales, plays tennis, flies to Vienna for New Year's. He dances until 2 a.m., sails in solitude, accepts awards gracefully. He attends boards of directors meetings, tells jokes and plays endlessly with his computers. He comes back from a trip on the *Queen Mary* in time for the Super Bowl. If life were fattening, Walter Cronkite would weigh 500 pounds."

Washington's favorite wit Art Buchwald had developed a shtick about how Cronkite's burning career ambition had lifted him upward from a Missouri cradle to the moon exploration and finally to being the Most Trusted Man in America. After Cronkite retired as anchorman in 1981, Buchwald maintained that the American people just couldn't find a suitable replacement for him. "With a population of only 220 million to choose from," Buchwald wrote, "it isn't going to be easy."

Being the Most Trusted Man in America while quasi-retired proved to be an unbeatable fund-raising ploy for Cronkite. What well-heeled liberal philanthropist wouldn't want to donate to a Cronkite-championed cause? In 1986, Cronkite raised over $300,000 for the Walter Cronkite Regents Chair in Communications at his alma mater, the University of Texas. It took a single night, during which he was roasted by some of his celebrated friends. Finding any faults to spoof was difficult—so comic Dick Cavett spoofed that very unusual personality trait: "I'm taking the easy way out," he said. "I'm going to use all the jokes I used at the Mother Teresa roast."

The kingdaddy of all honors Cronkite received was having the School of Journalism at Arizona State University named for him in 1984. Money was raised for the Cronkite School by Tom Chauncey, who in 1948 had purchased the radio station KPHO in Phoenix with his friend, cowboy icon Gene Autry. Chauncey was born in Houston and moved to Phoenix when he was thirteen years old. He was an early proponent of turning Cronkite's *CBS Evening News* broadcast from fifteen to thirty minutes, and then, once that was accomplished, he lobbied Black Rock for a sixty-minute nightly news broadcast. Being an advocate for longer newscasts was the perfect way to bond with Cronkite. The Cronkite family started visiting Arizona on mini-holidays.

Chauncey just loved old Cronkite, whom he called "The Commodore," like Ashford, even when the broadcaster was on a horse. Over drinks in Scottsdale one evening, Chauncey had talked with Bill Shover of the *Arizona Republic*, his son Tom Chauncey II, and other Valley of the Sun media leaders about doing something very special to honor Walter. There had been talk about building a new school of journalism at Arizona State University. Why not name it for the beloved anchorman? Chauncey telephoned Cronkite after his official retirement from the *CBS Evening News*. Could ASU name a new journalism school for him? A grateful Cronkite said yes. On April 27, 1984, the Arizona Board of Regents changed the name of the journalism program to honor the CBS legend. "We started answering the telephone the next day with 'Cronkite School,'" said Doug Anderson, who led the school for most of its first quarter century.

In 2004, Arizona State University decided to build a new home for the Cronkite School of Journalism and Mass Communication with Chauncey's financial help. At 235,000 square feet and six stories tall, the school, finished in 2008, instantly became a down-town Phoenix landmark. Once construction began in 2007, Cronkite, by then ninety years old, took a keen interest in the ASU project. Somehow it seemed fitting that while Murrow's legacy was being celebrated at Harvard-Tufts, Cronkite got Phoenix. He had always hoped that average Americans—more than elites—would celebrate his broadcasting career. "One of my biggest pleasures was that as the steel frames went up, Walter came to visit the construction site for an on-the-spot inspection," architect Stephen Erlich recalled. "He showed tons of excitement. But he was frail. He couldn't go up high. But boy . . . did he have a sparkle in his eye."

With the help of friends, Cronkite found his elder-statesman groove in the late 1980s. William Paley, whose own position in his company was shaky during the 1980s, ushered Cronkite onto the board in 1981. The intrigues at the corporate level in that decade became the stuff of media legend, as Thomas Wyman, a competent CEO of CBS, threatened to quit in 1983 if he wasn't given Paley's title as chairman as well. The directors tossed sentiment aside, ousted Paley after more than fifty years at the helm, and elected Wyman. Within a few years, the company was foundering, failing either to uphold its old prestige or to produce a strong response to new satellite and Internet technology. When the board members, including Cronkite, learned that Wyman's strategy for saving the company was a secret plan to sell it to the Coca-Cola

Corporation, headquartered in Atlanta, they withdrew their support for him. Wyman had no choice but to resign.

In 1985, Ted Turner, who founded CNN and became the dominant force in cable television, waged a serious takeover bid for CBS. Nicknamed the "Mouth of the South," Turner, the Atlanta-based media maverick, had a plan that called for the sale of CBS assets such as the record and book-publishing divisions to raise capital to pay for the purchase of the Tiffany Network. In the end, though, he promised to make the CBS television network the center of a cable television empire he had started with CNN. Turner loved the prestigious past of CBS à la Murrow and Cronkite, but he also understood the future of satellite television better than almost anyone in the world. "I tried to buy all of the networks," he recalled. "CBS was the one that was doable in the end; the math worked. Acquiring CBS wasn't an easy thing no matter how you slice it. And I engendered opposition." Cronkite had bonded with Turner at the 1977 America's Cup in Newport, Rhode Island, while on rare assignment for *60 Minutes*. It's no exaggeration to say that Cronkite was in awe of Turner's *Courageous* (an aluminum-hulled twelve-meter yacht). "Ted, how about letting me steer?" Cronkite asked. To which Turner snapped, "Sure, Walter, if you let me do the *Evening News*. (Cronkite never allowed Turner to sit in his anchor chair, but he did get a turn being captain of the *Courageous*.)

As Ken Auletta documented in *Media Man*, Turner had numerous enemies at CBS who wanted to squash his purchase of the network. Mike Wallace and Don Hewitt questioned Turner's "moral fitness" to own CBS, deeming him an unsophisticated redneck. Cronkite, by contrast, thought Turner the best thing since sliced bread. The directors followed Paley's lead in resisting Turner's bold bid to buy CBS. Within a short time, Paley found a willing billionaire, Laurence Tisch of the Loews Corporation, to help fend off the Turner incursion. Mostly, CBS foiled Turner by borrowing money and buying back its own stock, taking on a crippling level of debt in the process. As a result, the network was left with even greater financial problems than before.

After a short time, in 1986, Larry Tisch was named chairman of CBS. The sixty-three-year-old Tisch hailed from Brooklyn and made his financial fortune opening hotels in Atlantic City and the Catskills and, with his brother, overseeing Loews Theaters. With an impeccable business career, he seemed to be a white knight with the best intentions for CBS. He soon demonstrated, though, that he didn't understand the company at all, except as a vehicle to increase the wealth of savvy investors. In the time-tested and much-resented way of corporate raiders, he sold off CBS's assets—just as Turner had been expected to do. Tisch went further, however, eviscerating the workforce at the network while authorizing very little capital for the development of new programming or technology. CBS, which had been a leader almost from the start of the broadcasting industry, missed the opportunity to invest in itself in the cable era.

Cronkite, given a seat at the table, tried to interest the board in decisions regarding the fabric of CBS programming. With Paley's health wavering, he hoped that the board could step up and exert itself to uphold the CBS standard. Given his druthers, he preferred Turner to Tisch. At least if CNN and CBS merged, foreign bureaus wouldn't be shuttered. (Back in 1967, he had publicly insisted that news gathering had to be global.) He found, however, that his fellow board members were primarily interested in the accounting end of operations, not in what Cronkite called "the philosophy" of programming: its goals and its parameters. More specifically, he tried to argue that the board should insist upon a high standard of hard news on the *CBS Evening News with Dan Rather*, for the sake of higher ratings, if not journalistic integrity. Like an old bison left behind by the herd, Cronkite didn't make an impact at Black Rock. It was some consolation for him that Tisch didn't like Rather, and lobbied the new CBS News president to hire Bob Schieffer to replace Dashing Dan. "There was talk, which Cronkite was a part of, to fire Rather and have me take his place," Schieffer recalled. "Up until then, Dan liked me sitting in for him as substitute. It was Diane Sawyer at *60 Minutes* he felt threatened by. But now I was seen as Cronkite's guy, and that didn't sit well with Dan."

When Cronkite turned seventy on November 4, 1986, he was excused from further CBS board service, in accordance with a rule that had been recently implemented by Tisch. By odd edict, Walter Cronkite was considered too old to sit in the luxurious surroundings of a boardroom and discuss business issues. CBS under Tisch treated Cronkite, as the bluegrass standard puts it, as "Old and in the Way." This led to a dispute in 1988 about whether Cronkite would end up relinquishing his status as a CBS special correspondent. His contract would expire that year. Cronkite assured friends that his armor was strong, that the boot didn't hurt. But his assurances had a hollow ring to them. "There was a feeling that Walter was a man without a country," Andy Rooney recalled. "He started exploring all sorts of theories about World Federation."

Like many people hitting their twilight years, Cronkite took the time to try to mend various strained relationships. Because Friendly apologized for his role in the dethroning of Cronkite at the 1964 convention, all was copacetic. Often Cronkite and Friendly would go out to lunch or dinner to discuss the early days of TV news. Among their shared accomplishments was the "D-Day Plus 20 Years" interview with Eisenhower on Omaha Beach. Friendly held seminars at Columbia University, and Cronkite made a few unadvertised guest appearances. They discussed making another record about the 1960s in the vein of *I Can Hear It Now* (Friendly's historical album collaboration with Edward R. Murrow). "I remember us going to dinner with Walter and Betsy and the Rooneys, Andy and Marguerite," recalled Ruth Friendly, widow of the legendary television maverick. "Suddenly a young man came toward the table, seemingly wanting to meet Cronkite and Rooney, both TV celebrities. Instead, he came up and told Fred that he had changed his life by offering sound advice via a Columbia course. Walter and Andy were ignored. It was hilarious." At a wake for Gordon Mannings's wife, Edna, Roger Mudd suggested to Cronkite that they form a new network—the Old Guy Network (OGN News), staffed by codgers like Pierpoint, Herman, Benton, Reasoner, Stringer, Mudd, and Cronkite. According to Mudd, Cronkite was "amused by the prospect."

A great healing also took place between Paley and Cronkite in December 1989. The Museum of Broadcasting in New York held a gala celebration honoring Cronkite's extraordinary career. This must have been the fifteenth or twentieth such event Cronkite had endured since stepping down as the CBS anchorman. Paley, his body long ago having lost its vigor, had poured his heart and soul into writing a tribute speech worthy of Ted Sorensen. But instead of giving the JFK inaugural, Paley ended up, like Robert Frost, fumbling with his notes at the lectern, deviating from the script in an awkward way, even finding it hard to breathe. At eighty-three years old, Paley was having a senior moment. "I'm sorry," he said. "I can't read this."

He then launched into ad-lib mode, talking authoritatively about Cronkite's virtues, praising his sterling performance as CBS anchorman from 1962 to 1981. An honest feistiness burst forth when he acknowledged that CBS News was the house of both Murrow *and*

Cronkite. When Paley finished, the crowd went wild, stomping its feet and roaring as if Reggie Jackson had just whacked a grand slam over the right-field fence at Yankee Stadium. "Everyone was dying at the thought that he would humiliate himself," one guest recalled. "They wanted him to be *Paley*. When he saved himself, there was a thrill."

33.

Defiant Liberal

SPACE SHUTTLE DREAMS—CHALLENGER DISASTER—*ROLLING STONE* ADVISOR—DRUMMING AWAY WITH MICKEY HART—OFF WITH RATHER'S HEAD—FEUD OVER JFK ASSASSINATION ANNIVERSARY—SHIPPING OFF PERSONAL PAPERS— WRITING HIS AUTOBIOGRAPHY—IS THE *EVENING NEWS* DEAD?—KILL THEM ALL—FROZEN OUT OF HOUSTON—ANGRY AT DUKAKIS—BARBARA JORDAN AND THE DEFENSE OF LIBERALISM—ECO-WARRIOR REDUX—PULLING FOR SHAW—HARD DOVE OF THE GULF WAR—HITCHING HIS WAGON TO THE DISCOVERY CHANNEL—SALUTING CNN—TOASTING THE DEATH OF COMMUNISM WITH BUSH—CLINTON WINS—GOOD-BYE TO BUSH

When word reached Cronkite that President Regan would soon be was accepting applications from civilians to join a mission into space, he was among the first to say *send me*. On August 27, 1984, Reagan had announced that a new "Spaceflight Participant Program" would expand the group of individuals who could fly on the Space Shuttle to common citizens, including teachers, artists, and journalists. It was a way to excite taxpayers about the Space Shuttle. Around that time, Cronkite had narrated an IMAX film about the Shuttle, *The Dream Is Alive*, and was flush with excitement about possibly being the first journalist to orbit Earth. Due to his prominence, combined with a fine track record for promoting all things NASA, Cronkite thought he would make a superior civilian astronaut. On July 19, 1985, Vice President George H. W. Bush announced that a teacher—thirty-seven-year-old Christa McAuliffe of New Hampshire—would become the first civilian in space. But that the second billet would indeed go to a reporter. Cronkite was ready to flat-out win the competition. On October 5, NASA directed a Project Steering Committee to work with the Association of Schools of Journalism and Mass Communications (ASJMC) at the University of South Carolina in Columbia to draft a process for selecting a journalist to fly in space in the fall of 1986 as the second private citizen embedded on the Shuttle. NASA made the announcement of the "Journalist in Space" program on October 24, and on December 3, ASJMC started mailing applications to those that requested them. Cronkite, behaving like a high school student applying to college, eagerly filled out all the paperwork, determined to be chosen.

Cronkite knew he was in fine flying trim. His diet was going well, his heart was sound, and he lifted weights daily. Whenever possible, he played tennis with Andy Rooney, outdoors whenever the weather permitted. Welcoming a NASA physical with open arms, Cronkite filled out the ten-page NASA medical history questionnaire. NASA dubbed these potential new civilian astronauts "space flight participants" (SFPs). Eric Johnson, project director of the NASA recruiting program, told *People* magazine that there was "reasonably no age limit for the flight, only whoever is chosen has to have a good heart." If shortlisted as one of the first-round candidates, Cronkite agreed to undergo ninety-nine hours of vigorous training. In a "personal essay" for NASA, Cronkite wrote that the "principal thing" a reporter offered space exploration was the removal of "the last lingering suspicion" that the Space Shuttle was a boondoggle. Astronaut John Young was dismissive of the entire SFP program. "I sure want that first guy to be checked out by the FBI," Young told Michener, whose 1982 book *Space* was a bestseller, "I don't want to be babysitting some kook."

Cronkite's campaign to become a NASA citizen astronaut intensified during the summer of 1984. David Friend, who covered the space program for *Life* magazine and later went on to become an editor for *Vanity Fair*, caught wind of the rumor that Cronkite was vigorously pursuing the SFP voyager slot. Looking for a groundswell of publicity for his candidacy, Cronkite granted *Life* an exclusive interview and photo shoot in Edgartown. Hoping to get Cronkite in costume, Friend was able to procure an official light blue NASA space shuttle uniform from the Johnson Space Center. "So I got the space suit and flew up to Martha's Vineyard," Friend recalled. "I carried the astronaut helmet in my lap. Our half-baked idea was to have Cronkite pose in the uniform. The notion was that he was *really* ready for space."

To Friend's surprise, Cronkite snatched the space suit and helmet from him and charged upstairs to change into it. No questions asked. As Friend waited in the living room, Cronkite's nonagenarian mother, Helen, stood in the foyer expectantly. A few minutes later, Cronkite came clomping down the stairs dressed like John Glenn about to depart on a Mercury mission. "Oh, Walter," she exclaimed, "you look amazing!"

For half an hour, Cronkite paraded around Edgartown as if he'd leaped out of chapter four of Tom Wolfe's *The Right Stuff*, stretching credulity, posing for *Life* photos, waving to all the kids like a costumed Donald Duck at Disney World, proud to be a NASA astronaut for an afternoon.

On Tuesday January 28, 1986, *Challenger* lifted off from Kennedy Space Center and exploded. McAuliffe and the six astronauts on board died. Cronkite was vacationing in Santiago, Chile, at the time of the *Challenger* disaster but granted the Associated Press an interview. Full of stoicism, he insisted that the Space Shuttle program should continue regardless of the *Challenger* tragedy. "We have come a long way in Space, and there is still so much to be done out there," he said. "There are scientific, industrial, medical bounties to be reaped in Space. To diminish what we have done in the past would be to dishonor those who have lost their lives in that program on *Challenger* today." That May, when Walt Disney World in Florida opened the EPCOT Center attraction *Spaceship Earth*, Cronkite was selected to be the show's narrator. Having been chosen by NASA as one of the forty semi-finalists for "Journalist in Space" in July 1986, Cronkite used the EPCOT occasion to praise McAuliffe as a marvelous role model for American girls. But before long, while the Space Shuttle itself resumed operation, the "Journalist in Space" program was scrubbed.

For a *CBS News Special* in 1986 about the end of the cold war in Europe, Cronkite traveled to Russia, Hungary, and East Germany. "People are always calling up with things that sound interesting that I think I am going to have time to do," he explained to *USA Today* reporter Morten Lund. "I have never done so much wheeling and dealing. My wife, Betsy, has taken to standing over me on the telephone, shaking her head and mouthing, 'NO.'"

Imbued with a blind willingness to talk to anyone, even the proverbial potted plant, Cronkite labeled himself a "hangoutologist." Even if he were strapped to a torture rack, Cronkite would find a way to babble niceties about the exquisite chamber lighting or the dungeon stone. To such an extrovert, Manhattan nightlife was understandably one of life's exquisite pleasures. "When the new morality hit in the late 60s, early 70s— the singles bars and that scene—I would like to have dipped into that," Cronkite told *The Washington Post*. "I was interested in it. I don't mean as a sexual participant. But I'd have liked to have gone into some of the First and Second Avenue bars. I enjoy the tavern scene. It's a great way to meet people, talk to people. Hair's down. It's no longer possible because people surround me. They want to talk, but there is a little wall between us. They're talking to somebody they want to impress."

Ever since Hunter S. Thompson started excoriating Richard Nixon in *Rolling Stone* in the 1970s, Cronkite had become a fan of the rock-n-roll magazine. What he liked most about the *Stone* was its unflinching investigative articles about the four major dangers to civilization: pollution, depletion of natural resources, proliferation of nuclear weapons, and world hunger. Befriending the magazine's founding owner and editor, Jann Wenner, whom he first met aboard tycoon Malcolm Forbes's private plane (*The Capitalist Tool*) on a trip to France, Cronkite liked hearing Wenner's stories about Altamont, the Beatles, and Bruce Springsteen. A devilish Forbes thought it would be amusing for Jann and his wife, Jane, to spend four days at his Château de Balleroy in Normandy along with Reagan's friends Charlie and Barbara Zwick, Jay and Mavis Leno, and Jean MacArthur, the widow of Douglas MacArthur. "What a wonderful time we all had," Wenner recalled. "Betsy was a hoot, so funny, calling an ace an ace, a spade a spade. What surprised me was that Cronkite was much more than a gentleman—he was knowledge-able about everything."

A lucky break came Cronkite's way when he was given the opportunity to collaborate with pianist Dave

Brubeck—whose 1959 album *Time Out* was Cronkite's favorite—on an oral history project about West Coast jazz. When composer Irving Berlin turned one hundred, Cronkite emceed a gala celebrating the songwriter's career at Carnegie Hall. During the summers at Martha's Vineyard, Cronkite gladly sang for his guests. It was like a karaoke hoedown. After a few cocktails, he would lead sing-alongs to "Bill Bailey" and "I'm Gonna Just Sit Right Down and Write Myself a Letter." According to daughter Kathy, he "didn't have a good singing voice, but, boy, was he full of gusto." Cronkite *never* turned down an offer to help out the New York Opera—or opera companies in other cities. When John Adams and Alice Goodman were looking for a celebrity type to promote their new opera, *Nixon in China,* which premiered at the Houston Grand Opera in 1987, they turned to the veteran newsman for help. Cronkite volunteered to be emcee and promo man for the opera, which he thought was more fun than newsreels of his trip with President Nixon back in 1972.

Just how spontaneous and uncautious Cronkite became as an interviewee was on marvelous display in Jonathan Alter's *Rolling Stone* interview in November 1987. Cronkite was casual, funny, endearing, and unplugged. Cronkite had also befriended pop artist Andy Warhol in the 1980s. One evening the artist and anchorman sat down together barefoot at a black-tie dinner thrown by Yoko Ono. Cronkite had told *Rolling Stone* that Carter was the smartest cold war president—a minor dig at Reagan. It made for fun dinner conversation. Cronkite told Warhol that when he went to interview Richard Nixon in 1968, the GOP candidate's staff sat him outside the boss's door and he overheard the former vice president on the phone saying "piss" and "cocksucker" and "fuck." "Walter Cronkite thought it was a setup to have him hear all this so he would think Nixon was really macho," Warhol wrote in *Diaries*. "But then years later when the Watergate tapes came out he was surprised to hear Nixon talking like that all the time."

Grateful Dead drummer Mickey Hart became one of Cronkite's most trusted friends during the same period. In early 1987, Hart had been asked to score a Cronkite documentary on the America's Cup along with rock guitarist Stephen Stills. "While in the studio, I bumped into Cronkite," Hart recalled. "I told him I wanted to hear his narration so I could write around his voice." After they finished rehearsal, at which Stills had failed to show, it was getting to be late in the evening. "Hungry?" Cronkite asked Hart. "Want to go grab dinner?" Hart said sure. The seemingly unlikely duo ended up at the nearby CBS-favored diner, chatting unhurriedly about the 1962 America's Cup as if they were boarding school friends. Mutual admiration came easily for them. The Grateful Dead were scheduled to play a few sold-out shows at Madison Square Garden, and Hart invited Walter and Betsy to be his guests. The answer was . . . *you betcha.*

Cronkite and Hart shared an enthusiasm for sailing, an affinity for drums, and a deep commitment to save the world's rain forests. "Once I got away from the idolatry, I found Walter to be a real classy, straight-up gent," Hart recalled. "He allowed me in, and I allowed him in. My father was a common crook. Walter became the father I never had. His Vietnam dissent saved the lives of tens of thousands of people. He was a broadcast warrior. Walter walked the walk as well as talking the talk."

Whether in the San Francisco Bay area or Nantucket Sound, they often escaped the rat race together for a few days at sea. While Cronkite didn't become a Dead Head, he was something akin to an auxiliary member of the band. "We played drums together a lot," Hart recalled. "He started falling in love with music . . . it allowed him to be fluid and free. We would play all day, have mini-sessions. I was amazed one time to see that he had twenty drums set up in his living room. We'd regularly spend Thanksgiving together in New York. We'd play before dinner and after dinner. The music made him alive as he was losing his facility. The music connected him to life and the world at large. After a session, he was *really* articulate. The vibrations were therapeutic and meditative."

While the Grateful Dead might have been Cronkite fans, the ex-anchorman's stature at CBS News had faded to almost nothing, and his seven-year contract with the network expired in 1988. The darling of *Rolling Stone* and *Interview*, the disgruntled TV news star would be free to move to another network and publicly intimated that he just might do so. He was still openly critical of *CBS Evening News* (which intermittently regained the lead in the ratings race in the late 1980s and '90s). Sometimes it seemed that Cronkite, an ombudsman in exile, couldn't wait to renounce Rather. On September 11, 1987, CBS was forced to cut into the *CBS Evening News* when coverage of a U.S. Open tennis match between Steffi Graf and Lori McNeil ran long. Told that the broadcast would start fifteen minutes late and run on an abbreviated format, Rather stalked out of the Miami studio. "I was—and am—a great believer in Dan," *CBS Evening News* producer Jeff Fager recalled. "But when he walked out in Miami, I understood his fault. He put a strange pride over the organization. I remember thinking, 'Walter would never have done that.'"

Rather was widely criticized for the lapse of judgment in Miami, and Cronkite didn't pull any punches. Sounding like a rioter screaming "off with his head," he publicly claimed that he would have "fired" Rather outright for gross insubordination. Rather was understandably hurt by Cronkite's smackdown. How was it good, Rather asked, for CBS News to have Cronkite maliciously carping about him? "Walter, I long knew, was competitive down to his marrow," Rather recalled. "It was like he woke up in 1987 and saw me in his old job with successful ratings, making more money than he ever did—and I was relatively young to boot. He wanted to destroy me. I didn't know what to do. I kept wondering how to handle his venom. I decided I didn't want to fight him. So I hunkered down in the fetal position and just took it. I just let him take big chunks out of my ass."

Given the insularity of the upper management at CBS News, exactly who banished Cronkite in 1988 remains unclear. But Van Gordon Sauter (president of CBS News from 1985 to 1986) and Howard Stringer (president of CBS News from 1986 to 1988) seem to be left holding the bag. From 1962 to 1981, CBS News had ridden Cronkite's voice and work ethic to TV dominance. No more. The attitude toward him on West Fifty-seventh Street was an unspoken "get your mail and get out of here, old man." Why couldn't Cronkite go gently into that good night like Douglas Edwards? He should just go moor *Wyntje* in Sarasota, Florida, and stay put. The power circle around Rather maintained an oh-how-the-mighty-have-fallen disdain toward Cronkite. Peter J. Boyer of *The New York Times* published an article on June 8, 1988, about his dissatisfaction with being persona non grata at Fifty-seventh Street. Two former CBS News presidents—Van Gordon Sauter and Edward M. Joyce—acknowledged that Cronkite had been deliberately "shut out" of CBS News because they didn't want Rather to throw a tantrum.

What caused the Rather-Cronkite feud to escalate even further in 1988 was the twenty-fifth anniversary of the JFK assassination. Earlier that year, Cronkite had floated a detailed proposal to Sauter about hosting a prime-time *Special Report* on the anniversary of the Dallas tragedy. Everything would be looked at with fresh eyes, including Oswald's ties with Cuba, LBJ's fears of a conspiracy, and what the Warren Commission got wrong. Cronkite thought this was a no-brainer, the perfect special for him to host. Instead, the CBS network (not the news division) passed on it. Cronkite blamed Rather for dogging him out of the gig. Whenever an opportunity arose, Cronkite dumped Rather into the warlock's pot and stirred. "I think it's unfortunate that any other person feels about another as I do about Dan," Cronkite said. "But to me, I guess, Dan just reeks of insincerity."

What Cronkite never fully comprehended was that Rather wasn't the one who nixed his JFK special. No one at CBS News was getting an hour of prime-time TV in the 1980s—with vulture capitalist Larry Tisch as honcho—unless it was something like a *Challenger* disaster special. Rather himself could not have finagled an hour of such prime TV real estate; the very notion was laughable. Prime-time television was cage fighting—every ratings point counted. "He was pushing this Kennedy anniversary special ridiculously hard," Rather recalled. "Believe me, it was a complete nonstarter from the get-go. It wasn't even for a blinking instant a serious consideration. But Walter created this false scenario that I had somehow nixed his Kennedy special."

When CBS News broadcast a two-hour *Apollo 11* twentieth-anniversary special in 1989, it was hosted by Rather and Charles Kuralt. Cronkite was once again nixed from the entire nostalgic enterprise. Rather believed that only his resignation would have pleased Cronkite. Therefore, he just curled his mouth up and took whatever buckshot Cronkite fired at him. Over the summer of 1988, Black Rock determined that it was better to renegotiate Cronkite's contract than have him debase Rather for sport. If CBS paid Cronkite, they could at least guarantee in writing that he couldn't criticize company employees. After a protracted negotiation, CBS agreed to give Cronkite a ten-year contract. It was also a gag order, in the spirit of the old Arab proverb: "It's better to have the camel inside the tent pissing out than outside pissing in." The contract was nonexclusive, stipulating that Cronkite could work with most other media companies, the notable exceptions being NBC and ABC.

Getting his life in order, in 1988 Cronkite donated his papers to the Dolph Briscoe Center for American History at the University of Texas at Austin. He also asked Dr. Don Carleton, the center's director, to help him organize the research for his memoir, *A Reporter's Life*. A born-and-bred Texan—best known for his important anti-McCarthyism book *Red Scare*—Carleton conducted sixty hours' of recorded interviews with Cronkite. Within a relatively short time, Carleton became a trusted confidant. An amiable rapport developed between the two men, one that grew steadily in importance to Cronkite over the years. Like so many of the friends Cronkite made late in life, the two men shared the brotherhood of the sea. "Every three or four months for a period stretching over four years," Carleton wrote, "Walter and I met for two or three days, sometimes longer for me to interview him. . . . Those interviews were conducted in his office at CBS, his home in Manhattan, his summer residence in Martha's Vineyard and in the British Virgin Islands on his sailboat."

Cronkite didn't have much of a role in the 1988 presidential campaign that eventually pitted Vice President George H. W. Bush against Massachusetts governor Michael Dukakis. But he nevertheless had CBS News pay his way to the Iowa caucus and the New Hampshire primary that January. He circulated among the political stars—Bush and Dukakis included—with ease. One evening, New York magazine columnist Joe Klein joined Cronkite and Jerry Brown, former governor of California, for a drink at the Wayfarer Inn in Bedford, New Hampshire. "Walter was entirely shit-faced," Klein recalled. "He was slurring his words but having a grand old time." Suddenly, a very pesky right-to-life advocate interrupted their conversation with a rant against Roe v. Wade. This pro-lifer ripped into Governor Brown for being a faux Catholic, a promoter of abortion, a baby killer. After a few minutes of pontificating, her eyes locked on Cronkite for the first time. She was taken aback, thrilled to see the famous CBS News anchorman in person.

"Mr. Cronkite," she said, "don't you agree with me that abortion is wrong? What do you think?"

Whereupon Cronkite, with a dismissive wave of the hand and ironic expression, uttered the unutterable in his mellifluous voice.

"Kill them all," he said.

The woman gasped. Almost fainted on the spot. At loose ends as to how to respond to such a deplorable remark, she just walked away discombobulated. "That put an end to the haranguing," Klein said. "I don't know whether Walter meant it or it was just a ploy to get her to go. But we laughed hard."

On February 28, 1988, Cronkite went to Houston for the Democratic candidates' debate held at the George R. Brown Convention Center. The Sun Broadcast Group and the National Association of Television Program Executives International cosponsored the event. He had been chosen to moderate. The job was the highlight of his spring. On the day of the debate, he received a jolting call from Black Rock in his Four Seasons hotel room. Because the Democratic debate wasn't airing on CBS News—was in fact airing on NBC News—company lawyers argued that Cronkite would be in breach of his million-dollar-a-year contract if he moderated. This was a cruel, embarrassing blow to him. As a last-minute replacement, Linda Ellerbee filled in. Although Ellerbee had been an NBC reporter on the *Today* show, she had turned in 1987 to producing children's TV shows for cable channels. All Cronkite had for consolation was the press report that neither Dukakis nor Gephardt was going to participate in the Texas debate. "Cronkite watched," Ann Hodges of the *Houston Chronicle* reported, "just like you and me." Ellerbee, caught up in the moment, ignored Cronkite. All the press swarmed around Al Gore, Jesse Jackson, Gary Hart, and others, while Ellerbee was the toast of the town. Cronkite walked back to the Four Seasons alone, feeling old and useless. CBS had shot him down yet again.

His doldrums continued through the spring. That April, he joined forces with James Reston of *The New York Times* for a luncheon "conversation" with the American Society of Newspaper Editors. Every comment Cronkite made that afternoon in Washington had a curmudgeonly cast. Whether it was the Barbara Walters entertainment-as-news syndrome or the over-scripted presidential debates or the mixing of celebrity with politics, everything sickened him. And even though the communications school at Arizona State was named in his honor, he dissed the notion of going from college straight into TV broadcasting. "It's the glamour of the business that attracts them," he grumbled. "I think that what some of the schools are committing is fraud. They don't have to go to college to learn [the technical part] of TV news; they could learn that in a trade school in about three weeks."

Cronkite did offer political commentary for the *CBS Evening News* from the Democratic Convention (July 18–25) in Atlanta and the Republican Convention (August 15–18) in New Orleans, but it didn't add up to much. Bored by the 1988 presidential square-off of Bush-Dukakis, and dismayed that Mars exploration was not being embraced fulsomely enough by Congress, Cronkite decided that sailing his double-ended *Wyntje* around the Atlantic seaboard was the smartest thing to do. Although he personally liked Vice President Bush, whom he sometimes called "Poppy," and thought his extensive résumé as CIA director and vice president was impressive, Cronkite was aghast at the political tactics of GOP cutthroat Lee Atwater. He was disgusted with the anti-Dukakis smear ad centered on Willie Horton. (While Dukakis was governor, Horton, a convicted felon, was released from a Massachusetts prison as part of a weekend furlough program, during which time he committed rape and carjacking.) But he was just as livid at Dukakis for running a lackluster campaign, running away from being dubbed a liberal.

That July Cronkite visited his longtime friend (and producer since the 1950s) Bud Benjamin in a New York hospital; he was suffering from a just-diagnosed brain tumor. They held hands and reminisced about everything from *The Twentieth Century* to Watergate specials to *Westmoreland v. CBS.* On September 20, Benjamin died at age seventy. At the funeral in Scarborough, New York, Cronkite was a weeping mess. "Benjamin had been Walter's backstop," Andy Rooney recalled. "Living in a world without Bud wasn't easy for Walter."

Just a couple of weeks after Benjamin's death, Cronkite watched Dukakis implode in a televised debate with Bush. CNN anchorman Bernard Shaw had asked Dukakis, a death penalty opponent, how he would respond if his wife were raped and murdered. Dukakis mistakenly tried answering logically instead of emotionally. It proved to be a watershed moment in the campaign, and it buried Dukakis's White House odds.

Shaw: Governor, if Kitty Dukakis were raped and murdered, would you favor an irrevocable death penalty for the killer?

Dukakis: No, I don't, Bernard. And I think you know that I've opposed the death penalty all of my life. I don't see any evidence that it's a deterrent, and I think there are better and more effective ways to deal with violent crime. We've done so in my

own state . . . one of the reasons why we have had
the biggest drop in crime of any industrial state . . .
the lowest murder rate of any industrial state.

According to Rooney, Cronkite tossed a bowl of
popcorn in the air when Dukakis blundered. "Game
over," he said, and demanded the TV be turned off.
That November 8, Bush routed Dukakis, 426 electoral
votes to 111; the vice president carried forty states.
Bush had lambasted Dukakis with negatives, painting him as a big-spending liberal, wobbly on crime,
short on patriotism, detached from family values. To
Cronkite's chagrin, Dukakis never fought back. At least
when McGovern went up in flames back in 1972 he
had courage, defending New Frontier–style liberalism
and denouncing the Vietnam War with moral indignation. The Dukakis ship had sunk without a fight. An
incensed Cronkite was concerned that the Bush crowd
had turned *liberal* into an epithet.

Playing the Grand Old Man, Cronkite publicly came
out as a card-carrying liberal with an ACLU pedigree at
a People for the American Way's Spirit of Liberty dinner
honoring Congresswoman Barbara Jordan of Texas on
November 17, 1988. Dressed in a tuxedo with a hand-
kerchief protruding from his pocket, he looked handsome and dapper on the dais at the Roseland Ballroom

in New York City. Heading to the event that evening, in a taxi going down Park Avenue, he was in a discernibly feisty mood. His oratory that night, influenced by Sidney Lumet's touchstone movie *Network*, soared in a no-holds-barred "Defense of Liberalism." It was Cronkite's equivalent of Murrow's RTNDA speech of 1958 in Chicago. Roseland's multipurpose hall, with its purple and cerise tentlike décor, was Cronkite's favorite music venue. He had seen Harry James, Louis Armstrong, and Count Basie (who wrote "Roseland Shuffle") perform there. But on this night, a celebration of the pioneering Texas congresswoman Barbara Jordan from the Eighteenth District, it was Walter Cronkite's stage.

At the podium, Cronkite, spinning his thoughts in the low, rapid voice of a broadcaster just liberated from the rules of objective journalism, scolded Democrats to never again abandon the liberal tradition that Barbara Jordan represented. His spontaneous remonstrance was electrifying. Some people thought he was Maker's Mark drunk or brain-fevered. Perhaps he was a little of both. The soaring speech became treasured as Cronkite's political coming-out party:

> *The temptation is rather great at this point to digress into the defense of liberalism, but I shall fight off that temptation. No, I won't. I know that liber-*

alism isn't dead in this country. It isn't even comatose. It simply is suffering a severe case of acute laryngitis. It simply has temporarily—we hope— lost its voice. But that Democratic loss in the election. . . . It seems to me it was not just the candidate who belatedly found a voice that could reach the people. It was not just a campaign strategy built on a defensive philosophy. It was not just an opposition that conducted one of the most sophisticated and cynical campaigns ever. It was not just a failure to reach out to every section of our nation and every sector of our society. It was the fault of too many who found their voices still by not-so-subtle ideological intimidation.

For instance, we know that unilateral military action in Grenada and Tripoli was wrong. We know that Star Wars means uncontrollable escalation of the arms race. We know that the real threat to democracy is when half of the nation is in poverty. We know that Thomas Jefferson was right when he said that a democracy cannot be both ignorant and free. We know, we know, that no one should tell a woman she has to bear an unwanted child. And we know that there is freedom to disagree with all or part of what I've just said. But God Almighty, God Almighty, we've got to shout these truths in which *we believe from the rooftops, like that scene in the movie* Network. *We've got to throw open our windows and shout these truths to the streets and to the heavens. And I bet that we'll find that more windows are thrown open to join the chorus than we'd ever have dreamed possible.*

The uncorking at Roseland was restorative for Cronkite's sagging post-election morale. Never before had he spoken so candidly about his personal liberalism in public. Having built his house from the first brick onward as the objective journalist, the Roseland address planted him firmly in liberal-left soil. The charade of being Mr. Center was over. Something about the Bush ascension to the White House, the degrading of liberalism, had caused his spleen to rupture. Freedom of speech was his new talking point. A taste for the middling gave way to rabble-rousing. If Ted Turner was the "Mouth from the South," Cronkite became the "Missouri Mouth." *The New York Times* ran a long story about Cronkite becoming a scrappy left-winger who spoke his mind. "On television, I tried to absolutely hew to the middle of the road and not show any prejudice or bias in any way," he explained. "I did not believe the public was sophisticated enough to understand that a newsman could wear several hats and that we had the ability to turn off nearly, you can't say perfectly, but nearly all of our prejudices and biases."

On March 11, 1989, jarred by the Natural Resources Defense Council report *Ebb Tide for Pollution: A Program for Cleansing the Coast,* Cronkite returned to North Carolina to deliver a blistering speech about saving the state's pristine coastline. Sailing around Cape Hatteras National Seashore was to Cronkite a sacred endeavor. But on a return visit to North Carolina, inhaling a sulfuric stench, he saw poisonous water and decided to speak out. "Nowadays, you see more people, more houses, more development—on the barrier beaches and the coastline," he said. "You see oil scum and gasoline floating on the surface. And all the detritus of so-called civilized living—the throw-away wrappings and containers—above all the PLASTICS. The styrofoam, the used baggies—bobbing in the swells ubiquitously—sometimes as far as a hundred miles offshore. You see plastic waste floating all around you, and you find it hard to remember that all this plastic in our life is less than a half a century old—that there actually was a time when man managed to get along WITHOUT plastic—happy in the ignorance of what he was missing."

If Cronkite found any professional pleasure in 1989, it was, predictably enough, with NASA. He worked with Michael and Roger King of Houston on a documentary film about the *Challenger* disaster. When the twentieth anniversary of *Apollo 11* occurred that July, he hosted the star-studded black-tie gala at the Hyatt Regency Hotel at the Galleria in Houston. Surrounded by mural-size panoramas of the lunarscape, with a huge photograph of President Kennedy looming over the head table, Cronkite took to the podium. "I could drown in the nostalgia tonight," he said. "The waves of it are overwhelming." All three of the *Apollo 11* astronauts—Armstrong, Aldrin, and Collins—spoke from the heart that evening. The only sour note came from Cronkite, who was worried that Bush (unlike Kennedy) hadn't given a tight deadline or a strong financial commitment to Mars exploration. The Apollo program had cost the U.S. taxpayers $25 billion; to Cronkite, it was worth every damn penny. Without a similar cash outlay, he said, going to Mars would remain a pipe dream.

There were plenty of things President Bush did accomplish that Cronkite approved of throughout 1989 and 1990. None were more meaningful to the anchor emeritus than when the president met African National Congress leader Nelson Mandela in June 1990 and signed the Americans with Disabilities Act a few weeks later. Cronkite praised Bush for not gloating over the

United States' winning the cold war and overseeing the German unification process, but he was highly critical of the administration's defense of Saudi Arabia after Iraq invaded Kuwait in August 1991. Cronkite took the view that if the Big Three networks hadn't gutted their foreign bureaus in the late 1980s, the Middle East conflict might not have happened. In 1984, to Cronkite's eternal chargrin, Tisch laid off hundreds of CBS employees, including his correspondent buddies David Andelman, Fred Graham, Morton Dean, and Ike Pappas. Cronkite blamed Rather, who was signing off his *Evening News* broadcasts with one word— "courage"—for failing to stand up to Tisch. "*The New York Times* was reporting the [Iraqi] build-up on the border, but television gave the story slight attention," Cronkite believed. "Suppose network correspondents in Baghdad had been urging their evening news programs to put them on air with reports on the growing dangers?"

On January 9, 1991, the House voted 250 to 183, and the Senate 52 to 47, to authorize President Bush to go to war against Iraq. Cronkite was rife with dissent. When Bush ordered Operation Desert Storm to begin on the morning of January 16, 1991, in Washington (the morning of January 17 in Iraq), Cronkite made public noise. During those first tense days of the heavily televised

Gulf War, CNN, providing twenty-four-hour coverage, was the only news organization with the stealth ability to broadcast from inside Iraq as the U.S. bombing campaign got under way. Screaming missiles, F-14s taking off from aircraft carriers, antiaircraft flashes, night-vision cameras, tanks rumbling across the desert—the whole high-tech war was being beamed into America's living rooms on CNN. If Vietnam had been America's first living room war, then the Gulf War was cable TV's first real foray into the world of the three TV families. To a child, the CNN broadcast might have looked like a video arcade game or fireworks display; to Cronkite, the TV glow from the Middle East smelled of death.

The United States, with support from both NATO and the United Nations, aimed to kick Iraq's troops out of neighboring Kuwait. Cronkite, a war skeptic with highly tuned instincts for Pentagon anti-press shenanigans, was glued to his television, watching the CNN troika of Bernard Shaw, John Holliman, and Peter Arnett, who all braved the heavy bombing of Baghdad to broadcast from the war zone. CNN president Tom Johnson had previously negotiated a deal with the Iraqi government to permit the installation of a permanent audio circuit in their makeshift bureau in Baghdad. "The telegraph at the other networks went dead during the bombing," Johnson recalled. "So CNN had the

DEFIANT LIBERAL • 1021

only able service to deliver live reporting. There was a spell when Arnett was the only TV voice getting out of Iraq." At CBS News, only Allen Pizzey's fine reporting struck Cronkite's fancy.

Shaw had been promised another interview following his October 1990 session with dictator Saddam Hussein and publicly said he wouldn't leave Iraq until he got it. These CNN correspondents were the new Murrow Boys, cableteers deep in the Middle East maelstrom— only, their medium was television instead of radio. CNN captured on film Tomahawk missiles raining down on Baghdad *live* in a startling way. "The skies over Baghdad have been illuminated," Shaw reported in hair-raising fashion. "We see bright flashes going all over the sky."

Cronkite had telephoned Tom Johnson of CNN in Atlanta, worried that President Bush, known for a narrowness of vision, was going to blunder by prohibiting reporters from embedding with U.S. troops in Saudi Arabia for the slog to Baghdad. He urged Johnson to remember how President Reagan had censored the press in the Grenada invasion of 1983. The Pentagon was still trying to blame CBS News for losing the Vietnam War. "Walter," Johnson said, "why don't you tell the president yourself on CNN?" While CBS News used Cronkite only sparingly for Operation Desert

Storm, CNN used him often, through Johnson's intervention. There was still a weightiness to the Cronkite brand that CNN could profit from in 1991.

There was no virtuoso performance by Cronkite during the Gulf War. His voice on CNN was instead that of guardian of the fourth estate. While President Bush believed that the military strike had "started well" because no U.S. planes had been "lost in the first wave of attacks," Cronkite offered a different perspective. "There are Americans dying," he said on January 16, the first day of the war, "undoubtedly at this hour." Sounding like an antiwar pacifist of I. F. Stone vintage, he asked the Pentagon to make sure that reporters were given full access to the war, as in Vietnam under LBJ. Speaking on a four-wire link with Shaw, Arnett, and Holliman, Cronkite then oddly personalized the inherent dangers these brave reporters faced. "I suppose," he said, "there comes a point where it becomes foolhardy to risk one's life to do that job if it's almost certainly fated at the end. But I can't make that judgment for anybody today."

Sitting in New York, Cronkite was worried from the get-go about whether Shaw—who was reporting under a desk from the Al-Rashid Hotel in Baghdad as cruise missiles traced by—would survive the pounding. Shaw brought Cronkite into the mix in a meaningful way. He was now part of the network's coverage. A CNN truck had set up a makeshift studio at Cronkite's Eighty-fourth Street home so he could speak directly with Shaw in Baghdad. The net effect was that Cronkite became via satellite a sage advisor to the Baghdad boys, warning them not to showboat and to keep their helmets on. "It was so intense," Shaw recalled. "The historical irony of Walter and me covering a war together in such a modern Baghdad-to-New York fashion was lost on me. But we considered Cronkite a crucial part of our coverage when we were covering the war, and Cronkite was covering how the CNN reporters were covering the war."

Cronkite's old friend Herb Caen of the *San Francisco Chronicle* was in New York just after Desert Storm was proclaimed a whopping success by the U.S. media at the end of February. Walter and Betsy took Caen to dinner at Le Cirque on East Sixty-fifth Street. When talk about the Gulf War started up, Cronkite turned bitter. The very mention of the president made his face turn cold. "Bush said we were fighting the Iraqi leadership, not the Iraqi people," he remarked. "Well, we killed 100,000 of them and Bush has yet to offer one word of sympathy."

Besides the death of Iraqi civilians, the ordeal of CBS News' Middle East correspondent Bob Simon had

Cronkite gripped with anxiety. Simon was Cronkite's ideal of an outstanding foreign correspondent. Ever since they had met back at the CBS Broadcast Center water fountain in 1967, sharing laughs over a filthy joke, Cronkite had thought of Simon as kin. Simon, who served as a national correspondent in New York for CBS News from 1982 to 1987, was, Cronkite believed, among the finest TV reporters since Murrow. Whether Simon was reporting on Pope John Paul II's historic visits to Poland and Cuba, the prison release of Nelson Mandela, or the execution of Romanian dictator Nicolae Ceausescu, Cronkite approved. Simon, he would say, single-handedly saved the *CBS Evening News* from ruin during Rather's dismal reign.

So when Simon (along with three members of CBS News' coverage team) was captured by Iraqi forces near the Saudi-Kuwait border during the opening days of the Gulf War, Cronkite grew nervous, worried about the shakedown tactics of Saddam Hussein's thugs. At strange hours he would telephone Mike Wallace for information. Cronkite found out that CBS News was working all channels—the Vatican, Jordan's King Hussein, the PLO, and the Russians—to free the media hostages. After forty long days in solitary confinement, Simon and the others—Peter Bluff, Roberto Alvarez, and Juan Caldera—were released. The weight of the world was lifted off Cronkite's shoulders. The CBSers were safe and sound.

Simon returned to New York a flavor-of-the-week hero. Putnam, smelling publishing dollars, signed him to write a quick memoir, *Forty Days*, about being locked in solitary confinement, tortured by sleep deprivation, and ruthlessly interrogated. On his first day back at work, Simon found a handwritten letter from Cronkite waiting for him. "I'm so very proud of you," the note began. Cronkite praised Simon for having walked away from "pack journalism" during the Gulf War by covering the Saudi-Kuwait border and for his stoic bearing as a captive. "It made me cry," Simon recalled. "Can you imagine? Walter Cronkite was proud of *me*. . . . It left me numb just staring at the paper."

Cronkite's concern about the news media being thwarted by the Pentagon was overblown. Reporters such as Christiane Amanpour of CNN and Forrest Sawyer of ABC were able to detail U.S. troop actions quite ably from the pits of the Desert Storm action. And Cronkite's critique of the war as an unmitigated disaster for U.S. foreign policy was off base. While many Iraqi civilians did lose their lives in Operation Desert Storm, the Bush administration was widely applauded—even at the United Nations and NATO headquarters—for kicking the dictatorial Hussein out of Kuwait. Victory in the Gulf War translated into President Bush's scoring a 91 percent approval rating in *USA Today*, the highest ever for a U.S. president.

Political differences with President Bush over Iraq couldn't interfere with Cronkite's need for good contacts and summertime cordials. Many of his closest friends were Republican policymakers. At the Bohemian Grove in California, his campmate at Hillbillies was none other than George H. W. Bush himself. Much had happened since U.S.-led forces began air attacks on Iraq in January, ranging from the Rodney King beating in Los Angeles, to the EPA's announcement that the ozone layer was being depleted by pollution, to South Africa's repealing apartheid, to the Warsaw Pact's being dismantled. When the United States and the USSR signed the Strategic Arms Reduction Treaty (START I) on July 31, 1991, Cronkite fired off a note of congratulations to President Bush in Maine. The president responded with an invitation for cocktails and dinner.

Every summer, Cronkite—besides sailing from Martha's Vineyard out to Nantucket, or over to Cape Cod, or out into Buzzards Bay or the Elizabeth Islands—liked to head north and explore Maine's rock-ribbed coast. "Sometimes we would go visit Tom Watson, the head of IBM, at his place on Northeast

Island in Maine," nautical sidekick Mike Ashford recalled. "But this summer, Walter wanted me to meet with George and Barbara Bush in Kennebunkport, so we went."

At the Bushes' compound, Cronkite, Ashford, and a few others sat on the president's patio in the cool Atlantic breeze, watching the glorious sunset, relaxing and sipping Bush-shaken martinis. "Suddenly, there was an old-fashioned telephone ring," Ashford recalled. "President Bush went to take the call. He came back with the biggest smile imaginable on his face." A startled Cronkite had never seen Bush so "exultant" before. Soviet president Mikhail Gorbachev, who in 1990 had won the Nobel Peace Prize for his efforts to democratize the USSR, had just telephoned to let Bush know that the Communist Party had been disbanded in the Soviet Union. "What great news," Ashford recalled. "We all ceremoniously hoisted our glasses to toast the death of communism. For Walter it was the greatest news in the world."

On December 26, 1991, the Soviet Union dissolved following the resignation of Gorbachev on Christmas Day. To Cronkite it was the biggest event since V-J Day. The thought of a world rid of nuclear weapons seemed plausible. He spoke about that very real possibility with former secretary of state George P. Shultz on a number of occasions. Even with the Kremlin checkmated, Cronkite couldn't bring himself to back a Republican. But instead of criticizing Bush directly, he critiqued the entire electoral process. Like Tom Brokaw of NBC News, he lamented the "cancer of the sound bite" in which political candidates spoke in rehearsed five- to ten-second snippets aimed at making the nightly news cycle. "Naturally," Cronkite said, "nothing of any significance is going to be said in 9.8 seconds."

What Cronkite realized by 1992 was that the everyday American life stages had changed drastically since the black-and-white TV days of Douglas Edwards. With shopping mall stores staying open until 9:00 p.m. and some fast-food franchises operating 24/7, there was no longer a rigid nine-to-five workweek (particularly on the coasts). As Rather was delivering the *CBS Evening News* in 1991, potential viewers were at happy hours, workouts, ball games, and their children's extracurricular events. They weren't rushing home for suppertime news. Only in the Midwest and the Rocky Mountain states did the tradition of Big Three evening news seem to hold its firm footing in the age of cable TV. No longer was breaking news confined to the staid half-hour shows. Besides cable, the Internet was revving up to make the *CBS Evening News* even more disjointed and obsolete.

During the 1992 presidential election, Cronkite hitched his star to the upstart Discovery Channel. John Hendricks, the founder of Discovery who was raised on Cronkite broadcasts, approached the icon about rebroadcasting rights to *Walter Cronkite's Universe*. Hendricks, without hyperbole, credited the CBS science-environment show for being the galvanizing inspiration for his cable network. "I struggled for funding like mad in the 1980s," Hendricks said, "and then Walter came on board and everybody believed in it." Hendricks paid Cronkite to do long-form interviews of all the presidential candidates prior to the Iowa caucus. Hendricks also tapped him to host the Emmy Award–winning *Understanding Great Books*, whose title nicely described the program's content. "Walter became a friend, counselor, and mentor to me," Hendricks recalled. "If the story of the Discovery Channel ever gets made into a movie, Walter gets top billing. Without him there wouldn't today be a Discovery Channel."

While President Bush geared up for his reelection bid in early 1992, Cronkite continued circulating as the éminence grise of journalism. Whether he was hosting a dinner at the Pierpont Morgan Library in New York for author James Michener, or hiking the U.S.-Mexican border to study immigration, or lending his voice to Hollywood director Steven Spielberg's *We're*

Back animation about dinosaurs, or working on documentaries for the Discovery Channel about presidential politics, Cronkite was back in the mix. Nobody held his overt liberalism against him. But because he had denounced the Gulf War with such vehemence, fuming about the restrictive Annex Foxtrot memo (which stipulated new restrictions on the media covering the conflict), President Bush refused to participate in his Discovery Channel show. "I greatly regret that President Bush and his campaign managers have turned down our invitation," Cronkite lamented, "but I cannot help but note that all the others did find time for this."

One 1992 presidential candidate who didn't miss the opportunity to be interviewed by Cronkite was Arkansas governor Bill Clinton. The two became quite friendly on the campaign trail. Clinton would shout out "Hey, Walter" to Cronkite in New Hampshire or New York or Florida, like a grown-up kid seeing his teeny-bopper idol. But Cronkite became bored with the '92 campaign. His role seemed to be that of crotchety oldster, always telling the whippersnappers how much better journalism was back before Telstar. After the Democratic presidential debate in Dallas in early March, he held a round table forum on journalism ethics for the Discovery Channel, but the public service program fell flat with viewers. In an age of MTV videos and IMAX theaters, old-school public service programs were a cold curse to sponsors.

If Cronkite played a memorable role in the 1992 election, it was in taking a few well-placed swipes at third-party candidate Ross Perot of Dallas. But Cronkite agreed with Perot when he claimed at the National Press Club on March 18 that Washington was a town of "sound bites, shell games, handlers, and media stuntmen." Cronkite privately criticized CNN's Larry King—a dear friend—and others for always lobbing softball questions at the prickly billionaire founder of Electronic Data Systems. "Perot can stumble into an answer that is meaningful," Cronkite said. "But that can't go on forever. At some point he's going to have to sit down and discuss the issues with journalists who would be more persistent in their line of questioning."

On November 3, 1992, Clinton won 370 electoral votes to Bush's 168, with zero votes for Perot. It was a humiliating way for Bush to go down after brilliantly guiding the United States through the demise of the Soviet Union, German reunification, and the Gulf War. At a party that the actress Carol Channing threw, Cronkite was asked to sum up President-elect Clinton. Without hesitation he said, "Clinton has Carter's intelligence, Johnson's experience, and Kennedy's gonads."

It was Clinton's favorite shorthand summation of his style ever uttered.

Ever the loyal Democrat, Cronkite was glad Clinton had won, but oddly hurt for his Kennebunkport friends George and Barbara. They were among the finest, most patriotic people he knew. Just three days before Christmas, at the Kennedy Center honors, Cronkite, the emcee, suddenly launched into an unscripted moment. At the show's close, he pointed at President Bush and offered a high note of thanks. "There's one more honor to be paid tonight," he said, turning himself to look squarely at the president's face, "to an individual who has served his country in war and peace for more than a half a century who has joined us again tonight to pay tribute to America's performing arts. We offer him our respect, our gratitude, and we thank him for service to his country with honor."

President Bush got a long standing ovation, with a grateful Cronkite the last to stop clapping.

34.

"The World's Oldest Reporter"

EARTHQUAKE CHASING—CHECKING UP ON SHAW—
WELCOME TO THE CLINTON AGE—SEVAREID
DIES—HISTORICAL MEMORY—*THE CRONKITE
REPORT*—TIME FOR THE ORGY—GIVING ROSTROPO-
VICH A CHAIR— A SURROGATE FOR WORLD WAR II
ANNIVERSARIES—IN PRAISE OF 24/7 NEWS AND THE
INTERNET—STARTING UP CRONKITE AND WARD—
DEATH OF HELEN—CRONKITE REMEMBERS *A
REPORTER'S LIFE*—MOVING TO THE UN
PLAZA—GROWING MORE LIBERAL—INTERFAITH
ALLIANCE—TIME TO SAIL WITH THE CLINTONS—
JOHN GLENN IN SPACE—MILLENNIUM SPOTS—
SPOTTING TRUMP—WORLD FEDERALIST—*BUSH
V. GORE*

One evening in early 1994, the seventy-seven-year-old Cronkite was jarred awake from a sound sleep by a loud rumble. His hotel room was shaking. The lamp crashed, the desk drawer opened, and he was almost tossed from his bed. Los Angeles was in the midst of the Northridge earthquake, which measured 6.7 on the Richter scale. Cronkite instinctively headed to the lobby to find an emergency transistor radio. He heard Bernard Shaw talking to the Atlanta headquarters about the quake from his own L.A. hotel room. Quickly, Cronkite put on his suit and shoes, headed to the lobby, and flagged down a taxi, barking, "Go where it's the worst!"

While Shaw was reporting from a hotel room, Cronkite wanted to get the reportorial edge by seeing the damage firsthand. The itch of a newspaper reporter on the hunt for a quick lead hadn't left him. "He hadn't lost his drive to own a news story," Shaw later chuckled. "He outhustled us younger guys by immediately getting reactions from victims." There was no quit in old Walter. About a half hour later, having assessed the grim on-the-ground situation in downtown L.A., he tracked down Shaw, still at his hotel, telephoning him from the lobby. It was the reverse of 1961 at the Reef Hotel in Hawaii: Cronkite was now the stalker, while Shaw was the big-time CNN anchor.

"Are you okay?" Cronkite asked.

"Walter," an amused and touched Shaw said. "Is that you?"

"Yes!" he laughed. "I'm in your lobby."

"How did you know I was here?"

"I've been listening to your radio reports," Cronkite said. "Been riding around in a cab inspecting the damage."

Shaw was flabbergasted. Cronkite had the gumption to check out the devastation like an ambulance-chasing UP reporter and then swing by to check on him. He joked with Shaw that he still abided by the old wire service dictum: "Cover the goddamn news, get it on." Roving around Los Angeles, talking to quake victims, many of whom called him "Uncle Walter," became his quasi-missionary work for a week following the quake. During the New London school explosion in 1937, he had a job to do for the Dallas UP bureau. With the Northridge earthquake he was on the scene but had no media outlet for which to report. Rather wouldn't have him on his *CBS Evening News*. Having no byline or show was a terrible thing. "I think Walter was shaken by Northridge," Andy Rooney recalled. "Here he had been lucky enough to be smack in the middle of a natural disaster and he had no one to broadcast for."

No one saw Cronkite much on television anymore in 1994 unless it was a celebrity turn on the news-oriented CBS comedy *Murphy Brown* (as himself) or on CNN's *Larry King Live*. No longer was he needed for big conventions or terror attacks. He was largely an annoyance at CBS News and an out-of-steady-work legend everywhere else except at the Discovery Channel, which didn't do breaking news. But as the Northridge earthquake demonstrated, not for a second did Cronkite, a true workaholic and playoholic, want to retire from the fourth estate. Every day, he diligently followed a promising lead no matter that day's schedule. Producers in the 1990s who were successful in TV broadcasts with Cronkite—like John Hendricks and Jon Ward—knew that the magic words were "I want you to host" such-and-such news segment or documentary. Had somebody—for old times' sake—decided to create an "All Cronkite" network, like Oprah Winfrey did for herself in 2011, he would have said yes. "Walter was always open for business," Tom Brokaw recalled. "He never grew bitter or unapproachable. Walter got up every morning knowing who he was. Dan Rather woke up every morning trying to decide who he'd be that day. As a result, Rather didn't have a clue."

By the time Clinton was sworn in as the forty-second U.S. president on January 20, 1993, the world of journalism that Cronkite had grown up in was fast disappearing. No longer were newspaper rooms smoke-filled, resounding with the clatter of typewriters in every direction as corps of desk assistants dashed frenetically about. Carbon copies were unnecessary in the era of word processing. Confirming Cronkite's worst fears, cities that once had two or three newspapers were now lucky to have one. In television journalism, on the other hand, there were many more outlets. "People put their faith in what they see on television, and we all know there probably wasn't a night that went by that we didn't, somehow or another, badly, with no intent, distort a piece of news or make a mistake," Cronkite reminisced. "When we knew about it, we'd correct it. But, gee, to depend on somebody to tell you the absolute truth every night and give you The Word every night, that's a bad thing, a serious problem in a democracy."

Cronkite's cool, objective style (supported by vigorous fact-checking) could still be found on *The MacNeil-Lehrer NewsHour* on PBS, ABC's *Nightline* with Ted Koppel, CBS's *60 Minutes*, and a few other old-school holdouts. But such quality reporting had largely become obsolete in the accelerated world of 24/7 cable news. Cronkite, lo and behold, had come to represent a historical personage, a holdover from the golden age of

TV. Tabloid news had seized America's attention span and only Bill Moyers and Marvin Kalb seemed to care. "The fact that you can't find a new Walter Cronkite on television today is no fluke," Jack Fuller wrote in his seminal *What Is Happening to News*. "The dispassionate approach embodied by Cronkite does not attract the audience it used to. Walter Cronkite was lucky to have worked when he did. (And we were lucky, too, for he helped the country through some very difficult times.) Today he would be canceled. So, by the way, would Walter Lippmann."

Over the summer of 1992, Eric Sevareid died of cancer. He was seventy-nine years old. Ever since November 1964, when the long-established Sevareid joined Cronkite on the *CBS Evening News* to deliver two-minute end-of-broadcast commentaries, he had been an almost godlike presence on the airwaves. Always noble-looking, with his immaculate shock of silver-gray hair and Roman profile, Sevareid had been a unique figure in TV news. He had his detractors, but few begrudged him his high-altitude station as a sober journalist and urbane philosophical pundit. It was the superb irony of Cronkite's career that without Sevareid—the quintessential Murrowite—his famed *CBS Evening News* broadcast might never have surpassed NBC in the Nielsen ratings.

But that was then. When ABC News' Ted Koppel (one of Cronkite's favorite non-CBSers) retired from *Nightline* in 2005, after twenty-five years with the program, he told viewers about a spontaneous quiz he gave young interns hoping for a career in broadcasting:

"How many of you," I'll ask, "can tell me anything about Eric Sevareid?" Blank stares. "How about Howard K. Smith? or Frank Reynolds?" Not a twitch of recognition. "Chet Huntley? John Chancellor?" Still nothing. "David Brinkley" sometimes causes a hand or two to be raised, and Walter Cronkite may be glad to learn that a lot of young people still have a vague recollection that he once worked in television news. What none of these young men and women in their late teens and early twenties appreciates, until I point it out to them, is that they have just heard the names of seven anchormen or commentators that were once so famous that everyone in the country knew their names.

The dominant view, perfectly articulated by Koppel, was that a television broadcaster, at the end of the day, was only an ephemeral talking head. TV news epitomized transitory, disposable American culture. Sevareid's CBS News colleagues knew that "Eric the Red" helped bring down Joseph McCarthy, Spiro Agnew, and Richard Nixon. But history largely forgot his public influence once the Clintons moved into 1600 Pennsylvania Avenue. Cronkite never really warmed to Sevareid personally—he was put off by his conceit. But Sevareid's passing spelled the beginning of the end of the Greatest Generation of broadcasters raised on Murrow. "Eric was one of the best of that small number of news analysts, commentators and essayists," Cronkite told the *Los Angeles Times* obituary writer, "who truly deserved to be called distinguished."

No up-and-comer in the TV news business struck Cronkite's fancy during the Clinton years quite like Brian Williams. Cronkite had first encountered Williams on WCBS in 1993 and kept a watchful eye on him the way an NFL scout watches high school football talent in Texas or Oklahoma. When Williams went to NBC News in 1994, Cronkite caught his broadcasts regularly. He was impressed by the way Williams effortlessly grappled with the Clinton impeachment drama: with utter objectivity. When, in 1996, Williams anchored his own one-hour broadcast on MSNBC—a kind of AAA cable farm club for NBC News—Cronkite intuitively knew that the boy from Elmira, New York, was headed for electronic journalism stardom. Around that time, Williams wrote Cronkite "an obsequious letter," one that he hoped no historian would ever find. Williams told Cronkite that he was his "North Star" and invited his idol to lunch. Cronkite accepted, and a genuine friendship blossomed. "I couldn't believe I got to hover in the same sphere with him," Williams recalled. "We started seeing each other socially and talking on the telephone."

When Cronkite spoke at a library lecture series in Darien, Connecticut, named in honor of Richard Salant—who dropped dead of a heart attack on February 16, 1993, while giving a speech in Southport, Connecticut—Williams dutifully attended. A real journalism history nerd, Williams knew all about how Salant had raised professional standards as CBS News president from 1961 to 1964 and from 1966 to 1979. He knew how many duPonts and Peabodys the tireless Salant had earned for CBS News during Watergate and Vietnam. He was a huge fan. As prearranged, the Williamses—Brian and Jane—invited Cronkite to their New Canaan home after the library talk to tell Salant stories. "I was excited beyond belief," Williams recalled. "My one true hero was coming over to my house. If only my poor mother had been alive. I told my daughter that the older man with the white, fuzzy mustache was my idol, that he was like a Santa Claus figure. As he ate our lasagna, I thought that my mother would have considered Cronkite crossing the threshold of our Elmira home in the 1970s for dinner to be the single greatest event that could have possibly happened to her."

Susceptible to such flattery and warmth, Cronkite became even closer friends with Williams. Shortly after 9/11, the New York *Daily News* ran a little notice that Cronkite thought Aaron Brown of CNN was the Rolls-Royce anchorman in the news business. A shudder passed through Williams, the showman, who took mock umbrage at that tabloid endorsement. In full prankster mode, he wrote Cronkite a deeply comical, faux-blistering letter complaining that he had "been laid bare" and had his "feelings stomped on" by the revelatory embrace of Brown. "Walter cracked up about it," Williams remembered. "It became our running joke."

What Williams understood was that the Cronkites—Walter and Betsy—lived for humor. Practical jokes and clever asides consumed their days. With the kids fully grown, Betsy accompanied her husband on a dozen junkets in the 1990s. A case in point was working together on the documentary "Yellowstone Remembered" for PBS. At the gift shop near Old Faithful one day, the Cronkites split up, looking for souvenirs in different aisles. Suddenly, a woman came up to Betsy, tapped her shoulder, and whispered, "Doesn't that man over there look like Walter Cronkite?"

"Oh, no," Betsy said. "He's much too thin."

"You know," the woman said, now considering. "I think maybe he died."

"Yes," Betsy said. "I think that's right."

"Of what?" she asked.

"I think of thinness."

In February 1993, Cronkite hired Marlene Adler, a smart and savvy Bear Stearns broker working on Wall Street, to be his chief of staff. Tired of shadowy figures—booking agents, publicists, and advance men—Cronkite welcomed Adler as a great stabilizing force. Nobody was managing Cronkite's career in the 1990s—everything was catch-as-catch-can—so Adler seized the role. Cronkite had piles of unanswered speaking invitations on his desk at Black Rock. Adler turned that delinquency into business for Cronkite in a matter of months. Understanding the value of the Cronkite brand, Adler booked him for speaking engagements marketed as "audience conversations" with the CBS legend. The idea was to get "The Most Trusted Man in America" out on the road to meet people as you would James Brown ("The Godfather of Soul") or Bill Monroe ("The King of Bluegrass"). At journalism schools he'd hold

Q&As with students about everything from D-day to the mass killings in Bosnia-Herzegovina. They were usually overwhelmed to meet an icon. "He would always ask everybody he met, 'Where are you from?'" Adler recalled. "He'd be hands-on Walter with everybody."

On a couple of occasions, Cronkite traveled with Andy Rooney to deliver speeches or participate in conversations about journalism during World War II. By this time, both old codgers had become their own iconographers. At airports people would gleefully rush up to Cronkite and say, "You changed my life" or "Can I have your autograph?" Glad to accomodate everyone, Cronkite would *always* respond with, "Where are you from?" When that same fan noticed Rooney, the popular *60 Minutes* curmudgeon, standing next to Cronkite, they would offer a belated handshake or also ask for a signature. Rooney's stock answer was *always*: "Get lost!"

After New York City officially designated Cronkite a "living legend," he told Rooney he better do something philanthropic to live up to the honor. Always seeking publicity, he allowed himself to be auctioned off for four or five nonprofit events a year under the gambit "Have lunch with Walter Cronkite." Pay $10,000 to a charity and Cronkite would feast with you at the 21

Club or the Four Seasons. "This was Walter's way of getting to pig out on gourmet food for free," Rooney said, laughing. "It was shameless. Not only would he never pick up a tab willingly, he had now also devised ways to get the best free meals in the world while getting credit for being charitable. That made him, in my eye, the Smartest Man in America."

Trying to capitalize on Cronkite's broadcasting gravitas, the Discovery Channel launched *The Cronkite Report*, a new prime-time quarterly documentary series. John Hendricks paid Cronkite a goodly sum for his services. Discovery, in turn, received premium advertising revenue because of Cronkite's celebrity status. The first episode, "Help Unwanted," focused on unemployment; it featured both President Bill Clinton and Vice President Al Gore. The ratings were decent. *The Cronkite Report*—with Sandy Socolow as executive producer and Chip Cronkite as supervising producer—aired at 9:00 on Friday evenings. Channeling the ghosts of Murrow and Sevareid, Cronkite insisted that old-fashioned investigative journalism was a prerequisite in a democracy.

Looking for a consistent revenue stream, Cronkite, with the help of Adler, understood the enormous earnings potential of cable TV. In 1993, he cofounded an LLC called Cronkite, Ward and Company. Cronkite's partner in this pennywise operation was Jonathan Ward, a former producer at CBS News. Other founding producers were Sandy Socolow, Dale Minor, and Chip Cronkite. The company opened up offices in both New York and Washington (near Dupont Circle) and produced more than one hundred award-winning documentary hours for the Discovery Channel, PBS, and other networks.

But the rigors of a whirlwind press tour to promote *The Cronkite Report* for Discovery in mid-1993 caused Cronkite's health to buckle, as his old back problems resurfaced. At an interview session with Los Angeles *Daily News* reporter Ray Richmond, conducted at the Beverly Hills Hotel, Cronkite complained of severe back pain. He lowered himself down upon a chair with a slow, ponderous movement. He put on a good game face for Richmond, revealing his personal hatred of the syndicated *Inside Edition* tabloid-format show, and elucidating the toxic effects that such programming had on American society. When the hourlong session ended, he steeled himself to rise from his chair, Betsy offering a helping hand.

"Come on Walter. It's time to get to the orgy," she said.

"Oh golly, not another one. I don't know if my back can take it."

That summer of 1993, Cronkite was tied up with *The Cronkite Report* and sailing his beloved *Wyntje* to Maine. He did not meet up with Bill and Hillary Clinton, who headed to the Vineyard for an eleven-day vacation. But he did see Clinton at a White House function celebrating the arts in early September. An awkward moment occurred that evening when cellist Mstislav Rostropovich finished playing Tchaikovsky's *Nocturne* in the East Room and walked over to the circular dining tables, looking for his assigned seat. He didn't have one. All spots were taken. A snafu in protocol had occurred. Instinctively, Cronkite rose and offered Rostropovich his chair. It was the gesture of a gentleman. When Clinton spoke a few minutes later, he noted Cronkite's generosity. "You know, when I was a boy," Clinton said, "they used to say Walter Cronkite could get elected president by file-in, and now he's shown once again why."

The Clinton White House asked Cronkite to be the master of ceremonies for a slew of galas commemorating the fiftieth anniversary of the Second World War. This was much better treatment than being blacklisted by the USIA during Reagan's first term or dissed by Bush for an *Address the Nation* interview. Cronkite, at the invitation of the White House, was in Normandy with the Clintons on June 6, 1994, regaling the president with stories about zero visibility over fog-covered Omaha Beach on D-day. CNN likewise tapped Cronkite to co-anchor its D-day (Plus 50) coverage. "Any question I had about the Battle of Normandy," Wolf Blitzer of CNN recalled, "Walter had the fast answer."

In May 1995, CBS News—envious that CNN had used its old anchorman for D-day (Plus 50)—asked Cronkite to appear live from London on the *CBS Evening News* broadcast on the fiftieth anniversary of V-E Day. Cronkite, full of nostalgia about his days at United Press, agreed. He did a fine job. A couple of days later, he was on Bob Schieffer's *Face the Nation* (with Dan Rather) to discuss V-E Day. CBS News had erected a handsome set in London with Westminster Abbey as the backdrop for Cronkite. After Schieffer finished the *Face the Nation* broadcast that Sunday, Cronkite, without a job assignment, lingered with the London film crew, telling bawdy jokes about "Gunga Dan" Rather going to Afghanistan soon after the Soviet invasion in 1980 and donning a wool hat and shawl. Eventually, Cronkite, in the company of producer Al Ortiz, said good-bye to the technicians and left the studio. Walking down the hallway, Cronkite spotted the men's WC (his initials) sign and blurted, "Let's hit my place." At the urinal, the legend turned philosophical. "Let me give you three pieces of advice, Al," he said to

Ortiz. "Number one: never pass up a urinal; number two: never trust a fart; and number three: never, ever ignore an erection." Ortiz cracked up.

Just days after Cronkite turned seventy-seven years old in November 1993, word reached him that his mother Helen had died of congestive heart failure. Burying Helen took a toll on Cronkite. She was 101 years old, still dating retired U.S. Army officers. Somehow having his mother alive made him feel young and vibrant. What everybody, her only son included, had loved about Helen was her feisty vitality. At her hundredth birthday party, Cronkite had danced with his mom, but she seemed a little light-headed. "Walter, I think I need my medicine," she said, sitting down. Worried about her health, he quickly went and fetched her heart pills.

"Walter," she snapped, "who said I needed that?"

"You did, Mother," he said. "You said you needed your medicine."

And she replied, "I meant my martini."

Throughout 1994 and 1995, Cronkite grew discontented with how CNN, MSNBC, and the Fox News Channel interrupted broadcasts with "Breaking News" flashes for silly items like an L.A. freeway chase or another Clinton sex allegation story. He watched the 1996 presidential election between Clinton and Dole unfold with utter boredom. On November 5, 1996, when Clinton beat Dole by 379 electoral votes to 159, Cronkite celebrated with Art Buchwald and Andy Rooney. But politics no longer held much appeal for Cronkite. While the right wing was calling Clinton "Slick Willie," and allegations of adultery filled the airwaves, Cronkite told people that the president was indeed trustworthy, although he hedged his defense with faint praise. "Would I, at this lunch," he said to a reporter, "give him my wallet and ask him to pick up a few greeting cards and return the wallet this afternoon? I wouldn't have a problem with that."

When Cronkite's mother, Helen, died, one of the many condolence letters he received came from Joe and Shirley Wershba, his old friends from the Korean War days at WTOP-TV. Their card motivated Cronkite to telephone the Wershbas. "If you have time to write a condolence card," Cronkite told Joe, "you can help me finish my memoir." Since the 1950s, Cronkite had written up anecdotes and put them in a memoir box. But they all added up to a themeless pudding. "Walter sent us his notes and a long oral history he'd done with Don Carleton," Shirley Wershba recalled. "And we went to work. My job was organizing the material. Joe started looking up all the facts and statistics and dates. We did a lot of work, but it was Walter's book. We just helped."

Ultimately, though, Cronkite had to focus on doing some heavy lifting on the manuscript, and to that end, fate stepped in. After his knee replacement surgery in 1995, he was trapped in the house with little to do but work on his *A Reporter's Life* manuscript. He wrote every word himself (with a lot of editorial help from the Wershbas). The book finally appeared, four years late, in 1996, a year after Andy Rooney's memoir, *My War,* was published. Both appeared on the New York Times bestseller list, Cronkite's debuting at number two and hitting number one during the week of Christmas 1996. The same year, CBS broadcast the two-hour tribute *Cronkite Remembers,* which combined the network's vintage footage with family home movies. The concept was expanded the following year with an eight-hour version of *Cronkite Remembers* on the Discovery Channel. A few years later, NPR hired Cronkite to contribute radio essays for *All Things Considered,* his occasional features marking anniversaries of the major historic events of his lifetime. He was also seen frequently on cable television, hosting programs or granting interviews on current events. But his bread and butter, and the source of much of his income, was the marketing of his own life story in print and video.

An old Dutch proverb has it that the tulip that grows the tallest gets cut down. Cronkite experienced a taste of that folk wisdom in early 1997. His many TV interviews and the success of *A Reporter's Life*—including landing the front page of *The New York Times Book Review*—made him a target of the conservative movement. Everybody knew that he was liberal; that fact never bothered Cronkite's establishment Republican friends such as William F. Buckley and John Lehman. But midway through the *Cronkite Remembers* documentary, Cronkite postulated that the Soviet Union wasn't ever a dangerous threat: "I thought that we Americans overreacted to the Soviets, and the news coverage sometimes seemed to accentuate that misdirected concern," he said. "Fear of the Soviet Union taking over the world just seemed as likely to me as invaders from Mars."

Conservatives cried foul. Cronkite's recycling of the past had, with that whopper, become farcical. *The Washington Times* criticized Cronkite for a self-serving distortion of reality. "With newscasters like Mr. Cronkite," the *Times* scoffed, "who needs *Pravda*?" The gloves were off. Cronkite now became fair game. Tim Hughes, an Ohio blogger, created an anti-Cronkite website titled "Walter Cronkite Spit in My Food." It featured a cartoon Cronkite character drunk at Disney World, trashing former CBS colleagues, bragging about screwing another man's wife, and spitting in people's desserts. The *New York Post*—a conservative-leaning tabloid owned by Rupert Murdoch—ran a story about the website that caused Cronkite to throw a fit.

Instead of suing the Ohioan, Cronkite went on the offensive against the very "right-wing conspiracy" that Hillary Clinton, the first lady, once talked about on NBC's *Today* show. Refusing to clam up, worried that the GOP was trying to exploit God for political gain, Cronkite joined the Interfaith Alliance, an organization headed by Rev. C. Welton Gaddy, a Baptist minister from Monroe, Louisiana, that championed individual rights and promoted policies aimed to protect both democracy and religion. At Gaddy's request, Cronkite wrote an open letter denouncing the Christian Coalition of Pat Robertson and Ralph Reed for "wrapping their harsh right-wing views in the banner of religious faith."

Not that Cronkite wasn't in a praying mood. On April 1, 1997, after a routine cardiac stress test, Cronkite underwent quadruple bypass surgery at the New York–Cornell Medical Center (the operation was followed by knee replacement surgery). The operations went well. Because Cronkite was unable to walk for a while, Mickey Hart of the Grateful Dead—who was on the board of the Institute for Music and Neurologic Function—bought him seventeen different drums to play. If you visited the Cronkites for dinner, it was mandatory to launch into a drum jamboree. "The music seemed to heal his soul," Chip Cronkite recalled. "Along with medication, it was part of his recovery therapy."

That same April, Betsy had to have one of her knees replaced. It no longer made sense for the couple to live in a four-story town house with a lot of stairs. Reluctantly, they put 519 East Eighty-fourth Street— where they had resided for nearly forty years—up for sale; it was snatched up in four days. All the Cronkite kids were middle-aged: Nancy was forty-eight; Kathy, forty-six (with two kids); and Chip, forty (with two kids). It was time to move into the last phase of life. All of the books, commendations, and trophies in the large living room had been put in boxes.

How Cronkite decided to purchase a co-op at 870 UN Plaza (East Tower) was fraught with romance. The real estate agent was Joanna Simon, a beautiful, glamorous, and smart real estate broker from a well-to-do Manhattan family. A classically trained mezzo-soprano opera singer, she was married to Gerald Walker, the article editor of *The New York Times Magazine* from 1963 to 1990. Even though Cronkite was happily married, he had a crush on Simon. While he liked that the 25A co-op had almost an airplane-level look at the East River, the *real* purchase closer for him was Simon's charm. Quickly inspecting all the rooms with Betsy, he turned to Simon and said, "I'll take it." A few years later, after their friendship blossomed, Simon asked Walter about his impulse purchase. "I took one look at you," he said, "and I wanted you in my life at all costs."

After rummaging around closets for the best keepsakes, the Cronkites packed up and moved into UN Plaza, where they had doormen, elevators, and river views. Tom Brokaw remembered communicating with Betsy at the time of the Cronkites' move to UN Plaza. "It must be terrible leaving with so many family memories," Brokaw said. "What I'll miss is the backyard we had," Betsy said, "for I had a plot of land where I could bury all of Walter's plaques."

Although President Clinton remained popular with the American public during his second term in the White House, charges of perjury related to allegations of adultery brought forth impeachment proceedings in 1997. Cronkite watched in weary dejection as the PBS moderator Jim Lehrer heard the president denying he had "sexual relations" with White House intern Monica Lewinsky. Hadn't Clinton learned from Watergate that it's the cover-up that will get you every time? A *New York Times* reporter on religion who asked about Cronkite's beliefs was met with a firm "none of your business" from the broadcaster. That's the path Clinton should have taken. Independent counsel Kenneth Starr spent the spring of 1997 investigating Clinton. Lewinsky began to cooperate fully with the Justice Department. The word *impeachment* was bandied about. Amid the turmoil of the investigation, the Clintons, both Bill and Hillary, retreated to the Vineyard that August to heal.

After Clinton was elected and it became public knowledge that he and his family vacationed in Edgartown, Cronkite sent a note to the White House inviting them to go sailing with him. He never heard back about a solid time. Then, with impeachment looming, Cronkite received a telephone call from the White House social secretary, asking if the "wonderful" invitation was still open. Picking himself off the floor, Cronkite said yes.

"When can we do it?" she asked him.

Cronkite, a stickler for such things, calculated the wind and weather and replied, "Friday looks good." This conversation occurred on a Monday.

She said, "How about tomorrow?"

He said, "Sure."

With the exception of having a great future story to dine out on, Cronkite regretted going along with the yachting scheme. Within hours a slew of security details, including two drivers who spent the night guarding the *Wyntje*, arrived in Edgartown. Cronkite warned President Clinton that the paparazzi, even on the Vineyard, would be out en masse because of the Lewinsky crisis. "Somebody might take a picture of it," Cronkite told President Clinton, "but so what?" Clinton later joked that he never forgot that reassuring line: "At that time I could have done with a picture with Walter Cronkite."

The paparazzi and voyeuristic spectators indeed watched the Clintons board the *Wyntje* in the drowsy sunshine and shove off for the Atlantic adventure. Cronkite, for the first time in years, applied a little mustache wax to keep his bushy eyebrows tame. The outing—which included seventeen-year-old Chelsea Clinton and fourteen-year-old Walter Cronkite IV (grandson)—was an excellent strategic move by the Clintons. What better way to jump-start a personal rehabilitation campaign than to hang out with the Most Trusted Man in America? Although they sailed for only ninety minutes, never going very far off the island's coastline, the Clintons seemed to have a serene and healing time, plowing the great gray waters. After the *Wyntje* returned to Cronkite's private dock in Edgartown, they all stayed aboard and talked confidentially for a good hour. No leaks about the discussion occurred. Cronkite, having played family counselor to the Clintons, declined to report a single word. Cronkite did tell Sandy Socolow that "nothing much" happened on the short cruise. "Bill and Hillary didn't speak to each other the entire time," Socolow recalled Cronkite telling him. "Not a word."

An aftereffect of Cronkite taking the Clintons to safe harbor was an invitation to sleep at the White House. "On principle my dad never accepted that overnight offer from other presidents," Chip Cronkite recalled. "But both Mom and Dad saw it as an historic opportunity for young Walter—who would get to sleep in the Grant anteroom during the visit—so they said yes." Not only did the Cronkites sleep in the Lincoln Bedroom, but they gossiped for hours with Bill and Hillary as if they were at a co-ed slumber party. The president was extremely grateful that Cronkite had shown him such compassion during his darkest hour. "President Clinton was in awe of Cronkite," the former White House press secretary Dee Dee Myers recalled. "You know how your childhood heroes die hard in your heart? That's the way it was for Clinton with Cronkite."

Cronkite's main sustainable hero remained John Glenn. On January 17, 1998, NASA announced that the seventy-seven-year-old Glenn, the first American to orbit Earth, would become the first senior citizen in space. Desperately, Cronkite lobbied NASA to appoint him as Glenn's sidekick. After the *Challenger* shuttle had exploded in 1986, Cronkite had been reassured by NASA that he was still under consideration. But upon closer investigation, a NASA administrator nixed the possibility because of his 1997 heart surgery. Cronkite, carping that NASA was discriminating against octogenarians, telephoned Glenn in Columbus, Ohio, hoping to arm-twist the famed *Friendship* 7 astronaut and U.S. senator to help him fulfill his lifelong dream. "I told him if they wanted to test an older guy in Space, I ought to go," Cronkite recalled. "Or I could go with him, play canasta up there."

Just when Cronkite felt jilted by NASA, he got an unexpected telephone call from CNN Newsgroup chairman Tom Johnson. Always wanting to get Cronkite in the mix, Johnson had a wonderful offer. Would Cronkite co-anchor the Glenn mission live on CNN with John Holliman?

Oh boy, would he! Johnson had done a sweet thing. Throughout the summer of 1998, CNN correspondent Cronkite boned up on space. He regularly talked to Glenn by telephone, determined to "own" the story. When CBS heard that the eighty-one-year-old Cronkite had been poached by CNN for "Glenn's Second Trip into Space," it issued a short, funny comment as press release: "Gosh, we wish we'd thought of it." (At CBS, "gosh" and "by golly" were still considered lingering Cronkitisms.) Cronkite, in an effort to allay CBS News' concerns about him working for CNN, agreed to interview Glenn for an exclusive segment on *60 Minutes*.

When press wags suggested that the whole Glenn-Cronkite pairing was a giant publicity stunt, a way for NASA to milk more federal tax dollars, Cronkite bristled. "John Glenn going back into Space is serving the purpose of reminding a blasé public that we're still in Space," he said. "The flights of the shuttle have become so routine that newspapers don't cover them. Broadcasters don't cover them, really, we've almost lost track of the fact that we're making these flights on a very regular basis now. I think there's a whole generation out there, the under-29ers, who are hardly aware that we're in Space."

A deal was struck with NASA that Cronkite would get preferential treatment for the Glenn liftoff at Cape Kennedy, Florida, and then would fly to Houston to work for CBS Radio News. By once again linking Glenn's patriotism to Cronkite's performance, NASA was hoping to garner a tidal wave of great publicity. But a setback occurred. In late October, a week before the Glenn trip, Mike Freedman of CBS Radio News received a call from NASA asking for Cronkite's questions in advance. Although Freedman explained that this would violate CBS News policy, NASA insisted. Freedman telephoned Cronkite at the UN Plaza and outlined the NASA request. The phone went silent for what seemed like an eternity (but was likely about three or four seconds). In that instant the jovial Cronkite turned back into managing editor of the *CBS Evening News* and said in a stern, powerful voice, "Mike, if they want the questions in advance, fuck 'em. There will be no interview."

Freedman was proud of Cronkite, who was ready to give up the big scoop interview with Glenn live on CBS Radio rather than compromise his integrity or that of the network. When Freedman told NASA what Cronkite had said, it smartly dropped the insulting request. All systems were go.

On October 29, 1998, Cronkite played wise old man on CNN as Glenn returned to orbit, lifting off on *Discovery* STS-95 to study the effects of space on senior citizens. Cronkite reminisced about Kennedy-Johnson NASA efforts, seemingly teaching anchorman Miles O'Brien on the air about the history of space. It felt wonderful to be back at Cape Kennedy. He reminded viewers that during *Apollo 11* he was on the air for twenty-seven of the thirty key hours it took the astronauts to complete their mission. To help O'Brien and Cronkite out were former astronauts Buzz Aldrin and

Bernard Harris. A Florida reporter joked in the *Vero Beach Press Journal* that it was the "Cronkite School of Broadcasting and Space" on CNN. When Cronkite's buddy from the Bohemian Grove, Jimmy Buffett, stopped by the CNN booth he was immediately placed in the hotseat. "Walter waved me to sit next to him," Buffett recalled. "How cool was that? Co-anchoring a John Glenn mission with Walter Cronkite? It just doesn't get any better."

After broadcasting liftoff from Florida for CNN, Cronkite moved his show to Houston for CBS Radio. On November 4, his eighty-fourth birthday, Cronkite and Mike Freedman gathered for NASA's fortieth-anniversary luncheon. During the event, after everyone sang "Happy Birthday," Cronkite anchored what would be his final CBS News *Special Report*: a fifteen-minute conversation—from Earth to space—with John Glenn and the other astronauts on the mission.

Sounding for all the world like long-lost brothers thousands of miles apart, Cronkite and Glenn chatted about everything from weightlessness to the crew's release of the Petite Amateur Naval Satellite (which tested innovative technologies for the capture and transmission of radio signals). Then, for the last time in his life, Cronkite, milking his broadcast farewell like numerous other impresarios had done before him, used his signature close: "And that's the way it is, November 4, 1998. This is Walter Cronkite for CBS News in Houston."

Glenn's mission was merely a theatrical sideshow to the Clinton impeachment imbroglio. On the afternoon of February 19, 1999, when the impeachment came to its end, Cronkite was working with Freedman on a series called "Postscripts to the 20th Century" for CBS Radio News (short radio clips to help inaugurate the twenty-first century, also known as "Millennium" spots). Freedman suddenly got an inspired idea. Why not have Cronkite break the historical news of the Clinton verdict for the noon CBS Radio broadcast that would go out to all four hundred affiliates? "I asked Walter, and he looked a little surprised," Freedman recalled. "Then his eyes twinkled and he said, 'Sure.'"

And so it happened. The dah-dah-dah Teletype opening for the CBS hourly news alert hit the airwaves, and Cronkite spoke into the microphone from a booth at the CBS Network Radio Studio on Fifty-seventh Street. He opened the radio newscast crisply. "The impeachment case," he said, pausing a half second for operatic effect, "is about to finally come to the end." He went on to elaborate how the Senate Republicans didn't have a two-thirds majority to force Clinton to resign. Then Cronkite handed off the breaking news to the CBS News congressional correspondent Bob Fuss in Washington, D.C. "I had people from our affiliate stations around the country calling after that newscast like never before," Freedman recalled. "They were beyond thrilled. One guy in Wisconsin called and said 'UNBELIEVABLE! I drove off the road when I heard his voice.'"

Throughout the summer of 1999 at the Vineyard, Cronkite plotted with friends over how to stop real estate mogul Donald Trump from building an 861-foot residential tower on New York's East Side. It devoured all of his energies. Cronkite considered Trump-style unfettered development an abomination. Why did Trump need to build the world's tallest residential tower, which would "completely overshadow the United Nations and its beautiful gardens"? The Cronkite-versus-Trump squabble got heated in the tabloids. Trump claimed that Cronkite was a "totally preposterous" man who simply didn't want his rich-guy view marred. When a mediation meeting was held over the issue, Cronkite, walking into Trump's office with his NIMBY posse, was bowled over. Trump leapt out from behind his desk, came around with his arms outstretched and said, "Walter, it is soooooooo good to see you again!" Such breezy familiarity irked Cronkite because he had never met Trump before.

(The contentious issue was soon resolved in Trump's favor: construction started on Trump World Tower on First Avenue.)

In October 1999, Cronkite spent a week at the Jet Propulsion Laboratory (JPL) in Pasadena filming a Chip Cronkite–produced documentary titled *Beyond the Moon*, about the robotic devices of the future that would one day hopefully take astronauts to Mars. He flew back to New York from Pasadena in time to accept the World Federalist Association's Norman Cousins Global Governance Award on October 19 at the United Nations. Cronkite used the occasion to promote Earth Day, one world government, the United Nations, and the new George Soros book, *The Crisis of Global Capitalism*. This wasn't the accepted speech of a liberal. Cronkite had come fully out of the closet as a global-governance leftist, a political view more accepted in Copenhagen than Peoria. According to Cronkite, the notion of "unlimited national sovereignty" meant "international anarchy." It all got back to the picture that Bill Anders had snapped back in 1968 during *Apollo 8*: there was only *one* Planet Earth, and it had no borders.

At the UN, Cronkite uncorked his Interfaith Alliance–sponsored assault on the Christian Coalition and the religious right of the Republican Party. It was biting rhetoric aimed at Holy Roller crackpottery. The line between activism and journalism has always been imprecise, but Cronkite went off the Five Ws reservation at the UN with a shot of *Network* "I'm mad as hell" outrage reminiscent of his Roseland introduction of Barbara Jordan. "Their leader, Pat Robertson, has written that we should have a world government but only when the Messiah arrives," Cronkite scoffed. "Any attempt to achieve world order before that time must be the work of the devil. This small but well-organized group has intimidated the Republican Party and the Clinton Administration. It has attacked each of our presidents since [Franklin D. Roosevelt] for supporting the United Nations. Robertson explains that these presidents were and are the unwitting agents of Lucifer. The only way we who believe in the vision of a democratic world federal government can effectively overcome this reactionary movement is to organize a strong educational counter-offensive stretching from the most publicly visible people in all fields to the humblest individuals in every community."

How did Cronkite get away with such World Federalist rhetoric and not cause Republicans to collectively turn on him the way Fox News Channel would against Wall Street financier George Soros? For starters, he had too many GOP establishment friends, such as Roger Ailes, John Lehman, and George Shultz. It was also disconcerting to them that, after sounding like Paul Robeson at the United Nations, Cronkite headed to the Kennedy Center Honors in a tuxedo looking for all the world like Captain Kangaroo. Nothing about his kindly demeanor was menacing in the least. There is also, it must be said, an unwritten rule that once you pass eighty years old in America you have earned the right to pontificate without much penalty.

Election Day, November 7, 2000, redefined the term *political cliffhanger* in the United States. The square-off between George W. Bush and Al Gore seemed to be a dead heat. All the networks made predictions that Vice President Gore had won Florida that they were then forced to retract. Who actually won the 2000 election was eventually decided in Bush's favor by the U.S. Supreme Court. While most Americans worried about the breakdown of the democratic process, Cronkite kept his ire focused on his media colleagues. "I think it's up to the networks and the subscribing newspapers and press services to not call until all the states have closed," he said. "I don't understand the need for speed, although I was certainly one of the progenitors of the whole idea of exit polling. . . . The point is that nowadays, with the exit polling, we're calling these states so early that there are some three hours left of voting time out on the West Coast, and it seems to me that very probably it could work just as well to withhold returns until all the states have voted."

Just after Thanksgiving, Cronkite had surgery on his right heel to replace a part of his Achilles tendon. While the procedure went well, he was in terrible pain. With weariness and disgust, he canceled all his Christmas obligations, including serving as host of the Kennedy Center Honors. It wasn't like him to miss a gig, but his discomfort was very real. Gala producer George Stevens Jr. was shocked, saying that Uncle Walter was "irreplaceable."

That New Year's Eve—ushering in Y2K—a still recuperating Cronkite was forced to cancel his hosting of PBS's New Year's Concert at the gilded Musikverein concert hall in Vienna. The Cronkites instead celebrated with their oldest Kansas City friends, Frantz and Dorothy Barhydt. "I had to think more about the millennium than anyone," the eighty-three-year-old Cronkite would soon joke at a speech before the University of Wisconsin Medical School, "as the world's oldest reporter."

35.

The New Millennium

9/11/01 IN ITALY—CONSOLING AMERICA WITH
LETTERMAN—AROUND AMERICA—KING FEATURES
SYNDICATE COLUMNIST—ANTI-IRAQ WAR—SCOLDING
JOHN KERRY—MEMOGATE—THE FLUSHING OF DAN
RATHER—CHEERING UP MOONVES—DEATH OF
BETSY—THE LOVELY JOANNA SIMON—WC ARCHIVES
AT UT—WORKING WITH CARLETON—LEGACY IN
PHOENIX—CHALLENGING THE WAR ON DRUGS—
ATTACKED BY THE RIGHT—FADING AWAY—STANDING
FOR THE GENTLEMAN—TOM SHALES'S FINE GOOD-BYE

After watching the U.S. Open tennis tournament at
Flushing Meadows on September 7, 2001, Walter
and Betsy Cronkite packed their bags for an Italian

holiday. The last of the broadcasters from the golden age of TV was going to receive an honorary degree from La Sapienza University (founded in 1303 and still Europe's largest university). While in Florence, Cronkite heard the ghastly news of September 11: nineteen al Qaeda terrorists had hijacked four commercial planes and crashed two into the World Trade Center in New York City; the third into the Pentagon in Arlington, Virginia; and the fourth into a fallow field near Shanksville, Pennsylvania. Nearly three thousand people were killed in the most gruesome string of terrorist attacks in American history.

Cronkite was glued to CNN in his Florence hotel near the Uffizi Gallery, watching anchorman Aaron Brown broadcast the nonstop, commercial-free coverage. Scenes of people plunging to their deaths and plumes of smoke and ash rolling down Wall Street made Cronkite shudder. Scores of New Yorkers were fleeing from the crumbling towers with cloths over their mouths to avoid breathing in the smoke. Walter and Betsy desperately tried reaching their three children, determined to make sure they were safe. It took a while, but they eventually succeeded. "When Dad reached me, I suggested that he stay out of New York for a while," Chip Cronkite recalled, "but he was very anxious to get back to Manhattan. He wanted to get back to cover the story."

Marlene Adler was with the Cronkites in Italy, managing her boss's various entrepreneurial ventures when the news of 9/11 broke. "Get me out of here!" he demanded of Adler. When she explained to him that U.S. airports were in lockdown mode, planes grounded, he groused, "Then get me a private plane!" Adler frantically tried to book a flight, to no avail. With thousands of miles of sea separating him from New York, Cronkite told Adler in exasperation, "OK, then we'll take a boat." His impatience had become almost debilitating. It was the first time Adler had seen her beloved boss so demanding and rigid. His helplessness frustrated him terribly. "He *had* to see Ground Zero for himself while it was smoldering," Adler recalled. "He *had* to use his reporter's eye on the front line. Nothing would satisfy him until I got him to New York. Nothing."

Feeling useless and detached, Cronkite pottered around the Piazza della Signoria, pondering the gloom of 9/11. He wondered if World War III had started. He digested the gruesome reality that New York City, his adopted hometown since the early 1950s, was in a state of emergency. One supposes that a cramp of envy consumed him because Dan Rather of the *CBS Evening News* was anchoring fifty-three hours and thirty-five minutes of coverage. He felt again like a has-been broadcaster. Instead of canceling his La Sapienza

speech in Rome, though, Cronkite spoke to the Italian
audience, including in his remarks a brief interlude of
silence for victims of the 9/11 attack.

On September 12, Cronkite, still glued to CNN's
marathon coverage, telephoned Brown in New York,
urging the broadcaster to hold up under the intense
pressure. Even though seeing the jagged jawbone of
the smoking World Trade Center towers was trauma-
tizing, he nevertheless had the wherewithal to critique
Brown's on-air performance. "This is your Kennedy,"
Cronkite told Brown. "This is how people will think of
you." Brown said that "no call had ever meant more"
to him.

Once back in New York and reunited with his family,
Cronkite hugged all of his kids. Turning down dozens
of interview requests, he ultimately accepted an invitation from CBS's *Late Night with David Letterman*,
hoping to offer healing remarks about the 9/11 wicked-
ness. It proved to be a sentimental segment between the
great comedian and the great broadcaster. Letterman
and Cronkite, pros at banter, held a somber chat about
how the Bush administration shouldn't overreact to al
Qaeda's diabolical attacks. A sedate Cronkite admitted that his immediate reaction while in Italy had been
to "get even, for heaven's sake," with the murderous
foes. Retaliation, he said, was a natural instinct against

"Bin Lad . . . Bin Adam . . . whatever that idiot's name is. I'm trying to forget it already, as if that would help somehow." But rushing to war to get even wasn't the solution.

> *Letterman:* As someone who has seen and covered big stories all your life, when you heard of this, how did it feel compared to other big news stories in America?
>
> *Cronkite:* Well, how do you think it felt? I mean, how do you really think it felt? I think the question is acceptable, I'm not criticizing your question, except that I think we all felt the same way. I really think that's one of the unifying things about us. I don't think there was an American with a different thought except invoking the deity, "My God, how could this happen?" and the shock of it happening, the terrible awareness of our vulnerability, that a small band of fanatics, idiots could commit such mass murder in the middle of the greatest city in the world.

For a few weeks in the fall of 2001, Cronkite refrained from overtly criticizing President Bush, but the mute button wasn't on pause for long. He soon lost patience with the administration's false linkage of Iraq to the al Qaeda terrorist network. The unconscionable mistake that President Bush, Vice President Dick Cheney, and Secretary of Defense Donald Rumsfeld were making, Cronkite believed, was insisting that the United States needed a post-9/11 demonstration of war to prove national greatness. That October, Cronkite took to the CNN airwaves demanding that President Bush adhere to the War Powers Act, which required that the president seek congressional authorization before dispatching military forces abroad. That was just his opening shot. Cronkite decided in December 2001 to expose what he regarded as the Bush administration's warmongering and its false linkage of Saddam Hussein with al Qaeda. "I was hot under the collar about Bush overreacting to 9/11 with the Freedom Fries and all that," Andy Rooney recalled. "But Walter was hotter."

And Bush, Cheney, and Rumsfeld weren't Cronkite's only targets. He also lashed out at the evangelicals Jerry Falwell (pastor of the Thomas Road Baptist Church in Lynchburg, Virginia) and Pat Robertson (host of the 700 Club). In a TV Guide interview, Cronkite said that Falwell's remark about 9/11 (that the terrorist attacks were divine retribution for pagans, abortionists, feminists, and homosexuals) was "the most abominable thing I've ever heard." As Cronkite prepared to host the Emmy Awards in Los Angeles, he took his criticism of the Christian right a bridge farther. "It makes you wonder," he said of the evangelical's post-9/11 remarks, "if [Falwell and Robertson] are worshipping the same God as the people who bombed the Trade Center and the Pentagon."

With the November publication of his sailing memoir, *Around America: A Tour of Our Magnificent Coastline* (W. W. Norton), Cronkite attended book signings at what seemed like every Barnes & Noble, Borders, and independent booksellers from Marin County, California, to Portland, Maine. On the promotional stump, he saw his public role as championing America's pristine national seashores, such as Cape Hatteras, Padre Island, and Assateague Island . He fell in love with old Savannah: the buggy rides, fountains, and parks. As the "Air War Dean" of World War II journalism, he was thrilled to learn that an Eighth Air Force museum was being built near the airport. However, autograph seekers didn't want to talk about General Eaker or the Aransas National Wildlife Refuge's dwindling whooping crane population when newspapers headlined anthrax scares and whodunit theories about Saudi Arabian treachery. Everybody, it seemed, wanted Cronkite to compare 9/11 to Pearl Harbor or the JFK assassination or the Oklahoma

City bombings. So he did. Practically every time a TV viewer turned on CBS or CNN, Cronkite was holding court as the Great Eyewitness. "Somehow knowing that Walter was still around to put the terror acts in perspective," Katie Couric, future anchor of the *CBS Evening News*, believed, "was cathartic."

To the surprise of his family and friends Cronkite, riled up by 9/11, agreed to write a weekly column for King Features Syndicate, largely, it seems, to criticize President Bush. Ever since his Roseland speech in defense of liberalism, Cronkite told *The New York Times*, he had refused to be an "ideological eunuch." Since he lived to read the morning papers, Cronkite figured, why not write for them? Operating out of UN Plaza, using his laptop's search engine with great skill, he weighed in on the big foreign policy decisions facing the United States. What concerned Cronkite the most was that his two favorite papers—*The New York Times* and *The Washington Post*—were allowing the Bush administration to hype the unprovable notion that Saddam Hussein had weapons of mass destruction (WMDs). Cronkite had a deep and sickening feeling that the fourth estate, cowed by the intimidation tactics of the Bush White House, was failing spectacularly. To Cronkite, the whole class of American journalists, with a very few notable exceptions (namely the McClatchy chain and *The Nation*), had paved the way for Gulf War II by not asking the tough questions about the Bush administration's rationale for the war. Why didn't journalists explain the tension between the Shiites and Sunnis that was bound to keel into civil war?

Written with the assistance of Dale Minor, Cronkite's weekly column was picked up by 153 U.S. newspapers from August 2003 to August 2004. At eighty-eight years old, he had a platform once again. Refusing to be intimidated by Rush Limbaugh or Sean Hannity, who regularly took to the airwaves insulting antiwar liberal reporters like Ted Koppel, Cronkite promoted his secular, human rights–oriented, pro-NATO, pro-UN views of world affairs, with the conviction of Eleanor Roosevelt on the stump. Democrats lapped it up. His iconic status soared in deep blue precincts. "No longer was he trying to be Mr. Center," Couric recalled. "He wanted to be a vital voice of dissent on war-related issues."

The Cronkite of King Features Syndicate was a circumspect columnist who deftly wove fact, analysis, and morality. His liberal arguments—directed at President Bush in the spirit of bringing home the American soldiers from Iraq—were smart but homespun. "You might remember MAD—the Cold War policy of Mutually Assured Destruction in which the United

States and the Soviet Union each planned to obliterate the other in the event of nuclear attack," he wrote in his November 13, 2003, column. "Well, among themselves, the Democratic presidential candidates have triggered their own version of mutually assured destruction." Cronkite thought John Kerry, John Edwards, Joe Lieberman, Dick Gephardt, Wesley Clark, and Howard Dean—all vying to be the Democratic nominee for president in 2004—were committing "political fratricide." They needed to aim their collective fire at President Bush. The USA Patriot Act, Cronkite lamented, was stripping Americans of civil liberties guaranteed by the Constitution while Democrats were engaged in silly intramural schoolyard fights. There were many primary sources and pieces of classified information being acquired that raised questions about the casus belli. If American journalists had simply done their due diligence, they could have thwarted the Bush administration's hawkish moves vis-à-vis Iraq. It was the lack of any rigorous questioning that surprised and dispirited Cronkite. "Walter liked being in the ring," Minor recalled. "After decades of trying to be objective, the columns meant he no longer had to abide by any strictures."

Perhaps if the fourth estate had listened to Cronkite— their wise man—a trillion dollars and four thousand

U.S. troops could have been saved. But they ignored him as the out-of-touch author of *Around America*. While Cronkite's sustained hostility toward President Bush surprised even Socolow, Rooney, Wallace, and Safer—his four best friends in the media world—he pleased the progressive blogosphere to no end. In a column titled "Where Do We Go from Here?" (May 20, 2004), Cronkite suggested firing Bush on grounds of rank incompetence. Few other major U.S. media figures, except perhaps Michael Moore and Bill Maher, went after Bush with the impeachment vitriol of Cronkite. At Southern Illinois University that October, Cronkite, a gray-haired antiwar icon cheered as the ghost of John Reed, bluntly declared Bush's Iraq War the "worst policy decision this nation has ever made." The wire services transmitted Cronkite's insult around the world. The Bush Doctrine of preemptive strike was to Cronkite a jingoistic atrocity destined to bankrupt America morally and fiscally. "Bush is setting an example for every nation in the world," Cronkite carped. "If you don't like what's going on with your neighbor, it's perfectly all right to go to war with them."

Frank Rich of *The New York Times* praised Cronkite for trying to awaken America to the Bush administration's distortions. "At the networks, Cronkite's heirs were not even practicing journalism," an incensed Rich wrote. "They invited administration propagandists to trumpet their tales of imminent mushroom clouds with impunity."

If Cronkite thought one television broadcaster was brave during Mr. Bush's war, it was Christiane Amanpour of CNN. Amanpour had grown up in Iran and had never watched Cronkite broadcast as a child. When she emigrated to the United States in 1981, Cronkite was already poised to retire the *CBS Evening News* anchor chair. Always with an eye toward the female foreign correspondents, Cronkite developed a schoolboy crush on Amanpour as her star rose. Every time she appeared on CNN from Baghdad, he turned the volume on the TV way up, adjusting his hearing aid, not wanting to miss a word. To Cronkite, Amanpour had the guts of Murrow for blowing a hole in the famous "aluminum tubes" defense for the Iraq War featured prominently in *The New York Times*.

When the insurgency against Americans in Iraq reached full murderous throttle, Cronkite had Adler set up a "date" for him with Amanpour. They greeted each other like old friends. "We met in the restaurant of the Mark Hotel in Manhattan," Amanpour recalled. "He came alone, an elegant elderly dignified gentleman, walking slowly into the lobby. I think we both felt we knew each other, and there is a deep sense of camaraderie silently expressed between brothers- and sisters-in-arms. I myself had had a deep reverence for him and for everything he stood for. Anyway, after lots of chitchat over a couple of stiff whiskeys on the rocks, I asked him whether anyone today could do what he did back in Vietnam after Tet. And to my abiding disappointment, he gently told me, no, he didn't think so, because unlike in his time, there are multitudinous voices and channels out there today."

When it looked as if John Kerry had locked the Democratic nomination for U.S. president in the spring of 2004, Cronkite, instead of congratulating the Massachusetts senator, whacked him for ceding the "high ground" to conservatives and refusing to declare or even acknowledge his "liberal" principles. "If 1988 taught us anything, it is that a candidate who lacks the courage of his convictions cannot hope to convince the nation that he should be given its leadership," Cronkite wrote Kerry. "So, Senator, some detailed explanations are in order if you hope to have any chance of defeating even a wounded George II in November. You cannot let the Bush league define you or the issues. You have to do that yourself. Take my advice and lay it all out, before it's too late."

For the 2004 election season, Cronkite watched Tom Brokaw of NBC News during his final season as anchor.

The contrast between Brokaw's classy comportment and Rather's look-at-me arrogance told Cronkite who his *real* heir was. CBS News faced one of its darkest moments shortly after Labor Day: anchorman Rather claimed that President Bush had often been AWOL from duty when he was a lieutenant in the Texas Air National Guard from 1968 to 1973. Convinced that a document he'd obtained from Lt. Col. Jerry B. Killian's personal files was genuine, Rather took to the CBS airwaves on *60 Minutes Wednesday* (an offshoot of the original Sunday program) on September 8, 2004, and leveled the accusation at the president. Rather had broken Cronkite's cardinal rule of always confirming information before reporting it.

During his twenty-three-year career as CBS News anchorman—four years longer than Cronkite's stint—Rather, a gambler, often ran stories that were confirmed by only one solid source. His batting average of being right was high, but he was playing with fire. Eventually he had to get burned. The same razor-sharp investigative instincts that allowed Rather to help break the Abu Ghraib prisoner abuse story betrayed him on the Texas Air National Guard story just as the election year stakes were jacked up sky-high. President Bush was running against Kerry in a dead-heat contest for the White House. Questions were raised over whether

Kerry deserved the Silver Star, Bronze Star, and three Purple Hearts he had been awarded for his Vietnam service in the U.S. Navy. Vietnam had emerged as part of the 2004 presidential election fisticuffs. At a Museum of Radio and Television conference about "breaking news" around this time, Cronkite warned that a single false on-air report could destroy a brilliant career; Rather had just stepped on a claymore mine in a career-killing way.

When forensic experts determined that Rather's crucial *60 Minutes Wednesday* document could not be authenticated because of seemingly anachronistic typography, that it easily could have been cooked up by some forger out to damage Bush (or planted by GOP operatives to embarrass Rather), CBS News' obdurate anchorman was forced to offer a humble, almost indignant, retraction. "This was an error made in good faith as we tried to carry on the CBS News tradition of asking tough questions and investigating reports," Rather said, "but it was a mistake." Subsequently, Rather retreated from his apology, claiming he was coerced into making it. He then claimed he had nothing to do with the report itself, that he was only a talking head. Further, he denied that any mistakes had been made at all.

Rather, blaming everyone but himself, reluctantly announced that he would step down from the anchor chair in early 2005, while remaining at CBS News. Unable to emulate Douglas Edwards and just retreat to the graveyard shift show *Up to the Minute*, Rather fought like a wildcat to protect his reputation. For forty-three years, he had represented the CBS Eye tradition of Murrow. Now he was being dismissed as a pariah. Everybody at CBS News knew Rather had essentially been demoted. Not just for Memogate: *CBS Evening News* was sagging far behind NBC's *Nightly News* and ABC's *World News Tonight*. The Big Three anchors were Brokaw, Jennings, and way down the line, Rather. The *60 Minutes* gang wanted Rather publicly flogged for Memogate. Hewitt had built *60 Minutes* into an American institution and now Rather, looking for glory, had given the entire news-gathering operation a blinding black eye. Cronkite, refusing any connection to CBS's Judas, told a reporter that he didn't watch Rather's poorly produced show, just couldn't stand it. "There's nothing there," he said, "but crime and sob sister material . . . tabloid stuff."

A number of old-time CBS reporters—including Mike Wallace, Morley Safer, and Andy Rooney—recalled how jubilant Cronkite was that Rather's career crashed so dramatically that fall. "Walter's hip was bad," Rooney explained. "He couldn't move well.

But that ol' boy danced a jig when Dan went down."
Cronkite long knew that Rather's Achilles heel was his
tendency to jump the gun. What surprised him wasn't
Memogate but that Rather hadn't botched a story
sooner. What irritated Cronkite even more was how
Rather was going after some chicken-shit story about
Bush and the National Guard that had nothing to do
with 2004. For once, Cronkite actually felt some sympathy for President Bush.

Rather was insistent that his departure from CBS
had been illegal and filed a $70 million breach-of-
contract lawsuit against CBS and its former parent
company, Viacom. A New York state court of appeals
dismissed Rather's frivolous suit. Many historians
think Rather's *60 Minutes* blunder contributed significantly to President Bush's reelection in an extremely
close contest, with Bush winning 286 electoral votes to
Kerry's 251. Rather hadn't just had an oops moment.
He had self-immolated in front of seventy million *60
Minutes Wednesday* viewers. "It surprised quite a few
people at CBS and elsewhere," Cronkite said on CNN's
American Morning, "that they tolerated his being there
for so long."

Easing Rather out of the chair wasn't atonement
enough for Les Moonves. In early January, as Rather
was starting to clear his desk, Moonves asked four CBS

executives associated with Memogate—Mary Mapes, the story's producer; Josh Howard, executive producer of *60 Minutes Wednesday*; Howard's top deputy, Mary Murphy; and CBS News' senior vice president, Betsy West—to resign from the network. Moonves's decision was based on an independent study chaired by former U.S. attorney general Dick Thornburgh claiming that Team Rather had "myopic zeal" in trying to embarrass George W. Bush. Moonves thought Rather's use of "unsubstantiated documents" was the low ebb of CBS News history, a "black mark" against the reportorial house Cronkite, Murrow, and the *60 Minutes* gang had helped build. Determined to be the new Murrow, a crusader for social justice in the twenty-first century, Rather had inadvertently become the Soupy Sales of TV news gathering.

When Mike Wallace bumped into Rather in a CBS bathroom in the *60 Minutes* offices, a nasty verbal clash erupted between the men. Wallace called Rather, to his face, a shameless creep, a public disgrace, who instead of manning up for Memogate, allowed the fine talents of Mapes, Howard, Murphy, and West to suffer humiliation. Was that Rather's idea of courage? "We know it as the battle of the bathroom," longtime executive producer of *60 Minutes* Jeff Fager explained. "It's never been reported, but it was bad."

The day that Moonves undertook the dismissals, he asked that nobody disturb him in his office at Black Rock, then on the nineteenth floor, refusing even to take phone calls. Ensconced at his desk, a huge Peter Max painting of the CBS Eye behind him, listening to soft music, he was suddenly startled by a light rap on his door. Before he could get up, it cracked open. It was Walter Cronkite, white-haired and ruddy, his eyebrows raised like splayed brushes, fidgeting with his hearing aid and radiating a sympathetic warmth.

"Well, Les," Cronkite said, having charmed his way past the pool of secretaries, "you've just done the hardest thing a man has to do in his life. You let good people go. . . . But you had to do it for journalism, for fairness, and for the CBS brand. I just want you to know you did the right thing. I'm proud of you."

The suddenly unemployed Rather signed up as a producer with HDNet, a high-definition cable television station, and in October 2006 he began to host *Dan Rather Reports*.

For the next thirty or forty minutes, Cronkite and Moonves chatted about Memogate and what it meant to television history. The weight of the world had been lifted from Moonves's shoulders. For nights, he had suffered from insomnia, tormented at having to fire a bevy of longtime CBS employees. But Cronkite's generous gesture, completely unnecessary, much like

generous gesture, completely unnecessary, much like when he took the Clintons on the *Wyntje* during the Lewinsky scandal or wrote Bob Simon after his Iraq hostage ordeal, choked Moonves up. The CEO of CBS had long treated Cronkite with deference. Now he saw him as family. "You'll never know what that meant to me," Moonves later recalled, eyes clouding. "Everything came into focus. I'm getting goose bumps just talking about it. I went home able to sleep, able to feel whole. Walter said it was okay."

On March 15, 2005, the Cronkite family suffered a devastating blow when Betsy Cronkite, the auburn-haired beauty from Missouri, died of cancer just two weeks before her sixty-fifth wedding anniversary. Betsy had held her own in the New York–Edgartown social whirl without losing any sense of her own midwestern roots or taking on the pretensions of the nouveau riche. One had the impression that she and Walter would have been content living in a cold-water flat in Kansas City with an old Victrola playing Count Basie records for company. Betsy was so down-to-earth, she made forks drop at dinner parties with what Barbara Walters called her "wry and acidic" bluntness. Whenever anyone called Cronkite the Most Trusted Man in America, he would invariably offer the line, "They didn't poll my wife."

Now Betsy was no more. Feeling unprotected and lonely, he wondered whether he could persevere on his own. "Everything just crashed around him," Cronkite's daughter-in-law Deborah Rush recalled. "Betsy was the glue that held him together." Hundreds of people, including celebrities, attended Betsy Cronkite's memorial service at St. Bartholomew's Church in Manhattan. Rev. C. Welton Gaddy of the Interfaith Alliance gave the principal eulogy. All the other speakers were dwarfed and overshadowed by Hillary Clinton—who wasn't in the program but showed up unexpectedly. People gathered outside the church to offer Cronkite condolences and in the hope of catching a photographic glimpse of the first lady on their cell phones. To the surprise of Cronkite's kids, Dan Rather attended the service. That afternoon, Cronkite chatted with Joanna Simon, the real estate broker who sold him his UN Plaza co-op. Weeks later, Simon invited Cronkite for a drink. Her husband, Gerald Walker, had died the previous year of a stroke while working on the novel *Witness* (unpublished). "Walter was bereft and lost," Simon recalled. "His plan was to go to the British Virgin Islands, where *Wyntje* was moored for the winter months, with his kids for a week. And then he wanted to take me out on a date."

Coincidentally, Bill Small's wife died the same day as Betsy Cronkite. A few weeks after the funerals, Small received a telephone call from Walter. "Let's go commiserate together over lunch," he said. Upon arriving at a private midtown Manhattan club, the two old-timers were ushered into what was almost a private room to compare notes about losing their mates. Cronkite spoke of his deep grief and of sitting on his sofa at UN Plaza surrounded by a small theme park's worth of memorabilia. "I just wander around the apartment completely lost," he confided to Small. "All I do is puddle up and cry from morning to night."

When the conversation turned to Dan Rather's twenty-four-year career as CBS News anchorman, Cronkite stiffened, no longer convivial. He told Small horror stories about how Rather had purposely tried to humiliate him time and time again. He was glad that CBS had removed Rather from the chair. Cronkite relayed how the paranoid Rather had poisoned his well at CBS News by badmouthing him to other employees. "I don't believe that's true," Small told Cronkite. "My long experience with Dan was that if you had a problem he was always willing to listen. In fact, he was practically solicitous about avoiding bad blood or feuds."

"Should I call him?" Cronkite sheepishly asked. Small at first thought that was the right thing to do but then hesitated, understandably not wanting to play the middleman. "It's not a bad idea," he said, "but that has to be up to you."

Cronkite didn't call Rather for lunch. Instead, he remained hateful toward him till death. It can be said Rather was the only man whom Cronkite despised. "I could talk to Walter about anything," CNN anchorman Aaron Brown, a regular lunch companion, recalled. "But not [about] Rather." Both Cronkite and Rather had behaved badly toward each other. "Dan didn't have many friends," Jeff Fager recalled. "Walter had everybody on his side."

Nearing the end of his life, Cronkite decided to mend fences with all of his past CBS News colleagues—except Dan Rather. The very last special Roger Mudd did at the History Channel, where he hosted a show, was an interview with Cronkite at the Vineyard. Whatever disagreements they'd had in the past were either ignored or left unspoken. It was obvious how much they cared for one another. When Cronkite had trouble hearing, Mudd helped his old boss by devising a special feed (with the help of an expert soundman) that would get crystal-clear audio. He "was overjoyed." At the very end of the taping, with the cameras still rolling, he complimented Mudd for being a fine reporter, a gentleman, and a great American. Cronkite deeply regretted not having pushed for Mudd to replace him back in 1981.

One evening, just weeks after Betsy's death, two of Cronkite's good-time friends, Jimmy Buffett and Mickey Hart, were worried that poor Walter wouldn't know what to do with himself without his wife. They decided to take him out for a "cheer-up" night on the town in New York.

"Walter," Buffett said after they sat down, touching his hand for added compassion, "Mickey and I know what hell you're going through right now having lost Betsy. I've never known a marriage that worked so well, that was so close. We—"

Cronkite interrupted Buffett's spiel. "Boys," he said, beaming. "Stop! Stop! Stop! There's something you should know. I've got a new girlfriend."

Just weeks after Betsy died, Cronkite started dating Simon in earnest. Before long they moved in together. Chalk the romance up to loneliness and the hope of having a last hurrah. Marlene Adler joked that Simon had beat all the other "casserole ladies" to the punch. Joanna, the daughter of Richard Simon, founder of Simon and Schuster Publishers, was an Emmy Award–winning on-air arts correspondent for *The MacNeil-Lehrer NewsHour* before she became a Manhattan real estate broker in 1996. Her sister was the popular singer Carly Simon. Simon's first sale in 1997 was to Walter and Betsy Cronkite: their UN Plaza co-op. Widowed a year before Betsy Cronkite died, Simon soon became Cronkite's *girlfriend* (a term Simon thought belonged to high-schoolers only). They were regarded as an inseparable couple in New York, Washington, and Vineyard social circles until the end of Cronkite's life. *The New York Post* and New York *Daily News* both gossiped that she was Cronkite's new "gal pal."

In a perfect world, Cronkite should probably have waited longer to begin dating, out of respect for Betsy. Connie Chung remembered getting her nails done at a Manhattan day spa with Barbara Walters shortly after Betsy's death. Chung, admitting they were "terrible gossips," kibitzed about how tawdry the Cronkite-Simon relationship was. "Walter didn't wait very long to strike," she said, laughing. "How girls-day-out is that? Sitting in our pedicure chairs chatting about Walter's sex life."

When Peter Jennings of ABC News died in August 2005 from lung cancer, it deeply affected Cronkite. A life decision was made: he was going to go out in a blaze of glory with his lover Joanna at his side. Cronkite, the old-age survivor, enjoyed being around pretty women after Betsy's death. He offered them fatherly advice while getting to unspool the newsreel highlights of his eventful life. His old CBS News associate Carol Joynt became one of his closest friends (in a strange moment, when she was struggling financially, he proposed marriage to her). Beverly Keel, a young professor at Middle Tennessee State University, came to interview Cronkite at his Black Rock office not long after Betsy's death in 2005. "It was like I was reunited with my grandfather, I was so totally at ease," Keel recalled. "When he sat down in the chairs that we had placed close together because of his hearing issues we were about eighteen inches apart."

"My," Cronkite joked, "we're close!"

Feeling appreciated by Moonves at CBS, glad that Couric had replaced Rather as anchor of the *Evening News*, dating the sixty-five-year-old Simon (a teenager by comparison), enamored of Amanpour, and close to all three of his children, Cronkite entered his twilight years a happy man in the full flush of love. One night Cronkite and Simon walked to a Chinese restaurant on Second Avenue for dinner shortly after they moved in together. People kept coming up to Cronkite to shake the great man's hand. "You know, Walter," Simon said, "you really are American royalty." He looked at her lovingly and said, "As long as I'm your King of Hearts." Simon swooned.

While Cronkite didn't become a spaceman, NASA, as compensation for not allowing him into orbit with Glenn, presented him with an Ambassador of

Exploration Award on February 28, 2006. He was the *only* nonastronaut ever to win the honor, which he deemed "beyond anything I could have ever believed." As a token of appreciation, NASA also gave Cronkite a sample of lunar material encased in Lucite. This wasn't just any old piece of moon rock. It had samples of all 842 pounds of moon rock brought back to the Earth from the six Apollo expeditions that took place between 1969 and 1972. Instead of keeping this special present on his mantel in New York or Edgartown, Cronkite donated it to the University of Texas's Dolph Briscoe Center for American History, the archival home of more than three hundred linear feet of Walter Cronkite Papers.

Professor Don Carleton of the University of Texas continued to parlay Cronkite's years with *The Daily Texan* (1934–1935) into assets for UT's Briscoe Center. With Cronkite's help, Carleton acquired the papers of Morley Safer, Joe and Shirley Wershba, Harry Reasoner, Andy Rooney, Robert Trout, and other broadcast stand-outs to complement the Briscoe Center's existing holdings. All things dubbed Cronkitiana were welcomed. Cronkite, his fondess for Carleton growing over time, allowed the professor to become the custodian of his life. Together they would sail *Wyntje*, drink Maker's Mark, and discuss current events. Carleton conducted two extensive oral histories of Cronkite that are Studs Terkel models of genre excellence: one for the Briscoe Center (used as the basis for the 2010 book *Conversations with Cronkite*) and another for the Academy of Television Arts and Sciences (available online). Cronkite also parceled out his fading energies to helping the Walter Cronkite School of Journalism and Mass Communication at Arizona State University prosper. He had helped start the Cronkite School in 1984 and participated in the downtown Phoenix groundbreaking ceremony on February 21, 2007. What particularly tickled Cronkite was that the Arizona PBS affiliate would also be housed in the school, allowing students real hands-on learning about how to report on television.

Once Mike Wallace retired from *60 Minutes* after the most extraordinary career in broadcasting, he started spending quite a bit of time with Cronkite. Not only did they like the same quiet Manhattan restaurants, but they also had houses near each other on the Vineyard. One late afternoon in Edgartown, Cronkite and Simon had Mike and Mary Wallace over for cocktails on their enclosed terrace to gossip about friends and family. That's when Wallace dropped a bomb.

"Walter," he said, "don't you want to die? I've done everything I've wanted to do. How about you?"

Cronkite, taken aback, said, "No. Absolutely not! I want to live forever. I get one look at the water, the sunshine, the beach, and the trees here! Every day, Mike, is a blessing."

After the Wallaces left, Walter and Joanna mused about all the wonderful places they wanted to go to together. Life was intoxicating. In the coming year, they visited Portugal, Italy, Austria, Hawaii, and the Caribbean. With Cronkite as a guest lecturer, they went on a Silver Seas cruise, making scores of new friends. They spent a week with George Clooney at his home on Lake Como, speedboat racing and outfoxing the paparazzi. At the Vineyard, Cronkite would bang out "Stars and Stripes Forever" on the drums for friends while Simon sang the patriotic Sousa lyrics with operatic bravado. The whole scene was a hoot. In Manhattan, they dined out with friends four or five nights a week. The other two were spent eating meals on TV trays watching the *CBS Evening News* (pulling mightily for Couric), CNN's *Larry King Live*, and other news shows.

Cronkite realized that Simon was the perfect woman for him because, as an opera singer, she knew how to modulate her voice to decibels that he could hear. His pet name for her was "The Translator." Because he was taking various medications, he didn't handle his usual scotch well anymore. "Walter and I had a great romance," Simon recalled. "It came to us later in life.

I wish I'd met Walter when he was twenty-five and I was one."

Every celebrity adopts a nonprofit cause, and one of Cronkite's, surprisingly enough, was decriminalizing marijuana. Joanna Simon's brother, Peter, remembered in the late 1970s having Cronkite over for a party at Gay Head on the Vineyard. There were two cliques out side of year-round residents in the yard: on one side were hippies smoking pot and on the other was the boozehound establishment. "Mar-a-juana," he said to Simon. "I'm quite familiar with that drug." When offered a joint, however, he stoutly refused. "The fact that he didn't stereotype people into ilks or cults had a huge influence of me," Peter Simon recalled. "That was a lesson to me. He treated pot people as equals." Feeling he had one big fight left in him, Cronkite— who had earned cult status in the legalization of mari- juana movement because of his 1995 *The Cronkite Report* episode, "The Drug Dilemma: War or Peace?" on the Discovery Channel—had come to think that a little reefer was perhaps better than a lot of booze.

By 2006, Cronkite had become a warrior on behalf of the Drug Policy Alliance, a nonprofit advocating reform of the marijuana laws and alternatives to puni- tive drug war policies. Cronkite even lent his name to a *New York Times* ad promoting the use of medical marijuana and reduced incarceration time for drug offenders.

Cronkite's open letter was dated February 24, 2006. He put his reputation on the line for the cause of decriminalizing marijuana:

> *I covered the Vietnam War. I remember the lies that were told, the lives that were lost—and the shock when, twenty years after the war ended, former Defense Secretary Robert S. McNamara admitted he knew it was a mistake all along.*
>
> *Today, our nation is fighting two wars: one abroad and one at home. While the war in Iraq is in the headlines, the other war is still being fought on our own streets. Its casualties are the wasted lives of our own citizens.*
>
> *I am speaking of the war on drugs.*
>
> *And I cannot help but wonder how many more lives, and how much more money, will be wasted before another Robert McNamara admits what is plain for all to see: the war on drugs is a failure.*

What Cronkite was asking in his open letter—as was William F. Buckley of *National Review*—was whether arresting 1.5 million Americans a year on drug charges (half of them marijuana arrests) made sense financially to taxpayers. Weren't American prisons overcrowded enough? The Netherlands was his model of a modern society; it trusted its own citizens on whether to smoke pot.

By linking the failed Vietnam War of Lyndon Johnson to the failed war on drugs of George W. Bush, Cronkite caused a firestorm. A platoon of right-wing commentators attacked him with a new degree of animosity. The Fox News television host and commentator Bill O'Reilly—who personally liked Cronkite—challenged his Drug Alliance views on *The O'Reilly Factor* for being too soft on dope peddlers. He hoped to expose Cronkite as a man of the left and didn't pull any punches. "Listen, violent crime is induced by hard drug use, Walter," O'Reilly said. "I don't want to be too tough on you, you're ninety." But by the segment's end O'Reilly, truly agitated, couldn't refrain from jabbing at the legendary anchorman. "Now Walter Cronkite, the most trusted news broadcaster in American history [is] embracing every left-wing, crazy theory there is," O'Reilly said, "and now says drug dealers cause little or no harm to others. I mean, it's staggering! It is staggering!"

Cronkite, it seemed, attended more funerals than anyone else in America in the first decade of the twenty-first century. He was always flattered to deliver a eulogy. At the Briscoe Center, there is a fat file of Cronkite-penned "last words" for his friends and colleagues. When Sig Mickelson died in San Diego in 2000, Cronkite flew out to California to console his family. Old Sig had made it to eighty-six, the age at which Cronkite said you could celebrate a death as they do in New Orleans funeral processions: with a blues stomp party. When Ed Bliss, who shared the JFK assassination drama with him, passed away the same year, Cronkite was able to comfort the old CBSer's family with equanimity. He would do the same at Gordon Manning's funeral in September 2006. But when Ed Bradley died at Mount Sinai Hospital in Manhattan on November 9, 2006, from complications of leukemia, Cronkite collapsed at his stricken friend's bedside in grief. Ed was too young to leave the Earth. Cronkite was beyond devastated. During a twenty-six-year stint on *60 Minutes*, Bradley had interviewed everyone in music from Michael Jackson to Bob Dylan to Lena Horne to Ray Charles. Cronkite loved to hear the backstories of those music legends. "For Walter and I," Jimmy Buffett recalled, "losing Ed was impossible to endure. It left us numb."

In July 2006, PBS aired the ninety-minute documentary *Walter Cronkite: Witness to History* (narrated by Katie Couric). The program elegantly drew Cronkite's career into focus. Five months later, Cronkite had a flurry of health scares. On a couple of occasions, his daughter Kathy delivered public speeches he couldn't make. At long last he seemed to have slowed down. A condition called cerebrovascular disease—with symptoms that included personality changes, loss of consciousness, loss of memory, inability to speak, difficulty reading or writing, paralysis of body parts, changes in vision, and strokes—debilitated him physically. You could talk to Cronkite about anything at all: sometimes he'd respond with a non sequitur; at other times, he was completely lucid. Word got around Manhattan that Cronkite had a brain disorder. Newspapers started polishing up Cronkite's obituary. Holing up in the UN Plaza co-op with his two cats, Joanna, close friends, and family, he could tell stories about the Suez Crisis of 1956 but would forget that George W. Bush was the current president. "Sometimes, he would look out the window at the East River," Chip Cronkite recalled, "And say, 'that looks like New York. Not sure.'"

With Cronkite unable to run his calendar properly, needing more downtime than ever before, Marlene Adler, his chief of staff, screened visitors. She warned them that the CBS legend wasn't the bon vivant of old. Sometimes he had a vague, glassy look in his blue eyes—eyes that still viewed the crazy world with bemusement.

On bad days, it took all of Cronkite's concentration just to remember an old CBS colleague's name. Bernard Kalb, like many others, learned the hard way that Cronkite's memory was failing. Kalb recalled going to the May 2006 funeral of Abe Rosenthal, the executive editor of *The New York Times*. Cronkite was also at the service. Although Kalb wasn't personally close to Cronkite, having worked overseas for CBS News for most of the 1960s and '70s, they still had a lot of shared professional experiences. "I went over and said, 'Hi, Walter,'" Kalb recalled. "We shook hands, but he seemed perplexed and doddering. He didn't recognize me from Adam."

By late 2007, ninety-one-year-old Cronkite started contributing weekly editorials to Retirement Living TV, the Columbia, Maryland–based start-up channel where his son Chip worked. An awkward moment occurred at an anti–Iraq War convocation in Chicago in early 2008. With former *Times* (London) editor Harold Evans as moderator, a smart-persons panel was set up. While Cronkite couldn't be in Chicago, he was going to be beamed in from New York via satellite to pronounce his antiwar sentiments. What happened instead was that Cronkite appeared on a big screen furrowing and unfurrowing his brow, unable to hear a thing, desperately trying to get his hearing aid to cooperate.

"It turned into a ghastly moment," Caroline Graham, organizer of the event, recalled. "Harry had to just cut him off and move on." Cronkite understood that his days were numbered. Working with his friend Mike Ashford to establish a National Sailing Hall of Fame in Annapolis, he got testy about groundbreaking delays. "Let's get this thing going," he snapped, "so I can be at the opening."

Cronkite enjoyed staying in his UN Plaza apartment, reading newspapers and surfing the Internet, which offered him a world of information only a mouse click away. People started whispering about his forgetfulness, saying, "I told you so" when they heard he had been diagnosed with a variation of Alzheimer's disease. One afternoon, on a stroll in New York, a woman tapped him and politely said, "Did anyone ever tell you that you look just like Walter Cronkite before he died?"

Cronkite spent the Christmas season of 2008 with Simon, singing carols with her family. In the early winter of 2009, they escaped the New York cold and headed to Palm Beach for sunshine; he used a wheelchair or cane to get around. Back in New York, he and Simon were having dinner with Nick and Nina Clooney one evening. When their son, actor George Clooney, found out, he called the restaurant and surprised them all by picking up the bill. While the patrons at the restaurant recognized Cronkite, none bothered him. But as he left, everybody stood up. "They didn't applaud," George Clooney said, "they just stood up, because that's what you do when a gentleman is leaving the room."

Simon recalled that Cronkite had a real blast in London while making the World War II documentary *Legacy of War* for PBS. From the backseat of his limo, he would call out all his special sights: "That's where I first met Andy. . . . There is where Murrow used to eat. . . . There is the Park Lane Hotel." To Simon, there was a wistful lust in Cronkite wanting to remember the days when, as "Dean of the Air War," he wore the uniform of a United Press war correspondent. Somehow, Cronkite's working on that documentary rejuvenated his flagging memory. At night, Cronkite and Simon would read aloud from a book of extremely X-rated jokes they had purchased during a trip to the British Virgin Islands. "It was hysterical," Simon recalled, "because Walter read them with that serious Voice of the Century of his, as if he were reporting the news."

That April 2009, Tom Shales of *The Washington Post* wrote a wonderful review of Cronkite's *Legacy of War*. Cronkite had teamed up with British TV newsman Alastair Stewart to revisit places he had been from 1941 to 1945. At Nuremberg, TV viewers first saw an old picture of a young Cronkite as Unipresser back in 1945, with heavy earphones, receiving multiple translations of the Nazi war crimes trials. The camera then flashed to the ninety-two-year-old Cronkite, face swollen and teary-eyed. Shales, in his review, tellingly wrote, "It's Uncle no more, he's Grandpa Walter now." When Cronkite discussed the despicable Nazis put on trial in Nuremberg, a wave of anger suddenly flashed out of him. "I wanted to spit on them," he said, telling the viewers that Holocaust denial was a "dangerous crackpot venture." Horrific concentration camp film footage rolled on viewers' TV screens as Cronkite spoke about the extermination camps.

At one point in the hourlong documentary, Cronkite brought the British crew with him to the Cambridge American Cemetery in England, where 3,812 GIs rested in peace. Cronkite wandered respectfully among the Christian crosses and Jewish Stars of David in a scene reminiscent of the close in director Steven Spielberg's film *Saving Private Ryan*. His commentary was crisp as he made his way through the cemetery's white grave markers. But when Cronkite stood and studied a wall where the names of 5,127 GIs missing in action had been inscribed in memoriam, he broke into a gentle weep. "I'm thinking," he said, voice quivering, "my God, my God, my God. It's too damn much."

Epilogue
Electronic Uncle Sam

We have been present at the birth of the nuclear age, the computer age, the space age, the petro-chemical age, the telecommunications age, the DNA age. Together at their confluence flows a great river of change, unlike anything history has encountered before.

—WALTER CRONKITE, *A Reporter's Life*

On July 17, 2009, Walter Cronkite died. He was ninety-two years old. His health had been slipping for weeks. His children, Kathy, Nancy, and Chip, were at his side. Lying next to him were his beloved cats, Blackie and Kisa. "Everybody who loved Dad just surrounded him," Kathy recalled. "He was at peace with everything." During Cronkite's last days, Jimmy Buffett serenaded him at his bedside, strumming his favorite pirate songs on the ukulele like he'd done when Ed Bradley passed. Sometimes a weary and listless Cronkite would hum along, his throat rattling softly. "When we heard that Walter was dying, Mickey Hart and I would go visit him to cheer him up," Buffett recalled. "The music seemed to soothe his soul. He'd smile . . . at peace with the world."

That evening actress Deborah Rush was performing in the Noel Coward play *Blithe Spirit* at the Shubert Theater. A family friend, Angela Lansbury, was the star of the show. As Rush exited the stage, she learned from the security guard that her father-in-law had died. It was all over television. Out of the entire cast, only Lansbury knew she was married to Chip Cronkite.

"Are you all right?" Lansbury asked a numb Rush. "Can you go on?" Rush replied, "Yes, I'll be okay."

At that juncture, actress Jayne Atkinson came over to ask why both women were so downcast.

"Her father-in-law just died," Lansbury said.

"Oh, I'm so sorry," Atkinson said. "Did you know that Walter Cronkite just died, too?"

Everyone, journalists, politicians, astronauts, the Hollywood crowd, all called Cronkite the Most

Trusted Man in America, as if he never had a sur-
name. Basking in the warmth of public affection for
most of his adult life, he was eulogized as a patriarchal
figure, an honored constant at a time when television
had come to epitomize the disposability of American
culture. Entertainment television shows came and went
while Cronkite remained as durable as Plymouth Rock.
Thousands of ham radio operators saluted KB2GSD on
the airwaves; their tribe's chain had lost an important
link. "Cronkite Lives," one operator broadcast in pre-
Twitter fashion upon hearing the news.

The public voted through ratings, but the real
authority in TV was the scope of corporate executives.
If film was a director's medium and theater a writer's
medium, TV spawned business-suited managers with
highfalutin titles such as executive producer, vice president, president, and chairman. It was these corporate
capitalists like Dr. Frank Stanton and Robert Kintner
who set the tempo and taste of the post–World War II
times; their profit-seeking decision making defined
eras in television history.

But in the end, most Americans never heard of
these industry visionaries. Only Cronkite, Uncle
Walter, along with Murrow, earned a respect that
surpassed even that of some U.S. presidents. The
Cronkite brand, to the very end, stood for Straight

News truthfulness against the septic corruption of Vietnam and Watergate. From his CBS anchor chair in New York, one Everyman from St. Joe's, the Western plains, ably summed up a difficult world in a smart thirty minutes at suppertime. Although his trade was objective journalism, his product was fair-mindedness, judicial wisdom, and a moral compass that knew how to decipher right from wrong. "For an entire era," David Shribman insightfully wrote in *The Washington Star*, "Cronkite was—and this is what psychologists say is the greatest tribute to a parent—*there*." He was, as the *Los Angeles Times* and, later, the *Huffington Post* said, *paterfamilias*. "What can you say about him?" Ted Turner shrugged. "The one guy in TV history nobody ever got sick of."

Cronkite's death was a national embarrassment because of how badly TV journalism had fared in his absence. Back in 1978, a reporter for *The New York Times* questioned Cronkite about whether what he did was *really* journalism. Wasn't the essence of TV news *presentation*, not substance? Cronkite, usually jocular, turned defensive. He had helped invent TV news and wanted the medium considered worthy of comparison to Murrow's radio work. "We used to panic over bad notices in the newspapers," he said. "What's changed is that TV news is now respectable in the eyes of news people. We've built our own traditions, our own staffs. We have a self-confidence we didn't have in the beginning."

That was the year Cronkite brought Sadat and Begin together. By the time of his death, television news had been driven into Swamp Hollow because of its abandonment of public service values. With the exception of *60 Minutes*, *The MacNeil-Lehrer NewsHour*, and anything Christiane Amanpour did, there was a diminished return from watching TV news. What had once been just Cronkite making a cameo on *The Mary Tyler Moore Show* had descended into broadcast journalists thinking they were Hollywood celebrities. A cheesy and moronic boom industry, where entertainment imperatives and revenue streams had grown exponentially at the expense of educational television, had eroded the possible role of TV as teacher. More often than not, TV news rang the bells of the least common denominator. The marvel of Telstar in 1962 had turned into an orgy of Colosseum gladiators out for blood in 2009, broadcasters cheering on violence, pestilence, hurricanes, and gotcha moments because they were good for ratings.

In death, Cronkite stood as a defiant monument of what happened when a great news broadcaster had the sound, centrist judgment of the nation at heart.

Cronkite wasn't like ordinary TV narcissists and brag-garts. He didn't broadcast what the folks wanted. Cronkite instead wanted what the people wanted to be considered serious news. The difference was subtle, but sharp. With an inborn optimistic faith in America's constitutional principles, Cronkite ended up *mattering* in the annals of history. Being the CBS News anchor-man wasn't a sacred calling, but a public service. When the Vietnam War and Watergate threatened to tar and feather us all, Cronkite walked the plank for our nation. There was about him, *Texas Monthly* said, "a kind of innate, Calvinist honesty that can't be manufactured or affected, and certainly not perverted." He had become, in the summation of novelist Kurt Vonnegut, "our electronic Uncle Sam."

The Cronkite children held their father's funeral service at St. Bartholomew's Church in Manhattan, where their mother's service had been four years ear-lier. Cremation and a low-key ceremony followed at Kansas City's Mount Moriah Cemetery, attended by Walter and Betsy's surviving relatives and the Barhydt family. Any donations were directed by the family to the Walter and Betsy Cronkite Foundation (with contributions distributed to charities they both had supported). Marlene Adler, Cronkite's chief of staff, began planning his memorial service while handling hundreds of media requests. All the major TV net-works streamed in-depth stories of Cronkite as an eyewitness to history from the D-day landings to the election of Barack Obama. People from every walk of life offered the Cronkite family condolences. "He was the most important voice in our lives for thirty years," said the actor George Clooney. "And that voice made people reach for the stars. I hate the world without Walter Cronkite."

CBS News had properly prepared for the inevitable day of Cronkite's passing, filling the airwaves with well-edited obituaries and sound-bite remembrances for the better part of a week. All Cronkite's old colleagues offered tributes of unextinguishable devotion. From the *60 Minutes* crew, Mike Wallace said on CNN, "It's hard to imagine a man for whom I had more admira-tion." Morley Safer, noting Cronkite's reliable ability to distinguish truth from falsehood, dubbed him "truly the father of television news." Echoing this sentiment was Don Hewitt, Cronkite's first executive producer on the *CBS Evening News* back in 1962. "How many news organizations get the chance," he asked, "to bask in the sunshine of a half century of Edward R. Murrow followed by a half century of Walter Cronkite?"

Katie Couric, who held Cronkite's old dual jobs of *CBS Evening News* anchor and managing editor, spoke movingly about his extraordinary sense of "purpose and compassion," how he never committed a malevolent act. Couric had used Cronkite's recorded voice to introduce her *CBS Evening News* broadcast as an homage to her storied predecessor. (Cronkite's voiceover was not used by Couric's show when broadcasting his funeral.) On her first night as anchor on September 5, 2006, she humbly told viewers that she couldn't come up with a phrase close to match Cronkite's "And that's the way it is." In the end, she didn't dare try to compete with Cronkite, but simply closed with "Thanks for watching."

Barbara Walters used Sirius XM Radio to air a marathon tribute to Cronkite's illustrious broadcast career, based in part on a long interview they recorded around the publication of *A Reporter's Life*. Nobody, Walters believed, knew how to wrangle an interview like "wily old Walter." In a strange way, Walters missed her "infuriating" competitor more than anyone. Even Dan Rather, genuinely distraught, offered heartfelt praise to his old nemesis. "Walter had that ability," Rather told Rachel Maddow on MSNBC, "what we call in television the ability to 'get through the glass,' which is to say he could *connect* with people." Nobody ever felt that Cronkite was reading a TelePrompTer when anchoring. The TV viewer thought of him as a distiller, presenting the strong news reduced to its essence for the home audience. "There was nobody better than him," Rather said. "We had our differences, but my admiration for his accomplishment never wavered."

CBS News' *Face the Nation* did a marvelous job of putting Cronkite's wide-ranging career into focus. Harry Smith guest-hosted the Sunday program, with Bob Schieffer as éminence grise. Together they presented Cronkite as an arranger-editor and maestro of news delivery. He was that rare TV reporter who never tried to put himself over the story. Astronaut John Glenn warmly reminisced on the show about what Cronkite had meant to the Mercury, Gemini, and Apollo space shots: all cheerleader, all optimism, all ready with the hard-earned facts. "I feel like I'm almost sitting in for Wally Schirra this morning," Glenn said in eulogy. "Wally and Walter were a real team on those broadcasts, launch after launch after launch. You just expected to see them both."

Particularly eloquent was Schieffer, who perfectly answered Smith's question of why Americans trusted Cronkite so much. "Because everybody knew that Walter didn't get his suntan in the studio lights," he said. "He got it from being out on the scene, story after story. And that's why you liked to work for Walter. He knew that the news didn't come in over the wire-service machine. That some reporter had to go out there, somebody had to climb up to the top of the city hall steeple to see how tall it was, somebody had to do that. Walter knew how hard it was to get news because he had been there."

Every major TV journalist alive, it seemed, got into the praise-Cronkite action. Just as broadcasters during the Second World War strove to become Murrow Boys on radio, TV broadcasters wanted to be deemed Cronkiters. Tom Brokaw of NBC News, as always, cut to the core of Cronkite adeptly. Pointing out all the awards Cronkite had earned, from an honorary Harvard PhD to the Presidential Medal of Freedom, Brokaw said the accolades never swelled his friend's head. Cronkite was proud, more than anything else, to be a blue-collar reporter. "I always had the feeling," Brokaw insightfully wrote in *Time* magazine, "that if late in life somebody had tapped him on the shoulder and said, 'Walter, we're a little short-handed this week. Think you could help us on the police beat for a few mornings?' He would have responded, 'Boy oh boy— when and where do you want me?'"

Cronkite's death also prompted stories about the passing of the old guard. His storied rivals at NBC— John Chancellor, Chet Huntley, and David Brinkley— were long gone. Most of his great producers—Bud

Benjamin, Ernie Leiser, and Les Midgley—were gone. Roger Mudd's funny notion of the Old Guy Network (OGN News) wasn't even remotely possible anymore. It fell upon Sandy Socolow to be keeper of the Cronkite show's flame. Andy Rooney was still going strong, but when he tried to eulogize Cronkite at St. Bartholomew, he was overcome emotionally. "I feel so terrible about Walter's death that I can hardly say anything," Rooney wept. "He's been such a good friend over the years. Please, excuse me, I can't." Rooney died in 2011.

Mickey Hart of the Grateful Dead correctly asked people not to pigeonhole his friend as one of the old guard only. "He was the original social media guy," Hart explained. "Before Facebook or Twitter people depended on him being nice. Cronkite wanted to make a better, kinder world. He was a voice shaman. He had a powerful aura. The voice, glasses, pipe—they were perfect totems."

It was Cronkite's close personal sailing friends Mike Ashford and Bill Harbach who captured the freewheeling old sailor side of the famed newsman at the New York church memorial. Ashford said that when people asked him what Cronkite was *really* like, the stock answer was, "He's just the way you hope he is." The mourners broke out laughing as Ashford told how free Cronkite was steering the *Wyntje*, shouting, "Sensational!" as waves battered the yawl about. *Vanity Fair* once asked Cronkite what person or thing he'd like to be reincarnated as. Cronkite's answer was "a seagull—graceful in flight, rapacious in appetite." The genius of Cronkite, Ashford believed, was his own hurt for other people's misery. "He had an antenna sensitive to friends' pain," he said. "He knew the words to restore the fun, chase the worry and make things good."

When Harbach took to the altar, he spoke of Cronkite as a "one-off," an absolute original. No one knew how to separate the chaff from the grain quite like Cronkite. Seeing through shell games came naturally to him. Harbach, who had first met Cronkite in the late 1950s as a producer of *The Steve Allen Show*, sat at Cronkite's bedside as he lay dying at UN Plaza, reading him poetry. A favorite of Cronkite's was "Sea Fever," by John Masefield, and Harbach read it at the memorial service, changing the verse to the second person: "You must go down to the seas again, to the lonely sea and sky / And all you ask is a tall ship and a star to steer her by / And the wheel's kick and the wind's song and the white sail's shaking / And a grey mist on the sea's face and a grey dawn breaking."

After the memorial service, CBS News decided to hold a huge public celebration of Cronkite's career in September 2009 (when everyone was back in Manhattan from summer vacation). CEO Les Moonves opened up the CBS checkbook and threw a grand memorial service for Cronkite at Lincoln Center's Avery Fisher Hall. The task of making September 9 a historic event fell squarely on the shoulders of Linda Mason, the CBS News executive who had produced the *Cronkite Remembers* documentary back in 1997. Everyone in America, Mason soon learned, wanted to be part of the Lincoln Center event. A consensus had developed that in the history of broadcasting—both radio and television—nobody could run a big story alone like the Kennedy assassination or Nixon's resignation with Walter Cronkite's even keel. And no one begrudged him what he once told *Vanity Fair* was his greatest achievement: "Helping establish some TV news standards" (even though, as a corollary note, it was also recognized that television had, in the end, with one or two exceptions failed to maintain the Cronkite standard).

The standard was alive and well with Christiane Amanpour. While other broadcasters were lining up their limo rides to Lincoln Center, worried about their paparazzi shots, Amanpour had awoken in her Upper West Side home, gotten dressed, and pedaled her bicycle down Central Park. She wanted to *think* about Cronkite in the natural space. She parked her bike and locked it a couple of blocks away from Lincoln Center.

Cronkite had been amazed back in 1996 about how Amanpour managed to work full-time for CNN and also contribute five global reports for *60 Minutes* each year; he even had a DVD of all her on-air performances delivered to him at UN Plaza. "In my purple suede bolero jacket and black trousers," Amanpour recalled, "I felt like a cross between the Flying Nun and Mary Tyler Moore, but I got there in time."

Amanpour's written diary entry of Cronkite's memorial radiates the kind of warmth, humor, and intellectual reflection Cronkite would have loved reading. Watching a video montage of the great newsman— "This is Walter Cronkite in Paris . . . Moscow . . . the Great Wall of China and Beyond"—caused Amanpour to weep with pride. A journalist truly *could* make a difference in a world gone wrong. To Amanpour, just back in New York from Afghanistan (where she filmed the documentary *Generation Islam* about the lives of young Muslims), Cronkite's life wasn't about anchoring the *CBS Evening News.* He was the quintessential war correspondent of her lifetime. He had become her primary Fountain of Wisdom. No matter if she was covering ethnic cleansing in Bosnia, avoiding rape in Iraq, or comforting children with infectious diseases in Haiti, Amanpour always asked herself the same question: "What would Walter do?"

The answer was to seek the truth, keep people honest, explore the world, and laugh at the absurdity of it all.

Moonves invited President Barack Obama to speak at the memorial. Like everyone else, Obama had "grown up watching Cronkite," and he felt honored to be asked. Not only would the president speak at Lincoln Center, but he also ordered his White House staff to clear his entire afternoon schedule for the commemorative event. While CBS News didn't broadcast the Lincoln Center ceremony, it did stream the program live at the broadcast center on Fifty-seventh Street, via the corporation's internal feed. "Everybody in the building was glued to the ceremony," producer Armen Keteyian recalled. "We were riveted. All the speeches were great, but Obama really hit it out of the park."

To Obama—who stayed for the entire two-and-a-half-hour program—the anchor emeritus represented the high-water mark of TV broadcasting. It was hard, Obama said, to envision a world without Cronkite. "Journalism is more than just a profession," Obama said. "It is a public good vital to our democracy." What Obama respected about Cronkite was that he didn't dumb down news, shout, or act like an angry jackass. The president told the Lincoln Center crowd that

Cronkite was great because he understood that "the American people were hungry for the truth, unvarnished and unaccompanied by theater or spectacle." It was apparent that Obama used the memorial to send a strong message to the fourth estate that the Cronkite standard of clarity and truthfulness needed to be reinstated in a broadcast world where profit-fueled *Inside Edition* sensationalism was king. Obama was echoing what Cronkite himself had told a West Virginia audience earlier in the decade, when he blamed the decline in journalism standards on "mega firms" that viewed news as "just another profit center." Such conglomerates as Disney-ABC-ESPN, NBC-Universal-Telemundo, Time-Warner-CNN, and Rupert Murdoch's News Corp. spelled the end of wire service reporters like Cronkite being in control of the broadcast news centers of America.

Former president Bill Clinton—who sat next to Obama during the service—also spoke at the memorial, telling stories about how Cronkite reached out to him during the dark months of the Lewinsky scandal. Buzz Aldrin recounted that when the *Apollo 11* astronauts were in quarantine in 1969, they watched tapes of Cronkite's CBS moon broadcast to find out how the mission had transpired. "Storytelling was Walter's passion," Aldrin said, "just as flying in space was mine."

Music also conjured up the spirit of Cronkite that day. Trumpeter Wynton Marsalis and the Lincoln Center Jazz Sextet led a raucous New Orleans–style musical procession through the packed hall with horns blaring Dixieland. Mickey Hart used a wooden box as a drum. And Jimmy Buffett stole the day, strumming acoustic guitar and singing "Son of a Son of a Sailor," which Cronkite had adopted as his anthem. The thought of Commodore Cronkite listening to that Buffett song on *Wyntje*'s speaker system, sea breeze spritzing his face, was the lasting image from a day of music and remembrance at Lincoln Center.

The Cronkite attitude, stout and undaunted, combined with bedrock humility and compassion, gave the Missourian the ability to steady uncertain times. At the height of Cronkite's fame as CBS anchorman, he tried to identify that elusive quality in his DNA makeup, that defining ingredient that made him different, and somehow managed to explain it. "There are better writers than me, better reporters, better speakers, better-looking people and better interviewers," he said. "I don't understand my appeal. It gets down to an unknown quality, maybe communication of integrity. I have a sense of mission. That sounds pompous, but I like the news. Facts are sacred. I feel people should know about the world, should know the truth as much as possible. I care about the world, about people, about the future. Maybe that comes across."

In death, Cronkite was viewed as the polar opposite of tabloid news. In a 2001 interview with Larry King on CNN, the anchor emeritus had put his finger exactly on what was wrong with the TV news business. Instead of explaining vital news, networks operated like a pack of wolves, chasing after a tabloid story like Princess Diana's car crash or the O. J. Simpson trial ad nauseam, beating it to death. Cronkite's beef against pack news informed the spirit of Comedy Central's *The Daily Show* with Jon Stewart and *The Colbert Report* hosted by Stephen Colbert. What also worried Cronkite was that U.S. political campaigns were becoming reality shows instead of public teaching endeavors. "Nobody's asked me, which is strange, but I think the networks ought to be doing headlines," Cronkite had told Howard Kurtz of *The Washington Post* in 2007. "Drop that 'Your Pocketbook and Mine,' 'Your Beauty and Mine,' 'Your Garbage Can and Mine.' "

In July 2009, the Cronkite era, from any number of perspectives, ended. In the new world media order of twenty-four-hour cable news, sports, and business networks, and thousands of Internet news sites from the *Daily Kos* to the Drudge Report to the *Huffington Post* to a rushing flood of YouTube videos, there would never be one media voice so trusted again. No anchorman or reporter was likely ever again to command that much authority.

But, in perhaps the most meaningful tribute to Cronkite, CBS News, under the direction of its wunderkind president David Rhodes and veteran executive producer of *60 Minutes* Jeff Fager, started steering the network back to the seriousness of the House of Cronkite days. Not only was the first post-Couric anchorman Scott Pelley of Texas, who was all about hard news and a Cronkite worshiper, but the august Charlie Rose of PBS was also hired to anchor *CBS This Morning*. Cronkite's desk may have been turned to pulp wood, but his old studio's wall-sized Mercator projection of the globe was excavated from a New Jersey storage warehouse. It was reintroduced to the studio at West Fifty-seventh Street to serve as Rose's morning show backdrop. Cronkite would have felt flattered and vindicated.

Unafraid to flag-wave, but uncompromising when it came to exposing societal inequities of any kind, Cronkite, in last analysis, became the TV conscience of cold war America and beyond. His sense of comity at times of national crisis helped guide the country through tumultuous decades. "For a news analyst and reporter of the happenings of the day to be successful, he or she needs three things," Neil Armstrong, the first man to walk on the Moon, said of Cronkite when the anchorman died in 2009. "Accuracy, timeliness, and the trust of the audience." Cronkite had all three.

The essential thrust of Cronkite's life was captured by President Obama in his Lincoln Center eulogy. "He was family," Obama said, speaking as surrogate for millions of Americans. "He invited us to believe in him, and he never let us down."

Acknowledgments

I began this biography at the suggestion of the late David Halberstam. We were driving from New Orleans to Baton Rouge for the Louisiana Book Festival, drinking Starbucks coffee and swapping road stories, just killing time on I-10. Conversation turned to the relationship between the White House press corps and U.S. presidents in the age of television. Somewhere around Gonzales, Halberstam, whose *The Powers That Be* is the classic study of modern U.S. media history, made the bold claim that Walter Cronkite was the most significant journalist of the second half of the twentieth century. He felt that although Ronald Steel had written the definitive *Walter Lippmann and the American Century* and Joseph Persico had excelled with *Edward R. Murrow: An American Original*, no one had adequately tackled the life and times of Cronkite. I was intrigued. A few days later, I made a preliminary call to my agent of twenty-two years, Lisa Bankoff of ICM, to see if there was a Cronkite biography in the publishing world pipeline. She cast a wide net and came back with a no. I was off and running.

By happy coincidence, Cronkite had just donated his extensive papers to the Dolph Briscoe Center for American History at the University of Texas at Austin. Although Cronkite didn't graduate from UT—or any college, for that matter—he had spent two years at the school, from 1933 to 1935, taking classes and working for its student newspaper, *The Daily Texan*. His love for his alma mater was fierce. I telephoned the Briscoe Center's director, Professor Don Carleton, a first-rate historian, about the possibility of writing a biography of Cronkite. He was extremely enthusiastic about the idea. Someone, he believed, needed to take on the massive assignment. It was long overdue.

What made the Cronkite project appealing, other than Halberstam's belief that the CBS newsman was so historically significant, was the fact that the UT trove included such excellent artifacts as Cronkite's dozens of letters home from Europe during World War II; internal CBS memos; production materials from Cronkite series such as *You Are There*, *Eyewitness*, and *The*

Twentieth Century; private photographs document-
ing his early life, his United Press clippings from the
1930s and 1940s, personal scrapbooks and his reportorial notebooks from Vietnam; fan mail dating from
the 1950s to the 1980s; and personal correspondence
with the most famous journalists, political figures, and
entertainers of his day. Because Carleton is trying to
turn the Briscoe Center into a top-tier depository of
new media history, he has recently acquired the papers
of many of Cronkite's friends and colleagues, such
as Andy Rooney, Harry Reasoner, Joe and Shirley
Wershba, Robert Trout, Sig Mickelson, and Morley
Safer, as well. This made for great one-stop shopping.

While working on *Cronkite*, Carleton asked me to
serve as a fellow at UT's Briscoe Center—an honor
I gladly accepted. Office space, as well as a parking
spot, copy machine, and phone service—all the perks
a research scholar needs—were generously provided.
The staff at the Briscoe Center—led by Carleton—is
amazing. Thanks are in order to Margaret "the
Magnificent" Schlankey, Erin Purdy, Brenda Gunn,
Aryn Glazier, Roy Hinojosa, Amy Bowman, Stephanie
Malmros, Evan Hocker, and Teresa Palomo Acosta.
Don's daughter, Aunna Carleton, a close friend of my
family, helped find old *New York Times* stories and
checked out books from UT on my behalf.

In July 2007, I was hired by Rice University as a tenured professor of U.S. history. Every fall semester I teach three courses: History of the Cold War (HIS352); Twentieth-Century Presidents (HIS291); and U.S. Conservation History (HIS425). This leaves me free to research and write from January to August without classroom responsibility. Although Rice is in Houston, I own a home in the foothills of Austin, just a few miles from the Cronkite archive at the University of Texas. I'm frequently shuttling between Austin and Houston along Highway 71 and I-10—a commute of two and a half hours—which can be tedious. To pass the time, I listen to a lot of folk, jazz, and NPR. But there is a wonderful upshot. The Brinkley family can now claim personal friendships in two great communities: Austin (Westlake and Rollingwood) and Houston (River Oaks and West University).

Scores of producers, writers, reporters, executives, and archivists at CBS News are personal friends. They helped me in myriad ways. Bill Felling—the national editor—has been a dear and constant friend. (I hope he listens to the audiobook of *Cronkite* on his commute from New Jersey over the George Washington Bridge to midtown Manhattan.) I'm frequently on the *CBS Evening News with Scott Pelley*, *CBS This Morning* (with Charlie Rose, Erica Hill, and Gayle King), *CBS*

News Sunday Morning (Charles Osgood), and *Face the Nation* (Bob Schieffer). This association has enhanced my understanding of the frenetic work milieu at West Fifty-seventh Street. A special thanks to CBS News president David Rhodes (a Rice alum), Jeff Fager (chairman and executive producer of *60 Minutes*), Al Ortiz, Michelle Miller, Rita Braver, Charles Osgood, Bob Schieffer, David Farber, Jeff Glor, Bill Plante, Jim Axelrod, Byron Pitts, Bob Simon, Betty Nguyen, Steve Kroft, John Dickerson, Lara Logan, Norah O'Donnell, Bob Fuss, and Chip Reid.

To wade into Cronkite leavings in both New York and Austin, I tapped my longtime friend Julie Fenster of New York for assistance. I first met Julie back at *American Heritage* magazine many moons ago, and we have been steadfast allies ever since. She has been my committed partner on this biography, researching obscure facts, helping organize chapters, and offering her shrewd insights into the history of American journalism. Her editorial skills and historical judgment are awesome. I never could have sifted through the seas of Cronkitiana without her. She was indispensable.

Starting in the fall of 2010, Sara Haji, a recent graduate of the University of Texas at Austin, became my personal assistant. Sara, now a law student at the

University of California at Berkeley (and clerking for the Federal Trade Commission during the summers to boot), was recommended to me by my friend Katrina vanden Heuvel of *The Nation* (thank you, Katrina), and was a phenomenal asset. Sara worked with me at the Briscoe Center, rifling through boxes of material, collecting and compiling photos, and setting up interviews (all of which I personally conducted). She ended up naming her white Toyota "Cronkite."

In July 2011, I received amazing assistance from Virginia Northington, a recent graduate of the Plan II Honors program at the University of Texas at Austin. Virginia is blessed with a keen grasp of history, literature, and journalism that belies her young age. Her honors thesis at UT—"Literary Naturalism in the Interwar Novels of Jean Rhys"—is a revisionist study of the distinguished author of *Voyage in the Dark*. With Virginia, there was no learning curve . From the get-go, she helped me transform *Cronkite* from a diffuse first draft into the carefully copyedited final manuscript. Punctual, brilliant, and always in work mode, she made our collaboration one of the high-water marks of toiling on this book. Because Virginia has a great love for marine conservation, I look forward to working with her on *Silent Spring Revolution*, the third volume of my Wilderness Cycle.

A number of students at Rice University likewise pitched in from time to time to help me track down articles on the Internet. A tip of the hat goes especially to Natalie Lazarescou and Irena Popova. My colleagues in the Rice History are hugely supportive of my publishing career. Special thanks to Paula Platt and Rachel Zepeda for keeping our department shop running like Swiss clockwork. Because Cronkite grew up in Houston, I found the morgue at *The Houston Chronicle* (which has *Houston Press* and *Houston Post* clippings) to be a great resource. Special thanks to Jeff Cohen, the *Chronicle*'s executive vice president and editor, and his staff for helping me excavate old Cronkite-related clippings.

During the summer of 2011 I was a research fellow at the W.E.B. Du Bois Institute for African and African American Research at Harvard University. I have historian extraordinaire Henry Louis "Skip" Gates to thank for that.

It should be noted that I knew Walter Cronkite a bit. Along with his wife, Betsy, he attended my New York book party for *Dean Acheson: The Cold War Years, 1953-71* (a revised edition of my Georgetown University PhD dissertation that was published by Yale University Press in 1993). We had lunch a few times at the Century Club and I saw him occasionally at parties in New

York and in Massachusetts. He graciously provided a blurb for one of my books. But we were not close. Only through the intervention of Don Carleton did I get to have dinner with him at his UN Plaza co-op in December 2008, only months before he died. Cronkite knew I was writing his biography, but his brain disorder made it impossible for him to assist me in any substantial way. It didn't seem proper to include my conversations with him as interviews. He is not cited in the notes. Nevertheless, knowing him for over a decade, even a little, helped me better analyze his personality.

A considerable amount of energy was spent interviewing Cronkite's family, friends, and associates. Everyone in journalism, it seems—from Barbara Walters to Ted Turner to Brian Williams to Katie Couric—has riveting Cronkite stories. (See the laundry list of interviews I conducted on page 1404.) All three of Walter and Betsy Cronkite's children—Nancy, Kathy, and Chip—backed my work from the outset. They wanted me to write a truthful biography of their dad, warts and all. A scholar can ask for no more from a subject's family. I'm now close with the entire Cronkite clan (although we have our differences of opinion on a few family matters).

Likewise, Cronkite's significant other for the last years of his life, Joanna Simon, was amazing and forthright about her controversial relationship with the journalism legend. And Cronkite's chief of staff since 1991, the gracious Marlene Adler, served as my switchboard operator, putting me in touch with all kinds of people.

Three of my most helpful sources—Andy Rooney, Jeff Gralnick, and Bob Pierpoint—died while I was writing this biography. I'm sad they didn't get to read the final manuscript. Their observations and insights about Cronkite were crucial.

A special thank-you to Cronkite's longtime producer and friend, Sandy Socolow, is definitely in order. When I started the biography, Sandy came to visit me in Austin. It was the beginning of a productive friendship. We've spoken on the telephone probably one hundred times by now. In a number of key instances, he tracked down an old Cronkite friend for me to interview or found an odd document for me to ponder. Ditto for Cronkite's former scriptwriter Sandor M. Polster and producer Ron Bonn. And Dan Rather, whom Cronkite disliked, nevertheless spent quality time with me explaining all things related to TV news in the 1960s and beyond. He couldn't have been more candid and helpful. The great Roger Mudd is simply a prince.

Another crucial ally was Alfred Robert Hogan, a graduate student at the University of Maryland and a

TV news/space authority. I first met Hogan while signing my book *The Great Deluge: Hurricane Katrina, New Orleans, and the Mississippi Gulf Coast* at the National Book Festival in Washington, D.C. Out of the thin blue sky, Hogan presented me with a Cronkite for President campaign button. That was fun and strange. We exchanged telephone numbers and he mailed me his insightful M.A. thesis "Televising the Space Age—A Descriptive Chronology of CBS News Special Coverage of Space—1957–2003" (2005). Quite graciously, he also shared his own interview transcripts and documents with me. Among his many talents, he has started to compile a much-needed Cronkite broadcastography that attempts to list nearly every TV and radio appearance the icon made in his long public career. Once it's posted online, it will be *the* definitive reference guide on Cronkite.

A number of Cronkite's old friends proofread this book, helping me avoid embarrassing errors. Mervin Block, the great TV scriptwriter, meticulously copyedited chapters with fraternal good cheer. He is a mentoring mensch possessed of a razor-sharp wit and a pitch-perfect Maxwell Perkins pencil. Others who gave the entire manuscript a careful read include Roger Mudd, Bill Small, Chip Cronkite, Kathy Cronkite, Sandy Socolow, Don Carleton, Marlene Adler, and Robert Feder. Various specialists also weighed in on specific chapters: Ron Drez (World War II and Vietnam); Donald Miller of Lafayette College in Easton, Pennsylvania (World War II); Vivian Rogers-Price of the Mighty Eighth Air Force Museum in Savannah, Georgia (World War II); Gary Mack of The Sixth Floor Museum in Dallas, Texas (the JFK assassination); Lew Wood (*Eyewitness* and the JFK assassination); Daniel Ellsberg (Vietnam/Watergate); Don Fulsom (the Nixon administration); Gerald Posner (JFK assassination); Ron Bonn (space and the environment); George Abbey (space); and Bernard Shaw (the 1960s and 1970s).

No words can express how helpful two of the great CBS News correspondents of the Vietnam War era were in helping me understand the "Cronkite Moment." of February 27, 1968. Morley Safer and Jack Laurence are the *best* in the Murrow sense. They read multiple drafts of my Vietnam chapters, made shrewd editorial comments, and helped keep my morale high. My admiration for both men is boundless. I only wish I could have interviewed CBS news producers Ernie Leiser, Bud Benjamin, Sig Mickelson, and Gordon Manning (a close Cronkite friend). But, alas, they have passed.

Alan Weisman shared with me his marvelous 1981 diary from his trip to Sadat's funeral with Cronkite. Christiane Amanpour likewise offered me some personal diary pages. Don Michel, a legendary Illinois radio and television broadcaster, alerted me to the love letters of Cronkite and his high school sweetheart, Bit Winter. (They proved to be quite revelatory.) Brian Williams burned me a copy of the campy 1964 documentary *Anchorman*. The DVD provided an unvarnished look at Cronkite unplugged, cinéma vérité style. Former president of CNN Tom Johnson of Atlanta helped me track down people to interview, and sent me a stream of helpful e-mails. The brilliant Austa Shellace "Shelly" Austin provided essential counsel and suggestions throughout the writing process. And Shelby Coffey of the Newseum was a regular fount of wisdom.

At one juncture, this biography was considerably longer. Determined to keep the page count down to a manageable level, I received critical copyediting help from Trent Duffy of New York and Judith Steen of Santa Cruz. When this book needed hard cuts at the end of the line, Roger Labrie, a fantastic line editor, helped me slash anecdotes and tighten the prose for a final round. My friends Emma Juniper of Arizona and Kristen Hannum of Colorado always worked the graveyard shift on my behalf.

The keeper of the Nixon Tapes, Luke Nichter at Texas A&M University, directed me to relevant Nixon-Colson conversations, thereby saving me untold hours of labor. Everybody at the John Glenn School of Public Policy at the Ohio State University (including Senator Glenn) helped me perfect the Mercury program pages. The Paley Center for Media at 25 West Fifty-second Street has a fine collection of content broadcast on radio and television.

Chris Callahan, dean of the Walter Cronkite School of Journalism and Mass Communication at Arizona State University, provided me with reams of information pertaining to his outstanding program. It's hard to overestimate what a great place the Cronkite School has become for young people to learn the art of TV reporting. The school publishes *The Cronkite Journal*. Melanie Alvarez does a terrific job as executive producer of Cronkite NewsWatch. Aaron Brown, former CNN anchorman, now the Walter Cronkite Professor of Journalism at ASU, offered revelatory commentary to me about his old friend.

My friends at the American Society of News Editors, Carnegie Corporation of New York, National Public Radio, and the John S. and James L. Knight Foundation do so much to keep U.S. journalism history alive and well in America. All these nonprofits deserve our deep gratitude. As does Lally Weymouth of the *Washington Post*, for her stellar Fourth of July parties on the Hamptons.

Mark Updegrove, director of the Lyndon B. Johnson Presidential Library in Austin, helped me track down the original transcripts of the LBJ-Cronkite interviews. Karen Herman of the Archive of American Television in North Hollywood, California, provided me with important documents in their holdings. Gil Schwartz, personal assistant to CBS CEO Les Moonves, was exceedingly helpful on a number of occasions. Michael Freedman allowed me to participate in a very illuminating media conference at George Washington University, along with Marvin Kalb and Sam Donaldson. Freedman is a walking media history encyclopedia who shared numerous documents with me. Phil Gries's privately owned audiotape collection of landmark moments in TV history was a wonderful resource as well. Bill Whitehurst of Austin also deserves special mention for allowing me to use an amazing batch of Cronkite family photos that were originally given to him by Helen Cronkite (the CBS anchorman's mother).

Others on the honor roll include Stephanie Ambrose Tubbs, Debby Applegate, Doris Kearns Goodwin, Cindy Shogan, John Northington, Jim Powers, Bob Armstrong, Linda Aaker, David Friend, Graydon Carter, John Ross, Cullen Murphy, David Leebron, Howard and Suzanne Monsour, Daniel Kirschen,

Kabir Sehgal, Ed Forgotson, Lorrie Beecher, John Cole, Todd and Sharon Kessler, Walter Isaacson, Joe Klein, Frank and Mary Landrieu, Ellen Futter, Mark Madison, Gerry Goldstein, Jessica Yellin, Mary Walsh, Brian Lamb, Laura Leipert, Rachel Sibley, Tom Helf, Jimmy Buffett, Carol Blue, Yvette Vega, Mickey Hart, Jann Wenner, Will Dana, Wynton Marsalis, Jim Irsay, Duvall Osteen, Mac Lehrer, Doug Whitner, Mark Bilnitzer, Dave Morton, Scott O'Neill, Bob Asman, Susan Swain, and John L. Lewis. And to Linton and Jan Weeks (in loving memory of Stone and Holt).

My friends at HarperCollins did a terrific job preparing this biography for publication. President and CEO Brian Murray, a fellow Georgetown University graduate, was hugely supportive of my writing on Cronkite from the outset. Likewise, both publisher Jonathan Burnham and president and publisher Michael Morrison were always steadfast behind the project. The hyper-diligent editor Tim Duggan, a longtime buddy, oversaw all aspects of production. We've become a team with amazing shorthand. I admire him tremendously. He's the modern publishing industry's gold standard of excellence. His facile assistant, Emily Cunningham, operates much like a one-woman assembly line, keeping the process always moving forward with minimal complaints. She is a talented pro. Late in the game Duggan brought in Rob Fleder (freelance editor) to help pare down the manuscript; he was superb. In the production department, David Koral worked diligently with me on a series of draft manuscripts to make this book as error free as possible. He's an accomplished tradesman. Whenever I publish a book, I insist that Kate Blum be the publicist. She makes going on a national tour and doing media appearances fun.

My mother deserves credit for saving drawings I did as a seven-year-old in Atlanta, Georgia, depicting CBS News, Cronkite, and the Vietnam War. They serve as raw testimonials to the impact TV had on young people on the era. When we moved from Georgia to Ohio in 1968, my admiration of Cronkite stayed with me. There is a picture of me in the Bowling Green *Sentinel-Tribune* February 9, 1972, serving as anchorman for "News Six" (sixth-grade news). When asked by the reporter what I wanted to be when I grow up, my answer was "Walter Cronkite" or "a sports announcer." My sister, Leslie Brinkley, has been a TV reporter for ABC affiliate KGO in San Francisco since 1988.

Most of *Cronkite* was written in my home office in Austin. Every Monday to Friday after my wife, Anne, had dropped our three kids at Eanes Elementary School, she returned with breakfast and helped me for hours transcribing interviews and making travel arrangements. Whatever was needed. She is the best. With a surge of blood-pride rising from my heart, I hope our three children—Benton, Johnny, and Cassady—will get to read about the TV broadcaster who meant so much to Dad while he was growing up in Atlanta and northwest Ohio.

—Douglas Brinkley
Austin • Houston • Cambridge • New York
March 5, 2012

SOURCES AND NOTES

The Walter Cronkite Papers at the Dolph Briscoe Center for American History at the University of Texas at Austin are voluminous. They are kept in fairly well-organized files. Cronkite was a Depression-era packrat. He didn't throw out much, so scholars have to pan through the 263 linear feet of the collection to find the gold. Throughout the notes, I refer to this collection as WCP-UTA. It's truly astonishing how many interviews Cronkite gave over the years to reporters. To have cited them all or included them would have been an exercise in futility. The Rosetta Stone of the collection is clearly Cronkite's correspondence with his wife, Betsy, during World War II. Walter Cronkite IV (the anchorman's grandson), a recent graduate of New York University, and history professor Maurice Isserman are editing the correspondence into a book for National Geographic.

Two oral history interviews of Cronkite conducted by Don Carleton were extremely helpful. One was done for the Briscoe Center and the other for the Archive of American Television. Carleton is the co-author of the indispensable *Conversations with Cronkite* (2010). Out of all the books cited in the notes, Cronkite's own *A Reporter's Life* (1996) was by far the most valuable. A full bibliography would be far too long, but all the relevant secondary sources can be found in the notes. Every American should read three wonderful biographies of Murrow: Joseph E. Persico's *Edward R. Murrow: An American Original* (1988); Alexander Kendrick's *Prime Time: The Life of Edward R. Murrow* (1969) and A. M. Sperber's *Murrow: His Life and Times* (1986). In learning about Cronkite my admiration for Murrow grew leaps and bounds.

Stanley Cloud and Lynne Olson's marvelous *The Murrow Boys* (1997) should be mandatory reading in every journalism school and workshop.

Anybody interested in CBS News history should read Sally Bedell Smith's *In all His Glory: The Life of William S. Paley; The Legendary Tycoon and His Brilliant Circle* (1990); Ralph Engelman's *Friendlyvision: Fred Friendly and the Rise and Fall of Television Journalism* (2009); and Paul Gary Gates's *Air Time: The Inside Story of CBS News.* Six memoirs from old CBS News hands deserve special mention: Fred Friendly's *Due to Circumstances Beyond Our Control* (1999); John Laurence's *A Cat from Hue: A Vietnam Story* (2002.); Bill Leonard's *In the Storm of the Eye: A Lifetime at CBS* (1987); Leslie Midgley's *How Many Words Do You Want? An Insider's Story of Print and Television Journalism* (1989); Richard Salant's *Salant, CBS, and the Battle for the Soul of Broadcast Journalism: The Memoirs of Richard S. Salant*, ed. Susan Buzenberg and Bill Buzenberg (1999); and Roger Mudd's *The Place to Be: Washington, CBS, and the Glory Days of Television News* (2008).

The CBS News Reference Library in New York is an amazing depository of all things related to the history of the network. I received dutiful help, time and again, from Cryder Bankes and Carole Parnes. Here is where all of Cronkite's broadcast scripts and logbooks are kept. It's an amazing depository of the history of TV news. In addition to the WCP-UTA and the CBS News Reference Library, the following manuscript collections are important to those interested in Cronkite:

American University—Washington, D.C.
  Ed Bliss, CBS News

Columbia University—New York
  Fred Friendly, CBS News and public broadcasting
  Roone Arledge, ABC News and ABC Sports

Georgetown University—Washington, D.C.
  Frank Reynolds, ABC News

George Washington University—Washington, D.C.
  Richard C. Hottelet, CBS News
  Mutual Radio News holdings

Library of Congress—Washington, D.C.
  Eric Sevareid, CBS News

Lyndon Johnson Library—Austin, Texas
  Lyndon Johnson Papers

New Canaan Public Library—Connecticut
  Richard S. Salant, CBS News and NBC News

Saint Bonaventure University—New York
  Douglas Edwards, CBS News

Smith College—Massachusetts
    Pauline Frederick, ABC News and NBC News

Syracuse University—New York
    Mike Wallace, non-CBS interview material from
1959–1961

Tufts University—Massachusetts
    Edward R. Murrow, CBS News

University of Maryland—College Park
    Arthur Godfrey, CBS
    Neil Strawser, CBS News
    Plus the National Public Broadcasting Archives and
the Westinghouse Radio Archives

University of Michigan—Ann Arbor
    Mike Wallace, CBS News

University of North Carolina—Chapel Hill
    Charles Kuralt, CBS News
    Nelson Benton, CBS News

University of Wisconsin/Wisconsin Historical
Society—Madison
    Robert W. Asman, CBS News and NBC News
    Burton Benjamin, CBS News
    Jules Verne Bergman, CBS News and ABC News
    David Brinkley, NBC News and ABC News

Charles Collingwood, CBS News
John Charles Daly, ABC News
Chet Huntley, NBC News
H. V. Kaltenborn, NBC News and others
Edward P. Morgan, ABC News
Robert Pierpoint, CBS News
David Schoenbrun, CBS News
Howard K. Smith, CBS News and ABC News
Av Westin, CBS News and public broadcasting
Perry Wolff, CBS News

University of Wyoming—Laramie
Reid Collins, CBS News
Hugh Downs, NBC News, ABC News, and public
broadcasting

Washington and Lee University—Lexington, Virginia
Roger Mudd, CBS News and NBC News

Washington State University—Pullman
Edward R. Murrow, CBS News

Private Collections
Robert W. Asman—Washington, D.C.
William "Bill" Small—New York
Alfred Robert Hogan—Washington, D.C.
Bernard Shaw—Washington, D.C.
Ron Bonn—San Diego

Don Michel—Anna, Illinois

Robert Feder—Highland Park, Illinois

Michael Freedman—Washington, D.C.

Mervin Block—New York

John Laurence—Haslemere, United Kingdom

Morley Safer—New York

Lew Wood—Los Angeles

Brian Williams—New York

Sandy Socolow—New York

Alan Weisman—New York

Tom Johnson—Atlanta

Kay Barnes—Kansas City

Linda Ann Mason—New York

Christiane Amanpour—New York

Biographical Glossary

Adler, Marlene: Cronkite's chief of staff from 1991 until his death in 2009. She managed his post–CBS News career and was his adviser, confidante, and friend.

Aldrin, Buzz (1930–): NASA lunar module pilot of *Apollo 11*. In 1969 he became the second man to walk on the Moon after following Neil Armstrong out of the *Eagle* module to collect lunar samples.

Alter, Jonathan (1957–): Editor of *Newsweek* magazine from 1983 to 2011. After interviewing Cronkite for *Rolling Stone* in 1987, Alter became good friends with the anchorman and his wife.

Anders, William (1933–): NASA lunar module pilot of *Apollo 8*. He flew, along with Frank Borman and Jim Lovell, around the Moon ten times on Christmas Eve 1968.

Arledge, Roone (1931–2002): Chairman of ABC News from 1977 until his retirement in 1988. Arledge created *20/20* and *World News Tonight* for the network and was responsible for wooing David Brinkley from NBC to ABC in 1981.

Armstrong, Neil (1930–): NASA commander of *Apollo 11.* In 1969 he became the first man to walk on the Moon. After stepping out of the *Eagle* and onto the Moon, he uttered the famous line "That's one small step for man, one giant leap for mankind."

Ashford, Mike (1938–): Longtime owner of McGarvey's Saloon and Oyster Bar in Annapolis, Maryland, and Cronkite's frequent sailing companion from the 1980s onward.

Asman, Bob (1926–): Producer of CBS's *The Twentieth Century* from 1957 to 1961 and producer of special-events coverage for NBC News until his retirement in 1993.

Barnes, Ben (1938–): Former Speaker of the Texas House of Representatives from 1965 to 1969, lieutenant governor of Texas from 1969 to 1973, and lifelong friend of Walter Cronkite.

Barnes, Kay (1938–): Walter Cronkite's cousin. Cronkite helped Barnes campaign to become the first female mayor of Kansas City, Missouri, in 1999. She won the election and served as mayor from 1999 to 2007.

Bleckman, Izzy: CBS cameraman who worked with Cronkite for years. He accompanied Cronkite on his 1972 trip to China (as part of the Nixon administration's press pool) and worked on *Universe*. Bleckman also served as Charles Kuralt's cameraman for the entirety of his "On the Road" run.

Benjamin, Burton (1917–1988): Longtime writer, director, and producer for CBS News, where he worked for twenty-nine years until his retirement in 1985. He served as executive producer of the *CBS Evening News* from 1975 to 1978, collaborated with Walter Cronkite on *The Twentieth Century*, and was tasked with the internal investigation of the *CBS Reports* documentary "The Uncounted Enemy: A Vietnam Deception" in 1983.

Bernstein, Carl (1944–): Journalist who, along with Bob Woodward, did the most important news reporting on Watergate for *The Washington Post*. Cronkite relied on Bernstein and Woodward's investigative work during Watergate for his own *CBS Evening News* broadcasts.

Bibb, Porter (1937–): Former White House correspondent for *Newsweek* and the first publisher of *Rolling Stone* magazine.

Bliss, Ed (1912–2002): A second-generation member of the Murrow Boys and news editor for Edward R.

Murrow, Fred W. Friendly, and Walter Cronkite during Cronkite's twenty-five-year career at CBS.

Bonn, Ron (1930–): Journalist who served as senior producer of the *CBS Evening News with Walter Cronkite* for five years (most notably during its coverage of the Apollo missions and the 1968 Chicago convention protests) and helped to create *Universe*. Bonn worked for NBC News for twelve years and helped produce the Cronkite reports *The Drug Dilemma: War or Peace?* and *Family Matters: Or Does It?* for the Discovery Channel.

Bradley, Ed (1941–2006): CBS correspondent from 1967 until his death in 2006. He was hired by Bill Small to work at CBS's WTOP in Washington, D.C., in 1974 and reported for *60 Minutes* for over two decades (beginning when Dan Rather left the program to anchor the *CBS Evening News* in 1981).

Braver, Rita (1948–): CBS News correspondent hired by CBS's Washington, D.C., bureau in 1972 and a friend of Walter Cronkite. She, along with producer Bud Benjamin, accompanied Cronkite to a memorable 1977 inaugural ball in which he forgot his tickets.

Brinkley, David (1920–2003): Newscaster for NBC and ABC from 1943 to 1997. Brinkley cohosted *The Huntley-Brinkley Report* on NBC from 1956 until 1970.

Brokaw, Tom (1940–): Newscaster for NBC who hosted the *Today* show from 1976 to 1982 and the *NBC Nightly News* from 1982 to 2004.

Brown, Aaron (1948–): ABC correspondent from 1991 to 1999 and host of CNN's *NewsNight with Aaron Brown* from 2001 to 2005. He is best known for his coverage of the September 11 attacks, which occurred on his first day on air at CNN (and which Cronkite watched from Rome as the events unfolded).

Buchanan, Pat (1938–): Opposition researcher and speechwriter for the Nixon administration from 1966 to 1974. In 1973, Pat Buchanan's brother, Henry, sued CBS News for libel after the *CBS Evening News* aired a story accusing him of laundering money for the Nixon administration.

Buffett, Jimmy (1946–): Famous singer-songwriter and close friend of Cronkite's. He sang and played the ukulele for Cronkite in his final days and performed at his Lincoln Center memorial.

Carleton, Don (1947–): Executive director of the University of Texas at Austin's Dolph Briscoe Center for American History (the site of Cronkite's archive) and author of *Conversations with Cronkite*. He conducted a sixty-hour oral history interview with Cronkite in the 1990s that formed the basis of *Conversations* as well as Cronkite's memoir, *A Reporter's Life*.

Chung, Connie (1946–): CBS correspondent hired by Bill Small to work in the Washington bureau in 1971. She left CBS in 1983 to become an anchor on NBC, but returned to CBS in 1989 to co-anchor the *CBS Evening News* with Dan Rather until 1995.

Collingwood, Charles (1917–1985): CBS correspondent and host of *Eyewitness to History.* Collingwood was one of the Murrow Boys and the first U.S. reporter allowed into North Vietnam during the Vietnam War.

Collins, Michael (1930–): NASA command module pilot of *Apollo 11.* In 1969 he orbited the Moon in *Columbia* while Neil Armstrong and Buzz Aldrin made the first-ever landing on the surface of the Moon.

Colson, Charles (1931–): Special counsel to Richard Nixon from 1969 to 1973. Colson is heard frequently on the Nixon White House tapes, discussing Cronkite's coverage of the president and the Vietnam War. Colson served a prison sentence in 1974 for obstruction of justice in the Daniel Ellsberg case and went on to found the Prison Fellowship Ministries in 1976.

Cooper, Gordon (1927–2004): One of seven astronauts selected for NASA's Project Mercury. Cooper piloted *Mercury-Atlas 9* in 1963, spending more than thirty-four hours in space and orbiting Earth twenty-two times.

Couric, Katie (1957–): Broadcast journalist who co-anchored the *Today* show with Matt Lauer from 1991 to 2006 and often contributed to *Dateline NBC*. She replaced Dan Rather as the anchor of the *CBS Evening News* in 2006, but left the program in 2011 to develop her own daytime talk show for ABC.

Cronkite, Betsy Maxwell (1916–2005): Cronkite's wife, a graduate of the University of Missouri and a former journalist at the *Kansas City Journal-Post*. Betsy Maxwell and Walter Cronkite met in 1936 while both were working at KCMO, and they wed in 1940. They were married for almost sixty-five years and had three children together.

Cronkite, Helen Fritsche (1892–1993): Walter Cronkite's mother. Walter maintained a very close relationship with his mother throughout his life, especially after she filed for a divorce from his father in 1932.

Cronkite, Mary Kathleen (1950–): Walter Cronkite's second child, known as Kathy. An actress and author, she married lawyer Bill Ikard in 1980. The couple have two children, William Ikard and Jack Ikard.

Cronkite, Nancy Elizabeth (1948–): Walter Cronkite's first child. A yoga teacher.

Cronkite, Walter Sr. (1893–1973): Walter Cronkite's father. Walter Cronkite Sr., a dentist, and Helen Fritsche were married in 1915. They divorced in 1932 as a result of his alcoholism. Walter Cronkite's relationship with his father was strained for many years following his parents' divorce.

Cronkite, Walter III (1957–): Walter Cronkite's son, known as Chip. He and actress Deborah Rush married in 1985 and have two sons together, Walter Cronkite IV and Peter Cronkite. He was a founding producer of Cronkite, Ward and started Cronkite Productions.

Cronkite, Walter IV (1988–): Son of Walter Cronkite III and Deborah Rush and grandson of legendary newsman Walter Cronkite. He was hired by CBS's Washington, D.C., bureau as a broadcast associate in 2011.

Edwards, Douglas (1917–1990): First American network news anchor, anchoring *Douglas Edwards with the News* (later known as the *CBS Evening News*) from 1948 to 1962. Edwards was Walter Cronkite's predecessor and eventually moved back to CBS Radio.

Ellsberg, Daniel (1931–): Rand Corporation analyst who leaked the Pentagon Papers to various newspapers in 1971. Ellsberg sat down with Cronkite for a CBS News exclusive interview in June of that year, a move that was met with harsh criticism from the Nixon administration.

Fager, Jeffrey (1954–): Longtime CBS News executive. Fager served as the executive producer of the *CBS Evening News with Dan Rather* from 1996 to 1998 and then as executive producer of *60 Minutes* from 2004 to 2011, when he was named the first ever chairman of CBS News.

Feder, Robert (1956–): Founder of the Walter Cronkite Fan Club, who began a lifelong friendship with Cronkite. From 1980 to 2008, Feder was the TV/radio columnist at *The Chicago Sun-Times.* He is now the media critic for *TimeOut Chicaago.*

Freedman, Mike (1952–): Former reporter for *CBS World News Round-Up* and general manager of CBS Radio News. As general manager of CBS Radio News he produced the thirty-part series "Walter Cronkite's Postscripts to the 20th Century" and suggested that Cronkite announce the news of the Clinton impeachment verdict on CBS Radio in 1998.

Friendly, Fred (1915–1998): CBS News president from 1964 to 1966. Friendly and Edward R. Murrow created the documentary television program *See It Now.* He advanced public broadcasting, was integral to the establishment of PBS, and resigned from CBS in 1966 when the network replaced U.S. Senate hearings about the Vietnam War with an episode of *I Love Lucy.*

Gralnick, Jeff (1939–2011): Journalist who held major roles at CBS, NBC, and ABC. He was a founding producer of CBS's *60 Minutes,* reinvented the *NBC Nightly*

News, and produced news coverage for all NASA missions through *Apollo 11*.

Hart, Mickey (1943–): Drummer for the Grateful Dead from 1967 to 1971 and 1974 to 1995. Hart and Cronkite became close friends after Hart was assigned to score a documentary Cronkite was working on about the America's Cup. Hart performed, along with Jimmy Buffett, at Cronkite's memorial service at Lincoln Center in 2009.

Hewitt, Don (1922–2009): CBS television executive and producer of *60 Minutes*. He set an important precedent in 1960 by producing the first televised presidential debates.

Hottelet, Richard (1917–): Correspondent for United Press during World War II and one of the Murrow Boys. Murrow hired Hottelet to work at CBS in 1944. He remained with the network for forty-one years.

Huntley, Chet (1911–1974): Newscaster for NBC from 1955 to 1970. He hosted *The Huntley-Brinkley Report* from 1956 until his retirement in 1970.

Johnson, Tom (1941–): Executive vice president of LBJ's Texas Broadcast Corporation who allowed Cronkite to break the story of President Johnson's death in 1973. After LBJ's death, he served as president and publisher of the *Los Angeles Times* and then as president of CNN from 1990 to 2001.

Kalischer, Peter (1915–1991): CBS correspondent from 1957 to 1978. Kalischer won the Overseas Press Club award in 1963 for his coverage of the military coup that killed Ngo Dinh Diem, the president of South Vietnam.

Kuralt, Charles (1934–1997): CBS writer from 1957 to 1959 and correspondent from 1959 until his retirement in 1994. His is best known for his "On the Road" segments, which appeared on the *CBS Evening News with Walter Cronkite* beginning in 1967, and as the first anchor of *CBS Sunday Morning*, a position he held from 1979 to 1994.

Laurence, John (1940–): CBS News correspondent who covered the Vietnam War from 1965 to 1970. Cronkite regarded Laurence, who wrote *The Cat from Hué*, about his experiences in Southeast Asia, as one of the best reporters of the conflict.

Leiser, Ernest (1921–2002): Reporter and producer for CBS who helped the network in its expansion to television. He was key in selecting Cronkite as anchor for the *CBS Evening News*.

Leonard, Bill (1916-1994): CBS executive who oversaw the network's 1964 election coverage as head of a specially created Elections Unit before serving as president of CBS News from 1979 to 1982.

LeSueur, Larry (1909–2003): Correspondent for United Press during much of the 1930s and a CBS correspondent from 1939 until 1963. As one of the Murrow Boys, LeSueur covered the major events of World War II from Europe.

Lippmann, Walter (1889–1974): Journalist and author whose nationally syndicated column "Today and Tomorrow" won two Pulitzer Prizes. Cronkite read Lippmann's work while living in Houston in the 1930s and interviewed him in 1961 for a *CBS Reports* special.

Lumet, Sidney (1924–2011): Academy Award–winning director of *Network*, one of Cronkite's favorite movies. Lumet worked with Cronkite on *You Are There*, the historical reenactment TV series, from 1953 to 1957.

Manning, Gordon (1917–2006): Writer for *Newsweek* and later executive for CBS News from 1964 to 1974, where he was responsible for the Tiffany Network's reporting of Watergate, Vietnam, and Nixon's 1972 trip to China.

Midgley, Leslie (1915–2002): Executive producer of the *CBS Evening News* from 1967 to 1972. He produced many other CBS programs and won multiple Peabody and Emmy awards for his work.

Moonves, Les (1949–): Longtime CBS executive who became president of CBS Entertainment in 1995, president and CEO of CBS Television from 1998 to 2003, and chairman and CEO of CBS Corporation in 2003. His friendship with Cronkite ended the anchorman's years of relative inactivity at CBS beginning in 1995.

Mudd, Roger (1928–): Correspondent for CBS from 1961 to 1980. After Dan Rather was chosen to replace Walter Cronkite on the *CBS Evening News*, he left to join NBC News. During his tenure with NBC, Mudd served as co-anchor of the *NBC Nightly News* and co-moderator of *Meet the Press*.

Murrow, Edward R. (1908–1965): American broadcast journalist with CBS who came to prominence during World War II. He is noted within the field for his honesty and integrity and was instrumental in the censure of Senator Joseph McCarthy.

Paley, William "Bill" (1901–1990): Developer of the CBS radio and television networks. Starting with a collection of sixteen affiliates, he built CBS into a network that could compete with NBC by creating an independent news division in 1934, hiring Edward R. Murrow as director of talks in 1935, and promoting Frank Stanton to president of CBS in 1946.

Pierpoint, Robert (1925–2011): CBS News White House correspondent who covered six administrations (Eisenhower, Kennedy, Johnson, Nixon, Ford, and Carter) and was a part of the second generation of Murrow Boys.

Polster, Sandor M. (1942–): Reporter for the AP and *The New York Post* from 1967 to 1973, writer for *CBS Evening News* from 1973 to 1985, news editor for *NBC Nightly News* from 1986 to 1993, visiting lecturer to Colby College in 2004, and student adviser at Bowdoin College from 1999 to 2010.

Rather, Dan (1931–): CBS News correspondent from 1963 to 2006. He succeeded Walter Cronkite as anchor of the *CBS Evening News* in 1981, a position he held until 2005.

Rooney, Andy (1919–2011): Writer for *Stars and Stripes* during World War II and longtime CBS News commentator. Rooney became famous for his "A Few Minutes with Andy Rooney" segment on *60 Minutes* and was Cronkite's frequent tennis partner and longtime friend.

Safer, Morley (1931–): CBS News correspondent since 1964. He angered the Johnson administration with his broadcast about a search-and-destroy mission carried out by U.S. Marines on the village of Cam Ne and became notable throughout the conflict in Vietnam for his war reporting. Morley has hosted *60 Minutes* since 1970, when he replaced Harry Reasoner.

Salant, Richard "Dick" (1914–1993): CBS executive from 1952 to 1979. As president of CBS's news division, he built the *CBS Evening News* into a vehicle that could compete with the wildly popular *Huntley-Brinkley Report*, primarily by replacing Douglas Edwards with Cronkite in 1962.

Salinger, Pierre (1925–2004): Press secretary to JFK and LBJ. Salinger interfered in Cronkite's 1963 interview with JFK for the *CBS Evening News* in such a way that Cronkite's journalistic integrity was compromised, resulting in bad blood between the two men until the president was assassinated later that same year.

Schieffer, Bob (1937–): CBS News correspondent since 1969. He anchored the Saturday edition of the *CBS Evening News* from 1973 to 1966 and has moderated *Face the Nation* since 1991.

Schirra, Walter "Wally" (1923–2007): One of seven astronauts selected for NASA's Project Mercury. As one of the "Mercury Seven," Schirra orbited Earth six times in the *Sigma 7* spacecraft in 1962 as part of the manned space mission Mercury-Atlas 8. He was the commander of *Apollo 7* and served as a news consultant for the subsequent Apollo missions. In this capacity, he co-anchored the *Apollo 11* moon landing with Cronkite.

Schorr, Daniel (1916–2010): CBS News correspondent from 1953 to 1976. He won three Emmy Awards while at CBS and famously read Nixon's Enemies List (including his own name) on live television. After resigning from CBS in 1976, Schorr served as a news analyst for CNN from 1979 to 1985 and then as senior news analyst for NPR until his death in 2010.

Sevareid, Eric (1912–1992): CBS News correspondent from 1939 to 1977. He famously covered the surrender of France and the London blitz during World War II as a Murrow Boy and won several Emmy and Peabody awards for the two-minute segments he made for the *CBS Evening News* with Cronkite from 1964 until his retirement from CBS in 1977.

Shadel, Willard Franklin "Bill" (1908–2005): CBS Radio correspondent from 1943 to 1957 and ABC correspondent from 1960 until his retirement from broadcasting in 1975. He covered World War II for Edward R. Murrow before working at WTOP for the decade following the war. At ABC, Shadel replaced John Daly as the anchor of the network's evening news show, moderated the third presidential debate between Nixon and JFK in 1960, and covered John Glenn's Mercury-Atlas 6 flight in 1962.

Shaw, Bernard (1940–): Broadcast journalist for CBS News from 1971 to 1977 and for CNN from 1980 until his retirement in 2001. As a corporal in the U.S. Marines, Shaw met Cronkite, his idol, and expressed a desire to become a news anchor. After corresponding with Cronkite throughout his education at the University of Illinois–Chicago, Shaw became his colleague when he was hired by Bill Small in 1971 to work in CBS's Washington, D.C., bureau.

Shepard, Alan, Jr. (1923–1998): One of the seven astronauts selected for NASA's Project Mercury. Shepard became the first American to travel to space in 1961 when he piloted the *Freedom 7*, an event covered by Cronkite for CBS. He commanded *Apollo 14* in 1971, becoming the fifth person to walk on the Moon.

Shirer, William L. (1904–1993): CBS correspondent from 1937 to 1947 who worked closely with Edward R. Murrow to report on World War II from Europe. He left CBS after a public falling-out with Murrow and went on to publish the wildly successful *The Rise and Fall of the Third Reich: A History of Nazi Germany* in 1960.

Simon, Bob (1941–): CBS News correspondent since 1967. Simon has been a *60 Minutes* correspondent since 1996 and was won twenty-four Emmys, two Peabodys, and five Overseas Press Club Awards for his foreign reporting. He was Cronkite's favorite.

Simon, Joanna (1940–): Opera singer and real estate broker who began dating Cronkite after their respective spouses died within a year of each other. They were together from 2005 until Cronkite's death in 2009.

Small, William "Bill" (1926–): CBS News Washington bureau chief from 1961 to 1974 (during which time he hired Lesley Stahl, Connie Chung, and Bernard Shaw) and CBS senior vice president for news from 1974 to 1979. He left CBS to become president of NBC in 1979. After failing to overtake CBS in the nightly news ratings, Small was forced to resign in 1982.

Socolow, Sandy: Longtime producer of Walter Cronkite who was with CBS News from 1956 to 1988. He produced political convention coverage from 1960 to 1980, the *CBS Evening News* (under Cronkite and Rather), and CBS News coverage of NASA's various manned space programs. He was a founding producer of Cronkite, Ward from 1993 to 1997 and worked for Cronkite Productions from 1998 to 2002.

Stahl, Lesley (1941–): CBS News correspondent since 1972. She moderated *Face the Nation* from 1983 to 1991 and has reported for *60 Minutes* since 1991.

Stanton, Frank (1908–2006): President of CBS from 1946 to 1971, a period of significant growth for the network. Believing that the television networks had a public service duty, he helped orchestrate the first televised presidential debate in 1960 and risked going to jail for his role in the 1971 *CBS Reports* documentary "The Selling of the Pentagon."

Trout, Robert (1909–2000): Longtime CBS broadcaster who coached Edward R. Murrow for his career in radio and hosted the "European News Round-Up" for CBS immediately following the *Anschluss* in 1938. After Cronkite's ratings for the coverage of the 1964 Republican Convention came in behind Chet Huntley and David Brinkley's, Trout was called in to anchor the Democratic gathering. When he also failed to beat the NBC dream team, Cronkite was permitted to remain as the host of the *CBS Evening News.*

Turner, Ted (1938–): Media tycoon who founded TBS in 1976 and CNN in 1980. He made a failed attempt to buy CBS in 1985. Cronkite was a fan of CNN and even covered John Glenn's return to space for the network in 1998.

Vitarelli, Bob (1930–): Longtime friend of Cronkite's and decades-long employee of CBS. He started out in the CBS mail room in 1953 and eventually worked his way up to be named the director of the *CBS Evening News* under Cronkite and of *Face the Nation.*

Wallace, Mike (1918–2012): CBS correspondent and close friend of Cronkite who hosted an early iteration of the *CBS Morning News* from 1963 to 1966 and reported for *60 Minutes* from its inception in 1968 to his semiretirement in 2006.

Walters, Barbara (1929–): Broadcast journalist who got her start writing copy for CBS's *The Morning Show* (hosted by Walter Cronkite) and subsequently anchored NBC's *Today* show from 1961 to 1976, the *ABC Evening News* from 1976 to 1978, *20/20* from 1984 to 2004, and *The View* since 1997.

Ward, Jonathan: Producer of the *CBS Evening News* during the Cronkite years and founding partner of Cronkite, Ward, and Company, which produced hours of documentary footage for PBS and the Discovery Channel.

Weisman, Alan (1950–): Longtime producer, senior producer, and executive producer at CBS News, Time-Warner, PBS, and ABC who accompanied Cronkite to Cairo in 1981 to help CBS News cover the assassination of Anwar Sadat.

Wenner, Jann (1946–): Founder of *Rolling Stone* magazine who became friends with Cronkite during the anchorman's retirement from the *CBS Evening News*.

Wershba, Joseph (1920–2011): CBS News journalist from 1944 to 1988. He worked with Cronkite at WTOP in the 1950s and was one of the original producers of *60 Minutes*. Wershba and his wife, Shirley, helped Cronkite prepare his memoirs in the 1980s.

Wershba, Shirley: CBS producer and wife of Joseph Wershba who helped Cronkite ready *A Reporter's Life* for publication.

Weymouth, Lally (1943–): Daughter of Katharine and Philip Graham, publishers of *The Washington Post*, who conducted an interview with Cronkite in 1981 about his "Report from Vietnam"; she is now senior associate editor of the *Post*.

Zenker, Arnold (1938–): Manager of news programming for CBS in 1967 when he was asked to fill in for Walter Cronkite on the *CBS Evening News* during an AFTRA strike that lasted thirteen days.

Notes

Prologue

2 **"The actual crisis is upon":** Kurt Vonnegut, "A Reluctant Big Shot," *The Nation*, March 7, 1981.

4 **Cronkite trained himself to speak:** David Hinckley, "Walter Cronkite Remains Gold Standard for Journalists," *New York Daily News*, July 18, 2009.

4 **"God, mother, the American flag":** Harold Jackson, "The Age of Cronkite," *World Press Review*, April 1981, p. 46.

5 **"the calm eye of the newsgathering storm":** Doug James, *Walter Cronkite: His Life and Times* (Brentwood, TN: JM Press, 1991), p. 4.

5 **"I never spent any time examining my navel":** Walter Cronkite and Don Carleton, *Conversations*

with Cronkite (Austin: Center for American History, University of Texas at Austin, 2010), p. 7.

6 **"It can be said of three men":** John J. O'Connor, "Exit Cronkite, a Conscientious Superstar of TV News," *New York Times*, March 8, 1981.

6 **"He had the voice, calmness, and organic writing style":** Author interview with Roger Ailes, October 26, 2011.

7 **"Cronkite has the capacity to make people believe":** "1981: A Conversation with Fred Friendly," *Nieman Reports* (Winter 1999–2000), http://nieman.harvard.edu/reports/article/102 063/1981-A-Conversation-With-Fred-Friendly .aspx.

7 **"I don't suppose you'll see another Cronkite":** "1981: A Conversation with Fred Friendly," *Nieman Reports,* (Winter 1999–2000).

8 **"I guess Dad is leaving us":** Mary Battiata, "Anchor's Away," *Washington Post*, March 7, 1981.

8 **"In many countries during four such traumatic days":** "1981: A Conversation with Fred Friendly," *Nieman Reports* (Winter 1999–2000).

9   **"You've always been a pro":** "Ronald Reagan: Excerpts from an Interview with Walter Cronkite of CBS News," March 3, 1981, John T. Woolley and Gerhard Peters, *The American Presidency Project*, http://www.presidency.ucsb.edu/ws/index .php?pid=43497#axzz1hm0H9919 (accessed September 5, 2011).

9   **The banner read, "After Cronkite":** H. F. Waters, "After Cronkite," *Newsweek*, March 9, 1981.

9   **"Introducing Our Newest Correspondent":** William Leonard, *In the Storm of the Eye: A Lifetime at CBS* (New York: Putnam, 1987), p. 226.

10 **"Thank you, Walter" ads:** Steven Reddicliffe, "Tonight Cronkite Is the Big Story," *Miami Herald*, March 6, 1981.

10 **more media attention was being paid to Cronkite's departure:** "Cronkite Leaves as Anchorman," Sentinel Wire Services, March 7, 1981.

10 **"he looks like everyone's dentist":** Cleveland Amory, "What Walter Cronkite Misses Most," *Parade Magazine*, March 11, 1984, p. 4.

11 **"When it no longer appears at the anchor desk":** Mark Crispin Miller and Karen Runyon,

"And That's the Way It Seems," *New Republic*, February 14, 1981.

11 **Cronkite's wife, children, and agent watched the public adieu:** Tom Shales, "Anchor's Away: A Farewell from Walter Cronkite's Sign Off," *Washington Post*, March 7, 1981.

12 **"And that's the way it is":** Tony Schwartz, "Amid the Fuss, Cronkite Says a Quiet 'Good Night,'" *New York Times*, March 7, 1981.

12 **"As a parting gesture":** Nine-part oral history of James Wall, Television Academy Foundation's Archive of American Television, http://www.emmytvlegends.org/interviews/people/james-wall (accessed July 5, 2011).

12 **"School's out!":** Shales, "Anchor's Away."

One: MISSOURI BOY

16 **"My father and I went up in an old Curtiss-Wright":** David Friend, "Space Shuttle: Interview with Walter Cronkite," *Life*, August 9, 1984 (unpublished), David Friend Archive, Garden City, NY (hereafter Friend Archive).

16 **"begin with ancestors":** Clarence Darrow, *The Story of My Life* (New York: Charles Scribner's Sons, 1932), p. 1.

17   "We Dutch are a very pragmatic people": Walter Cronkite, "200th Anniversary of Friendship and Unbroken Diplomatic Relations with the Netherlands," August 18, 1981 (script draft), Box: M630, Folder: Dutch Filming, Walter Cronkite Papers, University of Texas at Austin (hereafter WCP-UTA).

17   Cronkite's pride in his Dutch heritage: Author interview with Kathy Cronkite, March 22, 2010.

18   "our Dutch ancestry is a valued legacy": Ibid.

19   Even Coca-Cola had to stop: David Dary, *Frontier Medicine: From the Atlantic to the Pacific* (New York: Knopf, 2008), pp. 271–302.

19   Honest and scrupulous, Dr. Cronkite made: James, *Walter Cronkite*, p. 20.

19   "Office and Cabatory of Dr. F. P. Cronkite": *Items of Interest: A Monthly Magazine of Dental Art, Science and Literature* 21 (1899): 586.

20   He and his wife, Anna, enjoyed a spacious home: George Gurley, "And Now the Newsman," *Kansas City Star*, January 30, 1997.

21   Helen Fritsche, a Kansas girl: "Helen F. Cronkite, 101, Mother of TV Anchor," *Washington Times*, November 11, 1993.

22 "It is unlikely that my parents": Walter Cronkite, *A Reporter's Life* (New York: Knopf, 1996), p. 6.

23 his father voted at the Frederick Boulevard firehouse for Woodrow Wilson: Ibid.

24 "Report for examination": "Walter L. Cronkite," Debra Graden, comp., *Missouri State Offices Political and Military Records, 1919–1920* (Provo, UT: Ancestry.com Operations Inc., 2001), p. 384, http://search.ancestry.com/search/db.aspx?dbid=5594 (accessed August 14, 2011).

24 The Cronkites took up residence in Sapulpa, Oklahoma: Cronkite, *A Reporter's Life*, p. 8.

25 "he acknowledged having known the chap": Ibid.

26 "I know exactly how they felt": Ron Powers, "Walter Cronkite: A Candid Conversation with America's Most Trusted Television Newsman," *Playboy*, June 1973.

27 Ninth Street trestle: Monroe Dodd, *A Splendid Ride: The Streetcars of Kansas City, 1870–1957* (Kansas City: Kansas City Star Books, 2002).

28 "I was always a researcher": Cronkite and Carleton, *Conversations with Cronkite*, p. 8.

28 **six blocks away was the Electric Park:** Cronkite, *A Reporter's Life*, p. 14.

29 **"They had horses":** "Walter Cronkite," *St. Joseph News-Press*, 1994.

30 **Besides peddling newspapers he also sold:** Cronkite, *A Reporter's Life*, p. 10.

31 **"I can't quite reconstruct today what led me":** Jim Poniewozik, "Walter Cronkite: The Man with America's Trust," *Time*, July 17, 2009.

31 **Dr. Cronkite was invited to join:** "About the School," University of Texas Health Science Center at Houston, Dental Branch, http://www .db.uth.tmc.edu/ (accessed July 22, 2011).

32 **so "grown-up" about moving:** Cronkite, *A Reporter's Life*, p. 26.

32 **often dreamed about Buchanan County's apple orchards:** Bob Slater, "Interview Provided Insights into Cronkite," *St. Joseph News-Press*, July 18, 2009.

Two: HOUSTON YOUTH

34 **Walter dutifully read up on Houston:** Richard Connelly, "Walter Cronkite's Houston, or What Is Left of It," *Houston Press Blog*, July 20, 2009, blogs.houstonpress.com/hairballs/2009/07/walter

_cronkites_houston_or_wh.php (accessed August 1, 2011). Also see Dyer, "Forgotten Houston."

34 **"I expected to see an ocean-going ship"**: Cronkite and Carleton, *Conversations with Cronkite*, p. 8.

35 **"We communicated by Morse code"**: Cronkite, *A Reporter's Life*, p. 26.

35 **"I might have grown up to help build the Lincoln Tunnel"**: Ibid., pp. 26–27.

36 **"And the job boom was beginning"**: Walter Cronkite, "And That's the Way It Was," *Houston Post*, March 31, 1985.

36 **"I hit a sparrow"**: Ibid.

37 **The Ku Klux Klan was thriving**: Writers' Program of the Work Projects Administration in the State of Texas, *Houston: A History and Guide* (Houston: Anson Jones Press, 1942), p. 115.

37 **"My natural sympathy"**: Cronkite, *A Reporter's Life*, p. 290.

38 **"'Helen, Walter, we're leaving'"**: Powers, "Walter Cronkite: A Candid Conversation."

38 **"I was horrified about the incident"**: Walter Cronkite interview with the Archive of American Television (transcript), April 18, 1998.

41   "It had a wonderful aura":   Walter Cronkite, "And That's the Way It Was," *Houston Post*, March 31, 1985.

41   "I guess the *Houston Post* was a small newspaper":   Ibid.

42   During summer breaks: David Barron, "With Houston Roots, Cronkite Left Mark on the World," *Houston Chronicle*, July 17, 2009.

42   "I could get more kids in that car":   "My First Car," *Parade*, October 14, 1962.

44   "We had actually run out of food":   Walter Cronkite interview, Archive of American Television, April 28, 1998, p. 6.

44   "Presbyterian–Lutheran kind of Calvinist background":   James, *Walter Cronkite*, p. 35.

45   "It's one of those gray areas, Walter":   *Parade*, March 23, 1980.

46   tales from the world of print: Cronkite, *A Reporter's Life*, p. 31.

46   "he was ordering me to don my armor":   Ibid., p. 32.

46   "He was so in love with his work":   Donna Sue Walker, "Army of Fans Enjoys 'Evening with Cronkite,'" *Tulsa World*, April 21, 1999.

46 **A typical news flash:** Joe Adcock, "Walter Cronkite," *Texas Magazine*, November 27, 1966.

46 **voted by his peers as best reporter:** *Campus Cub*, May 22, 1933.

46 **maintain a "high standard of quality":** San Jacinto High School Yearbook, 1933.

47 **"He was always running up and down the corridors":** John G. Rogers, "Walter Cronkite's Favorite Teacher," *Parade*, February 18, 1973, p. 23.

48 **as if he'd been "dipped in phosphorous":** Amy Henderson, *On the Air: Pioneers of American Broadcasting* (Washington, DC: Smithsonian Institute Press, 1988), p. 186.

49 **"an exalted copy boy":** Walker, "Army of Fans."

49 **"I had discovered journalism":** Cronkite, "And That's the Way It Was."

49 **"I could watch fellow passengers reading my story":** Ibid.

50 **"No corrections":** Walter Cronkite (clippings), WCP-UTA.

52 **"Tall, very Blonde—Good Dancer":** Cornelia "Bit" Winter scrapbook (1935), Don Michel Archive, Anna, IL.

52 **he couldn't afford to purchase a Balfour class ring:** Connelly, "Walter Cronkite's Houston."

53 **"the smartest person in the school":** Author interview with Fay Shoss, May 24, 2011.

53 **"the man Americans are most likely to buy a used car from":** "Press Club Hails Cronkite," *Houston Post*, October 27, 1973.

53 **"There's nothing I would like to have more":** Ibid.

54 **"how broke his mother had been":** Author interview with Andrew Goldberg, August 12, 2011.

54 **to honor Cronkite's mother:** "The Fun of Getting Your Senior Class Ring—70 Years Later," Balfour Press Release, June 22, 2004.

Three: LEARNING A TRADE

56 **"being the ham I've always been":** Walter Cronkite interview, Archive of American Television, April 28, 1998.

56 **he was on the Tube long before Murrow:** Lawrence Laurent, "Video Proves Nothing's as Exciting as History," *Washington Post*, December 13, 1953.

The Daily Texan was an amazing college newspaper: Don Carleton, "Cronkite's Texas," *The Alcalde* (September–October 2009).

journalism an extracurricular "flirtation": "Walter Cronkite: News Commenter," *Detroit News Magazine*, September 24, 1972.

58 Woodrow Wilson's closest advisor: Ibid., p. 27.

58 Determined to be the big man on campus: Ibid.

58 "the campus big shot of Fort Worth": Walter Cronkite to Helen Cronkite, 1934, Box: 2.325–E454a, WCP-UTA.

58 a "magna cum virgin": Art Buchwald, "Anchor's Away: The Life of Walter," *Washington Post*, July 17, 2009.

59 he and Bit resorted to letter writing: Don Michel to Douglas Brinkley, October 15, 2011.

59 "For Vice-President—WALTER CRONKITE": Box: 2.325–C130, WCP-UTA.

59 The only consolation he ever gleaned: Sharon Jayson, "And That's the Way It Was—Revered Anchor Cronkite Fondly Recalls His Days at UT, Daily Texan," *Austin American-Statesman*, October 1, 1999.

60 "I missed a lot of classes": Ibid.

60 **"I am experiencing great difficulty"**: Walter Cronkite, January 23, 1935, uncited photocopy, WCP-UTA.

61 **"She is genuine"**: Walter Cronkite, "Miss Stein Not Out for Show, But Knows What She Knows," *Daily Texan*, March 22, 1936.

61 **Cronkite secured a job**: Joe Adcock, "Walter Cronkite," *Texas Magazine*, November 27, 1966.

62 **"I'd never been in a place like this"**: Powers, "Walter Cronkite: A Candid Conversation."

63 **Cronkite learned that to his peers he was**: Walter Cronkite, undated [1935], Box: 2.325–E454a, WCP-UTA.

64 **steel-trap memory**: Carleton, "Cronkite's Texas."

64 **"the man who gets behind the campus news"**: Walter Cronkite, January 23, 1935, WCP-UTA.

64 **"One could tell a wireless faddist"**: Cronkite, *A Reporter's Life*, p. 35.

65 **warned Cronkite of misusing the airwaves**: Carleton, "Cronkite's Texas."

66 **"I could have been the Kaiser!"**: Author interview with Kathy Cronkite, September 18, 2010.

67 **"up with the pigeons"**: Carleton, "Cronkite's Texas."

68 **"I learned the principles of great journalism"**: Nancy Martinez, "Vann Kennedy: 1905–1924," *Corpus Christi Caller-Times*, April 19, 2004.

68 **"I have never found anything I like"**: Walter Cronkite, undated letter [1935?], WCP-UTA.

69 **"The columns to weekly papers"**: Walter Cronkite, undated letter home, WCP-UTA.

69 **After a year at INS, Cronkite was hired by *The Houston Press***: Michael C. Emery, Edwin Emery, and Nancy L. Roberts, *The Press and America: An Interpretive History of the Mass Media* (Boston: Allyn and Bacon, 1996), p. 221.

69 **"My duties consist of taking stories"**: Walter Cronkite, August 8, 1935, WCP-UTA.

70 **"the poor old wanderluster"**: Ibid.

71 **"Please don't forget me Bit"**: Walter Cronkite to Bit Winter, Don Michel Personal Papers, Anna, IL.

72 **But instead of marrying Cronkite**: Cornelia Winter Davis "funeral services" (invite), January 13, 1938, Don Michel Personal Papers, Anna, IL.

73 **he romanticized the City of Fountains**: Aaron Barnhart, "Walter Cronkite, 92, America's

Anchor, KC's Hometown Hero, Journalism's Conscience," *Kansas City Star*, July 20, 2009.

73 **"I have not met a really complete ass":** Thomas Hart Benton, *An Artist in America* (Columbia: University of Missouri Press, 1983), p. 275.

75 **Evans's father had been a student at the Kansas City College of Pharmacy:** Tom L. Evans, Oral History Interview, August 8, 1962, Harry S. Truman Library and Museum, Independence, MO, p. 22.

75 **"Simmons said, 'Here is a man with the best radio voice'":** Walter Cronkite to Helen Cronkite, circa 1936, WCP-UTA.

77 **Cronkite was asked what his greatest achievement was:** "Proust Questionnaire."

79 **"This is Edward Murrow speaking from Vienna":** Erik Barnouw, *The Golden We: A History of Broadcasting in the United States* (New York: Oxford University Press, 1968), pp. 77–78.

79 **The whole CBS News "Round-up" crowd:** Edward R. Murrow and Ed Bliss, eds., *In Search of Light: The Broadcasts of Edward R. Murrow* (New York: Knopf, 1967), pp. 4–5.

80 the art of what he called "reconstructed games": Cronkite, *A Reporter's Life*, p. 67.

81 It was fake sports: Hilts, "And That's the Way It Was."

81 "I didn't need many facts": "Walter Cronkite 1916–2009," *Sports Illustrated*, July 27, 2009.

82 "There were girls in most": Cronkite, *A Reporter's Life*, p. 52.

83 "I watched her coming down the hall": Walter Cronkite oral history interview, p. 48, WCP-UTA.

83 "It was," she recalled, "love at first sight": "What in the World," syndicated column, February 7, 1976.

83 "Betsy and I went from the studio": Barnhart, "Walter Cronkite, 92."

83 while earning As: Beverly Grunwald, "Capable Mrs. Cronkite," *Women's Wear Daily* news service, February 17, 1979.

84 "He used to be such a string bean": "What in the World," February 7, 1976.

86 Cronkite's sleuthing subsequently showed: Cronkite and Carleton, *Conversations with Cronkite*, pp. 18–19.

86 **"KCMO: Stupid Enough to Fire Cronkite":** Justin Kendall, "KCMO: Stupid Enough to Fire Cronkite, Downhill Ever Since," *The Pitch* blogs, September 10, 2009.

Four: MAKING OF A UNIPRESSER

88 **when it called UP a "scrappy alternative" to AP:** Donald Libenson, "UPI R.I.P.," *Chicago Tribune,* May 4, 2003.

88 **Most important for Cronkite's career:** Richard Harnett and Billy G. Ferguson, *UNIPRESS: United Press International—Covering the 20th Century* (Denver, CO: Fulcrum Publishing, 2003).

88 **Before long, UP, a worldwide news wholesaler:** United Press International, 1907–2007, http// www.100years.upi.com/history.html (accessed September 19, 2011).

89 **It is a business:** Stephen Vincent Benét, "United Press," *Fortune,* May 1933.

91 **Cronkite would hand Swayze:** Cronkite, *A Reporter's Life,* p. 78.

92 **"Good morning, John Cameron Swayze here":** Cronkite and Carleton, *Conversations with Cronkite,* pp. 27–28.

94 **He hitched a ride:** "New London Explosion," Depot Museum; http//www.depotmuseum.com/ newLondon.html (accessed July 28, 2011).

94 **"It is not easy," Cronkite quickly learned:** Cronkite, *A Reporter's Life*, p. 64.

94 **"Take oil from this town and nothing would be left":** Walter Cronkite, "Overton, Where Blast Occurred, Is in World's Richest Oil Field," UP, March 19, 1937.

96 **Harry Smith of *CBS Morning News* was preparing:** Author interview with Harry Smith, May 1, 2011.

96 **"I got some very good lessons":** Walter Cronkite oral history interview, p. 56, WCP-UTA.

96 **Unbeknownst to Cronkite, he was walking:** Walter Cronkite interview, Archive of American Television, October 18, 1999.

97 **"I used to think life wasn't worth living":** Lewis H. Lapham, "The Secret Life of Walter (Mitty) Cronkite," *Saturday Evening Post*, March 16, 1962.

97 **Cronkite came advertised on WKY:** Walter Cronkite interview, Archive of American Television, October 18, 1999.

98 **"It was really one of the lowest moments"**: Hilts, "That's the Way It Was."

98 **"If you're going to be doing an ad-lib"**: Walter Cronkite interview, Archive of American Television, October 18, 1999. See also Walter Cronkite oral history interview, p. 63, WCP-UTA.

101 **"I loved the United Press"**: Walter Cronkite oral history interview, p. 65, WCP-UTA.

101 **"The management had not been happy"**: Cronkite and Carleton, *Conversations with Cronkite*, p. 27.

102 **"Officials of airfields throughout the nation"**: Walter Cronkite, "Hunt for Plane in Which Flyer Was Kidnapped," United Press, *Oelwein (Iowa) Daily Register*, October 28, 1939.

103 **"State authorities appealed to airports"**: Walter Cronkite, "Seek Hoosier After Plane Fails Return," UP, *Valparaiso Vidette-Messenger.*

105 **"I began calling airports"**: Cronkite, *A Reporter's Life*, p. 74.

106 **"The general attitude seems"**: Edward R. Murrow, *This Is London* (New York: Schocken Books, 1941), p. 17.

107 **UP ended up sending 150:** Harnett and Ferguson, *UNIPRESS*, p. 134.

107 **Cronkite had, as he later recalled, all the "excitement":** Cronkite, *A Reporter's Life*.

Five: GEARING UP FOR EUROPE

112 **The church was bedecked:** *Kansas City Journal-Post*, undated clipping, WCP-UTA.

112 **the Cronkites went on a whirlwind auto honeymoon:** Author interview with Chip Cronkite, November 1, 2011.

113 **"We were traveling":** Walter Cronkite oral history interview, WCP-UTA.

113 **They became great friends with another young journalist:** Author interview with Deborah Rush, February 21, 2012.

114 **One of her additional duties:** James, *Walter Cronkite*, p. 45.

114 **"My journalism was really trivial":** Beverly Grunwald, "Capable Mrs. Cronkite Is Content with Life," *Women's Wear Daily* wire service, *Hutchinson, Texas News*, February 17, 1979.

114 **Cronkite's United Press bureau:** Gordon and Cohen, *Down to the Wire*, p. 11.

115   this led to five years of brutal occupation: Lance Goddard, *Canada and the Liberation of the Netherlands* (Toronto: Dundurn Press, 2005), p. 22.

115   "The Dutch people would never": Cronkite, "200th Anniversary of Friendship and Unbroken Diplomatic Relations with the Netherlands."

116   she ended up getting her pilot's license: Betsy Cronkite as told to Lyn Tornabee, "My Husband: The Newscaster," *Cosmopolitan*, May 1965.

117   Cronkite had been at: Benét, "United Press."

117   "If I hadn't been trained as a journalist": "What in the World," syndicated column, February 8, 1976.

118   TV was too much of a "technological toy": Henderson, *On the Air*, pp. 34–35.

120   "a perverse exhilaration to it all": John Maxwell Hamilton, *Journalism's Roving Eye: A History of American Foreign Reporting* (Baton Rouge: Louisiana State University Press, 2009), pp. 317–318.

120   "A searchlight just burst into action": CBS News Special Report, "London After Dark," August 24, 1940, CougarGA7, in collaboration

with www.archive.org and CBS News, http://www.freerepublic.com/focus/f-chat/2576828/posts.

121 **"Off to the east, searchlights poked":** Drew Middleton, "Eye-Witness to London Raid Finds People's Morale Good," AP, August 25, 1940.

122 **"There was an awful lot of clatter of showmanship":** Powers, "Walter Cronkite: A Candid Conversation."

123 **Carroll logged detailed stories:** Harnett and Ferguson, *UNIPRESS*, pp. 137–138.

124 **"a long year of waiting":** Walter Cronkite, "Remembering the North Africa Campaign of World War II," *All Things Considered*, NPR, LexisNexis transcript, November 8, 2002.

124 **Neither had ever been to the East Coast before:** Cronkite and Carleton, *Conversations with Cronkite*, p. 33.

125 **"New York is one of the finer spots":** Walter Cronkite to Helen Cronkite, January–February 1942, WCP-UTA.

126 **Cronkite was worried:** Harnett and Ferguson, *UNIPRESS*, pp. 138–40.

126 **he was a "nut animal-lover":** Walter Cronkite Roast in Phoenix, Arizona, November 15, 1985 (transcript), http://www.c-spanvideo.org/program/125802-1 (accessed July 7, 2011).

128 **Cronkite would not be among their ranks:** James, *Walter Cronkite*, p. 57.

128 **"to avoid getting into combat":** Powers, "Walter Cronkite: A Candid Conversation."

128 **"I occupied the admiral's cabin":** Walter Cronkite to Helen Cronkite, September 6, 1942, WCP-UTA.

129 **"They thought I was a chaplain":** Cronkite, "Remembering the North Africa Campaign."

129 **"a derelict merchantman wreck had been mistaken":** Walter Cronkite, "Biggest Convoy Sent from U.S. Reaches Britain," UP, August 24, 1940.

131 **"if I can fight it through censorship":** Walter Cronkite to Helen Cronkite, September 6, 1942, WCP-UTA.

131 **"United Press correspondent assigned to the Atlantic fleet":** Walter Cronkite, "Fire Guts Ex-Liner Manhattan," UP, September 3, 1942.

131 **UP was printing unrelated Cronkite-bylined:** Walter Cronkite, "British Expect One More

Blitz from Hitler Air Force," UP, September 12, 1942.

132 **"I was told to report to the battleship":** Cronkite and Carleton, *Conversations with Cronkite*, p. 38.

133 **By reporting on:** Harnett and Ferguson, *UNIPRESS*, p. 139.

133 **The UP that prided itself for "the world's best coverage":** "Shock-Troops of the Press," advertisement, UP, *Pittsburgh Press*, March 1, 1943.

133 **Cronkite was the new kid on the block:** Joe Alex Morris, "Five United Press Reporters Sent to Africa," UP, November 10, 1942.

134 **Cunningham was known to cultivate a chummy relationship:** Joe Alex Morris, *Deadline Every Minute* (Garden City, NY: Doubleday, 1957), pp. 260–261.

135 **Cronkite had filed thirteen UP stories:** Cronkite, "Remembering the North Africa Campaign."

136 **He had accidentally "hitchhiked":** Ibid.

138 **he explained every big scene and small nuance of his North African adventure:** Cronkite, *A Reporter's Life*, p. 90.

138 **"It was enough to make a young wire-service reporter"**: Cronkite, "Remembering the North Africa Campaign."

Six: THE WRITING SIXTY-NINTH

141 **"Walter would be at sea on Christmas"**: "Betsy Cronkite: Problems of an Anchorman's Wife," *Anderson* (Indiana) *Daily Bulletin*, November [nd] 1968, p. 28.

141 **it was determined to "compete toe-to-toe"**: Morris, *Deadline Every Minute*, p. 254.

142 **a voyage "abominable from every other standpoint"**: Walter Cronkite to Betsy Cronkite, December 30, 1942, WCP-UTA.

142 **whom Cronkite later called his "hero"**: Walter Cronkite oral history interview, p. 99, WCP-UTA.

143 **the high-heeled prostitutes, not the ordnance**: Don L. Miller, *Masters of the Air: America's Bomber Boys Who Fought the Air War Against Nazi Germany* (New York: Simon & Schuster, 2006), pp. 218–221.

143 **"I thought Walter was one of the big guys"**: Author interview with Andy Rooney, March 15, 2011.

143   **Rooney deemed Cronkite "a tough, competitive scrambler":** Andy Rooney, *My War* (New York: Times Books, 1995), p. 86.

143   **in a room he deemed a "cell":** Walter Cronkite to Betsy Cronkite, January 9, 1943, WCP-UTA.

144   **"Joe Morris and Ed Beattie were organizing":** Walter Cronkite to Betsy Cronkite, January 1, 1943, WCP-UTA.

144   **"What hours I'm going to be working":** Ibid.

145   **"I'm going through my meager funds":** Walter Cronkite to Betsy Cronkite, January [nd] 1943, WCP-UTA.

148   **about accompanying a Lancaster crew on its flight:** "James M'Donald, Times Reporter: Retired Correspondent Dies," *New York Times*, June 20, 1962.

148   **"Royal Air Force bombers transformed":** James MacDonald, "Fires Rage in City," *New York Times*, January 18, 1943.

149   **"Walter was a charmer":** Author interview with Andy Rooney, March 7, 2011.

150   **a "babble of tongues":** Walter Cronkite to Betsy Cronkite, January [nd] 1943, WCP-UTA.

151 **The Latrio disbanded not long after:** "Manhattan Merry-Go-Round," *San Francisco Chronicle*, March 6, 1991.

151 **"A Flying Fortress called 'Banshee'":** Walter Cronkite, "Flier Claims He Was First over Reich," UP, January 28, 1943.

153 **"It just seemed wrong":** Rooney is quoted in Michelle Ferrari and James Tobin, eds., *Reporting America at War: An Oral History* (New York: Hyperion, 2003), p. 53.

153 **"'Gosh, I wonder what Gladwin'":** Cronkite and Carleton, *Conversations with Cronkite*.

154 **"I don't know who decided to do it":** Ferrari and Tobin, *Reporting America at War*, p. 53.

155 **"wild elephants couldn't have kept Cronkite":** Jim Hamilton, *The Writing 69th* (Marshfield, MA: Green Harbor Books, 1999), p. 46.

155 **was "to hold a ticket to a funeral":** Harrison E. Salisbury, *A Journey for Our Times* (New York: Harper and Row, 1983), p. 196.

155 **"Walter came back all right":** H. D. Quigg, "Uncle Walter: Making of a Superanchor," *New York Daily News*, March 1, 1981.

156 **"For the past week six other correspondents and I"**: Walter Cronkite to Betsy Cronkite, February 6, 1943, WCP-UTA.

156 **"I don't know how that Writing Sixty-Ninth stuff"**: Author interview with Andy Rooney, March 15, 2011.

157 **"Walter was really the class clown"**: Author interview with Andy Rooney, March 15, 2011.

158 **"That's it"—the plane his movie would be based on:** Miller, *Masters of the Air*, p. 117.

158 **a curriculum that covered "first aid, the use of oxygen"**: Gladwin Hill, "Newsmen Train to Cover Raids in Bombers," *Schenectady Gazette*, February 9, 1943.

158 **"God help Hitler!"**: Miller, *Masters of the Air War*, p. 115.

159 **"There are ten of us here now"**: Hamilton, *The Writing 69th*, p. 46.

159 **"Listen, it happens"**: Rooney, *My War*, p. 121.

159 **Cronkite left Molesworth in a B-17:** "Bomber Command Narrative Operations, Mission No. 37—26 February, 1943, Target-Wilhelmshaven, Germany," WCP-UTA.

160 **"It was terrible"**: Quigg, "Uncle Walter."

160   The crew and the embedded Bob Post para-
      chuted: "Bomber   Command   Narrative
      Operations, Mission No. 37."

160   Cronkite saw German FW-190: Ibid.

160   the crew gave Cronkite a job: Ibid.

160   "I fired at an awful lot": Walter Cronkite oral
      history interview, p. 106, WCP-UTA.

162   "I had by far the best story": Ferrari and Tobin,
      Reporting America at War, p. 55.

162   Cronkite and Bigart felt lucky: Hamilton, *The
      Flying 69th*, p. 116.

163   put his hand on Cronkite's arm and moaned,
      "Y-y-y-y-you wouldn't":   Powers, "Walter
      Cronkite: A Candid Conversation."

163   "I swept the boards with my story": Quigg,
      "Uncle Walter."

164   "to get the smell of warm blood into their
      copy":   Carl Sessions Stepp, "Down to the
      Wires," *American Journalism Review* (August–
      September 2003).

164   "Bigart, Cronkite and Hill were badly shaken":
      Harrison Salisbury, foreword in Wade, ed.,
      Forward Positions: The War Correspondence

of Homer Bigart (Fayetteville: University of Arkansas Press, 1992), p. xiv.

165 **the best journalistic account:** Louis Snyder, ed., *Masterpieces of War Reporting: Great Moments of World War II* (New York: Julian Messner, 1962), p. 239.

165 **"The impressions of a first bombing mission":** Maurice Isserman and John Steward Bowman, *World War II* (New York: Facts on File, 2003), p. 131.

167 **"This is the story of Bob Post":** Walter Cronkite, "Bob Post," UP, February 25, 1943.

168 *The New York Times* **declared Post dead:** Hamilton, *The Writing 69th*, p. 123.

168 **"I was scared to death":** Author interview with Andy Rooney, March 15, 2011.

168 **"The Yanks are here":** Walter Cronkite, "Yanks in European Air Offensive in Full Force Now," UP, May 15, 1943.

169 **"We were all on the same side":** Cronkite, *A Reporter's Life*, p. 289.

169 **His November 19 dispatch:** Walter Cronkite, "Nazi Air Force Seen Beaten at Every Turn," *New York World-Telegram*, November 19, 1943.

169 **"We do not have the least idea"**: Morris, *Deadline Every Minute*, p. 254.

170 **"I'm embarrassed when I'm introduced"**: Powers, "Walter Cronkite: A Candid Conversation."

Seven: DEAN OF THE AIR WAR

172 **"It expressed the jargon"**: Walter Cronkite, "Dramatized WWII Radio Program 'Soldiers of the Press,'" *All Things Considered*, NPR, July 21, 2003.

172 **Murrow, a gifted talent scout, asked:** John A. Steuart, *Robert Louis Stevenson: A Critical Biography*, 2nd ed. (Boston: Little, Brown, 1924), p. 180.

173 **This group—which included:** Stanley Cloud and Lynne Olson, *The Murrow Boys* (New York: Houghton Mifflin, 1996), Author's Note.

174 **"I guess he was looking for cannon fodder"**: Walter Cronkite interview, Archive of American Television, April 18, 1998.

174 **"Well, he drove a stake"**: Walter Cronkite, oral history interview with Don Carleton, WCP-UTA.

175 **"He gave me a sales pitch"**: Ibid.

177 **"I don't think it cost him":** Walter Cronkite interview, Archive of American Television, April 28, 1998.

177 **"Murrow couldn't believe it":** Cloud and Olson, *The Murrow Boys*, p. 297.

177 **"a certain chill" pervaded Cronkite's relationship:** Stephen Miller and Sam Schechner, "Walter Cronkite, Broadcasting Legend, Dies at 92," *Wall Street Journal*, July 18, 2009.

178 **to worry about his Q factor with Murrow:** Alexander Kendrick, *Prime Time: The Life of Edward R. Murrow* (New York: Little, Brown, 1969), p. 275.

178 **Cronkite reliving the flight over Wilhelmshaven:** Walter Cronkite, "My Favorite War Story," *Look*, November 16, 1943.

178 **"Despite my turning down Ed's offer, CBS kept inviting me":** Cronkite and Carleton, *Conversations with Cronkite*, pp. 63–64.

179 **"a kind of orchestrated hell":** Belyn Rodgers, "Edward R. Murrow's 'Orchestrated Hell': A Rhetorical Analysis," University of Texas at Tyler, http//www.uttyler.edu/meidenmuller/publicomm/belynrogers.htm (accessed October 5, 2011).

181 "gratitude for getting us back": Photograph on the Writing 69th Home Page, Green Harbor Publications, http://www.greenharbor.com/wr69/wr69.html.

181 "That the first two years seemed to go": Walter Cronkite to Betsy Cronkite, March 29, 1944, WCP-UTA.

182 Cronkite conveyed how "broken hearted": Walter Cronkite to Betsy Cronkite, May 14, 1944, WCP-UTA.

182 "We've gotten a new mission": Walter Cronkite oral history interview with Don Carleton, WCP-UTA.

182 "It struck me": Walter Cronkite, "Cronkite Left in Fog on D-Day," New York Daily News, June 4, 1984.

183 Leyshon warned Cronkite that the flight would be at a very low altitude: Walter Cronkite, "R.A.F. Bombers Blasted Path for Invasion," UP, June 6, 1944.

184 "And then the order came to arm": Cronkite, "Cronkite Left in the Fog on D-Day."

184 "didn't seem to be room for any more": Cronkite, A Reporter's Life, p. 104.

185 **"Many of the German gun nests were blanketed"**: Walter Cronkite, "RAF Bombers Rip Coast," UP, June 6, 1944.

186 **"The planes come over closer"**: Erik Barnouw, *The Golden Web: A History of Broadcasting in the United States, 1933 to 1953* (New York: Oxford University Press, 1968), p. 199.

186 **"everything was anti-climax"**: Paul White, *News on the Air*, p. 356.

187 **Murrow was anointed president of the London-based organization**: Bob Edwards, *Edward R. Murrow and the Birth of Broadcast Journalism* (Hoboken, NJ: Wiley, 2004), p. 78.

187 **"I did fly the morning of the invasion after all"**: Walter Cronkite to Betsy Cronkite, June 12, 1944, WCP-UTA.

188 **"I think it was Omaha"**: Cronkite and Carleton, *Conversations with Cronkite*, p. 59.

188 **Cronkite got the opportunity to interview**: Stephen E. Ambrose, *D-Day: June 6, 1944: The Climactic Battle of World War II* (New York: Simon & Schuster, 1994), p. 583.

189 **"To think of the lives that were given"**: Walter Cronkite interview with Dwight D. Eisenhower,

June 6, 1964, *CBS Special Report*, CBS News Reference Library, New York.

189 **"I actually have been just as busy since D-Day":** Walter Cronkite to Helen Cronkite, August 15, 1944, WCP-UTA.

190 **"Hugh Baillie is coming":** Ibid.

191 **"There's no question that television has":** White, *News on the Air*, p. 372.

191 **He roundly disdained the rest of CBS's programming:** Conway, *The Origins of Television News in America*, p. 126.

Eight: GLIDING TO V-E DAY

193 **"I was unceremoniously crash-landed in a troop-carrying glider":** Cornelius Ryan, *A Bridge Too Far* (New York: Simon & Schuster, 1974), p. 216.

194 **silent glide into eternity":** Cronkite, *A Reporter's Life*, p. 10.

194 **"don't go by glider!":** Ibid.

194 **"I thought the wheels of the glider":** Ryan, *A Bridge Too Far*, p. 216.

196 **"Thousands of Allied parachutists and glider troops landed":** Walter Cronkite, "Arnhem," UP, September 18, 1944.

196 **Cronkite's upbeat Market Garden stories ran:** Walter Cronkite, "Sky Troops Fight as They Hit Earth," *New York Times*, September 18, 1944.

197 **"lame":** Ryan, *A Bridge Too Far*, p. 12.

197 **"I can see their chutes going down now":** Murrow and Bliss, *In Search of Light*, p. 84.

198 **Murrow's "That's the way it was" antedated:** Edward Bliss Jr., *Now the News: The Story of Broadcast Journalism* (New York: Columbia University Press, 1991), pp. 161–162.

198 **Cronkite reported on the battles to liberate:** Cronkite, "200th Anniversary of Friendship and Unbroken Diplomatic Relations with the Netherlands."

199 **"It looked like a gigantic skyrocket":** "Cronkite Believes He Saw V-2 Rocket," *New York Times*, December 2, 1944.

199 **with Downs as his constant companion:** Expansion of CBS war coverage from Columbia Broadcasting System 1944 Annual Report, March 24, 1945, pp. 20–21. Also see Bliss, *Now the News*, pp. 91–97.

200 **"I couldn't go around calling *your* name":** Bliss, *Now the News*, p. 162.

201 **"I was back in Brussels"**: Cronkite and Carleton, *Conversations with Cronkite*, p. 68.

202 **"During the early days of the Bulge"**: "Remembering the Battle of the Bulge, which took place 60 years ago this week," *All Things Considered*, NPR, September 27, 2004.

203 **"The heroic events of that Christmas"**: Ibid.

204 **"He really didn't deserve the credit"**: Cronkite and Carleton, *Conversations with Cronkite*, p. 68.

204 **the ability to say he'd been a war correspondent**: Mark Bernstein and Alex Lubertozzi, *World War II: On the Air* (New York: Sourcebooks, 2003), p. xiv.

205 **"Before you knew it, you could hear"**: Don Hewitt, *Tell Me a Story* (New York: Public Affairs, 2002), p. 32.

206 **"Downs, lying behind me, began tugging"**: Cronkite, *A Reporter's Life*, p. 114. Also, Edwards, *Edward R. Murrow*, p. 81.

206 **"They pelted us with tulips"**: Cronkite, *A Reporter's Life*, p. 123.

207 **"I got a lot of garlands"**: "Television: The Most Intimate Medium," *Time*, October 14, 1966.

207 **Cronkite was proud to be among the brave Dutch:** Ibid.

207 **"The sound of Allied aircraft":** Cronkite, "200th Anniversary of Friendship and Unbroken Diplomatic Relations with the Netherlands."

208 **"Through their tears of joy they couldn't wait to tell":** Cronkite, *A Reporter's Life*, p. 123.

209 **"There were a number of great stories":** Cronkite and Carleton, *Conversations with Cronkite*, p.74

209 **When Murrow took to the CBS Radio airwaves, he prayed:** Edwards, *Edward R. Murrow*, pp. 74–84.

210 **"You can't write horror stories":** Cronkite and Carleton, *Conversations with Cronkite*, p. 73.

210 **The Nazis had starved and beaten:** Goddard, *Canada and the Liberation of the Netherlands*, pp. 209–214.

211 **"There is absolutely no food":** Walter Cronkite letter, May 20, 1945, WCP-UTA.

212 **"It would serve America well to listen":** Walter Cronkite, "200th Anniversary of Friendship and Unbroken Diplomatic Relations with the Netherlands."

213 **Cronkite was able to buy wire:** Cronkite, *A Reporter's Life*, pp. 122–124.

215 **"I had a curious feeling of age":** Eric Sevareid, *Not So Wild a Dream*, p. 511.

216 **he was "in a kind of mental coma":** Ibid., pp. 511–512.

217 **He attended General Patton's funeral:** Cronkite and Carleton, *Conversations with Cronkite*, p. 77.

218 **The courtroom was an old German theater:** Joseph E. Persico, *Nuremberg: Infamy on Trial* (New York: Penguin Books, 1994), p. 132.

Nine: FROM THE NUREMBERG TRIALS TO RUSSIA

220 **"They had come into the dock":** Walter Cronkite, *The Nuremberg Trials* (transcript), PBS, *American Experience*, 2006, http://www.pbs.org/wgbh/amex/nuremberg/filmmore/pt.html.

221 **"We'd get drunk around the bar and debate":** Cronkite and Carleton, *Conversations with Cronkite*, p. 80.

221 **"The real skill," he recalled of Stringer:** Walter Cronkite oral history interview, WCP-UTA.

222 **"We got a lot of damn good front page sto-ries"**: Cronkite and Carleton, *Conversations with Cronkite*, pp. 79–80.

222 **procuring "new information"**: Walter Cronkite, "Goering's Wife Tells How She Helped Build Fortune," UP, July 9, 1946.

222 **"Göring displayed on the stand"**: Cronkite, *A Reporter's Life*, p. 126.

223 **"As soon as the defendants saw"**: Cronkite, *The Nuremberg Trials*.

223 **"There has been much criticism"**: Timothy White, "Walter: We Hardly Knew You," *Rolling Stone*, February 5, 1981.

224 **"I have a vivid memory of Walter coming to visit"**: Author interview with Kay Barnes, July 7, 2011.

224 **"I was chief correspondent"**: Walter Cronkite interview, Archive of American Television, April 28, 1998.

226 **Moscow was to Betsy Cronkite "a last bastion of empire"**: Betsy Cronkite as told to Lyn Tornabee, "My Husband the Newscaster."

226 **"They lived a dual existence"**: Author interview with Kathy Cronkite, March 22, 2011.

226   "Life at the Metropol was a little like": Harrison Salisbury, *A Journey for Our Times* (New York: Harper and Row, 1983), p. 255.

227   **With UP picking up the tab, the Cronkites spent a long weekend:** Earl Wilson, "A Visit with Walter Cronkite," *Houston Post*, September 11, 1955.

227   **"Sprawled in a snowbank this morning I heard":** Walter Cronkite, UP clippings, WCP-UTA.

229   **"The foreign correspondent in Moscow":** Walter Cronkite, "Newsmen in Moscow Run Get Their Stories on Papers," UP, March 23, 1948.

229   **"After the smashing of the German source of international reaction":** Walter Cronkite, "Red Commentator Says Truman, Marshall Head Aggression Rising," UP, September 25, 1947.

230   **Whatever veneer of excitement that had glossed:** Salisbury, *A Journey for Our Times*, p. 248.

230   **ending its policy of "limited friendship":** David Halberstam, *The Powers That Be* (New York: Knopf, 1979), p. 240.

231   **"If they had known we were newspaper people":** Cronkite, *A Reporter's Life*, p. 153.

233 **"the best masculine garb for the video camera":** Jack Gould, "Television and Politics," *New York Times*, July 18, 1948.

234 **needed to have a happy-go-lucky "anchorman":** There is a dispute concerning the coining of the term *anchorman*. Three different broadcasting executives have claimed provenance: Sig Mickelson, Don Hewitt, and Paul Levitan.

234 **"In a town overrun with eager beavers":** Gould, "Television and Politics."

Ten: INFANCY OF TV NEWS

238 **a pregnant Betsy had returned to Kansas City:** Walter Cronkite interview with Richard Snow, "He Was There," *American Heritage* 45, no. 8 (1994): 42–44.

238 **"I raced half way around the world":** "Walter Cronkite: TV Biography," Special Projects, CBS News, May 15, 1953, CBS News Archive, New York.

238 **"That's the way it was in those days":** Author interview with Nancy Cronkite, April 4, 2011.

239 **Cronkite theorized that he could pick up the slack:** *Detroit News Magazine*, September 24, 1978.

239 **"It was a very fine, responsible radio station":** Ibid.

239 **"Solid as a mountain":** Miller and Runyon, "And That's the Way It Seems."

240 **"When Walter got into radio":** Author interview with Bob Schieffer, July 13, 2009.

240 **"Cronkite is in Washington to establish headquarters":** Jim Carson, "Listen!" *Atchison Daily Globe*, January 9, 1949.

241 **Having the Missouri connection would give Cronkite:** White, "Walter, We Hardly Knew You."

241 **The Cronkites rented a small house:** Author interview with Nancy Cronkite, April 4, 2011.

241 **Edward R. Murrow was a semiregular guest:** Ann M. Sperber, *Murrow, His Life and Times* (New York: Freudlich, 1986), p. 225.

243 **"I couldn't believe that anybody was going to take McCarthy seriously":** Cronkite and Carleton, *Conversations with Cronkite*, p. 114.

243 **"Walter being Walter, he got to know Sam Rayburn":** Author interview with Andy Rooney, March 15, 2011.

244 **"The people who say TV will destroy":** Joseph E. Persico, *Edward R. Murrow: An American Original* (New York: McGraw-Hill, 1988), p. 301.

244 **"the Murrows, Collingwoods, Sevareids wouldn't deign":** Felicity Barringer, "Sig Mickelson, First Director of CBS's TV News, Dies at 86," *New York Times*, March 27, 2000.

245 **Murrow, along with producer Fred Friendly, had been doing:** Ben Gross, "Looking and Listening," *New York Sunday News*, June 28, 1953.

245 **Born in Ada, Oklahoma, in 1917, Edwards began a career:** Denis Hevesi, "Douglas Edwards, First TV Anchorman, Dies at 73," *New York Times*, October 14, 1990.

245 **"First it was *television*":** Conway, *The Origins of Television News in America*, p. 2.

245 **Edwards's fifteen-minute show on CBS:** Halberstam, *The Powers That Be*, p. 123.

246 **NBC started its own TV news program:** Barbara Matusow, *The Evening Stars: The Making of the Network News Anchor* (Boston: Houghton Mifflin, 1983), p. 60.

246 **Swayze could ad-lib a bit:** Frederick Jacobi Jr., "Video Newscaster," *New York Times*, September 10, 1950.

247 **"didn't know how to query me for information":** Cronkite and Carleton, *Conversations with Cronkite*, p. 101.

248 **"Ed said that not many guys get a second chance":** Ibid, pp. 102–103.

249 **"KMBC-KFRM Washington Correspondent has taken an indefinite leave":** Carson, "Listen!"

250 **Stanton was the provost type:** Holcomb B. Noble, "Frank Stanton, Broadcasting Pioneer, Dies at 98," *New York Times*, December 26, 2006.

251 **"'Go out and do five minutes on the evening news'":** "News Commentator Walter Cronkite," *Detroit News Magazine*, September 4, 1978.

251 **Cronkite drew arrows on the map:** Tom Wicker, "Broadcast News," *New York Times*, January 26, 1997.

251 **"We were still trying to figure out how to do news on television":** Cronkite and Carleton, *Conversations with Cronkite*, p. 104.

252 his was the only name CBS would promote: "Display Ad 28," *Washington Post*, November 7, 1950.

253 "Within six months he was the talk of the town": Shadel, "An Uncharted Career," p. 8.

254 "How do you do the news so perfectly": Author interview with Shirley Wershba, July 6, 2011.

254 "[Shadel] came every Wednesday night": Walter Cronkite, Foreword to Shadel, "An Uncharted Career."

255 "Walter Winchell drops a line to the effect that": Joe Wershba, "A Real TV Ace Doesn't Need a Script," *Washington Post*, January 23, 1951.

255 Cronkite and Lindley aired new combat footage: "Display Ad 60," *Washington Post*, June 24, 1951.

256 "I went on and I did the news": Walter Cronkite, oral history interview with Don Carleton, p. 198, WCP-UTA.

257 Murrow had been influenced by the immediacy: Persico, *Edward R. Murrow*, p. 300.

258 "The television performance," he admitted about the Kefauver investigations: William

Manchester, *The Glory and the Dream: A Narrative History of America* (New York: Bantam Books, 1975), p. 601.

258 **"This is an old team trying to learn":** Quoted in Persico, *Edward R. Murrow,* p. 303.

259 **His voice inflections always seemed:** Walter Cronkite, oral history interview with Don Carleton, p. 200, WCP-UTA.

259 **"a real slick job":** John Crosby, "White House Tour a Real Slick Job," *Washington Post,* May 10, 1952.

259 **"Do the clocks run":** Cronkite, *A Reporter's Life,* p. 170.

260 **"saw Cronkite as Douglas Edwards' successor":** Hewitt, *Tell Me a Story,* p. 55.

260 **"Walter Cronkite was not one of the Murrow Boys":** Halberstam, *The Powers That Be,* p. 238.

260 **they offered Cronkite a job as substitute host:** "Radio-TV Notes," *New York Times,* June 29, 1951.

261 **Cronkite, the substitute, became the host in 1954:** David Schwartz, Steve Ryan, and Fred Westbrook, *The Encyclopedia of TV Game Shows* (New York: Checkmark Books, 1999), pp. 106–7.

Eleven: ELECTION NIGHT AND UNIVAC

263 **"It seemed then that a revolution"**: Sig Mickelson, *The Electric Mirror: Politics in an Age of Television* (New York: Dodd, Mead, 1972), p. vii.

263 **"I used to see him fairly frequently"**: Jay Perkins, "Television Covers the 1952 Political Conventions in Chicago: An Oral History Interview with Sig Mickelson," *Historical Journal of Film, Radio, and Television* 18, no. 1 (1998). Perkins used sections from a number of oral histories Mickelson conducted from July 30 to August 2, 1993. Those interview tapes—recorded in San Diego—are on file at the Middleton Library at Louisiana State University in Baton Rouge. Two other Mickelson oral histories exist at San Diego State University and Columbia University.

264 **morphing CBS Radio and CBS TV**: Gary Paul Gates, *Air Time: The Story of CBS News* (New York: Berkeley, 1979), p. 59.

265 **"I held to my [pro-Cronkite] position"**: Perkins, "Television Covers the 1952 Political Conventions in Chicago."

265 **"I am not sure if that term was ever used"**: Ibid.

266 "political shell-game ... rigged, traded": Sperber, *Murrow, His Life and Times,* p. 385.

266 the idea was nixed as an illegal corporate contribution: Martin Plissner, *The Control Room: How Television Calls the Shots in Presidential Elections* (New York: Simon & Schuster, 1999), p. 35.

266 "I had little contact with Edward R. Murrow": Perkins, "Television Covers the 1952 Political Conventions in Chicago."

267 "all in the eyes": Michael A. Russo, "CBS and the American Political Experience: A History of the CBS News Special Events and Election Units, 1952–1968," PhD dissertation, New York University, June 1983, pp. 86–88.

267 The 1952 coverage of both Chicago political conventions: John Crosby, "Too Much Coverage?" *Council Bluffs Non Pareil,* July 13, 1952.

267 "TV had been radio's little brother": Plissner, *The Control Room,* p. 36.

268 "Those 1952 conventions were not only the first": Cronkite, *A Reporter's Life,* p. 182.

269 "We were young," Mickelson recalled: Perkins, "Television Covers the 1952 Political Conventions in Chicago."

269 **CBS planned to find a "common man":** Val Adams, "How Much Commentary Is Necessary?" *New York Times*, July 20, 1952.

270 **The 1952 Democratic Convention is remembered in the annals of U.S. political history:** Plissner, *The Control Room*, p. 36.

270 **"proclaiming that they favored television":** Reuven Frank, *Out of Thin Air* (New York: Simon & Schuster, 1991), pp. 55–56.

271 **"He ran a wire," Cronkite recalled, "up the outside of the hotel":** Cronkite, *A Reporter's Life*, p. 91.

271 **"ethical considerations did not deeply disturb us":** Mickelson, *From Whistle Stop to Sound Bite*, p. 37.

272 **CBS's convention coverage ran for 13.9 hours:** Plissner, *The Control Room*, p. 38.

272 **"Walter Cronkite," he wrote, "the slot man for CBS":** Crosby, "Too Much Coverage?"

272 **"Television," David Halberstam wrote of early 1950s journalism:** Halberstam, *The Powers That Be*, p. 130.

273 **"I am succeeding in maintaining objectivity":** Walter Cronkite to Don Michel, Michel Archive (personal), Dallas, Texas.

273   "we had really pulled off a revolution": Perkins, "Television Covers the 1952 Political Conventions in Chicago."

274   Cronkite had become "not just 'an anchorman'": Hewitt, *Tell Me a Story*, p. 55.

274   "you're famous now": Tom Wicker, "Broadcast News," *New York Times*, January 26, 1997.

274   "On the air Murrow treated Cronkite with collegiality": Edwards, *Edward R. Murrow*.

275   issued a press release naming him "anchorman": "CBS-TV's Plans for Nationwide Election Day Coverage," CBS press release, September 25, 1952, CBS News Archives, New York.

275   able to project election results from returns better than humans: James W. Cortada, *Before the Computer: IBM, NCR Burroughs, and Remington Rand and the Industry They Created, 1865–1956* (Princeton, NJ: Princeton University Press, 1993), p. 156.

275   "The novelty value of using UNIVAC: Mickelson, *From Whistle Stop to Sound Bite*, p. 138.

275   This left ABC news director John Madigan to lampoon: "Radio: Univac and Monrobot," *Time*, October 27, 1952.

276 **"Actually we're not depending too much":** Quoted in Chinoy, "Battle of the Brains," pp. 254–255.

276 **Cronkite was trying to gin up excitement:** CBS News Election Coverage, November 4, 1952 (eight-part transcription), Paley Center for Media, New York.

277 **"overly rich doses of high technology":** Mickelson, *From Whistle Stop to Sound Bite*, p. 134.

279 **"it may be possible for men and machines to draw":** CBS Election Night Coverage 1952 (transcript), Paley Center, New York.

282 **"Television has an X-ray quality":** Walter Cronkite, "Government by Hooper Rating?" *Theatre Arts*, November 1952.

282 **Ernie Leiser in Hungary:** Author interview with Morton Dean, September 14, 2011.

283 **Once Leiser and Cronkite had taped the royal pomp:** Sonia Stein, "TV's Coronation Spectacle Shades Space-Time Miracle," *Washington Post*, June 3, 1953.

283 **chartered plane:** Sonia Stein, "TV Is Rushing Films to U.S.," *Washington Post*, May 31, 1953.

283 **"gutted"**: Lawrence Laurent, "ABC Wins Sylvania Prize for Coronation Coverage," *Washington Post*, December 2, 1953.

284 **A broadcastography of Cronkite**: Alfred Robert Hogan, "Walter Cronkite Broadcasting Highlights/Broadcastography, 1943–2009," August 1, 2011 (unpublished transcript), Hogan Archive, Washington, DC.

284 **"Cronkite and Murrow didn't work well"**: Hewitt, *Tell Me a Story*, p. 70. See also "Peabody Honors Stations, CBS," *Broadcasting*, March 18, 1946.

Twelve: MR. CBS UTILITY MAN

286 **announcer would almost shout out, "You are there!"**: Tim Brooks and Earle Marsh, *The Complete Dictionary to Prime Time Network and Cable TV Shows 1946–Present*, 9th ed. (New York: Ballantine Books, 2007), pp. 1552–1553.

286 **Russell, refusing "dramatic license" in re-creating the past**: Lawrence Laurent, "Video Proves Nothing's as Exciting as History," *Washington Post*, December 13, 1953.

286 **"the premise of the series was so silly"**: "Walter Cronkite Dies," CBS News, http://www

.cbsnews.com/stories/2009/07/17/eveningnews/
main5170556.shtml (accessed November 3, 2011).

287 **"He's good," Dozier said, "he's effective"**:
Doug James, *Walter Cronkite*, p. 99.

287 **Cronkite's "serious demeanor"**: "Walter
Cronkite Dies," CBS News.

287 **"the history teacher"**: "St. Joseph Native
Narrates TV Series on 'You Are There,'" *Daily
Capital News*, February 10, 1955.

287 **"I was brought on as an actor"**: Walter Cronkite,
"Remembering 'You Are There,'" *All Things
Considered*, NPR, October 27, 2003.

288 **"Sidney Lumet's stock company"**: Walter
Cronkite interview with Richard Snow, "He Was
There."

288 **Russell wasn't willing to "play the blacklist
game"**: Cronkite, "Remembering 'You Are
There.'"

288 **"offered no shortage of ways to deal"**: Ibid.

289 **"man of all work"**: John Crosby, "Radio and TV
Comments," February 9, 1953.

289 **detonations at Yucca Flats**: Tim O'Brien, *The
Nuclear Age* (New York, Alfred A. Knopf, 1995),
p. 123.

290   **created signature sign-off lines such as "A good good-evening to you":** Les Brown, *The New York Times Encyclopedia of Television* (New York: Times Books, 1970), p. 66.

290   **Murrow wasn't Mickelson's "cup of tea":** Felicity Barringer, "Sig Mickelson, First Director of CBS's TV News, Dies at 86," *New York Times*, March 27, 2000.

291   **"The name which most viewers":** Mickelson, *The Electric Mirror*, pp. 159–160.

292   **"I think newsmen are inclined to side with humanity":** Powers, "Walter Cronkite: A Candid Conversation."

292   **"I thought he'd gotten the nomination":** Cronkite and Carleton, *Conversations with Cronkite*, p. 114.

293   **"CBS executives sensed a more immediate concern":** Walter Cronkite, "Civil Rights Era Almost Split CBS News Operation," *All Things Considered*, NPR, transcript, May 30, 2005.

294   **it would have been a career killer:** Author interview with Marvin Kalb, March 18, 2011.

294   **"A puppet," Cronkite said, "can render":** Michael Davis, *Street Gag: The Complete History*

of Sesame Street (New York: Penguin, 2008), p. 40.

295 a **"whimsical and frequently off-beat sense of humor":** Al Morton, "Martha Wright's Success Started with Song to Sow," syndicated, May 27, 1954.

297 **The gig went to Bill Shadel:** "TV Anchor Bill Shadel Dies; CBS, WTOP Radio Reporter," *Washington Post*, February 1, 2005.

297 **"serious broadcaster":** "Bill Shadel, 96, Nixon-Kennedy Moderator," *New York Times*, February 2, 2005.

297 **"I don't like the challenge":** Steven Scheuer, "Cronkite Likes Show Challenge," *Syracuse Herald-Journal*, October 20, 1955.

298 **"But I do believe in Walter Cronkite":** Al Reinert, "The Secret World of Walter Cronkite."

299 **"emerged wet but unhurt":** Lapham, "The Secret Life of Walter (Mitty) Cronkite," *Saturday Evening Post*, March 16, 1963.

300 **"You're our next Douglas Edwards":** Author interview with Phil Jones, October 21, 2011.

301 **"And then, one of the great compromisers said":** William Whitworth, "An Accident of Casting," *New Yorker*, August 3, 1968.

301 **"They received the critical attention:** "The Most Intimate Medium," *Time*, October 14, 1966.

Thirteen: THE HUNTLEY AND BRINKLEY CHALLENGE

303 **"dead pan":** Jack Gould, "In Retrospect; Some Random Reflections on Coverage of the Conventions by Television," *New York Times*, August 26, 1956.

304 **"The low CBS morale":** Eric Sevareid to Sig Mickelson, October 19, 1957, Box: 7733, CBS Records, New York.

305 **Cronkite even intimated:** Walter Cronkite to Sig Mickelson, October 14, 1956, Box: 7733, CBS Records, New York.

305 **naturally "clicked":** Gould, "In Retrospect."

306 **"While past attempts at using two anchormen":** Michael A. Russo, "CBS and the American Political Experience: A History of the CBS News Special Events and Election Units, 1952–1968," PhD dissertation, New York University, June 1983, p. 160.

307 **"It was a situation made to order":** Sig Mickelson, *The Decade That Shaped Television News*, p. 210.

307 **Cronkite's appearance on *What's My Line?*:** YouTube, "Walter Cronkite—What's My Line,"

www.youtube.com/watch?v=c6_RHxArgp8 (accessed August 13, 2011).

308 **"Mr. Brinkley's extraordinary accomplishment":** Jack Gould, "Witty Commentator: Brinkley Enlivens NBC Convention Coverage," *New York Times*, August 17, 1956.

309 **"We like the straight-news simplicity":** Sandusky *Register Star News*, August 8, 1956.

309 **"Walter thought that there were no":** Author interview with Brian Williams, September 2, 2011.

311 **The *Pick the Winner* series ran for eight weeks:** September 12, 1956, through November 5, 1956, CBS News Programming Logs, CBS News Archives, New York.

311 **CBS whipped the competition with a 25.3 rating:** Thomas W. Bohn, "Broadcasting National Election Returns, 1952–1976," *Journal of Communication* 30, no. 4 (Autumn 1980): 143.

312 **"my presence on CBS was confined":** Walter Cronkite, "How Sputnik Changed the World," *All Things Considered*, NPR, October 4, 2002.

312 **By 1958, CBS News had restructured:** "CBS at 75" Timeline—CBS News, CBS Archive, New York.

313 **Although Mudd's primary job was doing the 6:00 a.m. radio newscast:** Mudd, *The Place to Be*, pp. 20–21.

313 **"Although we all snorted about his gaffes":** Ibid., p. 344.

315 **Cronkite had "breached the shallow wall":** Walter Cronkite, radio broadcast, "The Mike Todd Party," *All Things Considered*, NPR, November 29, 2004.

315 **first and most well disguised ninety-minute infomercial:** Ibid.

315 **"Even the smooth-as-silk Walter Cronkite":** Fred Brooks, "Why Did I Keep Watching That Stupid Show," *Kansas Salina Journal*, October 23, 1957.

316 **the episodes immediately took a turn:** CBS News, *The Twentieth Century* (four-year report), October 1957–May 1961, Bob Asman Personal Papers.

317 **"We had lost the space race before we knew we were in it":** Cronkite, "How Sputnik Changed the World," *All Things Considered*, NPR, October 4, 2002.

317 **going to Cape Canaveral:** Walter Cronkite, "And That's the Way It Was," *Newsweek*, October 26, 1998.

320 his *The Twentieth Century* producer the "finest" documentarian: Walter Cronkite, Preface to *Fair Play: CBS, General Westmoreland, and How a Television Documentary Went Wrong* (New York: HarperCollins, 1988).

321 "In those days . . . I was temporarily": Harry Reasoner, *Before the Colors Fade* (New York: Knopf, 1981), pp. 37–41.

322 Reasoner blared out, "There she goes": Alfred Robert Hogan, "Televising the Space Age: A Descriptive Chronology of CBS News Special Events Coverage of Space Coverage from 1957–2003," master's thesis, 2005, Graduate School of the University of Maryland, College Park.

322 "It's difficult to remember now how impossibly dangerous": Walter Cronkite, "And That's the Way It Was," *Newsweek*, October 26, 1998.

323 He not only liked the role of space reporter: Ibid.

323 "Walter saw *The Twentieth Century* as a sly way to build": Author interview with Andy Rooney, March 15, 2011.

324 employees were forced to sign a loyalty oath: Jeff Kisseloff, "Televison/Radio; Another Award,

Other Memories of McCarthyism," *New York Times*, May 30, 1999.

326 **"conquest of space":** "NASA Honors Veteran Journalist Walter Cronkite," NASA.gov, February 28, 2006, http://www.nasa.gov/vision/space/fea tures/cronkite_ambassador_of_exploration.html.

328 **Thomas, an obviously serious man of good humor:** "Lowell Thomas, A World Traveler and Broadcaster for 45 Years, Dead," *New York Times*, August 30, 1981.

328 **"His almost forty-six years of reporting":** George Plimpton, *As Told at the Explorers Club: More Than Fifty Gripping Tales of Adventure* (Guilford, CT: Lyons Press, 2005), p. 431.

329 **"Everybody he met, as far as I know":** Ibid., p. 441.

330 **"If I knew, I'd be working for the Pentagon":** "U.S. Hungry for Know-How," Associated Press, January 20, 1958.

330 **Before long, Cronkite befriended the intellectual pundits:** Burton Benjamin, *The Documentary: An Endangered Species* (paper #6, Garrett Center for Media Studies), NY: Columbia University, October 1987; "The Documentary

Heritage," *Television Quarterly*, February 1962; "TV Documentarians Dream in Challenging World," *Variety*, January 4, 1961; "From Bustles to Bikinis—and All That Drama," *Variety*, July 27, 1960.

330 **"It's difficult for a celebrity":** Kenneth Barnard, "Korea Was Walter's Goal But He Got Sidetracked," *Hamburg Iowa Reporter*, April 12, 1959.

Fourteen: TORCH IS PASSED

332 **"Walter was the ultimate company man":** Author interview with Andy Rooney, March 15, 2011.

332 **"unprecedented" TV coverage of a presidential foreign trip:** "CBS to Give Ike's Trip Unprecedented Coverage," *New York Times*, December 4, 1959.

333 **"send me":** Maggie Savoy, "Cronkite Was Here," *The Arizona Republic*, April 5, 1961.

333 **"he trots the globe in pursuit of current history":** H. D. Quigg, "CBS Ready to Let Go Anchor-Man at Conventions," *Washington Post*, June 19, 1960.

333 **Cronkite, filling in for McKay, quickly became the TV master:** Robert J. Donovan and Ray Scherer, *Unsilent Revolution: Television News and American Public Life, 1948–1991* (Cambridge, UK: Cambridge University Press, 1992), p. 289.

334 **While he served as anchorman:** "Display Ad 110," *Washington Post*, February 18, 1960.

335 **Cronkite was accorded some historical credit:** "Saturday TV Program," *Washington Post*, February 14, 1960; "Thursday TV Highlights," *Washington Post*, February 14, 1960; "Television Previews," *Washington Post*, February 18, 1960; "Preview of Saturday's TV Highlights," *Washington Post*, February 20, 1960.

335 **Summer Olympics:** Jennifer Moreland, "Olympics and Television," Museum of Broadcast Communications, http://www.museum.tv/eotv section .php?entrycode=olympicsand.

336 **"We think of him as the on-air editor and coordinator":** Quigg, "CBS Ready to Let Go Anchor-Man at Conventions."

337 **"only Walter Cronkite had not been moved forward":** Walter Cronkite Fan Club *Newsletter* (June 1974), Feder Archive, Chicago, IL.

338 **raising money had become what politicians did:** Donovan and Scherer, *Unsilent Revolution*, p. 225.

339 **the two candidates first had to be chosen:** Theodore H. White, *The Making of the President, 1960* (New York: Atheneum House, 1961), p. 282.

340 **"We were on a shopping trip":** Dan Rather, *I Remember* (Boston: Little, Brown, 1991), p. 231.

341 **Paley hated being a number two:** White, *The Making of the President 1960*, p. 283.

341 **"This was supposed to be comeback time":** Author interview with Dan Rather, February 11, 2010.

342 **"I panicked and went to Sig Mickelson":** Don Hewitt, *Fifty Years and Sixty Minutes in Television*, p. 70.

342 **"Hewitt, whose judgment was normally impeccable":** Mickelson, *The Decade That Shaped Television*, p. 220.

343 **"One of the basic troubles with radio and television":** Sperber, *Murrow, His Life and Times*, p. xxii.

344 **"Murrow thought he was a larger historical personage":** Author interview with Don Hewitt, February 15, 1998.

344 **"I applauded it wildly":** Cronkite and Carleton, *Conversations with Cronkite*, pp. 137–38.

345 **The most notable Murrow documentary became "Harvest of Shame":** Kendrick, *Prime Time*, p. 505.

345 **"Walter was big":** Author interview with Dan Rather, February 18, 2011.

345 **"Murrow came and sat":** Ibid.

346 **"Who's supposed to do what?":** Cronkite and Carleton, *Conversations with Cronkite*, p. 140.

348 **"the pre-eminence of CBS in news":** Jack Gould, "TV's New Convention Look," *New York Times*, July 17, 1960.

348 **admitted in retrospect that it had been "a terrible idea":** Hewitt, *Fifty Years*, p. 70.

349 **CBS lost viewers to ABC:** "The Battle of TV News," *Newsweek*, September 21, 1963.

349 **"Cronkite was not blamed at all":** David Schoenbrun, *On and Off the Air: An Informal History of CBS News* (New York: Dutton Adult, 1989), p. 128.

350 **"Dr. Stanton courageously stood up":** Cronkite, *A Reporter's Life*, p. 186.

350 **"Walter Cronkite's a Republican, isn't he":** Halberstam, *The Powers That Be*, p. 414.

351 *Presidential Countdown's* **first telecast:** Brooks and Marsh, *The Complete Directory of Prime Time Network and Cable TV Shows*, pp. 1100–1101.

351 **"I came up with the idea":** Cronkite and Carleton, *Conversations with Cronkite*, p. 195.

356 **Cronkite threw unexpected questions at Nixon:** John P. Shanley, "TV: A Talk with Nixon," *New York Times*, September 13, 1980.

356 **The house had been a gift from Kennedy:** Pauline Frommer and James Yenckel, *Pauline Frommer's Washington, Part 3* (Hoboken, NJ: Wiley Publishing, 2007), p. 201.

357 **"When it was over, we thanked him:** Cronkite and Carleton, *Conversations with Cronkite*, p. 197.

358 **"I've got to talk to him":** Ibid., p. 195.

358 **They both saw "a fire in Walter's eyes":** Author interview with Ted Sorensen, May 14, 2010.

361 **"CBS is not the Ministry of Justice":** Schoenbrun, *On and Off the Air*, p. 129.

362 **CBS radio was in a position to start fresh:** White, *News on the Air*, pp. 22–23.

364 **And it was Cronkite, not Murrow, who was chosen as one of four reporters:** Sidney Kraus, *Great Debates: Kennedy vs. Nixon 1960* (Bloomington: Indiana University Press, 1977), p. 114.

365 **"The networks had insisted that the interrogators":** Sig Mickelson, *The Electric Mirror*, p. 211.

365 **CBS News spent a fortune taking out display ads:** "Display Ad 88," *Washington Post*, September 12, 1960, and "Display Ad 65," *Washington Post*, November 4, 1960.

366 **the show pro-Nixon:** Chris Matthews, *Jack Kennedy: Elusive Hero* (New York: Simon & Schuster, 2011).

Fifteen: NEW SPACE FRONTIER ON CBS

369 **"Our guys," Cronkite recalled, "were pulling cables":** Cronkite and Carleton, *Conversations with Cronkite*, p. 200.

369 **But all the CBSers were grumpy because they'd been outplayed by NBC News:** Val Adams, "News of TV and Radio—The Inauguration," *New York Times*, January 15, 1961.

369 **"I've been watching you and I have a big job":** Author interview with Robert Wussler.

370 **Are we *sure* JFK will be the youngest president?:** Thurston Clarke, *Ask Not: The Inauguration of John F. Kennedy and the Speech That Changed America* (New York: Henry Holt, 2004), p. 181.

370 **Born in Newark, New Jersey, in 1936, Wussler:** *Who's Who in America* (New Providence, NJ: Marquis, 1999), p. 5395.

370 **Wussler started helping Douglas Edwards:** Gates, *Air Time*, pp. 329–330.

371 **He ran the CBS News special events unit:** Hogan, "Televising the Space Age."

371 **"Men are going to fly in space":** Ibid., pp. 248–49.

372 **Cronkite himself had claimed that during the Second World War:** "Cronkite Believes He Saw V-2 Rocket," UP, December 2, 1944.

372 **The Cronkite-Wussler creative collaboration:** Russo, "CBS and the American Political Experience," pp. 305–13.

373 **"It was a little bit like being along for Columbus":** Robert Wussler interview with

Alfred Robert Hogan, March 13, 2003 (transcript), Hogan Archive, Washington, DC.

375 **Frank Stanton, working behind the scenes, had convinced the Kennedy gang:** Sandy Socolow to Douglas Brinkley, October 20, 2011.

377 **there would be a "prime-time examination" of where NASA (the U.S.) stood:** Author interview with Sandy Socolow, July 11, 2011.

377 **Cronkite and Marvin Kalb interviewed Gagarin:** Walter Cronkite/Marvin Kalb, "Down to Earth," CBS News, *Eyewitness to History*, April 14, 1961 (transcript), CBS News Reference Library, New York.

377 **"American prestige was jolted":** David Greene, "In Russia, Space Ride for U.S. Spurs Nostalgia, Hope," NPR News, July 15, 2011.

377 **"There was great pressure":** Cronkite and Carleton, *Conversations with Cronkite*, p. 233.

378 **"We were quite aware that the image that NASA was trying to project":** Gerard J. Degroot, *Dark Side of the Moon: The Magnificent Madness of the American Lunar Quest* (New York: New York University Press, 2006), p. 106.

379 **"I wasn't scared, but I was up there looking around"**: Gene Kranz, *Failure Is Not an Option: Mission Control from Mercury to Apollo 13 and Beyond* (New York: Simon & Schuster, 2009), p. 201.

379 **"We feared that Shepard's flight was premature"**: Cronkite, *A Reporter's Life*, pp. 274–75.

379 **"a man was going to sit on top of all that"**: "TV Looks at American in Space," *Christian Science Monitor*, July 19, 1974.

381 **When he praised the "depth of broadcast's contribution"**: Newton M. Minow, "Television and the Public Interest," National Association of Broadcasters, delivered May 9, 1961, reprinted in William Safire, ed., *Lend Me Your Ears: Great Speeches in American History* (New York: Norton, 2004), pp. 788–796.

382 **"You just saw the umbilical cord come away"**: Transcript of Walter Cronkite covering *Liberty Bell 7*, Gus Grissom Launch, Friday, July 21, 1961, CBS News Archive, New York.

384 **"captured the phenomenon of Eisenhower"**: Jack Gould, "TV: An Elder Statesman," *New York Times*, October 13, 1961.

384 credited Cronkite with conducting a "brilliant historical interview": Jack O'Brian, *New York Journal American* [nd], WCP-UTA.

384 Cronkite's CBS team focused on Boston's police: Bliss, *Now the News*, pp. 392–93.

385 "At this point, you may be inclined to say": Walter Cronkite, "Biography of a Bookie Joint," November 30, 1961, CBS News Archives, New York. The show was rebroadcast on March 20, 1963.

385 he was a "relentless adversary": Lapham, "The Secret Life of Walter (Mitty) Cronkite."

386 "There's no physical exhaustion": Joan Crosby, "Hectic Night Due for Anchor Men," *Abilene Reporter*, November 6, 1962.

386 identical to the Eisenhower administration, only "thirty years younger": Chalmer M. Roberts, "Kennedy Moving Ahead 'Decisively,' Lippmann Says, Lauding Crisis Acts," *Washington Post*, December 22, 1961.

387 For the Glenn mission, it had a team: CBS News, *Seven Days* (privately published), July 1962, John Glenn Papers, Ohio State University, Columbus.

387 "Space travel was so new": Author interview with John Glenn, October 27, 2011.

388 **"a glorified radio broadcast"**: Ron Bonn, "CBS News and the Landing of the Moon," speech draft, June 18, 2011, Bonn Archive, Naples, FL.

388 **At the CBS News control center**: "Cronkite Brings Enthusiasm for Space to CNN," *Houston Chronicle*, July 30, 1998.

388 **the orbit that "united the nation"**: Jack Gould, "Radio-TV: Networks Convey Drama of Glenn Feat; Give Dazzling Display of Modern Electronics," *New York Times*, February 21, 1962.

389 **"The best moment"**: Walter Cronkite, "Outstanding Moments During TV Coverage of John Glenn," *New York Herald Tribune*, April 29, 1962.

389 **"When President Kennedy comes to pin a medal"**: CBS News, *Seven Days*.

390 **"I think we have a lot more knowledge"**: "The Interpreters and the 'Golden Throats,'" *Newsweek*, October 8, 1962.

391 **it was "a one-up"**: Sacknoff, *In Their Own Words*, p. 194.

392 **"Can you imagine how great it would be to say"**: Joe Adcock, "Walter Cronkite," *Texas Magazine*, November 27, 1966.

392 **Cronkite outshone the competition:** Barbara Matusow, *The Evening Stars: The Making of the Network News Anchor* (Boston: Houghton Mifflin, 1983), p. 126.

393 **"instead of looking down despondently, we could look":** Sacknoff, *In Their Own Words,* p. 195.

393 **"This is not just Cronkite the old reportorial warhorse":** Cecil Smith, "Cronkite Flees NY—by Design," *Los Angeles Times,* May 22, 1962.

393 **Cronkite was treated as the new Murrow:** CBS News, *Seven Days.*

394 **"we all took to calling Walter 'Mr. Space'":** Author interview with John Glenn, October 27, 2011.

395 **"Just as Noah once sent out a dove":** "T-Minus 4 Years, 9 Months, and 30 Days," CBS Television Network, March 1, 1965 (transcript), CBS Research Library, New York.

Sixteen: ANCHORMAN OF CAMELOT

400 **"How many times have you been around?":** Lawrence Laurent, "Walter Does Get Around," *Washington Post,* March 27, 1960.

401 "Walter wanted to ride on the Kennedys' coat-tails": Author interview with Andy Rooney, March 15, 2011.

401 "first television president": Halberstam, *The Powers That Be*, p. 316.

403 Midgley was first hired by CBS in the mid-1950s: Douglas Martin, "Leslie Midgley, 87, Prolific TV News Producer," *New York Times*, June 20, 2002.

405 "Once Cronkite came to Newport with his director Vinny Walters": Author interview with Lew Wood, January 10, 2012.

405 "turned Cronkite onto the yachting world": Ibid.

406 "all the women who've made Cronkite men": David Friend, "Guess Who's Going Up in Orbit," *Life*, August 19, 1984 (unpublished interview notes), Friend Archive.

406 his CBS superiors were ready with the hook: Dennis Hevesi, "Douglas Edwards, First TV Anchorman, Dies at 73," *New York Times*, October 14, 1990.

407 When President Kennedy summoned Murrow to run USIA: Fred W. Friendly, *Due to*

Circumstances Beyond Our Control (New York: Vintage Books, 1968), pp. 126–27.

407 **Smith lashed out:** Harold Jackson, "Howard K. Smith," *The Guardian*, February 19, 2002.

407 **"All that is necessary for the triumph of evil":** Daniel E. Ritchie, ed., *Edmund Burke: Appraisals and Applications* (New Brunswick, NJ: Transaction Publishers, 1990), p. xiii.

408 **"I have heard all this junk before":** Howard K. Smith, *Events Leading Up to My Death* (New York: St. Martin's Press, 1997), p. 275.

408 **the days of Murrow's ACLU-infused mania were over:** Friendly, *Due to Circumstances Beyond Our Control*, p. 127.

409 **"Walter was in the studio sucking on cough drops":** Smith, *Events Leading Up to My Death*, p. 258.

410 **his love of Russian caviar and French espionage:** See Charles Collingwood, *The Defector* (New York: Ace, 1970).

411 **"Sig had begun at ground-zero and built":** Smith, *Events Leading Up to My Death*, pp. 268–69.

411 **"We were naturally terribly worried":** Walter Cronkite, "Reflections on Dick Salant," New

Canaan (Connecticut) Public Library, November 24, 1996.

412 **"We were," Cronkite recalled, "all depressed":** Walter Cronkite, "Salant Memorial Service," February 22, 1993, Museum of Television and Radio Archives, New York.

413 **the Wallace-Edwards team became fondly known as the "Cunningham Aces":** Susan Buzenberg and Bill Buzenberg, eds., *Salant, CBS, and the Battle for the Soul of Broadcast Journalism: The Memoirs of Richard S. Salant* (Boulder, CO: Westview Press, 1999), p. 37.

414 **"not the right image for an anchorman":** Schoenbrun, *On and Off the Air*, p. 143.

414 **nicknamed "one-take Walter":** Robert W. Butler, "From One Legend to Another, Good News," *Kansas City Star*, June 12, 1996.

415 **"We didn't pick Walter to anchor":** Buzenberg and Buzenberg, *Salant, CBS, and the Battle for the Soul of Broadcast Journalism*, p. 37.

416 **"That's the news":** Walter Cronkite, *CBS Evening News*, April 16, 1962 (broadcast transcript), CBS News Research Library, New York.

416 **"The suits—as we used to call them—went crazy":** Tom Watkins, "How 'That's the Way It Is' Became Cronkite's Tagline," CNN, July 18, 2009.

417 **"Over on CBS tonight Walter Cronkite takes over":** Cynthia Lowry, "Cronkite Won Respect of Rival Newscasters," Associated Press, April 29, 1962.

417 **"He was the father figure of television journalists":** Ben Bradlee, "Walter Cronkite, 1916–2009," *Newsweek*, July 27, 2009.

418 **"Doug Edwards used to brag that he had the highest rated newscast":** Author interview with Mervin Block, July 27, 2011.

419 **"knows the future of CBS news is riding on him":** "The Battle of TV News," *Newsweek*, September 23, 1963.

419 **Cronkite and director Don Hewitt:** David Schoenbrun, *On and Off the Air*, p. 84.

421 **"Cronkite would foresee the Next Big Story":** Ron Bonn to Douglas Brinkley, January 4, 2012.

421 **Cronkite as part of communications history:** Val Adams, "U.S. and Europe Exchange Live TV," *New York Times*, July 24, 1962.

422 Cronkite's profession had been revolutionized with the transmission of images: Ibid.

422 "The reality of live telecasts to Europe seemed so unbelievable": Ibid.

423 "He's nervous," Fred Friendly said: "The Battle of TV News," *Newsweek,* September 21, 1963.

425 "Turns out Helen was a swinger": Author interview with Bill Small, March 22, 2011.

425 "the half-hour news show was a communications creation": John Horn, "News—But Not Good News," *New York Herald-Tribune,* November 30, 1963.

427 "CBS is expanding Cronkite to a half hour": Frank, *Out of Thin Air,* p. 180.

427 CBS's news expansion "revolutionized" the American political process: Buzenberg and Buzenberg, *Salant, CBS, and the Battle for the Soul of Broadcast Journalism,* p. 43.

428 "Hewitt wanted to get all the kinks out": Author interview with Sandy Socolow, November 14, 2011.

429 script makers would "rip stories off the half-dozen wire service Teletypes": Ron Bonn to Douglas Brinkley, June 7, 2011.

429 **Having won a Peabody Award:** "Networks Divide Peabody Awards," *New York Times*, March 28, 1963.

429 **CBS had been chosen by lot to coordinate the pooled coverage:** Stephen C. Rogers, "March to Get Full News Goverage," *Washington Post*, August 25, 1963.

429 **"They called it the March on Washington for jobs and freedom":** Walter Cronkite, *CBS Evening News* broadcast transcript, August 29, 1963, CBS News Archive, New York.

431 **Not everybody at CBS thought Cronkite's coming to Cape Cod:** Richard Reeves, *President Kennedy: Profile of Power* (New York: Simon & Schuster, 1993), p. 586.

431 **"As I drove up to the motel":** Cronkite, *A Reporter's Life*, p. 246.

432 **"I was getting a little fed up":** Author interview with Robert Pierpoint, March 19, 2011.

433 **Cronkite—following questions about:** Harold W. Chase and Allen H. Lerman, eds., *Kennedy and the Press: The News Conferences* (New York: Thomas Y. Cromwell, 1965), pp. 484–86.

433 **"It is their war":** Kenneth P. O'Donnell and David F. Powers, *Johnny, We Hardly Knew Ye: Memories of John Fitzgerald Kennedy* (Boston: Little, Brown, 1972), p. 444.

434 **Salinger complained vehemently to CBS:** Reeves, *President Kennedy*, p. 589.

434 **the Kennedy administration was distancing:** Cronkite, *A Reporter's Life*, p. 244.

434 **"partial distortion":** Pierre Salinger, *With Kennedy* (Garden City, NY: Doubleday, 1966), p. 125.

434 **"Salinger was preparing a preemptive defense":** Cronkite, *A Reporter's Life*, p. 248.

435 **The features unfolded like articles in a glossy magazine:** John Horn, "News—But Not Good News," *New York Times Herald Tribune*, November 30, 1963.

435 **the shows didn't seem to offer anything more:** Ibid.

437 **his nightly catchphrase "caught on instantly":** Walter Cronkite interview with Archive of American Television (April 28, 1998, and October 18, 1999), Academy of Television Arts and Sciences Foundation, North Hollywood, CA.

Seventeen: THE KENNEDY ASSASSINATION

438   **eating a low-calorie cottage cheese and pine-apple salad:** Bliss, *Now the News*, pp. 335–337.

439   **he clearly did not have this forty-six-year-old *Newsweek* cover star in mind:** Alex S. Jones, *Losing the News: The Future of News That Feeds Democracy* (New York: Oxford University Press, 2009), p. 46.

440   **"Hell, yes, there's a battle":** Ibid.

440   **Flummoxed by his Florida experience, Wood recommended:** Lew Wood, "Dallas and JFK," *Reporter's Notebook* (blog), November 20, 2008.

441   **"loaded for bear":** Author interview with Lew Wood, January 9, 2012.

441   **"Dan Rather was downtown to cover the motorcade":** Ibid.

442   **"Hold on, Lew . . . don't go away":** Wood, "Dallas and JFK."

443   **"We figured there might be some good footage for Walter to run":** Author interview with Robert Pierpoint, March 19, 2011.

445   **"My God, they've killed Jack":** Smith, *Grace and Power*, pp. 447–48.

445 **"THREE SHOTS WERE FIRED":** Patrick J. Sloyan, "Albert Merriman Smith," *American Journalism Review* (May 1997).

446 **"DA IT YRS NY":** Small, *To Kill a Messenger*, p. 135.

446 **Although Rather's version of events has self-servingly changed:** In March 1964, Rather told author John Mayo that he was stationed along the expressway and saw the motorcade speed past after the shooting. This version of events was later published in Mayo's book, *Bulletin from Dallas: The President Is Dead*. Rather then stated in his 1977 book, *The Camera Never Blinks Twice*, that he was in fact next to Dealey Plaza (on the other side of a railroad overpass) when the shooting occurred. Wood insists that Rather was at KRLD-TV when Kennedy was shot. It's confusing. But Rather did great work.

448 **"Let's get on the air":** Cronkite and Carleton, *Conversations with Cronkite*, p. 202.

448 **but the cameras needed ten or fifteen minutes to warm up:** Walter Cronkite interview, Archive of American Television, April 28, 1994.

448 **the studio lights weren't "hot":** Bliss, *Now the News*, p. 336.

449 **"Here is a bulletin from CBS News":** "As 175 Million Americans Watched . . . ," *Newsweek*, December 9, 1963.

450 **"We beat NBC onto the air":** Cronkite, *A Reporter's Life*, p. 305.

450 **It was also Smith who first used the term** *grassy knoll*: Gary Mack (curator), "The Man Who Named the Grassy Knoll," Sixth Floor Museum at Dealey Plaza, mcadams.posc.mu.edu/ gk_name.htm (accessed October 31, 2011).

451 **As the crisis deepened, Eddie Barker, news director of KRLD-TV:** Small, *To Kill a Messenger*, p. 135.

451 **"Because of Barker and Rather," Cronkite claimed:** Cronkite and Carleton, *Conversations with Cronkite*, p. 202.

452 **CBS stayed live for fifty-five hours:** Small, *To Kill a Messenger*, p. 136.

452 **when a crisis occurred, "the adrenaline pumps":** "Cronkite Talks of Regents and Doing the Job," *Lancaster* (PA) *New Era*, April 12, 2000.

453 **"I don't even recall the spots":** "As 175 Million Americans Watched."

453 **"Walter ate all of this up":** Author interview with Sandy Socolow, September 18, 2010.

454 **Jackie Kennedy's pink Chanel suit being saturated with blood:** Gary Mack (Sixth Floor Museum) to Douglas Brinkley, December 25, 2011.

454 **"I was in shock":** Richard Goldstein, "Robert Pierpoint, 86, Dies; CBS News Correspondent," *New York Times*, October 24, 2011.

454 **"let them see what they've done":** Smith, *Grace and Power*, p. 442.

455 **He felt a "chill":** Bliss, *Now the News*, p. 337.

456 **"Even if you are right (and God help you if you are wrong)":** Rather and Herskowitz, *The Camera Never Blinks Twice*, p. 120.

457 **"Whoever said talk is cheap":** Sperber, *Murrow: His Life and Times*, p. 684.

458 **"I was really just a disreputable character":** Walter Cronkite oral history interview, p. 452, WCP-UTA.

458 **"From Dallas, Texas, the flash apparently official":** CBS News transcript, "The Assassination of President John F. Kennedy as Broadcast on the CBS Network," November 22, 1963, vol. 1, p. 24.

459 **"We knew it was coming":** Cronkite and Carleton, *Conversations with Cronkite*, p. 203.

459 **"It was touch and go there for a few seconds":** Cronkite, *A Reporter's Life*, p. 305.

459 **Cronkite explained that "the psychological trauma" didn't touch him:** Walter Cronkite interview, Archive of American Television, April 28, 1999.

459 **Unbeknownst to Cronkite, Vice President Johnson had been whisked:** Jim Bishop, *The Day Kennedy Was Shot* (New York: Funk & Wagnalls, 1968), pp. 269–70.

461 **"I think we just kind of intuitively knew what to do":** "JFK: Breaking the News," extended interview (transcript) with Eddie Barker, Online *NewsHour*, Public Broadcasting Service, November 20, 2003, http://www.pbs.org/news hour/bb/white_house/kennedy/barker.html.

461 **"When the news is bad, Walter hurts":** "A Man Who Cares," *Newsweek*, March 9, 1981.

463 **"This is Walter Cronkite, and you're a god-damn idiot":** Frank, *Out of Thin Air*, p. 187.

463 **"Unfortunately, that Park Avenue lady drove me mad":** Oriana Fallaci, "Walter Cronkite

Says What He Can't Say on Television," *Look*, November 17, 1970.

464 **"We were not challenged":** Author interview with Lew Wood, January 9, 2012.

465 **"It was an easy shot":** Wood, "Dallas and JFK," *Reporter's Notebook*, November 20, 2008.

465 **made history by airing a two-hour telecast:** CBS Television Network Program Logs, November 1–November 30, 1963, CBS News Archives, New York. Also A. R. Hogan to Douglas Brinkley, August 2, 2011.

465 **Cronkite steadied the 70 million friends of CBS News:** Miller and Runyon, "And That's the Way It Seems," p. 23.

466 **CBS News *did* have a camera at the Dallas police department:** Bliss, *Now the News*, p. 339.

466 **ABC didn't broadcast Oswald's death:** Gary Mack to Virginia Northington, November 14, 2011.

466 **"One of the great misfortunes at CBS was that we were off":** Cronkite and Carleton, *Conversations with Cronkite*, p. 203.

466 **"the national hearth":** George Rosen, "Television Responds with Its Finest Hour," *Variety*, November 27, 1963.

466 **93 percent of U.S. homes with televisions were tuned in:** Bliss, *Now the News*, p. 340.

467 **"to involve an entire population in a ritual process":** Marshall McLuhan, *Understanding Media: The Extensions of Man* (New York: McGraw-Hill, 1964), p. 293.

467 **"It is said that the human mind has a greater capacity":** "Cronkite Broadcasts: Moon Landing, JFK Death," MSNBC, http://today.msnbc.msn.com/id/31972354/ns/today-entertainment/t/cronkite-broadcasts-moon-landing-jfk-death/ (accessed July 3, 2011).

469 **"Walter was really in his element":** Author interview with Sandy Socolow, September 18, 2010.

469 **They'd go immediately to their Apple laptop:** M. G. Siegler, "In the Age of Realtime, Twitter Is Walter Cronkite," *TechCrunch* online, November 27, 2009.

470 **in his conjecture that Oswald acted alone:** Gerald Posner, *Case Closed: Lee Harvey Oswald and the Assassination of JFK* (New York: Random House, 1993), p. 450.

471 **"What fed the conspiracy notion about the Kennedy assassination":** Small, *To Kill a Messenger*, p. 36.

471 **dispelled the notion of an octopus-like conspiracy to get Kennedy:** Jack Gould, "TV: Useful View of Warren Report," *New York Times*, June 29, 1967.

471 **"We concluded," he said, "that nothing else could be proved":** Cronkite and Carleton, *Conversations with Cronkite*, pp. 204–5.

471 **"a rare and important experience in television journalism":** Rick DuBrow, "CBS Investigates Warren Commission," UPI, June 29, 1967.

472 **I'm not as happy as I once was with the Warren Commission":** "And That's the Way It Is," *Columbia Journalism Review* 19, no. 1 (May–June 1981): 50.

473 **an "international" conspiracy was at play:** "JFK Killing Left LBJ Doubtful; Cronkite: Ex-Prez Not Sure of Truth," *Philadelphia Daily News*, February 6, 1992.

473 **"A man lands on the moon":** "On the News Beat," *Newsweek*, June 1, 1964.

Eighteen: WHO'S AFRAID OF THE NIELSEN RATINGS?

475 **Lyndon Johnson's wife, Lady Bird, had purchased KTBC:** Robert Caro, *The Years of Lyndon Johnson* (New York: Knopf, 1990).

476 **"Their deep friendship went back a long way"**: Author interview with Harry Middleton, September 8, 2011.

476 **Before long, Lyndon and Lady Bird were making millions:** Jack Shafer, "The Honest Graft of Lady Bird Johnson," *Slate*, July 16, 2007.

477 **Johnson was a Pecos Bill–style folk figure in Texas:** Randall Woods, *LBJ: Architect of Ambition* (Cambridge, MA: Harvard University Press, 2006), p. 80.

478 **"LBJ and Frank Stanton were good friends":** Tom Johnson to Douglas Brinkley, September 18, 2011.

479 **The LBJ-Stanton relationship was so rock solid:** Lawrence Bergreen, *Look Now, Pay Later*, pp. 276–277.

479 **Cronkite knew that LBJ wasn't "Huckleberry Capone":** Author interview with Ethel Kennedy, November 5, 2011.

479 **"[Johnson] watched all the newscasts":** Cronkite and Carleton, *Conversations with Cronkite*, p. 225.

480 **"Walter, I called Bill Paley":** Frank, *Out of Thin Air*, p. 224.

481 **CBS, the largest advertising-based business in the world:** Leonard Wallace Robinson, "After the Yankees What?" *New York Times Magazine*, November 15, 1964.

481 **CBS broadcast fourteen of the top fifteen shows:** Deborah Haber, "They Still Remember Jim Aubrey (Shudder)," *New York*, September 9, 1968, p. 54.

482 **Defending Cronkite against Aubrey was Fred Friendly:** Bergreen, *Look Now, Pay Later*, p. 234.

483 **"He is the most competitive person I ever met":** Leslie Midgley, *How Many Words Do You Want? An Insider's Stories of Print and Television Journalism* (New York: Birch Lane Press, 1989), p. 244.

483 **"Douglas Edwards had been replaced with Walter Cronkite":** Buzenberg and Buzenberg, *Salant, CBS, and the Battle for the Soul of Broadcast Journalism*, p. 49.

486 **"He was the World's No. 1 purveyor":** William Lambert and Richard Oulahan, "The Tyrant's Call That Rocked the TV World: Until He Was Suddenly Brought Low, Jim Aubrey Ruled the Air," *Life*, September 10, 1965.

487 For a decade CBS had been—and would remain for years to come—the biggest advertising medium: Robinson, "After the Yankees What?"

488 set the tone "of its public relations image": Jack Gould, "Friendly to Head C.B.S. Unit," *New York Times*, March 2, 1964.

488 "If Paley could fire Aubrey and Salant with the snap of a finger": Author interview with Andy Rooney, March 15, 2011.

489 "getting Ed back here is my first order of business": Ralph Engelman, *Friendlyvision: Fred Friendly and the Rise and Fall of Television Journalism* (New York: Columbia University Press, 2009), p. 182.

490 "Friendly proposed that I cover every day": Mudd, *The Place to Be*, p. 141.

491 "We're going to cover this civil rights story": Author interview with Roger Mudd, November 14, 2011.

492 "Friendly deserved a lot of credit": Ibid.

493 "But we never felt that pressure on the news desk": Cronkite and Carleton, *Conversations with Cronkite*, p. 280.

494 **"It was like the dark side of the moon":** Author interview with Bill Plante, December 2, 2010.

494 **Cronkite served as host of the *CBS News Special Report*:** "The Summer Ahead," *Washington Post*, July 1, 1964 (Display Ad 241).

496 **"The Senate action came just before 8 p.m":** Walter Cronkite, "Mississippi 1964: Civil Rights and Unrest," *All Things Considered*, NPR, June 16, 2005.

496 **"Three young civil rights workers disappeared":** CBS broadcast transcript, June 22, 1964, CBS Archive, New York.

492 **having Mudd grow a beard:** Bill Small to Douglas Brinkley, March 5, 2012.

497 **"to reveal the anti-democratic hypocrisy of Jim Crow":** Author interview with Cornel West, January 10, 2012.

497 **a deeply isolated civilization that hadn't changed":** Cronkite, "Mississippi 1964."

498 **"I always considered CBS News an ally":** Author interview with Julian Bond, May 14, 2011.

499 **CBS "had the edge on other networks":** Leonard, *In the Storm of the Eye*, p. 136.

499 "He only made two visits back to Normandy": Paul Gardner, "D-Day Remembered," *New York Times*, May 31, 1964.

500 praising the "simple eloquence": "Eisenhower Recalls the Ordeal of D-Day Assault 20 Years Ago," *New York Times*, June 6, 1964.

501 "It may have been the most solemn moment": Walter Cronkite, "Eisenhower's Return to Normandy," *All Things Considered*, NPR, June 4, 2004.

502 "Cronkite personally tended to be on the side": Midgley, *How Many Words Do You Want?* p. 226.

502 far-searching documentary: Ibid., p. 187.

503 "nimbus of patriotic fervor": Walter Cronkite, "Gulf of Tonkin's Phantom Attack," *All Things Considered*, NPR, August 2, 2004.

503 acknowledged "supporting" Johnson's decision: Ibid.

504 "What do we really know about what happened": David Halberstam, *The Powers That Be*, p. 444.

504 "I was still living with my old feeling of sympathy": Powers, "Walter Cronkite: A Candid Conversation."

505 **Cronkite's "private feeling" after the Gulf of Tonkin:** Walter Cronkite to Bob Manning, April 3, 1987.

505 **He tried to maintain objectivity:** Walter Cronkite to Bob Manning, April 3, 1987.

505 **"I won't say he was hawkish":** Author interview with Morley Safer, September 9, 2011.

Nineteen: PALEY'S ATTEMPTED SMACKDOWN

507 **had callously said, "No comment":** Rick Perlstein, *Before the Storm: Barry Goldwater and the Unmaking of the American Consensus* (New York: Hill & Wang, 2001), p. 248.

507 **"a dad-burned dirty lie":** "Goldwater Rips CBS," Associated Press, July 18, 1964.

508 **"They haven't even the decency to apologize":** Ibid.

508 **"It's *February* that he can't say":** Author interview with William Small, March 22, 2011.

508 **"And it would work," Sandy Socolow recalled:** Brian Stelter, "Friends Recall Walter Cronkite's Private Side," *New York Times*, July 24, 2009.

508 **"Goldwater was a fervent hawk":** Walter Cronkite, "Gulf of Tonkin's Phantom Attack," *All Things Considered*, NPR, August 2, 2004.

510 **"The Germany story," Perlstein explained:** Perlstein, *Before the Storm*, p. 375.

510 **"A lot of people at CBS blew a gasket about the Goldwater-is-Nazi thing":** Author interview with Dan Rather, November 19, 2011.

511 **"You can say what you want about Goldwater's conservatism":** Stephen Shadegg, *What Happened to Goldwater? The Inside Story of the 1964 Republican Campaign* (New York: Holt, Rinehart, and Winston, 1965), pp. 152–54.

511 **Walter's favorite dish was veal stew:** "At Home with . . . Mrs. Walter Cronkite," *New York Post*, April 13, 1968.

512 **"Everybody including the trash man calls him Walter":** Betsy Cronkite as told to Lyn Tornabee, "My Husband: The Newscaster."

512 **"He had this great curiosity":** Bob Schieffer, television interview, *CBS Evening News with Katie Couric*, CBS, July 17, 2009.

513 **"Dear Mr. Cronkite, What do the astronauts do":** Pam and Margy to Walter Cronkite [circa 1962], Mervin J. Block Archive, New York.

513 **"Your complaint was justified":** Walter Cronkite to George H. Kenny, August 15, 1966, Box: 2M644, Folder: 1966, WCP-UTA.

515 **"By the time the Republican Convention rolled around"**: Leonard, *In the Storm of the Eye*, p. 108.

517 **"I saw your daughter Nancy"**: Drew Pearson, "Goldwater Interview Mystery," *Los Angeles Times*, July 19, 1964.

518 **"All of us have been the beneficiaries"**: "And That's the Way It Is," p. 50.

520 **"Cronkite was appalled"**: Cronkite, *A Reporter's Life*, p. 348.

521 **"Walter exploded"**: Leonard, *In the Storm of the Eye*, p. 109.

521 **That November Friendly named Sevareid a national correspondent:** "Sevareid to Washington," *New York Times*, November 16, 1964.

522 **"The only time Walter was difficult"**: Author interview with William Small, March 22, 2011.

523 **"If the old son of a bitch does that to me"**: Schieffer, *This Just In*, p. 182.

524 **"swallowing up great chunks of air time"**: Mudd, *The Place to Be*, pp. 161–162.

525 **"None of us did well"**: Author interview with Dan Rather, November 19, 2011.

525   **"The hell with Walter Cronkite":** Charles Mohr, "Chairman Chosen," *New York Times*, July 17, 1964.

526   **Brinkley and Huntley were routinely threatened:** Brinkley, *A Memoir*, p. 161.

526   **"The delegates," Brinkley wrote, "left their chairs":** Ibid., p. 162.

527   **"She was my first girlfriend":** Author interview with Chris Wallace, July 10, 2009.

528   **"Walter would just ignore directions":** Ibid.

530   **"Who do you think could replace Walter":** Leonard, *In the Storm of the Eye*, pp. 110–111.

531   **"One trouble with this business is it's like Hollywood":** Cronkite [unpublished notes], *Newsweek*, July 31, 1964, WCP-UTA.

532   **"every patient is owed the simple human dignity of being told the truth":** Tom Wolfe, "After the Fall," *New York Herald Tribune*, October 4, 1964.

532   **"The anchorman was hoisted":** Leonard, *In the Storm of the Eye*, pp. 110–111.

532   **"any contract is breakable":** Cronkite [unpublished notes], *Newsweek*, July 31, 1964, WCP-UTA.

533 **"Walter Cronkite—demoted!":** Tom Wolfe, "After the Fall," *New York Herald Tribune*, October 4, 1964.

533 **Sevareid and Reasoner would also play larger roles in Atlantic City:** Val Adams, "C.B.S. News Drops Cronkite As Convention's Anchor Man," *New York Times*, July 31, 1964.

533 **"We took a clobbering in San Francisco":** "Two-Man Team to Do Cronkite Job," AP, July 31, 1964.

533 **Cronkite might not be allowed to anchor Election Night:** Val Adams, "Cronkite's Role for November 3 Unsure," *New York Times*, August 1, 1963.

534 **"We've got a team here":** "Upstairs Was Unhappy," *Newsweek*, August 10, 1964.

534 **"I'm not bitter yet":** Cronkite [unpublished notes], *Newsweek*, July 31, 1964, WCP-UTA.

535 **"I kept thinking this is really going to screw up my relationship":** Author interview with Chris Wallace, July 10, 2009.

536 **Don Hewitt, in a show of solidarity with Cronkite, asked to be relieved:** Val Adams, "TV News Shows Added in Crisis," *New York Times*, August 6, 1964.

536　Lady Bird Johnson had agreed to do a *Person to Person*: Paul Gardner, "TV: From LBJ Ranch," *New York Times*, August 13, 1964.

537　"Once after Mudd had given the viewers some information": Dick West, "Wryness of TV Convention Coverage Noted," UPI, August 26, 1964.

537　Mudd's "rather desperate attempts at being funny": Richard Martin, "TV 'Backlash' Can Whip Convention," *Salt Lake Tribune*, August 26, 1964.

537　CBS garnered its highest share: Jack Gould, "TV: Huntley and Brinkley Retain Grip," *New York Times*, August 26, 1964.

538　Mudd considered a career change: Mudd, *The Place to Be*, p. 167.

538　"By brutally dumping and publicly humiliating": Brooks Atkinson, "Muddled Showmanship Is Degenerating Both Parties' Political Conventions," *New York Times*, September 8, 1964.

538　"Walter is so objective, careful, and fair": William S. Paley, *As It Happened* (Doubleday: New York, 1979), p. 301.

539 **"Walter said, 'I'm a newsman and I'm going to cover the story'":** Author interview with Chris Wallace, July 10, 2009.

Twenty: CIVIL RIGHTS AND PROJECT GEMINI

540 ***CBS Evening News with Walter Cronkite* ran its first color broadcast:** "CBS at 75" Timeline, CBS News, CBS Archive, New York.

541 **"No one has a larger stake in going into color":** Ben Gross, "Meet Walter Cronkite, TV Man of Integrity," *New York Daily News*, May 2, 1965.

541 **Raisky was the visual guru at CBS:** Alfred Robert Hogan to Douglas Brinkley, May 24, 2011.

541 **"A lot of New York designers steered clear of the newsrooms":** Author interview with Hugh Raisky, November 8, 2011.

541 **"There are no back pages":** "Television: The Most Intimate Medium," *Time*, October 14, 1966.

542 **"You better have it right":** Author interview with Jon Wilkman, January 6, 2012.

542 **The CBS workplace was notably small:** Alessandra Stanley, "An Appraisal; Cronkite's

Signature: Authority and Approachability," *New York Times*, July 18, 2009.

543 **"Good evening," Cronkite said:** *Anchorman* movie from Brian Williams's office, NBC Archives, New York.

543 **Along with Cronkite and Hewitt, the other essential facilitator:** Philip J. Hilts, "CBS: The Fiefdom and the Power in Washington," *Washington Post*, April 21, 1974.

543 **"We tried beaming propaganda into North Korea":** Author interview with Sandy Socolow, June 5, 2011.

544 **"Walter Cronkite wants to say hello":** Jay Fredericks, "CBS Strokes Victory with Walter," November 11, 1964.

545 **"LBJ's phone chat with CBS star newsman Walter Cronkite":** Walter Winchell, "Broadway and Elsewhere," November 17, 1964.

545 **"CBS by a Landslide:** Network's Coverage of the Election":** Jack Gould, "CBS by a Landslide," *New York Times*, November 4, 1964.

545 **Robert Pierpoint remained suspicious:** Ronald Steel, *Walter Lippmann and the American Century* (Boston: Little, Brown, 1980), p. 548.

545 **If CBS News thought they needed a knockout smear artist to anchor:** Cronkite and Carleton, *Conversations with Cronkite*, p. 216.

546 **"We used to call Walter 'Mr. Softball'":** Author interview with Robert Pierpoint, March 19, 2011.

546 **Cronkite wasn't the problem with the *CBS Evening News*:** Bob Foster, "TV Screening," syndicated column, November 18, 1964.

546 **"developing and innovating a new kind of news broadcast—the 'live documentary'":** Henry O. Wefing, *Cuetime* 6, no. 5 (October–December 1964).

547 **"I never pretended that we could do anything more":** Walter Cronkite, oral history interview with Don Carleton, p. 492, WCP-UTA.

548 **"Having survived the 1964 convention brush-up":** Author interview with Dan Rather, November 10, 2011.

549 **Throughout the segregated South, CBS in particular was denounced:** David Halberstam, *The Children* (New York: Ballantine, 1998), p. 486.

549 **"I couldn't do feeds from Dallas":** Author interview with Dan Rather, November 19, 2011.

550 **"If anyone got manipulated by King":** Donovan and Scherer, *Unsilent Revolution*, p. 19.

550 **"Cronkite was the voice of God":** Author interview with Julian Bond, May 14, 2011.

551 **"We felt totally out of sync with the racism":** Author interview with John Hendricks, November 12, 2011.

551 **"I tuned it in and, sure enough, Cronkite had given up a huge chunk of his time":** Donovan and Scherer, *Unsilent Revolution*, p. 21.

553 **"Back then you were really on your own":** Al Reinert, "The Secret World of Walter Cronkite," *Texas Monthly* (January 1977). See also Hughes Rudd, *My Escape from the CIA and Other Improbable Adventures* (New York: E. P. Dutton, 1966); and Sally Quinn, *We're Going to Make You a Star* (New York: Simon & Schuster, 1970).

553 **Cronkite's *CBS Evening News* stage manager was:** FN: "James (Jimmy) Wall, Captain Kangaroo's 'Mr. Baxter' and Longtime Stage Manager for CBS News, Dies at 92," October 28, 2010, Memo to CBS Employees from Sean McManus, CBS News Archives, New York.

554 **some liberals were irritated by the way the word *negro* was used:** Cathy [no last name] to Walter Cronkite, August 1965, WCP-UTA.

554 **"The report by Steve Rowan from Andrews AFB":** Mrs. Allie F. B. Stanford to Walter Cronkite, August 30, 1966, WCP-UTA.

555 **"Black people can detect prejudice in a person":** Author interview with Ed Bradley, December 21, 2004.

556 **"The content of the calls, invariably, was 'nigger'":** Author interview with Ron Bonn, June 7, 2011.

557 **Gemini had four primary and newsworthy goals:** John Noble Wilford, *We Reach the Moon* (New York: Bantam Books, 1969), pp. 84–85.

558 **"Jules Bergman of ABC and Walter Cronkite of CBS were the iron men":** Jack Gould, "Radio-TV: Gemini Flight's Drama Brought Home," *New York Times*, June 4, 1965.

559 **"I learn by doing; I don't learn by reading":** Terry Turner, "TV Channels: CBS to Use 'Helicopter Eye' in Gemini Shot," Chicago Daily News Service, March 25, 1965.

560 **In reality, he had more power than Murrow:** Joshua Meyrowitz, *No Sense of Place: The Impact*

of Electronic Media on Social Behavior (New York: Oxford University Press, 1985), p. 133.

561 **the heavyweight title of "Dean of Space":** "The Interpreters and 'The Golden Throats,'" *Newsweek*, October 8, 1962.

561 **"first golden age of broadcast journalism":** Frank Stanton to CBS News, April 27, CBS News Archives, New York.

561 **calling him "incandescent":** *CBS Evening News* broadcast, April 29, 1965.

561 **"He just didn't say a word about the death":** Author interview with Sandy Socolow, June 5, 2011.

561 **But Cronkite himself choked up:** Cynthia Lowry, "CBS Recalls Edward R. Murrow," Associated Press, April 29, 1965.

562 **"We all knew Walter owned Gemini":** Author interview with Roger Mudd, November 14, 2011.

562 **All three astronauts were asphyxiated:** Wilford, *We Reach the Moon*, p. xviii.

562 **"It was a great shock to Cronkite":** Author interview with Robert Pierpoint, March 19, 2011.

563 **Cronkite made his way to the West Fifty-seventh Street broadcast center:** Hogan, "Televising the Space Age."

564 **"at a time when we seemed to be coming apart":** Polly Paddock, "Cronkite Reassures as Always," *Charlotte* (NC) *Observer*, October 22, 1999.

565 **Wernher von Braun, who became a pliant collaborator:** Bob Ward, *Dr. Space: The Life of Wernher von Braun* (Annapolis: Naval Institute Press, 2005), p. 87.

565 **Journeys were made to Langley Field, Virginia, to experience firsthand:** Author interview with Sandy Socolow, April 27, 2011.

565 **"From the Moon we will truly step out into space":** Hogan, "Televising the Space Age."

566 **"much more of a cheerleader than a reporter":** Degroot, *Dark Side of the Moon*, p. 171.

566 **"We proved we could do it":** Walter Cronkite interview with Richard Snow, "He Was There."

567 **"My God, our building's shaking here":** *CBS News Special Reports*, Apollo 4, November 9, 1967 (transcript), CBS News Reference Library, New York.

Twenty-One: WHAT TO DO ABOUT VIETNAM?

569 **"Boy, did I get it from Dad":** Author interview with Nancy Cronkite, April 4, 2011.

570 **"Our foreign policy, simply stated":** Remarks by Walter Cronkite, CBS News Correspondent, to the Associated Press Managing Editors Convention (transcript), Buffalo, New York, September 29, 1965, WCP-UTA.

570 **"We are trying to prevent a Third World War":** President Truman's Address About Policy in the Far East (*American Experience* transcript), April 11, 1951, Public Broadcating Service, http://www .pbs.org/wgbh/amex/macarthur/filmmore/refer ence/primary/official docs03.html.

571 **"master politician":** Remarks by Walter Cronkite, WCP-UTA.

571 **"We are not about to send American boys nine or ten thousand miles away":** Marvin E. Gettleman, ed., *Vietnam and America,* 2d rev. ed. (New York: Grove Press, 1995), p. 241.

571 **"Cronkite gave great coverage and support to us":** Author interview with Joseph Califano, April 4, 2011.

573 **For Cronkite, it meant catching up with NBC News:** William Small, *To Kill a Messenger,* p. 109.

573 **Having just finished narrating "Abortion and the Law":** Jack Gould, "TV: Documentary Views Abortion," *New York Times*, April 6, 1965.

573 **Cronkite, at Bud Benjamin's suggestion, decided to film a report:** "20th Century to Focus Next Series on the News," *New York Times*, May 17, 1965.

574 **"It was a bitch in the field":** Ron Bonn to Douglas Brinkley, January 11, 2012.

575 **"One could not depend on things":** Cronkite, *A Reporter's Life*, pp. 250–51.

575 **"'How can we lose'":** Ron Bonn to Douglas Brinkley, January 7, 2012.

576 **"balls of steel":** Author interview with Ron Bonn, January 12, 2012.

576 **"Then I kind of lost the thread":** Cronkite and Carleton, *Conversations with Cronkite*, p. 207.

577 **"long, long, way yet to go—three, four years":** "Ky Outlines a Timetable for Defeating Vietcong," *New York Times*, July 19, 1965.

577 **"They're cowards!":** Author interview with Ron Bonn, January 9, 2012.

578 **"But the dumbest general really shook him":** Ron Bonn to Douglas Brinkley, January 7, 2012.

578 "Walter was too skeptical, too savvy": Morley Safer, *Flashbacks: On Returning to Vietnam* (New York: Random House, 1990), p. 109.

580 gave him a "grunt's-eye view of the world": Author interview with Morley Safer, September 4, 2011.

580 to counter all the "lies and bogus optimism": Safer, *Flashbacks*, p. 109.

581 "the five o'clock follies": Cronkite, *A Reporter's Life*, p. 252.

581 "The truths I told him didn't come as a complete shock": Author interview with Morley Safer, September 9, 2011.

582 "Some of the reporting I did pained Walter": Ibid.

583 "Frank, this is your president, and yesterday your boys shat on the American flag": Halberstam, *The Powers That Be*, p. 490.

583 "Well, I knew he wasn't an American": Pacifica Radio–UC Berkeley Social Activism Sound Recording Project: Anti-Vietnam War Protests in the San Francisco Bay Area and Beyond, University of California, Berkeley, 2005.

583 **Safer was a Canadian Communist:** Morley
Safer to Douglas Brinkley, February 12, 2012.
Also Ted Koop to Fred Friendly, October 20,
1965, CBS Memorandum, October 20, 1965, CBS
News Archive, New York.

583 **"It was after that broadcast that Friendly asked
me to take a break from Vietnam":** Morley Safer
to Douglas Brinkley, January 15, 2012.

584 **"Cronkite was out to get me":** Chester Pach,
"The Way It Wasn't: Cronkite and Vietnam,
History News Network (blog affiliated with
George Mason University), July 21, 2009.

584 **"We knew in 1966 and 1967 that the only group
who knew Vietnam was a lost cause":** Author
interview with Morley Safer, September 4, 2011.

585 **"redouble our effort to find the means of victory":** Remarks by Walter Cronkite, WCP-UTA.

586 **"You're interested in the drama of the news":**
"Newsmen Accuse Administration of Attempt to
Impose Secrecy," *New York Times*, November 1,
1965.

586 **CBS News was now treating Asia:** Author
interview with Lew Wood, January 9, 2012.

586 **"I returned from that first trip to Vietnam":**
Cronkite, *A Reporter's Life*, p. 252.

586 "courageous decision": Don Oberdorfer, *Tet! The Turning Point in the Vietnam War* (Baltimore: Johns Hopkins University Press, 2001), p. 248.

587 "American imperialism is the aggressor": "He Lists His Terms for Peace on U.S. TV," *New York Times*, December 7, 1965.

587 "This is the meaning of our commitment in Southeast Asia": Walter Cronkite, "Introduction," *Vietnam Perspective* (New York: Pocket Books, 1965).

588 objectivity: "If the World Goes to Hell": Author interview with Lew Wood, January 9, 2012.

589 His great achievement was getting President Johnson to read: "President Talks Twice for C.B.S.," *New York Times*, February 1, 1966.

589 "As field correspondents": Author interview with Bill Plante, November 7, 2011.

590 "CBS thought better of sending Cronkite": Morley Safer to Douglas Brinkley, January 15, 2012.

590 "Moyers had a very nasty streak": Author interview with Morley Safer, September 4, 2011.

590 "No. Johnson was riding high, wide, and hand-some": Cronkite and Carleton, *Conversations with Cronkite*, p. 210.

592 "every American ought to suffer": Ibid.

593 A livid Friendly deemed the Schneider move a "blackout": Richard K. Doan, "Friendly: The Academic Life," *New York Herald Tribune*, April 6, 1966.

593 Schneider, who became an opportune symbol of corporate greed: Engelman, *Friendlyvision*, p. 224.

594 Dick Salant, former president of CBS News from February 1961 to March 1964: Jack Gould, "Friendly's Farewell," *New York Times*, February 17, 1966.

594 Friendly's "brilliant, imaginative, and hard-hitting guidance": Rick Du Brow, "Television in Review," UPI, February 16, 1966.

594 "money changers in the temple": Engelman, *Friendlyvision*, p. 225.

594 *New York Times* even ran Friendly's res-ignation letter: "Text of Friendly's Letter of Resignation," *New York Times*, February 16, 1966.

595 **He wasn't sycophantic, but he valued the reasoned analysis of Stanton:** Engelman, *Friendlyvision*, p. 225.

596 **"I have been partial to CBS because of my friendship":** Dwight D. Eisenhower to Fred Friendly, February 15, 1966, Fred Friendly Papers, Rare Book Manuscript Library, Columbia University. Also see Engelman, *Friendlyvision*, p. 228.

596 **"ranked with God and Country in their scheme of things":** Leonard, *In the Storm of the Eye*, pp. 139–40.

596 **"Salant," Midgley recalled, "always preached":** Midgley, *How Many Words Do You Want?* pp. 236–37.

597 **His replacement was the soft-spoken Leslie Midgley:** Midgley, *How Many Words Do You Want?* p. 236.

597 **"If he saw some story on NBC":** Midgley, *How Many Words Do You Want?* p. 241.

597 **By 1964, Clark's pronounced antiwar views had led him to quit:** Eric Page, "Blair Clark, 82, CBS Executive Who Led McCarthy's '68 Race," *New York Times*, June 8, 2000.

598 **"Walter thought that Clark was too antiwar"**: Author interview with Andy Rooney, March 15, 2011.

599 **"I still have no idea why they selected me"**: Bob Greene, "Goodbye and Good Luck," *New York Times*, September 4, 2006.

600 **"I was shocked when Salant told me"**: Author interview with Arnold Zenker, June 27, 2011.

600 **"I did not go to work. And CBS pulled in this guy"**: Cronkite and Carleton, *Conversations with Cronkite*, p. 281.

600 **David Brinkley, for his part, was philosophically opposed**: Brian Lamb interview with David Brinkley, *Book Notes*, December 10, 1995 (transcript).

601 **nothing but "18,000 singers, dancers and jugglers"**: Robert E. Dallos, "Huntley and Brinkley United—Briefly," *New York Times*, April 4, 1967.

601 **Cronkite told reporters he remembered how hard it was**: Michael J. Socolow, "Anchors Away," *Journalism History* 29, no. 2 (Summer 2003): 50–58.

601 **Cronkite stayed out despite the *CBS Evening News* losing ground**: Jack Gould, "TV: Strike and Ratings," *New York Times*, April 1, 1967.

601 **"Chet Huntley Slaps at TV Strike" ran the banner:** "Chet Huntley Slaps at TV Strike," *El Paso Herald-Post*, March 31, 1967.

602 **"Good evening, this is Walter Cronkite, filling in":** Robert E. Dallos, "'Tonight' Goes on Without Carson," *New York Times*, April 12, 1967.

603 **Cronkite received louder, longer applause than Ed Sullivan:** Richard K. Shull, "TV's Celebrities Can Come from Any of Many Corners as Fans Mix Up the Media," *Arizona Republic*, June 25, 1967

604 **"It's not as though Walter were a movie star":** Betsy Cronkite as told to Lyn Tornabee, "My Husband: The Newscaster."

604 **"It is also irrelevant and inappropriate":** "Ax TV News Star System—Brinkley," *Press and Sun-Bulletin* (Binghamton, NY), February 16, 1966.

604 **"was a little like Lyndon Johnson attacking Texas":** Reston, "New York: Say It Isn't So, Fred."

605 **"It was about beating our rivals":** Author interview with Ed Fouhy, November 8, 2011.

606 **"This practice changed in 1967":** Jack Laurence to Douglas Brinkley [nd].

606 **Salant wrote a highly confidential memo:** Michael J. Arlen, *Living Room War* (New York: Penguin, 1982).

607 **"His expression was one of worry":** Jack Laurence to Douglas Brinkley [nd].

607 **"Spend," Salant snapped, "whatever it takes":** Author interview with Ed Fouhy, November 7, 2011.

608 **"Salant and Cronkite, by 1967, didn't think the war was going to end":** Author interview with Bill Plante, November 7, 2011.

609 **Kuralt's "On the Road" feature would run on a trial basis:** Charles Kuralt, *On the Road with Charles Kuralt* (New York: Fawcett, 1995). See also *Charles Kuralt's America* (New York: Anchor, 1996) and *Charles Kuralt's American Moments* (New York: Simon & Schuster, 1999).

610 **"two-minute cease-fires" from the tumultuous era:** "Travels with Charley," *Time*, January 19, 1968.

610 **As Midgley noted, Kuralt liked to talk to "oldsters":** Midgley, *How Many Words Do You Want?* p. 243.

610 **Together they toyed with the idea of buying a string of radio stations:** Author interview with Don Shelby, November 19, 2011.

611 **"controlled by the Vietcong":** Chester Pach, "The Way It Wasn't: Cronkite and Vietnam," *History News Network* (blog affiliated with George Mason University), July 21, 2009.

612 **"No one had a clear idea":** Morley Safer to Douglas Brinkley, January 13, 2012.

612 **"bird and Bobby watching":** Author interview with Andy Rooney, March 15, 2011.

613 **"where the end begins to come into view":** Larry Berman, *Lyndon Johnson's War: The Road to Stalemate in Vietnam* (New York: W. W. Norton, 1991), p. 116.

613 **"LBJ, just bypassing Stanton, would telephone Cronkite directly":** Cronkite and Carleton, *Conversations with Cronkite*, p. 215.

Twenty-Two: THE TET OFFENSIVE

615 **"I thought we were winning the war!":** Oberdorfer, *Tet!* p. 158.

616 **Johnson's "light at the end of the tunnel" drivel:** Powers, "Walter Cronkite: A Candid Conversation."

616 **"He now knew they were spot-on"**: Author interview with Andy Rooney, March 15, 2011.

616 **"Vietnam was America's first television war"**: Oberdorfer, *Tet!* p. 158.

617 **"mind wide open"**: Walter Cronkite to Robert Manning, October 7, 1987.

617 **"I wanted to be there for the clash"**: Mark Kurlansky, *1968: The Year That Rocked the World* (New York: Random House, 2005), p. 58.

618 **"try and present an assessment of the situation"**: Cronkite, *A Reporter's Life*, p. 256.

618 **The time had come to weigh in**: Matusow, *The Evening Stars*, p. 128.

618 **"Walter said he couldn't possibly do an editorial"**: Phil Scheffer to Jack Laurence, August 15, 2009.

620 **"You're getting pretty heavy"**: Kurlansky, *1968: The Year That Rocked the World*, p. 59.

620 **Salant and Cronkite settled on doing a prime-time *CBS News Special Report***: Author interview with Sandy Socolow, September 17, 2010.

620 **"It was an Orwellian trip"**: Halberstam, *The Powers That Be*, p. 512.

621   "Sphinx to pundit": Kurlansky, *1968: The Year That Rocked the World*, p. 59.

621   "see for himself what's happened in South Vietnam": "Cronkite to Present Views on Vietnam," *Lexington Daily News*, February 23, 1968.

623   **Cronkite and his team now headed to Hué:** Cronkite, *A Reporter's Life*, p. 256.

624   **"The battle was still on in Hué":** Cronkite and Carleton, *Conversations with Cronkite*, p. 211.

625   **the "real" meaning of Tet was coming into focus:** James S. Robbins, *This Time We Win* (New York: Encounter Books, 2010), p. 252.

626   **"It was quiet":** Miller and Schechner, "Walter Cronkite, Broadcasting Lengend, Dies at 92."

626   **Cronkite's best source in Vietnam was Abrams:** Halberstam, *The Powers That Be*, p. 513.

627   **"It was sickening to me":** Oberdorfer, *Tet!* pp. 249–50.

627   **"My decision was not difficult to reach":** Cronkite, *A Reporter's Life*, p. 257.

628   **"Walter said he wanted to know what was really going on":** Todd Gitlin, "And That's the Way It Was," *The New Republic*, July 17, 2009.

629 **"its soldiers were killing more of the enemy"**: John Laurence, *The Cat from Hué* (New York: PublicAffairs, 2002), p. 291.

629 **However, Laurence argued, the North Vietnamese weren't going to give up:** Jack Laurence to Douglas Brinkley [nd]. See also Halberstam, *The Powers That Be*, p. 513.

630 **"I watched the helicopter gunships circling the city"**: Cronkite to Manning, September 3, 1987.

630 **"He held his cards close"**: Jeff Gralnick to John Laurence, February 17, 2010.

631 **"You know, Walter was Mr. Unflappable"**: Author interview with Robert Vitarelli, March 8, 2011.

631 **"His calmness was eerie"**: Author interview with Robert Vitarelli, March 10, 2011.

632 **"It was Walter's writing"**: Author interview with Jeff Gralnick, June 11, 2010.

632 **"every word"**: Murray Fromson, e-mail to Sandy Socolow, February 17, 2010.

632 **In the course of the prime-time show Cronkite made a powerful case:** Daniel Hallin, "Vietnam on Television," Museum of Broadcast Communications, Chicago.

633 **Cronkite faced a personal crossroads in Vietnam:** Diane Sawyer, "A Challenge for Tomorrow," in Louis B. DeFleur, *Murrow Heritage: Challenge for the Future* (Ames: Iowa State University Press, 1986), p. 106.

633 **"we'd like to sum up our findings in Vietnam":** "Final Words: Cronkite's Vietnam Commentary," NPR, July 18, 2009, http://www.npr.org/tem plates/story/story.php?storyId=106775685.

636 **Apple had written a long article:** R. W. Apple, "The Making of a Stalemate," *New York Times*, Summer 1967.

636 **the public would turn against Johnson's war:** Michael J. Arlen, "The Air (On Television): Television's War," *The New Yorker*, May 27, 1967.

637 **"That short editorial helped":** Walter Cronkite, "Changing Attitudes Toward War in Vietnam," NPR, August 7, 2002.

637 **His opinion was quoted in the press, and it opened the door:** Jack Gould, "U.S. Is Losing War in Vietnam, N.B.C. Declares," *New York Times*, March 11, 1968.

637 **"The whole Vietnam effort may be doomed":** Kurlansky, *1968: The Year That Rocked the World*, p. 61.

637 **"When Walter said the Vietnam War was over"**: Frank Rich, "The Weight of an Anchor," *New York Times Magazine*, May 19, 2002.

637 **"I was very disgusted with the media, particularly CBS"**: William Westmoreland oral history interview, U.S. Army Military History Institute, Carlisle Barracks, Pennsylvania.

637 **As the CBS special aired that February 27, President Johnson was traveling**: Joseph Campbell, *Getting It Wrong: Ten of the Greatest Misreported Stories in American Journalism* (Berkeley: University of California Press, 2010), p. 89.

638 **"If I've lost Cronkite, I've lost the country"**: Douglas Martin, "Walter Cronkite, 92, Dies; Trusted Voice of TV News," *New York Times*, July 17, 2009.

638 **There are a few alternative versions of what LBJ supposedly said**: Kurlansky, *1968: The Year That Rocked the World*, pp. 61–62.

638 **"Believe me, the shock waves rolled through government"**: Small, *To Kill a Messenger*, p. 123.

639 **Gulf of Tonkin Resolution, which he now feared was "null and void"**: Barbara Tuchman,

The March of Folly: From Troy to Vietnam (New York: Ballantine Books, 1984), p. 352.

640 **"Cronkite's step out of character"**: Gitlin, "And That's the Way It Was."

640 **"Walter Cronkite sounds like a Pentagon spokesman"**: Brian Lamb, *Booknotes: America's Finest Authors on Reading, Writing, and the Power of Ideas* (New York: Times Books, 1997), p. 194.

641 **Bensley was wounded:** "CBS Man Wounded Twice," *New York Times*, March 5, 1968.

641 **Since Cronkite's visit, fourteen U.S. correspondents and cameramen had been wounded:** "Newscasting: The Men Without Helmets," *Time*, March 15, 1968.

641 **"Nowhere in Vietnam was safe":** Author interview with Russ Bensley, January 17, 2012.

642 **"It is only a matter of time before Chet Huntley and David Brinkley":** Jack Gould, "Should Huntley and Brinkley Don Leotards?" *New York Times*, February 11, 1968.

643 **Cronkite's analysis of Tet was premature:** Robbins, *This Time We Win*, p. 253.

643 **As Diane Sawyer noted, not since Murrow lifted Senator Joe McCarthy:** James Walcott,

"Round Up the Cattle!" *Vanity Fair*, June 2003, p. 86.

644 **"Johnson did talk about Cronkite going to Vietnam"**: George Christian, telephone interview with David Culbert, September 17, 1979, transcript, LBJ Presidential Library and Museum, Austin, TX.

645 **"We were held to such a rigid set of values"**: Author interview with Ed Fouhy, November 7, 2011.

646 **"It was an egotistical thing for us to do"**: Kurlansky, *1968: The Year That Rocked the World*, p. 63.

646 **"The doctrine required broadcast station licensees"**: Jack Shafer, "Why I Didn't Trust Walter Cronkite," *Slate*, July 21, 2009; http//www.slate.com/articles/news_and_politics/press_box/2009/07/why_i_didnt_trust_walter_cronkite.single.html (accessed December 6, 2011).

647 **"He asked me whether I had felt betrayed by him"**: Author interview with Tim O'Brien, August 15, 2011.

648 **Newsweek, echoing O'Brien, noted that it was as if Lincoln himself**: Harry F. Waters, "A Man Who Cares," *Newsweek*, March 9, 1981, p. 58.

648 **"that a war had been declared over by a com-mentator":** David Halberstam, *The Powers That Be*, p. 716.

Twenty-Three: CALM AND CHAOS OF 1968

652 **"You must announce your intention to run":** Frank Mankiewicz, "Vice President Walter Cronkite," *Washington Post*, July 25, 2009.

653 **" 'Walter, I'll run for president if' ":** Ibid.

655 **Instead of declaring it on the *CBS Evening News*, he did so:** "Scene Is the Same, But 8 Years Later," *New York Times*, March 17, 1968.

656 **"I shall not seek, and I will not accept the nomination":** "Lyndon B. Johnson," *The American Experience: The Presidents*, Public Broadcasting Service, http//www.pbs.org/wgbh/amex/presidents/36_1_johnson/printable.html (accessed December 11, 2011).

657 **"that the president himself would react like he did":** Walter Cronkite to Bob Manning. Manning had been editor of *The Atlantic Monthly* from 1966 to 1980. Cronkite wrote Manning this important reflection on a "Report from Vietnam" while Manning was working at the Boston Publishing Company.

657 "left me shocked, disbelieving and babbling": Mudd, *The Place to Be*, p. 231.

658 "I think that Johnson felt like most of the American people said": Cronkite and Carleton, *Conversations with Cronkite*, p. 213.

659 "Daddy and Walter stayed close": Author interview with Lynda Johnson Robb, November 16, 2011.

660 TV didn't just report events; it also helped shape: Kurlansky, *1968: The Year That Rocked the World*, p. 102.

660 He feared that the "middle-of-the-road folks": Donovan and Scherer, *Unsilent Revolution*, p. 102.

660 he'd socialize with Lady Bird: Author interview with Kathy Cronkite, March 22, 2011.

660 "You have been a great force for good": Lady Bird Johnson to Walter Cronkite, October 30, 2001, WCP-UTA.

661 "A lot of people were trying to connect Walter's Tet offensive report": Author interview with Sandy Socolow, February 18, 2011.

661 "It didn't quite happen that way": George Christian Oral History, Lyndon B. Johnson Presidential Library, Austin, TX.

662 **"What Walter was saying about Vietnam wasn't all that dramatic":** Author interview with Marvin Kalb, November 11, 2011.

662 **"I don't feel that a journalist's influence is so great":** Richard Snow, "He Was There" (interview with Walter Cronkite) (New York: *American Heritage*, December 1994).

663 **Dan Rather broke the news of Dr. King's death:** Jack Gould, "TV: Networks React Quickly to the King Murder," *New York Times*, April 5, 1968.

663 **"the apostle of the civil rights movement":** "Walter Cronkite breaks news of Dr. Martin Luther King's death," *Los Angeles Times* video archive.

663 **"I'd hate to be up on U Street tonight":** Cronkite and Carleton, *Conversations with Cronkite*, p. 281.

664 **Cronkite wanted to attend King's funeral services:** Alfred Robert Hogan interview with Joan F. Richman, October 22, 2003 (transcript), Hogan Archive, Washington, DC.

665 **"I'd left our New York newsroom right after reporting that primary":** Walter Cronkite, *Cronkite Remembers*, documentary.

666 **"Robert Kennedy was shot at 12:15 am":** "From the Vault: 'Robert F. Kennedy: 1925–1968,' " CBS News, video, June 22, 2007.

667 **politicians of all stripes considered him the fairest:** "Congress Backing of Agnew Is Found," *New York Times*, December 19, 1969.

667 **"the master of subtle variations in intonation of speech":** Jack Gould, "TV: ABC Still Seeking a Distinctive News Image," *New York Times*, June 17, 1968.

668 **"We got married in October '68":** Author interview with Morley Safer, January 16, 2012.

669 **"the best coverage is not necessarily the one with the best pictures":** Frank Stanton, CBS Memorandum to CBS Officers or Groups, Divisions.

669 **Covering the entire 1968 election cost:** Russo, "CBS and the American Political Experience," p. 467.

669 **"Avoid using lights when shooting pictures":** "Notes on meeting held on August 20, 1968," Re: CBS News Coverage of Civil Disorder, Box: 43700, CBS Records.

669 **"great, brawling sweatshops of American political history":** Walter Cronkite, "Recalling

the Mayhem of '68 Convention," *All Things Considered*, NPR, July 23, 2004.

670 **"We anticipated trouble":** Cronkite and Carleton, *Conversations with Cronkite*, p. 214.

670 **the blunt headline:** "Boring Convention Ignored by Viewers," *Washington Post*, August 9, 1968.

670 **Ultimately, American viewers preferred real drama:** Cynthia Lowry, "Networks Conceded Very Early," AP, August 8, 1968.

671 **"tanks in which to travel from A to B":** Frank Kusch, *Battleground Chicago: The Police and the 1968 Democratic National Convention* (Chicago: University of Chicago Press, 2004), p. 60.

672 **"All the executive producers were busy at the convention hall":** Author interview with Jack Laurence, January 16, 2012.

673 **"I was awful when I was growing up":** Kathy Cronkite, *On the Edge of the Spotlight: Celebrities' Children Speak Out About Their Lives* (New York: William Morrow, 1981), p. 60.

673 **many families were divided:** Cronkite, *A Reporter's Life*, p. 194.

673 **"I didn't like their attitude":** Walter Cronkite oral history interview, p. 551, WCP-UTA.

674 **Buckley "admired Cronkite's mind":** Garry Wills, *Outside Looking In: Adventures of an Observer* (New York: Viking, 2010), p. 157.

674 **"The anti-war demonstrators," Cronkite reported:** Walter Cronkite, "Recalling the Mayhem of '68 Convention."

675 **Cronkite, as usual, refused to wear an IFB:** Russo, "CBS and the American Political Experience," p. 405.

675 **"I think we've got a bunch of thugs here":** Dan Rather, *The Camera Never Blinks Twice*, p. 309.

676 **"only time in his long career that Cronkite displayed":** Gary Paul Gates, *Air Time: The Inside Story of CBS News* (New York: Berkley Publishing, 1979), p. 210.

676 **"Network media personnel such as Cronkite":** Small, *To Kill a Messenger*, p. 208.

677 **"We put it on the air":** Cronkite, "Recalling the Mayhem of '68 Convention."

678 **"The intellectuals of America," he declared:** R. W. Apple, "Daley Defends His Policies," *New York Times*, August 30, 1968.

678 **"I can tell you this, Mr. Daley":** CBS News *Special Report*, August 29, 1968.

679 **"It wasn't in him to climb all over Daley"**: Author interview with Brit Hume, August 24, 2011.

679 **"Daley took Cronkite like Grant took Richmond"**: Adam Cohen and Elizabeth Taylor, *American Pharaoh: Mayor Richard J. Daley: His Battle for Chicago and the Nation* (New York: Warner Books, 2000), p. 6.

680 **"He just didn't know how to interview Daley"**: Author interview with Stanhope Gould, November 9, 2011.

681 **"The pictures and sound of the Chicago police department in action"**: Apple, "Daley Defends His Policies."

681 **"My interview technique is not to have blood spurt"**: Gates, *Air Time*, p. 211. See also Cronkite and Carleton, *Conversations with Cronkite*, p. 216.

682 **The Justice Department would soon go after the "Chicago Eight"**: Michael R. Belknap, *American Political Trials* (Westport, CT: Praeger, 1994), p. 240.

682 **"I took your advice, you know"**: Dana Cook, "Walter Cronkite, 1916–2009," *Salon*, July 18, 2009.

682 **"the terrible sixties":** Cronkite, *A Reporter's Life*, p. 192.

683 **"This is something we've been aiming at":** Fred Ferretti, "Cronkite on Endurance: 'You Don't Think of That,'" *New York Times*, July 24, 1969.

Twenty-Four: MR. MOON SHOT

685 **Cronkite kept one intense eye fixed on the *Apollo* 7 flight:** "CTN Special Programs" logbooks at the CBS News Reference Library, CBS Space Log 1957–1960, CBS News Archive, New York.

685 **"Walter had grown very sick of the 1968 election":** Author interview with Jeff Gralnick, June 11, 2010.

686 **It was hard not to feel the healing and unifying effects:** David Woods and Frank O'Brien, "Day 1: The Green Team and Separation, TIMETAG 003:42:55," *Apollo 8 Flight Journal*, NASA Historical Center, Houston, TX.

686 **"We are the lucky generation":** Walter Cronkite, "Foreword" to William E. Burrows, *The Infinite Journey: Eyewitness Accounts of NASA and the Age of Space* (New York: Discovery Books, 2000).

687   **CBS News was now devoting more and more resources:** "CTN Special Programs" logbooks at the CBS News Reference Library, CBS Space Log 1957–1960, CBS News Archive, New York.

687   **"Never before had I seen Dad with such thick binders":** Author interview with Chip Cronkite, March 11, 2011.

687   **"Walter would have on a Hawaiian shirt":** Author interview with Norman Mailer, August 17, 2006.

688   **"We were given absolute freedom to report the story":** Walter Cronkite, "We Are the Children of the Space Age," *TV Guide*, July 9, 1969, p. 12.

689   **"Nobody ever said it because nobody had to say it":** Hewitt, *Tell Me a Story*, pp. 72–74.

690   **put a man on the Moon "before the decade is out":** Lawrence Laurent, "Space Show Gives TV Its Finest Hours," *Washington Post*, July 22, 1969.

690   **"We do not have an official or unofficial 'honorary astronaut' title":** Julian Scheer to Thelma Jones, March 18, 1969, NASA Archives, Clear Lake City, TX.

690   **moon exploration lifted the national spirit:** Leon Wagener, *One Giant: Neil Armstrong's*

Stellar American Journey (New York: Tom Doherty Associates, 2004), p. 15.

691 ***Reader's Digest* had distributed an astonishing 68 million:** Ibid., p. 16.

692 **"Now the moon has yielded":** Neil McAleer, *Arthur C. Clarke: The Authorized Biography* (Chicago: Contemporary Books, 1993), p. 230.

693 ***Apollo 11* presented some of the most "formidable challenges":** Robert Wussler and Richard Salant, Foreword, *10:56:20 PM 7/20/69: The Historic Conquest of the Moon as Reported to the American People by CBS News over the CBS Television Network* (Darby, PA: Diane Publishing, 1970).

693 **"we've been this nervous since back in the early days":** Wagener, *One Giant Leap*, p. 536.

694 **as "Walter to Walter" coverage:** Display Ad for *Apollo 12*, *Toledo Blade*, November 13, 1969.

694 **"There she goes! It's beautiful":** Wussler and Salant, *10:56:20 PM 7/20/69*, pp. 9–10.

695 **"Oh boy, oh boy, it looks good, Wally":** Walter Cronkite, *"Apollo 11* Liftoff," July 16, 1969 (tape), CBS News Archive, New York.

695 **"The principal let me go into his office to watch Dad"**: Author interview with Kathy Cronkite, May 17, 2011.

695 **"I had deep reservations"**: Author interview with Nancy Cronkite, May 16, 2011.

696 **"My previous *Apollo* experience"**: Author interview with Chip Cronkite, May 16, 2011.

696 **"I wanted to be able to say"**: Wussler and Salant, *10:56:20 PM 7/20/69*, p. 16.

697 **"not a big Lyndon Johnson fan"**: Alfred Robert Hogan interview with Joan F. Richman, October 22, 2003 (transcript), Hogan Archive, Washington, DC.

697 **LBJ might replace Schirra as Cronkite's new astrobuddy**: Wussler and Salant, *10:56:20 PM 7/20/69*, pp. 18–19.

697 **LBJ on the Great Society**: James Hansen, *First Man: The Life of Neil A. Armstrong* (New York: Simon & Schuster, 2006), pp. 5–6.

697 **"Our family never held a grudge against Walter"**: Author interview with Lynda Johnson Robb, November 16, 2011.

698 **whereby "anyone on earth could locate himself by means of a couple of dials"**: Arthur C.

Clarke to Andrew G. Haley, August, 1956, Clarke Archive.

699 **"Walter had so bought into Space":** Author interview with Bill Plante, December 2, 2010.

699 **What differentiated Cronkite from Armstrong was the effusiveness:** Hansen, *First Man*, p. 585.

699 **"No, I never did that":** Author interview with Neil Armstrong, September 19, 2011.

700 **"short-haired, white athletes":** Charles J. Shields, *And So It Goes: Kurt Vonnegut: A Life* (New York: Henry Holt, 2011), p. 264.

700 **"This was the first—and last, for that matter—time":** Captain Walter M. Schirra Jr., with Richard N. Billings, *Schirra's Space* (Boston: Quinlan Press, 1988), pp. 221–222.

701 **"Walter and his guests discussed the epochal events":** McAleer, *Arthur C. Clarke*, p. 227.

703 **he developed a condition "in which one's eyeballs become uncoordinated":** Dick West, "Go West for News on the Moon," *Bryan* (Ohio) *Times*, July 24, 1969.

703 **"were nothing short of remarkable":** Jack Gould, "The Whole World Sat Front-Row Center," *New York Times*, July 27, 1969.

703 **Kuralt spoke about the spiritual aspects of Space travel:** Wussler and Salant, *10:56:20 PM 7/20/69*, pp. 53–54.

704 ***"Eagle:* Roger, understand":** Ibid., pp. 74–77.

706 **"time had stopped in Studio 41":** Arthur C. Clarke to Neil McAleer, April 20, 1990, McAleer Papers, Baltimore, MD.

707 **"Wow," the great journalist said. "Oh, boy!":** Schirra Jr. with Billings, *Schirra's Space*, pp. 222–23.

708 ***"Cronkite:* There he is. There's a foot coming down the steps":** CBS-TV News Special Report (transcript), "Apollo XI," July 20, 1969, CBS News Archive, New York.

709 **"The step on the Moon was an awesome achievement":** Wussler and Salant, Foreword, *10:56:20 PM 7/20/69*.

709 **were "like colts" finding their footing:** Wagener, *One Giant Leap*, p. 522.

710 **"Hot diggety dog!":** Wussler and Salant, Foreword, *10:56:20 PM 7/20/69*.

710 **their attitude was oddly blasé:** Jack Gould, "TV: Lunar Scenes Top Admirable Apollo Coverage," *New York Times*, July 22, 1969.

710 "Man has finally visited the Moon after all the ages of waiting": Cronkite broadcast transcript, July 24, 1969, CBS News Archives, New York.

711 He hoped someday to touch the lunar rocks: Wagener, *One Giant Leap*, p. 545.

711 he never noticed the "fatigue factor": Walter Cronkite interview, Archive of American Television, April 28, 1998.

711 "seemingly effortless performance": *New York Times*, July 21, 1969.

711 *Apollo 11* would lead to the militarization of space: Bliss, *Now the News*, p. 368.

711 "History has never proceeded by a rational plan": Eric Sevareid, CBS TV, July 15, 1969 (transcript), CBS News Archives, New York.

712 An astonishing 94 percent of all American homes: John E. O'Connor, ed., *American History, American Television: Interpreting the Video Past* (New York: Frederick Ungar Publishing, 1983), p. 380.

712 "It was a wonderful story of achievement": Walter Cronkite interview, Archive of American Television, April 28, 1998.

713 **"I have always wished that I could have shared":** Buzz Aldrin, *Magnificent Desolation: The Long Journey Home from the Moon* (New York: Harmony Books, 2009), p. 54.

713 **CBS drew 45 percent of the audience:** Ferretti, "Cronkite on Endurance."

714 **"He's more popular than the astronauts":** Bernard Weinraub, "Tense Contractors Await Splashdown," *New York Times*, July 19, 1969.

714 **Cronkite shunned *Face the Nation*:** CBS News Archive, New York.

714 **Armstrong had written, "Deist":** Hansen, *First Man*, p. 33.

715 **"That's agency nomenclature":** *Face the Nation*, as broadcast over the CBS Television Network and the CBS Radio Network, Sunday, August 17, 1969, 11:30 a.m.–12:30 p.m., p. 24.

715 **"Walter told me that the biggest on-air mistake he'd ever made":** Author interview with Ed Bradley, December 21, 2004.

716 **But Armstrong didn't hold it against Cronkite:** Wagener, *One Giant Leap*, p. 268.

716 **there just wasn't a "one giant leap for mankind" moment:** *History of Manned Space Flight*,

NASA publication #75-24641 (Washington, DC.: National Aeronautics and Space Administration, 1975), p. 29.

716 **astronauts' wives watched CBS's coverage because of the "fatherly":** Jim Lovell and Jeffrey Kluger, *Lost Moon: The Perilous Voyage of Apollo 13* (Boston: Houghton Mifflin, 1994), pp. 272–77.

717 **"He had little vials":** McAleer, *Arthur C. Clarke*, p. 231.

Twenty-Five: AVATAR OF EARTH DAY

719 **he kept a framed photo over his desk:** Francis French and Colin Burgess, *In the Shadow of the Moon* (Lincoln: University of Nebraska Press, 2007), pp. 310–13.

719 **The Apollo program had been designed to visit the Moon:** Ibid.

721 **NASA employees developed "a new environmental appreciation":** Author interview with George Abbey, June 6, 2011.

721 **ended up canceling *Apollos 18, 19,* and *20*:** David R. Williams, "Apollo 18 through 20— The Cancelled Missions," NASA Goddard Space Flight Center, December 11, 2003, nssdc.gsfc

.nasa.gov/planetary/lunar/apollo_18_20.html (accessed December 2, 2011).

722 **"Of all humankind's achievements in the twentieth century"**: Cronkite, *A Reporter's Life*, p. 27.

722 **"The North American continent seemed ringed by oil slicks"**: Walter Cronkite, *Eye on the World* (New York: Cowles, 1971), p. 10.

723 **"When Walter said 'God damn it,' things happened"**: Matusow, *The Evening Stars*, p. 116.

723 **"We wanted to grapple first with air pollution"**: Author interview with Ron Bonn, June 1, 2011.

724 **Cronkite and Union Carbide as sponsor**: Author interview with Jon Wilkman, January 8, 2012.

724 **"Earth, you understand, wasn't in the palm"**: Ibid.

726 **The Santa Barbara oil spill of 1969 had become a rallying point**: *Los Angeles Times*, January 28, 1989, p. 123.

726 **the "environmental crisis" was "eclipsing student discontent"**: Gladwin Hill, "Environment May Eclipse Vietnam as College Issue," *New York Times*, November 30, 1969.

726 **The time had come, Cronkite intuited:** William O. Douglas, "The Public Be Damned," *Playboy*, September 1969, p. 209.

726 **"Once Cronkite got on the environment":** Author interview with William Ruckelshaus, August 2, 2011.

727 **"Walter was almost a nutcase about the environment":** Author interview with Sandy Socolow, May 28, 2011.

728 **"Uhmm, could we call that thing something else?":** Schieffer, *This Just In,* pp. 270–71.

728 **"This planet is threatened with destruction":** Oliver S. Owen, *Natural Resource Conservation: An Ecological Approach* (London: Macmillan, 1980), p. 859.

729 **"Science can reveal the depth of the crisis":** Barry Commoner, *Science and Survival* (New York: Ballantine Books, 1970), p. 157.

730 **"devoting extensive time and energy":** Gaylord Nelson to Frank Stanton, April 7, 1971, Nelson Papers, Wisconsin Historical Society, Madison.

730 **To hear Cronkite bemoan the "littered Earth":** Walter Cronkite, "Earth Day: A Question of Survival," CBS News, April 22, 1970.

730 **"I noticed that the mail increased"**: Matusow, *The Evening Stars*, p. 173.

731 **"The affiliates went crazy on Walter"**: Author interview with Sandy Socolow, June 5, 2011.

731 **When the anchorman started talking about bloodshed at Kent State**: Sean Kirst, "Kent State: 'One or Two Cracks of Rifle Fire . . . Oh My God,'" *Syracuse Post-Standard*, May 5, 2010.

733 **Michener, with Cronkite spurring him on**: James Michener, *Kent State: What Happened and Why* (New York: Random House, 1971).

733 **"We must not reject those among us who dissent"**: "Dissenters Should Listen, Be Listened to—Cronkite," *Columbia Daily Tribune*, June 3, 1970, p. 1; special thanks to Ron Kucera for bringing this to my attention.

734 **"The 1960s, when we first launched humans into space"**: Walter Cronkite, *The Infinite Journey: Eyewitness Accounts of NASA and the Age of Space* (New York: Discovery Books, 2000), p. 1.

734 **"how deeply interested Walter was in the environment"**: Author interview with William Ruckelshaus, August 7, 2011.

735 **"That is not doomsday rhetoric"**: Cronkite, *Eye on the World*, p. 1.

736 **The *Greening of America* advocated "choosing a new life-style"**: Charles Reich, *The Greening of America* (New York: Random House, 1970), p. 350.

737 **"Every year American power plants pour"**: Cronkite, *Eye on the World*, p. 3.

738 **in 1980 he would get to collaborate with Peterson**: Roger Tory Peterson et al., *Save the Birds* (Boston: Houghton Mifflin, 1989).

738 **the airing of occasional "Can the World Be Saved?" segments lasted until 1980**: Author interview with Ron Bonn, June 1, 2011.

738 **more than one thousand environmentally minded citizens stood up**: Ruth A. Eblen to Walter Cronkite, November 2, 1989, File: One Earth Award, Box: 2M609, WCP-UTA.

739 **"It's about your own relationship with Mother Nature"**: "Cronkite Talks of Regrets and Doing 'The Job,'" *Lancaster* (PA) *New Era*, April 12, 2000.

739 **"this little lifeboat floating out there in space"**: Ed Bark, "The Eyes of History: Cronkite Shares

Thoughts on Life in TV Journalism," *Dallas Morning News*, December 6, 2000.

Twenty-Six: THE NIXON-VERSUS-CBS WAR

741 "'This will tear the scab off those bastards!'": Author interview with Patrick Buchanan, June 20, 2011.

742 "that the networks were made more responsive to the views": Spiro Agnew speech, "On the National Media," November 13, 1969, Des Moines, IA.

742 President Nixon wasn't the first president to feel persecuted: John Tebbel and Sarah Miles Watts, *The Press and the Presidency: From George Washington to Ronald Reagan* (New York: Oxford University Press, 1985), pp. 500–513.

742 "This administration's antagonism had been": Powers, "Walter Cronkite: A Candid Conversation."

743 "their whole objective in life is to bring us down": Stanley Kutler, *The Wars of Watergate: The Last Crisis of Richard Nixon* (New York: W. W Norton, 1990), p. 175. "great vigor": Richard Reeves, *President Nixon: Alone in the White House* (New York: Simon & Schuster, 2001), p. 74.

743 **"dripped with vitriol":** Cronkite, *A Reporter's Life*, pp. 221–22.

744 **"To people in broadcasting, the picture of":** Bliss, *Now the News*, p. 409.

745 **"Perhaps we didn't react enough":** Cynthia Lowry, "Agnew Assailed by TV Analysts," AP, November 6, 1969.

745 **"gravest implications":** "CBS Head Warns of Press Threat," *Bridgeport Post*, November 26, 1969.

745 **"implied threat":** "Cronkite Says TV Won't 'Pull in Horns,'" AP, November 22, 1969; Christopher Lydon, "Burch Supports Agnew; Shift in F.C.C. Role Seen," *New York Times*, November 15, 1969.

745 **"dangerous to democracy in America":** Walter Cronkite, "Speech," International Radio and Television Society, May 18, 1971 (transcript), CBS News Reference Archive, New York.

746 **"They said I had no proof that the campaign":** Cronkite, *A Reporter's Life*, pp. 223–24.

746 **"A nothing!":** Reeves, *President Nixon*, p. 137.

748 **Whether the informant was telling the truth:** John Cook, "FBI Files Discuss Cronkite Aiding

Vietnam Protesters," Yahoo! News, May 14, 2010, old.news.yahoo.com/s/ynews/20100514/ts_ynews/ynews_ts2067 (accessed January 1, 2011).

748 **The FBI had also monitored Cronkite's work:** Ibid.

748 **"Nixon truly saw the press as the enemy":** Author interview with Patrick Buchanan, June 20, 2011.

748 **a White House travesty called "The Enemies List":** Kenneth Franklin Kurz, *Nixon's Enemies* (Los Angeles: Lowell House, 1989).

749 **"Nixon thought I was his number-one enemy":** Brinkley, *A Memoir*, p. 192.

749 **"Was this so-called 'anti-media campaign'":** William Safire, *Before the Fall* (Garden City, NY: Doubleday, 1975), p. 341.

750 **CBS reported in December 1969 that it had never received so much:** "Public Split on Television News Coverage," *New York Times*, AP, December 17, 1969; Daniel Schorr, *Clearing the Air*, p. 40.

751 **"there would be revolution in the streets":** Cronkite and Carleton, *Conversations with Cronkite*, p. 278.

752 **"I never got called on it":** Ibid.

753 **Lines like "people feel that":** Ibid.

753 **"The Cronkite-Schorr charge against my brother was false":** Cronkite, *A Reporter's Life*, p. 222.

754 **"Concentrate on NBC":** H. R. Haldeman to Jeb Magruder, White House Memorandum, Internet Archive, February 4, 1970, http://www.archive .org/stream/presidentialcamp10unit/presidential camp10unit_djvu.txt.

754 **"news coverage now seems to reflect an eagerness to please":** Untitled editorial, *New Yorker*, February 28, 1970.

754 **"I feel that perhaps subconsciously":** Nathan Miller, "Intimidation Succeeds: Anti-Nixon TV Curbed," *Editorial Research Reports*, March 31, 1970.

756 **"We broadcast the original story":** "Film of Atrocity in Dispute Re-Run," *New York Times*, May 22, 1970.

756 **Fulbright described incidents staged by the Department of Defense:** Lee Byrd, "Sen. Fulbright Demands End to War Films by Pentagon," AP, May 23, 1970.

757 **"an aggressive Communist tide has spread"**: "The $$$ Selling of the Pentagon," *Capital Times* (Madison, WI), March 15, 1971.

758 **"get that piece out of there"**: Mudd, *The Place to Be*, p. 263.

758 **"it would have been a part of the ammunition hurled"**: Leonard, *In the Storm of the Eye*, p. 164.

758 **"The Selling of the Pentagon" was the price he paid**: Garth S. Jowett, "The Selling of the Pentagon: Television Confronts the First Amendment," in John O. Connor, ed., *American History/American Television: Interpreting the Video Past* (New York: Ungar, 1983).

760 **"one of the anchormen most careful"**: Jack Gould, "TV as a Free Medium," *New York Times*, March 25, 1971.

760 **"There are a couple of hundred correspondents in Vietnam"**: Walter Cronkite before the Economic Club of Detroit, March 2, 1970.

762 **"the definitive observation on Dick Nixon"**: Cronkite, *A Reporter's Life*, p. 221.

762 **They sometimes arranged for all three**: Author interview with Chip Cronkite, April 4, 2011.

763 **"Dad explained to me all about how television works":** Kathy Cronkite, *On the Edge of the Spotlight*, p. 58.

763 **They were like a gigantic *National Geographic* field trip:** Cronkite, *A Reporter's Life*, p. 325.

764 **"Dad loved to snorkel and swim":** Author interview with Chip Cronkite, April 4, 2011.

764 **"Walter had broken a 'no, no, no' rule":** Author interview with William Small, May 17, 2011.

765 **"Walter Cronkite was one of the first people to come forward":** Dawn Withers, "For the Love of News," NewsWatch.com, February 13, 2002.

765 **"In doing my work, I (and those who assist me) depend":** Steven V. Roberts, "News Techniques Stressed in Trial," *New York Times*, April 5, 1970.

767 **"that President Nixon can escape responsibility for this campaign":** Roy Reed, "Agnew Finds Nixon Foes Unremitting," *New York Times*, May 19, 1971.

768 **"because of those years of indoctrination":** Pat Buchanan, *Right from the Beginning* (Boston: Little, Brown, 1990), p. 40.

Twenty-Seven: REPORTABLE TRUTH
IN THE AGE OF NIXON

770 **"Seventy-five percent of those group hate my guts":** Herbert S. Parmet, *Richard Nixon and His America* (Boston: Little, Brown, 1990), p. 585.

770 **Just how appreciative other journalists were that Cronkite stood up:** "A Times Reporter Wins a Polk Award," *New York Times*, February 17, 1971.

770 **The Polk Award coincided with Paley's announcement:** "Cronkite to Do Saturday TV Show for Children," *New York Times*, March 22, 1971.

772 **"I decided I would stop concealing that myself":** Daniel Ellsberg, *Secrets: A Memoir of Vietnam and the Pentagon Papers* (New York: Penguin, 2002), p. 291.

772 **"I don't want to hear it. Victory is not near":** Halberstam, *The Best and the Brightest*, p. 637.

773 **"A line kept repeating itself in my head":** Ellsberg, *Secrets*, p. 272.

773 **Colson started spreading rumors that Ellsberg was a sexual pervert:** Seymour M. Hersh, *The*

Price of Power: Kissinger in the Nixon White House (New York: Simon & Schuster, 1984), p. 385. See also Parmet, *Richard Nixon and His America*, p. 591.

773 **"Colson is a liar":** Author interview with Daniel Ellsberg, January 23, 2012.

774 ***CBS Evening News* covered the story heavily:** "Injunction on Times Studied," AP, June 17, 1971.

774 **Another reason NBC said no was that its news division was in flux:** Jack Gould, "N.B.C. News Ending Anchor-Teams Era," *New York Times*, July 19, 1971.

775 **"We wanted to interview Daniel Ellsberg":** Cronkite and Carleton, *Conversations with Cronkite*, p. 248.

775 **Frank Stanton was facing serious legal consequences:** James Reston, "The Unfairness Doctrine," *New York Times*, April 14, 1971.

775 **Stanton, in a heroic First Amendment stand, refused:** Author interview with William Small, May 18, 2011.

776 **Manning arranged an exclusive interview:** David Rudenstine, *The Day the Presses Stopped:*

A History of the Pentagon Papers Case (Berkeley: University of California Press, 1996), p. 252.

776 **Cronkite remembered the advance work differently:** Cronkite, *A Reporter's Life*, p. 334.

778 **"I was proud of Cronkite for his Vietnam stalemate report":** Author interview with Daniel Ellsberg, January 23, 2012.

778 **"homosexual pickup":** Cronkite and Carleton, *Conversations with Cronkite*, p. 248.

778 **"There were many amateurish aspects to the plot":** Cronkite, *A Reporter's Life*, p. 335.

780 **"present at some length to a prime-time national television audience":** Ellsberg, *Secrets*, p. 400.

780 **"We are seeing 1964 all over again":** Walter Cronkite interview with Daniel Ellsberg (transcript), CBS Reference Library, New York.

780 **A better question was how could Cronkite find Ellsberg:** Reeves, *President Nixon*, p. 336.

781 **"It is the anti-Nixon CBS-Establishmentarian":** *National Review*, July 23, 1969.

781 **"Never have I seen men so dedicated":** L. F. Williams, letter, *Kingsport* (TN) *Times*, April 16, 1971.

782 *The News Twisters* **begins by excoriating:** Edith Efron, *The News Twisters* (Los Angeles: Nash Publishers, 1971), pp. 1–2, 173.

782 **the book concluded that 31 percent of the material:** Efron, *The News Twisters*, p. 102.

782 **Cronkite was given a clean bill of health:** Les Brown, "Study at American University Disputes President on 'Distorted' Newscasts," *New York Times*, March 26, 1974.

783 **"I have watched Nixon spend a morning designing Walter Cronkite's lead":** John Ehrlichman, *Witness to Power: The Nixon Years* (New York: Simon & Schuster, 1982), p. 266.

783 **"by fiat, by assumption, and by intimidation and harassment":** Walter Rugaber, "Cronkite and Professor Differ on Press Freedom," *New York Times*, October 1, 1971.

784 **On December 10, 1971, Dick Salant, just in time for Christmas, promoted:** Richard S. Salant to CBS News Division, December 10, 1971, CBS News Archives, New York.

785 *Nixon:* **"Cronkite is one of the worst offenders":** OVAL 854-17, February 13, 1972, White House Tapes, Richard Nixon Presidential Library and Museum, Yorba Linda, CA.

787 **the added notation "absolutely not":** Author interview with Stanley Karnow, September 11, 2011.

787 **The Nixon trip became the inverse of the Enemies List:** "87 Newsmen Selected for Nixon's China Trip," *Washington Post*, February 8, 1972.

788 **"Suddenly, into the picture swaggered Walter Cronkite":** Henry Kissinger, *White House Years* (New York: Simon & Schuster, 1979), p. 1082.

788 **Cronkite had his physician inject him with gamma globulin:** "Cronkite's Pre-China Plans," *Waters/Watson, Barbi/Media*, February 10, 1972, *Newsweek* clipping file, WCP-UTA.

789 **"It was very much like landing on the moon":** Cronkite and Carleton, *Conversations with Cronkite*, p. 251.

790 **"Cronkite spent a lot of free time with Sevareid":** Author interview with Izzy Bleckman, February 14, 2011.

791 **"I'm a very quiet fellow in New York":** Herb Caen, "Cronkite on the Town," *San Francisco Chronicle*, February 17, 1972 (Newsmaker-Roeder wire report), WCP-UTA.

792 **"On a sexism scale of one-to-ten":** Ellen Goodman, "Cronkite 'Simply Cannot Interview Women,'" *Boston Globe*, August 30, 1976.

793 **George Herman of CBS News' *Face the Nation* deserves credit:** Louis Liebovich, *Richard Nixon, Watergate, and the Press: A Historical Retrospective* (Westport, CT: Praeger, 2003), p. 51.

794 **CBS News won an Emmy:** Albin Krebs, "C.B.S. Wins Major 1972 Emmys for News," *New York Times*, May 23, 1973.

794 **"We were pinching virtually everything":** Author interview with Stanhope Gould, November 9, 2011.

795 **"The program might well be called 'Cronkite and His Friends'":** William V. Shannon, "The Media Mob: 'Now Back to Walter . . .'" *New York Times*, August 16, 1972.

795 **"We had conversations about this":** Author interview with Warren Beatty, March 14, 2011.

795 **"I didn't really give it serious thought":** Author interview with George McGovern, June 27, 2011.

796 **"If we had picked Cronkite, I could have avoided":** Ibid.

797 **"You keep showing the wind-downs":** Author interview with Daniel Ellsberg, January 23, 2012.

798 **the Nixon administration's deal to allow the sale of wheat:** John J. O'Connor, "TV: C.B.S. Details the U.S. Soviet Wheat Deal," *New York Times*, October 12, 1972.

798 **"Walter decided the Russian wheat deal":** Author interview with Stanhope Gould, November 9, 2011.

799 **"the most encouraging development in electronic journalism":** O'Connor, "TV: C.B.S. Details the U.S.-Soviet Wheat Deal."

800 **"Everybody from Walter down wanted to make this look *different*":** Ron Bonn to Douglas Brinkley, January 1, 2012.

800 **"I'm going to save your ass in this Watergate thing":** Benjamin Bradlee, *A Good Life: Newspapering and Other Adventures* (New York: Simon & Schuster, 1995), p. 341.

801 **Cronkite was aware that the *Post* was under increasing pressure:** Stanley Kutler, *The Wars of Watergate: The Last Crisis of Richard Nixon* (New York: Knopf, 1990), p. 380.

801　the FCC tried denying licenses to *Post*-owned stations: Bradlee, *A Good Life*, p. 344.

801　**Dick Salant was taking a huge risk:** Buzenberg and Buzenberg, *Salant, CBS and the Battle for the Soul of Broadcast Journalism*, pp. 100–101.

801　**"Most of what is known as the Watergate affair has emerged":** Ibid., p.101.

803　**"There was great excitement in the bureau":** Lesley Stahl, *Reporting Live* (New York: Touchstone, 1999), pp. 18–19.

803　**"The broadcast troubled me":** Paley, *As It Happened*, p. 340.

804　**"We'll bring you to your knees":** Tebbel and Watts, *The Press and the Presidency*, p. 512.

804　**"I had called Paley on Nixon's behalf":** Author interview with Charles Colson, September 6, 2011.

805　**"Walter Cronkite," Salant recalled, "did not participate":** Buzenberg and Buzenberg, *Salant, CBS, and the Battle for the Soul of Broadcast Journalism*, p. 107.

805　**"If I thought [Salant] was responding to White House pressure":** Cronkite, *A Reporter's Life*, p. 312.

806 **"The Nixon administration calls these allegations false":** Buzenberg and Buzenberg, *Salant, CBS, and the Battle for the Soul of Broadcast Journalism*, p. 103.

806 **"When Cronkite aired the Watergate bits, the sun came out for me":** Author interview with Ben Bradlee, January 18, 2012.

807 **"Somehow the Great White Father, Walter Cronkite":** Bradlee, *A Good Life*, p. 342.

807 **"I think if Bradlee ever left the Georgetown cocktail circuit":** Ibid., pp. 342–43.

808 *Colson:* **"I talked to Paley yesterday":** WHITE HOUSE 34-92, December 15, 1972, White House Tapes.

809 **Nixon pejoratively deemed "intellectual people" who were against:** OVAL 837-4, January 10, 1973, White House Tapes.

809 **"Nixon wasn't wrong about the liberal media":** Author interview with Charles Colson, September 6, 2011.

809 **everybody knew it was Cronkite who decided what flickered blue:** Eric Pace, "Burton Benjamin, 70, Dies; Former Head of CBS News," *New York Times*, September 19, 1998.

809 **When he took time off around Thanksgiving 1972:** "Cronkite Is Recovering After Surgery on Throat," *New York Times*, November 21, 1972.

810 **Only NASA launches, Cronkite said, would warrant him leaving:** "Periscope," *Newsweek*, March 9, 1973.

810 **"But he tried to be fair to me":** Author interview with Henry Kissinger, January 31, 2012.

811 **"I'll be glad to wear the crown":** James Endrst, "Could Cronkite End Up at Large? It Depends on CBS," *Hartford Courant*, June 12, 1988.

811 **"it wasn't mere anchoring. It was addressing the nation":** Author interview with Brian Williams, September 2, 2011.

811 **"I was always offended by the fact that he put out an Enemies List":** Cronkite and Carleton, *Conversations with Cronkite*, p. 249.

Twenty-Eight: FAN CLUBS, STALKERS,
AND POLITICAL GOOD-BYES

813 **"We had Cronkite on the set":** Author interview with Bernard Shaw, June 10, 2011.

814 **"I was convinced he wouldn't show up":** Ibid.

815 was "pivotal ... seminal ... inspirational ... educational": Bernard Shaw acceptance speech for the Walter Cronkite Award for Excellence in Journalism and Telecommunications, November 16, 1994, Shaw Papers, Takoma Park, MD.

815 "My goal was to be at CBS working with Cronkite": Author interview with Bernard Shaw, June 10, 2011.

816 CBS also had a stable of correspondents whom Martin Luther King Jr. embraced: Cronkite, *A Reporter's Life*, pp. 292–293.

816 "I'll never forget the first story I did": Author interview with Bernard Shaw, June 10, 2011.

816 "We are a long way from perfection": Walter Cronkite to Bernard Shaw, October 29, 1971, Shaw Papers, Takoma Park, MD.

818 "I said I wanted a no-asshole staff": Author interview with Connie Chung, July 28, 2011.

818 "marvelous extemporaneous style": Walter Cronkite interview with Orville Schell, September 12, 1996, *San Francisco Chronicle* Herb Caen Lecture Series pamphlet.

819 "Betsy was proof that you could be": Author interview with Tom Brokaw, August 3, 2011.

819 **"I was a Cronkite groupie by the age of six"**: Author interview with Brian Williams, September 3, 2011.

820 **"I grew up in a CBS household"**: Ibid.

821 **"My guys were Tom Snyder and Howard Cosell"**: Author interview with Bill O'Reilly, September 23, 2011.

822 **"Pictures plus words plus personality equals believability"**: "Walter Cronkite: The Electronic Front Page," *Time*, October 14, 1966.

822 **he had created a fan club in the anchorman's honor:** Robert Feder, "Cronkite Was Hero, Role Model, Friend," *Chicago Sun-Times*, July 17, 2009.

822 **"I personally am appreciative of your loyalty"**: Walter Cronkite to Robert Feder, May 18, 1972, Feder Personal Papers, Chicago, IL.

823 **Correspondence continued between Cronkite and Feder:** Walter Cronkite to Robert Feder, December 19, 1972, Feder Personal Papers, Chicago, IL.

823 **"I don't go on a low-residue diet. I just don't feel fatigue"**: Walter Cronkite Fan Club National Headquarters, January 1975, Feder Personal Papers, Chicago, IL.

823 **Cronkite had become part of the popular culture:** "Walter Cronkite Fan Club Newsletter," September 1973, Feder Personal Papers, Chicago, IL.

825 **"the thirty-sixth president of the United States died this afternoon":** *CBS Evening News with Walter Cronkite*, January 23, 1973 (transcript), CBS News Archives, New York.

825 **"What always impressed me about that moment":** Author interview with Scott Pelley, May 11, 2011.

825 **"Walter loved the challenge of broadcasting Johnson's death":** Author interview with Brian Williams, September 3, 2011.

825 **Then it was CBS News' turn:** Author interview with Tom Johnson, May 24, 2011.

825 **"Cronkite had just been with LBJ at the ranch":** Ibid.

826 **Cronkite had been at the LBJ ranch only ten days earlier:** Jay Sharbutt, "Equal Rights Topic of Program," AP, February 1, 1973.

826 **While the five-part series wasn't dramatic:** John J. O'Connor, "TV: Johnson Interview," *New York Times*, February 1, 1973.

827 "Johnson was mad as hell": Author interview with Bob Hardesty, January 24, 2012.

827 "It burned the hell out of the president": Author interview with Harry Middleton, July 20, 2011.

828 "It was reprehensible": Tom Johnson to Douglas Brinkley, January 3, 2012.

829 "Walter got the first roll": Author interview with Bill Felling, July 6, 2011.

829 "He had simply conditioned himself to be the UP guy": Tom Johnson to Douglas Brinkley, January 3, 2012.

830 "Walter had been right after all. I dismissed him": Author interview with Sandy Socolow, July 8, 2011.

831 "These POWs were dressed in striped pajamas": Author interview with David Kennerly, May 28, 2011.

831 "a victim of a deliberate [media] campaign": Don and Val Hymes, "Target: The News Media," *Frederick* (MD) *News-Post*, October 12, 1973.

831 "I first met Spiro Agnew in 1967 and I liked him": Jay Sharbutt, "Radio and Television," AP, October 12, 1973.

833   Mark Allan Segal interrupted a Cronkite
       broadcast: "Gay Raiders Invade Cronkite News
       Show," *New York Times*, December 12, 1973.

833   "I sat on Cronkite's desk directly in front of
       him": Joe Openshaw, "Walter Cronkite and
       the Gay Rights Movement," *Birmingham Gay
       Community Examiner*, July 27, 2009, http//www
       .examiner.com/gay-community-in-birmingham/
       walter-cronkite-and-the-gay-rights-movement
       (accessed August 18, 2011).

834   "The police were called": Author interview
       with Mark Segal, August 21, 2011.

835   "the happiest check I ever wrote": Ibid.

836   "Network news was never the same after
       that": "Mark Segal, the Gay Raiders, and Walter
       Cronkite: That's the Way It Was," *Philebrity
       .com*, July 20, 2009.

836   "The homosexual men and women have orga-
       nized": Edward Alwood, *Straight News: Gays,
       Lesbians, and the News Media* (New York:
       Columbia University Press, 1998), pp. 146–47.

837   he boasted about being a champion of LGBTQ
       issues: Segal, "Mark Segal, the Gay Raiders, and
       Walter Cronkite."

837 **"if there is any criticism of President Nixon"**: Arthur Unger, " 'Vicious' TV Reporting? What the Anchormen Say," *Christian Science Monitor* service, January 2, 1974.

837 **"Walter liked presidents"**: Author interview with Dan Rather, February 18, 2011.

838 **Cronkite's fans and admirers, private and corporate, would send:** Author interview with Kathy Cronkite, March 22, 2011.

838 **"The Lenny Bruce cult certainly was (is) a strong one"**: Walter Cronkite to Lyle Stuart, August 22, 1966, Box: 2M644, Folder: 1960, WCP-UTA.

839 **"There's something in Walter's style"**: "Walter Cronkite Fan Club Newsletter," June–July 1973, Feder Personal Papers, Chicago, IL.

839 **"Why do you feel Mr. Cronkite has risen to the high position"**: Doug James interview with John Chancellor, December 18, 1974 (transcript), James Archive, Mobile, AL.

841 **Brian Williams and Diane Sawyer took a page from the Cronkite–Moore collaboration:** Alessandra Stanley, "An Anchor Loosens His Tie, Along with His Persona," *New York Times*, November 1, 2011.

841 **"I love *The Mary Tyler Moore Show*"**: Quoted in the "Walter Cronkite Fan Club Newsletter," August 1974, Feder Personal Papers, Chicago, IL.

843 **"You watched Cronkite on Kennedy's death"**: Author interview with Linda Mason, April 30, 2011.

843 **"I thought I had arrived"**: Ibid.

844 **He bought a summer house in Edgartown**: Clifford Terry, "Cronkite with Candor," *Chicago Tribune Magazine*, March 15, 1981.

845 **Friends considered him a "lunatic sailor"**: James, *Walter Cronkite*, p. 218.

845 **The 4,330-square-foot home also allowed Cronkite**: Sarah Kershaw, "Where a Media Icon Once Went to Play," *New York Times*, October 24, 2010.

846 **"San Clemente or San Quentin"**: "The Walter Cronkite Fan Club Newsletter," June 1974, Feder Papers, Chicago, IL.

846 **"The Chief Justice himself said he was simply following the dictates"**: "CBS Evening News with Walter Cronkite" (transcript), August 7, 1974, Box: 2M644, Folder: Warren, WCP-UTA.

847 **"magnanimous"**: Mudd, *The Place to Be*, pp. 328–29.

848 **"Did they consort in advance"**: Tom Braden, "Only Roger Mudd Saved the Day," *Modesto Bee* (California), August 19, 1974.

848 **"We should declare a honeymoon"**: "The Walter Cronkite Fan Club Newsletter," November 1974, Feder Personal Papers, Chicago, IL.

849 **"It's quite cozy," he said. "All of you are in a friendly circle"**: Stahl, *Reporting Live*, p. 48.

849 **"I thought he wanted to suck me dry of all my hard work"**: Author interview with Lesley Stahl, April 11, 2011.

849 **"He played all the roles in his stories"**: Stahl, *Reporting Live*, p. 48.

850 **Stahl also learned what a hoot Betsy Cronkite was**: Ibid.

850 **"He was very protective of his seat of power"**: Author interview with Tom Brokaw, August 2, 2011.

Twenty-Nine: A TIME TO HEAL

852 **Schorr, who had won Emmys for reporting in each of the Watergate years**: Alan Greenblat,

"Journalism Legend Daniel Schorr Dies at 93," NPR, July 23, 2010.

852 **whore:** Judy Flander, "CBS Rift Comes Out in the Open," *Washington Star*, July 14, 1975.

852 **At issue was Schorr's charge:** Daniel Schorr, *Clearing the Air*, p. 117.

852 **"sweetness and light":** Ibid.

852 **Brian Lamb, who later founded C-SPAN, was the publisher:** Author interview with Brian Lamb, May 30, 2011.

853 **"that executive orders at CBS News were handed down":** Daniel Schorr, *Clearing the Air*, p. 117.

853 **"Oh, that the son of a bitch had done it again":** Cronkite and Carleton, *Conversations with Cronkite*, pp. 262–63.

853 **Cronkite believed the feud began when Schorr was excluded:** Flander, "CBS Rift Comes Out in the Open."

853 **"There was always a Schorr version":** Cronkite and Carleton, *Conversations with Cronkite*, pp. 262–63.

854 **"I think the circumstances required a sort of decency":** Walter Cronkite oral history interview, WCP-UTA.

854 **"Our reporters would have to ad-lib all night":** Buzenberg and Buzenberg, *Salant, CBS, and the Battle for the Soul of Broadcast Journalism*, p. 115.

856 **"It is as wrong [for the media] to take on the role of nation-healers":** Schorr, *Clearing the Air*, p. 116.

856 ***The Washington Post* also declined a victory lap:** Douglas Brinkley, *Gerald Ford* (New York: Times Books, 2007), pp. 1–3.

856 **"Katharine Graham and Ben Bradlee issued a 'don't gloat' order":** Author interview with Bob Woodward, May 26, 2011.

857 **praising the ex-president's "overtures in international politics":** Barbara Haddad Ryan, "Cronkite Proves Adept on the Other Side of Question-Answer Sessions," *Denver Post*, July 18, 1972.

857 **he was "behind" Schorr "all the way":** Walter Cronkite to Robert Feder, May 31, 1976, Feder Papers, Chicago, IL.

858 **"that his only boss was his wife, Betsy":** Leonard, *In the Storm of the Eye*, p. 15.

859 **"assured," "unflappable," and "perfectly aimed":** Rather, *The Camera Never Blinks Twice*, p. 247.

859 **"God help us if NBC had a good story"**: Ron Bonn to Douglas Brinkley, June 7, 2011.

860 **"But as a managing editor, he was brutal"**: Author interview with Morley Safer, September 9, 2011.

860 **knew they could get their stories on the Cronkite newscast**: Roger Mudd to Douglas Brinkley, March 3, 2012.

861 **"Most newsmen have spent some time covering the seamier side"**: Powers, "Walter Cronkite: A Candid Conversation."

861 **One of his favorite phrases was "Find the facts"**: Ibid.

861 **"Walter Wants"**: Schieffer, *This Just In*, p. 270.

861 **"He took nothing for granted"**: Don Hewitt, *Tell Me a Story*, p. 74.

863 **"He was that kind of guy"**: "Ed Bradley, the Award-Winning Television Journalist Who Broke Racial Barriers," Associated Press, November 11, 2006.

863 **Cronkite interviewed Ford from the Blue Room**: Gerald Ford interview with Walter Cronkite, Eric Sevareid, and Bob Schieffer of CBS News (transcript), April 21, 1975, the American Presidency

Project, http://www.presidency.ucsb.edu/ws/index.php?pid=4855#axzz1jHKBIJlR.

863 **"Today, America can regain the sense of pride":** Charles E. Neu, ed., *After Vietnam: Legacies of a Lost War* (Baltimore: Johns Hopkins University Press, 2000), p. 27.

864 **North Vietnamese tanks rolled into Saigon:** Brinkley, *Gerald Ford*, p. 86.

864 **"Nothing was going to stop him from doing this broadcast":** Midgley, *How Many Words Do You Want?* p. 286.

864 **but he started the April 30 broadcast and made it to its end:** George C. Herring, *America's Longest War: The United States and Vietnam*, 2nd ed. (Philadelphia: Temple University Press, 1986), p. 265.

865 **"rather well":** Walter Cronkite, "Letter to the Editor," *New York Times*, April 5, 1985.

865 **"We embarked on this Vietnam journey with good intentions":** Russell H. Coward Jr., *A Voice from the Vietnam War* (Westport, CT: Greenwood Press, 2004), p. 168.

865 **"'We could have won'":** Cronkite, *A Reporter's Life*, pp. 264–65.

866 *Esquire* **put Cronkite on its cover:** *Esquire*, December 1975. Also see James, *Walter Cronkite*, p. 211.

866 **"too-much-the-toady":** Author interview with Ed Bradley, December 21, 2004.

866 **"Ford was probably the most personable":** Cronkite and Carleton, *Conversations with Cronkite*, p. 313.

867 **Cronkite broadcast** *In Celebration of US*: Frank Mankiewicz, "The Great Certifier," *Washington Post–Potomac*, October 21, 1976.

867 **"It was," Cronkite said, "a glorious, spontaneous upwelling of enthusiasm":** Cronkite and Carleton, *Conversations with Cronkite*, p. 316.

868 **with pickups from forty-two locations:** Les Brown, "'Rockets Red Glare,' a Gift from BBC," *New York Times*, June 2, 1976.

869 **Cronkite used the Bicentennial to tell Americans:** Mankiewicz, "The Great Certifier."

869 **"Walter came on the air and said, 'What a day'":** Author interview with Brit Hume, August 24, 2011.

870 **"He was a good party boy, a good mixer":** Author interview with William Small, May 3, 2011.

870   "Back then Cronkite set the tone and tenor":
      Author interview with Nick Clooney, September
      10, 2011.

871   **Too often Murrow was cited:** Midgley, *How
      Many Words Do You Want?*, pp. 244–45.

871   **"He was our industry's George Washington":**
      Author interview with Nick Clooney, September
      10, 2011.

873   **"His persona became so prominent in
      American culture":** Tom Shales, "And That's
      the Way Cronkite Was," *Washington Post*, July
      18, 2009.

873   **talked "to no more than 2,000 people":** Lee
      Dembart, "A Mudd Report on Candidates
      Rejected by Cronkite Program," *New York
      Times*, June 8, 1976.

874   **"cast television in a bad light by allowing itself
      to be manipulated":** Ibid.

875   **"We investigated the security detail issue":**
      Author interview with Sandor M. Polster, July 18,
      2011.

875   **"he's got one of the best brains of anybody":**
      Jonathan Alter interview with Walter Cronkite,
      Rolling Stone, December 10, 1987, p. 94.

875 **Sam Jaffe of ABC News claimed he had seen Cronkite's name on a top-secret list:** "Sam A. Jaffe, 55; Reporter for ABC, CBS," *New York Times*, February 9, 1985.

876 **Sig Mickelson had Cronkite (and other CBS reporters) receive a briefing:** Felicity Barringer, "Sig Mickelson, First Director of CBS's TV News, Dies at 86," *New York Times*, March 27, 2000.

876 **"To remove the stain on him":** Schorr, *Clearing the Air*, p. 276.

876 **the CIA confirmed that two *former* CBS correspondents:** Sharon Jayson, "And That's the Way It Was," *Austin American-Statesman*, Metro and State, October 1, 1999.

877 **"All of this is deplorable":** Walter Cronkite to Robert Feder, June 7, 1977, Feder Pesonal Papers, Chicago, IL.

877 **He called this the "foxhole":** Joel Swerdlow, "Stay Tuned for Vizmos," *Washington Post*, October 31, 1976.

877 **Carter won 297 electoral votes compared to Ford's 240:** *Congressional Quarterly's Guide to 1976 Elections* (Ann Arbor: University of Michigan Press,1977).

879 **"rolled over on the floor with the depiction of TV news":** "Sidney Lumet Remembers *Network*," AP, February 22, 2006.

879 **"None of us realized that it was prophecy":** Ron Bonn to Douglas Brinkley, June 7, 2011.

Thirty: LIVE WITH JIMMY CARTER

881 **"I'd go to help her with her coat":** Ron Powers, "Walter Cronkite: Knocking a Couple Back After the Show," *Chicago Sun-Times*, March 4, 1974.

882 **What Arledge didn't stress was that Walters received that salary:** Barbara Walters, *Audition: A Memoir* (New York: Knopf, 2008), pp. 284–86.

882 **"Walter was very nasty about me":** Author interview with Barbara Walters, August 24, 2011.

883 **"I'm not going to play the celebrity journalism game":** Author interview with Sandy Socolow, July 8, 2011.

883 **"Walter complained about me getting $1 million":** Author interview with Barbara Walters, August 24, 2011.

884 **"A million dollars is a grotesque amount of money":** "Will the *Morning* Star Shine at Night?" *Time*, May 3, 1976.

884 **what he privately derided as "happy talk":** Author interview with Rita Braver, March 18, 2011.

884 **"She has shown exceptional talent in interviewing":** Ibid.

884 **"He wasn't Uncle Walter to me":** Author interview with Barbara Walters, July 2, 2011.

885 **"We all felt honored when Cronkite came to town":** Author interview with Rita Braver, March 18, 2011.

885 **Benjamin had been Cronkite's alter ego:** Author inteview with John Lane, November 9, 2011.

886 **"about four people were waiting to sweep Walter away":** Author interview with Rita Braver, March 18, 2011.

886 ***Newsweek* called the event "Dial-a-President":** Peter Goldman, "Dial-a-President," *Newsweek*, March 14, 1977, p. 14.

886 **"you never get in a press conference":** Charles Mohr, "Carter Discusses Problems and Policies with Telephone Callers from 26 States," *New York Times*, March 6, 1977.

886 **none of the 900-code long-distance calls was pre-screened:** Goldman, "Dial-a-President," p. 14.

887 **"No matter how far out the question, he had in his head a textbook":** Cronkite, *A Reporter's Life*, p. 226.

887 **"My inclination would be to do this again":** Goldman, "Dial-a-President," and "America Gets on the Party Line," *Time*, March 14, 1977.

887 **"Mr. Interlocutor to President Carter's Mr. Bones":** Sander Vanocur, "The President Carter Show," *Washington Post*, March 13, 1977.

887 **"no one would be disrespectful" to him:** "Father Cronkite," 1977 [newspaper clipping, no date], WCP-UTA.

888 **NBC's *Saturday Night Live* did a hilarious spoof:** Author interview with Tom Davis, June 10, 2011.

888 **A deal was even struck for Cronkite to acquire a minority share:** Philip H. Dougherty, "New Pilots for Waterway Guide," *New York Times*, April 3, 1978.

889 **"We hit it off right out of the gate":** Author interview with Mike Ashford, June 3, 2011.

889 **"willing to go to Israel to talk peace":** Sandor M. Polster, "Friday, November 12, 2010," News Media Maven Blog, newsmediamaven.blogspot .com (accessed August 3, 2011).

890 **"Sadat said he could go [to Israel] within a week"**: "The World: Behind Cronkite's Coup," *Time*, November 28, 1977.

891 **"has a leader of Israel met with a leader of Egypt"**: *CBS Evening News with Walter Cronkite* (broadcast transcript), November 14, 1977, CBS Archives, New York.

891 **"It was later suggested by some critics that I had overstepped"**: Cronkite, *A Reporter's Life*, pp. 316–17.

891 **"There was a lot of desk-slapping"**: "The World: Behind Cronkite's Coup."

891 **"most dramatic cross-coupling ever"**: David M. Alpern and Betsy Carter, "The Cronkite Summit?" *Newsweek*, November 28, 1977.

892 **"Both sides have a vested interest"**: Ibid.

892 **"CBS ought to be congratulated"**: "The World: Behind Cronkite's Coup."

892 **"Walter, I'm sure Sadat would disagree, but dammit, I wish you'd retire"**: Alpern, "The Cronkite Summit," *Newsweek*, November 28, 1977.

892 **"It took Walter Cronkite of CBS"**: William Safire, "Cronkite Diplomacy," *New York Times*, November 17, 1977.

892 **"We played Sadat and Begin off of each other"**: Author interview with John Lane, November 9, 2011.

893 **"On the flight, I slipped Sadat a private note"**: Author interview with Barbara Walters, August 24, 2011.

894 **"We became, over time, very fond of each other"**: Ibid.

894 **"Marvelous Walter"**: Fred Ferretti, "What Do They Do When They 'Anchor' the TV News," *New York Times*, February 5, 1978.

895 **"it was extraordinary—a heck of an experience"**: Michael Gorkin, "Walter Cronkite: Why He's the Most Trusted Man in America," *50 Plus*, November 1979, p. 18.

895 **Why not quit CBS while at the top of his game?**: Author interview with Sandor M. Polster, July 18, 2011.

895 **"It'll be up to Walter to decide whether he wants to do more"**: Les Brown, "Incoming Chief of CBS News Describes Plans," *New York Times*, August 1, 1978.

897 **"What I rail against is the Action news"**: Eliot Ward, "Three on the Anchor," *St. Louis Post-Dispatch*, December 25, 1977.

897 **Salant was constantly asked in 1978 about who would replace Cronkite:** Buzenberg and Buzenberg, *Salant, CBS, and the Battle for the Soul of Broadcast Journalism*, p. 267.

897 **That bought CBS some wait-and-see time to decide:** "DuPont Broadcast Prizes," *New York Times*, February 16, 1978.

898 **"People who blame Rather for pushing Cronkite out":** Author interview with Richard Leibner, November 3, 2011.

898 **either Roger Mudd or Dan Rather would replace Cronkite:** Fred Ferretti, "And That's the Way It Is," *Family Weekly*, July 3, 1977.

898 **It was sort of Salant versus Cronkite:** Kevin Phillips and Albert Sindlinger, "Most Trusted–Most Liberal–Most Objective TV Newscasters," syndicated column, June 10, 1974.

899 **"I'd be a damn fool not to quit while I'm ahead":** Leonard, *In the Storm of the Eye*, p. 15.

899 **"In the grimiest commercial terms, each rating point gained":** Ibid.

900 **That year both Cronkite and Halberstam agreed to lecture:** Deirdre Carmody, "63 Top Figures to Lead Seminars at Columbia's

Journalism School," *New York Times*, June 15, 1979.

901 **"I'm not in the goddamn business of selling movie tickets"**: Tom Watkins, "How 'That's The Way It Is' Became Cronkite's Tagline," CNN Blog, July 18, 2009.

901 **"I think we did [Jordan] an injustice in reporting that"**: Walter Cronkite on CNN's *Larry King Live*, March 9, 2001.

902 **took fifty-two hostages**: William Shawcross, *The Shah's Last Ride: The True Story of the Emperor's Dreams and Illusions, Exile, and Death at the Hands of His Foes and Friends* (New York: Touchstone, 1988), p. 126.

902 **"It was always gnawing away at your guts"**: Jimmy Carter Oral History, White Burkett Miller Center for Public Affairs, University of Virginia, Project of the Carter Presidency, President Carter Session, November 29, 1982, p. 52.

902 **Cronkite would sign off with the number of days the hostages had been held**: Barry Rubin, *Paved with Good Intentions: The American Experience in Iran* (New York: Oxford University Press, 1980), pp. 337–64.

903 **Once again, Cronkite led the charge:** Robert A. Strong, *Working in the World: Jimmy Carter and the Making of American Foreign Policy* (Baton Rouge: Louisiana State University, 2000), p. 235.

903 **George Ball blamed Cronkite for starting a national TV soap opera:** John Dumbrell, *The Carter Presidency* (Manchester, UK: Manchester University Press, 1995), p. 168.

903 **"Night after night, the television news dramatized":** Rosalynn Carter, *First Lady from Plains* (Boston: Houghton Mifflin, 1984), p. 319.

904 **"We'd do it slowly," he told Gorkin, "across the Atlantic":** Gorkin, "Walter Cronkite: Why He's the Most Trusted Man in America," p. 19.

904 **Cronkite's *CBS Evening News* had topped the ratings:** Thomas Collins, "Good Night, Walter," *Newsday*, March 5, 1981.

904 **"I've spent thousands of dollars developing these bags":** J. Howard Williams, *Love at First Sight: A Lifetime of Sailing on Galveston Bay* (Bloomington, IN: iUniverse, 2005), p. 6.

905 **as being "perfectly ridiculous":** Jon Roe, "President Felt Left Out in Race for Alien Vote," *Wichita Eagle*, December 26, 1992.

905 **"We need courses, beginning in junior high, on journalism":** Cleveland Amory, "What Walter Cronkite Misses Most," *Parade*, March 11, 1984, p. 4.

905 **journalists could now make or break a candidate:** James David Barber, *The Pulse of Politics: Electing Presidents in the Media Age* (New York: W. W. Norton, 1980).

906 **Their focus was not on a local luminary:** Hugh Sidey, "The Presidency: A Revolution Is Under Way," *Time*, March 31, 1980.

906 **ripping Linus's blanket away from an electronic America:** Dick Williams, "End of an Era," *Atlanta Journal-Constitution*, March 8, 1981.

906 **"I'd like to be able to step out right now":** "Cronkite Reports '81 Plan to Leave CBS Anchor Slot," AP, February 6, 1980.

907 **the darkly handsome Rather would replace Cronkite:** Edward Diamond, "Television's 'Great' Anchors and What Made Them Rate," *New York Times*, March 23, 1980.

907 **CBS News refused to let Mudd out of his contract early:** Mudd, *The Place to Be*, p. 376.

907 **he was proud to call him his successor:** Author interview with Richard Leibner, November 3, 2011.

907 **"I've covered every inauguration":** Les Brown, "Dan Rather to Succeed Cronkite," *New York Times*, February 15, 1980.

908 **"Harrington tells Cronkite what is happening":** Robert G. Kaiser, "CBS's Big Feed: The Primary Reasons," *Washington Post*, February 28, 1980.

909 **Cronkite, amazingly, was suggested as a vice presidential candidate for Anderson:** John Anderson, "Cronkite Denies Interest in Running with Anderson," *Washington Post*, April 30, 1980.

909 **"he'd be honored if asked":** Plissner, *The Control Room*, p. 219.

910 **"To be among the best reporters and analysts of government":** Walter Cronkite, "You Heard It Here Second," *New York Times*, May 10, 1980.

910 **"that you were No. 2 for the No. 2 spot on the Anderson ticket":** Stephen E. Weisman, *Daniel Patrick Moynihan: A Portrait in Letters of an American Visionary* (New York: PublicAffairs, 2010), p. 413.

911   "It seems slightly mad," Reston wrote, "but it happens to be true": James Reston, "A Second Rescue Mission," *New York Times*, April 27, 1980.

911   Cronkite was "seemingly embarrassed" by the commotion: B. Drummond Ayres Jr., "Reporter's Notebook: Kennedy Takes Off His Gloves," *New York Times*, April 21, 1980.

912   the "preeminent figure" in contemporary journalism: "List of Those Honored at Harvard Ceremonies," *New York Times*, June 6, 1980.

912   "they believed you at a time when they needed somebody to believe": "1981: A Conversation with Fred Friendly," p. 165.

912   The big unknown was who would run with him: Mark Updegrove, *Second Acts: Presidential Lives and Legacies After the White House* (Guilford, CT: Lyons Press, 2006), p. 129.

912   A movement, somewhat unprecedented, was launched to have former president Gerald Ford be: Author interview with David Kennerly, May 23, 2011.

913   "scoop of scoops": Tom Shales, "Back to You, CBS," *Washington Post*, July 17, 1980.

913 **"and be a figurehead vice-president":** Author interview with David Kennerly, May 23, 2011.

913 **"Cronkite had me in a pickle":** Author interview with Gerald Ford, March 23, 2003.

914 **"Barbara and I had an argument":** Sandy Socolow to Douglas Brinkley, December 18, 2011.

914 **"She had planted herself right outside the door":** Author interview with David Kennerly, May 23, 2011.

915 **"suffered when Barbara twisted his arm to get him onto ABC":** Cronkite, *A Reporter's Life*, p. 238.

915 **"She said she was sorry":** Sandy Socolow to Douglas Brinkley, December 18, 2011.

916 **"an entertaining brawl with elements of farce":** Tom Shales, "The Last Hurrah," *Washington Post*, August 12, 1980.

916 **"I am overwhelmed," he said. "I really am":** "Unplugging the Miles," *Washington Post*, August 16, 1980.

916 **"teaching three generations of Americans the political process":** "CBS Retires Cronkite's Mike as He Anchors Last Convention," *Boston Herald*, August 16, 1980.

918 **"I don't believe there are any who distrust him"**: Jimmy Carter, "Medal of Freedom to Walter Cronkite," January 16, 1981 (transcript), CBS News Archive, New York. Also see Henry Mitchell, "Any Day," *Washington Post*, January 17, 1981.

Thirty-One: RETIREMENT BLUES

922 **"Keep it up, you're getting better"**: William Hickey, "Uncle Walter Departs," *Cleveland Plain Dealer*, March 5, 1981.

922 **"Walter Cronkite, television and radio newsman, died today"**: Albin Krebs and Robert Thomas, "Notes on People: In Cronkite's Mailbox," *New York Times*, January 21, 1981.

922 **In 1980, *Universe* ran four additional times**: Peter Goodman to Bill Leonard–Walter Cronkite, April 6, 1981, Folder: Awards 1981, Box: 2M609, WCP-UTA.

923 **"That little guffaw laugh of his wasn't around anymore"**: Author interview with Connie Chung, July 28, 2011.

923 **"We were impressed by his calm and physical courage during that hurricane"**: Gates, *Air Time*, p. 307.

924 **"This is shakier than cafeteria Jell-O":** Ken Auletta, "Sign-Off: The Long and Complicated Career of Dan Rather," *New Yorker*, March 7, 2005.

924 **"I'm a different person than Walter Cronkite":** Eric Mink, "His Challenge Is Replacing the Most Trusted Journalist," *St. Louis Post-Dispatch*, March 8, 1981.

924 **Cronkite's old beige set backdrop was repainted blue-gray:** Tony Schwartz, "Amid the Fuss, Cronkite Says a Quiet 'Good Night,'" *New York Times*, March 7, 1981.

925 **"But I broadcast the news from Walter's chair":** Author interview with Bob Schieffer, August 31, 2011.

926 **"'Socolow, he's standing up! He's standing up'":** Author interview with Sandy Socolow, July 7, 2011.

926 **"It was a near-catastrophe that will not be soon forgotten":** Sandor M. Polster, "The Empty Throne," Blog post, March 7, 2011.

926 **"What an asshole thing to do":** Author interview with Sandy Socolow, July 18, 2011.

927 **"I still can see Dan Rather perched on that typewriter table":** Polster, "The Empty Throne."

927 **"Dan looked like he was going to the crapper"**: Author interview with Bob Schieffer, August 31, 2011.

927 **"By the first commercial break he knew better and sat down"**: Author interview with Sandy Socolow, July 8, 2011.

927 **Chung nicknamed him the "Stealth Bomber"**: Author interview with Connie Chung, July 28, 2011.

927 **"Rather was determined to wipe out every vestige of Cronkite"**: Author interview with Morley Safer, September 17, 2011.

928 **"He told me he wasn't happy I got the job"**: Author interview with Jeff Fager, January 9, 2011.

928 **Ratings dipped by 9 percent at *CBS Evening News***: Peter J. Boyer, "Rather's Ratings Slip in First Week," AP, March 19, 1981.

929 **"Walter wasn't big on diplomacy"**: Author interview with Gordon F. Joseloff, June 19, 2011.

929 **"I'll never forget Walter's reaction as he heard those words"**: Gordon F. Joseloff, "A Westporter Remembers His Friend, Walter Cronkite," *Westport Now,* July 18, 2009.

930 **"America once again had Walter"**: Ibid.

931 **The Reagan assassination attempt put him in a deep funk:** "Cronkite Talks of Regrets and Doing the Job," *Lancaster* (PA) *New Era*, April 12, 2000.

932 **"It was a damn good interview; I'm very proud of it":** Cronkite and Carleton, *Conversations with Cronkite*, p. 342.

933 **his boneheaded decision to join the Pan Am Board:** Bob Langford, "Cronkite's Uneasy Retirement: Why Isn't There a Place for Uncle Walter?" *News & Observer*, April 13, 1992.

933 **Cronkite quit Pan Am to save his reputation:** Walter Cronkite to Pan Am Board, October 8, 1981, CBS News Research Archives, New York.

933 **"the Yankees when they had Murderers' Row":** Desmond Smith, "Is This the Future of TV News?" *New York*, February 22, 1982.

934 **Arledge was "like a boxer who smells the kill":** "TV After Cronkite," *Newsweek*, March 9, 1981.

934 **he visited the far reaches:** Arthur Unger, "Walter Cronkite in Retirement: A Tradition Winds Down," *Christian Science Monitor*, March 6, 1981.

934 **"crash courses at This-Is-the-World night school":** Author interview with Ed Bradley, December 21, 2004.

934 *Universe* **was conceived as a half-hour news-magazine:** Richard F. Shepard, "TV Weekend: 'Cronkite's Universe,'" *New York Times*, June 19, 1981.

934 **"The basic idea was to take subjects that could have a strong impact":** Author interview with Charles Osgood, April 17, 2011.

935 *Universe* **was akin to PBS's** *NOVA* **before its time:** CBS News Reference Library files; also, Daniel Einstein, *Special Edition: A Guide to Network Television Documentary Series and Special News Reports,1980–1989* (Lanham, MD: Scarecrow Press, 1997).

935 **he later flew over the Arctic Circle to see the aurora borealis:** "Cronkite's Show Takes Him Places He's Not Even Known," AP, June 10, 1982; Fred Rothenberg, "Cronkite Fesses Up," AP, June 7, 1982.

936 **"Walter essentially ran the camera on the** *Alvin* **himself":** Author interview with Isadore "Izzy" Bleckman, February 23, 2011.

937 **"I asked the owner about the fish":** Ibid.

937 **"Let's go drink at the Ritz Bar":** Author inteview with Charles Osgood, April 17, 2011.

938 "is not a genius at anything except being straight, honest and normal": Andy Rooney, "Good Ol' Walter," syndicated column, February 21, 1981.

938 "One would think that the grandeur of the universe needs no assistance": Neil Postman, *Amusing Ourselves to Death* (New York: Penguin Books, 1995), p. 123.

939 "It was our way of telling Walter thank you": Author interview with Dale Minor, August 16, 2011.

939 one of the producers wore a Failure Analysis ball cap: Ibid.

940 "Socolow and Cronkite were just banging the tom-toms against me": Author interview with Dan Rather, December 30, 2011.

941 a CBS News documentary: John Corry, "TV: A Cronkite Report, Children of Apartheid," *New York Times*, December 5, 1987.

942 It aired on December 5, 1987, and won both an Emmy: "Walter Cronkite . . . CBS News Special Correspondent," industry biography.

943 "You don't *have* to be the most trusted man in America": Author interview with Isadore "Izzy" Bleckman, February 23, 2011.

943 **"caterpillar in a jar"**: Kathy Cronkite, *On the Edge of the Spotlight*, pp. 17–18.

944 **"There were moments when reading this book"**: Walter Cronkite, Foreword, in ibid., p. 9.

946 **"But someone might recognize me"**: Alan Weisman, Diary notes, September 1981. The retelling of Cronkite's trip to Egypt comes directly from this diary.

947 **"Look at this. Nothing"**: Ibid.

949 **"Put that down"**: Author interview with Alan Weisman, January 22, 2012.

950 **"Deal"**: Author interview with Sandy Socolow, June 2, 2011.

951 **"You did it again!"**: Weisman, Diary notes.

951 **"It was a killer look"**: Author interview with Alan Weisman, January 22, 2012.

951 **the Carters held a grudge against him**: Ibid.

951 **"Wasn't that a time"**: Weisman, Diary notes.

952 **"strive valiantly"**: Donald J. Davidson, ed., *The Wisdom of Theodore Roosevelt* (New York: Kensington, 2003), p. 48.

953 **"He blamed CBS dissing him"**: Author interview with Connie Chung, July 27, 2011.

954 **"I very much regretted it because it didn't work out"**: Walter Cronkite oral history interview, pp. 681–82, WCP-UTA.

955 **"It was somewhere between awkward and a strain"**: Author interview with Dan Rather, December 30, 2011.

955 **Socolow learned that the desk had been pulped:** Author interview with Sandy Socolow, June 2, 2011.

956 **"has been putting dirt on me for years"**: Author interview with Dan Rather, December 30, 2011.

956 **So Brinkley quit:** Brinkley, *A Memoir*, p. 234.

957 **"I thought, well, the hell with them, if they want to pay me"**: Walter Cronkite oral history interview, p. 683, WCP-UTA.

958 **"Walter was bound to fail"**: Author interview with Bud Lamoreaux, February 28, 2011.

958 **"the Cronkite age is behind us"**: Smith, "Is This the Future of TV News?" *New York*, February 22, 1982.

958 **He was convinced that turning away from that kind of passion for news:** Peter Kerr, "Cronkite Now Critical of CBS News," *New York Times*, December 7, 1983.

958 **"Cronkite was always one step short of disillu-sionment"**: Author interview with Peter Kaplan, August 7, 2011.

Thirty-Two: STRUGGLING ELDER STATESMAN

960 **"I screened the broadcast"**: Bill Leonard, *In the Storm of the Eye*, p. 223.

961 **"blame on my back"**: Lewis Sorley, *Westmoreland: The General Who Lost Vietnam* (New York: Houghton Mifflin Harcourt, 2011), p. 129.

961 **the "definitive centrist American" and "every-body's uncle"**: Al Reinert, "The Secret World of Walter Cronkite," *Texas Monthly*, January 1976.

962 **"The total absence of privacy"**: Walter Cronkite, "Orwell's 1984—Nearing?" *New York Times*, June 5, 1983.

963 **"Walter blew his stack"**: Author interview with Dale Minor, August 16, 2011.

963 **had put Cronkite on its blacklist for being "too liberal"**: "USIA Blacklisted 84 from Speaking Program," *Los Angeles Times*, February 10, 1984.

964 **Reagan, who respected Cronkite, was embar-rassed**: Ibid.

964 **"The White House does not condone any blacklist":** Howard Kurtz, "Democrats Blast USIA Blacklist," *Washington Post*, February 11, 1984.

965 **"Everybody wanted to keep shaking Walter's hand":** Author interview with Missie Rennie, February 22, 2011.

965 **World War II veterans started asking Cronkite to blurb:** Walter Cronkite to Susan Wiant, March 13, 1989.

966 **"We all know, the shortest way home is through Tokyo":** "Interview with Walter Cronkite of CBS News in Normandy, France, June 6, 1984," The Public Papers of President Ronald W. Reagan, Ronald Reagan Presidential Foundation and Library, Simi Valley, CA.

966 **"Just tell them what we've done":** Ibid.

967 **"The convention pairing that garnered":** Maureen Dowd, "Reporter's Notebook; With Rather and Cronkite, That's the Way It Is," *New York Times*, July 18, 1988; author interview with Sandy Socolow, July 16, 2011.

968 **"Four years *is* too long":** "Cronkite's Corner," New York *Daily News*, July 12, 1984.

968   **CBS aired "The Legacy of Harry S. Truman" in prime time:** Gordon Walek, "Lots of Attention Given to Truman," *Chicago Herald*, July 18, 1984.

968   **"Walter was an excellent interviewer":** Author interview with Barbara Walters, August 24, 2011.

969   **"The main thing was that this hall listened":** Tom Starner, "Some Stars Were Brighter," *Syracuse Herald-Journal*, July 7, 1984.

969   **Cronkite was barely given a cameo on CBS:** "First Convention Since 1952 Without Cronkite," *New York Daily News*, July 16, 1984.

970   **"It was quite sad how CBS under Rather treated him":** Author interview with Bob Schieffer, August 31, 2011.

970   **"that all I'll have is a room with a monitor":** Peter W. Kaplan, "A Sequestered Cronkite Is on Call at Convention," *New York Times*, July 18, 1984.

971   **wondered why CBS had been cruel to his old rival and friend:** Author interview with Roger Mudd, May 25, 2011.

971   **"Being on the air five times a week from 1962 to 1982 created egocentrism":** Author interview with Dan Rather, May 29, 2011.

972 **"I would often come up with a cold":** Peter W. Kaplan, "The Longest Night for Television," *New York Times*, November 7, 1984.

973 **"Robert Redford. Maybe Walter Cronkite":** Bernard Weinraub, "Mondale, Assessing Defeat, Says He'll Leave Politics," *New York Times*, November 8, 1984.

973 **The first special was "Honor, Duty, and a War Called Vietnam":** Margaret Scherf, "Ex POW, Now Congressman to Visit Own Monument," AP, January 12, 1985.

974 **"Not all of us can emulate John Wayne":** Michael E. Hill, "Walter Cronkite," *Washington Post*, April 21, 1985.

974 **But to Cronkite, CBS News president treated him:** For the conflict with CBS, see Box: 2M632, Folders: BBC–PBS Space Shuttle Program (11/84–85/86) and Truman Library (4/86), WCP-UTA.

975 **"he had an appetite for both history and political bullshit":** Author interview with Ben Barnes, April 7, 2011.

976 **Cronkite was once challenged to a name-dropping contest:** Amory, "What Walter Cronkite Misses Most."

976   **"For Walter and me it's like the Dr. Seuss story":** Author interview with Brian Williams, September 2, 2011.

976   **"A big part of his lovability":** Author interview with Deborah Rush, February 21, 2012.

977   **Cronkite was a fan of painter Thomas Hart Benton's:** Author interview with Porter Bibb, January 30, 2011.

977   **A publisher had accepted my paintings:** Author interview with Ray Ellis, December 15, 2011.

978   **"He has the rapscallion look of a Welsh pirate":** Ibid.

978   **"Boating in the Pacific Northwest, in season":** Ray Ellis and Walter Cronkite, *Westwind* (Birmingham: Oxmoor House, 1990), p. 12.

978   **to give "the folks who live there hope to stave off":** Walter Cronkite to Robin Ann Chlupach, October 1, 1998, Box: 2M613, WPC-UTA.

979   **"I've been broadcasting for years":** Author interview with Ray Ellis, December 15, 2011.

979   **In the mid–1970s she married Gifford Whitney in New York:** "Nancy Cronkite Is Married to Gifford Whitney," *New York Times*, October 3, 1975.

980 **"Now we can just send the boat"**: Morten Lund, "Look Who's Back at the Helm," *USA Today*, July 25, 1986.

980 **"Mom loved Dad *so* much"**: Author interview with Kathy Cronkite, March 22, 2011.

980 **"I know a woman perfect for you"**: Author interview with Mike Ashford, June 3, 2011.

981 **"I'd get up to Martha's Vineyard to sail and check up on Walter's view"**: Author interview with Jimmy Buffett, September 18, 2011.

982 **"The greatest Old Master in the art of living"**: Andy Rooney, "It Takes Effort to Savor Life," syndicated, Tribune Media Services, January 28, 1986.

982 **"With a population of only 220 million to choose from"**: Buchwald, "Anchor's Away."

983 **Cronkite raised over $300,000 for the Walter Cronkite Regents Chair:** Guy D. Garcia, "People: May 19, 1986," *Time*, May 19, 1986.

983 **"I'm going to use all the jokes I used"**: "Roast for Good-Guy Cronkite Turns to Toast," AP, May 8, 1986.

983 **The Cronkite family started visiting Arizona:** Author interview with Kathy Cronkite, March 22, 2011.

984 **"We started answering the telephone the next day"**: Christopher Callahan, "Remembering Walter and His School," *The Cronkite Journal* (2010–2011), Arizona State University, p. 2.

985 **"Walter came to visit the construction site"**: Author interview with Stephen Erlich, April 4, 2011.

986 **"I tried to buy all of the networks"**: Author interview with Ted Turner, April 20, 2011.

986 **"Ted, how about letting me steer"**: Jim Flannery, "Cronkite: A Sailor, in a News Anchor's Chair," *Sounding*, August 31, 2009.

987 **"moral fitness"**: Ken Auletta, *Media Man: Ted Turner's Improbable Empire* (New York: Norton, 2004), p. 47.

987 **After a short time, in 1986, Larry Tisch was named chairman**: Ibid.

988 **Tisch went further, however**: Edward Rapetti, "A Look at TV News with Walter Cronkite," *Editor & Publisher*, October 14, 1967, p. 72.

989 **"There was talk"**: Author interview with Bob Schieffer, August 31, 2011.

989 **"There was a feeling that Walter was a man without a counter"**: Author interview with Andy Rooney, March 15, 2011.

990 **"I remember us going to dinner with Walter and Betsy":** Author interview with Ruth Friendly, November 8, 2011.

991 **Old Guy Network:** Roger Mudd to Douglas Brinkley, March 3, 2012.

992 **"When he saved himself, there was a thrill":** Sally Bedell Smith, *In All His Glory: The Life and Times of William S. Paley* (New York: Simon & Schuster, 1990), pp. 602–3.

Thirty-Three: DEFIANT LIBERAL

995 **there was "reasonably no age limit for the flight":** *People*, January 13, 1986.

995 **"the last lingering suspicion":** "Applications Are Flooding Space Journalist Program," AP, January 16, 1986.

995 **"I sure want that first guy to be checked out by the FBI":** David Friend notes.

996 **Cronkite's campaign to become a NASA citizen astronaut intensified:** Author interview with David Friend, February 6, 2011.

996 **"So I got the space suit and flew up":** Author interview with David Friend, December 7, 2010.

997 **proud to be a NASA astronaut for an afternoon:** Author interview with David Friend, May 11, 2011.

997 **"We have come a long way in Space"**: "Don't Forget Our Successes: Cronkite," AP, January 29, 1986.

998 **"People are always calling up with things"**: Morten Lund, "Look Who's Back at the Helm," *USA Today*, July 25–27, 1986.

998 **"When the new morality hit in the late 60s, early 70s"**: *Washington Post* Q&A, Cronkite-Katz, 1983.

999 **"four major dangers to civilization"**: Timothy White, "Walter, We Hardly Knew You: A Candid Conversation with America's Most Comforting Stranger," *Rolling Stone*, February 5, 1971, p. 76.

999 **"What a wonderful time we all had"**: Author interview with Jann Wenner, February 28, 2011.

999 **He collaborated with pianist Dave Brubeck**: Author interview with Chris Brubeck, September 18, 2011.

1000 **When composer Irving Berlin turned one hundred** : "Irving Berlin's 100th Birthday Celebration," CBS-TV, 2100–2300 EST, Friday March 27, 1988.

1000 **he "didn't have a good singing voice"**: Author interview with Kathy Cronkite, March 22, 2011.

1000 **Cronkite volunteered to be emcee and promo man for the opera:** Michael Broson to Walter Cronkite, February 22, 1988, Box: 2M632, Folder: Nixon in China, WCP-UTA.

1001 **Walter Cronkite thought it was a setup:** Andy Warhol, *Diaries*, ed. Pat Hackett (New York: Warner Books, 1989).

1001 **"While in the studio, I bumped into Cronkite":** Author interview with Mickey Hart, February 17, 2011.

1002 **"Walter walked the walk as well as talking the talk":** Ibid.

1002 **"We played drums together a lot":** Ibid.

1003 **" 'Walter would never have done that' ":** Author interview with Jeff Fager, January 10, 2012.

1004 **Rather was widely criticized for the lapse:** "Cronkite Criticizes Rather over Walkout," AP, October 14, 1987.

1004 **"Walter, I long knew, was competitive":** Author interview with Dan Rather, May 28, 2011.

1005 **acknowledged that Cronkite had been purposely "shut out":** Peter J. Boyer, "Cronkite Idea for Special Is Rejected by CBS," *New York Times*, June 8, 1988.

1006 "But to me, I guess, Dan just reeks of insincerity": Cronkite and Carleton, *Conversations with Cronkite*, p. 338.

1006 "He was pushing this Kennedy anniversary special": Author interview with Dan Rather, May 28, 2011.

1006 Cronkite was nixed from the entire enterprise: Ann Hodges, "CBS Offers Viewers the Moon with *Apollo 11* Salute," *Houston Chronicle*, July 12, 1989.

1008 "Walter and I met for two or three days, sometimes longer": Carleton, "Cronkite's Texas."

1009 "Kill them all": Author interview with Joe Klein, April 11, 2011.

1009 Cronkite would be in breach of his million-a-year contract: Robert Gillette, "Politics '88," *Los Angeles Times*, February 29, 1988.

1010 "Cronkite watched": Ann Hodges, "Cronkite Would Rather Not Comment About Colleague," *Houston Chronicle*, March 1, 1988.

1010 "It's the glamour of the business that attracts them": Eleanor Randolph, "Cronkite and Reston on the News Biz," *Washington Post*, April 16, 1988.

1012 **On September 20, Benjamin died:** Jay Sharbutt, "Burton Benjamin, CBS News President," *Los Angeles Times*, September 20, 1988.

1012 **"Benjamin had been Walter's backstop":** Author interview with Andy Rooney, March 15, 2011.

1012 **It proved to be a watershed moment in the campaign:** Author interview with Bernard Shaw, June 9, 2011.

1012 **"Governor, if Kitty Dukakis were raped and murdered":** Tom Wicker, *George Herbert Walker Bush* (New York: Penguin, 2004), p. 95.

1014 **"The temptation is rather great at his point to digress into the defense":** "Walter Cronkite Speech in Defense of Liberalism, Just Days After '88 Election," People for the American Way, http://www.pfaw.org/video/c3/walter-cronkite -speech-defense-of-liberalism-just-days-after-88 -election (accessed October 3, 2011).

1016 **"On television, I tried to absolutely hew to the middle":** Jeremy Gerard, "Walter Cronkite Speaks His Mind Instead of Just News," *New York Times*, January 8, 1989.

1017 **"Nowadays, you see more people, more houses":** Walter Cronkite speech to Natural Resources

Defense Council in North Carolina, March 11, 1989, File: NRDC, Box: 2M615, WCP-UTA.

1018 **"I could drown in the nostalgia tonight"**: Mark Carreau, "Memories Key Gala That Flies Crowd to Moon," *Houston Chronicle*, July 22, 1989.

1018 **to Cronkite it was worth every damn penny:** Ibid.

1018 **going to Mars would remain a pipe dream:** Ibid.

1019 *"The New York Times* **was reporting the build-up on the border"**: Cronkite, *A Reporter's Life*, p. 357.

1020 **Cronkite, a war skeptic:** Robert Wiener, *Live from Baghdad: Gathering News at Ground Zero* (New York: Doubleday, 1992), p. 3.

1020 **"The telegraph at the other networks went dead"**: Author interview with Tom Johnson, May 24, 2011.

1021 **"The skies over Baghdad have been illuminated"**: Bernard Shaw, "Baghdad Report," January 16, 1991, CNN Archives, Atlanta, GA.

1021 **"why don't you tell the president yourself on CNN"**: Author interview with Tom Johnson, May 24, 2011.

1022 no U.S. planes had been "lost in the first wave of attacks": James A. Baker III, *The Politics of Diplomacy: Revolution, War, and Peace, 1989–1992* (New York: Putnam, 1995), p. 384.

1022 "There are Americans dying": Tom Shales, "Television, Eyewitness on the Front Line," *Washington Post*, January 17, 1991.

1022 "there comes a point where it becomes foolhardy": Wiener, *Live from Baghdad*, p. 13.

1023 "The historical irony of Walter and me covering a war together": Author interview with Bernard Shaw, June 10, 2011.

1023 "Bush said we were fighting the Iraqi leadership": Herb Caen, "Manhattan Merry-Go-Round," *San Francisco Chronicle*, March 6, 1991.

1024 was among the finest TV reporters since Murrow: Author interview with Andy Rooney, March 15, 2011.

1025 "I'm so very proud of you": Author interview with Bob Simon, January 12, 2012.

1025 Victory in the Gulf War translated into President Bush garnering: Tom Wicker, *George Herbert Walker Bush* (New York: Viking Press, 2004), p. 166.

1026 **"Sometimes we would go visit Tom Watson"**: Author interview with Mike Ashford, June 5, 2011.

1027 **"President Bush went to take the call"**: Cronkite, *A Reporter's Life*, p. 355.

1027 **"We all ceremoniously hoisted our glasses"**: Author interview with Mike Ashford, June 3, 2011.

1028 **"nothing of any significance is going to be said in 9.8 seconds"**: John Tierney, "Furor Grows over Shrinkage of Sound Bites on TV News," *New York Times*, January 28, 1992.

1029 **"I struggled for funding"**: Author interview with John Hendricks, November 12, 2011.

1029 **Hendricks paid Cronkite to do long-form interviews**: Author interview with Dale Minor, August 18, 2011.

1029 **there wouldn't today be a Discovery Channel"**: Author interview with John Hendricks, November 13, 2011.

1029 **Cronkite continued circulating as the éminence grise**: "Newsmakers," *Houston Chronicle*, February 4, 1992; Neil Morgan, "Cronkite Turns Border Reporter," *San Diego Union-Tribune*, March 3, 1992.

1030 **"I greatly regret that President Bush and his campaign managers"**: "President Bush, Harkin Say 'No' to Special on Discovery," New York *Daily News*, March 7, 1992.

1030 **Cronkite held a round table forum on journalism**: Ray Richmond, "TV's Selling Power Puts Perot in Race," *Orange County Register*, July 5, 1992.

1031 **"sound bites, shell games, handlers, and media stuntmen"**: J. Michael Kennedy, "It's a Thankless, Slimy Job; So Why Is Perot After It?" *Los Angeles Times*, April 19, 1992.

1031 **"Perot can stumble into an answer that is meaningful"**: Ibid.

1031 **"Clinton has Carter's intelligence"**: Bill Zwecker, "As a Political Wit, Walter Cronkite Leaves 'Em Gasping," *Chicago Sun-Times*, November 22, 1992.

1032 **"There's one more honor to be paid tonight"**: Godfrey Sperlin, "Why Bush Lost," *Christian Science Monitor*, December 22, 1992.

1032 **President Bush got a long standing ovation**: *State Journal-Register* (Springfield, IL), February 22, 1997.

Thirty-Four: "THE WORLD'S OLDEST REPORTER"

1034 **Los Angeles was in the midst of the Northridge earthquake:** "The Magnitude 6.7 Northridge, California, Earthquake of 17 January 1994," *Science* 266, no. 5184 (October 1994): 389.

1034 **"He hadn't lost his drive to own a news story":** Author interview with Bernard Shaw, June 10, 2011.

1035 **"I think Walter was shaken by Northridge":** Author interview with Andy Rooney, March 15, 2011.

1036 **"Walter was always open for business":** Author interview with Tom Brokaw, August 2, 2011.

1037 **"People put their faith in what they see":** Gerard, "Walter Cronkite Speaks His Mind Instead of Just News."

1038 **"The fact that you can't find a new Walter Cronkite on television":** Jack Fuller, *What Is Happening to News: The Information Explosion and Crisis in Journalism* (Chicago: University of Chicago Press, 2010), p. 73.

1039 **"How many of you":** Ted Koppel's final *Nightline* broadcast, November 22, 2005, LexisNexis Academic transcript.

1040 **"Eric was one of the best of that small number of news analysts"**: "Eric Sevareid, Commentator for CBS-TV," *Los Angeles Times*, July 10, 1992.

1041 **"I couldn't believe I got to hover in the same sphere"**: Author interview with Brian Williams, September 2, 2011.

1041 **When Cronkite spoke at a library lecture series:** Bruce Lambert, "Richard Salant, 78, Who Headed CBS News in Expansion, Is Dead," *New York Times*, February 23, 1993.

1041 **"I was excited beyond belief"**: Author interview with Brian Williams, September 2, 2011.

1042 **"It became our running joke"**: Ibid.

1043 **"Doesn't that man over there look like Walter Cronkite?"**: Author interview with Michael Finley, March 1, 2010.

1044 **"He would always ask everybody he met"**: Author interview with Marlene Adler, December 9, 2011.

1044 **"Get lost!"**: Author interview with Andy Rooney, March 15, 2011.

1045 **"It was shameless"**: Ibid.

1045 **he insisted that old-fashioned investigative journalism was a prerequisite:** "Integration

Never to Be Realized," *New York Amsterdam News*, October 9, 1993.

1045 **confounded Cronkite, Ward and Company in 1993:** Terry Behrman, "Remembering My Former Boss Walter Cronkite," July 21, 2009, New Lantern blog for business innovation.

1046 **"Come on, Walter. It's time to get to the orgy":** Ray Richmond, "Cronkite Report: America's Most Trusted Man Still Sets Pace," *Los Angeles Daily News*, May 26, 1993.

1047 **"they used to say Walter Cronkite could get elected president":** Anne Gowen, "Down Home at the White House," *Washington Times*, September 14, 1963.

1048 **"Any question I had about the Battle of Normandy":** Author interview with Wolf Blitzer, September 7, 2011.

1048 **"Let me give you three pieces of advice, Al":** Author interview with Al Ortiz, May 12, 2011.

1049 **"I meant my martini":** Cronkite, *A Reporter's Life*, pp. 15–16.

1050 **"I wouldn't have a problem with that":** Verne Gay, "Cronkite on Credibility," *Buffalo News*, March 10, 1996.

1050 **"Walter sent us his notes and a long oral history"**: Author interview with Shirley Wershba, August 31, 2011.

1052 **"I thought that we Americans overreacted to the Soviets"**: Walter Cronkite, "The Cold War," Discovery Channel, January 16, 1997.

1052 **"With newscasters like Mr. Cronkite, Who Needs Pravda?"**: *Washington Times*, June 25, 1997.

1052 **an anti-Cronkite website titled "Walter Cronkite Spit in My Food"**: "Cronkite Not Amused by His Online Spitting Image," *Philadelphia Inquirer*, January 29, 1997.

1053 **"wrapping their harsh right-wing views in the banner"**: "Cronkite Attacks Religious Right," *Dayton Daily News*, March 6, 1997.

1053 **underwent quadruple bypass surgery on April 1, 1997**: John Carmody, "The TV Column," *Washington Post*, April 3, 1997.

1054 **"The music seemed to heal his soul"**: Author interview with Chip Cronkite, July 3, 2011.

1055 **"I took one look at you"**: Author interview with Joanna Simon, January 13, 2012.

1055 **"It must be terrible leaving with so many family memories"**: Author interview with Tom Brokaw, August 2, 2011.

1056 **Cronkite sent a note to the White House inviting them to go sailing:** Author interview with Sandy Socolow, October 16, 2011.

1057 **"At that time I could have done with a picture with Walter Cronkite":** President Clinton Speech at Cronkite's Memorial, 2009, Lincoln Center, New York.

1057 **No leaks about the discussion occurred:** Peter Johnson, "Cronkite Refuses to Talk," *USA Today*, August 2, 1998.

1058 **"Bill and Hillary didn't speak to each other the entire time":** Author interview with Sandy Socolow, July 8, 2011.

1058 **"historic opportunity for young Walter":** Author interview with Walter Cronkite IV, December 5, 2011.

1058 **"President Clinton was in awe of Cronkite":** Author interview with Dee Dee Myers, July 23, 2011.

1059 **"Or I could go with him, play canasta up there":** David Kronke, "Cronkite—A Look Upward at Space, Downward at the Demise of Television," *Los Angeles Daily News*, October 21, 1999.

1059 **Johnson asked Cronkite—still under contract with CBS News—to co-anchor:** "Walter

Cronkite to Co-Anchor CNN's Coverage," CNN transcript, July 29, 1998.

1059 **"Gosh, we wish we'd thought of it":** "CNN Beat CBS to the Punch," *San Jose Mercury News*, October 14, 1998.

1060 **Cronkite, in an effort to allay CBS concerns about him:** *60 Minutes*, October 18, 1998.

1060 **"John Glenn going back into Space is serving the purpose":** Dave Walker, "Cronkite Suits to Cover Glenn Trek," *Arizona Republic*, October 23, 1998.

1060 **"Mike, if they want the questions in advance":** Author interview with Mike Freedman, November 20, 2011.

1062 **the "Cronkite School of Broadcasting and Space" on CNN:** Bob Betcher, "Cronkite Tells Flight the Way It Is," *Vero Beach Press Journal*, October 30, 1998.

1062 **"Walter waved me to sit next to him":** Author interview with Jimmy Buffett, July 18, 2011.

1064 **"I had people from our affiliate stations around the country calling":** Interview with Michael Freedman, February 27, 2011.

1064 **Trump claimed Cronkite was a "totally preposterous" man:** "This Just In: Cronkite Slams

Trump Project," *Philadelphia Inquirer*, August 20, 1999.

1064 **"Walter, it is soooooooo good to see you again!":** Sandy Socolow to Douglas Brinkley, December 13, 2011.

1065 **spent a week at the Jet Propulsion Laboratory (JPL) in Pasadena:** Kronke, "Walter Cronkite—A Look Upward at Space."

1065 **the notion of "unlimited national sovereignty":** Myron M. Kronisch, "Toward a Democratic World Government," *Newark Star-Ledger*, January 14, 2000.

1066 **"Any attempt to achieve world order before that time must":** Walter Cronkite, "Speech Before the World Federalist Association" (transcript), October 19, 1999, WCP-UTA. Also see "Cronkite Champions World Government," *Washington Times*, December 3, 1999.

1067 **"I don't understand the need for speed":** "Cronkite Sees Good, Bad in News Gathering," *Charleston* (WV) *Gazette*, November 26, 2000.

1068 **Uncle Walter was "irreplaceable":** Jeannie Williams, "No Kennedy Gala for Cronkite," *USA Today*, November 30, 2000.

1068 **"I had to think more about the millennium than anyone":** "Names in the News," AP, May 16, 2000.

Thirty-Five: THE NEW MILLENNIUM

1070 **"I suggested that he stay out of New York for a while":** Author interview with Chip Cronkite, July 3, 2011.

1071 **"He *had* to see Ground Zero for himself":** Author interview with Marlene Adler, December 19, 2011.

1071 **Instead of canceling his La Sapienza speech:** "Cronkite Praises U.S. Broadcast Coverage," *Milwaukee Journal Sentinel,* September 15, 2001.

1072 **"This is your Kennedy":** Aaron Brown, "On Walter Cronkite," Walter Cronkite School of Journalism and Mass Communication, http://cronkite.asu.edu/node/689 (accessed July 9, 2011).

1072 **to "get even, for heaven's sake":** Walter Cronkite on *Late Night with David Letterman,* September 20, 2001 (video transcription).

1073 *Cronkite:* **"Well, how do you think it felt":** Ibid.

1074 **"I was hot under the collar about Bush over-reacting":** Author interview with Andy Rooney, March 15, 2011.

1075 **"if [Falwell and Robertson] are worshipping the same God"**: "Falwell = Terrorists, Says Cronkite," *New York Post*, September 28, 2011.

1075 **he saw his public role as championing**: *Kirkus Reviews*, review of *Around America: A Tour of Our Magnificent Coastline*, by Walter Cronkite, May 15, 2001, http://www.kirkus reviews.com/book-reviews/walter-cronkite/around -america/#review.

1076 **"Somehow knowing that Walter was still around"**: Author interview with Katie Couric, September 22, 2009.

1076 **"ideological eunuch"**: Gerard, "Walter Cronkite Speaks His Mind Instead of Just News."

1077 **Refusing to be intimidated by Rush Limbaugh or Sean Hannity**: Author interview with Marlene Adler, June 4, 2011.

1077 **"No longer was he trying to be Mr. Center"**: Author interview with Katie Couric, September 22, 2009.

1078 **Democrats engaged in silly fights**: Richard Zoglin, "10 Questions for Walter Cronkite," *Time*, October 26, 2003.

1078 **"Walter liked being in the ring"**: Author interview with Dale Minor, August 18, 2011.

1079 **"Bush is setting an example":** "Cronkite Condemns Decision to Go to War," *St. Louis Dispatch*, October 11, 2003.

1079 **"At the networks, Cronkite's heirs were not even practicing journalism":** Frank Rich, "And That's Not the Way It Was," *New York Times*, July 26, 2009.

1080 **"We met in the restaurant of the Mark Hotel in Manhattan":** Christiane Amanpour to Douglas Brinkley, January 17, 2012.

1081 **"If 1988 taught us anything":** Walter Cronkite, "Senator Kerry Shouldn't Be Afraid of Admitting He's a Liberal," *Ventura County Star*, March 18, 2004, from King Features Syndicate.

1083 **"This was an error made in good faith":** Josh Getlin, Elizabeth Jensen, and Matea Gold, "CBS Apologizes for Its Story on Bush Memos," *Los Angeles Times*, September 21, 2004.

1084 **"There's nothing there":** Howard Kurtz, "Osama Who?" *Washington Post*, January 24, 2005.

1085 **"But that ol' boy danced a jig when Dan went down":** Author interview with Andy Rooney, March 15, 2011.

1085   **What surprised him wasn't Memogate:** Sidney Blumenthal, "Dan Rather Stands by His Story," *Salon.com*, September 27, 2007.

1085   **"that they tolerated his being there for so long":** Walter Cronkite remarks on *American Morning*, CNN transcript, March 8, 2005.

1086   **Team Rather had "myopic zeal":** "CBS Ousts Four for Roles in Bush Guard Story," AP, January 10, 2005.

1086   **To Moonves, it was a "black mark":** Author interview with Les Moonves, June 10, 2011.

1086   **"We know it as the battle of the bathroom":** Author interview with Jeff Fager, January 10, 2012.

1087   **"I just want you to know you did the right thing":** Author interview with Les Moonves, June 10, 2011.

1088   **"You'll never know what that meant to me":** Ibid.

1088   **with what Barbara Walters called her "wry and acidic" bluntness:** Author interview with Barbara Walters, August 24, 2011.

1088   **"They didn't poll my wife":** Walter Cronkite remarks at roast in Phoenix, Arizona, November 15, 1985.

1089 "Betsy was the glue that held him together": Author interview with Deborah Rush, February 21, 2012.

1089 "Walter was bereft and lost": Author interview with Joanna Simon, January 13, 2012.

1090 "All I do is puddle up and cry from morning to night": Author interview with William Small, March 22, 2011.

1091 "It's not a bad idea": Ibid.

1091 "I could talk to Walter about anything": Author interview with Aaron Brown, September 7, 2011.

1091 "Dan didn't have many friends": Author interview with Jeff Fager, January 9, 2012.

1091 "was overjoyed": Author interview with Roger Mudd, November 14, 2011.

1092 "I've got a new girlfriend": Author interview with Jimmy Buffett, September 18, 2011.

1092 Just months after Betsy died, Cronkite began dating Joanna Simon: Kate Nocera and Erin Durkin, "Girlfriend Recalls the Way Walter Cronkite Was: As a Journalist Impartial, As a Human Passionate," New York Daily News, July 20 2009.

1092 **"casserole ladies":** Author interview with Marlene Adler, December 9, 2011.

1093 **"gal pal":** Author interview with Joanna Simon, January 13, 2012.

1093 **"Walter didn't wait very long to strike":** Nocera and Durkin, "Girlfriend Recalls the Way Cronkite Was."

1094 **he proposed to her:** Carol Ross Joynt, *Innocent Spouse: A Memoir* (New York: Crown, 2011), p. 258.

1094 **"It was like I was reunited with my grandfather":** Beverly Keel to Douglas Brinkley, May 19, 2011.

1094 **"As long as I'm your King of Hearts":** Author interview with Joanna Simon, January 13, 2012.

1095 **"beyond anything I could have ever believed":** "NASA Honors Veteran Journalist Walter Cronkite," NASA.gov, February 28, 2006, http://www.nasa.gov/vision/space/features/cronkite_ambassador_of_exploration.html.

1095 **he donated it to the University of Texas's Dolph Briscoe Center:** "The Briscoe Center for American History: The Walter Cronkite Papers,"

www.cah.utexas.edu/collections/news_media
_cronkite.php (accessed July 30, 2011).

1096 **Cronkite helping the Walter Cronkite School:**
"Cronkite Takes First Dig at School's New Digs,"
ASU News Now, February 21, 2007.

1097 **"Every day, Mike, is a blessing":** Author interview with Joanna Simon, January 14, 2012.

1097 **"Walter and I had a great romance":** Author
interview with Joanna Simon, January 15, 2012.

1098 **"Mar-a-juana":** Author interview with Peter
Simon, January 15, 2012.

1099 **"the war on drugs is a failure":** Walter Cronkite,
"Telling the Truth About the War on Drugs,"
reprinted by *Huffington Post,* March 1, 2006.

1100 **"Now Walter Cronkite, the most trusted news
broadcaster in American history":** Phillip
Smith, "Cronkite vs. O'Reilly: May the Most
Trusted Man Win," AlterNet, March 3, 2006,
http://www.alternet.org/drugs/33009/.

1101 **He would do the same at Gordon Manning's
funeral:** "Gordon Manning, 89, a TV News
Executive," *New York Times,* September 9, 2006.

1101 **"It left us numb":** Author interview with Jimmy
Buffett, July 18, 2011.

1102   **Cronkite had a flurry of health scares:** Author interview with Kathy Cronkite, June 3, 2011.

1102   **"Sometimes, he would look out the window at the East River":** Author interview with Chip Cronkite, February 20, 2012.

1103   **"He didn't recognize me from Adam":** Author interview with Bernard Kalb, February 26, 2011.

1103   **By late 2007, ninety-one-year-old Cronkite started contributing weekly editorials:** Brian Stelter, "Cronkite Joins Retirement TV," *New York Times*, November 15, 2007.

1104   **"It turned into a ghastly moment":** Author interview with Caroline Graham, March 29, 2011.

1104   **"Let's get this thing going":** Steve Samaras, "Sailing Hall of Fame Will Boost City," *The Capital*, March 9, 2008.

1104   **"Did anyone ever tell you that you look just like Walter Cronkite":** Polly Paddock, "Cronkite Reassures as Always—Former CBS Anchor Guides Charlotte Audience Through Century in Review," *Charlotte Observer*, October 22, 1999.

1104   **Cronkite and Simon went out for dinner with Nick and Nina Clooney:** "We Hear," *New York Post*, March 13, 2003.

1105 **"They didn't applaud"**: Matea Gold, "Obama Extols Cronkite at Memorial," *Los Angeles Times*, September 9, 2009.

1105 **"It was hysterical"**: Author interview with Joanna Simon, January 14, 2012.

1106 **"It's Uncle no more, he's Grandpa Walter now"**: Tom Shales, "Dear, Trusted Uncle Walter and the 'Legacy' of World War II," *Washington Post*, April 29, 2009.

1106 **"I wanted to spit on them"**: Walter Cronkite, "Legacy of War," PBS (transcript), April 29, 2009.

1106 **"my God, my God, my God. It's too damn much"**: Ibid.

Epilogue: ELECTRONIC UNCLE SAM

1107 **"Everybody who loved Dad just surrounded him"**: Author interview with Kathy Cronkite, June 3, 2011.

1108 **"He'd smile ... at peace with the world"**: Author interview with Jimmy Buffett, September 18, 2011.

1108 **"Walter Cronkite just died too"**: Author interview with Deborah Rush, February 21, 2012.

1110 "Cronkite was—and this is what psychologists say is the greatest tribute to a parent—*there*": David Shribman, "Can Viewers Kick Cronkite Habit?" *Washington Star*, March 2, 1981.

1110 He was, as the *Los Angeles Times* and, later, the *Huffington Post* said, *paterfamilias*: Reed Johnson, "Tethered in Technoculture," *Los Angeles Times*, December 18, 2005; Peggy Drexler, "Gasp! Katie Plays Rough," *Huffington Post*, September 11, 2007.

1110 "The one guy in TV history nobody ever got sick of": Author interview with Ted Turner, April 20, 2011.

1111 "We have a self-confidence we didn't have in the beginning": Ferretti, "What Do They Do?"

1112 "a kind of innate, Calvinist honesty that can't be manufactured": Al Reinert, "The Secret World of Walter Cronkite," *Texas Monthly*, January 1976.

1112 "our electronic Uncle Sam": Kurt Vonnegut, "A Reluctant Big Shot," *The Nation*, March 7, 1981.

1112 Cremation and a low-key ceremony, before burial next to Betsy: "Cronkite to Be Buried Beside Wife in Missouri," AP, reprinted in *Denver Post*, July 19, 2009.

1112 **Any donations were directed to the Walter and Betsy Cronkite Foundation:** Chad Butler, "Now Late Walter Cronkite to Be Buried Here in Missouri," *St. Louis Examiner*, July 18, 2009.

1113 **"I hate the world without Walter Cronkite":** Michael Essany, "George Clooney Weighs In on the Loss of Walter Cronkite," *Entertainer Examiner*, July 18, 2009.

1113 **dubbed him "truly the father of television news":** Valerie J. Nelson, "Walter Cronkite, Longtime CBS Anchorman, Dies at 92," *Los Angeles Times*, July 18, 2009.

1114 **his extraordinary sense of "purpose and compassion":** Brian Stelter, "Television Icons Reflect on Cronkite's Career," *New York Times*, July 17, 2009, http://mediadecoder .blogs.nytimes.com/2009/07/17/television-icons -reflect-on-cronkites-career/.

1114 **Couric had used Cronkite's voice to introduce her *CBS Evening News*:** Ed Pilkington, "Cronkite to Couric; CBS Weighs Anchor," *Guardian*, September 6, 2006.

1114 **"Thanks for watching":** Howard Rosenberg, "Katie Couric, News Anchors, and the Cult of Personality," *Los Angeles Times*, July 14, 2008.

1114 **Barbara Walters used Sirius XM Radio to air a marathon:** Cherie Saunders, "CBS RLTV and Sirius XM Announce Walter Cronkite Special," *Washington Examiner*, July 19, 2009.

1114 **"Walter had that ability":** "Dan Rather Reflects on Walter Cronkite," MSNBC.com, Saturday, July 18, 2009.

1115 **"There was nobody better than him":** Author interview with Dan Rather, May 28, 2011.

1115 **"I feel like I'm almost sitting in for Wally Schirra this morning":** *Face the Nation* transcript, Sunday, July 19, 2009, CBS News Archive, New York.

1115 **"Because everybody knew that Walter didn't get his suntan in the studio lights":** *Face the Nation* transcript, Sunday, July 19, 2009, CBS News Archive, New York.

1116 **" 'Boy oh boy—when and where do you want me?' ":** Tom Brokaw, "The Most Trusted Man in America," *Time*, August 3, 2009, p. 20.

1117 **"I feel so terrible about Walter's death":** Matea Gold, "Cronkite Eulogized as Newsman, Friend, Father," *Los Angeles Times*, July 24, 2009.

1117 **"He was the original social media guy":** Author interview with Mickey Hart, February 17, 2011.

1118 "a seagull—graceful in flight, rapacious in appetite": "Proust Questionnaire."

1118 "He had an antenna sensitive to friends' pain": Author interview with Mike Ashford, May 7, 2011.

1118 A favorite of Cronkite's was "Sea Fever": Author interview with Bill Harbach, January 24, 2012.

1119 Everyone in America, Mason soon learned, wanted to be part: Author interview with Linda Mason, April 30, 2011.

1119 "Helping establish some TV news standards": "Proust Questionnaire."

1120 "but I got there in time": Christiane Amanpour to Douglas Brinkley, January 23, 2012.

1120 "What would Walter do?": Christiane Amanpour, "Diary," September 18, 2009, Private Archive, New York, NY.

1121 Obama had "grown up watching Cronkite": President Barack Obama, comment to Douglas Brinkley, July 11, 2011.

1121 "Everybody in the building was glued to the ceremony": Author interview with Armen Keteyian, July 3, 2011.

1121 **"Journalism is more than just a profession"**: "President Obama," September 9, 2009, Lincoln Center Memorial (transcript), CBS News Archive, New York.

1122 **that viewed news as "just another profit center"**: Jim Wallace, "Cronkite Says TV News Fails to Tell Whole Story," *Charleston Daily Mail*, December 12, 2000.

1122 **"Storytelling was Walter's passion"**: Buzz Aldrin, "Cronkite Remembered," transcript, September 18, 2009.

1123 **"There are better writers than me, better reporters"**: Roger Vaughan, "Cruising with Cronkite," *Motor Boating & Sailing*, November 1976.

1124 **"Nobody's asked me, which is strange, but I think the networks ought to be doing headlines"**: Howard Kurtz, "Walter Cronkite Was the Last of the Towering Anchormen," *Washington Post*, July 18, 2009.

1125 **Cronkite's desk may have been turned to pulp wood**: Author interview with David Rhodes, January 7, 2012.

1125 **"For a news analyst and reporter of the happenings of the day to be successful"**: "Neil

Armstrong Statement on the Death of Walter Cronkite," *NASA Newsroom Press Release*, July 17, 2009.

1126 **"He invited us to believe in him, and he never let us down":** Todd Leopold, "Former CBS Anchor 'Uncle Walter' Cronkite Dead at 92," *CNN.com*, August 29, 2009, http://articles.cnn .com/2009-07-17/us/walter.cronkite.dead_1_walter -cronkite-huffington-post-egyptian-leader?_s =PM:US.

Author's Interviews

George Abbey, Houston, Texas • Marlene Adler, New York • Roger Ailes, New York • Buzz Aldrin, Washington D.C. • Neil Armstrong, Houston, Texas • Mike Ashford, Annapolis, Maryland • Bob Asman, Washington, D.C. • James A. Baker III, Houston, Texas • Joel Banow, Naples, Florida • Ben Barnes, Austin, Texas • Fred Barnes, Washington, D.C. • Kay Barnes, Kansas City, Missouri • Warren Beatty, Beverly Hills, California • Russ Bensley, Homewood, Illinois • Carl Bernstein, Washington, D.C. • Porter Bibb, New York • Izzy Bleckman, Vero Beach, Florida • Merv Block, New York • Julian Bond, Charlottesville, Virginia • Ron Bonn, San Diego, California • Ben Bradlee, Washington, D.C. • Ed Bradley, Woody Creek, Colorado • Rita Braver, Washington, D.C. •

Tom Brokaw, New York • Aaron Brown, Scottsdale, Arizona • Skip Brown, San Francisco, California • Patrick Buchanan, Rehoboth Beach, Delaware • Jimmy Buffett, Key West, Florida • Joseph Califano, New York • Don Carleton, Austin, Texas • Liz Carpenter, Austin, Texas • Nick Clooney, Augusta, Kentucky • Connie Chung, Glacier National Park, Montana • Charles Colson, Naples, Florida • Katie Couric, New York • Chip Cronkite, New York • Kathy Cronkite, Austin, Texas • Nancy Cronkite, New York • David Dary, Norman, Oklahoma • Tom Davis, New York • Morton Dean, Truro, Massachusetts • Sam Donaldson, Washington, D.C. • Daniel Ellsberg, Alameda County, California • Stephen Erlich, Los Angeles, California • Jeffrey Fager, New York • Bill Felling, New York • Michael Finley, Ashland, Oregon • Gerald Ford, Rancho Mirage, California • Ed Forgotson, New York • Ed Fouhy, Chatham, Massachusetts • Michael Freedman, Washington, D.C. • David Friend, New York • Ruth Friendly, New York • Rev. Dr. C. Welton Gaddy, Lake Charles, Louisiana • John Glenn, Columbus, Ohio • Andrew Goldberg, New York • Stanhope Gould, New York • Caroline Graham, Los Angeles, California • Jeff Gralnick, Weston, Connecticut •Phil Gries, Albertson, New York • Bill Harbach, Fairfield, Connecticut • Bob Hardesty, Austin, Texas • Mickey Hart, San Francisco,

California · Dennis Hayes, Seattle, Washington · Don Hewitt, New York · A. R. Hogan, Bethesda, Maryland · Brit Hume, Washington, D.C. · Tom Johnson, Atlanta, Georgia · Phil Jones, Naples, Florida · Gordon S. Joseloff , Westport, Connecticut · Carol Joynt, Washington, D.C. · Bernard Kalb, Washington, D.C. · Marvin Kalb, Washington, D.C. · Rick Kaplan, New York · Jay Kaufman, Atlanta, Georgia · Ethel Kennedy, West Palm Beach, Florida · David Kennerly, Los Angeles, California · Henry Kissinger, New York · Joe Klein, Washington, D.C. · Mathilde Krim, New York · Ron Kucera, Columbia, Missouri · Brian Lamb, Washington, D.C. · John Lane, Rye, New York · Lewis H. Lapham, New York · John Laurence, Haslemere, United Kingdom · John Lehman, New York · Jim Lehrer, Austin, Texas · Richard Leibner, New York · Norman Mailer, Austin, Texas · Frank Mankiewicz, Washington, D.C. · Wynton Marsalis, New York · Linda Mason, New York · Chris Matthews, Washington, D.C. · Jim McGillian, Carmel, California · George McGovern, St. Augustine, Florida · Megan McKinney, Chicago, Illinois · Don Michel, Dallas, Texas · Harry Middleton, Austin, Texas · Bill Minor, Phoenix, Arizona · Andrea Mitchell, Washington, D.C. · Les Moonves, New York · Patt Morrison, Los Angeles, California · Roger Mudd, McLean, Virginia · Dee Dee

Myers, Washington, D.C. • Al Neuharth, Cocoa Beach, Florida • Tom Noel, Dallas, Texas • Barack Obama, Washington, D.C. • Bill O'Reilly, New York • Al Ortiz, New York • Charles Osgood, New York • Scott Pelley, New York • Robert Pierpoint, Santa Barbara, California • Bill Plante, Washington, D.C. • Sandor M. Polster, Durham, Maine • Hugh Raisky, Newport, Rhode Island • Dan Rather, New York and Austin, Texas • Missie Rennie, Vero Beach, Florida • David Rhodes, New York • Lynda Johnson Robb, Austin, Texas • Andy Rooney, New York • William Ruckelshaus, Seattle, Washington • Deborah Rush, New York • Morley Safer, New York • Bob Schieffer, Washington, D.C. • David Schneider, New York • Jack Schneider, Westport, Connecticut • Mark Segal, Philadelphia, Pennsylvania • Doug Shadel, Seattle, Washington • Bernard Shaw, Takoma Park, Maryland • Don Shelby, Minneapolis, Minnesota • Fay Shoss, Houston, Texas • Joanna Simon, New York • Peter Simon, Edgartown, Massachusetts • William Small, New York • Richard Snow, New York • Sandy Socolow, Austin, Texas, and New York • Ted Sorensen, New York • Lesley Stahl, New York • Oliver Stone, Los Angeles, California • Mary Lou Teel, New York • Doug Terry, Washington, D.C. • Lee Thornton, Bethesda, Maryland • Ted Turner, Atlanta, Georgia • Ed Vebell, Westport, Connecticut • William

J. vanden Heuvel, New York • Bob Vitarelli, Chevy Chase, Maryland • Diana Walker, Washington, D.C. • Chris Wallace, Washington, D.C. • Barbara Walters, New York • Jann Wenner, Sun Valley, Idaho • Shirley Wershba, Floral Park, New York • Lally Weymouth, East Hampton, New York • Bill Whitehurst, Austin, Texas • Elie Wiesel, New York • Jon Wilkman, Los Angeles, California • Brian Williams, New Canaan, Connecticut • Lew Wood, Los Angeles, California • Bob Woodward, Washington, D.C. • Arnold Zenker, Weston, Massachusetts

About the Author

Douglas Brinkley is a professor of history at Rice University and a contributing editor to *Vanity Fair*. *The Chicago Tribune* has dubbed him "America's new past master." His most recent books are *The Quiet World*, *The Wilderness Warrior*, and *The Great Deluge*. Six of his books have been selected as *New York Times* Notable Books of the Year. He lives in Texas with his wife and three children.